T0368348

Gypsy
the Gem Dealer

Ivor Blimsworth

Order this book online at www.trafford.com
or email orders@trafford.com

Most Trafford titles are also available at major online book retailers.

Print information available on the last page.

ISBN: 978-1-4907-7146-5 (sc)
ISBN: 978-1-4907-7147-2 (hc)
ISBN: 978-1-4907-7148-9 (e)

Library of Congress Control Number: 2016904136

Trafford rev. 04/22/2016

 www.trafford.com
North America & international
toll-free: 1 888 232 4444 (USA & Canada)
fax: 812 355 4082

Dedicated to my beloved wife Sumalee who
recently passed away in 15th March 2016

INTRODUCTION

Enough time has now passed that this story can finally be told. Upto this moment, the telling of these adventures would have risked the safety of others or endangering the livelihoods of contemporary travelers.

But the world has now changed and even those from the old days who are still on the road now earn their living via other channels, the internet has put paid to many of the old ways and global trade on the internet has destroyed the small import export routines of many of the travelers and closed many of the old routes to make a living whilst being on the road. Nevertheless there are still parts that must remain untold, although all efforts have been made not to sanitise the story. The story that is told here is the story of a wild yet spiritual and curious individual on his search for truth and spiritual liberation and his adventures and experiences in his journey. He is in some ways a paradox of a character, feral and full of rage on one side yet spiritual, compassionate and humbly trying to learn all that he can, on the other. He is not conventional at all, in truth he is an anarchist, struggling against a system that he holds in total contempt and disgust. However, he is hoping to find a society that runs on higher principles than the one that he was raised in.

His journey starts at the age of 17 when he gets an invite from a cousin whom he has never met or even seen a picture of, to go and stay and work in Israel on the kibbutz where his cousin lives. From Israel, where he meets world travelers for the first time, he embarks on a quest to raise the money to get to India and the rest of the Far East beyond. It takes him many attempts and disappointments, but by the age of 21 he has made it to India and his real journey is only just beginning. ....he starts off green to it all, not quite knowing what is going on around him but ends up becoming streetwise enough to establish his own international method of trade and able to pay his way on the road without need to work for others. In this, the first book, his spiritual experiences are only just beginning, but nevertheless, he explores Judaism, Vaishnav

Hinduism and Buddhism from the inside....... This book tells the story of the genesis of our traveler where the foundation is built. Far wilder and deeper experiences are yet to come in book two. ......but I hope you enjoy this read. As to whether or not this is a true story, I leave that up to you to decide. . . . . --

FOREWORD

B orn in the shadow of the Malvern hills of Worcestershire in the early nineteen sixties, his first four years of life were full of wonder and enjoyment. His parents were horticulturalists and ran a small plant nursery where they grew house plants, selling these at county shows and agricultural events. The Three Counties Show was the biggest event of the year, but there were also the Tewksbury Mop and minor carnivals in the area. The boy enjoyed the excitement of the shows, staying in a tent and going to the mobile pubs that were set up on the show grounds with his parents. He liked the smell of beer and the freedom of wandering around the stalls on his own. . It must be said that even at this early age he preferred to be around adults, they were more interesting than the children of his own age whom he was expected to play with. He could learn things from them and satisfy his curiosity. Children of his own age had nothing to teach him and bored him.

At the age of two he experienced his first jet flight, flying on the then new Hawker Sidley Trident jet flown by British European Airways [later to become the part of British Airways that services European destinations]. The flight was from London to Nice. His father had driven to the south of France in their van in order to collect stock plants for the nursery and they did not think that he could handle the journey both ways at such a young age.

There he was: two years old and already a jet-setter. Looking down through the window at the earth below, flying in this incredible plastic molded and metal vehicle above the clouds, being served food on fancy trays......Mmmmmmh he liked this, it was good.

The plane landed into bright sunshine at Nice and he was soon running behind his mother through the terminal. His father was there to collect them with the van and soon they were driving to the camping site where his father already had the familiar tent pitched up that they used at the shows.

They were wrong about him not being able to travel easily. He took to it like a duck to water. They had a special seat made for him that mounted on the engine cover which sat between the driver and passenger seats. On following journeys he accompanied his parents everywhere. There were long drives on two lane roads all the way to the south of France; there were long journeys in England and there were journeys to the north of France, too. The boy enjoyed the journeys: sitting there in his comfy seat watching the scenery, enjoying the packed lunches and playing at the camping grounds.

On one occasion, his parents decided to fly the van over to France from Lyde airport in Kent to Latouquette airport in France.

The boy and his parents were looking out of the windows of the terminal as a British Air Ferries, Bristol Freighter was being loaded with vehicles. Suddenly their van came into view, being driven by one of the professional loaders. The boy looking and seeing that both of his parents were standing next to him thought that someone was taking their van away from them and started to cry while pointing towards the plane. The man who was running the snack-stand saw what was going on and came over towards him and gave him a bar of chocolate to cheer him up....... he need not have worried, soon he was sat in the passenger compartment at the back of the plane as they winged across the channel.

Then once more they were on their way along French roads, eating strange tasting French foods as they headed to the nurseries that were supplying them.

Then one day when he was four years old everything changed. Firstly his mother had given birth to his younger brother and secondly one of his two grandfathers had had a nervous breakdown and could no longer run his own plant nursery. He and the boy's maternal grandmother both lived in Sussex, so the family was going to move to the coast and merge the crops of the two businesses. His father was going to manage the whole business and his mother was going to manage the specialist crops that they had been growing in Worcestershire.

Just before Christmas in 1966 they drove from their place in Worcester down to the Sussex coast in the van which was loaded to the roof with their personal belongings and moved into a high ceilinged Edwardian semi detached large house. The furniture truck turned up the next morning and the contents were taken into the new house. Christmas happened a few days later by which time the house was semi functioning and there was a Christmas tree in the corner with presents stacked under it.

Just after Christmas his father turned up with a brand new car. The van had been replaced by a light blue Ford Cortina estate car. It was a company car and they did not directly own it.

Shortly after Christmas and the subsequent new year's party the boy started school for the very first time.....and thus began an eleven year nightmare.

He had never even been involved in a fight before and he got beaten up by older kids on his first day. He got shouted at by a teacher for running on the grass rather than staying within the confines of the tarmac covered playground and because he was made to wear shorts he was so cold that it was agony for him to be outside. When he got home he was so messed up from his horrible day that he accidentally broke a window when he ran one of his small toy cars down the banister of their new house. For this he was hit by his mother, shouted at and sent to bed. His sleep was full of nightmares and foul visions and his waking hours were not much better. How he hated school and his new environment. The people of the area were up tight and miserable, They weren't friendly and warm like the people of Worcestershire. There was a cold arrogant nastiness about them in this area....he got punished by his teacher but never knew for what or why. He tried to be good but was constantly being punished anyway. The nightmares continued every night and the horror of school continued every day. His mother had changed since they had moved into the house opposite her parents house. Often she was in grim moods and was constantly complaining about how horrible her mother was to her. . The mood in the house was not a happy one and certainly not for the boy. He was a child and resilient and so somehow got through it but never the less, the way that he was being treated filled him full of anger and rage and he longed for retribution. It was coming at him from all sides, from the other kids in the form of bullying and physical violence, from the teachers in the form of violent physical punishments and humiliation and at home from his parents in the form of shouting and beatings. Then at night, the horrible nightmares that were the projection of his horrible day. The people around him were ridiculous and nonsensical, they made a religion out of their petty rules and unwritten etiquette and were closed minded arrogant and pompous beyond belief. Yes he learned some stuff at school that was important, reading, writing and arithmetic for example, but always it had to be at their speed and never at the slower speed that was the best that he could work at. He was held out for ridicule in front of the class by certain teachers even when he was trying his very best. Certain other pupils then took it as a green light for bullying this smaller quieter boy.

He soon learned to fight back, his greatest ally and weapon being the blind fury of rage that he felt for anyone who would dare try and hurt him. Bigger and older children suffered when they tried it on. The boy did not know anything about rules involving fighting, anything was a weapon, all that mattered was to damage the opponent to the max and teach them to leave him alone. He got vilified for it but he messed up a lot of the bullies. He got scolded for what he had done to them but one thing was for sure, once they had fought with him they never came back for more. He became meaner and angrier as time passed on, yet still he tried to forgive. The parables and stories that the headmaster told during morning assembly had gone in and struck a note, but how he wished that those around him would wake up and wisen up.

It must have been in 1970 when he, his parents, his brother and a friend were on a summer camping vacation in central France when the big change happened. [It must have been 1970 because Mungo Jerry's "In the Summertime" and Credence Clearwater Revival's "Up Around the Bend" were the big favorites on the camp site juke box]. They were driving from the campsite to the local town when they encountered a procession. "What is it about?" the boy asked his mother and father. "It's a funeral" they replied. "What is a funeral?" This eight year old boy asked his mother. "Someone has died" his friend replied. "Does everyone die?" He asked once again "yes" they replied. "How long do people live for?" The boy asked his parents once more. "Maybe seventy or eighty years if you are lucky, some have even lived past one hundred" they answered "Then what happens after that?" He once again asked. "That's it, you are over and finished, nothing more" they replied. "That is not a very long time is it? I am already eight years old" he replied. "There has to be more to it than that otherwise what is the point?" "The religions all say that there is life after death but they are all deluded and cranky and untrustworthy. The Asians say that people live many lives and when one life finishes then you take birth again but we cannot be sure of any of this as there is no evidence" his mother explained.

On returning to England it was time for him to go back to school for the autumn term. The walk from the school to home was a distance of just under a mile. On the way there was a Catholic school with a Catholic church and behind it was a Catholic graveyard that was secluded in a tree shaded alley way. "There had to be something beyond death" he had concluded to himself. If he was going to find his answer then the best place to start would be the place where the bodies were buried.

On many afternoons after school he would go and sit in the graveyard among the head stones and crosses and see if there were any clues, any way of reaching across the divide. He would just sit there and contemplate death. Death scared him so the best way to deal with that was to face it head on and go and examine that which he feared and try to get to know it as best as possible and defeat the fear.

He became an avid reader of ghost stories and anything and everything about the unexplained. His dreams changed, yes there were still the horrible nightmares but now there were other curious dreams too. He saw himself in a muddy landscape full of poor but passive brown people, He saw himself wandering on a massive desert wilderness island that was covered in low bushes. So big was the island that he was wandering across it for days and there were very few people living there. He saw himself twice or more in a strange land riding in a narrow boat that was painted in bright colors. The people around him in the boat all had small heads and slant eyes and no one spoke to him. The place was very bright and warm and there were strange shaped buildings that were bright and painted in fantastic colors. Then there was the airport city where he saw himself flying in and out of on many occasions. And from there had been the hunt for the house of the golden dragon. The dreams were fantastic and technicolored, showing wonderful and strange places and his journeys in them. In other dreams he saw himself driving cars and trucks through massive expressway junctions, again in foreign lands. Meanwhile the nightmares were full of death, separation and great sadness and he saw things so real that they shook him.

At the age of nine his parents moved him to a different school, a private school and each day he had to take the train to get to the school that was some twelve miles away. There was something about many of the older teachers at this school that gave the boy the creeps. It was the way that they looked at the boys and the way that they behaved while all dressed up in the clothes of noble, respectable "ye olde England". Something just did not ring true. They seemed to get their jollies out of administering corporal punishment to the students. They would make up excuses to do it. They were a bunch of closet pedophiles. It was when one of the worst offenders brought his choir to the boy's village one Sunday when he saw his chance for retribution. Seeing his teacher's car in the church car park unattended he went and let the air out of one of the tires. He got caught by a local village man who reported him for it. The next day he was hauled up in front of the teacher who in a rage asked why he had done it. "because you are a sadist, you get your kicks out of administering corporal punishment, I let your tyre down to teach you a lesson" The boy replied "Why you ! how dare you, I could punish you right now, you should be careful what you say" the teacher threatened as he stood there red in the face, blustering and shaking with rage. But the boy just eyeballed him and stared him down and said "see what I mean? You prove me right". The teacher went from screaming red faced to a cowering shaking grey as the boy stared full rage and disgust at him. He had nowhere to go, his game had been named and now he was nervous and retreating. The boy had won that round.

It was at about this time that he asked his parents to move him to the local comprehensive school. It was 1973 and he was eleven years old. He hated the pompous snobs and the dodgy closet nonce teachers and sanctimonious headmaster at the private school. "I am paying your school fees and you will be staying at that school whether you like it or not" his father replied. "Right then, I will get myself thrown out, expelled if you won't move me voluntarily" the boy replied. And that he did.

His older friend was being picked upon by a fourteen year old whose father was obviously a good friend of the headmaster. The boy pulled him off and so he turned on him and attacked the boy instead. The boy gave him a taste of nasty down and dirty street fighting rather than the Queensbury rules bullshit that the snobs of the school expected. Later in the class the teacher had gone off to the toilet so the bigger kids from his class and the class above dragged the boy out to the toilet and made him face the bully in a fight. Once again his eyes glazed over and he turned incredible hulk as he let loose with full rage. He ran at the older boy, jumped up, grabbed his hair and pulled him over then lifted him off of the ground as he swung him around the room using his hair as the handle. The older boy was screaming and crying as the boy smashed his face into the toilet floor before holding him down in a headlock and attempting to gouge his eyes out with his nails.

The boy was dragged into the headmaster's study and was asked to explain himself. The boy explained that he had not started it and it had been self defence on his own part. "Don't ever let me see you in here again" the headmaster hissed at him. Outside of the door was a line of very nervous looking large black kids and at the end of the line the white fourteen year old bully who had started the whole problem. His face was gouged and bloody and he was still crying his eyes out, tears pouring down his face. The boy had inflicted the sort of pain on him that he had intended to. Served him right for picking on someone three years younger than himself but still the boy almost felt sorry for him as he stood there crying like a little girl after getting mangled by a boy three years his junior....sometimes the boy didn't know where his strength was coming from. He didn't want to be a bully but also he was not going to tolerate violence against himself...It was between that incident, facing down the closet pedo chemistry and maths teacher and vandalizing a British Rail train compartment on the way home that got him expelled but anyway, both he and the school were glad to see the back of each other and also he had taught his father a lesson regarding what was acceptable and what was not.

Now he was at the comprehensive which was far more relaxed. Like the difference between a highmax security prison and the most laid back of open prisons. It was still a prison but at least at this one there was space to breathe. The teachers were just normal people rather than a bunch of disgusting snob pedophiles hiding behind plummy accents, gouns and the ability to project arrogance. The facilities were good too and to add to this it was possible to leave the school grounds during the day to go to the shops. It was a mixed school and had some two thousand students attending it.

For four years everything went ok at this school until once more an angry bully wanted to start a fight. The boy had been enjoying the metalwork, technical drawing and woodwork classes, he was interested in both geography and history. In maths he could keep up and in other subjects he also could get by. He was enthusiastic and wanted to learn. He had taken up learning guitar and was most enthusiastic about that too. He had worked on the nursery during his school holidays, saved his wages and bought himself a second hand electric guitar, a red Hofner with two pickups and used to practice during his lunch breaks. It had taken huge persuasion to get his parents to let him learn guitar but eventually they relented and via a friend he was able to borrow a guitar to get started on and started attending lessons both at school and at home. He had also wanted to learn Karate but there was no way that he could persuade his parents to let him learn that, they point blank refused.

One day while on his way to the library another pupil blocked his way then kicked the boy when he swore at him…..once more the fight moved to the toilets and the boy just went berserk on him, grabbing him by the hair and ramming his face first into the wall and then the floor, kicking him and kneeing him as he went. He smashed the bully's face into the floor again and again until the bully was in tears and bloodied and then told the bully to leave him the hell alone….He went to the library to go research his homework but then a gang of other pupils came and dragged him out of the library while the librarian just looked on and did nothing. The bully wanted another fight and this time it was in the locker rooms. Once more the boy just went crazy and mangled his opponent until he was crying bitter tears of rage and pain. This time the boy just tried to make himself scarce, he did not want to be fighting, he just wanted to be left the fuck alone to research his homework. He went and hid in another part of the school but once more the so called friends of the bully hunted him down and dragged him out for another fight. This time they were holding his arms while the bully laid into him……..at this point something inside of him snapped and superstrength ran through his body. In one move he broke free of those who were holding him spread-eagled and with both hands in a flash he had grabbed the bully by the throat and squeezed hard until the bully made a horrible gargling sound and then fell limp to the floor. The boy was worried that he had killed the disgusting creature and so beat a hasty retreat looking for somewhere to get away from everyone. He made it to an area where he figured that he may be safe but then a mob of two hundred or more came running towards him and so he ran as fast as he could across the field in the direction of the staff room and offices as he figured that that would be his only place of safe refuge. One of them caught up with him and started punching and kicking as he ran so he grabbed him by the hair, held him down and ran along with this other kid screaming "let me go you bastard, let me go". The kid made a handy shield by which to keep the mob at bay. He made it into the offices and sought help from the staff room.

He explained his side of the story as did the other boy after he had been released from the medical room. The next day at the school there was a meeting and it was decided that because of the animosity towards him from other students he would have to stay away from school for two weeks. He had taken the other kid within half an inch of losing his life. However it had not been him that had started the whole damned thing so why the animosity towards him? and why was he the one being suspended? He was furious and disgusted. The teachers were cowards as were the mob that had tried to attack him. The only thing that he was sorry about was that he had not had a means of beating up, breaking the bones of or killing the whole mob at once. He did not even recognize half of the faces in it so why did they want to have a go at him?

Every weekend the boy worked for his father on the plant nursery in order to earn extra pocket money. It was at this time at the age of fourteen he began to find pubs where he could get served. Places with alcoholic landlords and a crowd of adults that didn't seem to mind his company. He had had enough of both home and school and needed somewhere to escape from both. All respect for the system was now out of the door. What did qualifications matter when they were dished out by such degenerate pieces of shit?.....what did they think he was? Some kind of performing animal at the circus? He wasn't there to prove himself or perform tricks for them, they could all go fuck off.

Soon he was starting to get up in the early hours of the morning to sneak out of his bedroom window and slip off into the darkness to go break into a school, a pub that wouldn't serve him, shops, businesses whatever. The whole system and the society that sustained it were his enemies, they had unjustly imprisoned him for nine years of his life, they had tortured him, they had forced him to fight and then vilified him when he won. They obviously wanted him to be their victim and were angry that he refused to lie down and play the role. Even if he couldn't find anything to steal he could still have a go at them by vandalizing their property.

Fuck did he hate them, all of them, there were no allies just useful acquaintances but no true friends. He had to watch them all, they would all do him down given half a chance. Every burglary was personal, not against the individual but against the system and society at large. He was furious and disgusted by them all. His alcohol intake was on average four pints a night and even for his age he was by no means a big kid.

Every school holiday he would work full time on the nursery business of his family, saving his money up for things that he wanted. Now all that he wanted was beer, whiskey and money for the juke box and pool table. The pub was the best place to help him to forget his sorrows, rage and anger. He was around mature people who were OK with him. At his favorite pub, the one that he could always get served at, the music in the juke box was his favorite with bands such as ELO, Slade, the Small Faces, and Boz Scaggs blaring out as they played pool. He was the only under 18 in the place but for some reason they didn't seem to mind him being there. He had balls just to go in there and try it at his age and he listened to the older folk in order to learn.

One of the workers on the nursery had a weekend job in the local market that paid handsomely and told the boy that there were more jobs going if he was prepared to get up early on a Sunday morning and peddle over there on his bicycle. It was some five or six miles from his house.

Soon the boy was working the market and putting an extra wad of cash in his back pocket every week. Eight pounds may sound like nothing today but back then a pint of Ind Coope bitter would cost 22p and a packet of cigarettes was less than 50p. Food was super cheap and combined with the meager amount that he earned on the nursery [£2.20] on a Saturday morning he had the means to pay for his drinking and smoking.

It was in his final year of school that Punk hit the scene. The music in the pub jukebox changed, now it was the The Jam, The Stranglers, Eddie and the Hot Rods, Space, John Michelle Jarre, Souxie and the Banshees and the Sex Pistols. At School things had taken a turn for the worse once more and the boy was hanging out with a gang that would skip off of school and go hang out down at the amusement park on the sea front on most days. Punk fashion was all the rage at school and kids were going around with safety pins through their ears, torn shirts and all manner of other bizarre attire. Fights were breaking out all over the place and the school was half way to a state of anarchy. The burglaries continued and he continued to hate everything around him, especially being at school. One day he got threatened by another pupil who was a bit of a gangster and he just got on his bike and cycled off. If he got into a fight he would need to pretty much kill the other kid and he remembered what happened the last time that he did that. The school had phoned his parents that he was missing and when he got home he just said "I am not going back there and no one is going to make me, I have had enough"

The school had no problem with him coming back but he did not want to, he had had enough of the fighting and bullying. It was only the drinking, the time out at the pub and playing his guitar that was holding him together. He longed to be working full time, school just disgusted him and he despised it and all that it seemed to stand for.

His parents sent him to a boarding school some forty miles away and he hated that place even more. He got caught by one of the staff when he returned back from an evening down the pub. The man shouted at him and told him how much trouble he would get him into in the morning and tried to belittle him.

Some Ten minutes later in the staff house where live in teachers stayed, it took no less than six staff members to hold the boy down when he launched himself at the staff member who had threatened him. He was swinging a six foot long log at the man's head and was in a state of full fury. He had had enough, the dog was off of the leash, all power trippers were fair game and the maximum damage that could be done to them the better. The staff member escaped unhurt but certainly not unshaken. It was probably the first time that he had experienced someone trying to kill him. He never once caused trouble for the boy again.

At the weekends the boy would come home from school and work the nursery and the market. He hated school but was supposed to be taking O level exams. His hatred of the system was such that he just didn't give a shit. The only reason that he had agreed to take them was as so that if he did pass then at least he could wipe his arse on the certificates and hand them back and tell them all to Go Fuck Themselves with their silly pieces of paper and their systems of judgment.

As it was he got drunk during the lunch break while taking his English O level and so didn't even need to worry about using such course toilet paper in order to voice his opinion of the system and it's adherents.

The day that he left school was by far the happiest day of his life up until that point. How he had loathed and despised his incarceration, The violence and hatred he felt towards his incarcerators was beyond imagining. By the time that he finally left school he was ready to explode. He would have burned the school buildings to the ground if he thought that he could find a way of getting away with it. These arseholes had stolen eleven precious years of his life. Not just that but people had told him that he would be a failure because he had left school with none of their precious qualifications. Well fuck them!, the boy would prove them wrong.

He went straight to work for his father and was most pleased with his first wage packet containing twenty four pounds. It was the most money that he had ever held in his hand at one time. Getting served in the pubs was now no longer a problem and he enjoyed his evenings drinking and watching live bands play. His mother came home one evening with a load of pamphlets from the local college of further education, telling him "just because school didn't work for you it doesn't mean that you cannot get an education" The boy replied "after what I have seen of the system, I want nothing more to do with it, I hate it, it disgusts me, I have zero respect for it and it has already stolen enough of my time, it can go fuck it's self" He then took the pamphlets, ripped them to pieces and threw them in the bin.

Bob Dylan was coming to play a festival at Blackbush airfield near London so Gypsy and the friend who had got him the market job went along to see him play. The day started with a reggae band called Merger then progressed to a very sleek and good sounding German band called Lake. They sounded like a cross between Supertramp and Genesis and were very smooth but with catchy riffs and good words. Then it was Graham Parker and the Rumor playing songs like Hey Lord Don't Ask Me Questions and Tear Your Playhouse Down. Then it was Eric Clapton and his Band followed by Joan Armatrading and then Bob Dylan playing an all electric set. Gypsy and his friend were right down at the front in a field with tens of thousands of people in it. While Dylan was playing they were able to slip through security and into the press area where they got to hang out at the bar. Dylan played an all rocking version of his earlier songs along with tracks from his latest album, "Street Legal".

During the early autumn the family were going to be taking a package holiday to Ibiza and Gypsy was invited. A package holiday in a hotel instead of the tedious camping trips to France that he had had to endure during his school years sounded like just the ticket. His parents left him alone to do his own thing and they were in a comfy hotel with a large swimming pool right next to the beach where buffet meals were served at set times. There were discos and bars, horse riding and much fun to be had. It was on this holiday that the boy resolved that he wanted to live in hot countries with palm trees and nice beaches.

Through the autumn a whole program of top bands were going to be playing the two largest venues in Brighton. The Boy made it to see 10cc, Eric Clapton with Muddy Waters, Frank Zappa, Bad Company, Wishbone Ash, Uria Heep, Rod Stewart and Thin Lizzy. Then through the spring he went and to see Fairport Convention with Bert Jansch playing support, followed by Rory Gallagher, The Squeeze, the Tubes and Steeleye Span on subsequent weeks. It was through the early Autumn that he first got turned onto the wonders of hashish and weed. He had got one of the guitarists in a local folk band to teach him some more guitar and at his house he had been offered a hit on a joint but had to decline the opportunity to try it as he had an evening job collecting used glasses and stacking the machine in the pub where the band played and he didn't want to be out of it at work. His weekend piss ups had reached epic proportions and he was too drunk to do anything after a Friday or Saturday night of it. Then one weekend some hippies from London had come down to camp at the local farm run campsite and they had a large bag of weed and some hashish. They invited the boy to come and join them for a smoke at their tent.

After the pub had closed they headed over the hill carrying half gallon take out cans of Watney's Red Barrel. Soon all nine of them were sat in the tiny tent as joints were busily skinned up and cans of beer opened and passed around. It was his first taste of hashish and he smoked a whole load before staggering off home where he spent a good half hour throwing up. It wasn't the hash or weed that he had smoked but the ten pints of larger that he had consumed at the pub along with six double whiskeys.

In the early spring his maternal grandfather had returned from a trip to Israel with an invitation from a distant cousin for the boy who was fast becoming a man to go and live and work on the kibbutz were he and his wife lived. The young man jumped at the opportunity and readily accepted the invitation. It was the spring of 1979 and the Young man had just turned seventeen. A date in early October was set and the boy's parents bought him a return on El Al from London to Tel Aviv. Meanwhile the young man saved what money he could. He bought himself a cheap but robust and reasonably good sounding folk guitar and a few other things that he figured that he would need. In the early summer he made it to his first three day music festival, the Glastonbury fair. Tickets were priced at five pounds and the event was being organized to raise money for the Unicef year of the child. Acts included Steve Hillage, Sky, Dennis Brown, John Martyn, Ovni, Nick Turner's Sphinx, the Leyton Buzzards and Peter Gabriel and Friends [including a very drunk Alex Harvey, Tom Robinson, Joe Partridge from Cockney Rebel, Steve Hillage and Nona Hendrix from La Belle Epoch]. The final act was an obscure synthesizer player called Tim Blake [it took the young man a couple of years to find out who he was and even longer to find any music by him] He played weird songs and had a fantastic laser show shimmering above the audience just for extra effect. His was an incredible and mind blowing act and the young man just stood and stared in wonder at what he was seeing. The act had started just after midnight and ran until two in the morning. He played songs such as Return to Crystal Island, Generator and Crystal machine and his synthesizer music sounded like it came from outer space or some weird distant planet.

The atmosphere at the festival was incredible, the most of the food was home made or made on hippie communes, there was an incredible area for kids with a giant inflatable psychedelic maze for them to play in and all sorts of other amusements for them. There were marquees with acts going on inside of them and also those who had not brought tents could sleep in them. The stage had a giant inflatable pillow shape held up on metal stands as it's roof. There was a general feeling of good will between people and it was a very uplifting feeling being there. This was also where the young man tried hashish for the second time and decided that he liked it.

Then after this a new friend from Germany came to stay for a month and work on the nursery. Barbara was from Essen in the Ruhr area. She was sixteen years old, she was beautiful and she was both very mature and very intelligent for her years. She liked the same music as the young man and also knew the alternative culture well. Things obviously were very different in Germany, this was not the first German that he had met and immediately taken a liking to. Children were obviously treated very differently in Germany from how they were treated in England. They seemed to grow up confident, non violent and well adjusted as opposed to either yobbish or snobbish with a severe attitude problem, violent malevolent tendencies and an ignorance of world affairs that they wore as a badge of honor, as they did in England.

The month that Barbara stayed for passed in a flash and then she was gone. She was just a friend but the young man had wished it could have gone further. She had a boyfriend back in Germany and so there was not much of a chance but none the less he really enjoyed her company.

The next big event on the summer schedule was the Knebworth Festival which Led Zepplin were headlining. They had Chas and Dave, Fairport Convention, Southside Jonny and the Aylsbury Dukes,

Commander Cody and Tod Rungrendt as support. The festival was just a one day event. There was none of the same atmosphere that had been at Glastonbury at the camp site and in the arena the next day it was an over organized and hemmed in feel that the place had about it. It was a not so pleasant vibe with not so pleasant food available. It was all about the money and nothing more. Never the less Led Zepplin put on a good performance even if Robert Plant did lose his voice on the last verse of Stairway to Heaven. Whole lotta love came out good and Jimmy page used his bow on the guitar on Nobody's fault but mine.

Gypsy worked on through the summer saving his money for his big trip, it would not be long until he was on his way to Israel. His mother, his uncle and his maternal grandparents had all told him stories about when they had either traveled or lived there.

The trip to Ibiza had given him the taste for sun sand and palm trees, he figured that he was going to like it, it had to be better than the life he led in England. The limits and social constraints of the time were totally suffocating. He was considered a subversive because he wore hippie clothes and smoked weed. Punk had been a reaction to the bullshit and at the time was in full swing. The hippies had been picked on and treated as rejects so here was punk just to show them how fucked up people can make themselves look if you are against people for just being a little bit different. The elections came in the summer of 1979 and the dumb populace went and voted for the monstrous Margaret Thatcher. The young man was too young to vote but he knew that he would never have voted Tory and certainly not with that horrible creature at the helm. The next night in the pub the others were all slagging off labor and singing the praises of Mrs Thatcher. The young man up until that point had no idea that people could be so collectively stupid. "You will regret it" he warned them. "She is no friend of the working classes, many of you will find yourselves out of a job, especially if she does what she said that she is going to do". They poo pooed him at the time but a few years later they would all be singing a very different song.

October was drawing ever closer and the young man was starting to pack his back pack in anticipation.

VOL 1

– ISRAEL

CHAPTER 1

His Father and Mother and two friends were in the car with him when they parked on the roof of the car park for Terminal 3 at Heathrow airport. Across the roof of the terminal he could see the tail fins of the jets, one stuck out in particular. The spiked tail of a Boeing 707 with a blue six point star painted on the top. He knew that this was the EL AL jet that would take him to Tel Aviv. He had never set foot outside of Northern Europe before this point and here he was, seventeen years old and off on his first big adventure to another continent and alone. Even those that he was going to be staying with were strangers to him even if they were all part of his big extended family.

He checked in and said goodbye to his parents and two friends and went through security, finding his way through the labyrinth of tunnels to his flight, knowing deep inside that nothing could or would be the same after this trip.

ISRAEL:

He along with the other passengers boarded the Boeing 707 and found their seats. The plane was dull and gray on the inside with designs featuring illustrations of ancient ruins in the holy land. He was somewhat disappointed that the plane was not a 747 with it's double gangway and ample space, but never mind, the most important thing was that he was starting his first journey alone to a part of the world where he had never set foot before.

A short while later the plane was pushed back and after a few minutes when the coupling had been taken away they started to Taxi out towards the runway to join the queue of other planes waiting to take off. After a line of other planes had taken off in front of them including several 747s and a Concorde it was their turn. The jet turned onto the runway, gunned it's engines and they were off. As the plane took off he felt a rush of exhilaration, no doubt similar to the exhilaration felt by a prisoner on a long sentence as he escapes from prison. It felt unbelievably good to be leaving England and all of the misery that that place had delivered upon him. He was looking forward to his new life abroad and was determined to make it work in Israel as so that he could stay out of England permanently. He had heard so many stories about Israel from his mother and grandparents, it sounded like it must be a pretty incredible place. It had been built out of the ashes of the world's worst known holocaust by supposedly the most intelligent people on earth, a people that he was one of.

The flight lasted four and a half hours. It in itself was nothing special but when the plane started to descend over the Mediterranean and he could see the coast of Israel, he felt excited. The plane flew low over Tel Aviv and he could see the lights of Jaffa off to his right. As the plane descended ever lower he could see cars buses and trucks on floodlit highways just beneath him. The plane touched down at Ben Gurion airport at Lod just outside of Tel Aviv.

As he stepped out into the warm night air and descended the steps onto the concrete below he hoped that maybe this country would be his new home. There were many jets parked on the apron but no air bridges, so they were bused to the terminal. There were many lines waiting to clear immigration and the place had a somewhat hectic and chaotic feel about it. They were in a high ceilinged modern glass and concrete hall. Customs was certainly not chaotic, they were checking everyone but quickly, they seemed to have it down to a fine art.

Having cleared passport control, collected his bags and cleared customs he stepped outside to find a scrum of grubby taxi drivers trying to hustle a ride. Having got past them, he looked until he saw a man holding a sign with his name on it "That must be my cousin", Gypsy thought to himself as he walked towards him. His cousin, a slim man in his sixties with a balding head and glasses could only speak German and Hebrew but his wife, Ora, a short and somewhat roundish woman spoke fluent English and did all of the translating.

They had another man from the kibbutz as their driver, a large Romanian fellow in his late fifties with gray hair. The air was warm and the sound of crickets was coming from all around as they drove north along the Israeli coast. It was all new to him and he didn't have a clue as to where he was but it felt good to be in a warm climate and he liked the smell and feel of the place already. Forty five minutes later they were at the kibbutz.

He stayed the first two nights in the small house of Ora and Yackob as he got acclimatized to the place and got to know a little of it's ways. They told him how things worked on the kibbutz and then over the next few days at Gypsy's request they told of their terrible experiences of Auschwitz death camp. Yackob and his mother had escaped at the beginning of the second world war by bribing a guard and disappearing off into the night. They had then made their way overland to a port on the coast of the Mediterranean Sea from where they boarded a clandestine refugee boat that took them to the shores of what was then British controlled Palestine. They were then landed in small boats on a beach in the dead of night and quickly taken and hidden on a kibbutz. The British were then in the habit of both deporting Jews back to Nazi occupied lands and blowing boats full of helpless refugees out of the water.

Ora's story was different. She had been found by the allies when they liberated the Auschwitz death camp. She was in the biological experiment wing, she had been operated and experimented upon by Hur Mengele and associates and as a result she could never have children of her own.

She had since become a vegetarian and worked with troubled children trying to help them on their way. Her disgust of Germany and what they had done to her was such that she said she would never speak that language again even though it was her mother tongue. "you cannot begin to imagine what it was like in that place" she said "it was indescribable, you could not believe that human beings could do anything so horrible. Because of this I will never speak the German language again, Yackob does but then his experiences were not the same". They had adopted two orphaned boys on the kibbutz who were now both fully grown and lived elsewhere. The older of the two of them had been a tank commander during the 1973 Yom Kippur War. Twice in one day, the tank that he was commanding was hit and blown up by enemy fire. In both of these disasters, he was the only survivor. After such bizarre and devastating experiences he got religion.

Becoming an ultra Orthodox Jew, he moved to a settlement on the West Bank.

The younger adopted son was working and living outside of the kibbutz, somewhere on the narrow coastal plain between Tel Aviv and Haifa.

Yackob elderly mother also lived on the kibbutz and though she was ninety two years old, she still went to work every day. She managed the kibbutz library and obviously only worked because she enjoyed being active. It was hard to imagine this frail old lady on the run across Europe escaping from the Nazis but she must have been tough, clever and lucky to have made it and then to have lived so long after as well.

The kibbutz consisted primarily of a village area with amenities within it, it also housed small, light industry. Then there were the farmland areas that it owned and which provided the bulk of it's income. The village sat high on top of a rocky hill, an ideal defensive position (which in Israel was imperative given the terrorist situation). At the bottom of the hill, first came the north south coastal road then the kibbutz land which stretched to the Mediterranean Sea some three to four kilometers away. The train lines and Tel Aviv to Haifa motorway crossed through the kibbutz land about 1 km before the beach. Tunnels under the rail lines and motorway kept the kibbutz lands connected.

The agricultural area included turkey farms, fish farms, banana and nut plantations, oranges, cut flowers, cotton etc. The farmland was laid out in large rectangles and was quite substantial in size and it was well mechanized too, with latest state of the art equipment.

In the communal and residential area of the kibbutz, there were immaculately kept gardens, a large swimming pool and a gymnasium, also there was a very large and smart looking building with large windows giving views of the coast and farmland below. This building housed the kitchens and a huge dining hall upstairs with a large movie theater, rest rooms and public showers below.

Married couples had their own small bungalows to live in, complete with a bedroom, living room bathroom and kitchenette. Singles would have a studio apartment. They did not need to cook for themselves as there were three buffet meals served up every day in the dinning hall, the kitchenettes were just for some extra luxury. From a young age the children of the kibbutz would live in special children's houses and only see their parents for a few hours each afternoon. This may seem like a strange and cold practice to some but it originated from when Israel was under serious attack from both Arab nations and terrorists. During such an attack the children would be kept together within the strongest, most fortified structure within the kibbutz, while the adults went out to do the fighting and defending. It still operated in much that same way at the time that is being written about. Terrorist attacks against civilians, including women and children were not at all uncommon in Israel in nineteen seventy nine. The kibbutzim of Israel were the only true to the letter form of Marxist communism in the world and unlike in the Soviet Union or any of the other iron curtain countries it worked well, but only because it only ran on a small scale.

With the typical kibbutz having a population of between five hundred and two and a half thousand people it was relatively easy to get the ear of the chief, if there was any sort of problem. In addition to this no one would be the chief of the kibbutz for more than one year, after which time he or she would have to go and work in the kitchens, washing dishes for one year to bring them back down to earth after having such a high profile job. Everyone who was a member of the kibbutz had not just a vote on anything major that was to be done, e,g, expansion of one commercial department, how to spend kibbutz profits, where to situate the swimming pool etc but would get an equal share of the spoils from the commerce that the kibbutz engaged in with the world outside of it's gates. As the people of the kibbutz liked to handle money as little as possible, on years when the profits had been good each member would get either a new color television or a high fi stereo or maybe even a two week holiday in Europe, complete with spending money etc. At other times, the profits would be put into leisure facilities that they could all use and enjoy but each time the decision would be voted upon by all members.

The first kibbutz was established by Russian Jews, who purchased land from the local Palestinians on the shores of the Sea of Galilee, in the year eighteen seventy nine. Due to their limited financial resources they pooled together in order to be able to farm and to feed themselves. Many of them were well educated and had read the ideas of Carl Marx and decided to give it a try at living as communists. It worked well for them and soon others were giving it a serious go too and kibbutzim were springing up throughout Palestine. It proved to be an effective model for bringing people up out of poverty. During and after the Second World War many refugees from the Nazi occupied regions turned up on the shores of Palestine with nothing but the clothes on their back. Many of them settled on kibbutzim and many new ones were formed at that time. With their own small micro welfare system on site, many lives were saved and the lot of all was improved rapidly. Each got according to their needs rather than according to how hard that they had worked. Of course there were always some lazy bastards who never pulled their weight, but for the most part people worked hard and generally enjoyed their work. If a member left the kibbutz, just like a share holder in a company, they would get given what was viewed as their stake in the kibbutz, in cash. Depending how many years they had lived there would determine what their stake was. Some who left would go to another kibbutz and live there for a couple of years, after which there would be a vote by the members of that kibbutz as to whether to accept them as a full member. Others would just go their own way and do their own thing, but on the whole the kibbutzniks were an insular lot and preferred the kibbutz way of life over life in the rat race outside of their gates. At the entrance to the village was a large car park and off from that, was a light industrial unit making rubber molds and lenses for glasses. Up a slight rise from there were the huts where the volunteers stayed. Kibbutz volunteers could be from anywhere and didn't need to be Jewish to participate, but many were. Anyone from eighteen to thirty five years old, who wished, could go to the kibbutz agency in Tel Aviv and get a placement on a kibbutz, where they would live and work as part of the community. Unlike a kibbutz member, they had no claim to a share of the place, but in return for working would get food, accommodation, free use of swimming pool, Movie Theater, etc plus some pocket money to buy essentials.

Further up the rise were three military style dorm blocks, each of them three storeys high, where people participating in a program called ULPAN stayed.

ULPAN was a set up to teach Hebrew to young people from foreign countries. They would work in the mornings and study Hebrew in the afternoons, the course was run on some of the other kibbutzim too.

After two days, Gypsy moved into the volunteer quarters which were in long wooden buildings on a lawn with shared bathroom facilities in a brick building at the end of the lawn. He was put sharing a room with an American Jewish fellow called Mike. He was from Sacramento and was in Israel, like Gypsy to check out his Jewish roots. He was a likable fellow in his mid thirties. He had a good sense of humor and made many dry remarks about what he witnessed around him. Also he liked the same sort of music as Gypsy and introduced him to the music of groups that Gypsy had not yet heard of. Gypsy at that time had never even heard of Sacramento and was surprised to be told that it was the capital city of California and was home to a famous university. So Mike told him about the place that he was from and what life was like there. From what he described, California sounded like a pretty amazing place to live, what with the good weather and the easy going lifestyle it sounded like it was a hell of a lot nicer to live in than England.

Gypsy's first job was working in the turkey farm cleaning and washing cages and other handling equipment. The other workers were friendly enough and he enjoyed working with them. For the first two weeks he worked in a shed doing the cleaning work, cleaning cages and feeding boxes. There was an old man who also worked there. He worked growing Stralitzia [bird of paradise] flowers and preparing them for market. He was talkative and told Gypsy about how he had escaped from Nazi Germany just before World War II. He had made it to England, where he had joined the Jewish Brigade of the British Army, fighting the Nazis. "After what they had done to us and our families," he said, "we didn't take prisoners, they could come out with their white flags and hands up but we would just kill them anyway, Just as they would have done to us, we gave them a taste of their own medicine."

He told Gypsy how most of the older members of the kibbutz were German Jews who had either escaped or survived the death camps, which helped to explain why Ora and Yackob felt so at home at this particular kibbutz. They had lived at one or two other kibbutzim before they had arrived at this particular one. They had at this time been full members for many years.

Also like Ora and Yackob had done, he told Gypsy how the people of this particular kibbutz had had to drain a swamp, which was located where the farm lands were presently. Many of them had died of malaria as they toiled and labored by hand, digging drainage ditches and planting Eucalyptus shoots [Eucalyptus puts down long roots quickly, thus stabilizing the ground, also they drink a lot of water and grow very quickly]. The land that the kibbutz was on had never been inhabited by Palestinians, as none of them had wanted to either live in the swamp or on the rocky hilltop above it. However that did not mean that they were safe from terrorist attacks and as such each morning at six o'clock when Gypsy went to work he saw military jeeps with large caliber machine guns mounted on them driving in from the beach. They were there every night and throughout the night, watching the coast, to make sure that no terrorists sneaked ashore in dinghies or wet suits. It was a serious problem and had happened before on other parts of the coast.   Two days after arriving in the volunteer quarters another American volunteer arrived. Kenny from New York, Kenny had been married to a Jewish woman from England and had been living in London for the past five years until she had walked out on him and asked for a divorce, ten days previously.

Despondent and not knowing what to do, he had jumped on a plane to Tel Aviv with what little money he had and went to the kibbutz office, from where he got placed at that particular kibbutz.

Kenny was a short heavy set man, who liked to talk a lot. Gypsy liked listening to his stories. He told Gypsy about his time in Vietnam as a conscript in the American Army. About being shot at and losing friends in action, etc. he told about one time when he had been out on patrol and ten of them had gone out but only four returned. He told about being shot at while putting telegraph wires up in the Saigon area. He also told Gypsy about how a few years after leaving the army he had been in Amsterdam and had bought himself for a couple of hundred dollars a ticket for a bus called "the Magical Mystery tour". It had slowly wound it's way through Europe, the Middle East and India before ending up in Kathmandu. He spoke about how life was in India and Nepal, this was when Gypsy first decided that he wanted to make a journey to India. Kenny's description of India had Gypsy totally intrigued, arousing the curiosity in him to go exploring.

After a week on the kibbutz, Ora and Yackob invited Gypsy for a trip to the West Bank to see their elder adoptive son on the settlement. His wife had just had a baby and they were going for the Brit Mila (circumcision) ceremony.

And so, Ora, Yakob, Gypsy and other friends and well wishers set out from the kibbutz in a minibus. First they drove along the coast road before joining the Tel Aviv Jerusalem highway. As they drove up through the Wadis, there were the remnants of burned out tanks and trucks by the sides of the road, twisted and mutilated from explosions and gun fire. "Those vehicles you see are from the 1948 War of Independence," Ora explained. "They have been left there as a monument to those who died trying to get supplies through to Jerusalem, in that war."

As the road climbed further, up through valleys of cypress trees, Gypsy began to see why it had been such a deadly corridor for the trucks, what with both hills and forests for the enemy to hide within.

As they passed through Jerusalem Gypsy caught a brief view of the old city and its famous gold domed mosque before the mini bus rounded a corner and travelled on into the West Bank. The land was barren and dry and there was a lot of military presence. They passed by the occasional Arab village on the modern and new road that they were on, but for the most part the view was of barren looking rocky ground and hills.

The settlement was a rocky barren area on top of a hill with high fences, watch towers and armed guards.

The settlers weren't welcome there by the locals, who were Palestinian and attacks were not uncommon. Inside the fence were newly laid roads and rows of mobile homes. The only stone building on the site was a Beit Knesset (Synagogue). Gypsy asked them what the plan was. They told him that they planned to build a town there. Although he did not agree that it was a good idea to colonize the West Bank, he had to admire their courage in taking on such a feat. These were very brave people, maybe misguided, maybe pigheaded, maybe chauvinistic, but certainly brave.

The ceremony was held in the Beit Knesset followed by the usual food and drinks. This being done outside as there was nowhere else to do it. Then in the late afternoon, they started the three hour journey home to the kibbutz.

Back at the kibbutz, Kenny and Gypsy were getting restless with no dope to smoke, as alcohol was not their favorite drug. One Friday night they made their way down the 1 km road to the coastal highway. From there, they flagged down a sheroot (collective taxi) to Akko, an Arab town north from Haifa. They spent the next several hours in Arab cafes and coffee houses, in dingy unlit alleys, trying to score the elusive weed, but all to no avail, it just was not happening that night. It was Gypsy's first experience of an Arab town and what with it being at night and with what they were trying to do, there was a bit of a threatening feel to the place. Dejected, they returned to the kibbutz, where they drank away their sorrows with a bottle of Israeli vodka.

Gypsy's grandfather had told him about his own time in that area when it was British controlled Palestine. He and two friends had taken the train across Europe to Genoa. From there they took a steamer to Jaffa and from Tel Aviv, which was only four streets at that time they headed north along the coast, looking for land to buy. The coastal strip was sparsely populated at that time, as it was either desert or swamp and not easy to farm. However it did have a good annual rainfall, so the three of them purchased a piece of barren sandy desert land from local Palestinian Arabs, near to the present day Israeli town of Hadera, which is more or less half way between Tel Aviv and Haifa. There, after drilling a borehole for water, they set about planting an orange, grove. They built a house for themselves and another for their workers. Gypsy's grandfather had stayed there from 1922 until some time in the mid 1930's, when parts of the local Palestinian population rose up and started using violence against the Jewish settlers. By that time he had a wife and young son [Gypsy's uncle], and not feeling that he could put their lives in danger, he moved them to England, where with help from his father, he set up a plant nursery. One of his partners had died but the other was alive and well and lived with his wife in a house, close by to the orange grove. An Israeli village had sprouted up next to the orange grove and Sam and Dina had their house in the village.

After a few weeks of working on the kibbutz, Gypsy took a day off to go and look up Sam and Dina. Their village was not so far from the kibbutz so Gypsy took a local bus. The village was small and it didn't take him long to find their house, from the directions his grandfather had given him. It was a small modest bungalow on a sleepy side road, lined with tall bushy trees that provided shade.

Dina was a tiny, slim red headed woman. She welcomed gypsy into their home and told Gypsy about the old times when his grandfather was there.

Sam arrived, sometime later and gave Gypsy a warm welcome, before telling Gypsy more tales from the early days, when his grandfather and the other friend and partner, Kaufman, had lived and worked there. There had been one time, when his grandfather had been worrying about one of the saplings that was not growing properly and asked the others what they thought about it, to which Kaufman had replied "of course it's not growing properly Jack, you keep walking around it and worrying about it all the time, you don't realize it but this is squashing the roots of the poor plant".

Gypsy's grandfather was a good soul with a good sense of humor and a heart full of compassion for even the most humble of life forms, but he worried and sometimes took things too seriously. He must have been at his best, when he was with Sam and Kaufman with them making sure that he did not take himself so seriously.

Sam was old but he was a giant of a man and fit, from his many years of working in his orange grove. He spoke slowly and had wisdom about him from the many experiences that he had lived through. He had fought in the war of independence and been there during the revolt against British rule. Since then he had seen many more wars and terrorist atrocities. However both he and his wife were still there, and their son too, they were survivors. Sam suggested that Gypsy take a walk along the lane and go and see the orange grove and the house that his grandfather had built.

So Gypsy wandered down the lane to the orange grove. His grandfather had shown him old black and white photos of the land, just after they had bought it and it was just sandy desert. So imagine Gypsy's surprise when he turned the corner and looked down a sloped dirt lane and there was a lush orange grove with large, mature and healthy looking trees that were full of fruit. There in the center of the orange grove, stood the ruins of the two houses that Sam, Kauffman and his grandfather had built, back in the nineteen twenties. The house that they had lived in, had a watch tower built into the roof, with gun slits in it. Both buildings were still standing, though the roof had collapsed on the house that was the workers quarters. They had apparently been abandoned for a long time and were over grown with local indigenous flora including bramble bushes.

Back at Sam and Dina's bungalow, sitting under the large porch in the afternoon heat, Sam explained how the watch tower had been necessary in the early days as settlers were sometimes attacked at night in their houses by wandering local bandits. But he pointed to a cot on the porch and explained that his Palestinian workers had given it as a present when their son was born, they had made it themselves. Sam obviously had no problem in getting along with the local Arabs and knew them as friends. He was a big man with wavy grey hair and a thick Hebrew/ Eastern European accent. He had seen and done a lot in his life and as such life no longer held any illusions for him. He was a happy and contented man, proud of what he had achieved with his life. He invited Gypsy for a tour of the fruit processing and marketing cooperative that he had helped to form, in conjunction with other local citrus growers. His son, Dodi was the manager of the processing and packaging plant, where the fruit was graded and packed accordingly.

13

The plant was set up inside a large industrial building and was almost totally automated. It was an impressive sight, with thousands, if not millions of oranges rolling along multiple conveyor belts, being stamped with the famous Jaffa stamp, before being auto graded and packed. Sam and his son were obviously very proud of what they had achieved with the cooperative.

After a meal back at the bungalow with Sam and Dina, Gypsy took a bus back to the kibbutz, happy with his day of discovery, proud to know that his own family had played a part in the creation of this incredible country.

Back at the kibbutz, Kenny had finally found some hash, so they found a quiet place to smoke it, while Gypsy told him about his day, and Kenny told Gypsy about how he used to deal hash in Germany before he got busted with two kilos of the stuff and ended up locked up in a German prison, for eighteen months. Kenny had lived a somewhat active life for his thirty one years and Gypsy was all ears when he would start talking of his past. He had grown up in Spanish Harlem, New York. "When my family moved there, the first thing that happened, was that the local street gang came to my door to check me out," he said. "So I handled it in the only way possible, for a long term good result. I walked up to the biggest one there and kicked him as hard as I could in the balls. They kicked the shit out of me for that, but I'd earned their respect and they weren't going to fuck with me in the future. In fact they invited me to join the gang, which I did, it was the only way to survive in a place like that."

Kenny explained how when he was eighteen years old he got drafted into the U.S. army and sent to Vietnam. He was a telecommunications specialist and would carry the radio, when they went on patrol. "We got shot at regularly and I lost friends in action. Sometimes we would get sent out on patrol and we would come back with less people than we started with. The hardest part of it was not only seeing someone getting killed in front of you, but that that person was your friend that you would drink and smoke weed with and you couldn't do anything to help him," said Kenny. (Kenny would often wake up in the night screaming from nightmares he had about the war). After the Army, he worked to save some money, and then travelled to Amsterdam, from where he bought his ticket on "The Magical Mystery Tour". The bus had ended up in Kathmandu before returning to Europe.

This is what he liked talking about the most, Gypsy was so intrigued about India and Nepal and especially the descriptions that Kenny gave of

Kathmandu. He had also seen one or two programs on television about the mountains of Nepal, while in England and so it was at this point that he made up his mind that he also would make this trip someday.

On some of his days off from work on the kibbutz, Gypsy would take the bus into Tel Aviv or Haifa and get to know his way around by walking everywhere, rather than using buses through the city streets. Haifa, he found rather boring compared with Tel Aviv, even though it was a more attractive place, with hills and large gardens. It also was the world centre of the Baha'i faith. The Baha'i religion originated in Iran several hundred years ago and is entirely peaceful and benign. On the side of one of the hills of Haifa are the Baha'i gardens with a shrine in the center.

Back at the kibbutz, he had managed to get a change of job (the foul smell of turkey shit and dead birds was getting to be too much to put up with) and now he worked with the gardening crew, up in the village.

He got on well with Haim, the boss. Haim loved plants and gardens. He spoke perfect English with an educated London accent and told Gypsy about his times in England, while serving in the British Army during World War II. He had been another German volunteer for the Jewish Brigade. He liked England and this was where he learned to enjoy gardening. He was also grateful to England for giving him the chance to fight Germans and avenge his murdered family. Having said this, Haim was a very kind and gentle man, a warm compassionate and quiet person. It was hard to imagine that he had been a soldier in both the British and Israeli Army and that he had probably killed many people.

Gypsy enjoyed working in the gardens, he liked the others that he worked with. They were more quiet and less arrogant and egotistical than many of the others and there were never disputes between them. In fact the only one who would ever get upset, was Haim's Basset Hound "Pico", who would howl and cry if someone forgot to share their lunch break sandwich with him.

Time passed and as Gypsy watched, he realized that this was not going to be the Shangri la that he was looking for. People still bitched and found reasons not to like each other. There was, despite the communist ideals of the place, intense competition between people, and with communism, no matter how hard you worked it was nigh on impossible to ever get ahead. It was a system that rewarded the lazy and the cunning, at the expense of its finest people. There was no freedom and it did not reward anyone for extra hours of work, or those who gave more than their fair share of effort. Gypsy saw all of this, plus a small stand off between the kibbutzniks and volunteers, over how the volunteers were being treated. Gypsy's disillusionment grew.

By the time Christmas came, it was cold and miserable at the kibbutz. Gypsy could think of nothing but getting away from the kibbutz, so he spoke with Ora and Yackob about going traveling. Also he was interested to start his spiritual search again, now that he would have the freedom to go exploring. Though he was Jewish by race, he knew very little about the religion and asked Ora if Judaism had any teachings about meditation and reincarnation. "Maybe", said Ora, "I'm not sure, but if you are interested in that, maybe it would be good for you to take a journey to India. I think you might find what you are looking for there."

"Whatever you do, don't go to Eilat," Ora warned him before he left the kibbutz. "Eilat is full of dangerous people and gangsters work there." Three days before the New Year of 1980, Gypsy, with a pack on his back and guitar in his hand, caught the bus from the bottom of the hill below the kibbutz village, to Tel Aviv. When he got off of the bus at Tel Aviv bus station he went and bought himself a bus ticket for the next available bus to Eilat. Despite what his relatives had said, Eilat was the only place in Israel where the weather was warm and also it meant a journey across the Negev desert. Gypsy had never seen a desert in anything other than movies and the news and wanted to see one for real. He then walked around to the scruffy stands around the outside of the bus station and bought himself a falafel to eat. While standing there munching it, a young Israeli girl came up to him and started talking, "Where are you going?" she asked him. "Eilat", he replied. "Me, too," she said. They were booked on buses at different times so they chatted for a time, before Gypsy got on his bus.

The buses in Israel, at that time were run, one hundred percent, by the state owned bus company, EGGED. It was a very well managed affair, with fast and frequent bus services to just about any far flung part of the country you cared to name. It was also cheap and the stations were clean and user friendly (even the toilets in the station were moderately clean).

The bus ride to Eilat was to take five hours. From Tel Aviv to the city of Bere Sheva, the land was green and full of orchards with small towns and villages dotting the way. Israelis at that time favored red roofed bungalows and whitewashed block like constructions. Each one throughout the land, would have a solar hot water heater upon its roof and a large shaded porch in the front where it could be said at that time that 80% of the nightlife in Israel, occurred.

Bere Sheva was a fast growing modern city. Like any Israeli town of that time, it was wall to wall with nondescript six to eight storey apartment blocks and new highways. The bus sped on through Bere Sheva, then after another twenty minutes, came Dimona, where Israel has its nuclear reactor.

After Dimona, there was nothing but pure desert, all the way to the red sea coast at Eilat. This was the first time that Gypsy had ever seen desert and he was mesmerized at how extraordinarily beautiful and peaceful it was. Every few kilometers or so, they might see a dry leafless thorn tree. There were wild camels running around or munching on the thorn trees. Occasionally they would see a patch of green, off in the distance. Ground water had been found and a kibbutz established and there they were, growing highly productive crops, when all there was around them, was bone dry desert. Also the most dirty polluting industries in Israel, had been relegated to the desert. So, at times they would also pass some large industrial set up, chucking out great clouds of smoke and dust.

Halfway between Beersheba and Eilat, they stopped and everyone got off of the bus to eat. Stepping off the bus, Gypsy enjoyed the deafening silence of the desert and knew he had made the right choice of direction.

After a piss, a cold drink and another falafel, everyone was back on the bus speeding towards Eilat. It was dark when the bus got in to town. Gypsy grabbed his pack and guitar and wandered off in search of a place to bed down. He found a cheap dilapidated hostel, with dorm beds, and checked in. He took a shower, before wandering out into the warm night air. He was happy to find Eilat was a major tourist resort, with a good choice of cheap food. He took a look among the food vendors, at a nearby outdoor shopping mall, called "The New Tourist Centre". Then finding a stall that he liked the look of, he sat down for something to eat. Later, while staring into a shop window, while eating an ice cream, he got a shock when someone kicked him in the arse.

He turned around to see the young Israeli girl that he had been chatting with at Tel Aviv bus station grinning at him. "Hi", she said, "I've just got in, where are you staying?", she asked.

She was sixteen years old and her name was Roni and she was travelling to Nuweiba, an oasis on the Sinai coast some hundred and eighty kilometers south of Eilat, where her friends were staying.

17

The next day, they hitched there together, getting there in the early afternoon. there was a Moshav there with its own tourist resort and a kiosk out on the public beach that sold food, drinks and basic essentials.

A Moshav was a collective farm, but unlike a kibbutz people took a ninety nine year lease on a plot of land, which usually would be two to three acres in size and farm it with the crops of their choice. Then they would market the harvest through the Moshav's on site cooperative, keeping the profit, minus all expenses, for themselves.

Wandering over the sand dunes, Roni soon found her friends. Gypsy couldn't believe it it was just like a pop festival, a hippy camp in the desert. Tens if not hundreds of other long haired travelers, were living in tents and home made shelters and sharing everything together.

Three people were sitting on top of a sand dune and jamming, one on guitar, one on a weird shaped clay bongo and the third one playing a solo on a flute. It was some of the best sounds that Gypsy had ever heard. There they were sitting on the sand dunes under date palms, with the water of the Red Sea barely ten meters away. It was mid winter in the rest of Israel, but here in Nuweiba, the sun was shining and a warm wind was blowing, at least in the day time, that was.

Food, drinks and joints were being shared around and the occasional Bedouin would wander over the dunes towards them, his camel in tow, loaded with dates, melons and other fruits that he was selling. It was late afternoon and the desert hills and mountains were turning to a deep red, it was a beautiful site. A fire was being made ready and Gypsy was jamming with the others on his guitar.

The sun went down and suddenly it was very cold, Gypsy had never been in a desert before and was totally unprepared. He had no sleeping bag or bed roll, let alone a tent or cooking gear. The fire was lit and food, joints, mugs of tea and cigarettes were shared around the fire. Even the guitars and other instruments circulated, as everyone was given a chance to jam. There were people from Israel, Europe, USA, Canada, Australia, South Africa and God knows where, sharing as friends, it was truly a magical night. When all the partying finished, Gypsy put on as many layers of clothes as he could. He had been invited by one group to sleep in their tent. Never the less, without a sleeping bag, he still woke up freezing and uncomfortable. He knew he couldn't do another night like that, he knew that he had no choice, but to head back up to Eilat. "I'm going north today", said one of the crowd. His name was Pico, he was sixteen

18

years old and was from Berlin. Gypsy wasn't tall but Pico was tiny. "Do you want to join me for the journey?", asked Pico. "Ok," said Gypsy and asked, "Where are you going?" "Jerusalem", said Pico. "Well, I've never been there before, to see it properly", said Gypsy. "I think, I'll join you, this sounds like an adventure."

The traffic was so sparse on the Sinai highway that they were forced to take the bus. A couple had been waiting three days, by the road and still had not managed to thumb a lift.

They got off the bus in Eilat and checked into the hostel. "Let me show you around Eilat", said Pico. "I've spent a bit of time here before", he explained. 'There's a bar here that you're going to like", he said. "It's called, Bollocks and it's run by some British guy called Henry."

So after wandering up from the beach into the town, they were standing in a courtyard full of shops and bars and there in front of them was a bar. Over the entrance in big gold letters, was the name of the bar, "BOLLOCKS".

Pink Floyd's, "Shine on You Crazy Diamond", was playing on the large hi-fi unit inside. This was the first time that Gypsy had ever heard this track, it blew his mind. It was the most incredibly beautiful piece of music he had ever heard. As the night wore on, the stereo gave him his first experience of Crosby Stills and Nash and much of the other hippy music from the sixties and early seventies that he had never heard before. By the end of the night, he had a whole list of albums that he was going to buy at the next opportunity. Gypsy and Pico got slightly drunk on Israeli beer and headed back to the hostel.

The next day, standing by the highway, they managed to thumb a lift, some one hundred kilometers out into the desert and then another lift from there to Bere Sheva. But it was getting dark by the time that they reached Bere Sheva, so from there to Jerusalem they once more had to use up resources and took the bus.

It was dark when they got into Jerusalem and took the local bus down Jaffa road to the old city, it was also considerably colder than Eilat and Bere Sheva. Entering the old city through the Jaffa gate they walked down the steps that make up David Street, until they reached the "Swedish Hostel" on their left (who knows why it was called this when it was owned by local Arabs). Checking in, they dropped their packs on their beds in the large but crowded dormitory and went outside into the semi deserted alleys of the Arab quarter.

"There's a place around the next corner that you're going to enjoy", said Pico. "It's a bit like Bollocks, in Eilat". As they came around the corner, there it was. "The Danish Tea House", with stained glass windows and a huge rack, full of vinyl LP's of rock and hippy music. Sitting beneath the high set racks that covered the wall, was George, an Armenian (Jerusalem has an Armenian Quarter inside the walls of the old city) sitting there with his hat, dark glasses and three days of stubble on his chin he could have been mistaken for a 'Blues Brother' (as in the movie) George was the house DJ and money counter.

The Danish Tea House consisted of three floors with very low arches and stained glass windows both internally and externally. It was necessary to practically crawl to get to some of the tables, as the archways were so low. The three floors were linked by a very narrow and steep curved stair case and rock music could be heard on all floors. The menu was basic and simple but the food was good and this was the place to hang out in Jerusalem for the travelers and hippies.

Gypsy spent the next two weeks checking out the wonders of the old city, getting to know its alleyways and markets and finding out how far he could bargain for goods. Having little money left, he lived mostly on a diet of falafels, they were cheap and healthy and available everywhere. His fellow Jews had warned him that Arabs were no good and dirty and could never be trusted, but Gypsy even at the young age of seventeen, knew far better than to believe a blanket judgment like that. He could feel in his heart, that such a judgment was wrong. He spent time talking with local Palestinians, trying to get to know them and the general way that they thought and how they viewed life. Spending much time at the Danish Tea House, he got to know Assad, the owner and would talk with him often. Assad was a very decent man, he let Gypsy know what his other job was [he was a detective, with the local Palestinian police force] as so that Gypsy knew not to light up a joint in or near his place. He had two prominent hand written notices just inside the entrance,… one said:

'IT'S NICE TO BE IMPORTANT BUT IT'S MORE IMPORTANT TO BE NICE'

and the other said:

'EXPECT THE UNEXPECTED'

Assad's mind was lively and he would spend a lot of time watching and pondering. Gypsy liked and respected him. He thought to himself, well there's one good Palestinian despite what anyone says. For sure the Arab quarter had its fair share of sleaze balls, but most of the people were just ordinary folk, just trying to get by. Yes there was definitely resentment at being ruled over by a foreign people and though in many ways the Israelis could be fair, they didn't understand the Palestinian people properly and would often offend the Palestinians without meaning to. The problem of communication was thus,

"A Jew tends to learn at school, being pushed by his ambitious parents, but in the process all his natural intuition, is verbally beaten and scrubbed out of him and replaced with just intellect. He will be an intellectual giant at the same time as being an emotional pygmy. Thus it was difficult for them, to be able to relate with others. Their heads would be full of nervous energy that stopped them from being able to feel empathy with others, thus the Jewish sickness.

The Palestinian child, on the other hand, will grow up in a house, with many other siblings. The mother stays at home looking after the children and the father has to work very very hard indeed just to feed and cloth them all. No matter how hard he works he will never be able to send them all to school, yet their religion tells them to procreate.

He himself, probably never attended school and learned all that he learned, in the markets and farms of his local area and by whatever his mother and father were able to teach him, in between taking care of the huge amount of work that each of them had to do, in order to keep the wolf from the door.

When people's lives are hard and painful they tend to move toward religion. However the trappings of religious vestments and uniforms are attractive to cunning and greedy types, as they can claw their way up the ranks of the social structure more easily when dressed up as a holy man. While dressed in the garb of the blindly revered and respected, they can get others to do their bidding for them. Thus, with so many uneducated people, in so much pain and looking for salvation, in the form of something to believe in, whether it be religion or nationalism, it is easy to see that even a mediocre but cunning fool might be mistaken for a national hero by such desperate people. When such fools control the education system and fill even the youngest and most impressionable children's hearts with hate then peace will be almost impossible to achieve. The Israelis don't help their own situation by being arrogant and looking down on the Palestinians and refusing to see them as humans, with souls and feelings, just like themselves.

To Gypsy, it made no sense whatsoever, to view another group of people in such a manner, in fact he felt in his heart that it was this failure to understand the indigenous population that was at the heart of the problem. Everyone, eats, drinks, sleeps, shits, pisses, farts, fucks, get's old, get's sick and dies in that we are all equal. We all have red blood in our veins and two arms, two legs and a head and we all understand how it is to feel pain, sadness, and sorrow. So, why fight over something as stupid as land? We don't live long enough to own land, if anything the land owns us, thought Gypsy to himself.

He enjoyed wandering in the souks [markets] of the old city. There were the tourist shops in David Street, selling clay drums, Arab kefirs, silver jewelry, T-shirts, etc. Then there were other areas, where food, such as dried fruits, beans, lentils and spices were sold, along with fresh vegetables and fish. The meat market was such that, one walk through it would turn the average person vegetarian in a heartbeat. The smell was truly something to behold, but the sight of the sheep's intestines and internal organs hanging up still semi attached to the mutilated carcass with clouds of flies hovering around it was just too much to look at.

Gypsy ended up down at the wailing wall (the last remaining wall of the original temple mount, built during the reign of King Solomon) on a Friday afternoon. A man in a black hat and a flasher's coat approached him and asked him, if he was Jewish. When he said, "yes he was", he was invited to a religious orthodox house, for Friday night Shabbat [Sabbath] dinner. On the kibbutz there was a Shabbat dinner every Friday night but this was just traditional and in no way religious. For the most part the kibbutzniks had been atheist or agnostic in their beliefs. Gypsy had had very little contact with and knew almost nothing of the ways of orthodox Jews, other than at the wedding of his maternal uncle where the rabbi rabitted on all through the afternoon and late into the night, making ceremony after ceremony and prayer after prayer. His only real knowledge of the ceremonies was that of the Passover, which he had attended once a year at the house of his maternal grandparents, when he was younger. That too, just like the wedding, would go on and on and on as if it was never going to end. So the only thing that Gypsy knew about the religion of his people was that there were lots of ceremonies which involved a lot of long winded waffling, wailing and praying. . There were other bearded, black hatted ones going around the huge courtyard, asking people if they also were Jewish and then inviting them for prayers and dinner. All those who had accepted the invitation, were invited into the enclosed space that was next to the wall itself and given a cardboard or cloth skull cap to wear. To the left of the wall were two arched caverns with prison like bars across them and doors, also made of bars. Inside these well lit spaces, were thousands of prayer books, the vast majority of which were written solely in Hebrew. Gypsy and the others that had been rounded up, were taken into the caverns and given prayer books that were printed in both Hebrew and English. Gypsy watched in stunned bemusement as the black hatted ones started bowing furiously at the wall, while chanting at speeds that a horse racing commentator would not be able to keep up with. The books were full of long winded, waffling prayers, about smiting the enemies of Israel.

Eventually, an hour or so later, the performance was over and the black hatted ones each chose some guests to take home for supper. Gypsy ended up walking up the steps into the Jewish quarter, with an old, grey haired rabbi and his entourage. They wandered through a labyrinth of pedestrian alleys, before they finally reached his house. The Jewish quarter had been entirely rebuilt since nineteen sixty seven but using much of the old stone and to much the same design that it had been configured in previously. However the houses now had all modern amenities, such as running water, electricity, double glazing etc. The Rabbi's house was modern and clean inside. The table was set and ready for dinner and everyone went and performed the Jewish hand washing ritual, then went and sat down ready for the next round of ceremonies and prayers. Thus it was after a lot of prayers, masses of ceremonies and a fair bit of waffling through large, unkempt beards, that they eventually got to eat something. He had never seen such a palaver in his life, as the prayers and rituals that an orthodox Jew goes through before he does even the simplest of tasks. He asked some of the black hatted ones at the table, as they lived right next to the Palestinians, if any of them had ever made friends with any of them. "No", they would reply brusquely, "You could never trust an Arab".

Gypsy was saddened by their attitude, as he knew that this way of viewing things could never lead to peace. He had met some good people from among the Palestinians and knew that it was incorrect to tar the whole people with the same brush.

Though the dinner had been good, Gypsy was more than glad when it was time to leave. The atmosphere in the house had been somewhat stifling with so many can'ts shouldn'ts and mustn'ts that he became nervous about doing even the simplest of things. Orthodox Jews took resting on the Sabbath to ridiculous extremes, to the point where they were not even allowed to turn a light bulb on or off. The lighting of fires and also putting out existing ones was banned [this meant that Cooking, smoking and driving were also banned], as was playing music or writing anything down, the carrying of any item was also banned as was so much else. He couldn't understand why someone would choose to live that way. . He wandered through the alleys of the Jewish quarter until he eventually found some steps that took him down into the Arab souk. Then he wandered up the steps of David street until he found the alley that led around to the Danish tea house. He went inside and went upstairs and sat down, lit a cigarette and ordered a beer.

Some days later Gypsy took the bus to Tel Aviv. When he got there, he took a local bus through the city, to Ben Yahuda street and found his way to the "Central Hostel", for which he had been given directions. After checking in, he took a walk to the El Al booking office to see if it would be possible to change his ticket, to leave on the following week, back to London, he was running out of money and didn't want to go and stay on a kibbutz again. He was lucky, there was plenty of availability at that time on the London route. He had caught the travel bug and wanted to come back to Israel, to just work and travel after he had made enough money to travel again, back in England. He went back to the kibbutz to say goodbye and thank you, to Ora and Yackob then headed back to Tel Aviv. Back at the hostel he got talking with some of the other travelers, they were a mixture of Americans, Europeans and Seth Efricans [Well at least, that was how they pronounced it]. Gypsy had never seen so many South Africans and white Rhodesians as he had seen in Israel. Obviously, there must have been a lot of Jews living in that area of the world at that time. . He was flying to London in the early morning, so decided to head out to the airport that night and bed down in the terminal. Ben Gurion airport was not a major hub of aviation and the terminal was small and simple, but there was good cheap food available from the cafes outside of the terminal building where Gypsy ate his supper. Inside of the building there were many other young people whose cash had run out. They too were bedding down on the terminal floor waiting for flights to Europe, America, and South Africa. The next morning Gypsy awoke early and after putting away his bed roll, he wandered over to the check in desk and waited. Soon he was checked in and he wandered through to security and went through a stringent search and a game of twenty questions before being allowed through to airside. Outside on the apron, a number of planes were being readied for departure. There were two Boeing 707s with TWA markings on their sides and tail, being fuelled and loaded for flights, with stops in Europe, before continuing on to New York and Washington D.C. There was a British Airways Tri-Star L1011 being readied for it's flight to London, there was the Israeli domestic airline, "Arkia" with it's many smaller propeller planes preparing it's fleet for the day's work and there was a large number of EL AL 707s and 747s, of both the freight and passenger varieties, preparing for departure to different destinations around the world. Gypsy sat back and relaxed as he waited for his flight to be called. It was a short while later that he was riding in a bus, squashed full with other passengers, as they were driven out to the plane. It was the first time that Gypsy was to fly on a wide body jet and he was excited as he leapt up the steps and into the EL AL 747 that was taking him to London.

Looking at it from outside, while standing on the ground, it was hard to imagine that such a huge chunk of metal could fly. It was truly enormous and the engines were huge, a man could stand up inside one of the air intakes and still have space above his head. Inside, it was spacious, bright and clean, with colorful abstract designs on the wall panels. It was a world of difference from the cramped and dismal cabin of the 707 that had brought him to Israel. Eventually the cabin doors were closed and the plane was shunted back. The engines were started and they taxied out to the runway and took off into a cloudless sky. Breakfast was served as they crossed the Mediterranean, towards the Greek coast. Two hours later they were passing over Athens. Looking down, he could see that it was a far bigger city than any that existed in Israel at that time. They were playing a movie on the large screen in front of the seating area and were renting out head phones for a couple of dollars a pair. They were the old hose variety, as electronic head phones at that time, were not available on flights. It was the first time that he had had such a treat on a flight. He enjoyed the flight and was looking forward to the next one, that would take him back to Israel.

The flight touched down at Heathrow. Gypsy collected his bag, cleared customs and headed for the underground station, guitar in hand, denim clad and carrying a bright orange external framed back pack. It was mid January and freezing cold. Making his way to Victoria railway station, through the underground metro then taking the train home, he walked the last mile to his house, surprising his parents with his arrival. He got home with just five pounds left in his pocket, which was enough at the time to keep him in cigarettes until the end of the week when he would get paid for the first two days of work for that week. He didn't rest but went straight to work for his father, he had no choice, as he had no money.

Gypsy worked hard for a month, he also got a decent tax rebate, as he had not been working in England for several months. He had saved three hundred pounds, in all. His parents helped him with a one way ticket back to Tel Aviv. He slightly delayed by a week, his departure date, as one of his favorite bands, 'Wishbone Ash', were playing at the Brighton Dome and he was not going to miss that for anything. The concert just like the last time he saw them play was excellent. Three hours of no nonsense rock, very little in the way of special effects except a mirror ball and the usual colored spot lights, but every track set on a completely different type of riff and with wild leads. All in all it was a very good night out and worth waiting for.

Just before leaving, Gypsy made a visit to the dentist, suffering from a pain under one of his front teeth "You have an abscess", the dentist told him. "I can't do this before you fly, it requires an operation where the gum will have to be cut and a hole drilled through the bone in order to remove it." Gypsy didn't want to delay his travel plans, so getting his dentist to write an explanatory letter, complete with x-rays, he decided he would fix the problem in Israel. The deciding factor had been when he found all flights to Israel were full for at least a month. The dentist equipped him with antibiotics, X rays and an accompanying explanatory letter to give to his chosen dentist in Israel and then he was off on his way.

CHAPTER 2

RETURN TO ISRAEL

So there he was at Heathrow checking in once again, at the EL AL counter, saying goodbye to his parents once more and off through to the flight. They would see him again in six weeks as they were coming out for a two week holiday come business trip. Gypsy's mother had been there when in her late teens in the nineteen fifties. She had also worked on a kibbutz and wanted to go back and see how much the country had changed.

This time he was flying back on a jumbo so the flight was far more comfortable than his first ride to Tel Aviv. Four hours later the plane passed over the glowing lights of Tel Aviv as it made its final approach into Ben Gurion airport. Gypsy stepped out into the cold night air and made his way down the steps and onto the airside bus. This time he was properly prepared. He had a sleeping bag and tent, plus a metal water bottle and cooking kit, he could live on the cheap while looking for work. He made his way through the usual airport formalities, then took an Egged bus to Ben Yehuda Street and back to the hostel he had stayed in previously.

ISRAEL:

The next day was spent in a video bar, on the beach as Gypsy chatted with some British Army squadies who were taking a break in Israel under the guise of 'Adventurous Training'. Since when was bar crawling considered adventurous training, thought Gypsy to himself. Pink Floyd's, 'The Wall' had just come out and was playing on the large video screen and speakers behind the bar. Gypsy just couldn't believe that it was Pink Floyd playing it. It sounded completely different to everything they had done before, more like a punk track than the progressive rock that they were so well known for. anyway he empathized with the lyrics, as they seemed to sum up his school days pretty accurately.

The next day, Gypsy made inquiries as to where to get the problem with his teeth fixed. "Well, there is one cheap place to get it done", someone told him. "If you don't mind having half a dozen medical students peering down your throat, as you lie there. Try the Hadassah teaching hospital in Jerusalem", he was told. So here was Gypsy, still green to the road, one week before his eighteenth birthday, about to head up to Jerusalem to get his teeth fixed, not knowing anyone there or the geography of the new city. "Still this is what travelling is all about, being self reliant abroad" thought Gypsy to himself.

The next day Gypsy was at Tel Aviv bus terminal. He had just bought a ticket to Jerusalem, when a young American man with long hair in hippie sweater and jeans, wearing a skull cap on his head approached Gypsy and asked him, "Excuse me, but what is the most important thing in your life right now"? "Sex", said Gypsy. "What about love?" said the other man. "When most people fall in love, its not love but infatuation", he continued. "Love takes time and is not instant. In fact the true definition of love is the appreciation of virtues in another and has nothing to do with sex", he spoke. This was the first time that someone had talked to Gypsy about this deep issue that already was bugging his thoughts, he was intrigued. He had witnessed men running around like packs of mongrel street dogs, while trying to get laid and there appeared to be only desire, to abuse and there was not a drop of empathy or love in them for the woman. And the women, likewise behaved in much the same way.

"So, you're Jewish", said the man. "What do you know about your roots and religion"? "Not much", admitted Gypsy. "I used to go to Passover at my grandparent's house as a child and my father who is not Jewish, used to read the old testament to me as bed time stories at night when I was seven and eight years old. Other than that, I know very little". "Well would you like to find out some more about Jewish philosophy and religion?", the man asked. "Yes, but I've just bought a ticket to Jerusalem", Gypsy replied. "No problem", said the man. "Just go to the kiosk and trade it back in or change the time or date".

After doing this, Gypsy was taken to a large house two streets from the station, where he met a group of young American hippies and students, who were now Orthodox Jews. They still were doing the health foods and had long hair and played guitars and the like.

Gypsy knew so little about his own people's religion, that he, like them, was interested to learn something about it. He spent the afternoon asking them questions about it, like, "Do Jews believe in reincarnation?" The answer was quiet interesting for this question as it was told to him. It was up to each person to make his or her mind up on this question for themselves, according to the Jewish law. The word for hashish was the same as the word for secret, in the Hebrew language. Gypsy became ever more interested. He was invited to have dinner there and stay the night, an offer he readily accepted. He had never forgotten his true goal in life, to find out what lay behind death. Here maybe would be a chance to discover something of the eternal truth.

Later in the evening their Rabbi was coming to give a talk on his path that he taught, called the forty eight ways. His talk was deeply philosophical and was about how the mind works and how not to be tricked by it. Gypsy's only experience of religion, up until this point, had been the usual Christian wet hypocritical bullshit, dished out in liberal doses as he went through the school system in England. This Rabbi with his sharp wit and deeper understandings, was a breath of fresh air in comparison. His school of religious learning was based in Jerusalem and was called Aish Ha Torah.

One of the residents of the house was going to Jerusalem the next day so Gypsy asked if he could join him. "Sure, come along, I can show you this real cool place, it's full of Jewish travelers and hippies from around the world, some of them have been out to India and other wild places. Now they are studying the 'Torah', (the first five books of the old testament of the Bible) they've got their own rock bands and the like, you might want to check them out."

So Gypsy spent a Shabbat at their strange institute of Jewish learning on Mount Zion, just outside of the walls of the old city. It was very stifling, you couldn't turn lights on and off or even light a match, they prayed in Hebrew before they did anything, including going to the toilet. It was all a bit too much. But on Saturday night their rock band played in a large catacomb like cavernous basement that had been turned into a gig hall. It was a strange sight, a group of black hatted bearded Orthodox Jews playing their own brand of rock, on electric guitars, bass, drums, violins and saxophone, with the audience dressed and dancing like the cast out of 'fiddler on the roof'. Nevertheless, Gypsy was not ready to stick around. At this point, he needed to take care of his tooth and the atmosphere at the Yeshiva was both too smart arsed and too uptight.

After checking into a hostel in the Arab quarter he went and found his way to the Hadassah hospital on the local buses and after an initial examination they gave an appointment for the operation in nine days time.

With nothing else to do and what with being stuck there in Jerusalem, he went down to the Danish Tea House and asked Assad if he could use a worker for a week. "Sure", he said, "We could use a waiter. Do you think you can handle trays of glasses up and down those stairs and under the arches?" "No problem". Gypsy replied. "I'm as sure footed as a mountain goat".

So Gypsy worked for Assad for the week, staying at the hostel dormitory that Armenian George, the DJ had, up the hill, in the Armenian quarter, as a side business. He didn't have many customers but it was clean and had hot water. Gypsy worked hard, doing a twelve hour shift each day. He made small money in tips but not enough to save, but he was enjoying himself and it wasn't costing him anything to live, which was what he needed at that time. There was snow on the ground outside and it was bitterly cold as icy winds howled through the alleys and markets of the old city. But in the Danish tea house at least, it was warm inside.

One day, George put on the most incredible piece of music that Gypsy had ever heard. It was a woman singing in Arabic. She sounded as if she was having multiple orgasms while she was singing, it was a truly beautiful sound.

Assad explained to Gypsy that the singer was an Egyptian woman, very famous in the Arab world for her songs. She had died two years previously and yes the song she was singing was about making love. Apparently the song had been banned from being played in many Arab countries.

Gypsy liked it and thought it was just about the coolest bit of music he had ever heard in all of his life. Her name was Urm Kulthom and when she sang live, on the radio, almost the whole of Egypt would stop what they were doing just to listen to her. One of her songs could last for up to two or three hours.

Working in the Danish Tea House, Gypsy got to know the local people a little better. He got to know and see them as people rather than as the enemy, which was the terrible mistake that so many of his own people made. The Muslim people, it should be said, see life from a different prism from that of those raised in either a Jewish or Christian society. Unfortunately there is a tendency among the adherents of each of the three main Semitic religions to think that only their particular angle is right and that anyone who does not agree with them is evil or stupid. Rather than looking to see what each could give the other, in their shared stated goal of giving themselves in service to God. "Who are these fools who stop people being friends with their neighbors?" thought Gypsy. "This phenomena could not be perpetuated on such a scale without some evil conscious conspiracy being behind it. All people seek happiness. The greatest happiness comes from making others around you happy, so what is this nonsense that is going on here? Peace should be easy to achieve, it should be the natural state, in a sane world." He thought to himself.

Gypsy finished his week's work and went to the hospital for his operation. Sure enough, there was a room full of medical students peering down his throat as the dentist worked, but it was only costing thirty quid and at a hospital with one of the best reputations on the planet.

So with a mouth full of stitches Gypsy had no choice but to rest for the week. He had just turned eighteen and drinking in a pub would never be so much fun again. He had moved to another hostel, "The Tabasco" on the "Via de la Rosa" [the route that Jesus was reputed to have been forced to carry the cross, on the way to his crucifixion]. It had a café downstairs, where Gypsy got to talk with other travelers. There were two guys from England, one of them had been to India. Gypsy asked him many questions about the place, he was now determined to go to India as soon as he could.

The next afternoon he and an American woman who was in her early sixties and staying at the hostel decided to share a Taxi to go see the Mount of Olives. The driver was showing them around and at one point took them into a small domed structure and pointed to a small off set rectangle of bricks set into the floor and proclaimed that this is the spot where Jesus took off from after the crucifixion. Gypsy could have pissed himself laughing, after nearly two thousand years and god knows how many wars, pogroms, migrations and transmigrations and other upheavals they still recon they know where exactly everything happened to such exactness?......"who the hell do they think that they are fooling?" he thought to himself.

Late in the afternoon after having been dropped back at the Dung gate near the wailing wall he got talking with the American woman, when he suggested his theory for the first time, that there must be a conspiracy against peace in the Middle East and indeed the world, perpetuated by very few people. He was interested and slightly surprised when she told him about a chapter in the New Testament of the Bible called, 'Revelations to John'. Even with all the Bible bashing he had endured at school, he had never heard mention of this chapter. The woman explained how an end of the world Apocalypse was described and that the conspiracy that Gypsy had sensed and reasoned must be there by the nature of physics, was described and named, as the Illuminate, a group who's consciousness comes from the bowels of hell itself. Humans with weak wills, who succumb to the lowest greed and fear based desires known. Influenced by vibrations from the lowest hellish dimensions of the astral. This group in their deep personal emptiness and fear, would seek to dominate and control all the wealth and peoples of the world and damn everyone to their own pathetic state of low consciousness. As with all pathetic dictators, they are frightened by anyone who is more intelligent than themselves. This struck a real chord with Gypsy as he could sense it and now he knew that he wasn't going mad, there were parts of his being that he had not been told about at home or at school in England and he would have to investigate further. Now his search for eternity was really beginning.

Across the old city in the Jewish quarter, Gypsy had made friends with two of the wildest people (by wild I mean feral) that he had met at the Yeshiva on Mount Zion. There was John the South African piss head and Tom, a young American who was up to trying any drug that anyone cared to place in front of him.

Gypsy called him Major Tom, the junkie, as he always was spaced out [as in the songs "space oddity" and "ashes to ashes" by David Bowie]

One afternoon while over at their desperately dirty squat while trying to locate some illegal green vegetable matter, he was informed that the city was once again dry and no one could find any anywhere.

John and Tom were in the kitchen grinding something up. "What are you doing there?" asked Gypsy curiously. "I read in this book that if you can eat enough nutmeg that it will take you on a trip", said Tom, "so we are grinding it up first so we can mix it with water and drink it. There's no dope in the whole city so we thought we'd make our own fun." That's desperate and sad", said Gypsy and left.

Apparently, according to both Tom and independent witness accounts recounted later, he and John spent the first eight hours vomiting with stomach cramps and then the next two to three days laughing and giggling like loonies while they tripped their brains out.

"I don't think that I want to try that one", thought Gypsy to himself, "it sounds a bit too extreme."

Gypsy was about to take a bus to Eilat when Pico showed up at the Tabasco hostel. "I've seen Roni and she says she wants to see you", he said. "Well I would like to see her too but right now I'm taking a bus to Eilat", said Gypsy. "I'll probably still be here when you get back", said Pico. "I'm here for a while and Roni lives here in Jerusalem so I'm sure we'll find each other in a few weeks or so."

The bus that Gypsy was riding left the Jerusalem bus terminal and drove down the Jaffa road before turning left, driving past, New gate then Damascus gate and then Herod's gate before descending down into the valley, then ascending the Mount of Olives and off through the winding roads of the West Bank, descending down through the Judean hills, to the Dead Sea. After a long descent the bus was driving along the coast of the Dead Sea, a truly surreal place.

The famous River Jordan, flows from a large lake called the Sea of Galilee, down along the start of the rift valley (the same one that exists in Kenya and Tanzania minus the sea in between) known as the Jordan Valley, until it reaches this lowest of low lying pans, just over one hundred kilometers to the south, called the Dead Sea, where not only no normal marine creature can live but even the river dies and flows no further.

The landscape around the Dead Sea was super surreal, with green wadis extending up into the hills complete with streams and waterfalls, at the nature reserve at Ein Gedi. There was the ancient hill fortress of Masada towering above the road. There were salt pillars sticking out of the water as evidence of how high the water had been before. There was a pillar of rock that was perhaps the same shape as a fat person in a long hooded cloak. It was called, 'Lot's wife'. [in the story of Lot, from the book of Genesis in the bible, Lot and his family were told by "God" to leave the city of Sodom where they lived, as so that God could destroy it without hurting them. However they were told that whatever happens they should not look back to watch the destruction. Lot's wife however, disobeyed this instruction and turned around to see what was happening and was instantly turned into a pillar of salt]. Sodom and Gomorra were reputed to exist at a location just to the south of where the dead sea presently ends. At the end of the lake, was a sign, pointing off to Sodom and Gomorrah, where the road forked off into totally inhospitable but beautiful landscape of solid rock canyons and volcanic alien realms. The canyons and weird landscapes continued until they met the main highway to Eilat, south of Bere Sheva and Dimona.

Again it was dark when he got into Eilat. He made his way down to the courtyard which housed both the 'red wine bar and Bollocks. Several people were lying on the ground outside of Bollocks in a semi conscious state and the Crosby, Stills and Nash song 'Long time coming' was blasting out from the stereo inside. The place was full of travelers and hippies. The aroma of hashish was evident from around the corner, as people snuck of from time to time for a spliff.

'Bollocks' was owned by a cockney Jew called Henry and his son Vince. Bringing his London humor with him and noting the Israeli inability at the time, to understand English slang, he got a kick out of watching just about everyone in the bar double up in fits of laughter every time an Israeli came into the bar and asked in all innocence, if they could please speak to Mister Bollocks. (Bars and restaurants in Israel at least at that time had a tendency to be named after their owners e.g. Finkelstein's, Cohen's, Levi's, etc).

A new notice had appeared at the bar offering a reward for information leading to the return of the hi-fi and album collection, belonging to Henry's son Vince, that had been stolen from his apartment along with a considerable quantity of cash. Apparently, he had got someone busted for smoking a joint, around the corner from the bar and someone had taken it upon themselves to teach the boy a lesson.

Later that night someone pointed Gypsy to the traveler camp on the beach. He went to put up the new tent that his family had given him, back in England but the fabric of the inner tent had rotted on him and fell into pieces. So taking a couple of branches, the fly sheet and the ground sheet, he made himself a shelter to sleep in.

The next morning he awoke to find himself in a camp of travelers and hippies, mostly living in makeshift shelters under a grove of trees next to the beach. The road to Sinai was on the west side of the trees and a large resort hotel called the "Red Rock", was to their south. They were right under the final approach of the flight path that led into Eilat airport as Gypsy was to find out early the next morning when he looked out of his shelter to see a Boing 727 in Dan Air Colors screaming in over his head.

Luckily it wasn't a very busy airport, with only two or three jets coming in each day. The rest of the flights being twin engined prop planes from the domestic airline, Arkia.

People were always sharing in the traveler community and anyone who worked in cafes and restaurants would bring food back to the camp after work to share with the others.

For the first few days Gypsy was just trying to find his feet in Eilat, he wanted to work but also he wanted to find the best paying job possible, but in the end his hand was forced by circumstances, All be it partly of his own making, as I shall reveal.

Gypsy had settled in well to tent city, what with his guitar and his self sufficient nature. He enjoyed sitting around and jamming with the others and with his only expense being food and drinks, he still had a few days in order to find a job before he was reduced just to a bus ticket north's worth of money in his pocket. He was still looking and asking questions as to how to find a job that paid reasonably.

Then one day a young Jewish man from London, who had been hanging out around tent city, although he wasn't staying there, came to Gypsy's tent begging him in tears for help. "I'll go to prison if I don't pay my bill by lunch time," he said. "Please, please help me. I need ten pounds. (These days £10 may not sound like much, but in those days Gypsy's wage packet in England would have been less than thirty two pounds for forty hours of work) In Israel, at that time he could live on between one and one pound fifty per day, as long as he stayed on the beach and didn't have to pay money for accommodation. "I'll pay you back in the afternoon", the young man pleaded. "My parents are sending me an emergency telex, it will be here by this afternoon and then I can pay you back", he pleaded. "Someone stole my wallet in the bar and I couldn't pay my bill. I'm in deep shit right now, they've given me until mid day to pay, or I'm in jail, please, please help me", "But, this is my last money", said Gypsy, "if I don't have this I'm fucked, I need to know that I have at least a bus ticket north to where I stashed the rest of my money". "Please, please, I promise you I'll pay you this afternoon", the young man pleaded. His name was Paul Rubens and he was from North London, close to where many of Gypsy's Jewish cousins lived. He gave Gypsy a photocopy of the first page of his passport and begged and pleaded until Gypsy, against his better judgment and unable to get rid of this problem person any other way, relented and lent the bastard the money.

By that evening the money had not shown up and Gypsy was getting nervous, he went and found Paul Rubens. "No the money hasn't shown up yet it should be here by tomorrow morning", he was told. The next morning there was still no money. Beating the hell out of Paul Ruben probably wouldn't help get his money back and anyway there was a chance that he may be telling the truth.

Gypsy no longer had a choice. Buried at the bottom of his pack was a clean set of clothes, and a bar of soap. Sneaking in through an unwatched door at the back of the hostel further down the beach Gypsy took a shower (his first non saline wash in a week) and got himself smartened up. On going back to his shelter to drop off his towel and dirty clothes, he was called by some others to join them. "Where are you all from?" asked Gypsy. "I'm an Israeli Jew", said the first one. "I'm a Palestinian Muslim", said the second one. "I'm a Palestinian Christian", said the third one. "Wow! And your all three friends and traveling together?" asked Gypsy. "Yes" they all replied at once. "This is what I've been waiting to see", said Gypsy. "This is how it should be. I wish there were more people like you in Israel, then there would be peace in this part of the Middle East".

"Where are you going dressed up smart like that?" the Israeli asked. "I've got no money, I need to get a job in a hurry", Gypsy replied. "Well you can't go looking for a job on an empty stomach" one of them said. "Come, we've just cooked a big pot of food, sit down and eat with us, then you can go and find a job".

Gypsy accepted the kind offer from these 'Three Wise Hippies', he was hungry and their cooking tasted excellent.

Gypsy scoured Eilat going door to door around the cafes, burger bars, restaurants and bars until he landed a job, working for a Belgian man at his fast food joint working thirteen hour shifts, seven days a week, for thirty pounds a week plus food. The plus food part really counted for something as Gypsy was broke, with not a pot to piss in at the time.

So away he slaved at 'Safari Burger', over the hot plate. Every night he would bring back whatever food he could, to the camp. There was a pregnant girl in one of the shelters, she wasn't able to work, so first he made sure that she had enough, and then shared the rest with the others. In the burger joint his work mate was a young Palestinian who he got on well with and who taught him efficient ways of working in a kitchen. All day they worked cooking burgers, chips and pancakes then at eleven thirty at night they started the clean up that took the best part of two hours. It was usually well after 2 am when Gypsy returned to the camp.

By the end of the week, with still no money from the despicable Paul Ruben, Gypsy, now with money in his pocket, tried to track him down. He was in town but remained most elusive, when Gypsy did manage to track him down, he had surrounded himself with ignorant bully boy types who made it clear that they weren't about to let anything happen to him, as he sat at the bar and still refused to give back the money. Gypsy could do nothing but feel rage at being ripped off by this foul and cunning overgrown spoilt brat. "This is the sort of behavior that causes anti-Semitism" thought Gypsy to himself.

After a couple of days, he took the bus north to collect the rest of his travel money. Also his parents were coming for two weeks to tour plant nurseries and find new suppliers. He thought it might be interesting to join them.

He made his way to Natania, a Mediterranean resort town north from Tel Aviv and found the hotel that they were staying in.

He would have been happy enough to use the local hostel but his father who is not Jewish has always been a generous type of person and insisted on getting him a room at the four star hotel that they were staying in. Being a fairly posh establishment the reception staff weren't sure what to make of this scruffy young traveler, with long hair, back pack and guitar, who had come in to their hotel and was asking to speak to two of their guests who had just checked in. But none the less they were friendly and helpful.

Soon Gypsy was checked in and recounting his previous six weeks of travel to his parents. The next two days were spent relaxing on the beach before the tour began. Gypsy's parents had hired a tiny little car, so first was a visit to the kibbutz to see Ora and Yakob followed by a visit to Sam and Dina. Gypsy's mother had not seen them in many years and it was a fond reunion.

Next, they drove to Jerusalem where Gypsy guided them through the maze of alleys that make up the old city. Then they drove on and down into the Jordan Valley, past Jericho, a city made of mud. Then north towards Galilee, where they checked in to a hotel by the shores of the lake. They stayed there for a couple of nights while visiting horticultural establishments in the area. They then drove further north to Kiriat Shmona (eight wells, in English) where they stayed as they toured the horticultural establishments of various kibbutzim of the area, making new orders for seeds and cuttings. Their tour had been partly organized by the Israeli government agricultural export service, 'AGREXCO', as their company was a regular buyer of Israeli cuttings and seeds.

Wherever they went they were treated like, not only valued customers but like friends who share a hobby. No one becomes a horticulturist to get rich, it is hard work and the margins are small while the risks are high. They do the job because they love growing plants. No matter how professional a horticultural business may look, you can be sure that the boss is doing what he is doing because it's his number one hobby. Consequently, all horticulturists like meeting other horticulturists, especially from different lands and climates as they are always interested to learn from each other how to grow different species.

At some of the Nurseries and seed gardens, there were tall cacti as high or higher than two storey houses, there were round button cacti as big or bigger than small cars. One of the seed gardens was managed and maintained by a quiet and happy man who took care of them and harvested the seeds. David Shahori was an American who had settled on the kibbutz a long while back, he loved his cactus garden and took good care of it. A small box of his cactus seeds, even at that time could bring in up to two thousand pounds and even though it was his hobby, it was highly profitable.

Saturday night in Kiryat Shmona was a very pleasant affair where children were safe walking around on their own until late into the night as people relaxed around the cafes and bars in the town plaza. The spirit of idealism still burned strong in the people of the more rural towns of Israel and there was very little violent crime in such areas and crimes against children where virtually unheard of. All ages mixed in a totally happy environment. Such a thing as this would be hard to imagine in either England or the USA.

The next morning people were all talking about the news. Apparently some terrorists had got across the border and penetrated the security of a nearby kibbutz, entering a children's house. They had killed a female child minder and injured a child or two before Israeli commandos arrived and eliminated them. Nevertheless the Israelis weren't about to let an incident like that go unpunished.

Later that day while following the road along the large fortified fence that marked the Lebanon border, they saw a column of twelve armored personnel carriers parked by the side of the road. There was a large number of Israeli soldiers, all sitting by the sides of the vehicles, studying maps in groups of five or six, while some of their colleagues were removing a small section of the border fence. It looked like some serious arse kicking was about to take place, north of the border.

They drove down through Haifa and around and past Tel Aviv and then turned onto the express way to Jerusalem going around the city, they once again took the road down to the Jordan valley. This time however they turned right and followed the road that ran along by the side of the Dead Sea. After a while they stopped at a beach near to Ein Gedi and got out and took a swim in the super buoyant waters. It wasn't like regular sea water, as when he got out and went back to the beach, Gypsy found that he was covered in a sticky layer of saline slime. After a wash down, under the beach showers, they got back into the car and drove back to the ruins of Masada where they took a cable car ride to the top. The settlement had last been occupied some one thousand nine hundred years previously, when a small community of Israelites, living on the small inaccessible plateau had held out against the Roman invaders for several years, before the Romans eventually built a ramp to get up on to the top, with a view to capturing the occupants and taking them off into slavery. However on finally reaching the top, they found all the occupants to be dead. They had committed mass suicide rather than allowing themselves to be enslaved by the "unclean" Romans. The ruins were remarkably well preserved and it was possible to see how they had lived, in great detail. There were huge underground cisterns that had been carved out from solid rock and even remnants of their food gardens were still visible. Many of the houses were still semi standing and down a couple of flights of stone steps, at a lower level there were the ruins of what had once been a small palace. The ramp that the Romans had built was still there intact and was most visible below. It was also possible to make out various marks from where their encampment had been, during the years that it had taken them to take the site. . After this excursion, they continued on their way across the desert to Eilat. Passing through the town they then took the coastal road south, into the Sinai Peninsula until they reached Nuweiba were Gypsy had stayed before. It felt weird to be staying in the resort instead of on the beach with the travelers and hippies. They stayed for three days at the holiday village on the Moshav. The comfort was a welcome break for Gypsy, although he didn't mind roughing it.

They headed north as Gypsy's parents trip was coming to a close, driving to Tel Aviv.

When they flew out Gypsy once again alone on the road, took the bus to Jerusalem to look up Pico and Roni.

He found Pico at the Tabasco hostel, he had been staying there for the whole time while Gypsy was travelling. They got talking and soon Roni showed up. "Hello", she said. "I've been wanting to see you. I want to go to England. Could I travel there with you?"

"Sure", said Gypsy. "I was thinking of buying a ticket to Athens so I can look for work in Greece, and then later, either hitching a ride or taking the magic bus back to England".

The next two weeks were spent in preparation for the trip. Roni got her money together and Gypsy went and checked out the hippie yeshiva on Mount Zion once more. He was still interested to see if there was anything profound to be learned from the religion of his own people. This time at the yeshiva he met interesting and more open minded people. They told him their stories of how they ended up there, after wild journeys across Asia and beyond and how they now thought that Judaism was the smartest and most correct of all the religions that they had checked out.

Soon Roni was ready and so they went and bought air tickets to Athens for the next day then caught a bus to the airport. After bedding down on the airport terminal floor they awoke early the next morning to check in for their flight on EL AL to Athens. As the bus dropped them off at the steps leading up into the 707 the mechanics had one of the engine cases up and were making adjustments inside. They climbed into the dismal black grey and off white decorated cabin and waited for the mechanics to finish their work and for bags to be loaded.

Soon they were off down the runway in the early morning sunshine. The flight took just over two hours and was barely half full. A rubber omelet and cardboard fried potatoes along with a stale bread roll were served for breakfast. Gypsy looked out of the window at the sea far below, occasionally spotting the odd ship in the distance. He had heard relatively good stories about Greece from many of the other travelers that he had met, but he wondered just how easy it would be to find reasonably paid work there.

The flight touched down at Athens International Airport and the two of them made their way through and out of the airport and on to a bus to Syntagma Square in the centre of Athens. Just by watching from the bus window Gypsy could see that Greece was not so clean or technically advanced as Israel. Also Athens was much bigger than any of the Israeli cities. The streets though were dirty and the skyline was full of billboards and unfinished and badly constructed buildings.

GREECE, ATHENS.

Leaving the bus in Syntagma square they wandered through the side streets in the direction of the Acropolis until they were in the 'Plaka' district, looking straight up at the Parthenon. There in a small plaza with ancient ruins at one end, they found a hostel, 'The Pericles, where for a very small sum of money (less than one pound per night each), they could sleep on the roof of the building. There were no beds or mattresses, just the cold stone and concrete, but both Gypsy and Roni had sleeping bags so for as long as it was dry, no problem.

Going up to the roof, they found that they were not the only ones to be sleeping up there. There was a whole colony of nearly broke travelers camped up there. Dropping their bags, they went out to check out the area and find some food.

There were large numbers of travelers coming from India, in Athens at that time. The revolution in Iran, which had kicked off at some point, in the spring or early summer of the previous year had forced some of them to buy air tickets and fly over the troubles. Others had come through on local transport, telling of wild adventures and difficulties getting through, as the newly formed revolutionary guard were somewhat hostile to anyone from the west. There were two female French junkies begging in the square down below, making quite a nuisance of themselves. They must have been desperately hungry as they would sometimes endeavor to stop people in the street who were eating while they walked. One would stop them and distract them from their food while the other one would launch herself sometimes mouth first like a dog, at any protruding morsel of food in the victim's hand. Gypsy was walking along a narrow side street, close by the plaza one day, chatting with an Australian traveler who had just come from India. He was eating an ice cream cone when the two French women stopped them and one of them demanded money. When she was told to piss off, she launched at the Australian, biting the top off of his ice cream, then she grabbed it with both hands and started desperately sucking on it, before the Australian was able, with great force to wrestle her off of it. (Some French people are such great ambassadors for their country when they travel).

Gypsy and Roni stuck around in Athens for a couple of weeks, but couldn't find any work or word of where to find work elsewhere. On a few occasions Gypsy hit the street with his guitar and went busking. On one occasion he had no choice, Roni had disappeared for the evening with all the Drachma (Greek currency) that they had and Gypsy was hungry. Two hours of bad Bob Dylan and Neal Young covers later and Gypsy was sitting down for a large Greek meal in a not so fancy looking café, in a side street. The food tasted good and he had made enough to pay for breakfast as well. He enjoyed busking, but it was a hard and unreliable way to make a living. Roni's moods were becoming more difficult to deal with and she wanted to go to England. She was only seventeen years old but she was wild and badly behaved and a bit of a spoilt brat. Unlike Gypsy she had never been expected to work and as such had not much of a clue about life and expected everything to be delivered to her on a plate. Gypsy on the other hand knew that if you wanted to make money then it was necessary to go and find a job. On realizing that he was not going to get any peace any other way, he got Roni to join him as he grabbed his pack and they headed three blocks down to Monastraki underground station from where they took the metro to Piraeus where the international port is located.

There were trucks from all over the place at the international truck park. There were trucks from the USSR and other countries behind the iron curtain. They all appeared to have minders on board, with them. There was a small group of British truck drivers. One of them by chance was from Gypsy's area in England and was the father of one of Gypsy's acquaintances. "You don't want a lift with me', said Roy. "I'm going up to Soviet territory to pick up a load of a dodgy diesel, then I'm coming back here to load up for a run down to Saudi". "You won't want a lift with me", said another. "I'm running to Baghdad". Most of the British drivers were basing at Piraeus for months at a time as they did run after run into the Middle East.

Eventually, Roni organized a lift but the driver said he would only take one person. With hardly any money left and Roni reverted to bitch mode Gypsy had to just let her go. She was only seventeen but she was Israeli, arrogant and headstrong. He was not going to be able to make her change her mind. Besides there wasn't enough money for two bus tickets, he would have to just trust that she would be safe. Roni said that she had changed her mind about going to England and would now go and see her cousin in Paris instead.

Well, thanks for nothing", thought Gypsy to himself as he took the train back to Monastraki.

There had been no chance of getting out from Piraeus, Roni had grabbed the only lift going north for the forseeable future. After dropping his back pack at the hostel he followed his nose to a travel agent he had spotted near to Syntagma Square. There for the grand total of twenty-eight pounds, he bought himself a one way ticket to London for the next day.

The Magic bus, at that time, used to run between London and Athens and London and Istanbul. It was also possible if you had all the necessary visas, to take another Magic bus from Istanbul to Delhi and even Kathmandu. In Athens and no doubt Istanbul too, a large number of copy cat operations were also flourishing with cut price services available to many parts of Europe including London. Gypsy was travelling on one such dodgy operation a Greek shoestring service.

It wasn't the smartest bus that Gypsy had ever seen and not just that but every seat was full. But when you are only paying twenty eight quid for a ride from Athens to London you know it won't be first class deluxe.

The bus headed out of Athens heading for Thessaloniki along a boring nondescript route. It took all afternoon and most of the evening getting there. In Yugoslavia Marshal Tito was on his death bed and people were commenting on what would happen if his death was announced while they were crossing the country. Would they seal the borders or do other crazy things? After all Tito made Yugoslavia. Without him maybe something really mad might happen.

At two o'clock in the morning the bus reached the border. First was the Greek passport inspection, then they drove to the Yugoslav entry point where a man in a peeked cap, jackboots and long tunic coat and a pencil mustache marched up and down the bus collecting everyone's passports.

The only thing missing were the swastikas, he was a visual carbon copy.

Gypsy looked at him feeling a little puzzled. He felt like saying "bloody hell, I thought you died in a bunker in Berlin in 1945", but thought better of it. The fellow didn't speak any English and even if he did, he might not have had a sense of humor. Anyway, what a great place for him to hide, when most of the world thinks he's dead, and the conspiracy theorists were focusing on South America. Who would know he was working as a humble border guard in Yugoslavia? However, he still might do well to get rid of the mustache!

Passports back and the bus was back on its merry way, rolling past large tracts of flat non descript farmland, as the sun started to rise.

The bus cruised on through the day. There was nothing much of interest to look at as they traveled. The scenery was depressing and the food at the roadhouses where the bus stopped was incredibly bad.

By the late afternoon the bus was rolling past the grey factories and other industrial buildings that marked the outskirts of Belgrade. There was a large billboard advertising JAT, (The Yugoslavian National Airline) it had a picture of a DC10 in the JAT colors. "Well at least the Slavs have enough sense not to be flying the crap that the soviets sell", thought Gypsy to himself. As a child he had wanted to be a pilot and still took a keen interest in aviation.

The bus continued north, into the night, crossing into Austria in the early hours of the morning. Gypsy breathed a sigh of relief, Tito hadn't died and he was back in a part of the world where the food was edible.

The bus cruised through Austria and the scenery improved. By mid morning they had crossed into Germany and were driving towards Munich.

When they stopped at a road house Gypsy changed money and got himself a hot meal, he was hungry, as after seeing the food that others had ordered at the road houses of Yugoslavia, he had decided that he would rather not bother. The food in Germany tasted good, like real good, but it was now time to jump back on the bus.

The bus sped on past Munich, Frankfurt and Colne, then up to Aachen and across the border into Belgium, through Liege, through Brussels, where two people got off the bus.

The bus drove on until it reached Zeebrugge on the Belgian coast. They all got off of the bus and boarded a ferry to Dover. The next three and a half hours were spent relaxing and sharing travel stories, as the boat made its way across the English Channel.

They then got back on board the bus at Dover port, for the short ride to customs. The bus was being driven by two young jovial Greek men who had done their best to make the journey as pleasant as possible for everyone. When the passengers had cleared the particularly sullen British customs and got back on the bus, a group of Kiwis at the back of the bus set about persuading one of the drivers to share out one of the two large bottles of duty free whiskey that they had seen him buying onboard the boat. So the drive to London turned into a piss up, with the

Kiwis singing out at full volume, a quaint old New Zealand rugby song, something about four German officers crossing the Rhine.

Two hours later the bus stopped at Victoria and everyone piled off. It was too late for a train so Gypsy bedded down on the floor in the station. He took the train home in the morning, once again getting home with just a fiver in his pocket to last out the week on.

CHAPTER 3

ENGLAND

MAY 1980

He got a good welcome home, his father had just expanded the business by buying a garden centre. He had kept the old manager on and he had said to Gypsy's father that it would be nice if Gypsy could work for him at the garden centre.

Gypsy enjoyed working at the Garden center and learned a lot. It was a world of difference from the scruffy tree and shrub department back at the main site. The staff had been trained to take great care to make sure each plant was clean, healthy and well presented, Gypsy liked this way of doing things.

Also there were not so many egos running around as it was an older crowd, thus Gypsy had his thoughts to himself as he worked. He thought about the road and about India. He was going to save up and hit the road to India as soon as possible, that was his plan.

Some days after arriving back in England, Gypsy was feeling relaxed and was enjoying his work. That was until he got a phone call from Roni, saying that she had just arrived in England and was coming to stay with him. She had been a complete bitch since leaving Jerusalem and he hoped that her ugly thoughts, words and behavior would subside on reaching her goal of getting to England. He almost regretted giving her his address, but she was young and alone, what could he do? he felt partly responsible for her being there. Roni arrived and was welcomed in by Gypsy and his family. She had no money so Gypsy's father offered her a job, working on the plant nursery.

For the next two to three weeks she bitched, moaned, shit stirred and threw the most infantile of tantrums and pretty much refused to work properly.

Not only had she caused Gypsy to lose face in front of his family and friends but she had pissed off everyone around her. She had such a demoralizing effect when she was working on the nursery that Gypsy's father had to sack her.

Even then, the family still tried to help her, offering her a domestic job instead, to which she not only refused but had another of her brat tantrums.

In the end the family could stand it no more, giving her some cash to get by on and the address of the Israeli Embassy in London, they put her on a train to Victoria, telling her, "It's impossible for us to help you given your bad behavior. Go to your embassy in London, they should be able to get you home." After this experience it helped Gypsy and his family to understand the causes of anti-Semitism all too well.

"As long as Jewish parents raise emotionally uneducated, non empathetic, dishonest, spoilt brats then how can it be expected for anyone to like them? The usual common, shrill, shrieking accusations of anti-Semitism leveled at people who don't appreciate the behavior that they are subject too by such spoilt brats rings pretty hollow in the eyes of any normal person. It should be explained to people who make the accusations, if you want to understand anti-Semitism, first look at your own behavior to see what it is that you are doing or not doing, that causes those around you to feel such offense. Accusing the whole world of being anti-Semitic is a most cowardly cop out".......Gypsy

Glastonbury festival wasn't happening that year so Gypsy hitched down to the Stonehenge free festival. It was much more anarchic than Glastonbury, with little or no organization. Bands just turned up and set up their own stage, sound system and generator and played for anyone who wanted to listen. The cops couldn't come onto the site so people could do pretty much, as they liked. Signs with the prices for weed, hash, mushrooms or acid were posted outside vans and tents. Nick Turner (of 'Hawkwind' fame) had set up his stage and let other bands perform on it until it was his time to perform with his latest band, 'The Androids of Mu'.

The atmosphere outside of the festival site was none too welcoming, with the cops pulling any person they saw walking alone that they thought might have anything to do with the festival. Gypsy was walking by the side of the road, when a cop car came screaming down the road in the opposite direction, they screeched to a halt and three cops jumped out and grabbed him then bundled him into the back seat, then sped off in the direction of the nearby village of Amesbury. They then bundled him out of the car and into the cop shop where they strip searched him and went through everything in his clothes and back pack with a fine toothed comb. He was carrying but they didn't find it. Gypsy at that young age may have been green to the road but he'd learned a trick or two in Israel where their security could be much tighter.

Back on site he saw a notice saying, "if you have been pulled by the pigs, please report it to 'Release', we are in a tent at the back of the field', so Gypsy went to their tent and reported the matter.

Inside was a group of young hippie lawyers who were working on a campaign to get cannabis legalized. It seemed like a good idea to Gypsy. He would take a joint over a beer any day. 'Cannabis doesn't make you do things that you will regret later. However it does make you quite hungry, but that was no problem, Gypsy wasn't prone to putting on weight.

The solstice morning saw a large procession of hippies, druids and assorted misfits and weirdo's making a procession from the festival site into the innermost ring of stones where they drummed and danced for several hours.

Two days later, with the Solstice over and no especially good music to stick around for, Gypsy pulled up his tent, packed his back pack and walked off in the direction of the highway.

He wasn't going to be able to hitch a lift easily, caked in mud as he was, so he took local buses to get home.

Back at work, he was moved from the garden center to the engineering workshop, at the main site where his modest skills were more urgently needed on general maintenance and repair duties. He enjoyed working with the engineers as they always had more intelligent things to talk about than the crowd who worked with the plants. They had a new worker helping them. The other engineers looked down on this new helper, as his approach to any job was brute force and ignorance. They had brute force when it was needed and were built like giants, But each of the three brothers were not only highly intelligent, but also highly trained in the skills of engineering. One had a 'City and Guilds Diploma in electrical Engineering', another had one in mining. They all knew how to weld, fabricate and erect any manor of building you cared to wish for. . Gypsy's friend, Barbara, arrived from Germany, for her month long stay and also three Italian girls of about the same age came to stay at the homes of the friends of Gypsy's family in the village. They too, were staying for a month and also would be working on the nursery. One of them was the grand daughter of an Italian friend of Gypsy's grandfather. They had probably met during the nineteen twenties while Gypsy's grandfather was making one of his numerous and regular journeys to Palestine. He was living in Yugoslavia up until the time of the Second World War and was immensely rich. However when the Nazis invaded, he being Jewish, had no choice but to take his family and run with nothing more than the clothes on their backs. Even then they had only just made it into Italy alive after crossing a lake in a small boat during the dead of night and in the depths of winter. Other Jews who had been caught crossing the lake to get to Italy had had weights tied to them and thrown into the depths.

Then With nothing, he had started over again and was the owner and founder of one of Italy's best known liquor brands. He had settled in Trieste after the war and had once again become immensely wealthy. One of his daughters had become a close friend of Gypsy's mother. Both Gypsy and his brother had been to stay with her and her family in Rome on different occasions. So now was the time to repay the favor, with her oldest daughter staying for a month with two of her friends in order to improve their understanding of the English language.

Gypsy would take Barbara out on trips into Brighton, sometimes the Italian girls would come too. Saturday night in Brighton in those days was an affordable and highly enjoyable experience, with hundreds if not thousands of highly affordable and good restaurants to choose from. Then bars, pubs, cinemas and night clubs were all there in plentiful supply. On top of that, as everyone knows, Brighton has a long beach with piers and pubs on it. So it was for the next month, every Saturday night was party time in Brighton.

Gypsy had been collecting albums in large numbers since he had returned from his second trip. Mostly he was looking for the music that he had heard in the Danish Tea House in Jerusalem and at Bollocks in Eilat. While Barbara and her new found Italian friends went searching for clothes and the likes, on a Saturday afternoon in Brighton, Gypsy would be scouring the second hand record shops, in the back lanes looking for albums by the likes of the Stones, Pink Floyd, Camel, Doctor John and John Mayall. Perhaps one of his favorites that he found at that time was an acoustic bottle neck solo album, by a guitarist called John Fahey. The album was called, 'The Transfiguration of Blind Joe Death'.

The month went by very fast and Gypsy was sad when they all went home.

On the nursery Gypsy's job had changed again and now he was on general labor but mostly he worked in the tree and shrub department. That was except for Friday mornings, when all hands were on deck, to help the Mushroom department.

Every Friday morning fourteen tons of horse shit mixed with straw would turn up on the back of a non tipping heavy duty truck. One of the staff from the nursery would be required to join the driver on top of this big, steaming, foul smelling, pile of shit, with a pitch fork. In the space of an hour and a half, they were expected to have the entire load forked off the truck and onto the first conveyor belt, of a large mechanized operation, that processed the compost for mushroom growing. (different processes were run on three consecutive mornings, each week, involving this machine, a fleet of electric forklifts, a spawning room and over ten growing houses).

It was a right of passage at the company, that any young man working on the company, on reaching his eighteenth birthday, would have to take a turn on this dreaded smelly and hard job. There were no showers at that time on the nursery and so doing the job also meant going around for the rest of the day smelling like a big pile of shit. This, of course did wonders for the man's popularity, as everyone avoided standing down wind of him.

The foreman who was also one of the three engineering brothers did not ask Gypsy to go on the load, although he had turned eighteen, as he was the boss's son.

Gypsy had to call out to him and said, "Wait a minute, John. I'm eighteen now, I'll take my turn on the load". It was an hour and a half of the most back breaking work he had ever done. By the time he had finished, he had broken bloody blisters all over his hands, but he had done it without slacking, even though it had been incredibly hot, standing on top of the steaming pile of crap.

It proved to be more than worthwhile, as the older workers all came up and shook his hand and said, "Well done lad". He had, by volunteering as he did, earned the respect of all of the workers. He may have been the boss's son but no one could call him a spoilt brat or coward. After going to the first aid cabinet in the office, to bandage up his bloodied hands, he was back, out working in the fields. Thankfully, his job put him at a good distance from the other workers.

On another day, he had been sent to retrieve some plants for an order. He noticed that the whole department, with thirty to forty thousand plants in it looked like it had been abandoned, with plants tipped over on their sides and a jungle of weeds growing over everything. Gypsy wasn't too surprised, as the charge hand in charge of that department, had a habit of wandering around the nursery, wasting the time of other people, as he tried to make himself look busy.

At lunch time Gypsy talked with his father about what he had seen and offered to single handedly rectify the problem. His father accepted his offer and gave him responsibility for cleaning up the department. Now Gypsy had his own department to take care of. He spent the rest of the summer and part of the autumn, cleaning, weeding, trimming, tying and applying fertilizers to the three acres of climber plants, in his department.

During the late summer, he had gotten busted with a small quantity of hash, at a not so large free pop festival on the South Downs and didn't want to wait around for the hypocritical, control drama queens of the local Magistrates court to play their pathetic waggy finger games with him.

While talking to one of his ex school teachers, who had now become a good and trusted friend, about his situation and how he wanted to earn the money as so as he could make the journey to India. His friend mentioned, how when she had been on holiday in Greece the year before she had stayed in a village on the Peloponnese peninsula, called Tolon. She said that she had met an Englishman there, who worked every autumn on the orange and grapefruit harvest and that he had told her that he had earned enough money from it to pay for a trip to India. Also he said that there was plenty of work to go around.

Gypsy was immediately interested and took down the details of where to find the man.

Back at work, Gypsy had completed the total rehabilitation of the climber department and now thousands of Halianas, Loniceris, Pafloras and Clematis, stood in clean lines, looking healthy, well trimmed and ready for sale, with not a weed to be seen. It was by now by far the smartest and cleanest department on the field, looking much like the garden center's clean, well laid out plant beds. . Gypsy, having finished his task, joined the rest of the tree and shrub team working under the direction of two charge hands, one of whom was the one who was meant to be looking after the climber department. Gypsy hadn't noticed it because he had been too busy enjoying his job, but workers from other departments, had been talking and taking the piss out of the two charge hands, asking why if one eighteen year old could look after a large department so well, did they fail with their whole team to keep the rest of the field in good stead. . In order to save money, the company was using used tomato grow bags, as part of its peat compost mix. Thirty, large, eighteen wheel, truck loads, of this muck, was due to arrive and had to be off loaded and stacked by hand, as no one at the time, had brains enough to think of loading it onto pallets at the point of dispatch.

The two charge hands had lost face at the company and sought to take their revenge. On one particular day ten trucks loads of broken, used grow bags turned up. While they rotated all of the other workers, on this back breaking, dirty job, Gypsy was kept on for every single load. By the end of the day he was so tired he could barely walk. On top of that a lorry had shown up at five o'clock and had to be loaded for deliveries as so that it was ready to leave first thing the following morning.

When his father asked why he was looking so very knackered he told him about the day's work.

The next day was entertaining to watch for Gypsy, he had never asked for special treatment and was treated as any other worker was, but there were limits, that had now been crossed. Gypsy enjoyed the spectacle of the two charge hands being made to unload the next ten loads on their own. "That will teach them", he thought, that should be the end of any troubles.

With the cops on his back, he bought himself a one way charter ticket to Athens, said goodbye to the family and took the train to Gatwick airport, carrying the usual back pack and guitar.

ATHENS, OCT 1980.

The plane left the terminal at three o'clock in the morning. That had been the reason the ticket had been so cheap. The flight was a British Airways 737 from their charter subsidiary. The seats didn't even recline, the flight was nearly empty, with some twenty or thirty people on board.

Three hours and forty five minutes later, Gypsy, bleary eyed and carrying his guitar was wandering across the apron at Athens airport. After clearing customs etc he took the bus into Syntagma Square and then wandered back through the Plaka to the Pericles hostel. Dropping his pack on the roof he wandered back out in search of some breakfast.

Greece at that time was not in what was then called the EEC, now known as the 'EU'

Food was cheap and even Gypsy, on his severely limited budget could afford to eat in restaurants and cafes. Gypsy liked Greek food with all that olive oil, garlic and goat cheese.

Breakfast consisted of two eggs fried in olive oil, a chunk of feta goat cheese, a stack of bread and a mug of coffee.

Gypsy had bought himself a map and located Tolon, it was near the town of Nafplion, on the Peloponnese peninsula, not far from Corinth.

The next day he took a bus to the town of Argos and from there to Tolon. He couldn't see where he might find a place to pitch his tent in the wild as all land around appeared to be in use. So he was compelled to use the camp site.

TOLON, GREECE

OCT, 1980.

Tolon was and probably still is a tourist village, with the whole place geared up for taking care of Northern European members of the bucket and spade brigade. It was a family oriented resort.

Gypsy put up his tent, then consulting his notes, he made his way to the village and found the bar described. Further to that on entering, he found the Englishman, described by his friend. "Yes, I do know where there will be work, but you're here way too early. You need to come back in a month or maybe longer" said the man.

Gypsy stuck around Tolon for a couple of nights and joined some young Germans on a hike. It was a nice place to be, but there was no work and Gypsy wanted and needed to work. He only had three hundred pounds and that was not even enough for a return air ticket from Athens to Bombay. (In those days Athens and Bangkok were the cheapest places to buy air tickets, which was why Gypsy had been so keen to go to Greece to work)

Gypsy headed back to Athens. He spent the next two weeks trying to track down any work that may have been on offer, but all to no avail.

There was a room on the roof of the Pericles hostel, all be it with no glass or wood in the windows and door. Rain had forced the others, to seek the comfort of the dormitory below. This left, Gypsy, English Steve and Munfred, who was from Germany as the only roof residents. They were each set up in their own space in the room, as rain had stopped play or the hunt for work for the day. Gypsy was lying on top of his sleeping bag reading a paperback by a writer by the name of Ted Simon. The book, 'Jupiter's Travels' was about a three and a half year journey that he had made, around the world on a Triumph motorbike. First he had crossed Europe and Africa until he reached Cape Town, then rode by ship to South America, he rode in a large loop around that continent, before heading up through central America and Mexico to California. From there he took another boat trip. This time he was heading for Australia. He looped the continent, then took another boat to Indonesia. Riding up through Java and Sumatra, he crossed to Malaysia and rode on up into and around Thailand. He then took one final boat trip with the bike, crossing to India for a loop of that place and then the long ride home, through Pakistan, Iran and Turkey etc. Gypsy was picking up vital bits of travel information and inspiration for future travels that he wanted to make.

Gypsy was two thirds of the way through his book and Steve and Munfred had spent the last few minutes talking about what a good breakfast they were having

"This is one of the best breakfasts I've ever had", said Steve. "Ja, it is zee good breakfast", said Munfred. Gypsy looked up to see Steve passing him a large cone shaped joint. Gypsy toked on it with pleasure. "Yes, you're right, this is a very good breakfast", said Gypsy.

Hashish and ganja in Greece, in those days were like the proverbial rocking horse manure and there were harsh penalties for those who were caught with it. So it was almost a miracle that any had been found at all.

Two more joints were shared, before Steve and Gypsy retreated in spaced out bliss, into the books that they were reading, while Munfred went off into the city to take care of some business.

Steve and Munfred apparently, lived in some caves at a hippie hang out on Crete and were in Athens taking care of business, e.g. visas, mail, etc.

Munfred returned from his mission, "Zat dope it really made me feel horny ja!!!" he said "I am valking tovards Syntagma Sqvare und as you can see I am vearing zees Indian trousers zat are so thin und I haf zis huge erection, I cannot help it! und zis old voman walks up to me in ze street und hits me on ze head vith her umbrella and calls me somesing bad in Greek. I sink zat she called me a pervert or somsing similar". Steve and Gypsy were rolling on the ground laughing like crazy as this large Deutschlander stood there with a helpless victim expression on his face. The rest of the dope was partied away that afternoon before a trip out for some good Plaka night life.

First, to a café, where all enjoyed chicken and chips, with Greek salad, feta cheese, bread and wine, at one pound (100 Drachmas) per head. Then to the 2001 club high up in the Plaka. It was possibly, the sleaziest disco in the area. On the way Gypsy ran into an old classmate from school who had joined the British navy and his ship was moored at Piraeus, or somewhere thereabouts. Gypsy joined him and his crewmates for a while as they partied, but it was just too embarrassing, watching the idiot antics that they got up to while on shore leave with evil disgusting Greek grog such as retsina and ouzo inside of them. So he wandered off to join Steve and Munfred at the 2001 club.

At other hostels, around that part of Athens, many other travelers were eking out their time, waiting for the picking season to start. Thus there was not even the whisper of a job going. At one hostel on one particular afternoon, Gypsy heard a group of British travelers slagging off Israel and Jews in general even though many of them had never been there. They were the normal types of uptight bullies, that Gypsy had so often the misfortune to encounter at school or down the pub, back in England. These were the sorts of people who could only attack another, while in a pack or gang.

Disgusted by their presence so far from their nasty homes in England, Gypsy sought to get as far from them as possible.

It was still a few weeks before the picking was due to start. He still had some money in his pocket. He took a bus to the airport and bought a return ticket to Tel Aviv on the first available flight, which happened to be with TWA.

In those days Trans World Airlines did two flights a day, to Tel Aviv. Both would be with a Boeing 707, that would have almost as many stops as a regional bus route. The flight would start out in some secondary city in the USA, somewhere like Baltimore or Philadelphia, for example, before flying to New York or Washington D.C. and then proceed on to Paris, Rome and Athens before the final destination of Tel Aviv.

And so it was, that after a night's sleep at Athens airport, Gypsy boarded a jet plane full of jetlagged and grumpy, middle aged, Jewish, American women (not an experienced to be recommended. Pass the Valium somebody please! - Prozac hadn't been invented at that point in time).

The flight was OK, as it only took two and a half hours, and the lunch with huge portions of food was great.

At Ben Gurion Airport Gypsy got through immigration and customs and jumped on a bus to Jerusalem.

On arrival in the city, he took a local bus down the full length of Jaffa road, to the Jaffa Gate, where he got off and walked through the gate, into the old city. He took a right turn and walking along past the Armenian quarter and following the road to the left, around with the contour of the old city wall, he continued on, until he reached the Zion gate, which leads outside the city walls, on to Holy Mount Zion. Gypsy turned right and walked through, walking straight in front the road forked. One way led through stone alleys to where the Yeshiva that he had visited before was located. The other way led to a synagogue, a Holocaust Museum and car parks and access to all other areas of Mount Zion.

Gypsy took the path through the stone alleyways, leading to an old Turkish fort, that was a remnant, left from the time of the Ottoman Empire. It had been converted into a rabbinical school of learning, called a Yeshiva.

The Yeshiva in question, was at the time, operating halfway between a hippie flop house and an institution of learning, thus Gypsy found no problem finding a place to bed down.

After finding a space in one of the stone rooms of the old fortress, Gypsy got talking to two of the other recent arrivals, they were Ephraim and Rick. Ephraim had flown from the States, straight to Israel and in the process of delving into his Jewish roots, decided to stay at the Yeshiva for a while. He was a carefree Californian who liked music, mysticism and hashish, all in equal measure. Rick on the other hand had taken a boat from Piraeus to Alexandria then travelled Overland down through Cairo, Luxor and Aswan to Wadi Halfa where he crossed into Sudan. From there he took a three day train ride to Khartoum (the trains are apparently always slow in Sudan). Then from Khartoum he took another train, that took something like two weeks, to get from Khartoum to the southern capital of Juba. He had spent a good deal of the journey, riding on the roof of the train alongside the local tribesmen and their goats. He described the people and way of life in southern Sudan as being wonderful and very welcoming.

Then after stopping there for some long while, he travelled on to Kenya. He spoke of many wonderful things in Kenya, especially an island offof the coast (that in this book shall remain unnamed, as Gypsy has not yet been there and wishes to visit it before the place turns into "Babylon central"). The island, he said, had to be seen to be believed. There was a town on the island that he described as being like an original Arabian Night's town, with exotic Muslim markets, etc.

After a trip around Kenya he had flown to Bombay and travelled extensively in India and Nepal. For part of his journey, he travelled with a monkey, who befriended him at one of the places that he had stopped at. The monkey, (a small brown Asian variety common in India) would ride on his shoulder and travel on the train with him and was his travel companion for several months. He had spent three months trekking in the Himalayas, starting from Kathmandu and Pokhara.

Then after India he had flown to Athens and then Tel Aviv and just like Ephraim and Gypsy, he was checking out his Jewish roots.

Gypsy spent the next two weeks, checking out Jewish study classes, about such things as the Talmud and the Gamora, which originally where the unwritten law of the Jews. Then at or before the sacking of Jerusalem, by the Romans, someone had decided that the unwritten law needed to be written down as so as not to be lost or forgotten.

Two commentaries were given on what that law actually meant and why. The Talmud is the writings of the unwritten law and the Gamora is the commentaries given by the two rabbis, Lamai and Hillel. The students of the Yeshiva would spend a lot of time debating the reasons for each small part of each law. While this would form a very good training for a lawyer, Gypsy was at a loss to understand what it could have to do with religion or mysticism. Apart from studying and eating and sleeping, Gypsy spent a lot of time with Rick and Ephraim, listening to their travel stories, as they sat smoking joints, among the trees, on the west side of Mount Zion.

The two weeks went by all too fast and Gypsy was soon flying back to Athens with fond memories of his two weeks on Mount Zion.

At Athens airport Gypsy took a bus straight to the bus station and then another to Corinth and then another to Nafplion.

It was on this night and the following morning, that Gypsy discovered the foul horrors of getting drunk on the Greek local tipple of Retsina, a wine with tree resin added for extra flavor.

Gypsy arrived in Nafplion's main square before the sun was down, it was full of travelers, no doubt all were waiting for the picking work to begin. Each one had a small bottle of a yellow, piss colored liquid that they were drinking from. Gypsy asked someone what it was. "Retsina" he was told "it's Greek wine and it's cheap" said one of the other travelers just thirty drakmas a bottle.

That night he got hammered on it. After several bottles, he staggered off, tripping over several railway lines on the way, while looking for a disused piece of land, on which to put up his tent.

He awoke in the morning to perhaps the most vicious hangover that he had ever had, his head throbbing with an evil headache. In his confusion he climbed out of the tent the wrong way, ripping a huge gash in it. He found that he had put up his tent in someone's orchard and he could hear voices not so far away. Quickly he took down his tent and packed it away along with his sleeping bag. He made his way to one of the bars where he had seen other travelers hanging out, for some much needed coffee. He sat there for much of the day, with needle and cotton, as he repaired his tent. One of the other travelers taught him how to double stitch, as so that if the thread was cut it wouldn't come undone.

By the afternoon, he had met some other travelers with tents and pitched his tent with theirs, next to the beach.

It wasn't the same sort of crowd that he had met in Sinai, Eilat and Jerusalem, this was a much more uptight and morose crowd. Gypsy stayed a few nights around the encampment, but it wasn't a comfortable feeling, being around so many uptight losers, projecting their psychosis.

"The weird thing about such people is how they gather in groups or clusters and attempt to project their own bullshit on others. Though they are angry and uptight themselves, they will go and find some quiet and shy person, sitting on his or her own and try to tell them that they are the angry and uptight one............Gypsy

After three or four days, Gypsy got together with three other travelers from England who were going to a secret location, on a cliff face to camp, just as so that they could get away from the wankers who had camped near the beach.

It was known as the secret site. The path up could not be seen as it was hidden from the main path by bushes and trees. It was so well hidden that at night, no one could see or smell their fire if they were walking on the main path below. They also had their own private beach that was hidden from view on the other side of the main path. The weather was still good and the water still warm, so while they waited for the work to start, they could relax a bit. Nafplion's skyline was dominated by a castle on top of a large steep hill with a long and winding stone stepped path leading up to it. The encampment was halfway up this hill, on a side not visible from the town. On one occasion they walked up the steps to the castle, while one of the group in his boredom, decided to count every step, (seven hundred and something steps). On another occasion, they practically climbed up the sheer cliff face, on to the top of the hill. A feets, that looking back on it, they must have been mad to have done without ropes and perhaps an experienced guide.

It was at the bar in the main square, while waiting for news of when the picking would start, when Gypsy got to hear the news from the other travelers, that John Lennon had just been shot and killed in New York by some pathetic American nutter. He had killed him apparently just because he wanted to make himself famous.

Gypsy felt disgust that a society could breed such vermin, with no empathy for anyone but themselves. Anyway why would he want to be famous? after all society only puts someone on a soap box when they want to throw rocks at them.

Gypsy was doubly spooked by this unfortunate event, as four years prior to getting this piece of news, he had had a dream or nightmare, that he was standing over John Lennon's grave with the other three Beatles standing there in mourning. The dream had been so real that he was surprised when he awoke in the morning and found that John Lennon was still alive, he wondered what it all meant.

Glasses were raised in the café and a minute's silence held as just about everyone there was a fan of the Beatles and John Lennon's solo work.

At the bar, it was a colorful crowd, with football hooligans from England, people on the run from the law, in their own and other countries, mercenaries, bikers and desperados, all waiting for the work to begin. Ironically, the best of the crowd in Gypsy's view, were the mercenaries and bikers as they always told it straight, as it was and would only get leery if someone really asked for it and wouldn't leave them alone.

There was one not so tall but hugely strong short haired Dutchman who spoke about opps that he had been on in the Belgian Congo in the French Foreign Legion and later as a mercenary, there were a couple of bikers from one of the well known British 1%er chapters [since to have been merged into Hells Angels UK] and a few other ex soldiers and wild men hanging around in the shadows. They were hugely strong and unlike the football hooligans and other inadequate types, knew that they didn't need to prove anything. Gypsy liked listening to their stories, they were certainly a more interesting crowd than any of the others there as they had all lived fully, running straight towards their fears rather than away from them. For Gypsy these types were a huge source of inspiration that stayed with him forever in the background and subconscious. To do what he had set himself as a goal in life he too would have to someday face his fears head on as a warrior.

A meeting was held between the farmers and the pickers representatives and a picking price of one Drachma per kilo was set, people were angry as they thought they should be getting more, but beggars can't be choosers, so everyone had to accept it.

The weather had gotten cold and everyone was moving into rooms in the town. Gypsy found himself sharing a cheap hotel room with four others. There was a German, he was the room joker, there were two Americans, who were the targets of the German fellow's jokes, on account of their brash and boastful behavior and there was one other traveler from the secret camp site. The room had four beds, (the Americans were a couple and shared one single bed) there was also a shower and wash basin, the toilet was out on the corridor.

Gypsy managed to get one day of work, at an olive oil pressing plant, beating mats to clean them, ready for the next pressing, for ten pounds (1000Drakmas) per shift of 12 hours.

The factory couldn't have been made more dismal if they had tried. There was nowhere to wash, not even an outside tap, and the work was hard and monotonous. Even the Eastern Europeans and Soviet refugees, who were used to tough conditions, had refused to work there and to cap it all, there was a man from England working there who by all appearances had lost his mind. He would jump up and down while holding out the mat and beating it clean, with a crazy manic grin on his face, while issuing fourth strange grunts, that sounded like a mixture of chimpanzee and pig noises.

Someone later told Gypsy, that the guy had been a university graduate before he went crazy. This left Gypsy feeling most disturbed, "how could a bright mind end up like that?" he wondered to himself.

Despite his need for money for his journey, one day at the olive oil plant was all that he could take and it was apparent, that only the most very desperate would even consider working there. Gypsy sat and waited with the others, until the time for work would come.

The work started in the last week of November. All of a sudden they were all getting up early and jumping onto trucks in the main square, from where they were taken in large gangs, to the surrounding orchards, where the ladders and buckets would be stacked, ready for use.

It was piece work, so no one was hanging about, the grapefruit trees that they were picking from had thorns on them and people's arms if they weren't covered would be scratched and bloody by the end of the day. Lunch was always provided by the farmers, in the form of a Greek plowman's lunch of bread, salad, feta cheese and olive oil.

It was hard to make money at this work, unless you were some sort of land dwelling octopus. No matter how hard he worked Gypsy found he was making barely enough money to pay his room and food bills.

The trouble with gang piece work comes, if one or two people decide to slack, then others have to work twice as hard to make up for them and with everyone else going as fast as they could this was not possible.

After three weeks of slogging, Gypsy found that he was no better off than the day that he had started picking. He was living as cheaply as possible, but after such a hard day's work, he was hungry and would wolf down a large quantity of food each night.

The atmosphere at the travellers favorite bar, on the plaza, was not pleasant and Gypsy figured that if he couldn't make money at this kind of hard work, then it was time to cut his losses and leave.

A knife fight had broken out one night between a group of Moroccan merchant seamen, whose ship was moored in the town harbor and some of the pickers. Alcohol and violence was becoming the way of things, in this small town, as everyone was trying to make money, but failing. Gypsy packed his bag and guitar and jumped on a bus to Athens.

It was cold in Athens when Gypsy arrived. There would be no sleeping on the roof this time. Gypsy checked into a hostel dormitory while he considered his options. There was a good crowd at the hostel and they went out into the Plaka one night, to a biker club, where a local band were doing excellent covers of tracks by Lynard Skynard, The doors, The Stones and Led Zeppelin. Outside was parked a long line of customized choppers, some with handle bars so high that it would be necessary to raise arms in a vertical position, to reach them. . Two days later, Gypsy was at Piraeus, trying to hitch a lift north. He had heard rumor of well paid laboring jobs in Germany and was wanting to check it out and see if it was true. There were no lifts available in Piraeus that day, at least not in the direction of Northern Europe. Gypsy had given up and was heading for the metro station to take the train back to Monastraki, when he met another would be hitcher that had reached the same conclusion.

The other traveler was an Irishman who had worked in Germany. Having been on a three month pub crawl around Crete and having spent half of the three thousand pounds that he had saved, he was now almost broke until he could get to Colne to retrieve the other half of his money. They both decided that it would be better spending the twenty five pounds cost for a ticket for the bus to Germany. They headed back into Athens to buy tickets on the next day's bus.

MAGIC BUS

ATHENS-COLNE

DECEMBER,1980.

Boarding the bus at mid day, a bag stacked with food and cold drinks each, Gypsy and Shaun, the Irishman, got on the ragged old bus that would take them to Germany.

Once fully loaded it pulled out from it's parking space and sped off through the streets of Athens and onto the road north to Thessalonica. The two drivers were a father and son team. Except that team was not the word, as the father would only let his son drive for two or three hours a day, as he and his container of little white pills did all of the rest of the work.

It turned out that Shaun was an ex-Catholic priest, who having done all the training, found that it was not his calling and he preferred just being a laborer and having his thinking time to himself.

The bus crossed into Yugoslavia at the ungodly hour of two o'clock in the morning and all travelers were awoken, first to hand their passports for checking and stamping on the Greek side of the border and then again on the Yugoslav side.

The bus rumbled on, through a dark, cold and uninviting, snowscape, as it headed north.

The bus stopped at 7:30 am for toilet and food break. The road house was the normal bleak looking hole, with food not worth eating that Gypsy had encountered before in Yugoslavia. So after a quick trip to the toilet Gypsy was back on board, eating food he had brought with him from Athens.

The bus rolled on through the foggy snowscape as it followed the signs for Belgrade.

They eventually stopped again for lunch at yet another nondescript roadhouse, again Gypsy ate on the bus. Half an hour down the road from the roadhouse and the bus was stopped by the police. It appeared that the drivers had forgotten to pay for the fuel that they had taken, back at the road house. Two hours were spent by the side of the road while one of the drivers hitched a ride back to the roadhouse to pay the bill.

A snowball fight erupted, once everyone was off the bus, and though it sounds silly, it was a good way for everyone to stay warm.

Thus the bill paid and driver returned, the bus rolled on, up past the ugly suburbs of Belgrade and North, towards Zagreb.   Again, at some ungodly hour, the bus reached the Austrian frontier. Passports out once more, and back into a land where the people knew how to cook good food. There was a road house stop at 7 am, but Gypsy again ate from his own stash of food on the bus. It wasn't worth turning any of his precious few travelers cheques into Austrian Shillings (the Austrian currency at that time) he would wait until they crossed into Germany and buy Deutsch Marks instead.

The bus rolled on past Saltsburg and across the border into Germany. As it rolled through the afternoon they passed first by Munich then north to Frankfurt.

The work was starting to take its toll on the old speed freak at the wheel as it got dark that night. He had been driving almost non stop the whole way and was now starting to let the bus drift across the road as he started to fall asleep at the wheel, even to the point of bumping the crash barrier in the central reservation. At this point people were starting to freak out and demanded that he take a break and let his son take over for a while. (like until London that was).

At roughly eight o'clock that night, the bus pulled onto the hard shoulder, near an ausfart [autobahn exit] and Gypsy and Shaun were handed their bags from the hold. The maneuver was totally illegal, the bus didn't even leave the autobahn, but both Gypsy and Shaun were relieved to have left the Grim reaper express alive and let it carry on on it's way to London. Even though they had been dropped off in the snow five kilometers from the city and late in the evening they were glad to be there. Walking down the exit and along the road, with their bags, they were soon able to flag down a passing taxi that then took them to the first U bahn station to appear on that road.

After a two train U bahn ride, they were at a bar at Barbarossa Platz, called 'Der Spiegel'. The first impressions Gypsy got of the Germans of his own age, was just how friendly and welcoming they were. Someone gave him an acid tab, which he took straight away. Shaun ran into a German friend in the bar, as they were sitting there, drinking. "Ja you can both stay at my apartment, there is enough room, no problem" he said.

They were out drinking until 6 am, so it was three very drunk and tired people, two of whom were carrying back packs, that staggered off to the apartment.

Gypsy and Shaun were immensely grateful, as without the invitation they would have been looking at crashing out in the U bahn.

When they awoke in the morning, they found themselves in a comfortable, hippie style apartment, complete with hi-fi and an excellent set of vinyl, much of which, they got to listen to, during their four day stay.

Shaun checked around his work contacts for Gypsy but couldn't help him find a job. "It's just too close to Christmas", he said. "No one is hiring new labour now, everyone is heading back to England or Ireland for Christmas. You might as well do the same."

It was not so far to go and see Barbara at Wanna Eikel, so Gypsy took a local train there. It was unfortunate, because Gypsy had caught the flu on the short train ride and by the time that he got there, he was feeling quite ill.

Barbara and her parents were taking a bus to the Alps that night for a skiing holiday. Gypsy was too broke to think of going skiing but he wished he could. He liked being in the mountains and the food and drink always smelled and tasted so good in those alpine regions.

Gypsy waved goodbye to Barbara and her parents as they got on board their bus, then he took the train back to Colne.

From Colne hopbahnhof, he phoned his parents and told them he was coming home.

"We'll be away in Italy skiing, you don't want to join us, I presume?" his father said. "I wouldn't mind, but I've got no money," said Gypsy. "Well if you want to join us then get yourself to England and await further instructions," his father told him.

The next day Shaun and Gypsy thanked their kind host once more, then made their way, via the U bahn, to Colne Hofbahnhof, from where they took a train to Calais, then a boat to England and then another train ride in to London.

Gypsy said goodbye and thanks to Shaun at Victoria station before taking a local train to his home village.

ENGLAND/SUSSEX

DECEMBER 1980.

He reached home four days before Christmas. He felt as sick as a dog with the flu and thus headed strait to the local doctors surgery for some medication. The family had already left and there was a letter of instructions, that had been left with his grandparents on how to join them skiing. There was also enough cash in the envelope to buy an air ticket to Munich and a train ticket from there to the Val Gardena station in the Italian Sud Tirol.

When he told his grandparents of his adventures and where he had been travelling, his grandfather who had also travelled extensively in the world said "wait a minute, I have something I wish to show you." He returned from his study with a stack of photo albums and then proceeded to show Gypsy a series of faded black and white photos of the same places that Gypsy had travelled, but taken between forty and sixty years prior. He told Gypsy about when in the early nineteen twenties he and his friends would travel by train in Europe and how on more than a few occasions, had taken the train to Genoa and then a ship across the Mediterranean sea to Jaffa. On some occasions, there had been groups of missionaries on board, who were travelling to the Holy Land with the express intention of converting Jews to Christianity.

His grandfather told of the delight he and his friends took in winding these fools up. Every morning, the missionaries would have a religious service on the open deck, at which they would sing hymns. Gypsy's grandfather and two friends had written parodies of each of the hymns and would stand behind the missionaries, during their hymn time and sing the parodies. Apparently the missionaries didn't appreciate the humor in this.

As his grandfather flipped through the album, Gypsy saw photos of Greece, Israel, Syria and most of eastern and central Europe, as they shared travel stories. When Gypsy told of how he had been working in Nafplion, his grandfather told him about when he and Gypsy's grandmother had stayed there, but unlike Gypsy, they had stayed in the fancy looking Xenia hotel, up on the cliff, opposite the castle.

He spent Christmas day with his grandparents, whose company he enjoyed very much. They were lively, intelligent and willing to listen to all ideas, even if they didn't agree with them. They would argue with intelligence rather than just raising their voices and adopting aggressive, arrogant postures, unlike certain other members of the family. Gypsy would always find this refreshing and relaxing.

On Boxing Day early in the morning Gypsy made a phone call to British Airways at Heathrow and booked himself onto a flight to Munich for mid day. With his bag packed and the envelope of money that his parents had left for him, he jumped into the passenger seat of his grandfather's Alfa Romeo for a breakneck race to the airport. His grandfather was known as a fast and wild driver. There was a joke in the family that though he never had accidents, his passengers often did.

In another life he could have been an excellent rally driver. Again, on this day, he was up to form, despite being in his seventies.

After a Stirling Moss like performance across the Sussex countryside, the car came to a halt outside the departure hall of terminal one at Heathrow.

Gypsy jumped out, thanked his grandfather and ran into the check in hall. Thanks to his grandfather's velocity habit he was just in time to take an earlier flight. Running through the tunnels to the gate, he was glad that he had only brought hand luggage with him, as there would have been no time to check in a bag.

The British Airways Trident taxied out to the runway and took off and Gypsy was able to relax and eat breakfast. An hour and forty minutes later, the plane touched down at Munich.

After clearing through the airport Gypsy took a bus to the Hofbahnhof where he bought a ticket and boarded a train to Sud Tirol in Italy. The train rolled for over an hour and a half across a flat snowscape towards Innsbruck from where it entered the mountains and climbed up through the Brenner Pass. Passing forests of pine trees, frozen waterfalls and semi frozen streams and rivers along the way. Three and a half hours later it was dark as he stepped off of the train at the 'Val Gardena' station and looked around for a public phone booth. After a wait of one hour, his father arrived with the car at the cold, snowbound station, to collect him. The car a Renault thirty was equipped with snow chains and as they took off up through the valley to San Christina Gypsy saw why. There had been a fresh fall of snow that night and the road had not yet been ploughed. It was covered in snow and ice and without chains there was no way that anyone could drive on those roads. . Gypsy was happy to see his family again and more than happy to be in San Christina, with its great skiing, excellent food and fantastic scenery. He enjoyed ten days of skiing with the family before it was time to leave, for the two day drive back to England.

Although his attempt to reach India had ended this time in failure he would try again to save the money to make the journey. The journey had ended on a good note, with the skiing holiday but now it would be time to go and stick his nose to the grinding wheel and make the money for some serious travel.

CHAPTER 4

SUSSEX ENGLAND

JANUARY 1981.

The first thing Gypsy had to sort out upon his arrival in England was the drug bust that had happened back in the summer. An arrest warrant had been issued for him as he had been absent from the country when the court date had been issued. So when he surrendered, it was run through the courts that same morning.

The arrogant cretin system demanded a penalty. Gypsy could tell from the eyes and gestures of the court officials and even the police that they knew what they were doing was neither fair nor honorable, but their hands were so very tightly tied by a rotten, corrupt system that would victimize any member of the establishment, that dared to point out that with regards to alcohol being legal and the terrible damage it does, the arguments about marijuana were hysterically ridiculous and much akin to the story of the Emperor with no clothes.

The court usher and a cop said as much to him in apology, as he left the court. "This law is ridiculous madness", said the cop. "I can see that you are not a problem or a danger to anyone, nor are most of the others who get into trouble for this", Small comfort given the fifty pounds fine, his wages after taxes, were only thirty two pounds a week at that time. How the hell was he ever going to make the money to get to India? he wondered.

Once again Gypsy had no choice but to work for his father, as Margaret Thatcher was in the process of ravaging the British job market. Though the pay was poor it was a God send to have a job at all at that time.

Gypsy's work in the climber department, plus his willingness to take a turn on the shit truck had certainly not gone unnoticed in the engineering department and he had been requisitioned by the engineers, as an extra pair of hands even before he had returned to England.

"We like him", the Chief Engineer told Gypsy's father. "He's clean and take's pride in his work, unlike those other scruffy so and so's in the tree and shrub department, who are always bringing in broken equipment.

Gypsy spent a lot of time cutting metal and salvaging parts from old heating pipes, from the greenhouses. The old pipes were rotten and had been replaced, but the hardened and cast parts, such as joints, elbows and valves were still in good condition, or at least could be repaired. Outside the workshop there was a large wooden bench with a large chain vice fitted on it. This was where he would spend much of the working day. The weather was good and he enjoyed the work and was happy as he wrenched the pipes apart with a small selection of different heavy hand tools and levers.

At other times, Gypsy would often find himself working with the youngest of the three brothers who was also the workshop and engineering chief. He was not only the company electrician but knew far more about engineering than his two elder brothers. He also knew how to keep the company's two massive steam boilers maintained and running, a vital necessity for the company, given that it had three or four acres of heated green houses.

MARCH 1981.

On and on he slogged day after day. He had paid off the fine, so now came, the uphill struggle to save some money. Agonizingly slowly, week after week, he saved. But it was such a small amount he earned, when compared with the cost of a ticket to India.

A friend suggested he start dealing some hash on the side. He decided to give it a try, using the small amount that he had saved. He bought four ounces on his first deal, two ounces of red Lebanese premium quality and two ounces of Himalayan charas. It was top grade and as rare as rocking horse manure, but the tight arsed imbeciles of Sussex couldn't appreciate, that fine things are worth paying for. As it was, he was very lucky to make a premium at all on the price that was being paid for the poisonous contaminated Moroccan shit that masqueraded as hashish in that part of the world. All he ended up doing was making enough for a moderately generous supply of hash for himself.

One day, after a near miss with the cops, which involved a cross country dash on foot to get away from two squad cars, Gypsy decided to lay low for a while. For a month or two he had been supplying a group of friends with such delicacies as Thai sticks, Nepalese temple balls and other quality smoke, but he couldn't afford any more trouble with the law.

He stopped dealing and just concentrated on his work. His father didn't let anyone but the most vital of workers do over time, so Gypsy was stuck with his small pay pack.

Gypsy carried on at work, greasing green house vents, cutting and preparing wood for van racks, cutting and welding steel, for plant moving layered trolley, etc.

APRIL 1981.

His music kept him from going completely crazy, but he was living at home and working a hard forty hour week, for a pittance.

One evening he was at his local pub watching his favorite local band, a folk rock outfit that played all sorts of music, and well. They would play music from artists as diverse as the incredible string band, Steeleye Span and Fairport Convention to Jeff Beck, Jimi Hendrix and the Grateful Dead. He was standing there talking to a friend, when someone from the village approached him and asked if he had any dope for sale. He told the guy that he didn't and that he had had to stop dealing, at least for a while, but he had a piece for personal use and he offered to make a joint to share with this guy and his friend. The offer was turned down so Gypsy continued to drink his beer and watch and listen to the band.

Two minutes later, as Gypsy stood peacefully watching the band, a fist came out of nowhere and hit him in the mouth. The guy who had asked to buy dope had got two punches in before Gypsy realized what was happening. He came to his senses rapidly and in a couple of moves, had the bastard pinned up against the wall by his throat while he asked the inbred cretin what this was all about. "You showed me up in front of my friend", the retard sniveled. "I was telling the truth", Gypsy told him. "I don't have enough to sell. I've only got enough for two or three joints".

To Gypsy's complete consternation, another man who Gypsy had gone to school with came up and indignantly began to ask why he had started a fight in the pub. "I didn't," retorted Gypsy. "This bastard attacked me, without warning and for no reason." They didn't throw the other man from the pub or even speak to him about it. Gypsy's father was rich, or so that was what most of the people in the village assumed. Never mind that the whole family, not only worked hard but shared their prosperity with those around them in a most generous way. The staff were all invited to use the family swimming pool during lunch breaks and after work. The garden and pool would be lent for free on numerous occasions throughout each summer, to host fund raising parties and discos for local charities and local people had been helped in numerous ways by them. Some had been lent workshops for free to help them when their businesses had collapsed, or had been helped get back on their feet in other ways after their life had collapsed. The family considered it a duty to be kind to those who were less well off than themselves or were in need of help. But never mind that, the ignorance, jealousy and resentment of the retards at the other end of the village knew no bounds and in their jaundiced view of life, they presumed that Gypsy had more than them. So therefore he should lose when someone started a fight with him.

Gypsy just didn't see things that way, he worked as hard as anyone else for his meager pay pack and he had proved himself as brave as or braver than any of them. He wasn't some sort of wet middle class spoilt brat and he wasn't about to be pushed about by any of them, least of all by a low quality, inbred piece of dog shit like that.

In Gypsy's village there were so many imbeciles. There were the aspiring classes, who would hang around his parents and attempt to crawl up their arses, while doing them down behind their back. There were the uptight snobs on their private estate who walked around feeling too pleased with themselves and would talk in such a way that you might think they had a large legume stuck in their rectum.

Then at the other end of the scale were the council estates (Government housing projects) where a lot of no hopers lived. These were the ones who started fights in pubs and elsewhere and caused over ninety percent of all trouble in the village. Hidden between all of these were some good souls but they were hard to find. Gypsy was wondering how he was going to cope with living in this spiritually dead zone for the next year, until he had saved up enough to get out of this purgatory and hit the road to India.

MAY 1981.

Gypsy's mother was going into Brighton with his younger brother. Gypsy asked if he could get a ride into town and would take the train home.

They were walking down the hill from a car park near the station together when they spotted an advert in a travel agent's window. 'Holidays for people between the ages of eighteen and thirty years old, at 'Camp Africa' in Morocco, a two week package for one hundred and eight pounds'.

Gypsy's mother turned to him and said, "You've been down in the dumps lately and looking like you're going to get into trouble if you carry on being friends with the people you've been hanging around with. That holiday looks like an amazing bargain. Would you like to go if I pay for it for you?" "Yes, please", said Gypsy. "Maybe it will help you stop smoking pot", his mother said.

She obviously didn't know too much about Moroccan culture or export products but Gypsy wasn't complaining. Two weeks of sun in a Third World Country sounded like just what he needed to wipe away the miserable England blues. He accepted with gratitude this kind gift.

Gypsy had been waiting to poke the cops in the eye ever since they busted him. He was angry with them for enforcing unjust laws. They could argue all that they wanted that their hands were tied but Gypsy's view was different, Hitler could not have delivered the scale of murderous destruction on the world that he did, without people who were just doing as they were told and being good little robots that just followed orders. Each person must take responsibility for their own actions, if they upheld a law that they themselves knew to be unjust, then, at the very least Gypsy was going to blow smoke in their faces, without them being able to touch him.

All through his life, with the exception of one village copper who used to patrol the village on a bicycle and spoke well to everyone, all of the cops he had met had been gruff, rude, aggressive and threatening, even when he was doing nothing more obtrusive than asking directions. There was no law in England against having long hair and wearing hippie clothes but you wouldn't know it by the way the establishment treated the people who so much as dared to dress differently.

Gypsy went to the airport with his usual back pack and guitar, he checked in and went through passport control to air side. There in the bar were loads of others just like him, long haired rockers and hippies, going to Morocco for the sun and smoke.

Gypsy had brought enough dope to the airport to make four or five well loaded joints. He made his first one and lit it up, to the shock of those around him. "Aren't you scared about the security in the airport?" said one of the hippies. "Look", said Gypsy, "the undercover security agents aren't going to blow their cover over something as trivial as a joint and if the tit headed, blue meanies come, I can see them coming from a mile away. There's only one entrance and I can see it well from here. If I need to I can swallow the dope and if necessary I can eat the joint.

He smoked two more joints, while people came up to him and asked sheepishly for a couple of tokes, before running off in fear of being seen by the cops with this miscreant.

With the last piece of dope hidden in his right hand, he went and asked two cops for directions to the flight information desk. "You look like you might be on drugs", said one of the cops. "Come this way. We are going to search you." Gypsy had become accustomed to such behavior, as such, he put his last piece of dope in his mouth and chewed and swallowed it.

He felt totally relaxed, as now he was clean. He spent the next thirty minutes winding up the cops and having a laugh at their expense. "What do you think of the Blair Peach case?" he said with a grin on his face. (Blair Peach was a New Zealand national who had been clubbed to death at an anti fascist demo by two or three cops, in an unprovoked attack. It was causing a big stink for Scotland Yard, at the time and was in the press daily) at this he had the cops snarling, but they could do nothing.

In the end, when they had finished searching him and with steam coming out of their ears, from having suffered the piss being taken out of them, all be it in a polite educated voice that Gypsy modulated for the occasion. Gypsy turned to them and said, "Look while it's been very nice, meeting you all. I now hold you all responsible for making sure that I don't miss my flight. Being as it is, that you didn't find anything. I think we had better move quickly, if you don't wish to be purchasing me a new ticket to Tangier."

The cop who had decided to pull him was given the job of giving him a fast escort through security to the boarding gate while the flight was asked by the police to wait. The cop was obviously not happy at not having found anything and gave the impression of not liking young people in general, let alone hippies, rockers and punks. Gypsy wound him up all the way to the gate, all be it in a polite voice and manner. He had now had a part of his revenge, even if it had not been at the expense of those exact same sons and daughters of whores who had busted him. These ones however had been equally fascist and deserving.

The flight taxied out to the runway, gunned it's engines and took off into the darkness. It was an ageing Dan Air (fly the Grim reaper) Boeing 727 (Dan Air later helped raise the safety average, cut the mortality rate and reduced the rate of crashes by British based airlines, by going bankrupt). Three hours later they were disembarking into the warm night air at Tangier airport.

ASCILLA, MOROCCO.

MAY 1981.

From there, they were taken by bus, some thirty kilometers, south along the coast road, to the holiday resort, near a fishing village of Ascilla.

On arrival, before being assigned their huts, they were all brought into the restaurant, where one very stoned, egotistical, smart arse, who was the leader of the British team who worked there, jumped up on the stage and gave a very stern lecture about how there was strictly to be no dope smoking in the resort. He was stoned off his tits so everyone just took the piss out of him.

It was easy to see how the holiday had been so cheap, accommodation consisted of a mattress inside a small hut that you could not quite stand up in, a roof made of palm thatch and a door that could only be crawled through. But there was a bar and a disco and the restaurant food was almost edible. The resort was right on the beach itself, inside a large bamboo fence, with large prickly pear cacti making an extra protective hedge.

Gypsy and a group of the others, immediately set about scoring some of the local hash. He got burned on his first attempt to score, something that had never happened to him before. He had made the mistake of paying first. When Gypsy said, "Hey, man, this isn't hash."

The Moroccan pulled a knife on him and got all his nasty friends to stand with him. It was his first encounter with a Moroccan in their own country and already he was starting not to like them. Hassan who had been one of his closest friends at school, had been different, he was wild, yes, but he was not a cheating coward who hid behind his friends with a knife when he got called to answer for something. But then, Hassan came from a village hundreds of kilometers away to the south, near to Fez. It was possible that the people there were different.

Other encounters with locals were equally unpleasant, the people of this area were generally dishonest, with an overtly hateful and aggressive stance towards foreigners.

Going out into the village to look for some hash, with three hairy members of a British heavy metal band they were invited to lunch at the house of some local dealers. It was a decent lunch of local bread and fried fish with salad.

Sitting in an old stone room with rugs and carpets covering the floor the negotiations started for the price of the hash, different grades were put in front of them. The Moroccans had some mad assumptions about how much they were going to get for their smoke and started jumping up and down, shouting and hissing threats when they were told that that was not the price that anyone in the group was willing to pay. The group held their ground and the Moroccans backed down.

Gypsy was starting to like the locals less and less. They had no redeeming qualities, they were dishonest, aggressive, bullying cowards and knowing the reputation that they had, probably engaged in unsavory and unnatural sexual acts with each other as well. They certainly behaved like people who harbored unexpressed feelings of deep self-hatred and revulsion, something that is caused by indulging in such acts, especially in people who have had a religious upbringing.

After a trip into Tangier, that brought them into contact with much the same sort of people they all took a bus back to the resort village and went to one of their huts, smoked some joints and decided that they would stay in the resort for the rest of the trip. The Moroccans that they had met so far were by far the most foul and contemptuous people that anyone in the room had ever met and it wasn't worth going out to suffer further abuse from them.

Anyway, the disco was fun and the dope plentiful and Gypsy got to do an all night rock and folk recital, in front of a crowd, on his folk guitar when the disco closed early one night.

It was in many ways, a typical eighteen to thirty year old holiday, with people getting drunk and vomiting in the bushes and flower beds at night, groups of dyed blonde secretaries, students and the likes dressed up each night and posing in the disco looking for a fuck. But at least, at this particular resort a sizeable proportion of the tourists had long hair, liked rock music and liked smoking dope to the max.

The holiday came to an end and though he couldn't say that he was looking forward to going back to England, he was certainly glad to be leaving Morocco. That was one country that Gypsy was hoping he would never have to visit again, it almost made Yugoslavia look appealing in comparison.

The jet took off and Gypsy was in the air between two places where he did not wish to be, in a plane that was owned by probably the worst airline in Western Europe, it was not a good feeling.

ENGLAND

The jet touched down at Gatwick without Gypsy or any one else on board, being added to the Dan Air, Grim Reaper score board of statistics and Gypsy took the train home.

The next day, after an argument with one of the family, Gypsy had had enough, he had some savings of six hundred pounds, that his mother had put aside for him to use if he wished to go on to further education. It would have broken her heart if he had taken it to pay for a trip to India. Besides there wouldn't be much spending money left after buying the ticket, so he decided once again to go back to the Yeshiva in Jerusalem. His mother wouldn't be too upset if he spent the money going to learn about the Jewish religion.

He had arrived back in England on a Monday. By that Friday, he was sitting on board an EL AL Jumbo, taxi-ing out to a runway at Heathrow.

ISRAEL

JUNE 1981.

The jet took off and Gypsy felt that now so familiar rush of freedom and excitement, that he got from leaving England. He was definitely a space alien in that country and felt like he didn't belong there. . It was always a pleasure to be leaving England's shores.

Four and a half hours later and the plane touched down into a hot night at Ben Gurion airport. Gypsy cleared through the airport procedures and hopped on a bus straight to Jerusalem. Taking the same old route down Jaffa road and through the gate, he walked around the inside wall to Mount Zion and in to the Yeshiva. He quickly found his two friends, Rick and Ephraim who helped him to find a disused room to sleep in.

Much had happened since he had been there last, eight months prior.

Ephraim had gone for a holiday in Ashkelon, a town south of Tel Aviv and near the Gaza strip. While walking on the beach, he found a tire that had washed up on the tide. Inside was approximately twenty six kilos of hashish. Ephraim couldn't believe his luck and quickly grabbed himself two or three kilos and ran off quickly while no one was there to see him do it. Returning to the guesthouse with a large package wrapped in an old piece of plastic, that he had found on the beach, with a large shit eating grin on his face aroused the suspicions of the guesthouse proprietor who thought it might be a bomb that he had. She called the police and Ephraim was busted. For months, they didn't believe his story as he languished in prison. That was until more tires rolled up on the beach. It appeared that further down the coast in Gaza, hash deliveries were done using tidal currents to roll the tires in on the sea floor, by getting the weight ratio in the tire just right. However, sometimes the deliverymen of Lebanon, missed their target and the tires would wash up in an Israeli town or village.

With a lot of effort from the Chief Rabbi at the Yeshiva, Ephraim had been freed after only three months and instead of prison was given community work, one day a week for a year, shitting out the monkey house at the Jerusalem city zoo.

He had found religion and become totally serious and boring. Gypsy couldn't wait to get out of his company, what with the bullshit moralizing lectures and all.

Rick on the other hand, was still his usual laid back self, yes he was trying out the religious life, but there was nothing forced or guilt driven about his approach to it, it was something he did quietly for himself.

Gypsy didn't want to be a freeloader while he stayed at the Yeshiva, so he would go to the kitchen and volunteer to help chop vegetables and meat and to clean tables and wash dishes and pans. He would go to one or two Yeshiva classes on Torah (the first five books of the Bible) and Talmud, but soon he found himself working full time and for free. He didn't mind, as he enjoyed being there and felt good living on Mount Zion.

One day a French traveler by the name of Philippe, landed a job in the kitchen, he was getting paid US$180 per month, plus food and accommodation and he wasn't even Jewish.

"Wait a minute", said Gypsy to the man in charge of the kitchen finances. "I've been working full time in your kitchen for two months for free, if you're going to pay him that much, isn't it right that you pay me the same as well? After all that's all I am doing here, is working."

"Don't you worry, Gypsy, you're Jewish like us. We'll look after you" Said the man. Gypsy trusted him, after all he could see no reason not to. He and Philippe got on well and would share joints and drinks after work., both of them, unlike the Orthodox Jews at the Yeshiva, felt more at home in East Jerusalem, among the Arabs than ever they did in the Jewish quarter, with its uptight, scowling beardy mad hatters.

Everything went merrily until pay day when Philippe was handed his pay of US$180. Gypsy was handed only US$35, by an Orthodox beardy, with a smart arsed grin on his face. As if that wasn't enough of an insult, the next day he had gone to the shower, leaving his wallet, with the thirty five dollars in it in his jeans, on the bed. He came back to his room to find the money missing. Only Orthodox Jews came into this area so it was one of them or one of the spoilt Jewish brats, who had been sent here to study by their parents. Anyway, it was beyond selfish and spiteful, each one of them studying got a financial allowance either from their families or through a trust fund. They didn't need Gypsy's meager wages as well.

Gypsy was somewhere past livid at this double insult. He went out and changed a traveler's cheque. He couldn't find out who had ripped him off, though he had some ideas. There was a smart arsed, narcissistic, spoilt brat, from New Jersey who was totally in love with himself, another Paul Ruben (as mentioned in Chapter 2) who had been floating around the area at that time. He was a mean, selfish spiteful brat of a man. But Gypsy could not prove it. If he confronted or even threatened the scumbag he would of course have denied it, there were no witnesses.

Gypsy went into the new city and bought himself a bottle of cheap arrack. (for the uninitiated arrack is an aniseed drink, much like Ouzo and pernod). Gypsy was just so pissed off that anyone who called themselves a religious person could do anything as low as this.

In a rage, he downed the bottle in ten minutes flat and then proceeded to stagger about the city raging abuse and pissing in door ways, much like any normal Glaswegian on any normal Saturday night. By the time he had finished his staggering and raging he was half way to Bethlehem. Some secular Israelis in a car saw him and stopped, "Hey, man. It's dangerous for you out here. Let us give you a lift back to town", one of them said. Gypsy, his rage now burned out at least a little, accepted the kind offer. On the way into town, he told them what had happened, to get him into this state. "Yes, most of those religious Jews are bastards", they all agreed. They make all the trouble in this country, throwing stones at cars that drive on Saturdays, etc. and making settlements on the West Bank. Then they don't want to serve in the army. One sect, the Naturi Karta don't even recognize the state of Israel, while simultaneously demanding use of all of it's services, including the protection and security that the army and police force provide. They take everything and give nothing but trouble.

They dropped Gypsy near the Jaffa gate, from where he staggered down and around the Armenian quarter, until he wound up back in his bed on Mount Zion. He awoke the next day, with a horrible hangover, it felt like some small person had crawled inside his head with a hammer.

Despite all that had happened Gypsy continued working in the kitchen. After all he had nothing else to do and now that he knew what sort of level of honesty to expect, he didn't care much for studying their religion. What's more after what had happened, he was thinking of moving on.

However two events happened that caused confusion to his plans and drastically changed everything.

Gypsy's boss, Carl was a codeine addict, Phillipe had been the one to spot it. Phillipe had, in the past travelled to India and in the grand French tradition, had got himself hooked on smack (heroin). Though he was at this point clean, any junkie or ex junkie, automatically recognizes another junkie, from eyes, skin and behavioral patterns.

Carl looked and behaved like a real life, but aged version of 'Yosemite Sam' (from the bugs bunny cartoons). He had the great big mustache and American accent and further to this, would jump up and down screaming abuse, at and about people at the drop of a hat. It was some of the most irrational behavior Gypsy had ever seen from a man (women of course, where another story). Carl was the sort of cook that could probably even give prison food a run for it's money in an inedible slop competition. Nevertheless, Gypsy and his immediate superior in the kitchen, a large muscular American Jew who had served in the US army, did their best to compensate for Carl's numerous short comings. On more than one occasion, they got themselves to the kitchen on Friday morning to help prepare the Shabbat (Sabbath) feast, only to find Carl not there or sick from his codeine tablets. Then they would find it was just the two of them preparing two meals for one hundred or so people, in the space of six or seven hours. One morning Carl had been having one of his Yosemite Sam tantrums, ranting and raving about a mad Polish woman who studied in the woman's side of the Yeshiva. She was not the most attractive of creatures in any way, shape, or form, but more than that she had come into the kitchen and interfered with the cooking when people's back's had been turned. In doing so, she had rendered whole pots of food useless forcing not only unwanted wastage on the kitchen, but unwanted extra work on the cooks too. Carl on this day though was right. "No one but kitchen staff is to enter the kitchen area", he said. "And whatever you do, don't let that mad crazy bitch inside the door, at all costs keep her out". Gypsy took Carl's words to heart and carried on working. Soon he found himself working on his own after both Carl and Surya, the number two in the kitchen (Phillipe had already left on his travels) had gone off to do other things. As luck, or should we say, as bad luck would have it, 'the mad crazy Polish bitch' came to the kitchen. "No one but kitchen staff can come in here", said Gypsy to this ugly creature who for some strange reason always seemed to have strips of sellotape stuck to her face. At this point, she started physically pushing and shouting, "No, I'm coming inside".

Gypsy held her at bay and explained that he wasn't allowed to let anyone in, especially not her. "You destroyed our cooking, when you've been in here before. I don't want to do extra work because of your interference', he told her. "And besides, you are banned from inside the kitchen. Please go away and let me do my work. I've got a meal to prepare". At this point the young miss ugly decided to go completely crazy, gouging, kicking and punching as she tried to fight her way in. Screaming and shouting, how it was her right to go into the kitchen. Though she was behaving in a way that warranted sterner action, Gypsy pushed her to and out of the door as gently as he could and blocked her way from returning. "Right", she screamed. "I'll go and get an Arab to come here and kill you". Gypsy thought nothing more of it and carried on working, preparing the evening meal.

Ten minutes later, madam loony returned, accompanied by a large alcoholic Israeli, who being above six foot tall and muscular, was not someone that Gypsy could take down without a weapon. Before he knew what had happened, this monster was in the kitchen trying to push him around and shouting and bellowing. "You have no business on Yeshiva property behaving like this", Gypsy told him. "What happens here is none of your business".

He started pushing at Gypsy, the only thing that Gypsy could have done, would have been to have used one of the kitchen knives on him, but that would have probably landed him a long prison sentence. Anyway, he didn't want to stab anyone. It would make the kitchen dirty with all that blood on the floor.

He decided, discretion was the better part of valor and backed off until this cunt had burnt out his energy and fucked off.

The alcoholic soon tired of barking and raving and went back to his bench outside the entrance to the Turkish fort. Gypsy locked the kitchen and went to tell Surya what had happened. Surya jumped to his feet and Gypsy took him to where the drunk was hanging out. Surya approached the drunk and told him to stay the hell out of the Yeshiva kitchen and not to threaten any of the kitchen staff. At this point, the drunk launched himself at Surya. He put up one hell of a fight before Surya could land a punch on him that put him down. Despite his drunkenness his Israeli army training had shown through. But then so had Surya's US army training been evident. Gypsy had been right to give this monster a wide birth, anyway, Surya now had the bastard pinned down, at least for the moment. "Gypsy, go get the cops. I just saw a patrol jeep pull into the car park, before this started" Surya yelled. "Maybe they are still there." Gypsy ran down the hill to the car park, the cops were still there and Gypsy approached them and told them, that there was a problem.

They took the drunk, Surya and Gypsy to the police station at Russian compound, off the Jaffa road. Gypsy and Surya both gave statements concerning what had happened. both of them told the honest truth, so imagine their consternation when the cops let the drunk go and told Surya and Gypsy that they would have to spend the night in the slammer. Gypsy asked me at this moment if he could add some words of his own about this incident.

This is a common problem for travelers, especially when outside of E.U. countries or Australia and New Zealand where policing is moderately fair. If you are a foreigner, even a foreign Jew in Israel (as this case demonstrates) then you are automatically wrong in any dispute with a local in the eyes of the law, even if they are the ones who attack you, for whatever or no reason. I warn all intrepid travelers to be aware of this phenomenon, in the hope that you will learn to walk lightly and carefully as you travel. I myself as a traveler am disgusted that people who live in their snug, little, immobile, static communities are so cowardly as to use a foreign visitor to their country as a scapegoat and cash cow in this way. Even when it is plain as the light of day that it is one of their own that is the villain of the peace. (This is why I travel, in order to stay out of the company of such cowards, within the community that I was raised in). When I do have a base (which has happened many times in the last thirty years) then it will tend to be in a place where many other international travelers congregate. There is a decidedly lower number of cowards among the traveler community and thus less problems of bickering, backstabbing and shit stirring. Travelers tend to have lively inquisitive minds, that lead them to have many interests in life. Many of us have a spiritual outlook on life, realizing life's impermanence. We are not so much interested in owning so much in the way of material possessions, as we are in where our next adventure will be and how we will get there.

A warrior will always run towards his fears, when as a coward will always run away.

Surya turned to gypsy and said, "Look, their backs are turned, lets walk". The two of them quickly disappeared from the room and off down the corridor and out into the city and off into the night to find a place to lie low.

Once again, the crazy bitch and her spite, had sabotaged the cooking. Now Gypsy and Surya would have to keep their heads down and wouldn't be able to cook for the students at the Yeshiva. The cops didn't come that night, so the next morning when they had also not come they figured that they were in the clear. At about mid day, a dope deal showed up and Gypsy and Surya where with one other person, cutting up the deal, when they heard the loud shout of a rabbi, who was a good friend of theirs, from a distance saying, "This is their room officers". It was fortunate that there was a friend to give a warning. Surya and Gypsy scrambled out of a window, onto a ledge three stories above a wide stone and cement path, while the other person ate his hash. Surya had made the unfortunate mistake of dressing as a mad hatter that day, as a disguise, complete with black coat and Selisia cowboy hat. The mad hatters had been rioting in another part of the city that day over one of their many demands.

Grabbing hold of an overhead water pipe, each of them went in different directions. "Hello Shalom", said the cop to Surya as he leaned over the wall where Surya had met a dead end. "Oh, shit", Surya mumbled under his breath. Gypsy dressed only in jeans, T-shirt and sneakers was far more light and nimble. He had made it around the corner and shinned up another pipe, onto another roof, where he could hide behind the domes. He had his share of the hash deal with him so he decided to hide it in a crevice in a wall. He waited silently on the roof for half an hour or more, before he shinned slowly and quietly back down the pipe and snuck off through the twists and turns of the passages of the old fortress to find out what had happened to Surya. The cops returned several times through the day looking for him (like it was such an important case in a city that suffers more than its fair share of corruption and terrorism), each time Gypsy hid.

After a day of hiding from the pigs, Gypsy had had enough, he went looking for the rabbi who had shouted the warning and asked if he might know how to help fix this gross injustice. The rabbi took him to the house of a friend of his in the Jewish quarter of the old city (Mount Zion sits outside of the walls at an elevation, but is close by the Jewish quarter)

He was an American Orthodox Jew who had learned much about Israeli law and been successful in using it very much to his own advantage, he offered to help Gypsy.

"You'll have to hide for a few days while I go and negotiate with them on your behalf" he told him. "I know someone who could use some help, if you like working".

Gypsy spent the next three days helping a man who was renovating a house in the old city's Jewish quarter. Hacking out channels in the rock, to lay water pipes through and shovelling up piles of rubble, it was the kind of work that Gypsy enjoyed. Also, it helped to keep him well hidden from the cops as the place could only be reached via a labyrinth of alley ways.

When it came time to go to the police station, it emerged that the best Gypsy could hope for was to surrender his passport and he would have to pay one hundred and twenty pounds to get it back (a fortune to Gypsy at that time).

This was totally outrageous, Gypsy had done nothing to warrant this injustice, but he was stuck, what could he do? The cops wouldn't give up and had been looking for him constantly for the last few days at the Yeshiva and surrounding areas. He had no choice he had to go and surrender his passport to the pigs, but boy, did he hate and despise them for it.

The next thing to happen to Gypsy that would change things, started when he was summoned into the administrative office by the chief rabbi's wife.

"You've been here for several months and we know very little about you", she said. "Have you got any documents with you, we need to register you in our book". Gypsy handed her the receipt for his passport, which in addition to his passport details, the paper contained his home address. "Is this the same address as the rest of your family live at?" she asked. "Yes", said Gypsy. "Good", she said.

"Right", she snarled. "You've been here for some months now, what have you contributed?"

"I've been working full time in the kitchen", said Gypsy. "And that's all I've had the time to do". "Do you get paid for it?" she asked. "Of course, I do. I'm working for you, but it's only a small amount like just a living allowance". "That's wrong, you should be paying us for being here". (a typical piece of Jewish, asshole, chutzpa logic). She shouted and screamed and writhed her big ugly Yabba the Hut of a body in a most threatening manner. Gypsy was sad that he did not have his camera with him at the time, as he was wondering if he had just discovered an entirely new and unknown species of invertebrate. Again and again, he tried to explain to this member of the Lee sisters (as in Uglee Beastlee and Gastlee) that he had been working and if anyone should be getting some money it was him for the hard work he was doing in the kitchen. All to no avail, this foul ugly fat pig of a woman just got more angry and fierce. "No come on you give a donation. NOW!, don't you know that this Yeshiva is a charity?" she screamed, slamming her fat ugly tentacles on the table.

This was the kind of monster that the censors would have banned "Hammer house of horror" from portraying in one of their movies for fear of causing a vomiting fit amongst the audience. She was worse than foul, and her logic obviously came from barking loony land. "I want you to give a donation right now" she roared.

In the end, Gypsy buckled under the pressure and gave her thirty pounds from his now meager resources before she started to read him some Vogon poetry (aka Hitch Hikers guide to the Galaxy). She also told him that she would be sending a letter to his parents asking for, or more like, demanding money from them, for him being there. Gypsy was furious but powerless to do anything more than phone his family and warn them not to send anything to this ugly swarm of parasites. He had more than worked his way since he had been there and now instead of rewarding him for his service they were demanding money.

Q: Did you hear about the Jewish child molester?
A: No.
Q: Want to buy a sweetie?

Gypsy packed his bag. He wanted to get as far as he could from this group of greedy, hypocritical parasites as possible. He could not believe the outrageous behavior and arrogance that he had witnessed while staying on Mount Zion. Never before in his life had he met so many people who had so very few if any redeeming qualities. They even made the Moroccans look good in comparison.

He had very little money and no passport and so his choices were limited as in fucking limited. He took a bus to Eilat and set about looking for a job. He had little choice but to sleep on the beach as resources were so tight. He kept running into a catch twenty two situation, he couldn't get a job without a passport and he couldn't get his passport back without a job.

Eventually, he got a job as a dishwasher in a hotel kitchen. He had to work twelve hour shifts for some absolutely piss poor wages, but at least he had food and accommodation with the job, which at that moment counted. Many people came and only lasted a few hours on the job. It was not pleasant work twelve hours a day of dirty dishes and no natural light.

Gypsy got on well with the Palestinians who were working there, they were just ordinary people trying to get by and what's more they were friendly and helpful and never once caused Gypsy any problems.

The work was so foul that he only lasted a week at it. But it was his Palestinian supervisor that made sure he got paid when the Jewish boss didn't want to pay him. He threatened to take the whole kitchen staff out on strike if Gypsy didn't get paid.

Gypsy had heard Jews ranting and raving bad things about the Palestinians, in fact try as he might, he found it extremely hard to get a Jew to say one nice thing about them. But now with his own eyes he witnessed more good Palestinian manners and sense of fair play than he ever had encountered from his own people. He was beginning to wonder who might be the real villain of the peace in the Israeli-Arab dispute, especially given the outrageous, spoilt brat behavior that he encountered from so many of his fellow Jews.

With a little money in his pocket, Gypsy went back to the beach to contemplate his prospects. There were some workers from Thailand who had a day off from work and were sharing their food with all the others who were also sleeping on the beach. They were very friendly even though they couldn't speak any English.

Gypsy decided to put their country on his list of places that he wished to visit.

After a search around Eilat, he couldn't find any more work and phoned his family in the hope of getting some financial help to get his passport back. He was told by his mother that they had sent money to his bank account in Jerusalem and he was to go there and take it out and give it to the yeshiva and no they couldn't sort out money for Gypsy to help get his passport back until they knew more.

Gypsy felt totally betrayed by his own family, he had told them not to send money to these people who had ripped him off. Now, here they were, believing a bunch of corrupt mad hatters who they had never met over the word of their own son.

Gypsy took a bus to Jerusalem, he figured at least he could retrieve his thirty quid back before dispensing with the distasteful task of handing the money of his parents to that foul group of Silesia bandits [Silisia is a town that was part of Germany before World War Two but is now part of Poland and is where the mad Hatter penguin outfit of the orthodox Jews seem's to have originated from].

He got to Jerusalem and went to Bank Mizrahi, in the Jewish quarter of the old city where he held an account. The money hadn't come there so he went to the Yeshiva to find out if it had gone to them directly. It had and he was angry, but he didn't show it. All of a sudden, "Jabber the Hut" had gone from being a foul screaming violent monster, to being over friendly, like she was greasing up to him for some more of that oh! so lovely money.

This creature's motives and behavior were so blatantly transparent that it was disgusting. Gypsy wanted to vomit, he had never seen anyone in his life so lacking in self- respect or moral dignity or so consumed by material greed, except as a ridiculously exaggerated character in a pantomime. Even Fagin from "Oliver Twist" did not come close. Even if it was for a charity, the end doesn't justify the means.

Gypsy felt defiled just by being in the presence of such a low fallen being. He had not even seen an animal behave in such a foul, groveling, simpering manner.

Not just that but now he was fucked, he had no passport and no chance to make any money and his family seemed more interested in throwing large amounts of cash at the mad hatters and bad hatters of Jerusalem than in helping Gypsy who was their son. What he was asking for was a much smaller amount than what they had sent to these parasites and for a much more valid reason. He wasn't asking for them to support him, on the contrary, he wanted to work for his living.

It was all so damned unfair and utterly ridiculously disgusting, what was happening to him. All he ever wanted or tried to do was good, so why was he getting kicked from all sides?

Now he was beyond anger, why would nothing work well for him. He went to an Arab doctor in East Jerusalem and got a large prescription for Valium. Then after scoring the script and buying a bottle of strong liquor, he took a bus to Ein Gedi by the Dead Sea. He lay down on the beach with a bottle of gin and did a packet of the Valium, taking over one hundred milligrams of the stuff. He just lay there as his thoughts and body went into slow motion. Now he was really beginning to understand the rage felt by the Palestinians and what may have been the cause of so much anti-Semitism in the world.

Gypsy had collapsed, given up and wanted to die. He could see no way out of his mess. He could do all the hard work he wanted, in this country but it wouldn't get him anywhere. Now all he wanted to do was go to India, but he couldn't see how. He didn't mind working, but the pittances that he was able to earn, meant that he would have to live like a fucking hermit for at least two years doing a job that he didn't enjoy, working with people and their bullshit gossip and sniping that he also did not enjoy. He would go crazy well before he saved enough for the trip. He was trapped he could think of no way out and besides, with every effort he made blowing up in his face, what was the fucking point.

EIN GEDI/ISRAEL

He phoned his parents and gave them an earful of abuse. "I told you not to send them money", he said. "And what do you do?" "I told you what I am doing here is my business. Whatever these people have told you, I was working for them full time and not just did they not pay me properly, but one of them even stole the little bit that they did pay me. What is so unbelievable, is that after that they had the cheek to demand that I give them money. I told you not to send them money but you will never believe me will you? I could have used some of that money to get my passport back. Anyway, you bastards, I've just taken a packet of Valium and I'm going to take a whole heap more before I bed down on the beach for the night, I also got a full bottle of gin to wash them down with. With any luck, I won't have to wake up into this shit world with its shit people ever again. I hate you for what you have just done, but most of all I hate you for not believing me."

Gypsy did another packet of valium and bedded down with a bottle of cheap Israeli Gin just for good measure. He was by now so angry that he just hoped that he wouldn't wake up.

zzzzzzzzzzzzzzzzzzzzzzzzzzzzzzzzzzzzzzzzzzzzzzzzzzzzzzzzzzzzzzzzzzzzzzzzzzzzzzzzzzzz
zzzzzzzzzzzzzzzzzzzzzzzzzzzzzzzzzzzzzzzzzzzzzzzzzzzzzzzzzzzzzzzzzzzzzzzzzzzzzzzzzzzz
zzzzzzzzzzzzzzzzzzzzzzzzzzzzzzzzzzzzzzzzzzzzzzzzzzzzzzzzzzzzzzzzzzzzzzzzzzzzzzzzzzzz
zzzzzzzzzzzzzzzzzzzzzzzzzzzzzzzzzzzzzzzzzzzzzzzzzzzzzzzzzzzzzzzzzzzzzzzzzzzzzzzzzzzz
zzzzzzzzzzzzzzzzzzzzzzzzzzzzzzzzzzzzzzzzzzzzzzzzzzzzzzzzzzzzzzzzzzzzzzzzzzzzzzzzzzzz
zzzzzzzzzzzzzzzzzzzzzzzzzzzzzzzzzzzzzzzzzzzzzzzzz

But he did!, Waking up slowly the next morning, the Valium's pleasant effect still strong. The sun had been up for a while and the air was warm and pleasant. He got out of his sleeping bag, stripped off down to his underwear and walked into the warm, still, waters of the Dead Sea.

He sat floating for some time. It felt as if the salt was cleansing him from his previous day's experience.

He eventually left the water and washed off the salt under one of the showers available on the beach. Getting dressed, he took another half packet of valium and lay back down on the beach, on top of his sleeping bag and drifted through his thoughts.

The Valium and Vodka cocktail hadn't killed him, so he would have to pick himself up and fight back. . . Honesty and decency had no place with these bastards but somehow without breaking his own code of ethics, he would find a way to win.

There was nothing more to do at Ein Gedi, so he packed his sleeping bag, got dressed and had some breakfast, then took a bus back up to Jerusalem. His parents had given them a whole heap of money and he owed them absolutely nothing, so the least these black hatted cockroaches could do was give him some food and a roof over his head in his hour of need.

JERUSALEM/ISRAEL

NOVEMBER 1981

To their credit, there was no problem with this. But they wanted him to study in the Yeshiva, instead of working in the kitchen and they wanted his parents to pay them money for the privilege.

This was not the least bit what Gypsy wanted or had in mind. Right from the start he had believed in working his own passage, which was why he had gravitated straight to the kitchens. It was the one place that he saw physical work going on and where he could make his own contribution.

To trick him and involve his parents, felt like they had destroyed his independence and cut his balls off. And for his parents to go along with them against Gypsy's wishes was utter and total betrayal. Gypsy's balls were in a vice, no passport no job, no job no passport, there was nothing he could do, he was trapped.

He went busking with his guitar but he could never make more than what was needed for basic necessities. Gypsy still wasn't a brilliant guitarist and even a good musician could starve while busking in Israel. They are like their reputation, to them there is no such thing as spare change.

93

Gypsy's mother came to visit and help him get his passport back. He warned her about the games going on at the Yeshiva, how all they wanted to do was part her from copious quantities of her money. They went to the British Consul in Jerusalem (Gypsy had already been to the main consulate in Tel Aviv, but to no avail). Gypsy explained all that had happened (minus the dope deal of course, as no one was wise to it anyway). The consul was a typical British civil servant. He spoke in one of those British uptight posh accents. Sounding, looking and behaving as if he had just rammed a large Israeli cucumber up his arse. He talked down to them and tried to make it seem as if Gypsy had done something wrong. He refused to help in any way shape or form. He must have felt quite at home among the Israelis, as he too, like many of them, (especially their police force) was having a deep and intense love affair with himself.

There was nothing else that they could do, they would have to pay the pigs.

Just the principle of paying these useless arseholes, who had failed in their job of getting the local drunk to behave himself and instead punished two absolutely innocent victims of the creature's violent behavior, turned Gypsy's stomach.

"There is little point in having a separate Jewish state if our own police force are to become the same sort of ugly, fascist persecutors that the elders of this country had run here to get away from", said Gypsy to his mother. "Now, now. Don't be like that", she patronized him. This just made his blood boil more. Whatever he did was wrong, even when he was right he was wrong in all of their eyes. This was disgusting. "Hitler must have been Jewish", thought Gypsy to himself. "Only living in a community of these people with all their nasty little head games, control dramas and fraudulent trickery, could make someone hate them enough to drive them to commit the sort of atrocities that Hitler and his cohorts had done".

His mother, much to his consternation, believed the mad hatters and negotiated a deal with them behind Gypsy's back, that involved trapping him at the Yeshiva. . Ok, he had his passport back but all that had happened had drained his cash reserves dry. His back was jammed most firmly against the wall. . There was one particular Orthodox Jew from Seth Efrica who for the duration of this book shall be given the name: Fagin (though according to Gypsy this character was far greasier and more dishonest and smug than poor old Fagin from the Oliver Twist story).

From the moment Gypsy's mother appeared at the yeshiva, this slithering greasy penguin was there, trying to pretend to be Gypsy's best friend, putting his arm around him, which Gypsy quickly repulsed, "What are you doing?", said Gypsy as he tried to fend off this nasty parasite of a creature. But all to no avail the penguin kept persisting in much the same manner as a fly or mosquito would. Even a dog would have got the message by now that it's company was unwanted.

This vile creature was interested in one thing only, (Gypsy was to find out later that he was the chief fund raiser for the Yeshiva). This vile parody of a jewish crook, if you had to rate his level of dignity or self respect on a scale of one to ten, would probably have scored minus eighty five. The blatant, in your face, dishonesty of this creature's behavior was truly breath taking.

There is a word in Yiddish that describes this most accurately. The word- CHUTZPA-

The most accurate definition of this word is given as a story about a boy who kills both of his parents and then throws himself at the mercy of the court on the grounds that he is an orphan.

The use of defective logic was what made Fagin behave in such a foul manner, thinking if he lived and cheated for God it was OK. To be on this particular spiritual path then it is not for you to pick and choose which of the Ten Commandments to follow or not.

To his total shock and disgust his mother fell for this cheap trick, even as he tried to warn her what was going on. The greasy penguin was able to connive with her into blackmailing him into staying at this bullshit institution of dead learning.

LIVING WITH PSYCHO PENGUINS

"Look, you stay here and we'll send you some money (eighty pounds) every month", said his mother. "You can stay here and study and learn. We'll pay for you to be here". She had not listened to a word that he had said. She had made up her own mind about what she thought he should be doing and backed him into a corner and emotionally blackmailed him into doing something that he didn't want to do. And all this while he was down and in no position to fight back.

Gypsy did the only thing he could do at that time and went along with it. He could do nothing for now and would have to bide his time. But somehow he would get his strength back and build up cash reserves again and be free of these foul creeps once and for all.

Feeling like an animal in a cage he went along with what the mad hatters wanted, at least to a certain extent, but often he would take off his yamaka (small Jewish hat)and put it in his pocket and go off down into the Arab quarter and visit his friends, George and Assad at the Danish Tea House. He, unlike the other Jews felt quite at home in the Arab shouqs of the old city and would often go and sit on the steps outside Damascus gate in East Jerusalem and drink Arabi mint tea and watch the flow of humanity going about their daily business. The food and the spices was part of what kept drawing Gypsy into East Jerusalem. Another reason was that he knew that there was just no way on earth that the Palestinian people as a whole could be as bad as the Jews portrayed them as being.

It wasn't mathematically probable in any way or sense. A whole people can't be that bad and anyway shouldn't there be at least some respect for the fact that these people and their forefathers generations had been occupying this land for hundreds and possibly even thousands of years?

Gypsy wanted to find some educated Palestinians to befriend as so that he could hear their side of the story. Whenever he did meet one of them that would talk about the issues they were very angry and bitter about how they had and still were being treated, a bit like Gypsy's feelings towards the Orthodox Jews he had met thus far. He understood them. Sometimes the Israelis were just too arrogant and could piss anyone off to the extreme, even a saint. They just didn't get it, as if they were blind and could only see anything through a prism of jaundiced thoughts and views, influenced by their religion and upbringing.

One of the first groups of friends that Gypsy made in East Jerusalem was an international group of Christians who ran the garden tomb, which some say was the tomb were Jesus was buried after the crucifixion. . It was right below the hill where the crucifixion was meant to have happened. It was a tomb carved in the rock, with a large rolling stone wheel that was meant to be rolled across the entrance to the tomb once its occupant had been placed inside. The tomb had been found empty so it was thought that this could be the tomb, rather than what was proclaimed to be the tomb of the holy sepulcher, inside the walls of the old city. After all, the garden tomb was just below the hill which it was said the crucifixion happened upon and was of a style used at that time in that part of the world.

The people who ran and looked after the garden around the tomb were invariably friendly and relaxed about their religion, unlike the Orthodox Jews, Muslims and many of the other Christians. Gypsy found these people to be the truest and most spiritual of all in this weird city of tensions. Unlike all of the others that he encountered, they had not got lost in dogma, ritual and scriptures but cut straight to the truth. If God is love then the best way to praise him isn't to go banging your head up and down against the western wall or making salah in or near a mosque, what use is this? The best way to praise God is to be a good ambassador for him and demonstrate good qualities in daily life. Be kind, helpful and compassionate in dealings with others and show humility and a willingness to learn from others as even a fool has things to teach us, all is God's creation.

These people lived, spoke and acted in a way that reflected that thinking, so Gypsy always enjoyed visiting them. The level of peace and goodness was as such, in the area of that garden, that Gypsy wondered if this was the real tomb and possibly Jesus left some of his celestial energy behind there. It was by far the most calming place in a very mad and dysfunctional city. They knew that Gypsy was Jewish but didn't try and convert him or shun him. He was open minded and wanted to listen to their point of view. He was looking for the truth so there were no taboos in this regard. He had no absolutes or dogmas and would listen with interest, he would even pray with them. Their prayers were like meditations, asking for help for others in need and for the strength to only do good unto others. These were clean and wholesome prayers, normally only conducted with just those who were present at a place together.

Gypsy made friends with one man in particular, he was an ex- British army officer who had seen service in the second World War. After the horrors that he was witness too, he turned to the church as a way to do some good and help heal the world in any way that he could. He had trained and become a Church of England priest and had worked as a missionary in different parts of the world.

He was a most genuine, honest, humble and decent man a good ambassador for his country, his god and his faith. His name was Terrell Boise and his wife was from America.

Gypsy would see him from time to time when he made a trip to the tomb and on one occasion made a trip with him and his wife to the Church of the Nativity in Bethlehem.

If the Looney penguins had heard about that they would probably have given themselves a cardiac with the gibbering and clucking fits that they would have gone into.

FEBRUARY 1982.

Back at the Yeshiva, the prayers were all about smiting the enemies of Israel or about performing this rite or that rite or groveling for being so fucking unworthy (this last part really had become self-fulfilling).

Gypsy on hearing that the whole of the Yeshiva was funded by sending begging parties to the Jewish communities of Europe and America, suggested that it would be good if they could at least do something at the Yeshiva to produce something, much as Christian monasteries and other spiritual communities do. Gypsy suggested that one idea would be to grow herbs, especially the ones used and spoken about in the 'Torah', and sell them to visitors and tourists who came to Mount Zion. The Rabbi liked the idea and gave the go ahead for it to start.

Gypsy and Fagin, who was holding the purse strings went and found a supplier for peat moss, pearlite and vermiculite plus other additives. With the peat delivered, Gypsy set about clearing and removing all the rubbish in one of the disused tunnels under the old fortress to use as a store room and potting shed. His labors had taken him almost a week. He had found some wood, a saw, a hammer and some nails and built a potting bench. he was just about to build the cold frames to start the seedlings and cuttings off in when out of the blue with no prior warning, a bearded penguin with a big smug grin on his face, accompanied by an entourage carrying furniture, barged past gypsy and proceeded to fill up the space which Gypsy had labored so hard to clear, with unwanted household junk. When Gypsy said, "Hey, what are you doing? I spent a week preparing and cleaning that space for my own use". They all just grinned smugly at him, and walked away without saying a word. They obviously thought they were very clever for shitting on Gypsy in such a manner. Gypsy wasn't going to be deterred so easily and set about building his cold frames. He wanted them to be mobile, as so as to use spaces that weren't being used by anyone else, for short times e.g. 3 months or less. He found some old bed frames that had no springs to use to make the main structure. Putting a wooden ridge across the centre, he then proceeded to cover the outside in polythene.

There was a totally abandoned and disused volley ball court near the Beit Knesset (Synagogue or should it be spelt Sinner Gog????) so Gypsy asked the Chief Rabbi for permission to use it to start the growing. Permission was given and he duly moved the frames there, after first having cleared enough of the weeds that were growing up though the tarmac.

Again there was a problem, it was the same penguin who had handed him thirty five dollars for a month of hard work in the kitchen, the same mother fucker who watched him clean out the catacomb and then filled it with his own junk. Now he was complaining that now that gypsy had cleaned the volley ball court of its weeds he wanted to use it to play volley ball.

With steam coming out of his ears Gypsy was persuaded that he had to now move the frames to a different location. So this time he moved them up onto the roofs of the old fortress.

This time they were sabotaged and broken by someone, one of the mad hatters no doubt, as no one else had access to the roof.

Gypsy knew now that whatever he did would be sabotaged by these retards. It was as if they were deliberately trying to send him mad or make him give up. "Label Gardner", who was the penguin who had done these things to sabotage him obviously got a kick out of winding Gypsy up, judging by the big shit eating grin on his face each time that he pulled one of his tricks. Gypsy just could not get his head around why a grown man with his own family would choose to play such infantile and destructive games. To Gypsy's way of thinking, such games were pathetic and totally beneath his dignity even to contemplate, and he was only nineteen years old at the time. Label was already in his thirties and still pulling kindergarten tricks.

Gypsy gave up in disgust and went back to helping Yosemite Sam in the kitchen. He didn't like not to be working, it gave him a good feeling of self worth to be producing something with his hands.

MARCH 1982

The Yeshiva had effectively kidnapped Gypsy, with the collaboration of his mother, and now was trying to impose their will on him. They wanted to turn him into a penguin, ...fat chance of that happening. He did go to some study classes but he found that it had very little to do with anything that could be called spiritual. It had more to do with ritual and dogma than anything that might be helpful to the elevation of the soul.

However, he did make some friends. One of these was a trainee Rabbi called Wolf. Wolf had been a traveler before he came to the yeshiva and had been overland to India. He had stayed in Pakistan for quite a while and had converted to Islam, even to the point of going to Mecca on the Haj. But after he got to Israel he reconnected with his Jewish roots.

He said that part of what started to put him off of Islam was when he entered Saudi Arabia as a true Muslim convert and the officials at passport control spat at him for having a vaguely Jewish surname.

One day, Wolf and some other friends asked him if he wanted to go with them to the 'Mikve'. "What's a 'Mikve'?", asked Gypsy. "It's a ritual cleansing bath in natural untreated water that Jews often take before Shabbat, just like a hot spring", Wolf explained. "It's a large hot tub that is used by the community." "I can't go", said Gypsy. "Why not?", they asked together. "Because I have never been circumcised", Gypsy replied. "In case you're wondering, my father is not Jewish, that's why." "Well we had better help you deal with this situation", said Wolf. "But for right now, it won't be a problem at the Mikve. Go get your towel and come along".

Gypsy phoned home and arranged for all relevant papers to be sent to him.

Once he had them Wolf accompanied him to the Beit Din (Religious Court) where he presented his papers to prove that he was Jewish. Job done and they could now go and look for a place where he could get circumcised.

Sharad Tzedik Hospital was expensive, so Wolf suggested a far more humble clinic that he knew of, in the Maer Sharim Ultra Orthodox district, where Soviet Jews went on arrival from the USSR [Jews in the Soviet union had been banned from getting circumcised].

It was certainly far cheaper at the clinic and it was also clean enough.

The job was done under local anesthetic and Gypsy just closed his eyes and tried hard to imagine that he was somewhere else, preferably in a different body. "Just don't think about women", he kept telling himself.

After what felt like an eternity to Gypsy, the job was done and he came out of the surgery to find two old men from the Lubavich sect, also known as the 'Chabbads' waiting to greet him with several large bottles of vodka, gin, arrack. They poured several large glasses, handing one glass to Gypsy, they held out their glasses and recited yet another ritual prayer (there had been who knows how many prayers said already by the Rabbi in the operating theatre during the past medical proceedings). Then everyone downed their generous sized shot. That was followed by one or two more very large shots just for good measure.

The two old boys had obviously been quite busy helping people to celebrate on that particular afternoon, as they were now rocking and staggering around the corridor while laughing and speaking incoherently.

Wolf had come along as moral support and in case Gypsy wasn't in a good state to walk home. They were just leaving the building when nature, or should I say the vodka called and Gypsy had to make a dash for the toilet. His prick was wrapped in bloody bandages which took some opening and closing procedures before he could take a leek, Thus it took some time. Wolf called out "hey Gypsy what are you doing in there?" Gypsy yelled back, "I can assure you of one thing Wolf, I'm not jacking off". When Gypsy finally came out, Wolf was hanging onto the wall laughing like a madman, tears streaming down his face. Back at the Yeshiva he was still laughing and telling everyone about what Gypsy had said.

One of the people that Gypsy had befriended at the yeshiva

was a British percussionist who had performed with many underground British bands including Nick Turner, Here and Now and Hawkwind.

He had got interested in his Jewish roots and was now an Orthodox Jew studying at the Yeshiva. He told Gypsy who the mystery final act at Glastonbury '79 was, that he had been looking to find out about. He was a personal friend of this guy and not just that but he had a bunch of studio demo tapes of him. His name was Tim Blake and he had been the synthesizer pianist in one of the earliest underground acid bands 'Gong'. He gave Gypsy two tapes of Tim Blake and other assorted obscure music that he thought Gypsy might like. (Gypsy still has these two tapes in his archive store room in England, though he says he played them so many times that he's not sure if they still work).

He was right, Gypsy did like the tapes and played them regularly, they became his favorite choice of music.

This friend who we will call 'E' for the duration of this book, was waiting for his Dutch wife to convert to Judaism and then they were going to have a proper Jewish wedding.

The problem was that he was stone broke (a condition often affecting musicians and artists of which he was both). There was a whip round to collect enough money to pay for the food and drinks and Gypsy and another friend agreed to do the cooking for free.

It was a very good wedding possessed of a totally organic and earthy nature, no one was dressed too smart as this was a phenomena all of its own, try and imagine an Orthodox Jewish hippie wedding that looked like it belonged in Lord of the Rings, Woodstock and Fiddler on the Roof, all at the same time. The setting also helped. The reception was a night of feasting and dancing on the stone courtyard in the middle of the Turkish fort that formed much of the Yeshiva. It was amazing that such a large and happy wedding had been put together on such a small budget. And as far as Gypsy was concerned it knocked the living shit out of all of the stale and stuffy high budget weddings that he had been unable to avoid going to.

There were many weddings through that spring as loads of poor, ignorant bastards signed away their rights to a peaceful and happy life. It could be said that this was the Yeshiva's way to hang on to its people and dare I say, funding. Weddings invariably were between two people of the same Yeshiva, at least as far as this one was concerned.

Gypsy was starting to think to himself that if ever he had seen a typical cult, then this was it.

Some poor bastard even married the mad and nasty Polish bitch with the sellotape on her face. Gypsy wondered who and what the poor so and so was going to think about while he closed his eyes while making love with her. The poor bastard had to be the looser of the century and was probably going to die from a bad case of henpecking and harassment.

Jerusalem was in the grip of a terrible dope famine and it was getting to be almost impossible to score anything at all. Gypsy was at the Danish Tea House with a friend from the Yeshiva when another Englishman called to him thinking he was someone else. "I'm sorry", the other man said. "I thought you were someone I know from Nuweiba, his name is 'Animal' as in the drummer from the Muppet show. He looks, acts and talks like you, that's why I thought you were him". "Wow, you mean there's another like me, like an identical twin?" asked Gypsy. "Yes", said the man. "Why don't you take a seat with us?"

They were sitting outside talking and soon became friends. His name was Alan and he had been living the hippie life on the road for the past ten years, travelling to India overland, etc. He had long hair, big, bulging eyes and a manic grin and looked not unlike a Muppet himself.

Sinai was about to be given back to Egypt as part of the Begin/Sadat Camp David peace accords. As such, Alan who was Jewish was looking to relocate himself to Jerusalem.

Back at the Yeshiva, another British Jew by the name of Pessach turned up. Within a short space of time he and Gypsy were friends. Pessach was a tall but very gentle and kind man with a self mocking sense of humor. He could have a whole room in stitches while recounting the endless stream of crazy disasters and unfortunate happenings that he had through little or no fault of his own found himself in. The main reason he found himself in so many disasters, was his honesty. He was a very trusting person and as such usually got roped in by some not so scrupulous or incompetent individuals who were looking for either moral support or a patsy to take the fall when they eloped the scene of their activities.

Pessach, like Gypsy had to make the trip to see the Moyle. (Circumcision doctor with religious training - it is often a full time profession in large Jewish communities around the world, though the Moyle is often also a rabbi) as his father, also was not Jewish.

Pessach didn't have such an easy time of it, wherever he went, disasters seemed to follow him. It was as if he had a big neon sign on his forehead saying 'kick me'. To his credit he had taken to laughing about it, what else, could he do? it didn't seem like it was going to change anytime soon. A few days after his circumcision Pessach ended up back at the clinic, being given all kinds of pills and antibiotics for an infection that he got. However, after a time he did get better.

Gypsy was still hammering away on his guitar and was trying to teach himself how to play 'Stairway to Heaven' among other songs. He would sometimes go to the bus station and busk in the pedestrian subway tunnel. He didn't ever make much as Jews is Jews, as far as spare change is concerned. As they see it there is no such thing as spare change.

Q: Do you know how wire was invented?
A: No. Tell me.
Q: It came about after two Jews had a fight over a penny.

The Palestinians sometimes don't think clearly. Rather than wasting all of that time, money and effort to make and place bombs they could achieve their objective with far less trouble by just going into a Jewish neighborhood and rolling shekels in front of the fast moving trucks and buses.

One day while going to the subway to play, he met another busker who had already set up and was playing. The other busker cleared his case of the change he had made so far and invited Gypsy to join him busking for a split on the takings.

They didn't make so much but that wasn't the important thing that happened that day. Gypsy had made a new friend who was to later help Gypsy towards the path of his greatest interest. His name was Yitzhak and he was a French/Algerian Jew who had immigrated to Israel.

Gypsy always enjoyed the company of other guitarists and musicians and so he invited him around to visit at the Yeshiva.

Yitzhak accepted and came around. He lived only a couple of kilometers away which was an easy walk. All was good, but when he offered Yitzhak some food Yitzhak said "thanks But I can't eat it as I am vegetarian". He then explained to Gypsy that humans don't need meat to survive and it is not a good idea for many reasons to eat our fellow animals.

Gypsy was interested and asked Yitzhak if it was also for some reason of religion that he was vegetarian. "Well it's not exactly religion as you would know it, but yes I have a spiritual path, I do yoga and meditation and I have a teacher who is a yogi, he is from India, you can come and meet him if you would like". So that afternoon he went back with Yitzhak to where he lived. He lived in a Spartan room with virtually no furniture, explaining he needed the space to do yoga and anyway on the search for the truth not much in the way of material possessions were needed.

Baba, his Indian yoga teacher was from Bombay and of Jewish descent. However, he was not interested in the Jewish religion as he had been learning his spiritual path from Hindu yogis and now was acting as a yoga instructor and spiritual guide within that framework of understanding.

Gypsy was very very interested indeed. He wanted also to get involved in yoga and meditation, it was a large part of why he wanted to go to India. Gypsy was already on his search for truth but was not getting so far with Judaism. He knew from deep within that the Indian paths would take him much closer to his goal than anything else that he had ever heard of.

He joined Baba and Yitzhak for a session of yoga and meditation (something he was to do on many occasions in the future). No one had taught him any techniques for stilling his mind and it was hard if not almost nigh impossible, to stop it wandering all over the place. Never the less he tried.

After meditation, Baba cooked a wonderful hot and spicy Indian vegetarian curry. Gypsy was thinking that he could become vegetarian immediately if he could have food like that everyday. It was not dissimilar to the wonderful vegetarian food that his grandmother would cook, it was just that Baba used more fiery spices. Gypsy wanted to go vegetarian, so he bought his own stove and took to cooking in his room. He had since the age of sixteen, noticed what a foul, barbaric and wrong thing it was, to eat animals. He could see that animals too had feelings, consciousness and thoughts, not unlike humans. All that it had taken was some reassurance, which this time came from Yitzhak and Baba, to get him to the point where he would buck the trend around him.

The Orthodox Jews, especially Fagin, tried to tell him that it was a 'Mitzvah' (a good deed) to eat meat on a Friday night and that it is said so in the scriptures. This it may say, in some writings from some later time, after the fact. But in the Book of Exodus, from the Torah, when the Israelites were travelling through the desert and being fed manna from heaven they demanded of their God to be allowed to eat meat.

Their God allowed it but warned them that there would be heavy consequences and punishments for doing such a thing. Even so, their God had shown them the least bad way of killing the animal, observed Gypsy.

Gypsy had involved himself in reading while he was trapped at the yeshiva. He read not only the Torah but most of the Old Testament. Through the next eight months he read a book that documented the formation of the modern state of Israel, a very large thick volume titled 'A History of Modern Israel'. He also read a history of the Israeli air force, 'The History of the Mossad', which was a most fascinating read, full of stories of extreme bravery, brilliance and daring. He also read Menachim Begin's autobiography about his time as the leader of a freedom fighter/terrorist group called the 'Irgun Zvi Leumi'. They were the ones who copped the blame for the bombing of the King David Hotel, though it was likely that that particular act was carried out by a more radical splinter group called the Stern Gang, named after their assassinated founder, Abraham Stern. The book was called, "The Revolt" and described Israel as it went from the British mandate ruled Palestine to the state of Israel. As told through the eyes of this individual, as he went from Polish soldier, to Russian gulag inmate, to refugee to freedom fighter, to politician, to peace maker, with Sadat. This was the story of a truly incredible man, tough, strong, at times hard in his approach. But at the same time with true good ethics and under it all he had compassion and wanted peace more than anyone, just it must be with justice first, otherwise there is tyranny.

> There are some things that are more important than life.
> And other things, more horrible than death.

> -Menachem Begin

The list of books, nearly all of them non fiction that Gypsy devoured during his time at the Yeshiva goes on and on. He would forever be borrowing, buying or swapping books with people.

One such book that he chanced upon was called, 'The New Dark Ages Conspiracy' and detailed how a powerful group of bankers and industrialists were working to develop a disease that would kill drug addicts, homosexuals and hemophiliacs to start with, before going on to develop other diseases that they could later use to thin out the human population. Gypsy and many other people he was meeting had a feeling that someone or something malevolent was manipulating things on the planet at the time, so it came as not so much of a surprise to read this. Three years later AIDS was just starting to make its presence felt around the world.

Gypsy could see how easy it would be, given the right state of consciousness to make a paradise Utopia right here on earth. It was something that all of humanity craved and some even dared to dream about it. It made sense to him that there was something consciously fighting against such a thing taking root. Whether it was an entity or a conspiracy by some very fallen souls, incarnate here on earth or both, he couldn't say. But exist it surely did, otherwise people's natural intelligence would no longer be retarded and they would see and understand, what it is that would make them truly happy and just get on with creating it.

Another two friends that Gypsy made were Yackob and his American wife. Yackob was originally from London, but had been living in Los Angeles and San Francisco for many years, where he had worked as a lawyer in the rock and roll/hippie scene. He now worked as a teacher of scriptures at the Yeshiva. He was into rock music and liked to smoke a joint or two, thus he and Gypsy hit it off immediately.

Gypsy could study with Yackob, as with him unlike many of the other teacher/lecturers there was a genuine humility in his own thirst for knowledge. Thus from him would come quiet insights that might be missed by some of the more egotistical and delusional manic street preachers who thought that the study table was their pulpit.

Gypsy would walk out when someone of that nature would come to lead a class but Yackob was more open minded and Gypsy could enjoy to study with him. Yackob had a friend in San Francisco who was a landscape gardener. He offered to help Gypsy get fixed up with a job working for him over there. Gypsy liked the idea of living in the place where the whole hippie thing had started, it would no doubt be fun and what's more on American wages it would be easier to save the money for a really good trip around Asia.

Gypsy's father was coming out on a business trip to see his Israeli suppliers. Gypsy met him at the airport and joined him for the trip.

They first went to a large carnation nursery, that did most of its business supplying cuttings to nurseries in Europe, where the actual flower would be grown. The nursery even had a high tech laboratory, where they worked with the inner stem of the plant to create disease resistance in the varieties that they grew.

They toured the northern part of the country visiting many nurseries and were even given a full tour of AGREXCO's giant air conditioned and refrigerated agricultural cargo terminal at Ben Gurion airport. Apparently it was responsible for filling a number of El Al's cargo fleet of jumbos, on a daily basis. . .

His father also took the time to visit the Yeshiva. Gypsy had spoken with him about the possibility of a job in San Francisco and had asked if he could return to England and work on the nursery once more, to earn the money for the ticket, to get there.

Before going to the Yeshiva he warned his father about the foul, dishonest, bullshit, of 'Fagin' the weasel and asked him not to be fooled by his act. The main thing he would seek to do would be to discredit Gypsy and get him to join Gypsy's mother in conspiring to keep Gypsy trapped there so as to be able to get their hands on some more money.

Gypsy's father to his great discredit also allowed himself to be made a mockery of by Fagin.

> It is truly amazing the tricks, that a con artist in a religious
> uniform, can pull on an agnostic atheist, it truly is.........
> Gypsy

Gypsy's father turned to Gypsy, after a couple of hours of listening to the weasel and said, "I tell you what, you stay here at the Yeshiva until the autum, instead of going to San Francisco and I'll put up half of the money for you to make a trip to either Africa or India. You can come and visit us for a month in the summer if you like, as well".

Gypsy knew that it would be better to go along with it as if he didn't and his own plan failed he would have to deal with an infinite number of 'I told you so's' and it would discredit him further, in the eyes of his family. Anyway, it sounded like a good deal. "I'll be needing at least twelve hundred pounds to make the trip", he told his father. "So you'll be good for six hundred pounds, is that all right?". "Yes, that will be no problem", said Gypsy's father. "Promise?", asked Gypsy. "Promise", said his father.

After the trip to the Yeshiva, Gypsy suggested they make a trip to Ein Gedi and go for a hike up the wadis where streams flowed. The area was a nature reserve, with streams, waterfalls and pools of which some were big enough to swim in.

It was a hot day in a hot desert, as they climbed up and up. By the time they got to the top pool, along the first wadi, the beer in their day packs was warm and almost undrinkable. On seeing the pool, Gypsy stripped off to his underwear and jumped in, in order to cool off. But to no avail, as even the water was hot in this small dip pool. Later they dropped down to another wadi and climbed up to a much bigger pool. Gypsy jumped in once more and this time was able to swim. The water was almost as hot as a bath. Gypsy had never swam in water so warm. Then a sand storm started up and they had to beat a hasty retreat down the wadi, to where the car park and facilities were located.

After a couple of cold beers in the café at the car park, they were back on the road again, driving back to Jerusalem and onwards to Tel Aviv.

MAY 1982.

It was the end of his father's trip and Gypsy went with him to the airport to say goodbye before taking the bus back to Jerusalem.

He had taken to drawing, using acrylic pens and had amassed a collection of his own works that people were starting to talk about. All of his pictures had a somewhat surrealist psychedelic nature about them, influenced by his three favorite artists, Magrette, Picasso and Escher. Many of them were representations of the shapes and forms of the old city skyline that he would see daily but many more just sort of drifted out from his dreams and imagination and wound up on the paper. There was an Orthodox Jewish doctor from Strasburg, France who really liked his works and offered to help him set up with an exhibition in the new city. Gypsy was obviously excited at the idea and set about making mounts for his pictures.

But then disaster struck and he got sick the week of the exhibition. Bed ridden with a raging fever, cold shivers, hot sweats and a throbbing headache, he asked Pessach and two friends to take the pictures to the exhibition. They went into town but couldn't find the place and gave up, bringing the pictures back to Gypsy's room with lame expressions on their faces and lame excuses. By the time Gypsy was better the exhibition was over and Gypsy was too pissed off for words, he ripped up and burned the pictures in disgust.

He had been commissioned by a man who did handwriting analysis and lived at the Yeshiva to draw a picture of a man writing, for his business cards. He did the drawing But as per usual he never got paid.

Gypsy threw away his pad and pens and stopped drawing. It would be many years before Gypsy would draw like that again.

Alan as in Alan from the Danish Tea House came to see Gypsy one day. He had a problem. His non-Jewish German girlfriend Ingy had been arrested at the airport, for the most heinous, serious, crime imaginable. She had arrived in Israel without enough wonga in her purse.

The authorities wouldn't take Alan's word for it that he would look after her on account of him being a penniless hippie.

The word of penguins carried a lot of weight in Israel and even though Gypsy was not a penguin, himself, the fact that he lived among them and his address was at a penguin sanctuary, would help. Alan wanted Gypsy to write a letter of character reference for Ingy.

"No problem", Gypsy replied. "but, I don't see how a letter from me can help much".

"Well, it's worth a try, you're the only person that I know who lives among the Orthodox", said Alan. "Ok, no problem", said Gypsy. "What do you want the letter to say?"

A few days later Ingy was free, and as a mark of gratitude Alan invited Gypsy to visit him at the hostel that he worked at. Over lunch he connected him with a dealer of hash who was willing to supply him to sell in the Yeshiva and around the Jewish quarter. Gypsy was more than willing. There had been a bit of a dope famine in Israel at that time and everyone was looking for a smoke, especially all those ex-hippies turned penguin. The Shabbat or Sabbath each week was a time of interminable boredom when Orthodox Jews were not allowed to play music, work or even turn light or electricity switches on or off. In fact the few things they were allowed to do included religious study, prayer and eating for the unmarried and procreation for married couples. . Thus just before shabbat got started on a Friday afternoon there would be loads of penguins blasting away on Bong's chillums and joints. Gypsy could see the business opportunity in this and besides, if he couldn't get them to pay him when he did honest work then he would take their money in dope deals. . The dealing at the beginning was small and there was no problem running it across the old city from Damascus gate to Mount Zion. . Yitzhak was playing a concert at a hotel one evening, he asked Gypsy if he would like to come along. Gypsy came along and helped them set up then operated the mixing desk for them. He had never done this before, but he coped with it well enough to make all concerned, happy. After they had finished the gig and packed away the equipment Gypsy was most pleasantly surprised when Yitzhak turned around and handed him some money for his help. It had been fun and he had learned something new from it and to be paid for it as well was just a bonus.

JUNE 1982.

The whole town of Kiriat Shmona had been living in bomb shelters for the previous six months under a barrage of Palestinian rockets that were being fired from southern Lebanon. Meanwhile the Israeli military was gearing up for a strike, to deal with this menace, once and for all.

The Israeli ambassador to England was assassinated in London a week before Gypsy was due to fly to England.

Meanwhile, just prior to this, in the south Atlantic, Argentina had invaded the Falkland Islands and Britain had sent a battle group to the South Atlantic to take them back and a bloody war had ensued.

In the days that followed the assassination in London Israel invaded Lebanon. |Pushing on the first day to Tyre and on the second day to Sidon.

The world, at the beckoning of the oil exporting Muslim states took turns at criticizing Israel, as per usual. But when Margaret Thatcher took her turn to wag her finger, Menachim Begin who was the Israeli Prime Minister at that time laughed at her.

"You dare to criticize Israel for doing something to protect the people of Northern Israel from constant rocket attack. Yet you go eight thousand miles to fight a war over some windswept isles that most people in your country have probably never even heard of" he told her.

Gypsy flew from Tel Aviv back to London arriving to a country in a frenzy of nationalistic jingoism in the aftermath of the British military having just kicked ten tons of living shit out of the Argentinean military.

JUNE 1982

It shouldn't have been too hard. The Argentineans are a strange bunch, being mostly of Italian descent, with German names and speaking Spanish. A condition that has them in confusion and in that confusion they have gained Delusional ideas of their own grandeur which in turn led them to pick a fight that in their confused condition could never have hoped to win.

Gypsy went back to work on the nursery, saving all the money he could.

Then after the first week, came Glastonbury, it was now being run by CND (Council for Nuclear Disarmament) who had been sparked into action by the conservative government's plans to allow the Americans to store land mobile nuclear missiles in England.

The festival had expanded massively and the money would be going to a very good cause. It wasn't quite the spiritual occasion that his first visit to the Glastonbury festival had felt like back in '79 but it was still good, with a good vibe, except for of course, the post midnight visit around the campfire from the occasional spun out speed or coke freak jibbering in their delusional paranoid state about how the cops were raiding and people were getting busted. Those sorts could put a real dampener on a good gathering.

There were four stages and a movie tent and the green field had just come into its own as an expo of alternative living. The whole festival had been that back in '79. There was now a permanent stage in the shape of a pyramid with a CND symbol on the top. Acts such as Aswad (a reggae band) and Osibissa performed on the main stage along with Richie Havens, Incantation (a south American Andino style band with panpipes and charangos), Fairfort Convention and the Chieftains.

It was a good three days of fun where Gypsy met many like minded people, also on the search for their own truth. When Gypsy told them what he had been checking out while he lived in Jerusalem they were invariably interested and wanted to ask questions.

The festival was over all too soon and Gypsy headed home and back to work. Through the next few weeks he saved all the money he could. He wanted to buy a Fender Stratocaster or Gibson Les Paul to sell back in Israel, where good electric guitars could be sold at quite a premium on the British price.

An American friend from the Yeshiva called Avraham came to stay for a while. He also worked on the nursery but it must have been hard for him as he had done very little physical work in his life. He did have a skill however and had a juggling act that he would perform at weddings and parties. He would juggle with both fire torches and knives and would keep Gypsy's friends and family entertained.

After a month of hard graft Gypsy had some money saved. He made a trip to London and stayed with some cousins in Finchley. From there he went into Central London to Tottenham Court Road and Denmark Street. After a long search through all of the guitar shops of the area it was there at the last shop that he entered which was the famous 'Andy's Guitar Workshop' that he found what he was looking for. He picked it up and played it, it was not only affordable but it played like a dream, allowing Gypsy to perform tricks that he could never have done on his old Hofner Galaxy. He decided that this was the one and paid for it. He now had an American made Fender Stratocaster. Also it came with a hard case which would help in getting it back to Israel.

Back at home, Gypsy busied himself in stripping a speaker cabinet he had, of two of it's individual speakers. It was a set of four Goodman, twelve inch speakers in the cabinet. He packed the two speakers carefully in his suitcase along with an H/H 100 watt two channel amp and a set of tweeters and crossovers that he had bought. The year of pennance at the penguin institute would be over in a few months and he would need to find half of the money for his big trip. He had a plan.

With cases all packed, the family gave him a lift to the airport and dropped him off. His case was full and heavy, loaded down with musical instruments and equipment. He checked in at the EL AL desk in terminal three. Soon he was sitting by a window on board the plane as it sped down the runway and up and out in a south easterly direction.

JERUSALEM/ISRAEL

JULY 1982.

Five uneventful hours later Gypsy was in the process of getting his not insubstantial luggage onto a bus to Jerusalem.

On getting to the Yeshiva, he found out that the penguins were having a twelve day festival of gloom, mourning and guilt trips to mark the time that the Temple of Jerusalem was destroyed almost two thousand years prior. They weren't allowed to wash for the whole twelve days and when Gypsy got to his room, which he shared with two other students, the place was starting to stink like a kennel.

Gypsy soon found out why. There in his alcove, where he slept and stored his things, lying on his bed, was the filthiest foulest, fat penguin that he had ever seen. This creature was disgusting and not just that, he spoke no English and refused to move and let Gypsy put his things away. He was forced to use another bed that night and had no choice but to watch as this foul, wretched, foul smelling creature screwed up his clean sleeping area.

The bare faced arrogant cheek of the mad hatter penguins never ceased to amaze Gypsy. But then, anyone who sincerely believes that the world is only 5,700 years old and that God put the dinosaur bones and fossils in the earth to fuck up the unfaithful, Isn't quite living in the real world are they? Why let the truth get in the way of a perfectly good dogma?

It took several days to have the fat penguin removed from his sleeping area. It took the threat of physical violence and a large wooden club to achieve this, as the other penguins told Gypsy that he would just have to put up with this intrusion.

Having cleared his area and cleaned all things that had been fouled by this dirty smelly animal, Gypsy went into town and bought a large sheet of ply and some black paint that he then had delivered to his room at the Yeshiva. He had a hammer, a screw driver, a hand powered drill, a saw, some sand paper and a paint brush. With this small tool set, he set about building two speaker cabinets, as so he could turn the speakers and amp head into a P.A. system. .

In a house in the old city, several of Gypsy's friend were helping an old (but not nearly as old as he looked), man from New York, 'cold turkey' off of heroin. He had been a 'smack head' for over fifteen years and now wanted to kick his habit. He had rented or borrowed this fancy two bedroomed house in the most sought after area of the smart and renovated jewish quater.

Gypsy joined Stanley's team of minders. Part of the job would be to block the door or pin him down every time the pain got to the point that he couldn't take it anymore and he wanted to go running out looking for a fix. Another part of the job which for some reason had become very difficult, was to go out and try and score some hash to at least dull the pain for him a little.

As Stanley told his story it became clear that he was a career criminal back in New York. "It's absolutely against my ethics to do honest work", he said. "the mere idea of it makes me shudder". However, in Israel he was going to behave himself. . Two or three weeks previously his friends had apparently turned up at his apartment, grabbed him, dragged him into a taxi and whisked him off down to JFK airport. They had then thrust a ticket to Tel Aviv in his hand. "Get on the plane and go, you are about to be busted, the cops are watching some of the people who you are working with" they told him.

Stanley was protesting all the way to the airport that he was safe but luckily for him they insisted and even escorted him down to the plane (which used to be possible even for international flights, at American airports prior to 911) to make sure he got on it. Stanley was the master forger for a fraud outfit running tricks in the New York/ New Jersey area.

A few weeks after arriving in Israel, the busts started happening back in New York and it was all over the news that his gang who had been forging American Express cards complete with glowing X and other security features had been busted and further members were of the syndicate were being rounded up. Stanley was glad that his friends had done him such a service. Of course one could take a more cynical view and say that maybe these friends were involved. What could any self respecting fraud outfit hope to achieve without its main component, the 'master forger'? You could afford to lose a lot of people from the operation, as positions could be filled with relative ease, but master forgers of Stanley's caliber were an extreme rarity and it was in everyone involved's interests to help not only keep him out of jail but to keep his nose clean. As the next time a batch of dodgy 3 ½ dollar notes show up on the police radar they don't want the buggers knocking on Stanley's door, as he could be doing work for them at the time and they couldn't afford to let his cover be blown. . Stanley, for all intents and purposes looked like a piano teacher, an accountant or maybe a vicar from a small quiet village in Ohio or Missouri or somewhere else that's too boring to be worth going to. He certainly did not look like some smack head gangster which was why he had stayed out of prison for most of his life, despite having such a 'respectable' traditional Jewish trade. . In between screaming fits and attacks of the shivers etc as he went through 'cold turkey' he told of other exploits that he had been involved in, including hash runs to India. They had dressed as businessmen, then flown to Bombay, stayed at the famous Taj Mahal hotel, then flew back to New York with twenty kilos in each of their bags. Back in New York, he was so crooked that he didn't even pay for his phone or electricity. Instead he found ways and places to tap the lines outside his apartment without being noticed. . Not only was he a fraud artist, he was also a good artist in his own respect and turned out several highly saleable, fine works from his own imagination while incarcerated in the apartment. The style was later to inspire much of the sketches and graphic designs that Gypsy would produce from time to time as he travelled. . Though Gypsy did some of the minder work at the house, because of his various connections in the Palestinian areas and the fact that he was the only one not afraid to go into East Jerusalem, even late at night meant that his main job was to take care of hash supplies.

All his main people were out of town and he was down to street scoring and begging for leaves and the occasional bud from various friends who had their own domestic horticultural endeavors. It was serious hard work that took long hours of searching as the crowd with the reliable connections were all back down in the Sinai Oasises of Nuweiba, Da Hab, Sharm el Sheik and Ras Mohammed. . The Sinai had been handed back to Egypt some months prior and the various people who had lived there when it had been under Israeli rule wanted to find out what their visa status would be if they wished to return there to live after the area had reverted to Egyptian rule.

After covering just about all areas that he knew, where it might be possible to score something with Stanley's money (a search that lasted 5-6 hours), Gypsy returned to the apartment with a measly two and a half grams of Lebanese hash.

They were all sitting around in the living room while Gypsy and another man in the room put joints together.

All of a sudden there was a loud knock at the door. The apartment did not have a spy hole, so one of the nervous occupants called out, "who are you?" POLICE!!. OPEN THE DOOR!!!, came the loud aggressive reply.

Gypsy ate the joint that he had just rolled and one of the others was about to jump from a second storey window with the remaining, precious piece of hash.

Then they opened to find both Stanley's doctor and a rabbi laughing like two madmen at the mayhem and panic that they had caused, in the apartment.

They were all sitting in the apartment, the doctor and the rabbi included, when a young Palestinian man came and knocked on the door. It was one of Gypsy's connections but he didn't have full confidence that he would come through. However the Palestinian man came in and handed over a large piece of decent quality hash that was then taken and used to make a large quantity of joints.

It was an interesting and diverse group of people in the apartment that night, with a group of innocent American Jewish hippie kids, one experienced traveler, a New York con artist, a young Palestinian, a doctor and a rabbi. What was so interesting was to see people coming from so many different lines of thought, sitting down and talking with each other.

Then the young Palestinian asked the doctor what he thought about the war in Lebanon that was in it's third month at that time.

The doctor was an Orthodox Jew, so Gypsy was surprised at his answers, the man had an intelligent, long sighted, liberal, point of view. His reply was this, "I think it is a bad idea for everyone. Sooner or later the two sides will have to make peace and find a way to live with each other, this is inevitable. So why not get on with it now instead of wasting all these lives, destroying so much infrastructure and squandering so much money on something that ultimately will not solve the problem?". That was an answer that no one in the room could honestly disagree with, including the young Palestinian who had asked the question. He nodded in agreement as the joints were being passed around.

It was a scene that Gypsy remembered well and recited to me with joy and relish as he said it was the first time he had seen Orthodox Jews and hippies partying with one of the indigenous locals. It made a welcome change to see them getting on well together and to see them accept a Palestinian as a fellow human being instead of vilifying them all and dehumanizing them which was what is so much of the problem and misunderstanding between the two peoples was all about.

Gypsy was later to hear from another friend, that the doctor had been responsible for bringing young Jews and Palestinians together to get to know each other and to play music together. If true, then it was a very good idea indeed, a good way to break down the barriers and get friendships started.

"When religion makes not just walls but wars between people then it can only be said that people are not understanding of their religion in a correct manner and need to go and reflect deeply and honestly on what motives, madness and psychosis is making them feel so correct in doing such wicked evil things".

-GYPSY

AUGUST 1982.

Meanwhile, back near the Damascus gate things had got a whole lot more interesting. Alan and friends had just returned from a prolonged trip to Neweba in what had once again become the Egyptian Sinai.

Alan was now running the hostel where he had been working and it had an in house dealing operation going on. What's more due to the progress of the war in Lebanon huge quantity of Lebanese hash were being liberated with each P.L.O. base that was being taken. It was likely that most Israeli soldiers were carrying at least two kilos each in their back packs when returning to Israel. That made for a pretty cheap supply, at least at wholesale price that was. With the steady drop of the price of hash at dealers prices and word of such things having not reached the insular world of the toker penguins, Gypsy was starting to make good with the dope dealing.

Pessach had met himself a really nice girlfriend from an area of Jerusalem called Katamon. There was a large Kurdish Jewish community there, from which she came.

They were deeply religious people but unlike the penguins, their ways were a lot more natural and relaxed.

Soon Pessach was engaged and a wedding day was set. Apparently, even when he proposed to her the situation had the usual Pessach tragic comedy about it.   At the time Pessach was walking down the road with her he had been fine and he was about to propose to her. But he must have eaten something bad at Yosemite Sam's hall of fine hygienic dining (ahem!). All of a sudden, as he got down on one knee to propose to her his guts dropped and he had stomach cramps that brought tears to his eyes. Anyway his girlfriend mistook his tears of pain for tears of love and immediately and enthusiastically said yes. That was followed by Pessach making his excuses and running off, in desperate search of a toilet. A bush behind a wall was all that he could find, so he jumped behind it, dropped his cacks and breathed one massive sigh of relief. Then going back to his fiance, he had to make up a very inventive story as to what he had been doing, as his lady was now staring at him with a puzzled look on her face.

SEPTEMBER 1982.

Pessach soon got married and moved to Katamon. Gypsy and Efraim, an American friend from the Yeshiva, went to his wedding, but none of the other penguins from the yeshiva were there. It was a good and simple wedding with most of the catering taken care of by his wife's extended family.

Pessach had only been married for a couple of weeks when Gypsy went to visit him.

His wife's family was so happy with Pessach that they thought it would be a good idea to get one of their other daughter s married to another Englishman.

Pessach was laughing when he told Gypsy what was going on. His wife's sister was in the next room tarting herself up ready to see if she could catch Gypsy. Gypsy was deeply flattered that this sweet young woman found him attractive and he wouldn't have minded perhaps a brief fling or night in bed with her. But the trouble with women who are deeply religious is that they want to play for keeps and the very very last thing that Gypsy wanted at that point was to get tied down and trapped in anything like marriage especially if it meant being tied to a dogma religion where he would be expected to pray umpteen gazillion times a day.

Q: Why do Jewish women close their eyes when they make love with their husbands?
A: Because they hate to see him enjoying himself.

That particular joke came from George, the Armenian Blues Brother at the Danish Tea House.

Meanwhile back at the Yeshiva, apart from the main band, who played their regular Saturday night gig at their own gig hall on Mount Zion there were also two or three other bands playing Penguin rock. .

Gypsy would work as the road crew for these other semi liquid bands that used to form according to which musicians were available and who liked jamming with who. He would get to the venue early with a hired P.A. system and mixing desk, set up the system and then with a friend or someone on the mike, strumming guitar and hitting drums, endeavor to have the mixer set ready as he could before the band arrived. Gypsy got to be a part of the gig wherever they were playing, sometimes lending his own equipment to help improve the quality of the sound coming out of the naff old unit that they had hired that afternoon. The gigs were in a variety of places around the city from gig halls and community centers to five star hotels. . On one occasion they were to do a gig in one of the large reception rooms at the world famous King David Hotel on the hill opposite Mount Zion. It was a smart place with a classic, antique and very expensive vibe about it. Gypsy particularly enjoyed that gig, as the equipment actually functioned well for a change. The musicians who were playing were all friends of Gypsy and gelled well in their music and their performance. The hotel staff were exceptionally decent and helpful, which at the time was a great behavioral rarity in Israel. So all in all it was a very good night.

Meanwhile, Gypsy's speaker cabinets were coming together well, especially considering that his tool collection was limited to five or six pieces. He had the boxes together and now he wanted to make sure that the speakers would fit perfectly. The woofers were inset back inside the cabinet, while the tweeters were mounted inset through a board on the upside of the front of the cabinet. They fitted and Gypsy took them out, ready to paint the cabinets.

Then a young American from California, who lived in the next room, came in. His father in America sent him plenty of money to use as opposed to the £20 pounds per week that Gypsy would get by on. He had rented a car and wanted to know if Gypsy wanted to bring some joints and go for a spin.

They took off in the small car, first into the West Bank, taking the road down to the Dead Sea. On reaching its shores they took a left turn and drove towards Jericho. It was nine o'clock at night but it was still unbelievably hot there at the lowest point on earth.

They drove on, heading north past Jericho and up to the sea of Gallilea and Tiberias, a town on the lake. They stopped for a beer or two and then got back in the car and drove up over the hills to the coast. They stopped for another beer or two more, in one of the bars that was still open in Haifa. It was now 1:30 am, the only bars to be found still open were in a rough area down by the port.

They were just about the only two people who were in the bar apart from the barman and a couple of semi conscious men sitting in the corner. This was no fun so they took off down the highway to Tel Aviv.

It was motorway all the way and they were there in less than an hour. Driving around, looking for any form of nightlife was a fruitless exercise, there was not a bar or club to be seen open at 3 am. So they gave up and drove back to Jerusalem, getting back at 4:30 am, having travelled most of the north of the country in a single night.

There was a condemned part of the old fortress that was in need of serious renovation, it had been married quarters for some of the families that lived at the Yeshiva but now stood empty and was only accessible through an upper floor window from the roofs of the fortress.

This did not stop an intrepid Spaniard whose name was Miguel from turning the place into a squat. He and Gypsy soon became friends and would meet on the roof to cook food, drink vodka and smoke joints.

The apartment that Miguel had taken was a large place and soon Gypsy moved in with his amps and guitars and it became the secret party venue for certain chosen people. A few nights after Gypsy had moved in, a man by the name of Haim crawled through the window and introduced himself. He had escaped over the wall of the local looney bin the night before arriving and was just the sort of person to make the party more interesting.

He was crazy but he knew it. He also had a brilliant mind, full of insights into the nature of people and what motivates them to do some of their insanities. Gypsy and Miguel enjoyed listening to him talk, he was someone to learn from and like them he was also a musician.

There was a concert stage set up at an open air venue in the bottom of one of the valleys that surrounded Mount Zion on three sides. The venue was called 'Sultan's Pools'. On several occasions there were to be large concerts with world famous jazz/rock fusion musicians playing.

The first gig was the American keyboard player Chic Corea. Miguel and Gypsy who were both financially limited at the time, managed to probe the fence until they found an area with lax security where they were able to enter the arena unseen and for free, not just that they were backstage and with a perfect view. At the end of the gig they even got to meet the artist, Chick Corea, in person. There were enough people around backstage with long hair that neither of the two of them stood out. Israeli security at that venue was not so watertight as perhaps they would like to have believed it was.

Back at the squat Gypsy and Miguel's many hippie friends who were living in either Israel or Egypt would stop by. Invariably they would be looking for something to smoke.

Gypsy's runs across the old city were getting to be more and more regular. As a result his own personal stash had grown to the point that he supplied the regular residents of the squat for free and still had masses to spare.

They would do silly things like rolling a twelve inch, fat sausage, using umpteen papers. It would take almost an hour to smoke as it was passed around the room.

Sometimes there would be a whole crowd playing guitars, electric guitars, flutes and drums, as the joints went around.

A regular visitor to the squat was a friend called Rene who lived down in the Sinai, at Da Hab. He was from Switzerland. He had lost a foot and part of his lower leg in one road accident and a finger in another. He had a car that had been specially adapted for him. He worked at the one business still functioning in Da Hab at that time, the diving centre. He would cross the border at Taba regularly and drive up from Eilat to Jerusalem and visit them, staying in the squat for two or three nights at a time.

Gypsy would sort him out with his hash needs and then they would relax and talk and play music.

Back in the other room that Gypsy used to sleep in before, the speaker cabinets were coming together well. He had finished the structural work and was now giving them a coat of paint. They were starting to look good.

Across town in East Jerusalem things were more interesting and Gypsy would spend more time there at the hostel. Gypsy was gearing up for his trip to India. Alan had been there before, having driven there in a mini bus and had many stories about the place that Gypsy was eager to hear. He wanted to get as street wise as he could before he arrived there.

Gypsy had made friends with a Palestinian who he used to smoke joints with along with other friends, under the trees and bushes between the New Gate and Damascus Gate. A group of them would meet at Damascus gate on the amphitheater like steps, where they would sit and drink Arabi tea with mint leaves inside, served by a man with a large classic middle eastern tea urn over one shoulder and glasses in a bucket in his other hand.

It was always interesting to watch the flow of humanity as the Pedestrian traffic flowed through the Damascus gate. There would be porters carrying out heavy objects of furniture and even fridges on their backs. There would be donkey carts laden with produce going into the market. The people would be wearing anything from western attire to full Arab Bedouin clothes. There would be tourists with cameras, in tour groups and alone. There were Christian nuns, monks and priests of every denomination imaginable. There were the shop owners and the constantly busy money changer, who was a young blind Palestinian who Gypsy knew. Despite being blind he was very intelligent and exceptionally good at his job. Among all this throng of humanity and color, would also appear groups of scowling four eyed mad hatter penguins with their noses in the air as if they owned the place. They were some of the residents of the ultra orthodox, fanatic lunatic 'ghetto' district of Maer Sharim. They would cut through the Arab quarter several times a day, on their way to the wailing wall were they went to go and grovel before their God. The shortest route went through the Arab market.

Yerushalime as it is pronounced in Hebrew means 'City of Peace' but that was the last thing that Jerusalem was. The politics were very complicated. The Palestinians despised the Israelis, who are of a different religion to them. Also many of them were of European or Turkic descent with white skin.

The Orthodox Jews have no problem with Islam, as like Judaism it has just one God. However, they despise Christianity and much like the Monty Python team say, they think that he was not the Messiah, he was a very naughty boy. (by chance the place that Gypsy got to see 'The Life of Brian' for the first time, was Jerusalem. Gypsy laughed because it was so damned accurate in its portrayal of the ridiculousness of the place. He told me that Jerusalem politics are just so far gone as to be beyond parody). To continue, The Muslims for their part accept Jesus as a prophet and the old testament as gospel, but the first chapter of the Koran, 'The Cow' is spent slagging off both the Jews and the Christians for their hypocrisy and other bad ways.

The Christians for their part generally like the Jews but also tend to feel that it is their duty to convert the Jews for their own sakes to Christianity. This is something that the Jews despise them for. The Christians don't like Islam as a rule and view it as the devil's religion, as it was founded in the year 666 A.D. 'the number of the beast', according to a chapter in the New Testament called 'Revelation to John'.

To add another complexity to the situation, the men in women's dresses at the Vatican at that time had no diplomatic relations with the

123

state of Israel and instead backed the Palestinians, a minority of whose number are Christians of various denominations and sects.

So here it was, Jerusalem, a city where many people from a wide variety of places rubbed shoulders in the street while despising each other in unimaginable ways.

Gypsy had caught the friend who stayed at his place in England before stealing from someone and jumped on him for it, saying "is it too much to ask that you keep by the most basic of the Ten Commandments while you wear that religious uniform of yours?' The friend turned and said, with a smug shit eating grin on his face, "Oh, that rule only applies between Jews, it's ok to steal from a non Jew." Gypsy hit the roof with rage. "Mother fucker. My father is not Jewish and he gave you a job and a place to stay while you were in England. Do you think that it would be ok to steal from him too?" Gypsy snarled at him in disgust. "You are not a friend of mine if that is how you think".

At Yitsak and Baba's place one evening, an American yogi, who was also a commercial pilot working in Jordan was also staying. Originally he had been a hippie before being introduced to yoga. He still had a long, platted pigtail down his back but now his passions were flying planes, yoga and meditation.

Gypsy sat and tried to mediate with them but he still did not have a clue as to how to still his mind.

Back at the Yeshiva, Gypsy was at a study class on Kabala which is the mystic teaching of the Jews. Many of the mad hatter penguins who Gypsy had asked about Jewish beliefs regarding the nature of the soul had hunched up their shoulders and grinned smugly and said only Jews have a soul and only Jews have an after life. Gypsy knew that this was utter bullshit because he could see and feel this could not possibly be true, he could even see the soul in animals and he had seen it in most people who he met. But here it was, also in the mystic teachings of the Jews. Every living being, that means every human, every animal, every fish, every plant, and every insect has a soul and is a part of God and eventually all returns to God.

There it was, as clear as the light of day, deep within the Jewish teachings was that which Gypsy knew in his heart to be true. No one could now dispute it with him. No more smug grins, no more bullshit.

It was on one rain soaked Saturday afternoon that Gypsy had jumped into the doorway of the Beit Knesset to get out of the rain. There were many people inside praying and they had the Tora scroll out on a reading bench. One of Gypsy's two room mates at the room where he was building the speakers was the Gabbai (keeper of books and ceromonies) in this particular synagogue.

He called Gypsy up to read from the Tora scroll. "What do I do? I've never done this before", said Gypsy. "You're joking", said the Gabbi. "No", said Gypsy. "This is something I've never done before. I didn't grow up in or near a Jewish community".

"Well this is going to be your Barmitzva then", he told Gypsy. "Oh, is that what a Barmitzva is?", said Gypsy. "I thought it was just when some obnoxious spoilt brats were given a mountain of expensive presents".

So Gypsy, with help and instruction, read from the Tora and was then Bar Mitzvad and everyone in the synagogue then made lots of noise and had a good old dance and sing song. And that was Gypsy's Bar Mitzva.

There was a much more laid back groups of young Orthodox religious hippies that would come and hang out in the jewish quater from time to time. Their Rabbi 'Shlomo Karlabach' was known as the singing rabbi. He played guitar and was into peace, he had helped form a collective farming community called Moshav Modien, that produced organic whole foods, and many of the Moshav members were vegetarian.

He would come to do performances regularly in Jerusalem and afterwards would gather with his hippie followers in a house in the old city's Jewish quarter to talk further and play his guitar. Gypsy would go and listen sometimes but though he spoke as if what he was saying was so profound there wasn't anything of true universal profoundness in what he was saying. Nevertheless, at least unlike the penguins, this guy had a more benevolent and peaceful approach to life, even if he didn't seem to have so much wisdom to speak.

Back at the Yeshiva, Gypsy had finished his speaker cabinets, having bought a soldering iron to connect the speakers and the crossovers and plugs. Though with only two channels, it was only suitable, as it stood, for a solo vocalist and instrument. That was not going to be a problem in Jerusalem, a city full of one man acts. Besides, a mixing desk could always be added.

Most of the people at the yeshiva, both penguins and the only half twisted, looked on in admiration at the fancy and professional looking

P.A system that Gypsy had put together and with just the most basic of hand tools too.

Soon he had work offers flooding in. he first wanted though to sell his guitars and amps, including the P.A. and all pedals and extra equipment to help him raise the half of the cash that his father said that he would match him for to pay for his trip to India and the Far East.

Gypsy's endeavor to turn his old guitar amp into a P.A. had caught many people's attention and as the job offers came flooding in members of the Yeshiva establishment began to get worried about losing this particular source of income.

Fagin came to Gypsy and asked how much he had been offered to work for some of the others who wanted his work. Gypsy exaggerated ever so slightly the amount that he had been offered to go and work abroad by certain people.   Fagin offered to pay him more, or more to the point he promised that the Yeshiva would pay him more.

Gypsy had now become accustomed to the dishonest trickery of the mad hatters and in his caution he made them sign a binding Jewish religious document that would be applicable at any beit din as part of his employment contract.

This was something that no matter how hard they wriggled or twisted or turned they would not be able to get out of. To Gypsy's surprise, they actually signed. This could have been a result of Fagin's smart arsed incompetence or optimism about how much money they could screw out of Gypsy's gullible parents.

OCTOBER 1982.

Anyway, Gypsy now had the buggers over a log and there was just no way that they could back out. Those Talmud and Gamora classes hadn't been a total waste of time after all.

Gypsy was commissioned to build up a workshop for the Yeshiva, to repair various wooden items and build new pieces of furniture. He was on a high wage among a group of people who wouldn't know what a day's work was if it came and kicked them in the arse.

The Rabbi had blocked the sale of his musical equipment to his primary target market. That market was the musicians at the yeshiva, whose needs Gypsy understood and tailored his buying and creativity too. At least that was what Gypsy had been told, that a certain person who wanted to purchase various pieces of Gypsy's rig had been told not to, in order to keep him trapped at the Yeshiva.

However it was rewarding to watch the pissed off rage on the Rabbi's face once a week when Gypsy waved the contract under his nose and forced him to hand over a pile of loot. The Rabbi would slam each note down on the table, almost spitting with disgust, that a student had done this to him. Him a rabbi, being forced to be honest and keep his word, huh! How dare he?

Under a bush, between the New Gate and the Damascus Gate, on a pile of rocks. Gypsy and his Palestinian friend from the PLO were sitting and smoking a joint when a loud but muffled explosion was heard from inside the old city walls. They turned their heads but carried on smoking their joint, it was probably someone doing a controlled demolition or something. A couple of moments later two young men ran down the hill and disappeared into the taxi rank.

Five minutes later the first of some twenty ambulances started to arrive, sirens blazing and lights flashing. They were just finishing a second joint when the Palestinian said how much it made him happy to see his own people making such attacks.

Gypsy had to stay quiet he was disgusted by this attitude, but if he wanted to argue about it it would not change anything now and could possibly get him killed in this part of the city. Nevertheless, it was a deeply sad tragedy that had happened. Not just for those hurt or killed but also for their families too.

It turned out that the victims were a group of Italian Christian pilgrims who had absolutely nothing to do with any of the troubles and were causing no offence to anyone, they were absolutely innocent victims. The terrorists had thrown a hand grenade amongst them. Gypsy wondered what sort of mental contortions the terrorist group claiming responsibility would go through to justify their attack or to twist it around and blame Israel for it. It turned out later that one person had been killed and some twenty others had been injured.

Back at the squat the crowd of residents was growing and the price of hash at wholesale rates was going ever lower. Another visitor at that time was another Jewish traveler by the name of 'Chai'. He had been all across Asia and knew his way around everywhere, from India to Japan.

"If you want the 'Ultimate Asian Experience' then you should go and see Japan, that country is as ultimately Asian as it can get" said Chai.

He told Gypsy much about India, Thailand, Malaysia, etc. Gypsy for his part listened. Asia proper would be a totally different experience from all that he had known before.

Stanley was walking down the hill into the car park below the Holocaust Museum, accompanied by the orthodox Jewish, French doctor, when he saw Gypsy. Gypsy had asked him if maybe he could score an extra prescription of some of the weird Psychotropic pills that the doctor had given him to help him quit his smack habit.

Stanley turned around to face Gypsy, "I've just remembered the names of those pills that you said that you wanted to try", he said. Gypsy didn't know which way to turn to hide his face, this was embarrassing and not just that but now he would never get a chance to try this stuff. But to Gypsy's amazement, upon hearing the names of the pills, the doctor said, "ah you want to try Fiton and Hypnoderm?" He pulled out his prescription book and quickly wrote Gypsy up a prescription. "Is there anything else that you would like?' he asked. "Well it might be nice to have some valium", said Gypsy. "No problem", said the doctor and wrote it onto another prescription. "You are intelligent enough to know the experiences that you wish to try, it is not for me to obstruct you", he said.

That afternoon, Gypsy and Miguel went out and scored the prescriptions. It was the evening when they decided to open the first packet of Hypnoderm. They were walking along the Jaffa road in the direction of the new city when Gypsy turned to Miguel and said, "How many of these do you think we will need to pop to get a result?"

"Dunno", said Miguel. "Try two or three". Gypsy tried three and passed the packet to Miguel who also popped three. After fifteen minutes with no result, they both decided to pop another five each.

A short while later, they were aware that they were walking like drunks with a confused sense of where gravity was meant to be happening. However, apart from a deeply relaxed feeling, they both had their faculties of perception working.

The others were in the squat when Gypsy and Miguel wandered back in through the upstairs window. They introduced the others to their new high and soon the squat was looking like an opium den or a dimazepam party, as one by one, everyone in the room turned into conscious but motionless zombies.

There was a particularly obnoxious young Parisian penguin who without invitation or provocation had been jumping around and wagging his finger at everyone in the most manic street preacher act ever seen on Mount Zion He had been prancing around outside the Beit Knesset telling everyone how very very, waggy finger bad it was, to have sex outside of marriage.

As everyone was lying around the squat, motionless but conscious, on various mattresses and couches, the lights turned off, but the incense still burning and music still playing, two shadows entered the squat. Gypsy could make out one of them was a female, by her clothes it was obvious that she was an Orthodox Jew.

Convinced that everyone in the squat was asleep or unconscious, Froggy, the penguin then proceeded to fuck his girlfriend on the floor in the middle of the room in front of everyone, oblivious to the eyes around the room watching them. It is indeed interesting what some people do when they think that those around them are not watching.

> Forget about prayer, study or good deeds. Hypocrisy is the number one activity of those who hide behind religious uniforms.
>
> -GYPSY

Sergio Mendez the Brazilian musician, was giving a concert at Sultans Pools. Gypsy and Miguel got back to their old trick of probing the fence for an area with slack security. Though they had missed the first two or three songs, after a short while they were sliding down a slope under cover of some bushes and into the backstage area once again.

It was a fantastic concert of Latin jazz and happy Brazilian sounds. After the concert Gypsy and Miguel were allowed to enter the stage with the other backstage people and got to talk with the stars of the show including Sergio himself. Sergio was a very friendly and happy person with zero in the way of rock star ego or arrogance about him. He was just like the interesting intelligent friends that they had who it was such a pleasure to spend the company of an evening with.

Gypsy carried on working, building a workshop for the Yeshiva and every week the rabbi would be compelled by the document that his deputy weasel had signed, to hand over a large sum of shekels. He really didn't like it and made it obvious. But he and his weasels had pulled a multitude of underhanded tricks upon Gypsy and that was not going to be allowed to pass without sufficient retribution being taken against them.

Fagin had some deal running with a house down on the coast, just outside of the resort town of Natanya and he wanted Gypsy to go there and do some work on it. Gypsy took the bus from Jerusalem, arriving in Natanya in the early evening, just after dark. He found his way to the expensive estate out on the cliffs overlooking the sea and found Fagin's pad. He spent the next five days working, fixing small things around the house and swimming at the beach below.

The beach was a religious one and as such, males could only swim in one area and females could only swim in another area. Further down the beach, was just a regular tourist mixed beach, but here penguins could be viewed in their unnatural environment.

Gypsy at this time phoned his father, about keeping his promise to help him to make his trip to India, "What promise?" Gypsy's father retorted in denial. He then went on to deny having made such a promise, refusing to admit to what he had given his word to back in April.

Gypsy hit the roof, he didn't know what to do now. What with the Rabbi blocking the sale of his musical equipment and now his very own father bullshitting him, wasting his time and sabotaging his plans.

Back in Jerusalem, Alan invited Gypsy to "come over and spend the night at the hostel". Gypsy readily accepted the invitation, it would be good to be in a place with no mad hatters around and what better place for that than the Palestinian area.   It was a world of difference there, with not the tiniest sliver of Jewish religion or dogma to be seen. That night Gypsy met a beautiful Austrian hippie girl and her pet dog, a large German shepherd called, Bello.

Gypsy and Eva shared a blotter tab of 'California Sunshine Acid' and then smoked joints and tripped the night away in a secluded room at the back of the building. After some rest Gypsy eventually made it back to the squat the following afternoon.

NOVEMBER 1982.

The place looked as if a bombed had hit it with large burn marks on the table and floor rugs, but not a soul to be seen there.

Apparently Haim (from the nut house) and Randy, a particularly self centered, Canadian, over grown spoilt brat, had been left on their own in the squat. Haim had built a fire on the coffee table and was dancing around it looking like the yeti in the rutting season. While Randy, oblivious to all was strumming away on one of Gypsy's guitars playing nauseous songs about himself and his feelings (well at least that's what he must have been playing as that was all that he seemed to know).

All of this strange activity and what with large flames coming from the coffee table and flickering in the window, the police were alerted and summoned to find out what was going on.

To their credit they found their way to the concealed window entrance, entered the squat and doused the flames. They then proceeded to remove the two retards from the squat.

At least Gypsy's guitars and amps were safe. He just could not follow how two grown men could behave in such a pathetically self centered and destructive manner. He moved his equipment out of the squat and into a safe location. This was going to be a large portion of what would be paying his way to India.

There had been large chunks of hash lying around under the furniture and mattresses in the squat and it was lucky that there had not been a major bust. The lack of electricity in the place at that time had probably helped.

Now that the squat was known about, it was too dangerous to use. So at Alan's invitation Gypsy started living at the hostel. The dope deals were getting ever bigger and soon a few kilos would show up in an evening, all neatly wrapped in 250 grams sacks.

Security being what it was in Israel, the air would be electric when a large delivery was made. That was of course before Gypsy and the others had their pieces to run to their various different neighborhoods, where they sold. Then when there was only a small amount, enough only to take care of local friends and in house needs, then everyone could relax. There were various other small dealers picking up from there. There was English Steve who used to sell to Israelis in one particularly laid back part of the city. There was an Israeli called Mordechai who sold to his fellow artists. Some others who worked at different hostels in the city would come by and pick up orders for their guests and of course Gypsy was banging it out to the penguins of Mount Zion along with the odd, lost, wandering hippie who had lost his way while returning from the Mount of Olives. It always made the others at the hostel laugh that Gypsy was busily engaged in banging out ounces and the likes to rabbis and penguins. They just didn't look like the types to have their head down, over a bong.

Another character that needs to be mentioned and who was the only other one who would hang out in both the Yeshiva and the hostel was Daryl who was a somewhat burned out acid head from California. Most of the time he would just mumble incoherent thoughts to himself, but sometimes he would speak some astute observation that would leave everyone present, spellbound. He looked as if he had just walked out of a hallucination from one of his own acid trips. He reckoned that he had done a couple of thousand trips in his time. He was the sort of innocent and oblivious soul that one could imagine being one of the sole survivors of Armageddon. Not just that but he appeared to live in another world or dimension. Nevertheless, after all was said and done he was one of the world's better people and a regular and welcome guest at any smoke party.

One of the reasons that Alan, a Jew, was able to get a job working for a Palestinian boss as his hostel manager, was that it made a good cover for the owner to come and hide behind in the evenings when he and his friends wanted to get together for a quiet drink or three. Being Muslims they were limited about where they could hide for a few glasses of Arrak while dressed in their traditional Arab attire.

The upstairs terrace of the hostel was an ideal venue for him and his friends. They could see the street, the Gate and their shops, while no one in the market would look up and notice them.

Abu Gazi who was an old shop keeper from the market and the blind money changer from inside the gate itself would be regular visitors.
One night the money changer was feeling very pleased with his work. The shekel had taken a hit against other currencies, most notably the dollar. However it had been massively over sold and like a pendulum, would inevitably swing back. So Ahmed had bought masses of shekels at super low rates and now that the shekel was back where it belonged, possibly even a bit higher. Ahmed had cashed into Dollars and Jordanian Dinars and pocketed a somewhat large profit.

Now that Gypsy was living at the hostel he would be required to participate in the work routine which consisted of throwing the guests out at 9:30am, then each of the crew would take a chore which would usually take the best part of forty five minutes to complete. Job done and one of the team would take a large bowl from the kitchen and some money from Alan and go down to the cafe near the hostel entrance where the bowl would be filled with Houmous, ful and salt pickles.

The bowl, along with a very large stack of pitta breads in a bag would be brought back to the hostel kitchen where everyone (that means staff and selected special guests) would be sitting around and smoking joints and making and loading chillums from broken bottles, sometimes there would also be a bong doing a circuit of the room. The stereo would be blasting out anything from Led Zeppelin to Fairport convention and the incredible string band and even on occasion, Mozart and Bach.

The moment the first joint was lit the hostel rat catcher would jump up onto the very highest shelf in the room and sit there sticking her nose out as she sniffed the fumes. After a short while huge clouds of billowing dope smoke was wafting up in her direction and the cat, just like everyone else in the room was stoned out of her mind and enjoying it. It must have either been an Arab or a hippie in its previous life.

After the smoke session everyone sat down in a group to eat, all eating from the same bowl and using the pita bread to pick up the hummus and ful.

After food Gypsy would go to his room on Mount Zion and continue his work. It was hard to focus however, with the Rabbi still blocking the sale of his musical equipment and his father still going into absolute denial about the promise that he had made.

Even other things that he was doing were constantly being sabotaged by penguins and others. He kept trying to get his father to keep his word but all his father did was sneer at him and send him a ticket for a fixed date charter flight back to England which Gypsy told him where to go and stick.

In the end Gypsy was pushed to the point where he snapped, they had even stopped him from using the gig hall for having a private jam even though he had set the bands up and run the mixing desk for free on a number of occasions.

The final straw came when after letting loose with a string of expletives about what he thought of the yeshiva and penguins in general a large stocky Rabbi who had previously been a pimp in Toronto and was still reputed to sell blue movies on the side attacked him in the street. Gypsy picked up a couple of rocks and ran straight at his attacker roaring and snarling like a wild animal.

Up until this point Gypsy had no idea that penguins could run so damned fast. He chased the pimp penguin up the hill, through the Zion Gate and to the Beit Knesset on Mount Zion, using one of the rocks to knock out a back window of the hypocrite's meeting house (the sinner gog). He raged on and on until eventually the Rabbi gave in, after all it had started to get dangerous now with the consequences of their actions coming back at them. He stopped obstructing Gypsy's musical sales and in a matter of two or three days all of the amps, guitars and pedals were sold. Now Gypsy had half the money for his trip so it was time now to raise the other half.

Stanley's doctor offered to help as he had met both of Gypsy's parents at different times. They had a lot of respect for him, he was a doctor who wore a suit, was an Orthodox Jew and had a French accent, no less. The doctor underneath the disguise was as much of a hippie/anarchist as ever Gypsy was. But people are so easily fooled by accents, titles and uniforms.

Gypsy had told the doctor, all that had taken place. The doctor agreed that this was totally unacceptable behavior on the part of Gypsy's father and offered to help.

One night in a house in the Jewish quarter of the old city, the doctor asked Gypsy for his parent's number which he dully gave him. The doctor then phoned his parents and proceeded to berate them for breaking their word and told them just how much anger and stress they had caused. He then told them to keep their word. "Now I will hand you over to your son and he will tell you what he needs", he finally told them. "I need six hundred pounds", said Gypsy. "The same that was agreed before, deposited in my bank account in Sussex. I'll be needing to come home and sort my health out soon, after what I've been through and before going to India", he told them. The stress and sleepless nights of all that had happened had messed with Gypsy's health badly.

ISRAEL

DECEMBER 1982

He decided that before leaving for England he would take up the invitation that Eva the Austrian girl had made in order to try to unwind a bit. She had invited Gypsy to join her and her dog Bello on a trip to Sinai. Before leaving they made a trip into town to get some supplies.

Though Bello was a big dog, he was so very well behaved that she could allow him to be off of his lead for much of the time and he would walk along beside them as any other friend would.

This would produce an interesting set of reactions, among the penguins. On seeing the dog walking free, they would at the least hurriedly cross the road with a frightened look on their faces, or even shout, run or scream, or all three at once if you can imagine the spectacle. However on this particular day as they walked along there was a penguin coming in the other direction. On seeing Bello walking along nonchalantly with his two friends the penguin let out a piercing scream and ran, [yes, I said ran and not climbed] up the first available tree, which he was then clinging too while shaking like a jelly, teeth chattering in mortal fear as Eva, Bello and Gypsy walked casually by beneath. All the while while staring with puzzled looks on their faces at this weird creature up in the tree.

Ok, Bello was a large German shepherd dog but he was well behaved and by no stretch of the imagination could he be confused with a big bad wolf character. So why all the fuss, Bello was one of the crowd of friends at the hostel, never mind that he was in a dog's body. Never once did he start a fight with another dog and he certainly always behaved well around humans. The only bad doggy habit he had was….

Q: Why do dogs lick their own balls?
A: Because they can!

Gypsy, Bello and Eva got out and on the road by late the following morning. Walking out past St. Stephen's gate and past the end of the old city walls, Eva stuck her thumb out and soon they were all riding in a light delivery vehicle up over the Mount of Olives and on further into the West Bank with a friendly young Palestinian driver. The next lift was with Israelis and that took them almost to the shores of the Dead Sea. Then the lift after that was on the back of a pickup truck as it followed along the road that ran by the shore of the Dead Sea.

They were standing there with their thumbs out by the shore when an empty bus stopped. The driver was a Falasha, [Falashas are the black Jews from Ethiopia] "Come on jump aboard this ride's free", he told them. He also stopped and picked up all the other hitch hikers he saw along the road.

135

By night fall, they were close by an Israeli army check post near to where the road fork's with one road going to Eilat and the other going to Sodom and Gomorra. They informed the guards of their presence and were invited to make camp at the guardhouse for extra safety.

The next morning they got back on the road and started to hitch across the Negev desert towards Eilat. They got several lifts on trucks, servicing the industry and kibbutzim in the middle of the desert. Then they got a lift from an older couple who were into archeology and classical music. "We're going to Eilat and we can take you the whole way if you don't mind making an archeological de tour with us to go and see King Solomon's mines". Both Gypsy and Eva eagerly agreed, they had not the finances nor the means in any way to make a trip to such a remote location on their own.

The car turned off from the main highway and drove off into a desert moonscape, going through large valleys, they entered a huge crater like area.

Apparently the area had been mined for its copper since ancient times and was still being mined to the present day. King Solomon's workers had also come to this strange desolate place to mine copper and there was archeological evidence of their presence having been there.

After a look at the rock formations and surreal landscape it was back to the comfy air conditioned car with Mozart on the stereo, for the drive to Eilat.

They slept on the beach that night, but not before a visit to the 'Peace Café' which had taken over as the traveler and misfit hangout after Bollocks got closed down (apparently someone on the local council had learned enough English to figure out what the strange name meant).

Gypsy by chance bumped into someone who he had done the dishwashing with a year before. He had been a sergeant in the British army and had to take retirement at the age of 47. He was offered half of his pension in one lump sum of twelve thousand pounds. This was a lot more money then than it would be today.

To cut a long story short he had spunked the lot in six months of living the high life in five star hotels while going out on pub and bar crawls, wherever and whenever he felt like it. When Gypsy had first met him he had just blown his last shekels and was working with Gypsy on a hotel's industrial scale car wash style dish washing machine.

Now here he was, the retired ex-sergeant turned hippie and living the hippie life, it was a good omen for the future. He had got himself a job on some of the building work going on in Eilat and was making a good living in a nice warm place and that was enough for him.

The next day Eva and Gypsy, along with supplies of food and water headed on foot, off down to the Egyptian border at Taba, it wasn't such a long way.

After clearing border formalities, they changed money and headed for the bus. But there was a problem. The driver of the bus did not let dogs on his bus. Not even well adjusted and well mannered hounds such as Bello, they had to get off of the bus. "What were they going to do now?" Gypsy wondered.

There was an open backed medium sized truck parked near by with two men sitting in it.

Gypsy asked where they were going and when they said Sharm El Sheikh a price was negotiated for a lift. Then Gypsy, Eva and Bello jumped onto the back of the truck and the truck was soon out on the road and rolling south at speed.

EGYPT/SINAI

DECEMBER 1982.

Through the daylight hours as the wind buffeted them they could see beautiful wadis with the odd plant growing in its shade, wild camels running free or tucking into those oh so tasty thorn trees that grow in the desert while tending to look more dead than alive, except to a camel that is. There was the occasional Bedouin encampment with the usual herds of goats and ever so occasionally a building down by the beach where someone was trying to start a tourist or traveler oriented business. They passed the gas station at the Nuweiba turn off and carried on down the road as it got dark.

As anyone who has been there knows, the desert can get very cold at night. But it is the initial shock as it suddenly goes from being warm and pleasant to being frigid cold in a matter of just a few minutes that catches everyone out as one goes from admiring the sunset to racing to put on socks and proper shoes, sweater, jacket and scarf. Soon Gypsy, Eva and

Bello were shivering under a blanket as they sheltered behind the cab of the truck as they sped on into the darkness.

After another hour and a half of riding on into the cold dessert night the truck stopped at a Bedouin encampment and everyone got out and off the truck to eat. Gypsy and Eva were also invited to eat, they were all sitting on a mat or blanket in the dark, eating bread, cheese and olives with the camels sitting ten or fifteen feet away, grunting, groaning and making camel noises, a large Bedouin tent just a couple of meters behind them.

With food finished, they jumped back on to the back of the truck and were once again rolling towards Sharm el Sheikh. For another hour and a half they sped on through the darkness, shivering under the blanket as the cold started to really bite. Then lights came into view and half an hour later they were getting off of the truck. They were now in Sharm el Sheikh.

There was not much there at the time. Only what the Israelis had left behind. there was a housing estate on the top of a hill consisting entirely of apartment blocks, an airstrip, a hospital a petrol station and a bakery.

It had only been handed back to Egypt one year previously and as of then there were no families living there, only young men who had been sent there to work and get the place ready for whatever use the place was to get in the future.

Gypsy and Eva found an empty patch of ground (of which there was plenty), found some wood and dead branches and made a fire. Eva cooked some food for Bello (fish and rice) and Gypsy noticed some activity at a building not so far away. He took a walk to find out what it was. It was a bakery and though it was past nine o'clock in the evening it was not just open but in full swing, producing fresh hot bread. Many people were coming by to purchase supplies. Gypsy bought a stack of bread and headed back to camp. After eating they talked for a while then unrolled their bedrolls and crashed out for the night.

The next morning, they awoke to find themselves on a flat area beneath what had been the Israeli settlement of Ofira.

A local Egyptian man who now occupied one of the apartments, approached them and introduced himself. He was very friendly and on hearing that they had been on the road hitching for several days, invited them to his apartment for something to eat and a shower. He then invited some friends to come around and meet his new traveler friends.

After some food and cups of tea they all invited Gypsy and Eva to come snorkeling with them from a nearby rock, where they said the water was exceptionally clear. So off they all walked, out across the desert rocks to the diving spot. They spent the whole day out there before returning to the apartment. The new friends wanted to invite them to stay the night in the apartment, which was a nice offer. They had given Gypsy and Eva and for that matter even Bello, an excellent day out and been such a pleasure to be with. But Gypsy and Eva liked sleeping outside in the desert. With no clouds or light pollution it was possible to see so many stars and also it felt good being outside in the vast emptiness of both desert and sea. Night in the desert is so wonderfully quiet, with no human nor animal or even insect sounds at night. The only sound would be that of the wind, if it was not a still night.

Gypsy, Eva and Bello thanked their kind hosts and made their departure, wandering off into the desert to make camp.

The next day after some breakfast, they packed their bags and decided to hitch north to Da Hab. They got a lift in a truck to the Da Hab turning and another one that took them the last nine kilometers to the beach and Da Hab proper.

There was a Bedouin village made of tents and pieces of wood, etc. There was also a large grove of date palms full of abandoned huts and cafes. The grove went right to the tide line on the beach and had obviously been the hippie hangout when the Israelis had occupied the place. Now it was abandoned and in disuse. Other than the Bedouins, the only other signs of life were around the diving center.

Gypsy went there to see if maybe Swiss Rene was about but he was not. He was out on a journey, possibly in Israel.

Though Da Hab was beautiful there was no way of staying there, as there were no shops nor anywhere to buy food, unless that was, someone had the money to buy a goat from the Bedouin. Da Hab was more like an abandoned ghost village than anything else and it felt desolate and forgotten.

The next day again they packed their bags and headed to the road to stick out their thumbs. There was hardly any traffic but the one truck that came to Da Hab that morning did stop and give them a lift as far as the highway.

Then as they stood there by the side of the road, about to stick their thumbs out once more, they were treated to the most strange of spectacles to see in this strange unpopulated place. A convoy of thirty or forty cars and SUV's came swerving and bouncing down the road, lights flashing and horns blaring, they were coming from the south and just before they reached where Eva and Gypsy were standing they all turned off the highway and drove down to the empty nothingness that was Da Hab at that time.

They couldn't have thought much of it because half an hour later the sound of blaring horns coming back in the direction of the highway could once again be heard.

Gypsy stuck his thumb out as they approached. He didn't expect anyone to stop as they were in convoy and looked busy. But to both Gypsy and Eva's amazement and disbelief, the first car of the convoy stopped and with it all of the other cars stopped too.

The rear window wound down and the man inside introduced himself. He was the Governor of South Sinai. It was the one year anniversary of the hand over, he was taking the press and other concerned parties on a tour of the area under his jurisdiction to show them the progress that was being made in developing the area.

Though Gypsy and Eva were just two scruffy hippies with backpacks and a dog, he spoke very nicely to them, welcoming them to his country and offering them a lift in one of the other vehicles of the convoy.

The press jumped out and snapped a load of photos of them with the Governor, and then they were offered seats in a SUV with the Governor's public relation's chief.

He also was friendly and they spent a lot of the journey to Nuweiba talking.

About ten or fifteen kilometers before Nuweiba, the convoy swung off the highway and drove for approximately three kilometers down a narrow road to a collection of buildings and tents that were just back from the beach. The convoy stopped and everybody got out.

The place was a fish restaurant, run by local Bedouins. To their surprise and delight Eva and Gypsy were invited to join the large party for lunch. There was hardly any tourists in Sinai at that time as there were virtually no facilities, so it was amazing that this place, away from even the smallest population centers and three kilometers off the highway, could survive.

Lunch was a rather good fish curry and rice. Both Gypsy and Eva were somewhat hungry and to their pleasure there was more than enough to go around. After lunch, everyone got back into their respective vehicles and they were soon rolling along the highway, in the direction of Nuweiba when the convoy ground to a halt.

There, just off the highway, on camels and in battle dress, where the elders of the local Bedouin tribe. They had came out to meet and greet the Governor.

The Governor got out of his car and walked out to where they where, a couple of hundred feet from the road. The camels sat down and the elders dismounted. Then they all sat down, in a large circle on the desert sand, the Bedouin in their colorful ceremonial attire and the Governor in his suit.

Gypsy had a small but high quality camera with him and was busy taking all the shots he could of this amazing event, he couldn't imagine an official from England behaving in such an unpretentious way. This man looked like he knew his job, he came across as both humble and compassionate, a good ambassador for his religion and his people. In fact many of the Egyptians that Gypsy had so far met were also good ambassadors for their country and their people. They had invariably shown themselves to be kind and helpful and what's more there was not a hint of ulterior motive, they were just really nice, genuine people who knew the pleasure of friendship and enjoyed helping others.

The meeting soon drew to an end and the Governor got up, dusted himself off and walked back to his car. After a short drive down to the old moshav of Neviot They dropped Eva, Bello and Gypsy near the beach at Nuweiba.

The kiosk, holiday village and Moshav were no longer operating as such, but things were going on in the Moshav compound and there was a shop there that was open, selling food and basic essentials. The only change to the hippie area over the sand dunes and under the date palms was that there was hardly anyone there. There were a few small encampments but nothing on the scale that had been there before. They spent the night camped under the palms after the first dune. The next day Eva said she wanted to stay longer in Nuweiba while Gypsy felt restless and wanted to travel back to Jerusalem and get anything sorted out that he needed too.

He took the bus alone out of Nuweiba that morning back up to the border at Taba. He had enjoyed Egypt and couldn't believe what a very nice and friendly people they were. Sadly however it would be many years before he would find himself back in Egypt again.

He got off the bus and walked to the border crossing. After twenty minutes he had cleared through the border formalities and was back in Israel. He then walked to Eilat where he stopped for the night at the hostel.

The next day he took an early morning bus back to Jerusalem, where he headed back to the hostel near Damascus gate.

JERUSALEM/ISRAEL

DECEMBER 1982.

After telling Alan and the others what had happened on the trip, Gypsy headed back over to Mount Zion. An American called Zev had just turned up in the area. Having just flown in from somewhere in East Asia. Although he was not a naturalized Israeli and still held only an American passport he served in the Israeli army as a volunteer or something.

He had just been taking care of some other business in Asia and had just arrived to lend his hand to the Israelis for the ongoing war in Lebanon.

For the next week or so he hung around at the Yeshiva. There was a plump woman from New York who had been coming on to Zev and Gypsy and one or two of the other wilder or more straight up of the male crowd around the Yeshiva. But no one had yet left their glasses behind or been drunk enough to go there with her. That was until Gypsy ended up having a vodka and arrak session with Zev and some other friends, when she showed up.

The others all left, one by one. Gypsy was most definitely drunk and he had been left alone with this desperate young woman.

He awoke the next morning with his mouth feeling and probably tasting like the inside of a wrestler's armpit in a seedy room in the most seedy, sad disgrace for a hotel in East Jerusalem, lying on top of her. This was most definitely a coyote situation, but too late she was already awake.

In the early morning with not so many people around, he walked her back to the Jewish quarter. She was not a bad person but she most definitely was not Gypsy's type and he did not feel good about what had happened. Now she would be chasing after him all the time and that was the last thing that Gypsy wanted or needed. He already had Pesach's sister in law chasing him, dreaming of a wedding huppa (ceremonial outdoor structure used for Jewish weddings) not to mention the attention of a rather pretty Israeli girl at the Yeshiva. But although the attention was quite flattering, the last thing that Gypsy wanted or needed was to get stuck in a marriage to some domineering, power tripping Jewish woman. That looked to Gypsy like what it was: Pure hell on earth.

Gypsy headed back to the hostel and had a jam on his one remaining guitar, he was teaching himself to play 'Stairway to Heaven'.

CHAPTER 5

ISRAEL

DECEMBER 1982.

One of the crowd at the hostel, an American, who liked Gypsy and his music asked him if he would like to make a trip to Tel Aviv, to help him carry a hi-fi unit to a friend's apartment. Gypsy agreed to go. So off they went, down to the bus station, with different parts of the unit in bags over their shoulders.

On the bus, they chatted about music, eastern philosophy and Gypsy's planned trip to India. After getting off the intercity bus at the main station they took a local city bus to a block close to the apartment.

Having found the apartment and been welcomed in by the woman whose apartment it was, the hi-fi was set up and drinks and joints passed around. It was a relaxing vibe inside the apartment and for the first time in a long while Gypsy felt safe to drop his defenses and relax. There were no ego or power trip vibes coming from anyone in the apartment and Gypsy actually felt safe.

Just sitting there in the chair in her living room, suddenly Gypsy had let go of the anger and stress of the last year or so. It was a good feeling, being in the safety of good honest company and not having to be on his guard for the next weasel trick.

SATORI

In this wonderful relaxed state something totally incredible happened to him. It was as if he had suddenly woken up from a bad dream. He

144

was seeing but not with the physical eyes he has in this world. He was having spiritual vision. He could see that all souls continue and have no beginning or end. And how all, get chance after chance for life after life until they get it right.

He could see that most of the food available in the markets and shops throughout the world was poisonous and was more likely to cause sickness than anything else. He could see that the Jews were wrong in both thought and the practice of their religion.

He could see ways forward on his search for enlightenment and none of them involved wearing silly hats or dressing up like a penguin. He could also see that all those that had messed with and manipulated him on his path had been wrong and deserved nothing more than to be ignored.

What was also obvious was that yoga meditation and vegetarianism were all going to be essential and helpful tools on his way to India, where he could really begin his search for the truth and thus eternity.

There were no hidden voices speaking to him, this was just pure vision, like a deep inner knowing. This was the first time it had ever happened to him, showing him how that every soul is eternal and all life forms have a spirit soul at their centre, as a necessity of them being alive.

Gypsy got Messiah complex for all of thirty seconds before he clicked, that if all souls attain enlightenment then enlightenment was something very ordinary and he knew that he was not even enlightened. He had just had glimpse of divine truth, but even that was enough to clear out any dogmas or wrong thinking that may have subconsciously been lurking in any unlit part of his subconscious.

The experience had the effect of helping to clear all of the penguin shit and fears from his mind.

"Jefferson Airplane's" 'Somebody to Love' was playing on the stereo as Gypsy tried to articulate to the others in the room on the vision and awareness that he was having.

It was strange because Gypsy felt as if others in the room were also having their own experiences of a similar nature at the same time, because as he spoke others in the room seemed to understand what he was talking about.

The music changed to "Brian Eno's" music for airports and Gypsy stayed with the experience as much as he could, he wanted to absorb it within himself and be in that state of clarity all of the time. The night carried on and Gypsy, still in a higher state, fell asleep on the couch in the living room.

Waking up the next morning, he said his goodbyes and walked across the city to the bus station. He was still in a highly aware state and didn't want to get on a bus until he had too. The only things that he could find to eat along the way that weren't contaminated, were some fruit and some nuts. Raw food was what the body was designed to digest and it was essential to be vegetarian.

Gypsy eventually reached the bus station and jumped on a bus back up to Jerusalem.

Zev had suddenly donned a kaki uniform and with an assault rifle over his shoulder, was last seen getting on board a bus to his base as so that he could join up with his unit in Lebanon.

With nothing much more to do Gypsy prepared to leave and go back to England to sort his head and his health out before his trip to India. However, the El Al pilots were on strike and British Airways were fully booked for the foreseeable future.

Gypsy had stopped wearing his skull cap a while before, but after the Satori [enlightened experience] he would not even wear one inside of the Yeshiva or its environs. He explained to them how it had been shown to him as a detriment and not as a help on the road to enlightenment, but predictably, all they did was give him filthy looks and walk away.

"There is nothing that the self imprisoned hate the sight of more, than that of the self liberated who are at ease with themselves."----Gypsy

Gypsy eventually found a cheap flight back to London with Swiss Air.

After saying his goodbyes to his friends, especially the ones at the hostel, he headed for the airport. Alan and several other friends had pledged to join him on the trip to India that he was planning to make in several months time.

Along with a British girl who had been staying at the hostel he checked in on the Zurich bound flight. For once it felt good to be getting out of Israel. He had had quite enough of all of the bullshit and now all he wanted was to get fit and ready for his trip, and most of all he craved some solitude.

TRANSIT TO ENGLAND

DECEMBER 1982.

The plane, a DC 10, taxied out to join the queue of aircraft waiting to leave. Eventually it was their turn. The plane turned while gunning it's engines, then sped off down the runway. Then they were airborne, climbing up through a heavily clouded sky and heading northwest to Zurich. It was the best flight that Gypsy had ever been on, having, for the very first time free drinks and headphones. The food was good, too. Three and a half hours later the plane was on the tarmac at Zurich International airport.

Gypsy along with the others disembarked and got on the bus to the terminal.

The terminal was smart and had a fantastic delicatessen inside selling all sorts of teas, coffees, cheeses and smoked fish products. Gypsy went in and stocked up on goodies before heading to the main duty free to get the whiskey and tobacco.

The flight to London was on a smaller plane, a DC 9 and took an hour and a half.

Gypsy got off the flight, feeling as sick as a dog, he had caught a throat infection somewhere along his journey and was now going to need some medical attention.

ENGLAND/SUSSEX

He made his way home from Heathrow to the Sussex coast. His family were away so he went to see the doctor who gave him a course of antibiotics. He went home and started doing the medicine. Now he was not broke but he couldn't work until he was better, which would probably mean a week or so. There was a letter from the yeshiva addressed to his parents. He would never normally open other people's mail but given the circumstances he was curious to know what had transpired between them regarding how they had connived against Gypsy behind his back.

The letter made for some interesting reading. The yeshiva was trying to demand money from Gypsy's family for all sorts of things including paying his wages while he worked for the institution as a handyman. They also said some rather nasty and untrue things about him, calling him a junkie and trouble maker and painting him up to be a bit phsycho. what was breath taking was the huge amounts of cash that they were trying to demand.

Soon the family returned from their skiing holiday. Gypsy was still sick and though they were glad to see him, his mother was furious that Gypsy had found a way to make his father who was strangely quiet about the matter, keep his promise.

JANUARY 1983

ENGLAND/SUSSEX

It was fortunate that there was an empty caravan mobile home on the nursery land a quarter of a mile from the family house. It was a very old single wide, with a small living room, a kitchen a small bedroom and a tiny bathroom with a very small bath tub. It had with it a very large garden with a high hedge around it, giving it a measure of privacy.

Gypsy moved in and furnished it with whatever he had or could find. He started working on the nursery again, back in the engineer's workshop. He was happy to have the freedom and independence that living in the caravan gave him. He could do pretty much anything that he wanted to as long as he was at work at eight o'clock each morning.

The first thing he wanted to do, was find out more about the enlightened experience that he had had. He wanted to find out if others had also had similar experiences. A few weeks after returning he saw a magazine in a news agent's rack, called 'yoga today' and bought a copy. He was surprised to see from the articles, that many people were getting similar vision as a result of yoga practice and meditation.

Gypsy soon surrounded himself with books on meditation and mysticism, reading about the commune at Findhorn in Scotland and about Indian Philosophy. With the money he earned on the nursery he bought himself a good acoustic guitar for one hundred and seventy five pounds. It was an Ibanes jumbo with an underside cutaway and a built in bridge pick up. It played like a dream and Gypsy really liked it. Soon his playing improved as a result of constant practice.

FEBRUARY 1983.

Something very sad had happened to Gypsy's local friends that he used to hang out smoking dope, listening to music and rambling around the local countryside with.

Yes, everyone in the group had tried varying different drugs, from dope, acid and mushrooms, to coke and speed, but nothing had prepared them for what happened next.

One of the group, had walked in one day with a bag of smack (heroin) and like the clever bunch of Charlies that they were they nearly all got hooked on it. Within weeks, they were skin popping it (injection technique) and then they moved on to banging it straight up their veins.

The next phase came when they ran out of money and the burglaries started. Soon after they were starting to be regular faces in the local magistrate's court. Their crimes were too small and pathetic to earn them the jail time that they would have needed to do a proper cold turkey and get free from it, so the wheel turned and turned as they all sank into the morass of their addiction.

It was when one of the group, stole his parent's antique silver cutlery collection to sell as so as he could buy a fix that Gypsy could stomach his friends no more. They had gone from friends to fiends in a very short space of time. One of them said to Gypsy, "You can't judge this stuff unless you try it". Gypsy said, "I can see what it is doing to you and that is enough to tell me that it is not what I wish for myself. However, I'm willing to try it just once, just so that I can understand why you like it enough that you would throw your life away over it". The 'friend' gave Gypsy a small wrap of the stuff and suggested that he snort it.

Gypsy waited until the next day to try it. He had promised himself that no matter how good it made him feel, that he would do it just this once. Even if he felt mad cravings for it, he must not do it again.

There were and still are many hysterical uninformed opinions about not just heroin but all drugs that are pompously spouted by the ignorant and fearful and because in their irrational terror they scream and shout more loudly than the more calm and objective members of the community their opinions are taken to be fact by society at large. Gypsy knew this and was pretty sure that it would be nigh on impossible for an aware person such as himself to be turned into a messed up junky from just trying it the once. He had too much to do with his life to waste it doing something like that.

After snorting the smack, Gypsy felt as sick as a dog for half an hour or so, he went to the toilet and vomited violently. Then when his stomach was empty he felt light and relaxed, he felt no pain or aches from his day at work and it was very relaxing. But that was it, no more.

The next time he saw the 'friend' that had given him the bag, he asked Gypsy what he thought of the buzz. "It's a pain killer", Gypsy told him. "Why are you making such a mess of yourself for a pain killer? Hash and weed I understand because it frees the mind and gives you the space to see things that we normally miss, but this is nothing, no wild thought or visions. Doing smack is like trying to climb back into your mother's womb to a place where everything is safe and painless, that's not what I look for when I take a drug. I like adventure and discovery, not this painless safety that you are obviously after".

With great sadness, Gypsy cut off from that group of friends, he couldn't believe that they could be so stupid, it was truly sad to see them not only destroy themselves but also the people who loved them, such as their families.

There were however two other friends from the group who also did not fall into the mess and Gypsy spent more time with them and one or two of the other freaks and hippies of the area.

Ron and Black Tony would visit Gypsy at his trailer home. Both of them were skilled people and had high paying jobs. They too were talking of making a long journey, they wanted to go to Thailand and Australia.

They would normally meet up on Friday and Saturday nights and go for a night out with other friends in Worthing or Brighton. They would go and do the usual thing of smoking a few joints and then go and see bands playing in pubs or trying [without much success] to find some women to party with. Inevitably like so many millions of other young men in England they would end up at the Indian or Chinese take away with a heavy attack of the munchies, order far more than they could possibly eat and head back in Ron's car, to one of their pads to listen to music, smoke joints, eat the food and possibly drop a tab of acid each.

MARCH 1983

An old acquaintance resurfaced in England, after several years of living in Holland. When his beautiful Asian girlfriend left him he developed a smack habit which he had then had for over three years. He was staying in the village and now he wanted to cleanse himself and go through cold turkey.

Gypsy had already had the experience of helping Stanley go through the process back in Jerusalem. so he offered his friend a place to come and chill out at while going through the process, without any lectures or judgments being put on him and where his situation would be fully understood. He told him that he would be welcome around at any time of the day or night.

The offer was taken up and used. The friend would come around often and Gypsy would get him stoned and listen to his stories. Sometimes he would run out of the front room, into the garden and vomit. Often he would have the shakes during the initial two weeks of the "cold turkey," but full credit to him, he stuck it out and made it through and never once touched it again.

Gypsy's interest in mysticism and Asian spiritual paths was manifest and growing but it was extremely hard if not almost impossible to find anyone in the area that didn't think that he was crazy and had lost it for being interested in such things. He had learned both from watching television and from reading books that many people when put under hypnosis could remember about past lives and even some archeological discoveries had been made as a result of such research.

Gypsy became interested as he had felt that many of his personal problems in life were there as a result of something or things that had happened before this life. He had a very long memory and could easily remember many things from when he was only two years old so he was pretty sure that whatever had both traumatized him and made him so very different from those around him had happened in a previous life.

He used to have horrible, gray, miserable dreams and nightmares on a regular basis [until he discovered hashish, that was]. Also as a child he would hear voices telling him to do all manner or crazy things. He fought them off and made sure that he did not do any of the madness that they were trying to persuade him to do. But it was annoying as a child and even later, in his early adulthood to have to waste energy and attention on these unseen saboteurs rather than concentrating his attention on matters of learning and study.

Gypsy got hold of a number for a hypnotherapist in Harley Street in London and phoned and booked an appointment.

He took the train to London and found his way to Harley Street. and thus the hypnotherapist's practice. He told the hypnotherapist what his thoughts and intuition was telling him. That his problems were past life related and asked If the hypnotherapist would be either willing or able to help his memory regress far enough back, as so he could at least shed enough light on what had happened as so as with consciousness the healing could begin.

The hypnotherapist with an expression on his face as if he had just smelled a bad fart, told Gypsy he was missing a few screws and should go and see a psychiatrist. Then he demanded his payment of fifty pounds [which was more than a week's wages and then some, to Gypsy at that time] and told Gypsy to get out of his practice quickly.

Gypsy was totally pissed off and disgusted by the way he had been treated by this foul, avaricious, narrow minded little man. People like that always seem to think that only they with the limited shit that they have poisoned their heads with, could ever possibly be right. Such people always think that they have more rights than the people they disagree with. So why are people so stupid as to see such creatures as respectable on account of their plumy accents, suits and bits of paper from so called schools of learning?

APRIL 1983.

ENGLAND/SUSSEX

Back at work, Gypsy had just been handed a letter with Israeli stamps on it. It was just past eight o'clock in the morning and Gypsy had just clocked in and was walking from the packing shed to his place of work, in the engineering workshop. As he walked he opened and read the letter.

"What's the matter with you this morning?" the chief engineer asked. "You're as white as a sheet. What's wrong?" Gypsy waved the letter in the air and explained how he had got drunk one night in Jerusalem and how his friends had dumped him in the company of this fat little garlic breathed Jewish girl from New Jersey and how he had woken up hung over and on top of her in a seedy Palestinian hotel in East Jerusalem with very little recollection of what had happened or how he got there.

Someone must have given her his British address because she had just written to him to say that she was planning to come and stay with him.

The chief engineer had a field day, taking the piss and winding Gypsy up as Gypsy tried to plot his way out of this mess. "Ah there will be the sound of wedding bells soon", the engineer said chuckling and sniggering away. "Will this be a shot gun wedding or do you think you can run fast enough", he continued. Gypsy just stayed quiet, he could see the funny side of the situation but right now he needed his head clear to plot his way out of the mess without causing offence to the poor girl. She wasn't a bad person and if she lost some weight she would be rather good looking but her thoughts and interests were light years apart from Gypsy's and she wouldn't be able to fit into the world that he lived in.

At lunch time Gypsy got on the phone and got through to Fagin's wife in Jerusalem. The girl had been hanging out at their house and Gypsy was hoping that they might have a number where she could be reached. Fagin's wife told him that she would try and find a number for her and told Gypsy to phone back in twenty minutes.

By the end of his lunch break he had the whole situation sorted. He felt like a rat at having to lie as he did, the girl had been in tears when he told her that it wasn't possible to stay as he wouldn't be there, as he was hitting the road in a couple of days.

Gypsy was then able to relax, a disaster had been averted and he could carry on track towards the big adventure.

The chief engineer spent the whole afternoon grinning and making jokes about Gypsy's averted problem, but now Gypsy could also laugh about it.

Gypsy made all sorts of new friends at this time. There were some other young people working at a nursery nearby who specialized in renting out plants to offices and Gypsy liked to go and hang out with them after he finished work to smoke joints and listen to music with them.

MAY 1983.

There was an ageing brother and sister in their fifties or sixties who had been made homeless so had moved into a disused greenhouse on an abandoned nursery. Gypsy liked them for being different to most other people. He also felt sorry for them being forced to live in such circumstances and would take them food on occasion.

Eddie, the friend who had just gone through cold turkey, was getting himself sorted out and had found a girlfriend. He introduced Gypsy to the woman's sister and a friendship formed. Gypsy liked her, but much as she liked Gypsy, he scared her, with his focus so much on mysticism and travel, and as such the relationship that they both would have liked never quite happened.

At work Gypsy was placed back in the tree department. There wasn't enough work to keep him busy in the workshop so he was told to take a tractor and trailer and drive around the field clearing rubbish and dead plants. He enjoyed the job as he was working alone and had time to dream and think about his forthcoming journey.

His younger brother was now seventeen years old and at a college of further education preparing to take his A levels. At home their parents would push him hard to study, etc. He would be so stressed when he visited Gypsy that the air inside the trailer home would be almost crackling.

Invariably Gypsy would roll a large joint and light it. Then, after taking a couple of large tokes would pass it to his brother. Within five minutes, his brother would be relaxed and feeling like a normal person once more.

He and his brother had not got on well as children but now there were no problems between them and Gypsy would even take him along when he went into Brighton at the weekends.

JUNE 1983

It was Glastonbury time once more and Gypsy with his customary back pack and tent hitched west to Somerset for the annual pilgrimage. After getting dropped off in street he and a bunch of other festival goers hiked the nine miles to Pilton then went around through various other fields and climbed over the fence. The main acts that year were Judy Tzuke, Curtis Mayfield and UB 40. Gypsy had his usual three or four days of fun and relaxation with people of his own type and interests. Many of his friends, including Eddie and his old guitar teacher were there and Gypsy felt good.

Back at home, Gypsy made it to several good concerts, including Steeleye span, Curtis Mayfield and Wishbone Ash. The summer was turning out to be a lot of fun.

There is not much to write about during this time, as although Gypsy was mostly enjoying himself and working to save as much for his trip as possible, nothing of great significance had happened. Gypsy continued to read books on mysticism and travel and people around him continued to view him as crazy and dangerous.

Eddie told him about a bar in Worthing that was the hang out of the area's misfits.

Gypsy wasted no time in finding it. It was a good place to score hash and acid and it was one of the few places in the area that he did not feel out of place. The crowd from the bar would also get together for after closing time beach parties.

CHAPTER 6

THE GREAT JOURNEY

ENGLAND

SEPTEMBER 1983.

The night before he left on the journey his mother was angry and nervous. She didn't want him to go to India. But Gypsy was a grown man of twenty one years old and she could do nothing now to stop him. There were no longer any Rabbis or penguins that could be called upon to thwart his progress. And besides, Gypsy had sworn that he would either make it to India on this trip or he would die in the attempt. He was furious at how others always seemed so absolutely determined to fuck up all of his plans and he was at the point where he would have been ready to kill anyone who would even think of blocking his path. His father also caught flak for not doing anything to stop Gypsy making the trip.

The next day Gypsy said goodbye and took a train to London, where he was to stay with some of his cousins for three days. He used the time to buy himself anything he might need for the trip including travelers cheques, a walkman and an ultra light sleeping bag. He now had one thousand, three hundred pounds. He left five hundred pounds safely in his UK bank account and took the remaining money with him.

The night before he left England he went to see Peter Tosh in concert at the Dominion Theater on Tottenham court road. The music was good but the vibe was angry, with Peter Tosh playing a guitar made in the shape of an M16 assault rifle. The crowd didn't mix or speak to each other, unlike any of the other gigs Gypsy had ever been to. It was a world away from the Curtis Mayfield gig that he went to in Brighton where everyone was up and dancing with joints being freely shared among the crowd.

TRANSIT: LONDON-ATHENS

SEPTEMBER 1983

The next day after saying goodbye to his cousins he took the tube to Victoria where he boarded a bus to Dover, along with an oddball mix of travellers and Greeks who were returning home. For thirty five quid he had bought a Magic bus ticket from London to Athens).

The bus arrived in Dover some two hours later, where it deposited them all at the boat, which they then boarded. Gypsy was celebrating finally being back on the road again and in so doing got drunk on the ferry. An hour and a half later they all got off the ferry in Calais where they boarded another bus that had just come from Amsterdam.

Gypsy woke up the next morning, in his seat with his head throbbing and his mouth feeling like it was full of dirty old socks. Reaching for his bag he pulled out a bottle of water and gulped it down. They were on the road to Leon.

At Leon they picked up two more passengers. They passed the bright lights of Nice late in the night and soon afterwards, Gypsy nodded off. He awoke early the next morning just as the bus was passing through Trieste. Then they were at the border, crossing into Yugoslavia. It was uncanny, it had been warm in Italy, but the moment that they stepped into Yugoslavia the air was freezing cold, as if the land were under some strange, sinister curse. The bus soon stopped for refreshments and although the landscape, architecture and people looked the same suddenly there was no good food available and the vibe had changed. Gypsy knew about Yugoslavia from previous trips and as such had a well loaded bag of food on board the bus. He only got off of the bus to stretch and use the toilet. Once again declining to consume the pigswill that masqueraded as food at Yugoslavia's grim transport cafes.

On the bus he had the dubious pleasure of sitting next to a fat, uncouth, smart arse from Glasgow who snored and kicked in his sleep. He was on his first trip abroad and like his five friends who he was travelling with, was heading towards Israel to go and work on a kibbutz. They, like Gypsy were planning to take the boat to Israel from Piraeus.

The bus passed close by Zagreb and continued on its way to Belgrade. On and on they rolled. The two drivers had two tapes of the "J. Gilles band" which were played repeatedly, way past the point of annoyance and they would not play anyone else's tapes. The journey was getting to be somewhat tiresome for Gypsy.

The bus passed Belgrade and some hours later he was asleep. He woke up at the Greek border. The bus crossed into Greece, through the usual formalities and rolled on down the road, to Thessalonica. Some four hours later a whole group of maybe twenty or twenty five normal straight Greeks got off the bus.

Then the bus, with its remaining crowd of hippies and travelers, carried on to Athens.

Depositing them, some five hours later on the street near Syntagma Square. The bus then went off on its merry way. The Glaswegian and his crowd of friends, all being new to the road asked Gypsy and another traveler from Mexico to help them find accommodation and show them around.

GREECE/ATHENS

OCTOBER 1983.

Gypsy went off into the Plaka area but to his disgust, the area had been tarted up and all of the hostels had been closed down by government orders as so as to make the place more attractive to uptight wankers who didn't like hippies and travelers.

The Mexican had been in Athens more recently than Gypsy and knew of some cheap hotels near Amonia square. So they all hopped on a bus down to Amonia, an area notorious for having some of the fattest and ugliest hookers on the planet. It wouldn't matter how many glasses or bottles of ouzo you were to drink, nothing could possibly make any of them look the least bit attractive. A man would have to be a seriously twisted and pervert to even consider having sex with one of them.

Anyway, to cut a long story short, the Mexican found a grotty little hotel that he knew and they checked in, sharing four to a room. The rooms were basic and clean but that was it, there were only two beds in each room and Gypsy despite having helped in finding accommodation, found that he was one of the ones who would have to sleep on the floor.

That night Gypsy took them all for a tour of the Plaka but all of his favorite bars and clubs had been closed and replaced with many twee little and not so little tourist restaurants. There was not even a glimmer of the fun and the energy that had been in the area when Gypsy stayed there last.

Eventually Gypsy gave up and took them to a shop selling liquor and wine and introduced them to the dubious pleasure of drinking Retsina, while warning about the hangover that would follow if they guzzled a whole bottle of the shit. So of course 'Fat Bastard' (the character from the Austen powers movie could have been based on this slob) and his obnoxious friends threw away their corks and started necking the foul tasting piss colored liquid.

Later that night while walking back to their hotel Fat Bastard in an inebriated state attacked Gypsy in the middle of the roundabout at Amonia. Gypsy had had to put up with sitting next to this revolting slob for three days and nights on the bus, now this.

Gypsy lost it and laid into him in a fit of rage. Fat Bastard managed to get a wrestling hold on Gypsy but made the grave mistake of putting his fingers in Gypsy's mouth, a mistake that almost cost him the ability to jerk off. Gypsy couldn't believe what an opportunity he had been given and almost chewed the bastard's fingers off. Fat Bastard was screaming in agony. Gypsy knocked him to the ground and the others dragged Gypsy off before he got the chance to vent the full force of his fury on this sad fool.

Fat bastard towered over Gypsy's skinny frame so all of a sudden they were all looking at Gypsy with wary sideways glances. The next day Gypsy did what he could to avoid them. The ferry to Haifa would be leaving on the next night and he was just bidding his time until then.

Unfortunately he bumped into Fat Bastard and his friends in a bar in the Plaka. Fat Bastard had been getting into more infantile troubles, having managed to get himself slung out of one or two bars that afternoon and been attacked and given a hard slap by a local for his ignorant rudeness. He was still sniveling about what Gypsy had done to him the previous night and nursing his swollen, bloodied fingers.

It made Gypsy ashamed to be British, when he looked at this sorry shower of halfwits and he certainly didn't think he could put up with another three days in their company on board the Haifa ferry without launching at least one of them to the sharks.

There was nothing else for it, he went back to the room packed his bag and left. He took a bus to the airport and hunted for and then waited for the first available flight to Tel Aviv.

Sixteen hours later he was on an Olympic Airways A300 heading down the runway and off into the dark evening sky en route to Tel Aviv. The flight was completely full and he had been lucky to get a seat.

It was nine o'clock in the evening when the wheels hit the concrete at Ben Gurion Airport. The plane taxied to it's allotted parking spot. The engines were turned off and the steps, generator and baggage handling equipment was placed around the plane. As they were walking across the apron towards the terminal Gypsy was pulled from the crowd and taken into a security van for questioning. "Look, mate I can tell you you're wasting your time with me. I'm a Jew just like you. If you want to check it out, my papers proving it are lodged with the Beit Din in Jerusalem", he told them. "Now, why don't you let me go and go catch some real villains?", they checked out his papers and passport and eventually let him go. "Sorry", they said. "It's just that you just look kind of dodgy", "great" thought Gypsy to himself. "I look dodgy. What the hell does that mean?"

He took the bus to Jerusalem, he looked forward to seeing Alan and Ingy and the crowd again. He had phoned them regularly from England and on the last call they had assured him that they were almost ready for the trip to India. He had sent them mail from England with cassettes containing the collected works of Syd Barratt and viewed them all as his best friends, so nothing could have prepared him for what was to come.

When he first got back to the hostel, everything was fine and he was welcomed back like family. He got back into his old routine of selling hash in the penguin quarter and all seemed fine.

One Friday afternoon when Gypsy came back to the hostel, from a walkabout in the old city, one of the others looked at Gypsy and said, "How come you look so stoned man?" "It's Friday", Gypsy answered. "Ah he's been over in the Jewish quarter banging out dope to the Rabbis before Shabbat starts. You know how boring Shabbat is for an Orthodox Jew, a lot of them like to get bombed out before it starts", Alan explained to the others. "Did you sell a lot this afternoon?" Alan asked. "Cleaned out", Gypsy replied. Everyone in the room was laughing and trying to imagine a bunch of penguins having Bong and Chillum parties.

Gypsy still found amusement in the situation, as the bullshit and the drivel that comes out of people's mouths late at night around a campfire, as the joints go around can sound a might similar to the mad rantings of religious nutters. He wondered if he would also be able to bang out some acid to the penguins too. But then he thought better of it, those kooks were dangerous enough anyway without sending them off to the mad hatter's tea party on California sunshine or pentagrams.

Soon Gypsy noticed that things had changed. Alan was uptight and forever fighting with friends. Sometimes he had the shakes too. He was always fighting with others about money and never seemed to have any, he was not his usual cheerful Muppet like self.

It was when he saw Alan sitting in the kitchen and gouching out that his suspicions were confirmed.

He confronted Alan about it and asked how this had happened. Alan then explained, that a few weeks prior to Gypsy's return to the hostel Howard, an American, Jewish hippie who had been at the hostel and part of the scene for a long time, had walked in with a bag of smack. Like his old crowd of friends back in England the silly sods had all merrily got themselves hooked on the stuff. They had already spunked all of their India money on it and had now taken to stealing from guests to fund their habits.

Gypsy had a fall out with Alan about what was going on but Gypsy had already moved out of the hostel and was staying elsewhere in the city. He needed to sell his beloved Ibanez folk guitar now to help fund his ticket to India. He was loath to do it but he had no choice, he needed the money.

There was no one with the money at hand in Jerusalem who wished to buy it but one man who took a particular like to it asked Gypsy if he could wait for two or three weeks for him to get the money together. As he was the only taker Gypsy didn't have much choice but to wait.

He took the bus down to Tel Aviv and landed himself a job as a cook, working twelve hours a day in a British pub called BBC (Bernies Bottle Club). It was at the end of Dissengorff Street in a nightlife area known as Little Tel Aviv. He worked at the pub for two weeks and slept, either on the beach or on the floor of a friend's apartment, depending on circumstances. The job wasn't so bad and Gypsy found it quite bearable

Israel and India had to go to Athens or another European capital and pay one hundred dollars at the Indian consulate, for a three month visa).

ISRAEL

NOVEMBER 1983.

After two weeks of cooking baked potatoes and greasy fry ups for twelve hours a day and sleeping rough Gypsy was on the bus back up through the hills to Jerusalem. ....Howard had been blamed for everything and had been thrown out of the hostel by Alan. He was now working at another hostel in the new city for the man who wanted to buy Gypsy's guitar. Gypsy checked into the hostel and waited. His wait lasted several days, during which time he grew more frustrated and pissed off that he had wasted precious and limited resources coming to this energy draining hole. He wished that he had flown immediately from Athens to India, then he would still have his guitar. The man bargained him down on the price of the guitar to the point where he made nothing on it. This was something that had been urged on him by his smug, hunched and grinning, smart arsed, American, Jewish, boss, who had nothing to do with the deal and nothing to gain from it either way.

Gypsy jumped on the first bus available to Haifa with the money and his bag. He got to the port and bought a ticket to Piraeus. The ship was due to leave in less than an hour and there wouldn't be another sailing for at least another three days.

TRANSIT TO PIRAEUS-SOL OLYMPIA

NOVEMBER 1983.

Once on board the boat, Gypsy was able to relax. The ticket cost him fifty dollars, which was dirt cheap even back then for such a long journey. The ship, 'The Sol Olympia' was a truck and car ferry, it had duty free liquor and tobacco shops, restaurants and canteens, a night club and a casino on board among other things. The lounges were full of travelers heading to Athens to take the bus or train home. Most of them had wanted to make it to India but like Gypsy in years gone by, they had failed to make any money working in Israel and were now heading home, promising to themselves to make it there on their next trip.

Gypsy watched the Israeli coast recede into the distance as the ship put out to sea. He was not sorry to see the back of the place and didn't care if he never went there again. Jerusalem had an uncanny energy that seemed to trap him and glue him there as if the city did not just have mere physical walls around it. He had felt that if he did not fight with all of his energy he would have become trapped there again. He had developed a pathological hatred for the place and despised the dysfunctional obstructivity of many of the diaspora Jews who had emigrated there.

As the last piece of the coast had disappeared from view, Gypsy made his way to the duty free shop and bought himself a liter bottle of scotch to celebrate getting out of Israel with his cash reasonably intact. Like many of the other travelers, he was walking around the deck and drinking. He had a lot to celebrate. He would be going to India in a few days, one of only three others on board who was going to East Asia directly from Athens.

There was no hash or weed on board so everyone had liter bottles of spirits and soon it turned into a bit of a swap party as bottles were shared. Soon many of the occupants of the seats in the lounges were wasted and passed out. . The next morning the ship pulled into the harbor at Limasol in Cyprus. Gypsy got off of the ship and went for a walk, but there wasn't much to see and he was soon bored and besides, he didn't want to spend any money, so he went back to the ship and just waited for it to leave. . That afternoon the ship pulled out of harbor and set course for Rhodes. . A storm kicked up in the night and the ship was rocking about a bit. The morning came and many people were throwing up over the side. Gypsy was OK, he had good sea legs but the sight of all those throwing up, was enough to put him off of food for the morning. . The ship pulled up to the harbor wall at the old city at Rhodes and Gypsy got off the ship once more for a walk about. . Though the old city was beautiful it seemed that if you didn't want to buy duty free alcohol or tobacco then the place had nothing to offer. Again Gypsy was soon back on the ship and waiting for it to pull out. Again it left port in the afternoon and then sailed to

Piraeus. . The next morning Gypsy disembarked at the international port and made his way to the metro station, from where he took a train to Monastraki and found a cheap hostel to stay at near the Plaka.

ATHENS/GREECE

DECEMBER 1983.

After dropping his bag in the hostel, he went out looking for somewhere cheap to buy his ticket to the east. He found a budget ticket office on a road off from Syntagma Square and went inside to ask about a ticket to India.

The travel agent was British and asked him if it was just India that he wished to visit.

When Gypsy said, "No, I want to go further" the agent looked at him and smiled and said, "I've got just the ticket for you, if you would like. Have a look at this, it goes from Athens to Bombay, then on through Dhaka and Rangoon to Bangkok. You can make stops where you like and I can give you a one way for three hundred dollars, how's that?"

"I like it", said Gypsy. "I'll take it. By the way, which airline is it with?" "Bangladesh Airlines", the agent replied. "Has the plane got engines or will I have to pedal?" Gypsy asked.

"No, don't worry, they're flying DC10's and they must be reasonably safe as they are allowed to land at London. In fact that's where the flight you'll be on originates from on this route" the agent replied with a wry grin on his face.

Gypsy bought the ticket and then went out to the markets near to Monastraki looking for cheap digital watches and other things that he could sell at a profit when he got to Goa, which was where he was planning on heading for first. He had been told by many of the older travelers that it was easy to sell cheap electronic items, gold, whiskey and western brand cigarettes at a good profit in India. He bought a bunch of cheap two dollar digital watches and some other cheap items, such as radios and the like. He already had a second hand SLR camera that he had bought from an Australian woman who had been on the ship and was about to fly home to Sydney and he planned to buy cigarettes at the airport.   . Two nights later, now with just two hundred and thirty dollars in his pocket and a one way ticket to Bangkok, Gypsy rode the bus out to the international terminal at Athens international airport. He got into the building and found the right counter and checked in. There wasn't much of a queue and it wasn't long before he was going through security to airside. After stocking up on items to sell on arrival at duty free he sat down in the lounge and waited. There were other travelers who were not only waiting for the same flight but were also, like Gypsy, planning to take the steamer from Bombay down the coast to Goa. They all got talking, Gypsy included and decided that it would be a good idea if they all shared a taxi from the airport to the harbor. Then as they looked out of the huge windows towards the apron, they saw their flight pull in from the taxi way and pull up at its allotted parking space. Gypsy watched as the ground crew who were already waiting, surrounded the plane and set up the various equipment. It is a very interesting thing to watch, the competence and clockwork like way that airports operate. It was something that fascinated Gypsy.

None of them had been to India before and they were all excited to be going there. The plane was not due to take off for over an hour so a bus brought some of the passengers from the plane to the terminal building. Among the passengers were five tall, young Dutchmen, who proceeded to pull frisbees from their bags and play frisbee across the length and breadth of that part of the airport. The amazing thing was that no one came and stopped them. If they had tried a similar stunt at an airport in northern Europe there would have been much wailing and gnashing of teeth over it. It was obvious were these guys were heading so the crowd of travelers who were waiting at Athens for the flight got talking with them. Sure enough they too were heading for Goa, The flight had stopped in Amsterdam on it's way from London and that was where they had got on board.

Riding the bus across the airport apron to the plane, Gypsy felt excited. At last, at long last, he was truly on his way to India and nothing was going to stop him now. He had taken the trouble to buy enough things that he had heard were unavailable in India to sell when he got there. He had packs of duty free cigarettes, whisky, digital watches, pocket calculators and an SLR camera.

TRANSIT TO INDIA

DECEMBER 1983

The flight was surprisingly OK and the in-flight meal was a nice hot curry. The flight was mostly full of British Bangladeshi restaurant owners and their wives and children. They were mostly heading to Silhit, to see their families and take a break from their tandoori restaurants. The crew were pleasant and it wasn't a bad flight, unlike Gypsy's visions of what a Bangladeshi airliner might look like or be like to travel on. And unlike airlines from many Muslim countries, they served alcohol on board.

Six hours later the plane started it's descent into Bombay and fifteen minutes later as the plane was almost over the city a foul smell like a big stale fart wafted into the cabin, it smelled like a giant open sewer. Then looking out of the plane window they could see mile after mile of shanty town slums. The airport was located in the middle of it all.

The plane landed and pulled up to a modern looking terminal, complete with air bridges. Gypsy and several other passengers disembarked and cleared passport control, collected their bags and then went through customs.

In 1983, Indra Gandhi was still the Prime Minister, India was socialist and people from commonwealth countries were automatically given a forty nine year visa on arrival.

Customs and passport control had been fast and easy and now Gypsy and the other travelers from the flight were all standing outside of the terminal building in the airport car park. Nearly all of the cars looked as if they were from another era, with just ancient fiats and Morris Oxfords making up the vast majority of cars in the car park. As Gypsy looked on, two white Indian holy cows walked nonchalantly across the car park. Now Gypsy knew he was in India for real.

BOMBAY/INDIA

DECEMBER 4, 1983.

They negotiated a rate with a couple of taxi drivers for a ride to the Goa boat and somehow they managed to squeeze six or seven of them into each of the not so big fiat taxis and took off across town, their bags strapped to the roof. It was 6:30 in the morning and people were just waking up. For mile after mile it looked like a mixture of the day after a pop festival and a scene from Dante's inferno, with tens of thousands of people sleeping by the side of the road and obviously, millions more living in the shanty towns, with huts made out of anything from cardboard boxes to flattened tin cans. There were streams and ponds of raw sewage, the stench was truly something to behold.

They all stared out of the window, wide eyed and speechless. Never in all of their lives had any of them seen such harrowing poverty. Not just that, but there were people with horrific deformities as well, just there lying in the street instead of in a place where they could be taken care of. There was also the occasional dead body lying there, covered with a cloth or sack. people were pissing and shitting out in the open, there were no proper toilets. The whole place looked like a bomb had hit it. It was a disaster zone. Amongst all of the mud, shit and filth there were Hindu temples and shrines and Mosques too. People were getting up and going to work, just like in any other town or city on this earth and their wives were taking care of the living space. There were grotty little local buses, jeeps, mopeds, grotty antiquated home made looking trucks, taxis and larger buses on the roads but not many personal cars.

The taxi eventually made it into the center of Bombay. Even there the pavements were covered in sleeping bodies and improvised shacks and the like. Eventually they reached the Goa boat terminal and got out and stretched themselves after the claustrophobic taxi ride, then after paying the driver, they all headed into the boat terminal. . Paying seventy rupees each [which at the time was about seven and a half dollars], they bought tickets for the middle deck.

There were three decks on the steamer, upper which was all cabins, middle which was just open deck and lower which was also open but more close to the engines and more cramped.

After paying for their tickets they entered the waiting room which was a cage like room with a row of jail like bars on the gates leading out to the harbor.

Gypsy clocked these with interest as he had never seen anything like it before in a waiting room.

There was a chai stand in the corner and soon they were all standing around drinking cups of chai with other travelers who had just come from the north of India, as they waited for the steamer to arrive.

There were porters, dressed in red shirts and turbans who kept asking them if they wanted their services to get them a space on the deck. Gypsy just had one medium sized shoulder bag and a water canteen and didn't need or want any help.

The boat pulled in and he went to watch the activities at the steel bar, cage doors. It was all new to him and even though he had now been making long journeys for the past four years, this was nothing like anything he had ever seen before. Even the most mundane of tasks was being done in a completely different way and with different and weird looking tools, it wasn't so much like being in another country as being on another planet in another dimension.

INDIA/GOA STEAMER

DECEMBER 1983.

The ship tied up, then the gang planks were lowered and a whole mass of people with their bags descended down the ramps from the ship's middle deck, they were dressed in all manner of fancy dress outfits and colors. It was indeed impressive how fast the ship was cleared of its passengers and then cleaned ready for the next lot.

Gypsy watched and readied himself for the race up the gang plank to find himself a good space to sit and lie down on for the journey. After watching the hyperactive way the ship had disembarked he figured that he now knew why the waiting room had such tough cage like doors and besides, he was used to bad mannered scrums from living in Israel.

The porters were given a twenty second head start, as they leapt on the ship from all directions swinging and climbing on ropes etc like a bunch of kids playing pirates in a school gymnasium, while at the same time carrying the heavy bags of their customers.

The cage doors were then flung open and Gypsy like everyone else, ran like a Looney up the gang plank and tried to find an empty space to put his bedroll and bag down.

He found a space under some steps that led up to the next deck. He spread his bedroll out and lay down on it, waiting until the gang planks were pulled up before getting up to walk around.

The others from the flight had all managed to park themselves close by, as such, each could watch each other's bags.

Eventually, some forty five or so minutes later the boat gave a honk of its horn and pulled out from its mooring berth. Gypsy got up to walk around. He had seen a group of hippies with a sitar on the other side of the boat and went over to check them out and see if one of them was going to play the instrument.

They had some good Indian hash and they were smoking a chillum, they were Italians and they invited Gypsy to sit down with them and smoke. He stayed for several rounds of the chillum pipe and then wandered back to his bedroll and bag. It was now ten thirty in the morning and Gypsy having not slept much on the flight, fell into a deep sleep.

Awaking after dark, he went for a wander around the boat and found the canteen where he sat down to a plate of vegetable curry and rice.

His mind was still blown from what he had seen in Bombay. He had previously never even imagined that such a scale of poverty and squalor existed anywhere on the planet, it looked like a living hell.

But here he was in India, the place he had heard all the incredible stories about, the place he had for so long dreamed of travelling in. he would just have to keep looking until he found that incredibleness that he had heard and read so much about.

Through the night, the boat pulled into several different unlit coves along the coast and stopped to pick up and drop off passengers. They would row up to the side of the steamer in long boats and drop off one lot of passengers and take another lot aboard via the lower deck, before rowing to shore.

The steamer chugged on through the night making its drops and pick ups and Gypsy went back to his bedroll and went back to sleep. He awoke with the dawn and looking from where he was lying he could see a coastline lined with forests of coconut palms. This was the first time that he had ever seen such trees in anything other than a photograph in a book, a glossy magazine or a Movie.

At around nine o'clock in the morning, the steamer pulled into the estuary at Panjim (the capital of Goa state) and they all disembarked. Gypsy was planning on heading up to Anjuna Beach where there was a flea market where he could sell his goods.

But in the group who had flown from Athens there was a Greek woman called Hariklia who proceeded to persuade Gypsy to join her in going to Calangute (another beach, south of Anjuna and north of

Panjim). She also had never been to India before and was clearly frightened by what she had seen so far.

They walked the short distance to the bus station. It was a scene of madness with people running everywhere, hustlers trying to make a rupee from everyone who passed and bus conductors shouting out a cacophony of different destinations like a bunch of parrots on amphetamines. They took a bus to the town of Mapusa in the North and then another bus to Calangute.

Mapusa [pronounced Mapsa] was a small scruffy place, full of old Portuguese colonial buildings with a market in the center of town and not much else. The ride down to the beach was a lot more pleasant.

As he got talking with Hariklia it transpired that she was a tour guide back in Greece who specialized in giving guided tours in English around the various archeological ruins of her country. The reason she was in India was that her boyfriend had become a junkie and his family had blamed her for his predicament (even though she was clean and never touched the stuff). He had run off to Goa with a stack of cash and now his family had paid for her ticket and given her some cash and asked her to go and rescue the idiot from himself.

At Calangute, they found a room where they dropped their bags and then went out to find a place to eat. There were no shortages of places selling food but the place was a hole. There were large quantities of smack heads from all over Europe, most notorious were the French in their dirty, once white Gandhi outfits sitting alone and in squatting groups, smoking brown sugar down a strip of tin foil with a pipe.

On the beach Gypsy found a stand selling hot freshly made samosas, he bought a plate of them and they tasted delicious.

There were cafes and bars selling Indian beer. They only had one brand, it was called Kingfisher. They also sold a local drink that came in two flavors, either coconut or cashew. Fenny was perhaps the most disgusting drink that Gypsy had ever tasted. It was like drinking paint stripper or something equally caustic.

Calangute, at that time was a small village. It had some relatively fancy modern looking, tourist accommodation on the beach and a roundabout and car park surrounded with restaurants and cafes. Some of them were nothing more than a bunch of hessian sacking stuck up on bamboo poles with tables and benches below. Their kitchen's normally consisted of one or two kerosene, pump up stoves and a couple of buckets to wash the plates and vegetables in.

It was primitive. Other than soda there was no bottled water and it was nigh on impossible to make an international phone call from anywhere but perhaps Panjim or Bombay. There were no western brands of drinks like Coca cola or Sprite available and instead they had their own Indian brands, like Thumbs up, Campa cola, Limca and Gold spot. Television had only just started in India and at that time was largely unknown. Dope was legal in many if not all states and was sold in government licensed shops. India was another world, like a large step back in time. All of the motor vehicles were of the type that they had stopped making in Europe many years previously and the trucks, well Gypsy had never seen trucks like that before, neither in books or museums, they looked like a large botched D.I.Y attempt, possibly the most ungainly looking trucks in the world.

But the most disturbing aspect of this place came to his attention the next morning when he went out to use the toilet.

The toilet was a white cement stand alone structure several meters from the house. Inside was a large bucket of water, with a much smaller one inside and a hole in the floor leading to a Shute, that went to a puddle outside. There were pigs wandering around the area just as freely as the cows. When one of them spotted him entering the toilet it came running over all excited and stuck its snout up inside the Shute. Gypsy was inside having a dump and found it more than a little disturbing to watch this grunting snout beneath him, eating his shit as it landed. He had already resolved to go vegetarian while in India but this just helped him to not to crave bacon or pork sausages. . Wednesday was flea market day at Anjuna and Gypsy and some others had decided to walk there. They all had things for sale and the flea market was a good place to sell, so Gypsy had been told.

They walked along the beach, north to Baga, then at Baga they waded across the creek and started to climb up along the cliff side, following the trail to Anjuna. After a short walk, they were starting to drop down to the beach at Anjuna. The flea market was right in front of them under the palm trees, just off from the beach. There were already a few stands set up on blankets on the sand and with clothes hanging on strings tied between the trees.

Gypsy and the others set up their stands as each of them put a blanket out with their wares on it. Gypsy had a good day trading, there were maybe thirty or forty stalls other than the local ladies, with their mobile, pack down chai stands.

Most, if not all of his customers, had been Indians, mostly tourists and honeymooners from Bombay. They obviously liked what Gypsy had brought as they didn't hesitate in paying for the goods.

Gypsy wandered back along the cliff with some of the people he had come there with. It was sunset time and he was happy as he enjoyed the view. He had taken money and that was good. They dropped down to Baga as it got dark. The tide had come in and now they had to use the punt ferry to get across the creek, which was a small open fishing boat with a man with a punt stick operating it. They walked back along the sand from Baga to Calangute and found food before going somewhere peaceful to smoke chillums. There were so many people strung out on smack at Calangute at that time that it was not funny. Even the waiters in the cafes would be spending more time hidden behind a screen chasing the dragon than they would be serving the tables and were either shaking or gouching out.

There were young British travelers hooked on it and older Germans who had been travelling for years. But if someone's room had been broken into to steal money, everyone could be pretty sure it was done by one of the French junkies who sat under the trees with their candles and tin foil.

Local transport to and from parties, normally involved motorbike taxis that like the cars were painted yellow and black and were invariably Enfield 350cc Bullets. They regularly carried two or three passengers at a time and could be a scary ride through the narrow country lanes of Goa at night.

Gypsy, Hariklia and some of the other travelers from the house where they were staying made it to some of the famous Goa parties.

This was in the days before rave and techno, so there would be rock bands from the west performing and disco parties with music from the Talking Heads, Monsoon and the Rolling stones. Hundreds of the local women would set up chai stands on bamboo mats on the ground where they would sit and sell chai, cakes and cold drinks. The parties were often held in disused paddy fields if not on the beach itself.

At a party at Calangute one night things turned ugly when some local Goans started making moves on the girlfriend of a Black man from

France. He in turn let off a canister of CS gas or something similar in order to get them away from her.

The locals then chased him down to the beach, cornered him and then pelted him with rocks. It was the most brutal, merciless and cowardly attack that Gypsy had ever witnessed. It was amazing that they hadn't killed him. Even when he was lying on the ground they were still running up and throwing large rocks at him with force, they then stole all of his money and documents.

It all happened so fast that many people didn't realize what had happened until it was over. Gypsy on his own, could have done nothing to help him fend off the attackers and anyway, it was over almost as fast as it had started. A couple of other travelers got together with Gypsy to at least get him to a hospital. He was staggering around and crying, blood oozing out from his many wounds.

However the local lads were standing like a bunch of cowards on any bit of high ground they could find and threatening any driver that offered to help. The other travelers were of no use either as they lamely stood around like so many wildebeest as one of their own was getting devoured by lions and hyenas.

Eventually up on the main road they were able to get him a taxi to the hospital.

Gypsy was absolutely disgusted by what he had just witnessed. What a foul, revolting shower of faggot, cowards, not just the locals but most of the travelers too. Where was their heart? how could they just stand there and do nothing to help the poor fucker? Their inaction to help was cold, heartless, cowardice and Gypsy was shaken to see what utterly low quality people he was surrounded by.

"Attacks like that should be saved for, rapists, child molesters, kidnappers, and murderers only", thought Gypsy to himself. "Letting off a can of an offensive substance of that type might have warranted a couple of hard slaps and ejection from the party but nothing repeat nothing on the scale of what was meted out on this poor guy.

Gypsy's favorite café was one of the hessian sack wonders that lined the car park. The food there wasn't bad and it was run by an educated man and his wife. He spoke fluent English and had previously worked as a jazz musician in Bombay before coming to Goa to try and get his own business started.

His only waiter was a raving junkie who was always running around the back to smoke more smack and spent a lot of the rest of the time gouching or shaking. He wasn't much different from the other waiters or for that matter, their clients.

Gypsy and a minority of the other travelers stayed clean as did the restaurant, café and guest house owners, but not so their male staff.

Gypsy did a couple of more runs over to Anjuna for the flea market and Hariklia found her boyfriend and started to work on him, to persuade him to go home. Gypsy in order to make his money last a bit longer, moved to a smaller room. A couple of times, he got a day of the Indian horrors when he spent the whole day rushing out to the toilet to vomit and shit at the same time. It was at such times as these when his toothless ugly old hag of a land lady would come and harrass him mercilessly and endlessly for the day's rent. She was as benevolent, intelligent and tactfull as she was good looking [it can be a little difficult when you are vomiting and shitting at the same time or doubled over with stomach cramps, to also reach for your wallet and count out money]

It rained through Christmas Eve, Christmas day and Boxing day but that did not stop Gypsy enjoying himself.

INDIA/GOA

DECEMBER 1983, CHRISTMAS.

He had met some people of his own age from Kerala and as they sat in a chai shop under a plastic sheet awning they pulled out a bag of fine smelling Kerala grass and skinned up some joints.

Also at the table was a traveler of dual Dutch and Austrian nationalities by the name of Steve. He had a bottle of Indian rum that he shared with everyone, while Gypsy had cigarettes and hash.

Steve, like Gypsy was planning to travel on from India to Thailand and further, he was on the run from national service in both Austria and Holland and had no intention of going back to Europe any time soon.

It was only a small gathering but that wasn't what was important, all of the people at the table were of high quality and lived by a code of ethics, unlike the lame, weak arseholes at the party that Gypsy had attended not a hundred yards from the same chai shop that they were sitting in. The guys from Kerala were university students and spoke

English fluently, they were intelligent and each had his own view on things around them. Gypsy felt comfortable and at home with them as he listened to what they had to say.

The Kerala weed was so good that it tasted almost like hash and the Indian rum was doing its trick. And a good night was had as Steve and Gypsy recounted travel stories and the Keralans told them about life in Kerala and joked about the way that things worked in their country.

Christmas had passed and Gypsy wanted to find something new. Calangute was a smack riddled shit hole full of junkies and hateful greedy locals. All in all it was not a place to be hanging out.

Gypsy took a bus to Panjim with his bag, he had had it with the Goa scene, from Calangute to Shapora in the north, neither the travelers nor the locals were people he wished to associate with. He took another bus to the town of Margao, an hour and a half to the south.

Getting off the bus with some other travelers, they headed for a nearby beer garden and sat down for a drink. A scruffy Indian man who none of them had met before followed them into the place and sitting down with them proceeded to order something.

The next thing anyone knew three waiters showed up carrying large plates of food in each hand, "Who ordered this?" everyone asked each other. It turned out it was the scruffy Indian sitting with them and not just that but he expected them to pay for it. The cheek. The food was sent back and the scruffy man ejected from the garden.

It should be mentioned at this point that in India prior to the mid nineties when things began to change, there were many people who suffered from chronic iodine deficiency in large sections of the population. This led to Cretinism which meant that poor India had absolutely no shortage of fools and idiots running around its countryside buggering the place up. That was of course until one of India's biggest business families, the Tatas realized that the government wasn't going to do anything to change the circumstances and took it upon themselves to provide the cure in the form of Iodine reinforced salt. It has been part of the backbone of India's recent economic success]. The other travelers all eventually disappeared on their way to wherever, leaving Gypsy sitting there alone. He wandered out of the bar and found a bench in the town square garden to sit down on while he gathered his thoughts and wondered how he was going to get himself down to Colva.

For some reason, back at the bus station Gypsy ended up on the wrong bus, instead of going to Colva beach as he had planned he ended up in the somewhat scruffy port town of Vasco. He had a little money on him so he got himself a room for the night at a cheap hotel. It was the first time in all of his travelling life that he had ever had a room with it's own toilet and shower, OK the shower was cold but Gypsy was certainly not complaining, the room had only cost him twenty seven rupees for the night [there were nine point something rupees to the dollar and fifteen point something rupees to the pound at that time].

The next day Gypsy took a bus back to Margao and then another that this time got him to Colva village which was one kilometer from the beach.

In Colva Gypsy landed on his feet. He found a wonderful old Portuguese colonial house where they had a cheap dormitory in an old ballroom come banqueting hall. For eight rupees per night he got a mattress on the floor in this nice, large cool room.

The owner of the house was a man of mixed Portuguese and Indian ancestry. His name was Albert and he was a very genuine and kind man who never hassled his tenants about the rent, preferring to wait for them to come to him and pay when they were ready.

Gypsy was desperately short of money and the camera that he had bought back in Athens had broken and needed fixing before he could sell it. He didn't know much about cameras and it appeared that the Aussie woman who had sold it to him had pulled a fast one on him and sold him a dud.

He started chatting with another young traveler from England about ideas for making money. He was wondering about knocking up an alcoholic fruit punch and selling it from a container to people at the beach. The other traveler took him around to meet a Scottish man who was living there. He had done a deal with the local baker for part time use of his oven and was at that time supplying one or two of the local cafes with his cakes. He suggested that Gypsy could go and buy himself a basket and then he could load him with his cakes to sell. This was a great offer and Gypsy wasted no time in getting himself set up and ready. He went to the local market the next day and bought himself a plastic rectangular basket (like a shopping basket at a supermarket) and a clip on shoulder strap.

He went and found Davy the Scotsman and got the basket loaded with cakes and a list of what he had with prices. He then wandered down to the beach and started selling to the travelers who were sitting there. (there were no Western tourists as such in Goa in those days, just travelers and hippies who would be there for months at a time).

Though people complained about the prices of the cakes (three to four rupees each) he still managed to empty the basket, before going back to Davy's place to give him his share of the money. It was a fair deal and now it was working and Davy told Gypsy what time he should come to the bakery the next day to collect his load.

Across the road from Albert's house, was a garden café called Umatis restaurant, run by a happy and friendly man. He also sold Davy's cakes, but also he did a rice plate for three rupees, it was a whole meal, consisting of dahl, rice, vegetable curry salad and a papadom. Gypsy lived on these as they were so cheap and tasted pretty good too. . In the garden for most of the day, would be sat a bunch of older travelers who were mostly from England. Most of each and every day was spent passing chillums and pipes around and telling travel stories. The oldest and most travelled of them was a Yorkshire man called Fred who had a huge handle bar mustache and looked and sounded as if he belonged on the cover of the Beatles album, 'Sergeant Peppers lonely hearts club band'. He was travelling now, with his French wife, Anne and their children. He had his own smoking implement that he had made for himself and was very much attached to and always travelled with. It was a water pipe made from an empty 'John Masson' California wine carafe, with two thick sticks of bamboo coming out through a large cork in the top of the bottle. There was a diagonally set pipe with which to inhale from and a vertical pipe with the burn bowl on the top. The pipe would stay constantly hot throughout the day, as it made countless circuits of the table.

Gypsy would go and sit and smoke with them while waiting for Davy to finish the baking.

For the next few days Gypsy would load up and inevitably return before sunset with an empty basket and the money. As such all concerned were happy. Then one day Davy started making hash cookies for Gypsy to sell. Although Davy was a Scotsman, he was not mean with how much he put in each cake. Putting a gram of Himalayan charas in each slice. Gypsy wasn't going to try one of them. They looked too strong and he didn't want to be totally wiped out, he had no money and needed to work. Instead he would go into Umatis garden and get blasted on pipes and chillums, with the others before wandering off to the beach, where he would wander and stagger down the beach calling out in a loud voice, "hash cookies …hash cookies". It was even easier to empty the basket with this stock and the money was better. He was now making thirty five rupees a day, and saving half of it. He wanted to go to Kathmandu and was trying to save up to make the trip.

The hash cookies should have had a warning posted on them, they were just too strong for one person to eat on their own. Gypsy had effectively wiped out half of the traveler population at the beach for four days. People were lying there in the sand throughout the night unable to move as they were so stoned. It took most of them three or four days before they were recovered and back to normal.

Gypsy still managed to empty the basket each day, but now the customers stopped complaining about the price and started doing only half of a cake each which only fucked them up for two days at a time. In the end it was agreed by most of the beach crowd that one cake between four people was more than enough for anyone.

There was another baker from abroad, who was also busy at work and selling his products on the beach at that time. Chris from New Zealand made breads, all sorts of different ones, with different flavors and ingredients, he made different fruit breads and onion bread, garlic bread, herb bread, Ganja bread, etc.

He would peddle his bicycle along the beach, selling his bread from a wicker basket strapped to his back rack. His products were different from that that Gypsy sold and there were no conflicts or problems with them both selling in the same areas. Colva beach is one of the longest tropical beaches on earth, stretching approximately thirty kilometers from end to end and lined with coconut groves the whole way. Most of the tourists however, at that time were concentrated in a three or four kilometer area, close to Colva village, the other areas were still only used by fishermen and holy cows who enjoyed the view and the sea breeze.

Gypsy continued his selling work, staggering down the beach each day shouting out "hash cookies…..hash cookies" at the top of his voice. Newly arrived travelers would look at him and say, "wow, he's stoned out of his mind, those cookies must be good" and then proceeded to stop him and buy some.

Inevitably, even though he had warned them not to eat it all in one sitting he would come by the next day doing his rounds to find them still lying in the sand from the night before, with big silly grins on their faces and still unable to move to do anything more than reach for their bottle of water and even that was hard work for them.

At Umatis garden one day Fred started talking about one of his many overland journeys to India. He and Anne had been living in an apartment in Paris, from where some activities involving hash had been going on. One night, the flat got raided by an armed gang who figured that there was money in the place. They were right, but Fred and Anne had got their wits about them quickly and made it out of a window unseen as the gang was distracted by other people in the other rooms.

They had with them the cash, their passports and the pipe.

Deciding that with an incident like this happening right in their front room it was too dangerous to be hanging around in Paris any longer. So they jumped on a bus to Istanbul. From there they took buses across Turkey and crossed into Iran at Bazaar Gann and took a bus to Tehran and then another to Marshad from where they went to the Afghan border. On the Afghan side of the border, on seeing Fred with his hubble bubble pipe the customs officers ordered him into the customs shed and told him and Anne to sit down.

The shelves around the customs shed were lined with huge quantities of confiscated hashish and Fred and Anne wondered what they had done wrong that they had been ordered to stop here, after all they only had the pipe but nothing to load it with at the time.

The customs chief gave some money to a small boy who was loitering around and sent him across the road to buy some cold drinks from the vendors shacks. He then pulled down a couple of blocks of hashish from the shelf and proceeded to crumble a large quantity into the bowl of Fred's pipe. He then lit it and took a large toke before passing it to Fred. The rest of the customs officers then pretty much deserted their posts for the afternoon as they sat around inside the shed, incinerating large quantities of the confiscated contraband. They had never seen a pipe quite like Fred's and wanted to give it a try.

In the late afternoon with a large piece that the customs officers had given them as a going away present, they wobbled up the road to catch a bus to Herat and onward to Kabul.

Fred had many good stories about Afghanistan and said how friendly and kind the people were. Alan, back in Israel, had also given similar accounts of the place, it was a shame that it was then off limits, on account of the Soviet occupation and ensuing guerrilla war.

Gypsy enjoyed listening to other people's travel stories, they informed him of other places to check out on his own journey and he would want to ask questions so as to learn more.

Fred then spoke about the legendary psychic woman who worked for Indian customs on the Pakistani border near Amritsar and the psychic boy who worked on the Afghan border in the Khyber Pass. Fred had been backwards and forwards between Europe and India on the overland trail many times and knew his way. However, he said that although he liked Afghanistan and it's people it also had a side to it that was brutal and stone age. It wasn't at all uncommon in those days for a headless body to be found in one of the alleys of Kabul for example. It would usually be that of a French junkie who in their total ignorance of the culture or the mentality of the people of that area had ripped off or otherwise seriously offended one of the locals, then paid the ultimate price for it.

There were other nightmare stories too from places such as Mazaar el Shariff in the north.

One involved a young couple from Europe who didn't have a clue about the customs and dress codes of the area. They were driving along the road to Mazaar el Shariff when their jeep broke down. The man went on foot to try and find help leaving the woman who was wearing just shorts and a bikini top with the jeep.

A mad mullah and some of his retarded followers were walking along the road and saw her. The mullah apparently flew into an even more mad state than he was already in.

The man came back to find his girlfriend's severed head by the side of the road next to her body.

Gypsy continued to save money and work, each day. That was until he got sick. All of a sudden he was in incredible pain with stomach cramp. Then the Indian horrors set in and he found himself running to the toilet umpteen times in a day and vomiting and shitting all at the same time. He must have eaten something bad.

That night, Albert took him to the local doctor, Doctor Umesh who proceeded to give Gypsy huge quantities of every type of gastro intestinal medicine known to man and even gave him injections.

Gypsy and Albert headed back to the house and Gypsy rested for a couple of days and took the medicine. But it did no good and Gypsy felt even worse than ever. He continued the courses of medicine to the end but after a week he was still getting up in the middle of the night to run to the toilet and the stomach cramps were unbearable. Albert would come to check up on him and try and help him stagger back to his bed.

He tried the folk cures and other things that Fred and the others recommended but all to no avail. Eventually he borrowed a bicycle and cycled to the next village, Benalim where another doctor worked. His name was Robinson de Costa and after Gypsy described the symptoms and told him what Doctor Umesh had given him he gave Gypsy just one pack of medicine and said, "Do this to the end of the course and you will be better".

Gypsy did as he was instructed and this time he got better. He had spent most of what he had saved while he had been sick and for the last few days someone else did his round with the basket.

While he had been sick he had spent time chatting with a beautiful German woman by the name of Gabi. She was an artist and designer and rented a room from Albert for months at a time, each and every year. She let Gypsy use her paints. He knew that he had seen everything that was around him including the slums of Bombay in a series of dreams, as a small child. It had been many very long and crazy dreams that had shown him the journey he was presently making.

In Gabi's room, he sat down and painted a picture of a building that he had seen in the next part of the dream that related to where he was, a building with a brightly colored yellow, orange and red roof and sharp pointy angular structure. He left the picture with Gabi as he had no way to carry it with him on his journey.

He went back to selling his cakes, sandwiches and hash cookies along the beach and also added tolas of hash to his sales items (a tola, in hash terms, is always ten grams but for all other products, bar opium, the measure is eleven point sixty six grams).

There were women who would go along the beach selling fruit from baskets on their heads, they would laugh when they saw Gypsy, a white man from the west working just like them for similar money. They were always giving him fruits and sometimes he would share cakes with them (the cakes were a lot more expensive than the fruit).

One evening there was a bus parked down near the beach, it was from England and had West Yorkshire Express, World Travel, written neatly on it's side and had colorful wind breaks and tents around it. There was a large stereo blasting out Rolling Stones tracks. The people at the bus signaled Gypsy to come over.

They were a mixed race group of travelers from England who used their own bus to go too and fro from India to Europe, as they wished, moving all manner of people and products each way in order to make a living and stay travelling. Gypsy stayed there for a while with them, smoking joints as they got up and danced to jumpin jack flash and street fighting man.

Although it was very nice staying at Albert's house and Gypsy really liked Colva, this was not what Gypsy had come to India for. He was interested in Hinduism and mysticism. Goa being Christian, had very little of either.

He was walking along the road one afternoon when he realized that he didn't know where he was going or why he wanted to go there. It was time to leave.

Within ten minutes he had his bag packed, paid Albert, said his goodbyes and hit the road. He took a bus to Panjim and checked into a grim hostel dormitory and waited for the steamer that would be there in the morning. The next morning he joined the crowd on the steamer and set off for Bombay. He was not the only one with no money, there were two British travelers who also were broke. They were planning to use V.T.[Victoria terminus] station to sleep in until they could get some money sent or find a way out of India.

Apart from the worry of surviving in Bombay with hardly any money it was a nice journey, sitting on the deck chatting with some men of his own age who were from Bombay. They were all of different religions and talked and debated about their opinions of each other's faiths without anyone getting angry or feeling upset. They were good company and Gypsy joined them in the canteen for dinner as well.

The steamer made its usual stops at the bays and coves along the way and the long boats rowed out to meet them. Late in the evening the boat honked it's horn and another boat honked back. It was the other steamer that was going in the opposite direction. The Bombay to Goa steamer ran daily from each end and was serviced by two boats.

BOMBAY/INDIA

JANUARY 1984.

The next morning, the steamer pulled into its berth at Bombay. Things hadn't been easy for Gypsy, what with having hardly any money, the camera breaking and getting sick for so long.

As he came down the gang plank he made a silent prayer, "OK, I know I'm in India to find out the truth about life, the universe and everything. Show me the path and I will try to follow it."

He spent the day getting organized. First, he went to the Thomas Cook office and changed what little he had in foreign currency.

That money would have to be used for food only. Next, he went to the British Consulate to get some instructions as how to get money sent from his bank account in England. Then he went to a bank to get instruction sent to his bank.

That night he went to V.T. station to find the two from the boat. It would be safer to stay in a group with other travelers if he was going to have to sleep on the station floor.

On the way into the station, he was approached by a British man. He looked really straight and was dressed more smartly than Gypsy or the other travelers. He had greased back short hair and just carried a small straight looking bag. He approached Gypsy and asked him where he was going. He had a slightly posh London or home counties accent and could have been a businessman or diplomat. "I'm going to find some people I met on the steamer from Goa. We've got no money and are going to sleep here in the station" Gypsy told him. "I'm doing the same", said the man. "Do you mind if I join you and your friends?" "This was really freaky. What was a straight geezer from England doing crashing out in a station in Bombay?" Gypsy thought to himself.

The man followed Gypsy up through two flights of stairs, he found the two travelers from the steamer along with half a dozen other penniless travelers. They were setting out their bed rolls next to one of the stations buffet rooms that at the time was closed.

Gypsy pulled his bed roll from his shoulder bag and to his surprise, the straight looking guy pulled out an Indian sheet from his bag and stretched out under it and went to sleep on the hard floor.

The next morning at around seven thirty Gypsy woke up gradually, followed by the others. The canteen was open so they wandered in with their bags and had breakfast.

The canteen was self service but the food was good with lots of nice spicy dishes and snacks available.

The two from the steamer, Gypsy and the straight looking guy were sitting and chatting. Then the two from the boat got up and headed off to the port to see if they could find a ship where they could work a passage to Europe or Egypt or somewhere in that region.

This left Gypsy and the straight guy talking in the canteen. "So how long have you been in India for?" Gypsy asked him. "Ten years", replied the man. "Wow. Ten years. What do you do for work?" asked Gypsy again. "I do armed robberies", replied the man. "But if you've been in India for so long have you ever checked out any ashrams, spiritual places or teachers?" Gypsy asked. [Having lived in Israel for so long and now gotten moderately acclimatized to India he was not easily shocked by people or their ways] "Oh yes", he replied. "By the way, my name is John. I have spent most of my time in India in Ashrams where I learned about Vedic history and religion. What I'm doing now is something different from anything I've done before. I'll explain later." Gypsy went and bought two more chais and some snacks at the counter. When he returned, John, at Gypsy's prompting started to explain the Hindu concept of creation, which to put it in a nutshell was that:.... It is not a universe but a multiverse that we live in. And that Vishnu the ultimate God lies in the sea of Ambrosia sleeping. As he breathes he blows bubbles out of his mouth, each bubble is a dream of Vishnu and a universe too. All is made of Vishnu, so in effect we are God having a dream, according to this interpretation.

John then said, "If you would like we can go into town. I know some good places to eat, have you ever been to a thali house before?" "No", replied Gypsy. "Well, come along then, It's cheap and it's good. It's where a lot of office workers go to eat." On the way out he showed Gypsy where a bag deposit was, where he could leave his kit for the day. They then headed out into the city to find a thali house.

The streets were full of people and there were many street stands selling everything from clothes to imported electronic contraband goods (India in those days had very strict import rules and very high taxes for any item brought in for local consumption). There were London style red double decker buses plying their routes, some being pulled by articulated trucks and all manner of people dressed in all manner of fancy dress outfits.

They made their way to a thali house near the Hong Kong and Shanghai bank building. It was a huge and crazy place with several floors of people sitting down and eating. As soon as one person finished eating another would sit down to take his place. This place was feeding people on an industrial scale, conveyor belt style. Some of the different floors had to be reached via ladders and not one bit of space went to waste, with tables and benches crammed into the tiniest nooks and corners. In the main dining halls, there were hundreds of people sitting at many tables and long benches, all eating with their right hand, without cutlery. There was only one dish on the menu. 'Vegetarian thali' and a full thali would cost four rupees at that time.

Gypsy had never seen a plate of food like this before, it was incredible. There were three different kinds of curried vegetable dishes, two different dahls, yoghurt, a mound of rice, a stack of fresh hot puris (like a fried chapatti), a dollop of hot pickle and a dessert of rice pudding with cardamon. This was all laid out in small stainless steel bowls on a large high edged stainless steel plate. It looked, smelled and tasted wonderful, like the best food that Gypsy had ever tasted in his life. It would be worth sticking around Bombay for a while if only to eat thali twice a day, not to mention some of the other great food that he had seen, smelled or tasted.

During the afternoon they went and sat in a park. John then asked Gypsy if he could spare twenty ruppees to go and buy a bag of weed with. Gypsy sat and waited while John went off to score the bag. He returned after a short time and as they talked John hollowed out a bidi [Indian cigarette made from a small tobacco leaf rolled into a cone, stuffed with tobacco and held together by a piece of fine cotton looped around it] and filled it with weed. As they smoked it John continued to explain the Hindu understanding of life and death. "According to the scriptures and visions of yogis, a human birth is rare and most people because of their state of consciousness or lack of it, are doomed to come back as animals. Eating animals, especially cow is a bad idea, they have the same kind of consciousness as humans and also have a family life", he told Gypsy.

Gypsy had noticed this in Goa while watching a family of rats walking across one of the beams of the roof of Albert's veranda. "The natural state of the soul is bliss", John continued. "Yet most people live in misery. Look at the people walking along the pavement. Look carefully and see how many of the faces are smiling or look happy."

Gypsy stared at the passing crowd for a full five minutes. And although hundreds of people passed by, virtually none of them looked happy or relaxed. Most were walking quickly with worried or otherwise unhappy expressions on their faces.

John was right, most people do not have happy lives and now Gypsy could see it for himself. He had not noticed before but now he could see how most people live very unhappy lives.

"Anyway", said John, "No matter what. There are four miseries that are there for all and unavoidable. They are; birth, disease, old age and death. This planet is a hellish place and by no means is it the home of the soul.

That night the other two came back from the port, they had had no luck and were going to try again the next day.

For the next few days, Gypsy sat and listened to John and asked questions about Hindu and Vedic thought and beliefs. He was perhaps the only person that Gypsy would have listened to at the time. He was still furious about how he had been treated by his parents, the Yeshiva, the schools that he had been incarcerated in in England and the unforgivable way he was treated by the British in general for not living the sort of life that they thought he should. He saw all that was around him in the west as his enemy, because after all, that was how they had treated him, putting him down, disapproving of him and ridiculing him no matter what he did.

John was an outlaw and didn't fit to any of society's nasty moulds. He looked like David Niven in his role as the phantom in the 'Pink Panther' movies. Most of all, unlike that bunch of pompous, arrogant, aggressive, snobbly narrow minded types who's company he had the misfortune to be in during his time in England, John was interested in divine truth and had been out of the west for over ten years. He didn't poo poo questions of any type and his answers, though different from anything he had heard before seemed to make sense.

The next day they jumped the train with no tickets, up to Poona on the Deccan plateau and used the benches at Poona station as their digs for that night.

They tried to use a cheap guest house but when they went to the door, an Indian hustler followed them in and tried to claim the credit for bringing them to the place in order to claim a commission. As such, John cursed him in Hindi and they walked out and back to the station in disgust. When they went to a local thali house, one of the imbecile, cretin waiters, started trying to mock them, thinking that they wouldn't understand him, they walked out of there too. As they left John cursed the manager in Hindi for employing such a rude and stupid waiter. This was almost certain to have cost the waiter his job, which was the idea.

Back at the station they went to the station café and asked for two cups of chai. The man serving was dressed in religious clothes with a large Shiva symbol painted on his forehead. He was obviously someone deeply involved with his religion.

He slammed the two cups down and barely filled a third of each cup as he splashed the tea carelessly between the counter and their cups while all the while giving them hateful and jealous scowling stares. When they asked him to fill the cups properly, he splashed a drop more in each cup while snarling and showing his teeth. "You may wear the clothes of a holy man but you behave like a fallen soul", John told him in Hindi as they walked away.

It seemed that there was a hostile attitude towards foreigners in Poona and Gypsy asked John why. It was explained to him that some of the people who had come from the west to the Bhagwan Shri Rajneesh Ashram which was barely a mile from the station, had no idea about sensitivity to local ways and customs. Rather than keeping some parts of their spiritual practice to the confines of the Ashram or their own private accommodation they were doing things in public that would be deemed offensive enough to get them arrested and taken to court even back in the west. However they expected the locals to put up with anything and everything that they did.

In those days, the Rajneesh people or 'Sanyasins' as they called themselves, were easy to spot, as they all wore a uniform of orange clothes with a black malla around their neck, with a photograph of the Guru, 'Bhagwan', in the center.

They had at that time mostly left Poona and gone to a huge ranch that they had bought in Oregon, USA, where sporadic reports of excesses and madness emanated from and into the local Indian press. There were still however a small number who had stayed on, mostly Indian, but also one or two Westeners at the Poona Ashram, just to keep the light burning there, as it was. Gypsy had seen two of them passing through the station.

John explained to him how the different spiritual paths worked and what result each was likely to achieve. The path that he followed was called "Bakti" (devotion, in English), the path of love, devotion and surrender to the ultimate Godhead, the personalization of the supreme God or fountain of goodness.

There were other paths too, John explained.

The path of the impersonalists was one of them. It focused on union with the one energy, or Brahman, which according to him was just the effulgence around the God head. The Rajneesh path according to him was one of these. "You may reach this through hard work and sacrifice, you may be able to stay there for a while, like twenty or thirty thousand years. But after a time the soul will become restless, as it intuitively knows that there is more and it will have to leave and re enter the material dimensions, in order to find it's way home" John explained. He also said that the natural state of the soul was to be in total devotion and service to the Godhead. He went on further to say that the reason that we find ourselves in this screwed up, painful world is that when we were in the spiritual dimensions beyond the bubble dream of this universe, that we somehow fucked up and became jealous of the Godhead and in so doing the consciousness/awareness found it's self in this strange foul dream that we call life.

He continued to speak about the nature of the soul, explaining how we have three bodies, one physical, one astral, that is made of mind, memory and karma, which is effectively a ghost body, existing within other dimensions of this universe (somewhere within the so called 'dark matter') and thirdly the celestial body, the soul, which is effectively non-existent within this universe, but is the watcher and awareness behind all life, the dreamer watching the dream, so to speak.

He also explained that according to Vedic thinking or knowledge, beyond the bubbles of the different universes, lies the spiritual sky with infinite stars and planets, where beings live in a functional way, beyond time or space or good or bad as we know it. This universe is as if we have fallen asleep and are having a nightmare. "Nothing is satisfying, or at least not for long. A man has a million dollars but it is not enough, he wants twenty million dollars but again when he has it is not enough, he wants a hundred million and so on, like a hungry ghost. But it is madness, because he can only sleep in one bed at a time and eat only three meals a day or drive one car or ride one horse or motorbike at a time. People try to own all manner of things but in so doing, the paradox is that they become a prisoner to that which they own, always afraid of losing whatever it is that they think they own. In truth we own nothing, not even our bodies, which we occupy for such a short amount of time before they degenerate back into the earth.

This world that looks so very encompassing is to all effects and purposes an illusion, a dream. The secret is to be able to wake up and see it.

They jumped the train back to Bombay the next day. On the way, John told Gypsy how he had been a Hari Krishna monk for many years, but one day he just snapped and left it all behind as he could no longer stand to go without sex. Since leaving he had fucked his way around many of the brothels of India as he made up for lost time (AIDS was not yet on the radar back in that time).

When they got back to Bombay, John offered to give Gypsy a tour of Bombay's infamous red light area.

That evening they took the train from V.T. station to Dadar and then another train to Bombay central station, where they dropped their bags at the luggage deposit and then walked to the 'cages'. It was called this because in days gone by the pimps would kidnap young girls from rural areas and bring them to Bombay where they would be held against their will, in cages. At that time, in the eighties, it was believed that this practice had been largely put to an end.

They reached the cages area after a short walk through muddy half made up streets, passing the usual industrious small street sellers and cafes along the way. It was a bizarre sight, with the area being wall to wall brothels and nothing much else. There were still cages in the area but for the most part the doors were open and the women were out in the street, trying to catch clients. There were however one or two shop fronts with closed, locked, cage doors, with young women sitting behind them. There were clubs with dancing women and the like and a lot of men walking around with guilty and worried expressions on their faces, similar to that on a pet hound that has just eaten the main ingredient for a family dinner, he knew that it was wrong but he couldn't help himself.

It was most amusing to watch the quick glances they all gave in each direction to make sure no one they knew was watching them, before they leapt like greased lightening through the door of their chosen whore house. It was like watching scenes out of an old black and white comedy or a Peter Sellers movie such as the "Pink Panther".

Most of the buildings went up three to four floors and John took Gypsy up for a tour of a couple of them. There was room after room full of women who would try to beckon them in.

Often the place for performance was just a bed with a curtain around it. It was perhaps one of the most dirty, unhygienic and smelly places on earth. Some of the women looked good but the surroundings were not exactly a turn on. Besides, Gypsy was broke and could not even afford their modest fees even if he had wanted to. After getting out of the rancid buildings they took a walk nearby to Falkland road, which was a smaller version of the cages. This place was even more foul as one side of the street was just normal dirty Indian brothels with women. The other side of the street was too dodgy to walk on as it was lined with 'Hijaras' (eanuchs) who were men who had done half a D.I.Y sex change operation upon themselves and were dressed as women. It was a stomach churning and highly disturbing sight. Both Gypsy and John beat a hasty retreat back to central station. After that strange spectacle they stopped to drink a chai at a chai stand on the street.

"You mean that you've been screwing around in places like that?', asked Gypsy. "You must have caught a dose a bunch of times". "Yes, I have used places like that", John replied. "And as far as diseases go, I've been lucky and only caught one forty eight hour dose, which I cleared up with penicillin and nothing more. "Bloody hell the smell alone was enough to put me off", replied Gypsy. "Wouldn't it just be better to find just one good woman and stay with her?" he asked. "Yes, but then your freedom is gone as you get pestered and nagged. With hookers everyone gets what they want and I don't lose my freedom. Besides, I want to try hundreds of different women, not just one and this way of doing it is better and perhaps, more fair for all concerned".

After retrieving their bags from the luggage room they pulled out their bedrolls and crashed out on the station, along with several thousand other people.

The next day they took the local train back through Dadar to Churchgate station, which was another terminus like V.T. (Victoria terminus) and 'Central'. It was located maybe one kilometer from V.T. and was more close to the Colaba area, which houses 'The Gateway of India', the Taj Mahal hotel and the famous Leopold's bar and eatery. .

Just past Leopold's bar and following the pavement around to the left, then crossing that road and taking the first turning on the right, John showed Gypsy a good place to get breakfast or a snack. The shop made spicy potato dishes and samosas. A plate of two potato cakes with curry sauce or a plate of two samosas with chutney would cost two rupees. It tasted incredibly good, as did just about all the food that Gypsy had tried in Bombay.

One of the other great delicacies of Bombay that Gypsy also developed a fondness for was pav baji (pronounced, pow baji), this was often sold on the street from hand carts. For those who don't know this dish, it is like a potato and tomato curry, a bit like dahl but generally both more greasy and spicy, it is normally served in a snack like portion with toasted bread rolls.

Even though his money was very low the price of food was so low even in Bombay where accommodation was exorbitantly high, that he knew that he would be able to survive for a few weeks, as long as he didn't have to pay for a room. There were free showers in the second class waiting rooms of all the major stations of the city and he could normally gain access to them.

John asked him to join him doing either begging or a fraud, but although Gypsy was in a kind of desperate situation [especially if there was a problem with the bank transfer, that in India could (and did) take weeks]. He just could not bring himself to do such things. He had worked whenever he wanted or needed something, even in Goa. Begging or fraud were so far beneath where his self respect was prepared to go as to be totally incomprehensible to him.

He still had the camera however and John knew a place where he could get it fixed and he also knew another place to sell it. So off the camera went for repair.

They sat and talked in a park for the rest of the day while John hollowed out countless bidis and filled them with weed, while continuing to explain about such things as the Vedas and other books of ancient knowledge. Apparently, some of the books spoke of life on other planets and stars throughout the universe and also in other dimensions. In some of the books, flying machines and missiles of war were described. Gypsy asked John about the many Gods of Hinduism. "There is only one true God even in Hinduism", he explained. "The one true God or Godhead is expressed in many forms e.g. Vishnu, Krishna, Ram, Nasringadev,

Narain etc.". "There are others who are demi Gods or to put it more accurately, powers or the intelligence behind them, within this universe".

Some of them by the descriptions given sounded like they were extra terrestrial or extra dimensional beings.

He went on to say that according to the Vedas, the age that we are now in is known in Sanskit as Kuli Yuga (age of ignorance, in English) and that prior ages have seen far greater technological advances than we know today. There was knowledge of life on other planets and dimensions and possibly the ability to journey there. There was great knowledge of science, medicine and astronomy etc, of which all the books that today are available are just a poor shadow.

According to many of the books, in days gone by they had not only flying machines but also other tools that gave them incredible powers. Also human life and highly advanced societies were described as being here on earth for millions of years. The history taught in the west was both wrong and extremely limited.

Then he started to speak about reincarnation and how a mixture of karma and desire guide the soul to its next body. "What a person is thinking of at the point of death in one life will be what guides them, along with their karma, both good and bad to the body of their next incarnation. For example, a woman who likes lying around and posing a lot might come back as a tree, a man who likes to eat animals is likely to come back as one, as are people who like dogs and cats or other pets or animals at risk of retuning as such animals in their next life. Equally a man who dies, thinking of his wife or girlfriend is likely to return to this world in the body of a woman, as is a woman who dies thinking of a man or boy that she loves, likely to return as a man. This according to Hinduism is the explanation for the phenomena of homosexuality and lesbianism.

Walking from Colaba to V.T. that evening, among exotic looking Hindu and Zorostrian temples, chai shops and the sea of humanity in their different and varied colorful outfits and costumes, Gypsy's head was swimming from all that John had spoken. It all, or at least most of it, seemed to make sense of life a lot more than any other ideas he had ever heard before on this subject and there seemed at least, to be no ugly loose ends or contradictions, unlike Judaism or Christianity.

Nevertheless, he had very little money and was sleeping on railway station floors and now his whole concept of reality was being blown clean, out of the door. And here he was in this strange land, so far from anything that was familiar. It was all a bit mind blowing.

Back at the station that night the two would be sailors were back. They were having no luck at finding a ship that would take them on. Gypsy told them about the trip to Poona and the trip around the cages. When he spoke about the cages they became interested and asked if they could see it as well.

So off they all trotted, down to the platforms below and took a train to Dadar, then another one to Central station, then they walked through the filthy streets to the cages. They went up and down through the hot smelly buildings as John led the tour.

But it was on Falkland road where one of them nearly got himself into trouble. Gypsy and John had forgotten to warn them about what was on the other side of the street,

figuring that they had eyes and would be able to work it out for themselves. Wrong! One of them had to be grabbed by the other three and dragged away to safety. "But she only wants eight rupees for the whole night", he whined as they dragged him down the road. "Yes, but can't you see it's not a woman You cheapskate bastard?." Gypsy told him. "Are you sure? It looked real to me". He carried on. After that near misadventure, they headed back to Central and took the train back to V.T.

The next day, again Gypsy sat and asked questions while John explained more on Hindu understanding as he spoke about the Bagavad Gita and Maha Bharata, while his hands worked with nimble speed, filling bidis with weed. Finally Gypsy asked him where the best Ashram would be to learn the practice of techniques that could take him to Enlightenment. "I recommend that you at least take a look at the Hare Krishnas", he said. "They are the cleanest and most true to Vedic teachings that I have found, They may look like a cult but here in India they are one of the most highly respected spiritual groups that there are, their traditions go back through history and are true followers of the Vedic dharma".

The next day they parted ways and Gypsy wandered around central Bombay in a daze. With all of his previous concepts of what was important in life completely blown away he no longer felt sure that he knew who or what he was. Here was a whole strange, completely new way to see things that however seemed to make a whole lot more sense than anything that he had heard before, it was the first tine he had come across a religion that spoke about reincarnation, life on other planets and what lies beyond the universe.

He had wondered as a child if this existence was not a dream. What's more many of the other things that he had heard over the last four days had struck chords deep within him too. Before he had made that prayer as he got off of the Goa steamer he had a feeling that learning the truth would be a rather mind blowing and bizarre experience, which was why it had taken such extreme circumstances to drive him to make that ultimate prayer. He had prayed to know the truth, but it was truly uncanny how quickly such a learned teacher had presented himself. He had never had a prayer answered like that before. He knew that it could not have been a coincidence, as John had been the sort of person that could earn Gypsy's respect and attention, more than even an Indian yogi could have. He spoke in a way that Gypsy could understand too.

He couldn't think straight as his mind tried to digest all that he had heard in the past four days, his old self had been totally destroyed and in it's place was a different person, as if he had been reborn. There was still the same watcher behind the eyes, but he could no longer even remember how his concept of life had looked before this very long conversation.

He wandered around feeling totally fucked up and with virtually no money in his pockets, in this strange city. He saw dead bodies lying in the street and people dying there too. There were people with chronic deformities begging, there was a group of Tanzanians who had got there by stowing away on ships. They slept in a park and were mostly addicted to smack. There were children begging and living on the pavement. Bells rang in temples, as worshippers entered, the aroma of incense floated in the air, mixing with both the aroma of food being cooked and the smell of open drains too. And around all of this, for the most part, life just went on, as people went about their daily lives and their work.

After a few days, John appeared again and they collected and sold the camera. John took a ten percent commission for fixing the deal and Gypsy had some extra survival money. After three weeks of sleeping in various railway stations and with no money arriving at the bank, Gypsy felt desperate enough to ask for some help. He had wanted to make this journey without any help from home but this was beyond a joke.

He went to the central telephone and telegraph office, booked his place in the line and filled out the details on the form. The place was heaving with people but he was the only foreigner who was there that day. It was a long wait of maybe eight or ten hours before he got his turn for a call and even then someone cut in on the line after only two minutes, but he had enough time to explain his predicament and asked to borrow two hundred pounds and for it to be sent to the Thomas Cook office in Bombay.

Two days later, he had the money and went and checked into the salvation army hostel, which was the cheapest clean accommodation in Bombay, with dorm beds then costing fifty rupees a night.

There was a large notice by the reception desk saying, "No alcohol or hashish smoking in the rooms". When he got to his allotted bed on the third or fourth floor a Frenchman in a Gandhi outfit on the bunk below his own had just finished making a large cone shaped-joint, laced with opium. As Gypsy climbed up on to his bunk, the Frenchman lit his joint. After a few tokes he passed it up to Gypsy who took several tokes before passing it back and lying very still. The irony was not missed on him, the notice downstairs had neglected to mention opium. It felt good to be in a normal bed after three weeks of station floors and the opium took all of the aches from his body, it was good to have a moment out from the stress and pain.

He met some other travelers at the hostel who were heading north to Udaipur. Gypsy figured that he'd join them and use it as a way to get to Kathmandu.

The next day his money turned up but not before a wild goose chase around the city. The money had turned up at the wrong bank.

Anyway, Gypsy now had some money in his pocket and was ready to join the others travelling to Udaipur.

That night they caught a train out of Bombay to Ahmadabad in Gujarat. Travelling second class with no reservations they slept on their bags or stretched out on the carriage floor in the odd spaces available.

Early the next morning before dawn the train pulled into Ahmadabad station and they all piled off and changed platforms to the narrow gauge lines.

After a wait of almost an hour an antiquated steam powered locomotive came chugging along the tracks pulling a line of carriages behind it. It slowed down and stopped in front of them, letting out a loud whistle as it did so. This was the train to Udaipur. They got on board and soon the train was pulling away slowly out from the station. For the first few hours they were too tired to do anything but sleep. The train was almost empty at that time (which in India was an extreme rarity) so they were able to stretch out on the seats. As the morning wore on, the train made stops and more people got on board but the train was not even half full (quarter full by Indian standards) by mid day. The stations that it stopped at were small and almost deserted with not much sign of human habitation in the immediate area.

At one o'clock the train stopped for lunch at an almost deserted station between two hills with arid desert type plants growing around the immediate vicinity. Most of the people on board got off and made a queue where a man was serving up steaming hot curry and chappatis.

Gypsy joined the queue, he felt more than ready for some lunch. It was served on a plate made from pressed leaves (possibly the most organically disposable plate in the world) and chai was served in disposable terracotta cups. It all tasted good enough and soon they were back on the train as it pulled out of the station and chugged its way up through the arid Rajasthan hills, making its regular stops at the small stations that lined the route.

From the train, they could see monkeys jumping through the dry and leafless under growth. The occasional chai walla got on board, at different stations along the way, with a giant hot teapot and a galvanized steel bucket that was full of cups. He would then chant out that famous Indian mantra, "chai chai garam chai", then dish out hot chai in china cups to people before coming back afterwards to collect the empty cups and the money.

The toilets on board were of the usual Indian high tech variety, the cubicle had a hole in the floor through which the tracks could be viewed, at least it stopped the cubicle from smelling too bad, that was unless a train stopped to take a long break somewhere. Then the smell from the tracks would waft up through the hole and the cubicle would start to smell like a kennel.

The train pulled up at Udaipur station in the late afternoon and they all got off covered in soot. The carriage windows had been open the for the whole journey. The doors had been open the whole way and They had all been sitting in them watching the wildlife as the black smoke had been blowing around them.

They took a horse buggy to a place that one of them had read about that was Several kilometers out of the city. Pratap Country Inn was owned and run by a Maharajah and he provided horse riding facilities and bicycle rentals to his guests. Despite this, the place was neither snooty nor expensive and catered to travelers rather than tourists. The Maharajah had graying hair and was obviously in his fifties. Despite this he seemed to attract the attentions of his young foreign female guests, this was something that he obviously relished and who could blame him?

Out on the road near the guest house men could be seen riding camels with large piles of hay also loaded on their humps. It was a strange sight to see; a camel with a haystack on its back and a man balanced on the top of the haystack who was trying to steer the camel.

The next day after they had arrived, they all went into town together. Everyone wanted to go and see the famous lake palace that had featured in the last James Bond movie, 'Octopussy'

Taking a boat out to it, they ordered the most expensive pot of tea that any of them had ever had in their lives. It was just a regular pot of tea, nothing special. It was just that everything in the place was ridiculously overpriced. There was no doubt that the palace was beautiful and that incredible work had gone into building it but that still did not justify the outrageous prices. If they had stayed for lunch, then they could have kissed goodbye to large junks of their travel budgets, and that would have been for just dahl, rice and chapattis.

After a brief look around, they decided to take the boat back to the shore and went for a walk along the lakeside and into town. Gypsy had been travelling when Octopussy' was released and had never seen it, but it was nice to see the lake palace, anyway. Later while walking back from town on his own, an Indian man on a bicycle stopped and offered Gypsy a lift on the back rack. There was only one guest house on that road, tourism was not a big business and as such the locals were still very friendly and helpful. Walking along the road, people would smile and wave all of the time. The locals were mostly farmers who lived much as their ancestors had done, probably for millennia.

The cyclist dropped Gypsy off outside of the guest house and smiled and waved goodbye. Gypsy stayed for a few more days at the guest house, but it was blowing dust storms for a lot of the time which sometimes made breathing difficult and they would wake up in the morning choking from it, it was a most unpleasant feeling. After a while Gypsy didn't think he could take a moment more of the Rajasthan dust and decided that it was time to get out of Rajasthan quickly if he did not want to choke to death in his sleep. He would have to abandon his plan to go to Kathmandu via this route for now.

He went into town to find a ticket back south, he had paid his bill at the guest house and had his bag with him. There was a travel agent's shop window with adverts for bus services to a variety of places. He knew of an Ashram a hundred kilometers from Bombay, that Chris the baker had told him about back in Goa. So he bought a ticket to Bombay and then the travel agent took him to the bus on the back of his vespa.

It was a hairy ride with the hairy, bearded, Sikh travel agent swerving, stopping, dodging, etc at such a pace it was incredible. Gypsy had never seen anyone drive in such a manner. It was amazing that there weren't crashes along the way. After his ride with Evil Kanevel across the city Gypsy boarded the bus to Bombay on a muddy lot by the side of the road. It was described as a super deluxe video bus. Though the seats were reasonably comfortable when compared with wooden benches, it was not exactly what anyone could by any stretch of the imagination call luxury. But hey, this was India.

The video part however, was true and non stop Hindi Bollywood movies were shown on a television set hooked to a VHF video machine, which was set up in a glass compartment above the door to the passenger compartment. Through the day and the night the videos played at full volume as so as to distort the sound grotesquely, occasionally the tape got stuck in the machine which would cause the picture to go into contortions and the sound to wail repeated screaming noises that were even worse than the noise of the Indian actress's singing or dub, as it probably was. The multiple cacophony continued through the night as the bus rolled and bumped it's way along the potholed roads to the big city.

They arrived in the early morning and Gypsy went to V.T. station to find out about trains to Igatpuri. After some breakfast in the station and a wander around he went and found his train and was soon on his way.

The train went north east up the tracks, stopping at various stations where an assortment of different colorful people got on and off the train at different stops, with the usual chai wallas and people selling nuts, bananas, sandwiches, samosas and all sorts of assorted snacks, among them. It was like being on board a mobile bazaar. The train would pull to a stop outside of a village where there was no visible sign of a station and honk its horn. At which point a colorful collection of villagers would come running out from the buildings and climb aboard. Gypsy was sitting on his bag on the floor. There was a Baba (holy man) sitting on the floor near him. Gypsy pulled out a packet of Bidis taking out one for himself, he offered one to the Baba who took it and smiled back, it was a moment of communication that needed no language. India had taken a hold on him and he was starting to feel at home with this culture in a strange way that he could not verbalize, not then and still not even now. Even at the time of writing India gave him something, a kind of freedom that he just did not feel anywhere else on earth.

The religious and spiritual paths were certainly a part of it. For the most part there was harmony between the different peoples of different paths and faiths. Hinduism was so tolerant that it honored each and every other religion and as such, India through millennia, had welcomed in people of many different faiths. There had been the Parsis and Jews from the Middle East along with both Shia and Sunni Muslims, some coming in as refugees. There were Christians and various sects of Buddhists. The last great influx of refugees had been the Tibetans in the nineteen fifties, who were fleeing the Chinese invaders of their country. Nehru who was at that time the Prime Minister of India welcomed the Dalai Lama and all of his people and gave them plots of land to establish as refugee camps, even giving the Dalai Lama a place to set up a government in exile. The Indians didn't have a pot to piss in but they still shared with others in need. In India there is a freedom to debate on all subjects without people getting cranky or intolerant, as much as they might in the lands to the west. Dogma holds no credence or respectability in the Hindu/Vedic culture. Science and religion are not opposite forces, but one and the same in a Hindu's eye. It is all about the search for the truth with objectivity being a key ingredient.

The train eventually stopped at Igat Puri station shortly after dark. Gypsy got off and walked into the village and found a guest house. He dropped his bag and went out and found the ashram. It was a Goenka, Vipassana Ashram that offered two week and ten day silent retreats.

Mr. Goenka was a businessman from India who discovered the benefits of the Buddhist system of Vipassana meditation (putting the awareness with the breath or watching the breath as it goes in and out in order to still the mind. As it is only when there are no distractions and the mind is still, that the truth can reveal it's self to the seeker). He then went about setting up centers throughout India, like the one at Igat Puri that offered two week silent retreats on a regular basis to all comers. The fee was a donation from the heart or whatever anyone wished or could afford to give. Not just that but no one was allowed to give until they finished the course.

There was not going to be a retreat for a while but the people there were friendly and offered him some dinner of dahl sabji and chappatis. They told him that he would be welcome to come and join the retreat when it was due to start, in a couple of weeks time. They also suggested some local sites to see, such as Nasik which was an hour or two away by train and the Ajanta caves that were less than a day away.

Gypsy went back to the guest house and went to sleep. The next day he jumped on a train up the tracks to Nasik and enjoyed a couple of hours on board the great railway bazaar, as swarms of vendors descended on the train at every station, often jumping on board before the train had pulled to a stop. They would almost run through the carriages desperately shouting out their sales pitch or the names of the goods that they were selling. A couple of hours later Gypsy jumped down from the train at Nasik station.

Nasik was a holy town with ghats by its small river. Gypsy took a wander around but after seeing the place, he decided that there was nothing that he could see that made him want to stay there for the night. It was a typical scruffy and dirty little Indian town with the same sorts of shops and same rubbish lining the streets as anywhere else.

He went back to the station and bought a ticket to Aurangabad, which is near to where the Ajanta caves are located and then waited for a train going in that direction.

Once more, he was on board the mobile bazaar sitting on his bag in the corridor of yet another overcrowded carriage. While sitting there he pulled his map from his pocket and asked someone where the final destination of this train was.

When he was told that it was going to a city in the centre of the country that was halfway to the Nepalese border, Gypsy decided that he would miss Aurangabad and the caves and instead ride the train north and then find a route via buses and other trains to Kathmandu.

He was busy looking at his map and plotting the best possible route to Kathmandu when the train stopped at a large station where he was meant to change trains if he was to go to Aurangabad. He was sitting there waiting for the train to pull out and head north when a ticket inspector which in those days were something of a rare sight, jumped on the train and pushed his way through the crowded compartment until he was in front of Gypsy who was sitting on his holdall bag in a quiet corner almost out of sight. "Where's your ticket? Where are you going?" he almost shouted, Gypsy showed him his ticket and tried to explain that he wanted to stay on board to the end of the line and would be happy to pay the difference, but the man both didn't understand him and wouldn't understand him. He was already fixed in his tiny little mind about what he wanted Gypsy to do and was now operating on automatic pilot and refusing to wake up and take notice (one of the annoying symptoms of iodine deficiency). "No, no", he said. "You must get down here and change trains." Try as he might to explain, the only way to get rid of this cretin was to get off of the train and walk away.

At this point Gypsy was in no doubt that some unseen force was at work to stop him reaching Kathmandu and that it would be pointless and only invite problems and disasters to continue to pursue this track. At first as he got off the train pursued by this arsehole of a ticket inspector he was laughing hysterically like a madman. He could of banged his head on the ground with frustration. Why had this mother fucker pushed past everyone else to reach him? He probably couldn't even see Gypsy, he was sitting down low and his face would not have been visible from the window. It was beyond bizarre or uncanny how many times that he had been thwarted from his goal of reaching the hippie rainbow's end of Kathmandu, Nepal. In disgust and anger at whatever unseen being or energy it was that kept playing these tricks on him, he went to the ticket office and bought a ticket with a sleeper berth on the next train available back to Bombay. He had had enough and decided that if he couldn't get to Kathmandu at this time then it was time to leave India and travel on to Thailand.

It wasn't long before his train to Bombay arrived. He had been so very pissed off by what had happened that he had decided to pay the extra and go first class. It had not been expensive and he needed it at the time, as he really didn't want to be in a cramped carriage with hundreds of other people stepping over and on him through the night again.

First class was very pleasant with four sleeper berths in each closed door compartment and no crowds or vendors, just a polite steward who would bring chai and food as ordered. He was sharing the compartment with an elderly Parsi couple who were on their way home to Bombay from a trip to see friends. They were both educated and spoke fluent English. Gypsy enjoyed a conversation with them about the religions of India and life in Bombay before they all went to sleep.

Early in the morning at about 5:30 am the train pulled into Bombay central. Gypsy got down off the train and walked to the local metropolitan lines and jumped onto a local train to Santa Cruz, near the airport and took a taxi to the international terminal. But there was no one at the Biman Bangladesh counter or even at their upstairs office. He had no choice but to go into the city and wait for their main ticket office to open. It was still very early so he decided to walk back to Santa Cruz station. It was a distance of several kilometers. But when he got there he still felt like walking, so he walked up the line past several more stations in the direction of Dadar before getting onboard a train into the city.

Later in the morning, he found the Biman Bangladesh office and went in and asked if he could miss the stops in Dakkar and Rangoon and book straight through to Bangkok. There was no problem with that but he was told that they could only book him through as far as Dhaka and that he would be wait listed from Dhaka to Bangkok, he was booked on the flight that would be going in two days time.

He checked himself back in at the Salvation Army hostel and with nothing else to do went out to explore more of the city and find something to eat.

He had noticed a synagogue in the Colaba area and as it was just before sunset on a Friday afternoon, for some strange reason he decided to go in and join the Shabbat prayers. He was still feeling bewildered by everything and wanted to reach out for something familiar, even if it was his Jewish roots that he now felt unconnected to.

The synagogue was upstairs above several shops. Inside, even though it was both ornate and large there were barely twenty people there. They were mostly of Baghdadi origin. Their ancestors had moved from Iraq to India for whatever reasons centuries before, but now their numbers were low as most of them had emigrated to Israel.

The Friday night prayers started and Gypsy joined in as they read from page after page of Hebrew prayer texts. Eventually it was over and Gypsy along with the one other foreigner who was present, a New York Jew, were invited for Shabbat dinner at a nearby house. It was a very opulent place and had smartly dressed servants who served the food at the large table that they were sitting at.

The house was owned by a middle aged woman who throughout the excellent dinner spoke about how good it was to be living in India and how well the Indians treated the Jewish community. "I couldn't wish for a better place to live", she said. "There is no anti-Semitism and the Indian people are just so polite and courteous and it's genuine".

The American was in Bombay because he wished to adopt a street child to raise in America as his way of doing some good in the world. It was explained to Gypsy that apart from the Baghdadi Jews, Bombay had a far more ancient and larger Jewish community called the 'Benai Israel'. They had only recently been discovered and recognized by the world Jewish community. Israel and the Jewish agency sent them money to support them but as they did not suffer any form of persecution, they were told by the Israeli authorities that unless they could afford their own way to Israel then they would have to wait in India until those suffering religious and racial persecution such as the Soviet and East European Jews plus the 'Falashas' from Ethiopia were assisted in resettling in Israel first. In the meantime, the Jewish agency gave each family a monthly allowance to help them stave off poverty (Yes, believe it or not, there are some poor Jewish communities scattered around the planet, contrary to popular beliefs)

Soon the excellent dinner party was over after cognac and coffee and everyone headed off into the warm night air of Bombay.

The next evening before heading to the airport to wait for his early morning flight he went back to the synagogue for end of Shabbat prayers.

To his amazement he bumped into an old acquaintance from Israel. Zev, the American was there when he arrived.

"Hi, so you made it here to India then" said Zev. "Where are you heading for now?" he asked. "I'm going to the airport to get a flight to Dhaka and if I'm lucky I should be able to get a flight from there to Bangkok. I've been wait listed, I just hope that I don't get stuck at Dhaka", Gypsy explained. "Ah, that's good, we can go to the airport together. I've got $5,000 worth of rupees that I made from acting in Bollywood movies and I need to change it into a more useful currency, before I leave the country" said Zev.

He explained to Gypsy that when the war in Lebanon started to wind down, he had left and gone back to India where he had been living before. For a time, he had been in Afghanistan as a volunteer fighter with the Mujahidin, fighting against the Russians. He told Gypsy about how he had been at the Mujahidin bases that were inside huge caves inside the mountains where whole convoys of vehicles could be hidden. "It was incredible, they could drive vehicles inside and apart from arms dumps and accommodation they had hospitals and all manner of things in the tunnels and caves" he said. The prayers started and they stopped talking and joined in. Half an hour later prayers were over and they resumed talking.

Gypsy grabbed his bag and they headed out to the airport. There were heavy currency restrictions in India at that time and the not so good value black market was the only way of changing money if you didn't have certificates from banks showing that you had changed at least that amount into rupees while in India.

Zev had another idea. At the airport he got Gypsy and all of the other travelers who were willing to help him, by using their unneeded certificates to change the money for him into dollars.

By the time that Gypsy had checked in and was about to go through passport control Zev was well on the way to getting all of his money converted.

That was the last time that he ever saw Zev but he still couldn't get his head around Zev's story, it didn't add up, fighting for both Israel and the Afghan Mujahidin and movie acting?. If he was coming from Afghanistan, with that country being in the state of anarchy that it was, there were many ways that he could have made that money. It would not have surprised Gypsy if Zev worked for the spooks. Possibly he was a CIA operative or asset. Anyway he said goodbye and wished him well then went through passport control and waited to board his flight out.

The flight from London and Athens arrived and hooked up to the sky bridge.

Gypsy was both relieved to be on his way again and apprehensive at the possibility that he could and was likely to get stuck at Dhaka. He boarded the flight and soon after they left the terminal and taxied out to the runway.

The plane took off and started gaining height as Gypsy looked down on Bombay from his window seat position. Yes Bombay was in many parts a dirty smelly shit hole, but the place had a soul. It was alive and vibrant and despite its super inflated costs for accommodation the place was quite welcoming and without a shadow of a doubt had the very best tasting and best presented food that Gypsy had ever had in his life.

Though he was glad to be moving onwards on his journey he knew that one day in the not so distant future he would have to return to this incredible land and explore it's wonders further.

After two and a half hours, the plane started to descend and as Gypsy looked out of the window he could see huge rivers and countless rice paddies below. The rivers, judging by the height of the plane, must have been a good three to five kilometers wide and not just that but there were many of them. This was the Delta of the mighty and massive Bramahputra River that flows from its many tributaries in the Himalayas across Tibet and down through Bhutan, Nepal India and Bangladesh and out into the Bay of Bengal.

The plane made it's final approach then came in and landed at Zia international airport. Gypsy was surprised to see that the terminal was a clean modern building, instead of the crumbling colonial building that he was expecting to see. There were three wide body jets and a Fokker, small regional jet painted in the Biman colors standing on the apron along with a Saudia L10/11 Tristar. Despite the huge size of the population, because of the far reaching poverty very few could afford to travel abroad and as such the airport was of a size similar to that of a small regional airport, back in the West. Gypsy along with the other passengers made his way down the steps and across the apron to the terminal building. In the terminal, he went and handed his passport and ticket in at the transfer desk and stood and waited.

To his amazement, after a few minutes he was handed back his passport and ticket, with a boarding pass, he had been expecting to be told to wait or to go into Dacca and wait for another flight. However when the flight went to board there were several angry people who had confirmed onward bookings but had been bumped off of the flight. It seemed that there had been a mix up at the transfer desk. Gypsy just kept quiet and walked out to the plane. Dhaka was not on a list of places that he wished to become too familiar with.

It was not until the plane took off that he dared to relax. Luck had been on his side that morning. The flight was more comfortable than the one from Bombay, with both good food and free drinks. This was the first time on this trip that he had been offered free drinks on a flight.

Looking at his options Gypsy knew that he needed to work soon. The three most obvious options were: 1. Go back to India after Thailand then slowly make his way back to England. "Yuck, no way am I going back to England or even Israel or Greece if I can avoid it", he thought to himself. 2. Go to Japan and teach English etc. "Well, I don't speak Japanese and I don't know yet how the ways of East Asia are and I could fall down by making mistakes. I need time in the area to get familiar with it before starting to work there" he thought to himself. 3. Go to Australia and work there, they speak English and pay well. "Well, I've liked the vast majority of Aussies that I've met and it's a big place with many opportunities. Yes, I think I'll see if I can get a visa and go to Australia" he decided.

BANGKOK, THAILAND

FEBRUARY 1984.

The plane started to descend and was soon low enough that Gypsy could see rice paddies and busy motorways below, as the plane made its final approach into Don Muang airport. Gypsy looked out of the window and across the paddy fields to a building just like the one that he had painted back in Gabi's room at Colva in Goa.

It was a Buddhist temple Gypsy was later to learn. The plane landed and taxied to the large terminal building. Out of the window he could see people tending the grass by the side of the runway with what looked like lamp shades on their heads. "Yes" he thought to himself "he was definitely in the Orient".

Coming off the plane through a sky bridge into the large high ceilinged terminal, he went through passport control, collected his bag and went to go and find a bus to Democracy Monument in the centre of the city. . Then as he went out through the automatic doors it hit him. All the while that he had been inside he was in an air conditioned area, now his clothes suddenly were stuck to his skin and it was as hot and as humid as a steam room at a spa. The trucks were all painted in bright Technicolor designs and the people were miniature and with very different faces from any that Gypsy had seen before. The place was clean and to his amazement after being in India, things were modern and seemed to work in similar ways to things in the West, at least when compared with that other dimension or planet that was India.

Gypsy got on the bus number '39' as he had been instructed by the people at "tourist information" but after a long rid, he got down at

Victory Monument as he was informed by the driver that this was the end of the line.

There were two American Mormon missionaries on the pavement with a religious picture on a stand, trying to convert the local Buddhists to their particular sect. Gypsy went and asked them for directions and ended up on another bus that this time got him to Democracy Monument. After asking directions he found his way to the Kowsan Road, which at that time was only just starting to take over from the Malaysia Hotel district as the main place for travelers to hang out. It was not at that time the mad circus that it has since become. Most of the shops were involved in making furniture for temples and shrines. There were however ten to fifteen guest houses in the area, most of them concentrated near a long, old, wooden, two storey building mid way along the road. There were five cafes selling Thai and Chinese food but with the menu written in both English and Thai. There were also two shops that sold tobacco, cold drinks and ethnic clothes and souvenirs. There was also one travel agent, 'Ronny's'.

Gypsy checked into the Bonny Guest House which was in a side alley that ran through the middle of the wooden building. It was another world after India. It was spotlessly clean and was a traditional Thai style of building with wooden floors and glassless windows.

Gypsy, because of his huge travel ambitions and microscopic budget decided to save money and use the dormitory that they had. Even that was clean, with a mosquito net over each bed.

He was only granted a two week visa on arrival and didn't have a moment to waste. He left the hostel almost immediately after dropping his bag and seeking directions he headed to the opposite end of Kowsan Road from where he had entered. He then crossed Samsen Road and cut through the grounds of a Buddhist temple in the direction of the river, crossed the road on the other side of the temple grounds then found the alley way leading down to the boat pier. From there he took a river taxi to the Royal Orchid hotel, from where he walked to the Central Post Office and phoned his family to let them know that he was OK, he was in Bangkok and was planning to get a visa and head for Australia next.

His mother told him that he had cousins in West Australia, which was where he was planning to land and said that she would try to get their address for him. Gypsy was most definitely not on a family visiting trip, especially with memories of Israel still fresh in his mind. But their address could prove useful in helping him attain a visa.

Gypsy left the post office absolutely amazed at how little time it had taken to get his call through (three minutes), especially after the Laurel and Hardy show that he had had to endure in Bombay in order to get a call out.

Though in so many ways, Thailand was different from the West, it was modern, efficient and clean and not just that but it was almost as cheap as India. Gypsy stopped and ate at a Muslim café next to the post office and then headed back to the river from where he took another river taxi back to the Bang Lam Po area where the Kowsan Road is situated.

There was so much to look at on the river, with all manner of temples and strange wooden houses on the banks. But on the river itself so much was going on, with tiny tug boats pulling huge great trains of barges, tourist boats, river taxis and long narrow dragon boats. The Dragon boats were something else again, they had huge great engines on a pivot on the back of the boat, with a propeller on a long shaft sticking out of it. The boat operator would stand on the back and maneuver the engine until the propeller was in the water. Then with a heavy foot on the gas, it would take off across the river at high speed and into one of the klongs (canals) with between twenty to thirty passengers on board sitting two abreast on tiny wooden seats along the long narrow craft. In between all of the rest of the boats on the river ran the many cross river ferries (passenger only) and it was a testament to the skill of the boat operators that there were not masses of accidents and collisions on this overcrowded piece of water.

That evening around the guest house and outside in the nearby cafes, Gypsy got talking with other travellers. Some of them were going up to the north of Thailand, to go hill walking in the then lawless zone of the "Golden Triangle". There were travel agents offering guided opium sampling tours through the villages of the region. It sounded like fun, but if he was to make it to Australia on his highly limited budget then he would not be able to make any side trips at this time.

The next day he made his way to the Australian embassy on the busy Sathon Road. It was a fancy looking modern building of three storeys, covered in yellow tiles and was positioned up on concrete stilts and with a bit of a tropical jungle growing around it. Inside he bumped into Steve who he had celebrated Christmas with back in Goa. He was also applying for a visa for Australia and also had very little money. They both planned on applying for six month work visas. There was a group of young Americans in front of them who were also applying for work visas. But they were turned down and given one month tourist visas instead, despite being young enough to be eligible for work visas.

Gypsy and Steve got talking about this and decided to leave and come back the next day. If they weren't giving out work visas so easily it would be necessary to change tack and try something else in order to get in for a long stay.

On their way back to the river they both decided that it would arouse less suspicion and be easier to go and apply for six months tourist visas. They could always make up an identity and work on the black when they got there.

So the next day back at the Aussie embassy and armed with his cousin's address, he engaged in that most ancient of Australian art forms and bullshitted his way through the pre visa interview, telling them a load of old bollocks about how much money he had and what he was planning on doing in Australia. The woman interviewer said, "OK, as long as you can show me that you have a ticket back out, I'll give you a visa."

Near to the Aussie embassy was the Malaysia Hotel and in the area surrounding it were many budget travel agents, so Gypsy went around them all searching for the cheapest ticket he could find. Though it was also a traveler area it was not a pleasant place, with masses of dirty noisy traffic. The ticket prices, also were too high.

He went into a bar where some other travelers were. One of them, an American had a young Thai girlfriend who was sitting on a bar stool and sucking a cold drink through a straw. She was young and looked happy to have someone looking after her. He was wearing a fancy silk embroidered waist coast and had just come from Kathmandu. Gypsy sat down to listen to his stories about the place, he had been sad not to get there himself. Later Gypsy took a walk back down to Sathon road. He was hungry, he had noticed a lot of street restaurants set up on the pavements of Bangkok where someone either had a wheeled trolley with their kitchen set up on or they would have a scooter and side car. They just seemed to park anywhere that they wanted to and set up their tables and chairs across the sidewalk. There were many people eating in them so when Gypsy clocked a particularly large one with it's own tent roof, set slightly back from the road and full of people he went and sat down at one of the tables and waited. A beautiful young woman in a school uniform turned around from another table and said "excuse me but would you like me to help you to order?" Gypsy could speak not one word of Thai so he gratefully accepted the offer from this English speaking young lady. "Yes please, that would be great, this is my first full day in Thailand" he replied, "can you order me vegetable noodle soup please?" she ordered it for him in Thai then smiled at him and left.....he would have liked to have chatted with her more but she was in school uniform and he did not wish to get himself into any trouble. She looked and talked as if she was older than 18 years old but looks can be deceiving....at this time however he did not realize that women at university in Thailand were also required to wear school uniforms. What is significant here is that in many years time Gypsy is going to meet this woman again, not in this story nor the one after that or even the one after that one too but in a book in the future you will one day read about this woman again. Her name will not be told until such time.

After eating Gypsy took a tuk tuk [auto rickshaw] back to the river. Even the auto rickshaws were smarter in Bangkok and looked sleek and fast when compared with the black and yellow monstrosities that plied the streets of Indian cities. Their engines roared and crackled as they took off at speed across six lane carriageways and down narrow back alleys. Back at the Royal Orchid Gypsy took the river taxi back to Bang Lam Po. There was a total of three travel agents in the Bang Lam Po area including one at the Royal Hotel at Suam Luang, near the Temple of the Emerald Buddha.

Ronny's on Kowsan Road had by far the cheapest and best fare that Gypsy was able to find and what's more, his cheap tickets to Australia were on Singapore airlines. The only drawback being, that to catch the flight Gypsy would have to take a bus nearly a thousand miles to the south, to Penang in Malaysia. But even after that it would still be the cheapest way of getting there.

Steve was staying at the central guest house. It was in a side alley at the opposite end of Kaowsan Road from the temple. Gypsy went to join him for an evening of drinking Mekong whiskey. Steve had been told the same as Gypsy at the embassy. Show a ticket back out and get a visa. The local travel agents were only too happy to front a receipt to help. Gypsy informed Steve about his trip around the travel agents and his conclusion that Ronny, down the road there had by far the best deal.

Steve was on the run back home in Austria having refused to do national service and now was hoping to eventually immigrate to New Zealand where he had relatives. Gypsy wanted to work and make enough money to come back to East Asia and have a good look around. He also wanted to find a way to stay in Japan for a while, being that he really liked Japanese art and design and wanted to have the opportunity to learn more about their culture by living in it.

Later, back at the guest house some of the other travelers wanted to go out to Pat Pong (Bangkok's main red light area) and see the banana show, which apparently featured women firing bananas up to a height of two meters from between their legs. It sounded pretty funny but Gypsy couldn't afford to squander the tiniest bit of his precious resources before getting to Australia and finding a job. He was sailing very close to the wind, trying to do what he was doing on the budget he had available to him. The others took off to Pat Pong in a tuk tuk and Gypsy went to bed and slept. He would need to be on the ball the next morning, his visa was for only a short stay and he needed to be ready and out before it expired.

The next morning Gypsy was sitting at a table, out on the pavement at one of the open fronted cafes on the Kowsan Road. He was having a breakfast of muesli, tropical fruit and curd (yoghurt) and reading one of the local English language newspapers.

Thailand was a strange and interesting land. The people were devoted to their king as if he were a God. He certainly seemed to look after his people and guide them well judging by how clean and well organized the place was and the excellent, intelligent religion that they have (Buddhism). The people were generally friendly, tolerant and courteous, but under all of this also lay something dark and mysterious and not very pleasant at all. In the paper were stories of crimes of such a horrific nature that Gypsy could not even begin to understand how anyone could do such things.

A gang or several gangs had either kidnapped or bought severely disabled children and put them out onto the streets of Bangkok, begging for them. They fed them a basic survival ration and kept them imprisoned when they were not begging. The police being what they were, which was highly corrupt, did nothing to stop this cruelty. But a kind woman who ran a special charity saw their plight and took them in straight from the street and housed them. At her charity care house, the children were given not only food and accommodation but also specialist care and education. Most importantly they were given their dignity back.

The gang who had been abusing these vulnerable children however weren't taking this lying down and had taken to riding around the care home on scooters, firing off guns, throwing bricks through the windows and threatening to kill the woman proprietor and her staff. All of this they were doing with impunity as the police appeared to be doing nothing to stop them, obviously they must have been on the take.

Gypsy just couldn't believe it, how could anyone degrade themselves by behaving in such a foul, cowardly and greedy way? Why had the local community not got together and grabbed these foul devils and either lynched or severely and permanently disabled them, for their crimes? Also why had the police and judiciary refused to do their job properly?

It was unimaginable for him, that a society could let a crime like that go unpunished. In the 1970's Thailand had got rid of the death penalty from its statute books. The country was Buddhist and killing people is not something that Buddhism is in favor of. However, the murder rate had jumped through the roof during that brief period of time and the powers that be, all be it with reluctance and great sadness, felt that they had no choice but to bring it back in order to protect the public at large.

Though in Thailand wonderful and saintly people could be found, and there were plenty of good and simple people just trying to get by, there was a significant minority that had real ugly devils running untethered in their heads. Thailand was so very corrupt that it would have been hard to get justice against such bad people, as they always seemed to know how to use and abuse the law to their own advantage better than their victims ever could dream of. And when that didn't work they resorted to other means.

Anyway, Ronny, the travel agent was one of the many good ones among the Thai people. He happily fronted Gypsy a receipt for full payment of the ticket and Gypsy went back to the embassy with it and waited while his passport went in for inspection and hopefully a visa.

In the waiting room there was a whole row of Aussie men sitting and waiting, next to each one was a Thai woman. Each one of them, Gypsy could see from their eyes, were just using the man to get into Australia. Their eyes were as cold and as hard as any that he had ever seen, they looked like hookers and probably were. Either these fellows had got suckered into a package holiday with a mail order bride thrown in or they were being paid to escort in a fresh batch of hookers for an Aussie whore house. It could have been a bit of each.

Anyway as he watched the Aussies and their "girlfriends" and the body language of these two desperate groups, with amusement, he was called to the counter and was given his passport back with a tourist visa for six months on a sticker inside. The words "WORK STRICTLY PROHIBITED" were printed in large letters across it but that was not going to stop him. Now Gypsy could relax ever so slightly. He walked across the road and turned and walked along a small side street leading to Silom Road where he walked along looking at the street stalls and markets and the big Hindu temple at the far end of the road. He had no camera nor the money to buy one, so he was unable to photograph what he saw but he would be back here again after Australia and then he would have money and a camera and could take all of the photos that he wanted to.

He once again took the river taxi back up the river towards Bang Lam Po enjoying once more the wonderful views of river activity and the architectural wonders on the banks. He got down at Sunam Luang, the stop for the Emerald Buddha.

There were dragon boats at the jetty and he noticed that there was one of them filling up with people as if it were a bus. Since seeing them he had wanted to take a ride in one and here was his chance. He jumped on board into one of the narrow, cramped, two abreast seats. Soon the boat was full and the operator started the engine. They backed out of the mooring and shot at high speed across the Chapaya river and into a wide klong [cannal] on the opposite side. They went past the boat house were the royal barges are kept and up past houses, temples, shops and gas stations that all faced onto the river there were small and large boats operating as mobile shops, there were people washing, swimming and cleaning the pots and pans in the river. There were people fishing, transporting goods to market, brushing their teeth, riding dragster like personal boats, washing their clothes, selling fruit and veg from their small boats as they rowed and paddled between houses, it was more than just a road made of water, it was a whole way of life to those who lived along it. Gypsy watched in wonder, there was something so beautiful and exotic about this way of life, it was totally different to anything that he had ever seen before. He stayed on the boat until the end of the line, watching as the boatman dropped people directly onto their own verandas as well as at the jetties. At the end of the line was the usual clutter of food stalls. Gypsy bought a couple of sticks with barbecued chicken skewered to them and walked along eating it. He was outside of the city on one of the many side canals that crisscrossed the area. There was nothing more to see here but he wished that he had a camera as so that he could get some shots of life along the river. He took a boat back down the canals and into Bangkok, once more arriving at the Sunam Luang jetty.

Wandering out into Sunam Luang he was confronted with a whole market in front of him that was very much a part of the boat terminal. It was full of all manner of exotic goods including herbs, spices, strange smelling hot food, silk, jewelry etc etc. He wound his way out through this cramped Bazaar and walked along by the high white walls of the temple complex until he found an entrance. Wandering inside, he went through a courtyard until he was going through another gate that was guarded by two huge colorful concrete or stone demons. In the temple in front of him was the temple of the Emerald Buddha....in fact it is not made of emerald but from a particularly fine piece of green aventurine. Gypsy went inside to see it. It was a very special carving made from a very special piece of stone but what was more impressive was the whole architecture of the place, it was psychedelic design with psychedelic colors, a place of incredible beauty, a Buddhist wonderland. Like Disney World on acid or mushrooms. This and the river boat trip were things that he had seen in his dreams as a child.

Back at the Kowsan Road, he paid Ronny for both the air ticket and for a seat on a bus to Penang leaving the next night. The flight would leave for Perth the night after that. He was given a receipt and told that he would have to collect his ticket from a mister Singh in Georgetown Penang. Ronny wrote out the address and drew a map with directions on a piece of paper then handed it to him. The guest house employed a young woman who's job it was to clean the place and generally help run the guest house. She would sleep on a small foldable mattress on the reception floor. She was a good looking young woman in her late teens or early twenties.

Gypsy awoke the next morning to see her pulling the hairs on his arms with a puzzled expression on her face. East Asian people generally have no hair on their bodies apart from head and genitalia, that is. She had probably just come from a village and had not seen many westerners before, certainly not many with hairy arms and legs.

In many ways the Thai's were uninhibited and innocent, like children and in a rather nice way were not in the least caught up in the nonsense of western style stand offish etiquette. They did however have a few strange rules of their own that all of the travelers had to be aware not to breach. Most of them involved the Buddha, the King and where people chose to place their feet.

Gypsy got up and went and washed, before going out for breakfast. It was going to be a very busy day. He went to see Steve who had just got his visa and was planning on flying to Sydney. Gypsy was flying to Perth but firstly would be taking the bus to Penang later that day. They said goodbye and good luck to each other once more.

Then after taking care of everything else, he went around the corner to Ronny's and collected his bus ticket. "You like drink whiskey?" Ronny asked. "Sure", said Gypsy. "You go collect your bags and come here and I get bottle of whiskey", said Ronny. Gypsy paid his guest house bill and returned with his bags. Ronny was waiting with a bottle of Mekong and a bucket of ice. They sat down and chatted and drank as Gypsy waited for the bus that was to collect him and take him on the twenty four hour drive to Penang. Gypsy had told Ronny previously of his situation and his plan. The reason Ronnie had invited him for a drink was out of respect. Ronnie was also a go getter and told Gypsy how he had started in the travel business by selling Aeroflot tickets from an attaché case around the cheap hotels of the city. He had built himself up into a travel agent with his own office and shop front. He made it clear that if he was in Gypsy's position he would be doing exactly the same thing. They finished the bottle and Ronnie asked, "You like drink some more?" "Sounds like a good idea to me", said Gypsy.

An hour later with the second bottle almost empty, the bus arrived and Gypsy thanked Ronny and staggered outside with his bag, climbed aboard, found his seat and went to sleep. He woke up after dark when the bus stopped at an outdoor tent roofed restaurant on a patch of dirt by the side of the highway. An evening meal was included for free with the bus ticket.

All of the passengers were sitting at two very long tables. Everyone was given a plate with rice on it and the main dishes were placed in large pots in the center of the tables for each to help themselves from.

They were in a tent like structure set back from the road. Once again the local women had not seen too many westerners and came up to Gypsy and started pulling the hairs on his arms and giggling. They kept on wanting to touch the hairs and couldn't believe they were real. Gypsy could see that he was going to enjoy Thailand if he could come back here with some money. The women were totally uninhibited and beautiful and what's more, most of them gave the impression that they were looking for a white man.

After twenty minutes everyone got back on board the bus and on they rolled through the night, down the Thai coast to the Malaysian border. Eventually on the following day at noon the bus passed Hat Yai and then shortly afterwards they were there at the border. Everyone got down and took their bags and walked through the border formalities, first getting their exit stamps on the Thai side and then getting stamped in on the Malaysian side.

Gypsy had given his bag an extra check to make sure that no one else's contraband had found its way into it on the journey. As on the Malaysian side of the border was a notice saying "DEATH TO ALL DRUG SMUGGLERS", "KNOW WHAT YOU CARRY", "YOU HAVE BEEN WARNED". This was written inside of a picture of a noose. As such Gypsy was taking no chances.

On the Malaysian side of the border they were collected by a different bus that was to take them the rest of the way. They were now Driving past yet more paddy fields and farmers with lamp shade hats, walking with or riding their water buffaloes among the palm trees and banana plants that grew by the side of the road.

They reached Butterworth on the mainland and from there they took the ferry across to Penang. There had been a couple of other travelers from the west on board the bus and Gypsy had got talking to one who had a guide book for South East Asia. "What does it say about dirt cheap accommodation in Penang?" he asked. "Well you can come along with me if you like because that's where I'm going. To the cheapest place available", he replied. When they got to the island they shared a trishaw, (which was like a rickshaw but with the passenger seats at the front) to the New China guest house, where they checked in to the dormitory. Gypsy then went out to go and find Mister Singh and collect his ticket. The trishaw rider brought him to just a regular office rather than a shop front, it didn't even have a sign on the door to say that it was a travel agent's office. However there was no problem, the friendly, smiling Sikh man handed him an envelope with the Singapore Airlines ticket inside of it. There it was marked on four separate coupons;- Penang, Singapore, Perth, Singapore, Penang. The Sikh man invited Gypsy to stop for a chai and they talked a little as the Sikh man explained how his family had emigrated there from Punjab some sixty years previously.

PENANG/MALAYSIA

MARCH 1984.

Going out later to eat Gypsy noticed it was a bit like Bangkok, with its street stands and noodle shops and the same strange strong smells. Penang was far smaller and more laid back, but it still had strong Chinese influences and that same exotic and interesting way of doing things. Gypsy was only just starting to get the hang of how to eat rice and noodles with chop sticks and there were other strange things to get used to. For example, the Chinese men would sit around for the whole day in pajamas or string vests, they always looked like they were only half dressed. And even in Penang they would eat some of the strangest and smelliest of things.

Gypsy did however enjoy the bowls of noodle soup, the night markets and the smell of incense around their temples. Penang was a colorful and fun place to be.

The next morning Gypsy got to work in a hurry. He bought himself two pairs of fake Levis and a very 'touristy' looking shirt, he also bought himself a smart looking matching set of two holdalls (one for hand luggage) of a dull color, and a smart looking set of trainers. He then took the jeans to a tailor for adjustment and found a barber and got his hair cut short enough that he could pass as Mr. Straight. He then went and collected his jeans and returned to the guest house where he repacked his kit into the new bags and changed clothes. He was flying into Australia with no more than three hundred American dollars in his pocket and without a work permit. The last thing that he needed was to get stopped at the airport and turned around and sent back for not having enough money. Painful though it was, he would have to dress up to look like some sort of idiot, straight tourist until he was out of the airport at Perth.

TRANSIT TO PERTH

MARCH 1984.

He took a bus to the airport and checked in. He looked so straight that Malaysian customs became suspicious of him and took him in for a drug search, thinking that maybe he was a mule. Gypsy if he had been a customs officer would also have pulled anyone looking as straight as he did on that day. It was embarrassing, but he knew that it would work far better than his usual scruffy appearance to get him into Australia unhindered.

The first flight that took him to Changi airport at Singapore lasted an hour. He was excited to be going to Australia but he was also dreaming of when he could return to Asia with a big enough budget to get around and see the place properly.

The plane landed at Singapore after dark and the passengers disgorged from the Airbus and up the tunnel and into the terminal. Gypsy had his onward boarding pass so he took a look around for the information board to find out when and from where his flight was leaving from. That established, he then went to the bar and allowed himself a celebratory couple of drinks.

The waiting passengers were called to board the flight, a 200 series Boeing 747. However the plane was almost empty when it left the gate and the stewardesses came around and asked everyone which drinks they would like when the plane was off the ground. The plane took off and started gaining height. Soon the seat belt signs went out and Gypsy sat back and relaxed across the two empty seats next to him. One of the hostesses came by with the whiskey and beer that he had requested. For five hours at least he could relax and feel like a rich man on this almost empty jumbo with it's presently under worked hostesses. Unfortunately he couldn't indulge as he would have liked from the drinks trolley as he was going to need his wits about him at Perth, not only to get through the airport but to find a place to bed down when and if he got into town. The scheduled time of arrival was 2 a.m. and he at that time had less than three hundred dollars in his pocket as he jetted towards the unknown, without so much as a guide book or address for direction.

The plane landed on time. The flight was the only one that had arrived for hours and with so few people getting off of it and such a bored looking bunch of customs officers waiting to search people, Gypsy knew that he had done the right thing by dressing up like a prat. If he had come through in his hippie clothes with long hair, they would have had a field day with him. They would probably have taken him to pieces and then finding out how little money he had, put him on the next plane back to Penang.

As it was, he looked so straight that they didn't look at him twice and out he went into the cool night air. He was forced to use some of his precious cash on a taxi into the city as there were no buses running and so few cars about at that time as to make it impossible to hitch a ride.

PERTH/AUSTRALIA

MARCH 1984.

The taxi driver knew of a cheap hostel and he dropped Gypsy off there. It had a self check in system for late night arrivals, which was find an empty bed, crash out and pay in the morning. The next morning Gypsy awoke on their living room couch and found his way to the kitchen.

The place was full of bratty, young straights from England, America and Canada.

There was a fucked up American girl who was either in her late teens or early twenties with a line of twenty to thirty different vitamin and supplement jars in front of her, It looked as if she had just robbed a pharmacist. This obviously was her breakfast. There was a po faced bespectacled prat from England who looked as if he sucked lemons for breakfast. He was a student type who had learned that ancient British pseudo educated art form of looking down his nose at other people. There were also a bunch of other backpackers who were about as interesting as the dull pastel wallpaper that decorated the house.

There was not one real traveler or interesting person amongst them, which made Gypsy feel quite lonely. Later that afternoon, he wandered to the city center and tried to get himself oriented. There was a crowd of long haired young Aussies playing guitars, busking in the middle of the pedestrian area. Gypsy was missing having a guitar with him but what could he do? He certainly couldn't afford one now.

There was one guy standing there with a 'Hitler European Tour' T-shirt on and another with a T-shirt with a picture of Hitler giving a fascist salute with a ganja plant under his hand and a speech bubble saying, "My plants are this high".

He was starting to really like the Australians, they liked taking the piss out of things and weren't in the least bit uptight, he knew he was going to be OK here.

He got chatting with some of the people who were hanging around watching and listening to the buskers. He asked them if they might know where he could go if he wanted to find work. One of them told him about a town some two hundred or so kilometers south from Perth called Donnybrook. They grew apples there and the crop would soon be due for harvesting and they needed pickers.

Back at the hostel, the owner arrived and Gypsy paid her. He also asked her if it would be a good idea to go to Donnybrook if he wanted to find work. "Oh, yes", she said. "That's your best chance. There's a recession in West Australia right now and jobs are hard to find, but they always need workers on the picking".

The next day he took a local bus out of the city and found a good position on the highway to hitch from. He got lift after lift very quickly and people were both helpful and friendly all the way, telling him about other places where he might find work after the apple picking finished. The area was very sparsely populated but the countryside was green all the way, like northern Europe except for the different plant and animal life.

DONNYBROOK, WEST AUSTRALIA

He made it to Donnybrook in the mid afternoon. There was a hostel in the village that was easy to find as the place had just one street going through it and if you blinked you would probably drive straight through not realizing you had passed the place. The hostel was in a small side road that led to a dead end shortly after, at the entrance to a household driveway.

The hostel was full of people waiting for the work to start. There were both Australians and an international crowd too. There were a lot of British and Irish who had flown straight to Australia from England and there were just a few who had been on the road in Asia before getting to Australia.

The next day Gypsy went out and hitched up and down the highway visiting each and every farm in his hunt for a job. He was told that he would be welcome to come back and start work at one farm in a few weeks when their crop was ready and in the meantime he landed a job working at another farm starting the following week.

Back at the hostel, he found himself sharing a room with a tall thin blond haired man from England. He had also been travelling before getting to Australia but not in India.

They told each other of their journeys getting there and Gypsy told him about his time in Bombay living in the railway station and his conversations with John, about the Vedic teachings. "Oh, all of that stuff is bullshit. I don't believe in any of that stuff, religion, mysticism or psychic stuff it's all rubbish". "You think so, do you?" asked Gypsy. "Yes", said the man. "Well what if I could show you a way that you could see your own faces from previous lives that you have lived?" asked Gypsy. "Bullshit. It's not possible", replied the man once more. "Well, you know you can never be sure about the statement that you've just made, so I suggest an experiment. It can't hurt you and I will not be involved. In fact, I will need to leave the room and let you do this for yourself alone." "Okay, what's the technique?" asked the man. "Right", said Gypsy. "If you want to find whether I am right or not you will need to do exactly what I tell you". "Ok, go on", said the man. "I want you to sit and stare into your own eyes in that mirror on the wall, do not blink whatever you do. Tears will well up in your eyes but you must not blink, just let them fall. Do not lose focus on your own eyes. If you do this correctly it should only be a few minutes before you start to see what I am telling you about."

Gypsy left the room to let him try the technique and went around to the local pub for a drink where a lot of the other pickers were hanging out.

When he returned to the room later he saw the man sitting reading one of Gypsy's books on mysticism. "I thought you said all that stuff was bullshit", said Gypsy. "You were right", said the man. "I just tried your technique and had a rather strange experience, I saw myself as a black man". "Well, that explains why you're almost albino white this lifetime doesn't it?" replied Gypsy. "What do you mean?" asked the man. "Well if you had been black before, then you probably suffered racism from white people and you were most probably poor, unlike the whites. So it is only natural that you would have wished with all your heart that you could be as white as white could be, so as you would not have to suffer as you did. This wish would have been so ingrained in both your conscious and subconscious mind that at the moment of your death it would have registered and brought you to incarnate in the body that you presently inhabit. You must have some good karma as you could have also come back as a white cat or dog or even as a polar bear".

The picking work started and Gypsy found that he had the misfortune to be working for a man with very short arms and very deep pockets. He was getting paid by the hour at a low rate rather than by how much he picked. He tried to negotiate with the man but he was one of those tricky types that never stopped looking for ways to get something for nothing. He was a man whose whole life was dedicated to the service of his own meanness and greed.

Gypsy moved on and found a farm where he got paid according to how many boxes he filled. This was better and gave him a chance to save some money. It was hard work but that was not something that Gypsy was frightened of.

The whole place had the same atmosphere as Nafplion in Greece did, with pickers getting picked up in the morning in pick up trucks and being driven out to the orchards, the same drinking after work and a basically non cohesive crowd of misfits who were only brought together by the need for money.

After two weeks they had cleared the orchard at the farm that Gypsy was working at. He hitched out the twelve miles to where the farm that offered him the job that wasn't ready to start at that particular time, was located.

They were now ready and asked Gypsy if he could find one more person to join him in the work. They were offering a reasonable hourly rate and had cherry picker machines to do the job with.

Back at the hostel, there was a British man who had his own vehicle, a Ford Falcon that he slept in the back of. He was looking for a job and Gypsy asked him if he wanted to join him on the work at the farm. It was advantageous that he had wheels in that it would save him having to hitch to and from the farm every day.

They started work the next morning and all was well, as they set in to three weeks of labour. The other fellow had just finished several years of service in the British army as a second leftenant. He had a posh

Sandhurst accent and being that he had spent the previous five years in the paratroop regiment, had very little else to talk about. He was indeed an odd sight on a job like this. He had only seen active service in Northern Ireland but talked incessantly about the Falklands war.

All carried on well and they each saved their money. St. Patrick's Day was celebrated in Donnybrook as it had a lot of people of Irish descent living around the area. One of the "Paddies" from the hostel went out in the night and painted green footsteps across the zebra crossing on the highway and a regular large piss up was held at the local pub.

The work on the farm was coming to an end and Gypsy was thinking about where to go to find more work. He had heard about work at a town to the south called Pemberton where there was vegetable picking work.

Job finished and Gypsy packed his bags and went out to the highway and stuck out his thumb. By the early afternoon, he had reached Pemberton and was hiking the several kilometers on a dirt trail to the local hostel which was out in the woods.

He got there and checked in, and asked the manager and guests if anyone knew about picking work in the area. He was told that it was all finished and not only was there no work but the town had a redneck population and that it was not advisable to drink in the local pubs if you didn't want to be involved in a fight.

The next morning he was back out on the road heading back north. The third lift that he got was from a couple of hippies in a battered and dented Holden station wagon. They lived in a hippie commune on a sandbar just outside of Bunbury. They got talking and Gypsy ended up at the commune with them. It was called Belvedere and had a population of several hundred grey kangaroos living there as well as fifteen to twenty people.

There was an A-frame house that no one else was using so Gypsy was told that he could bed down there. The houses were all sorts of weird and wonderful homemade constructions that had been assembled mostly from other people's rubbish.

It was a gathering of people who each did their own thing but helped each other out. They had launched a protest against an American company's policy of dumping radio active effluent in open pits several miles further along the sand bar. The American company instead of thinking about cleaning up their mess, responded by strong arming the local authorities into harassing the inhabitants of the commune and trying to use all sorts of obscure by laws to get the commune closed, even though it was on private property with the owner, Wally, also actively participating. Gypsy stuck around for a while and even joined the others in blagging a welfare check off of the local authorities He could do an Aussie accent so well that no one could ever even suspected that he was a Pom. He blagged the check only once only to prove to himself and the others that he could do it.

Time was of the essence if he was going to get some money in his pocket and get back to Asia.

ON THE MOVE
WEST AUSTRALIA

APRIL/MAY 1984

He left the commune one morning and hitched north, passing Perth and heading north up the coast road towards Geraldton, where he stopped and spent several days looking for a job. He got lucky in Geraldton in terms of accommodation when he got turned onto a hostel for young Aussies who were traveling and looking for work. He had only saved six hundred Aussie dollars on the picking work and even though it was cheap staying at the hostel his money was diminishing and time was going by, he needed to make money in a hurry.

He could find no work in Geraldton and so hitched another five hundred kilometers north up the coast to Carnarvon where he tramped around every farm in the area looking for a job. It was warm in Carnarvon and most of the farms were growing bananas, but none of them needed an extra laborer. He scouted around in town to see if maybe he could get a job on a fishing boat, but all to no avail.

There were two families on holiday with caravans and being of the friendly type, they invited Gypsy to join them for a beer or two. On hearing that he was going to take his bedroll and sleep outside in the bush they invited him to use the tent porch on the side of one of their caravans.

The next day they invited him for a trip out into the bush in one of the 4x4's that they had. Everyone was hoping to run into someone else's secret ganja plantation, so the first couple of hours were spent checking around the areas where there were water holes. There were a lot of wild horses around and quite a few water holes, but no ganja. A part of the afternoon was spent shooting tin cans off of logs with hunting rifles before they headed back into town and back to the campsite for a barbecue and some more beers, which Gypsy again was invited to.

The next day Gypsy stood by the side of the road for the whole morning and much of the afternoon trying to hitch a ride north to Port Headland. He went and asked the road train drivers at the filling station and anyone else that he could see who he thought might have been heading north, but all to no avail.

In disgust, he gave up and crossed the road and stuck his thumb out again. Within ten minutes he had hitched a ride in a truck heading south, it was ridiculous, there were just as many vehicles going north as south but again he felt like he was being thwarted, just like when he tried to go to Kathmandu.

Two lifts and several hours later and he was back at Geraldton. He went back to the nice and friendly workers hostel where he had stayed before.

The next day he got chatting with a group of men who worked as crew on the fishing boats and asked them if there was any chance that they needed an extra deck hand on one of the boats. Gypsy wasted no time waiting for them to get him an answer and went into town looking on all of the notice boards that he could find, until he found a job advertised for a tractor driver. That was a job that he knew how to do and so he jotted down the number and went and found a public phone.

That evening he was collected and taken out to a large farm sixty kilometers out of Geraldton, directly inland.

The job involved driving a large tractor with double tires on the rear around huge five hundred and thousand acre fields with a super spreader on the back, loaded with fossilized bird shit (phosphate) spraying it out across the fields. Food and accommodation was thrown in but the shifts were twelve hours long and the pay was just two hundred dollars per week.

Gypsy worked as hard as he knew how but things would just keep going wrong, he caught scabies in the bunk house and had to miss half a day while he went to a doctor, some forty or so kilometers away.

The brakes failed on first application, while driving a truck around a bend and by the time he had pumped some life into them he had had to swing wide to avoid rolling the vehicle and hit a gate post instead, knocking out a front light. Also it was difficult following tracks around the fields accurately when they tended to branch out in many directions. He did his best to keep the correct distance but with virtually nothing to line up on and the tracks disappearing altogether regularly, he would often have to guess the right way and re-adjust his position when he could again make out the faint, weed covered tracks.

The farm covered some twenty thousand acres and was split between sheep and arable crops. The arable crops consisting of wheat and lupines that were shipped to Singapore where they were used as cattle feed. In addition to the fleet of normal farm sized tractors they also had two monster sized Steiger, centrally articulated tractors that had two 2 meter high wheels on each corner and air conditioned cabs with eight track stereos. These giant machines would pull huge gang ploughs and planters behind them and would be in operation twenty four hours a day during planting season. With two drivers doing twelve hour shifts each. However, the huge costs involved in buying and maintaining the equipment and the poor nature of the land, meant that the family had to keep planting more and more land each year, just in order to break even.

UNA, WEST AUSTRALIA

MAY 1984.

Things kept going wrong, as if to tell Gypsy that this was not the place that he was meant to be. After three weeks the old owner of the farm said, "I'm sorry but this is not working. I'll have to let you go." He paid him and gave him a lift into Geraldton. Gypsy had worked hard and done his best and he was familiar with the machinery but whatever he had touched out on that farm had turned to shit in his hands.

Gypsy stayed the night at the hostel and was hoping to look for a job on a fishing boat the next day. But the next morning someone in the room was smoking a joint, he offered it to Gypsy who took a couple of hits and passed it back. Later he got caught by the hostel manager and got thrown out, but not before he ratted out Gypsy for taking a couple of hits which meant that he had to leave as well.

So with no other choice Gypsy hitched back to Perth where he found a different hostel to stay at than the one that he had first used.

He went to the main C.E.S office (Commonwealth Employment service) but there was nothing in the way of manual work on offer. Just to clear his head he took a local train to Freemantle and took a walk about and relaxed. He went to a local museum and took a look at the exhibits and was able to read more about the barbaric behavior of the British, in times gone by. Along the railway tracks, on an overhead bridge, someone had written in bold white graffiti, "Are you a good little Robot?" which was the best bit of 'wake up' graffiti that he had ever seen. The hostel that he was staying at was exceptionally cheap and run by a Christian group. They were very kind and helpful and even tried to help Gypsy find a job, but it was no good, there were hardly any positions vacant in Perth.

Gypsy made one more visit south, to the commune at Bunbury. The American company was going all out to have it closed down instead of disposing of their rubbish responsibly. Gypsy wanted to help as he really liked the commune while absolutely despising this foul American company that had moved in to someone else's country and then misbehaved in such an outrageously arrogant and underhanded way. However, his visa was not for long enough that he had time for such activities and he knew that he was now going to have to move fast if he was to make money before his visa expired.

Leaving out of Belvedere, he knew that he was going to have to head east to find work. He hitched to and around Perth until he was on the Kalgoorlie Road and carried on hitching. He made it to a small town just before Southern Cross by sunset and stopped and checked in to a cheap guest house. He was tired and it was cold outside. Even though he was down on his last money he was exceptionally tired and needed a good place to rest on that particular night.

The next day he got out on the highway to start hitching when two cops pulled up and wanted to check him over. He showed them his passport but still they wanted to check his bags. "No problem", he told them. "I don't have anything that a self respecting thief would wish to take, let alone anything that would interest your lot". He passed them his bags. They searched them and then asked him where he was trying to get to. "Sydney", replied Gypsy. "What do you want to go there for, it's a rat race, you'll do better staying over here with us lot mate. It's much more laid back", said one of the cops. "Anyway, you have a safe journey" they told him.

Walking further down the road, he met another hitcher heading for Sydney. It's not a good idea for two men to hitch together as many drivers would have second thoughts about stopping for two male strangers so Gypsy wandered a few kilometers further along the road before stopping to thumb a ride.

After about half an hour a Ute (pickup Truck) came down the road swerving and running across both lanes before stopping in front of him. He opened the door and the owner in a drunken slur said, "Get in mate, here's a beer for you". The other hitcher was also in the truck. Gypsy got in slinging his bags in the back and off they rolled towards Koolgardi.

The driver was from Tasmania and was heading home. He was as pissed as a fart and the Ute had no working foot brake.

A couple of hours later they stopped in Koolgardy which would have been best described as a one horse town were someone had shot the horse. The Tasmanian devil then turned around and said, "You two buy a case of beer and I'll get everything else". After paying for the beer, Gypsy had the grand total of fifteen dollars in his pocket.

Koolgardy was a small place that looked like the town that time forgot. It looked like a place from the wild west gold rush, with wooden buildings and bars that looked like saloons from a John Wayne or Clint Eastwood movie. The main street ran down a hill and off from it was nothing but residential shacks and houses. Even out on the main street it was none too busy apart from a bit of passing traffic, there were not many vehicles parked and even fewer people walking.

With supplies gathered they jumped back into the ute and headed out of town and on down the highway to Norseman which is where the road forks and the main highway heads out across the Nulabore desert. The road went through great forests of Eucalyptus with no wide open views to be seen, Gypsy had expected this area to all be desert. It was wilderness but it certainly wasn't desert.

An hour or two later at the filling station at Norseman they stopped and tanked up before heading out.

On the Nulabore Road the Eucalyptus forest continued up past the first filling station after Norseman which was some 250 kilometers along the road. After that there was one filling station every two hundred or so kilometers and nothing in between apart from bushes and kangaroos.

Riding off into the evening, they reached the first filling station and road house after dark. The tank was topped up and they drove off into the cold winter night.

Each one of them took a turn behind the wheel as they drove on through the night. The highway was covered in road kill for much of the way, at times almost becoming a carpet of mangled and mashed marsupials. There were road trains passing in the opposite direction every few minutes, each pulling two or three long trailers behind them and there was the odd pickup truck or beaten up old Holden interspersing them. There was even the occasional biker on a chopper with his kit in a roll on the back seat of the bike but all in all it was not such a busy road at that time of the night. The Tasmanian devil was so drunk that he managed to mince a big red kangaroo without even seeing it, the other two had shouted a warning but to no avail. They got out to look at the mess. The roo was dead and it had buggered the roo bars on the front of the Ute, severing one of the couplings, but otherwise there was no damage to the vehicle.

Gypsy was driving when they reached the one and only hill on the highway. The Tazmanian devil cried out in alarm when Gypsy used the hand break to slow down, "No, no, don't use that, it's got a problem and can only be used when the truck is at a standstill". "Oh, great", thought Gypsy to himself. "What an excellent truck". "It's a good job there are no cops about out here as I don't even have a license".

They rolled on into the dawn. What had surprised Gypsy so much about the Nulabor was that he had expected to see nothing but dry flat desert, but instead by the sides of the road eucalyptus trees and all manner of exotic looking shrubs were growing that people back in Europe would have to pay good money to buy from their local garden center. To Gypsy it was like driving through the biggest exotic garden on earth, it looked like a giant shrubbery and he recognized many of the plants from either the nursery back in England or from the kibbutz gardens in Israel.

Just after dawn they stopped at a roadhouse on the other side of the road, directly atop cliffs that made up part of the Great Australian bite. "You don't want to go swimming in there", said the other hitcher. "Why's that?" asked Gypsy. "Because those seas are absolutely writhing with sharks, that's why", said the Tazmanian devil as he joined the conversation. "There is a higher concentration of sharks in those waters than anywhere else around the Aussie coast", he continued.

It was an incredible place to be standing, on the edge of a desert, atop the cliffs and looking straight out to sea, knowing that the next nearest land mass in that direction was Antarctica.

They carried on on their way and by eleven o'clock that morning or there abouts, they passed the village of Penong which looked a bit like Koolgardy but without the shot horse. It was a tiny place in the middle of nowhere. A couple of hours after that they reached Ceduna, the first town after Koolgardy. It was a place with a very high percentage of the populace being aboriginal. The place was fine in the mornings before the pubs and liquor stores opened but it was not the place to be on a full moon or Friday or Saturday night and certainly not the place to be on welfare cheque day.

They stopped in town to pick up supplies and then carried on down the road.

Then in the late afternoon just after going through a small village, a horrible noise came from inside of the engine. There was a mechanic just a mile or two back, in the village that they had just driven through and so Taz turned his pickup truck around and limped it to the garage.

The mechanic came out and took a look under the hood and then removed the rocker head cover and got Taz to start the engine. "Yep that's not going to get you far like that", he said as he rubbed his hands together with a grin on his face. "I won't be able to do it today. I'll have to order parts first".

The Tasmanian devil was now stuck and said that first he would have to phone his sister in Tasmania and get her to wire him some money. Gypsy however was not stuck but with only fifteen dollars in his pocket he had to move fast. He said goodbye and thank you to the Tazmanian Devil and the other hitcher and moved off down the highway to find a good hitching place.

By nightfall he did not have a lift and a bitterly cold wind was blowing. There was no way out there to get out of the cold and he could find no sheltered place to sleep. He had passed a Greyhound stop with bus times written on a board outside. A bus was due in at nine in the evening that would be going to Port Augusta. When by eight thirty he had still not managed to thumb a ride, he went to the bus stop and waited, Then when the bus came by he parted with his last fifteen dollars for a ticket to Port Augusta.

He was warm on the bus and could relax a little, he still had some dried food and a couple of tins in his bag to keep going on but it wasn't much, he was going to need some help from somewhere to get out of this mess.

The bus pulled into the station at Port Augusta and Gypsy got down with his bags and went and looked for a sheltered place to bed down for the night.

He hadn't slept the night before, as they rolled across the Nulabor and was now desperately tired, it was an extremely cold night for that part of the world, with the mercury not up much above zero.

After a search around the area the only building that he could find open was a public toilet. Desperate times call for desperate measures. His thin sleeping bag, although it was lined with a reflective thermal blanket, was not really up to the job, certainly not for sleeping outside in that temperature.

He locked himself in the cleanest of the cubicles and took out his bedroll. Luckily the cubicles did not have a gap under the door and he was able to sleep until eight in the morning undisturbed. He then got himself cleaned, packed and ready to move. At least he didn't have far to go to take a dump and a leek that morning, not to mention a wash and a cleanup, before hitting the road.

Out on the highway he didn't have to wait long for a ride. Two aborigine men in an old saloon car stopped for him. They were decent and friendly types and at that time sober. They drove down to Port Piery chatting all the way. When they got there the elder of the two of them said, "Here, come and join us for a beer, mate". "I would like to but I can't. I've got no money", Gypsy replied. "No problem. I'm paying", the older of the two men replied.

After several drinks Gypsy must have either fallen asleep or passed out because when he awoke he was lying on the back seat of their car and just the older of the two of them was in it and was driving. It was as if the nice decent person who had stopped for him and chatted away all the way to Port Piery had vacated his body and the spirit of some terrible monster had taken over. He was driving like a lunatic and snarling, growling and showing his teeth like an animal in attack mode. The moment the car stopped at some traffic lights Gypsy opened the door, grabbed his bags and ran. He just shouldn't have gone for a drink with them. He had heard the stories but had forgotten, never drink with aborigines, it's dangerous.

Well at least he had now learned from experience and the mistake would never be repeated.

In town Gypsy met another homeless man and when he explained that he had nothing, the man took him to the town mission. They didn't have facilities there so they gave him a bus ticket to Adelaide and the address of a homeless shelter run by a Catholic group called St. Vincent de Paul. Gratefully, Gypsy took the ticket and address and thanked them before setting out for the bus station.

Getting off the bus in Adelaide Gypsy asked directions and then made his way to the shelter.   When he explained that he had nothing they were very kind and gave him a meal and a bed with clean sheets. It was in a large dormitory, but he didn't mind that. He had nothing worth stealing except his passport and ticket from Perth to Penang. It was a luxury to sleep in a proper bed after such a long journey and he woke the next morning feeling much better.

One of the other homeless and broke men at the hostel took him around with him that next day and gave him a tour of the places where he could get a free meal. Apparently a lot of the fruit pickers and seasonal laborers fell on hard times from time to time and many of those in the shelter were looking for work, just as Gypsy was when the cash ran out.

It still did not sit easy with him, relying on charity to stay alive but until he could find a job, there was nothing else that he could do but be grateful for the help.

The next day he saw a man busking with a guitar but he was not making much, Gypsy wandered over and listened. When he stopped playing, he asked Gypsy if he was a guitarist. "Yes, I can play", said Gypsy. The man handed him his guitar and asked Gypsy to play something.

Gypsy had learned some songs from an Australian folk rock band called Redgum, most of their songs involved taking the piss out of politicians and their corrupt activities and about public attitudes. He had learned the songs at the commune on a borrowed guitar. His rendition of a track called, "Doesn't Matter To Me", impressed the busker, who asked him to play some more. Gypsy played on for a while. Then the busker said, "Here, mate we're not making any money at this. Want to go for a beer, instead?"

Just then, a voice shouted out. "Hey! Gypsy. What are you doing here?" He looked around to see Steve from the hostel at Damascus gate in Jerusalem. He had gotten married to an Australian woman who he had met in Jerusalem and was now living in Adelaide. They stopped and spoke for just a short while and Steve rushed off. He gave Gypsy his number but Gypsy never got a chance to use it.

The busker had been waiting patiently and Gypsy turned around to him and said, "I'd really like to join you for a beer but I'm broke and staying in a homeless shelter."

"No problem", said the fellow. "I'll pay, it sounds like you've got an interesting story and I want to hear it". So they went into a pub and sat down. The busker went and got the beers and then Gypsy told him about his previous travels and the journey that had brought him to Adelaide.

The man said, "If you like, I can help you". "Yes please", said Gypsy. "If you know were I can get a job, that would be the best help possible". "Yes, that was what I was thinking", said the man. "I have some friends who live in a wine making town a couple of hours from here, they often have jobs going in the vineyards. Also there's no work in Adelaide at the moment unless you've got a skill and even then it's not easy. I think that this will be your best bet". "Sounds good to me", said Gypsy. "Well I was thinking of driving there this afternoon. Want to come along. I'm sure that my friends will be happy to put you up".

NOORIUPTA
SOUTH AUSTRALIA

MAY 1984

That afternoon, Gypsy rode with the man in his car to Nooriupta. The man was another long haired hippie like Gypsy. What's more he had a bag of weed from his own crop and they smoked pipe after pipe of ganja for the whole journey.

They arrived at the house of his friends an hour or two later and he introduced Gypsy to them and explained his predicament and asked if they could put him up while he found himself a job.   The woman was an Australian but her husband was from England and worked in the wine industry in a technical aspect. They readily agreed to put him up and help him. They had a relaxing evening together and the man left Gypsy with his friends before driving off to his house in a more remote area.

Gypsy spent the next five days scouring the area looking for a job, but all to no avail. The couple were really kind to him and fed him and gave him a warm place to stay, but it was no good for them to have him staying for too long and he knew it. So he thanked them for their kindness and left in the direction of Sydney.

The first three lifts took him along the Murray River but the fourth lift was in a truck that took him all the way to Sydney.

The driver was a decent type and told good jokes. He had been a driver all of his life and knew his way around much of the country. He had been diagnosed with a non curable form of cancer and had been given only two or three years to live by his doctor. He had decided to keep on working just so as to keep his sanity. They rolled on through the afternoon and into the night. The driver stopped at midnight and they both slept. There were two bunks in the truck and Gypsy was told he could use the upper one.

He awoke at about six in the morning, by which time the driver was already behind the wheel and the truck was rolling down the highway.

On and on they went, through forests of eucalyptus and the turn off to broken hill, then on towards Canberra. Though this area was still sparsely populated it didn't seem that way after west and south Australia. Eventually they reached the turn off for Canberra and kept on driving on the Sydney highway. Soon they had reached the Blue Mountains and Gypsy could see down into the canyons with rivers and streams flowing through them as they rode along the highway.

Soon after they were in Sydney and the driver dropped Gypsy off a few miles from the city center. From there he used some small change that he had, to catch a local bus into the city. Before he did anything else he had to go and see the bridge and the opera house, after making such a journey even if he had no money he was still going to go and enjoy the view.

After a good look at all that was down there on the harbor front, he wandered off and asked some other destitute looking people where he could find a homeless shelter. They pointed him towards the Salvation Army and he wandered off there and got fixed up with a bed and a meal.

Later that evening he was wandering about in the King's Cross area of the city when he came upon a Hare Krishna restaurant. Not just that but it was free to eat at.

Remembering what John in India had told him about the Hare Krishna's Gypsy went inside and had another meal and got talking with them about their religion. The food was excellent, he much preferred vegetarian food to anything else anyway. After a while talking with the monks and because he had expressed such an interest in their path, they asked him if he would like to try out the type of life they lived at a farm that they had on the Colo River, just past Wollongong to the south. . The next day Gypsy got a lift with some of them in a mini bus to the farm. It was down in a valley by a wide creek, there were fruit trees and lush green fields all around. The Hare Krishna farm had orchards and fields with cows roaming around them. There was a milking shed in one corner that was a corrugated iron and wooden post construction that was open on two sides. The road through the valley ran through the middle of the farm and the ashram, which included living accommodation, a library and the temple, which was located in the farm house that stood on a rise on the south east side of the road. It was a different routine and lifestyle to any that he had come across before that the monks lived. Rising at three in the morning to wash and shower. That was followed by several hours of prayers, devotions and chanting of the Hare Krishna mantra. After that came breakfast, then a sermon and then to work on the farm.

The strange thing was that many of the monks were just straight up, tough, working class Australians. One night when some local oiks came by causing trouble and throwing things at the animals, they were confronted by a group of big, heavy skinheads in Indian robes who were brandishing shot guns and rifles. "But you are monks" the oiks sniveled "you're meant to be peaceful and non violent" "we are when people are not threatening us or the animals in the fields" one of the monks replied. The oiks had been given the scare that they needed, they took off down the road shaking, having just had powerful loaded guns pushed in their faces.

The main animals on the farm were cows as the Hare Krishna's are big on both cow protection and milk products. Krishna had been from the Yadav caste, who were cow herders. As such cows have a very special place for them. According to Vedic teachings a human has three mothers. First is the biological mother, then there is mother India and then the cow, who gives us so much without taking anything from us in return. There were also peacocks and other animals but the cows were the most in number. It was a strange sight to see but whenever the monk who did the milking went to the milking shed the cows would all wander over and form a queue as they awaited their turn to be milked. There was a big old bull who was the father of all of the calves on the farm, his name was Dharma Raj.

The young Bullocks were all taken to a coral, one at a time for training to pull ploughs and carts. Sometimes in order to get them to move, it was necessary to hit them on the arse with a stick. At which point Darma Raj, who was standing outside of the coral, would start snorting and baying with rage. As if to say, "Don't you dare hit my son".

Gypsy read books and asked many questions during his stay. Being a Jew, it was hard to accept that they used statues to represent their God. As in the Jewish books It speaks harshly against such practices. But he had prayed and asked that the truth be shown to him and this is what he got shown as being the truth, or at least a chunk of it.

It was hard work keeping to the routine, especially the long prayer and chanting ceremonies and getting up at three in the morning, but he persevered on for over a week. But soon the worry about his visa became too much and he explained his predicament to them. They told him that if he became a Bramachari (monk), that they could take care of everything for him. But Gypsy was not at the point where he could even imagine such a life. He wanted to pursue his path to the truth and enlightenment, but giving up his freedom and taking on that lifestyle was totally beyond him. Besides, their description of heaven sounded remarkably hellish to him in certain ways.

He got a lift back to the city and made his way to the St. Vincent de Paul night shelter.

The next day he managed to get accepted for a job with commission based pay doing door to door sales. It was a scam, in that they were pretending to be working for a nonprofit organization that was helping young people. The job involved talking people into buying various different items of stationary from them. The only young people benefitting from this were the ones selling the stuff.

Gypsy got the job because when they asked about his sales experience he told about how he made his living in Goa. "If you can sell cakes on a beach in India, you've got all the sales experience necessary" the boss told him.

The next day he arrived at the office with his kit and waited. There were two groups going out selling. The older ones, who were around

Gypsy's age were going north to Coff's harbour, but Gypsy got placed with the younger ones who were going south. They were given a station wagon full of stationary and told to hit every area of population that they could find on the coast road south of Sydney.

So off they went. They hit the housing estates south of Wollongong and carried on south. Gypsy made the second highest score that day out of a team of seven. They phoned in to give the day's results to the boss who congratulated Gypsy for almost doing as well as his best bullshitter on the team and said, "I want you doing even better tomorrow".

They rented a caravan on a park that night and rested up. One of the team had brought a bag of weed with him and so Gypsy joined him and one others from the team to indulge in a smoke.

The next day they got dropped in an area where many of the houses were only used at weekends or for holidays. It was a disastrous morning where each one was lucky if they had made five dollars. They drove down the coast further to a more occupied area and had a better afternoon, but it still was not brilliant.

That night they stopped again in a caravan park. Then one disaster struck them after another. The car broke down out of town and they had to call in help. A cop came to the trailer and caught two of the crew with a bag of weed after noticing that one of them had a turn handle cheese grater that reeked of skunk. He searched Gypsy's kit and found two different I.D.'s with two different names but both with Gypsy's photo inside. "How do you explain this?" he asked. "deed pole", Gypsy blurted out. "I changed my name but I still haven't changed all of my documents." The cop took down the details and went away with the two that he had arrested. Gypsy was shitting himself over the I.D.'s he had had to forge a different name onto one of them, in order to be able to cash his pay cheques under the dodgy name he was using when he worked. He decided to use the name of the biggest asrsehole that he had met in Australia, who was one of the apple farm owners back at Donnybrook. "If anyone should get an unwarranted visit from the authorities then let it be him", thought Gypsy to himself.

Thankfully when the cop called in both names and found that there was no record of any trouble from anyone of either description, he let it go. The two who were in charge of the trip went to go and get the two guys out of the slammer. In the meantime the car was broken into and a load of the stock was taken or destroyed. The next morning they drove back to Sydney in a different rental vehicle after retrieving what stock was left in the destroyed station wagon. The trip had been a disaster. The two who had been busted would have to go and appear in court, no money had been made and Gypsy could see that trying to pursue money by this means would be futile.

He returned to the St. Vincent de Paul shelter. He had thirty five dollars to show for the last three days of work. He went up to the King's Cross area, up on the hill above where he was staying and got talking with some of the other travelers at the back packer hostel, which was located there, to see if anyone knew where he could find a well paying job. He needed it desperately. Time on his visa was getting short.

He was desperate and depressed as he told some other travelers about his seven thousand kilometre search for a job. "You've come this far now. You mustn't give up. You've got to pick yourself back up and go out there and do what you came here to do", a black girl from England who had been listening to his story told him. Gypsy was at the point of giving up and laughing in crazy hysterics at all the shit he had been through and the disasters that had happened, each time that he had looked for or even found work. But then he thought, "I'll give it one last go and it just better fucking work this time or else...if one, just one more fuckup happens I will abdicate any responsibility to behave reasonably and then anything is game".

The black girl had done Gypsy a huge favor because now he was fired up he was angry but now he was focused.

He went to the CES office on the opposite side of King's Cross and looked around the boards until he found a manual unskilled job advertised that offered a high wage and plenty of overtime. He took the card down and went to the desk and asked how to apply for the position. They gave him a number and a phone and he phoned the company. They told him that he could come for an interview the next day. He went back to the St. Vincent de Paul shelter and told the people there of his predicament. That he had a job interview but no clean or smart clothes to wear for it. They took him down into the basement where there was rack after rack of donated garments and let him select a couple of changes of clothes.

The next day at the interview, there were some fifteen or twenty other applicants in the waiting room. Gypsy looked and gulped with shock when he saw just how many other applicants were there. They were of many different nationalities. However when Gypsy went in and explained how he had hitched from Perth to find a job and that not only was he raring to go but that he also wanted every last bit of over time that they could throw at him and he was already accustomed to doing hard work and long shifts. To his delight he got the job.

The next morning after taking the train from Kings Cross for a twenty minute ride and then a bus ride of another twenty minutes to work, he was on parade with the other workers at 6:30am. One of the other workers showed him his cleaning round and then he just got on and did it.

It was the easiest job that he had ever had but he wasn't slacking. He just put his head down and put his best into it. At five hundred dollars a week it was the highest paying job that he had ever had, so he really, really wanted to keep it. As such, he tried to make sure that his area was the cleanest in the whole factory. Even so he would still finish an hour or two before the others and go and help them. His boss Domingo, a man from Chile would tell him to go and hide and take a break.

Because he worked so hard and never caused anyone a problem he got on well with everyone that he worked with and was happy in his job. The factory was like the United Nations with almost all of the world's nationalities represented and working there. The staff for the most part were a happy and easy going bunch and as long as no one made trouble nobody got any trouble. Everyone, bar for a few "winging poms" who complained unceasingly, were delighted to be living in Australia. It was so very much different to working in England.

At the end of the week with his first wage packet of three hundred and fifty dollars after taxes, he was able to move out of the shelter and into a shared room at an overflow house belonging to the 'Backpackers' hostel in King's Cross.

He would eat at the Hare Krishna restaurant each night, it was not just the opportunity to eat for free, he was still very much interested and dedicated to finding and understanding anything that would lead him to his goal of the realization of enlightenment. He had prayed and his prayer had led him to this group, so he wanted to listen and read what they had to say.

Most of what they spoke made sense but there were areas that didn't but it was probably something that had got lost in translation, as many of the Vedic teachings when looked at in depth, resonated with mathematics and science. This was more than could be said about the Semitic religions to the west. For example, the Vedic concept of the birth of the universe was remarkably similar to that of Steven Hawkins and many of the top physicists and mathematicians who are specialists in this field. Except that the Vedas go further, not just describing other planets within this universe but also what is outside of the bubble that this universe sit's within.

Further to this, it explained the nature of existence and what it is that bonds our awareness to this world. The great thing about the Hare Krishna organization was that the basis of their way is taken exactly from the teachings of the Vedas, Upanishads, Maha Barata and Baghavad Gita, which are some of India's most respected books of knowledge and wisdom.

In India, the organization was highly respected and there have been Hare Krishna monks there for at least the past five hundred years and possibly much longer. As such they were an organization of great integrity and one that warranted listening too, even if Gypsy did feel a little uneasy about some of their interpretations of what was being said in the books.

Back at the hostel Gypsy was staying in a downstairs room of the house which had two sets of bunks beds in it. The other two who were also occupying the room at the time were also working and like Gypsy, used the place to sleep and wash only. It was the cheapest short term accommodation available. It suited him as he had far too much that he wanted to do other than lounging about and sleeping.

He had set his target at saving two hundred and fifty dollars a week and he wanted to save three thousand dollars in total before leaving Australia. (at that time the US and Aussie dollar only had a ten to fifteen percent difference between them)

To save the three thousand dollars Gypsy would need to extend his visa by at least six weeks. This was not an easy thing to achieve as the Aussies were not in the habit of dishing out visa extensions without a very good reason, but Gypsy had an idea.

He got his six week extension but by a method that won't be elaborated on in this book. It had something to do with his two different I,D,s but that is all that I am allowed to say.

Away he worked in the factory each day and as he did so he got to know the people who worked on the production lines better, he was surprised to discover that not only did he have one of the most pleasant and easy jobs in the factory but because of the overtime, he was earning vastly more than the other workers. He liked being at work for such long hours because not only was he earning more but after work he was too tired to go out and spend any of it.

August 1984

He spent his evenings, mostly at the Hare Krishna temple and spent time reading their books after eating. On a couple of occasions he went out with them when they went out on the streets singing and dancing, to help them in their goal of giving out free books to the locals or anyone else who would like to have a read on Indian philosophy.

Some of the local self-declared Christians would come and rage and scream abuse at them. Some of them would first take a book and then rip it up while staring rage and hate at all who were there. The Krishna's just shrugged and smiled and carried on and gently suggested they would do well to have a read of the book before passing judgment on its content. This enraged the so called Christians even more and they would inevitably end up hissing, spitting and making ridiculous threats as they continued to be such wonderful ambassadors for their religion. "My church is going to take over this city" one of the delusional nutters raged. The Krishnas just looked at him and smiled in both amusement and pity, which made him even angrier. He stomped off looking furious and humiliated, as he muttered and snarled over his shoulder.

There was a lot of good will towards the Krishnas from many quarters, as many had experienced the excellent food at the free restaurant and takeaway at Kings Cross. It was surprising how much interest there was in Vedic philosophy among just the average ordinary working Australians. It was a testament to their open mindedness. Speaking in general terms, the Aussies were perhaps some of the most non judgmental and progressive people, in the world.

Gypsy was also interested in another Indian spiritual group who had a presence in Sydney. The Bramakamaris or Raj Yogis as they are also known as. He and an Australian friend went and checked out their place and tried doing their meditations with them for a couple of weeks. But though they were a beautiful group and their meditation was very peaceful, Gypsy just could not share their view of history and their technique of meditation was too subjective too and had more in common with techniques of self hypnosis than an objective search for the truth.

The weeks were going by and the money in Gypsy's pocket was slowly starting to build up. Soon he dared to start dreaming of the trip that he wanted to make into North East Asia. He started borrowing other people's Guide Books for the area and started jotting down addresses of cheap places to stay, in the main centers that he was planning to visit.

He only worked a half day on Saturdays and would spend the afternoon after work in Paddington, which was easily within walking distance of Kings Cross. Firstly he would go to the market and then later, he would go to one or several of the rock performances that were going on in the many pubs of the area. The music was invariably good as most of the bands were doing covers of Eric Clapton, Led Zeppelin, Steely Dan and Lynard Skynard tracks, with the odd bit of Jimi Hendrix thrown in for good measure. Sundays were spent, firstly in the morning, down in front of the opera house, by the waterside, were a rather good folk rock band called 'Hat trick' would perform. The band featured two really hot female violinists who could perform an absolutely brilliant version of the Mason Williams track 'Classical Gas'. Then after their performance finished at about noon, Gypsy would either take a wander across the bridge to the north shore, or wander up into the nearby botanical gardens and then later walk to Hyde Park and listen to people having a good old rant and rave at speaker's corner. Some of the speakers were both funny and informative, as they stood on their step ladders and soap boxes taking the piss out of anything and everything, from people's attitudes towards sex, on through to the dodgy activities of the clergy and local politicians.

There were the delusionary Christians who had dreams of founding a church in their own image and in the meantime, used speaker's corner as their pulpit. Then there was Charlie. He was there every week, standing up there on his step ladder, a fat man in his mid sixties he gave his opinions on everything and anything. He was a man of limited education or experience in life, but he knew that he knew more about everything than anyone else on earth. If he were of working age today no doubt the Murdochs would have given him a highly paid job on Fox News 'alongside Bill O'reilly'.

It was all so very entertaining and educational watching people being uninhibited and speaking their minds to all who wanted to hear. And of course the funniest of all was watching Charlie going off pop and swearing and cursing at the many people who were smarter than him and would ask questions that he didn't have answers for. He would call them stupid and go red in the face and curse and splutter at them and then change the subject, just like one of the anchor's 'on Fox News'. It's a pity that the man must certainly be dead by now as he would have been so perfect for the job. Bill O'reilley eat your heart out, you've got nothing on this guy. Come to think of it, he would probably have been old enough to have been O'reilley's father. You don't suppose......?

After they all started running out of wind and things began to wind down Gypsy would normally walk back up to King's Cross and take a detour up and around the corner into the main street, sometimes stopping at the aptly named fish bowl pub that had all glass on three sides providing no privacy, but good views of what was happening in the area. King's Cross is or at least was at that time, the red light area of the city.

So from the Fishbowl it was possible to watch all sorts of goings on. Some nights it could be better than television and as it got later and people got more inebriated the funnier it would get. The Aussies, as everyone knows are an uninhibited bunch anyway but when they're drunk it's something else again.

At the Cross, there also was a number of Lebanese takeaways. humous and falafel were still among Gypsy's top favorite foods so a visit to one of them several times a week was essential. He would order one of the long tubular wraps that they made, using a large Bedouin style pita, wrapped around, falafel, hummus, ful and tabuly (salad).

The rest of the time however, he pretty much only ate food from the Hare Krishna temple. They had a free takeaway at the back of the building that was not just for the needy but for all who wished to take food. The food in the Hindu Vedic context was all 'Prasad' (food that had been offered before God). According to Hindu/Vedic understanding such food carries a higher vibration and is used as a way of spreading a higher spiritual energy to the masses. These Hare Krishna's had the dream and goal of turning the whole city on and causing a spiritual awakening, through free books and free holy food.

Gypsy had absolutely no problem with this at all. If he could get enlightened just by eating really nice food then the more the better and he would get his lunch for the next day, the night before, at the take away. It had been cooked with the idea of offering it to God before being given away. So it always tasted wonderful.

The idea behind Prasad could be presumed to be effective as Gypsy had some of the happiest times of his life during those three months while he lived and worked in Sydney and lived almost exclusively on Hare Krishna food.

He enjoyed his job and the company of the people he worked with. They were nearly all immigrants. There were Germans, Hungarians, Peruvians, Chileanos, Brazilians, Russians, Indians, and all manner of south East Asians and pacific islanders. Everyone was extremely happy to be in Australia except that was for a small group of po, faced analy retentative uptight British women who ran the canteen who really needed to go down to the local hospital and have large legumes surgically removed from their rectums. They made Gypsy ashamed to be British. Everyone else could see that they were living in the best city on earth, in a wonderful huge country, populated, all be it sparsely, with some of the most friendly and straight up, genuine and exuberant people on earth. Social services were on another level compared with any other country outside of Scandinavia and Switzerland and the weather was pleasant too. Not only that but with the Medicare bank they also had one of the most intelligent socialized medicine systems in the world.

The only thing, truth be told that these women had to complain about was in their adoptive country there was nothing much to whine about. It could also have had something to do with the fact that in Australia, curtain twitching is neither considered a sport or a respectable past time. They were probably becoming a source of mirth for the neighborhood in which they lived. Such types expect to be taken seriously and become furious with rage when this does not happen. When Gypsy was speaking with them one day, during the lunch break, he said, "you must love it here in this country, it's so much more relaxed than living in England, I would emigrate here if I could, it's the best country that I have ever seen". "Oh no" they replied, with screwed up expressions on their faces "we don't like it, we miss England and wish that we could move back there". This was a sentiment that Gypsy just could not get his head around. How the hell could anyone miss England, with it's nasty weather, uptight attitudes, malicious officious, screwed up beaurocracy and depressive people? Besides that, England at that time was in the process of being totally destroyed by Maggie Thatcher and her incompetent, sexually deviant and totally corrupt minions.

Gypsy's job was easy enough that he had time to stop and have a quick chat from time to time with people along the way who were working on the production lines. The large Hungarian man who ran the paint shop was one of his favorites to chat with. During the uprising against communism in Hungary he was involved and was only just out of range of the Soviet tanks when he made it to the border and escaped into Austria.

Also there was an old German man in his sixties who ran the stores department. He had worked for Qantas for many years as an aviation mechanic and was an intelligent man who had stories worth listening to.

Generally, throughout the factory, people were interesting, as they had come from so many varied places. Some of which were places that Gypsy planned to visit in the very near future. He would ask them about their homelands, as to help him plan his journey better. It was better than reading a guide book. He would make brief notes of the most important things, like place names, areas of a city that had cheap accommodation and interesting historical and spiritual places that were not on the main tourist routes.

In the evenings, now that he had saved over two thousand dollars, he started to plan his route to Japan. Even with three thousand dollars it was still going to be a tight squeeze, to do all that he wished to do with it. He sat down and planned a realistic budget for each stage of the journey, according to the local costs in each country and then added on a further fifteen to twenty percent for unforeseen costs and fuck ups.

SEPTEMBER 1984.

He made a visit to a dentist and had no less than six fillings put in in one afternoon. It was the one and only time that he had taken time off of work and then only because it was unavoidable. As such he got the whole job done in one sitting. The dentist was a lady from Czechoslovakia and she seemed to really know how to do her job well. Never the less he walked around for the rest of the afternoon with his whole mouth numb from the novacane.

what with his work, the good pay, the Hare Krishnas and the good natured ways of the Aussies he was enjoying himself so much that he was able to give up smoking cigarettes.

Back at the room at the 'Backpackers', an Aussie by the name of Greg had moved into the room. He, too, like Gypsy, had hitched from West Australia. He was from Kalgoorlie and had worked in the mines there. His father had died when he was thirteen years old and straight after the funeral his mother had run off with another man, leaving him and his younger brothers to fend for themselves. He had gone to work in the mines in order to put food on the table while his two younger brothers finished school. He was self- educated and very straight up, without being in the least bit pushy or arrogant. But one thing he was determined to change was the complete lack of partying by the others in the room. He got himself a job doing building work and soon had his first week's pay. "Come on you lot", he said. "You may have to get up for work early but at least let's go out for a beer or two".

So up they would go to the Fishbowl or another pub and laugh at the crazy antics going on out in the street.

Another friend of Gypsy's who would sometimes join them in the pub, was an ageing bearded drunk by the name of Bill. Bill had a wicked sense of humor and probably had a P.H.D. in 'taking the piss'. They were watching as two ugly creatures in skirts walked past, everyone was trying to guess whether they were just really ugly women, transexuals or trannies. When Bill yelled out at them. "Excuse me, but what sized school uniforms do you wear?" it became very obvious what they were, as the two transvestites turned around and gave him a highly effeminate and bitchy earful of abuse.

People up and down the street were laughing so much at the response that they had tears rolling down their faces. Some were trying to hang on to the wall or lamp posts for support as they fell about the place laughing as the two trannies stalked off in their stilettos with sodomized expressions on their faces.

On another occasion when Greg returned to the room at five thirty in the morning after a night out and Gypsy was just about to leave to go to work, Greg turned to Gypsy and said, "Your mate, Bill, he's twisted, he is". "Why do you say that?" asked Gypsy. "Well, I was walking through the cross just now and there he was sitting down on the pavement leaning up against a rubbish bin with a can of beer in his hand laughing and taking the piss out of half the people that walked past him. I think he's taken to regarding the street as his home. I wonder if he give's that particular rubbish bin as his address when he goes to collect his welfare cheque".

At work, to Gypsy's and everyone else's relief, the most winging and sadly infantile of all of the Brits working the shop floor managed to get his nasty self sacked for taking an uninvited grope of one of the women working at the factory. She was an extremely beautiful and well dressed, married Indian woman from Fiji and she wasted no time in raising a complaint. As such the bastard was pretty much immediately ejected from the factory premises. It was indeed good to see the back of him and no one was sad to see him go. The Indian woman always smiled sweetly at everyone in the fractory but that was by no means an invite type of smile, it was just a nice friendly, innocent smile but this arsehole had chosen to totally misinterpret it in his tiny little mind.

One Saturday afternoon, Gypsy went to the Singapore airlines office and paid the difference and booked a seat as so that he could fly from Sydney instead of Perth back to Singapore and made a booking to leave at the beginning of October.

The Manly Jazz festival happened, and so on that sunday Gypsy took the ferry across the harbour to go and see it. There was even a trad jazz band playing on the ferry as they went across. He spent several hours listening to and watching several jazz rock fusion bands perform. It got him inspired as that was the type of music that he liked best and he wished that he could play it on guitar.

On another Sunday, he borrowed a camera and went and bought a roll of 35mm film and walked around Sydney taking photos of the various different sights. Sadly it was the only film that he was able to shoot in Australia. He wished that he could have taken photos of many things, including his journey across from Perth, but at least he would have this as a memory of this fantastic country.

On another occasion, one Saturday night, Greg and the other three went down to a nightlife area of Sydney known as the rocks, where they went to see the Australian Blues Brothers in concert, at a large club. It was an amazing performance and they looked, danced and sounded just like the real thing, with a full band behind them. There was one fat one and one tall thin one Dressed in the outfits, complete with dark glasses and hats, doing the singing and the doing the same dance acrobatics as in the movie and singing the same songs as in the movie. It was a very good night out.

Back at work that Monday morning however there was some pretty heavy news in the papers and on the television. There had been a shoot out in a pub on the outskirts of Sydney the day before, involving two motorbike gangs, the Banditos and the Comancheros who were reportedly aligned with the Hells Angels. Seven or so people had been killed, some of them being innocent bystanders. It had been like a scene out of the Mad Max movies according to some who had seen it happen. It was all over the news that day and for the next two weeks and it was all that anyone was talking about. There were rumors in the press that bikers from America from both the Banditos and the Hells Angels were planning on flying in for an all out war between the two gangs and Australian immigration was on alert to stop them from entering the country. But in the end nothing more happened at that time. Never the less one innocent young girl lost her life as did six other people, some of whom were only in the pub to enjoy a quiet drink on a Sunday lunch time.

All of Gypsy's kit was falling to pieces, he had had to sow patches on his jeans to hold them together and the cheap travel bags that he had bought back in Penang were not up to the job ahead. Further to this the 'high tech, super light weight, thermally lined, sleeping bag' that he had purchased back in the UK had proved disastrously ineffective and he needed a replacement.

Though he tried to avoid buying much in Australia where things were expensive, he went to an army surplus store and bought a tough canvass hold all and a warm, hollow fill sleeping bag that was good for sleeping outside, down to a temperature of minus eight degrees Celsius.

Things were coming along well, his visa extension meant that he could stay long enough and work to reach his target of three thousand dollars.

Meanwhile At the hostel, there was a room upstairs occupied by two young Brits and an Israeli. The Brits were a couple of wankers (as was par for the course) when one of them was smoking a joint one day and there were just a few hits left, Gypsy asked if the guy could spare a hit on it. So the wanker threw the joint out of the window and grinned spitefully as if Gypsy had done something wrong to him or spoken to him wrongly. He was just pissed off that Gypsy had the cheek to ask for such an outrageous favor. The behavior of so many of the British could be held up in sharp contrast with that of the Australians or New Zealanders. Indeed, it was difficult to understand why so many of the young British at that time were such a resentful, hateful, spiteful and infantile bunch of prats. It was at that time, the end of the punk rock era and the British youth culture was full of snivel and piss. But why oh why did they always have to follow the lowest path of behavior possible like a bunch of sheep or a pack of dogs?

Eli, the Israeli was a super patriotic type and if anyone ever dared mention anything about the shortcomings of his country then he would jump to his feet and launch a vigorous verbal defense with his strong blocked nose Israeli accent that could be an absolutely hilarious sight to watch, at least from a distance. Gypsy was chatting with the Two British wankers one Sunday afternoon and Eli was lying on his bed asleep. Gypsy asked them which airline they had used to get to Australia. They told him that they had used Malaysian MAS. Gypsy then said, "I managed to get a ticket from Penang on Singapore Airlines" and then added in a loud voice, "of course they were much better than EL AL". and then watched with mirth as Eli jumped from his sleep in one spring like movement landing upright on his feet at the foot of his bed and demanded to know in his blocked nose Israeli accent, "What do you mean they are better than EL AL?. What is wrong with EL AL?" "Well for starters there's free drinks on Singapore Airlines", said Gypsy. "Are you crazy? there is free drinks on EL Al, too", he carried on. "You get free fruit juice and tea and coffee". "Yes", said Gypsy. "But you have to pay for alcohol and head sets for watching the movies". Eli continued to splutter and argue. He would not have known a piece of objectivity if it wacked him in the face.

The joke had been had and now it was getting boring, even though he could still not understand that Gypsy had just been winding him up and taking the piss.

The occupants of that room helped remind Gypsy, that he neither wanted to see England or Israel, in the foreseeable future. At work, Gypsy had given his bosses two weeks notice of his plan to leave and was getting ready to be in Asia once more. However so determined had he been to make sure that he kept his job that he had worked as hard as the most dedicated workers in the factory. This was something that had not gone unnoticed by the management. They called him into the office and asked him if he would reconsider his decision to leave. "You've hardly missed any time from the job, we hear reports of how hard you work and how well you get on with the other staff and not only that but you have been here for every overtime shift. Are you sure you won't reconsider? We don't come across staff like you very often", the personnel manager said. "Well,

I'd love to but I can't. I've really enjoyed working for you and you've paid me well, but I have no choice. I have things I must be doing that will take me travelling once more", Gypsy explained. His visa was to run out the day that he was booked to fly out and he was doing overtime right up until the night before. But he couldn't tell anyone his true situation. They didn't even know his real name as he was still working with dodgy I.D. as he didn't have a work permit.

He could and did fake the accent so well that he would engage his bullshitting skills and either say that he was a British immigrant who had been in the country for years or at times he would just bullshit his way as an Aussie and get away with it without anyone suspecting differently. However pulling it off over a longer period of time was harder and so thus the immigrant story was safer and a helpful cover in case of any slip ups.

OCTOBER 1984.

Just before leaving, who should show up at the Hare Krishna temple but Steve from Goa and Bangkok. Gypsy had not seen him since that last morning on the Kowsan road in Bangkok. He told Gypsy that he had used Ronnie's travel agent too, but when he got to Penang where he was to collect his ticket from a travel agent, all sorts of mayhem broke loose before he finally got his ticket. He had left shortly after Gypsy out of Bangkok and had also been working in and around the Sydney area. He was heading to New Zealand with the idea of immigrating to that country. It was good to see him again but now each would head out on different roads as Gypsy's only wish was to return to Asia to travel and live there.

On the morning of leaving Gypsy had already incinerated his fake I.D. He had just over three thousand dollars in cash and travelers cheques. However, he wanted to at least be able to leave the country with it all intact. So with the few possessions he had, that he did not wish to take with him and his canvass bag over his shoulder, he walked to the main Backpackers hostel where he was able to raise a further fifty one dollars selling off his old kit (e.g. bags, sleeping bag, books, cassettes, etc) to the other travelers, in fast but cheap sales.

Then he took a bus to Kingsford Smith international airport.

The airport was a strange triangular shape and it was certainly not one of the nicer airports on the planet. With service at its most basic and only hard, uncomfortable plastic seats to sit down on, he sat down and waited. Out on the apron and connected to the airbridges were jumbos with Lufthansa, British Airways, Japan Airlines, Thai, Air France, Alitalia and of course Qantas markings. There were containers with Air Nauru and Air Pacific markings and a DC10 marked in the colors of Continental airlines.

No matter, the flight was soon to board and actually it was good that there was nothing at the airport to tempt the money out of his pockets. Gypsy was feeling good, he was about to return to East Asia. The day before, the personnel manager had summoned him and given him a letter of recommendation and told him that he would have a job if he ever wished to return to the factory. He had more money in his pocket than he had ever held in his hands before and all being well, he should have enough, just about and by the skin of his teeth, to travel on the route he had chosen.

Australia had been really good to him and he had taken a strong liking to the people, with their straight up and friendly ways. Unlike England, there was no nastiness and bullying in the work place and people were contented with their lives. Aussies just liked to get on with other people. That didn't mean that they didn't like to take the piss, it just meant that it was given and taken in a good natured way.

CHAPTER 7

TRANSIT TO SINGAPORE

OCTOBER 1984.

The passengers were called, to board the flight. It was one of the new Boing 747 300 series with extended upper deck that only Singapore airways, Swiss Air and a couple of other airlines had. Shortly after boarding they taxied out to the runway and took off. The plane gained height and headed out in a north westerly direction that took them diagonally across the centre of Australia. Looking down from the plane window they were greeted by a most unusual sight for Australia. It had been raining in parts of the outback for several weeks and an area that was for most of the time bone dry desert was now covered in huge but temporary lakes.

Gypsy had been living like a hermit monk for an exceedingly long period of time while he endeavored to find a job and also while he had been working, not to mention on his journey from England. But now he had money and was free of commitments and on a flight with free grog. He was not going to let this opportunity slip him by. The flight was full but the service was good as was the food and the drinks. Seven hours and forty minutes after take off the plane touched down at Changi Airport, taxied in towards the H shaped terminal and pulled up to a waiting airbridge. Gypsy staggered off the flight, long haired, drunk and looking for all the world like a penniless swag man. Somehow he managed to make his way out of the airport without a problem. (in those days the Singapore immigration officials would make men with long hair take a visit to their in house barber shop before being allowed into the country). Several South East Asian countries had no hippie policies. At Bangkok they had a rather comical list at immigration, "Ten ways to spot

254

a hippie" and Indonesia had the infamous S.H.I.T. stamp which stood for: Suspected Hippie In Transit. If they put that stamp in your passport it meant that you had twenty four hours to get out of the country. It was worn as a badge of honor by any of the travelers who had been unfortunate enough to get one. Straight society was viewed very much as the enemy at that time, on account of the non acceptance, hostility and hatred that was constantly dished out against hippies, travelers and anyone else who did not fit into their nasty little moulds. It had become a bit of a sport to wind the tossers up, especially any of them who were on a real power trip.

SINGAPORE.

Jumping on to a shuttle bus he made his way into the city. He had been told that Singapore was a smart place but he didn't realize how smart until he saw it with his own eyes.

All the way from Changi into the city, which was a few kilometers away, along by each side of the highway and also in the wide central reservation, were beautiful and sculpted tropical gardens. Even inside of the city every available bit of space, no matter how small would have gardens of climbing and hanging plants.

Gypsy got off of the bus on Orchard road and then sought directions to Ho Mantin Street where the cheap hostels were located. Somehow even in the inebriated state that he was in he managed to find his way to a hostel and drop off his bag before going out to a bar to further celebrate his return to Asia.

He Woke up the next morning in a large dormitory with a throbbing head and vague recollections of the past night's activities, including getting very drunk, falling over and going to sleep underneath a table in a bar. But how he got back to the hostel safely after that, he had not a clue, his memories ended when he fell under the table.

Sitting on the next bed and puffing nonchalantly on a large joint, was a traveler from the Philippines. "You sure look like you could use a hit on this my friend", he said as he leaned over with a grin on his face and offered the spliff to Gypsy. "Thanks", he said. "Yes, I could sure use a few hits on it to kill this hangover". Gypsy took several large tokes and passed it back. "Isn't it dangerous smoking weed here in super fascist Singapore?" Gypsy asked. "Sure", said the Philippino. "But I'm not going to let that stop me from enjoying a smoke". Gypsy took a few more tokes and then went to find some breakfast.

He wandered around through old Singapore with its two storey white terraced houses and its small shops selling exotic smelling spices and strange looking soft drinks.

He came across several half finished food centers, that though the building work had not been completed, the halls had food stands within them. Gypsy went in and looked around until he found a stand selling noodles and vegetables that he liked the smell of. Having spent the last several months in the company of the Hare Krishna's each evening, he had become a strict vegetarian with the exception of eggs and dairy products. Finding food that he could eat was not so easy. He got chatting with a local couple about heir country, they were of Chinese descent but Singapore being first world they thought in a similar way to Europeans in many ways but not all.

After eating, he wandered over to the counter to pay but to his pleasant surprise was told that the couple had paid for his food for him. "What a kind, generous gesture" he thought to himself. He then wandered off in the direction of the new part of the city. Soon he was checking out the electronic emporiums on Orchard road, as he looked for a good deal on a camera and a walkman.

Eventually after having checked out the wares in some thirty or forty shops in five or ten emporiums, he met a man who was ready to cut him a good deal. For one hundred and fifty U.S. dollars which is what he had budgeted for it, he was able to buy a Minolta X300 semi automatic SLR camera with a 30mm lens and a 70 to 210 mm zoom complete with cases. For another thirty dollars he bought a Sanyo, walkman type, tape player and a small set of speakers, again for what he had budgeted for it. Now he was set up with what he had stopped in Singapore for.

He spent the next day exploring Singapore and taking photos with his new camera. Singapore was not so full of great sights so he barely used up one film. he spent that evening in the night market buying bootleg cassettes of some of his favorite music and drinking beers in the sidewalk bars with travelers from Australia and New Zealand. He went to go and see Bugis street but he was too early, the evening's entertainment had not begun. Apparently one of the best laughs in the whole of Singapore was to go and watch the transsexual hooker market taking place on Bugis street from one of the local sidewalk bars and watch the crazy antics

By the end of the next day Gypsy was bored shitless with Singapore. Yes it was beautifully clean and people were generally friendly, helpful and honest and it was full of elegant gardens and the like but it was too much like the west in some ways but more so. What with it's strict rules and plentiful punishments for transgressors and the strict orderly way of doing things, it was a bit claustrophobic. So after a couple of hits from the Philippino's latest joint he headed out to find a travel agent. He didn't have to look too far. On the next block he found one and went in. They were very helpful, he still had a ticket to Penang and they booked him onto the afternoon flight.

He went back to the hostel, packed his bags, paid his bill and then sat with the Philippino smoking joints until it was time to leave for the airport. Once again but this time in a sober state and in daylight he rode the bus along the road full of sculpted tropical gardens to Changi Airport. The place looked beautiful but it was so heavily controlled and sterile and Gypsy longed for the scruffier third world beyond its borders, where things were more relaxed.

Gypsy checked in and went through passport control. He found the bar and stopped for a couple of drinks. The airport also was incredible, with climbing and hanging plants decorating columns from out of giant tubs. There were also two waterfalls, coming from the next floor up into large pools that were set above waist height in the main departure lounge. He eventually wandered from the bar to the gate where his flight would be departing from. Soon he was boarding his flight, a Singapore Airlines A300, for the one hour flight to Penang. The plane doors were closed and shortly after, the plane was pushed back. It then taxied out to one of the runways and took off into a clear sky. Lunch was soon served, followed by a couple of rounds of drinks.

The plane started its descent into Penang and as the plane flew ever lower Gypsy could see the green island, covered in jungle and coconut plantations. It looked like somewhere out of an exotic adventure movie with it's scenic hills and tropical vegetation. Then they were landing amid the coconuts and cassava. The plane taxied to an air bridge and soon after Gypsy was standing at passport control with its stark warning posters:

'DEATH TO ALL DRUG SMUGGLERS, KNOW WHAT YOU CARRY, YOU HAVE BEEN WARNED.', with a picture of a noose, to emphasize the point.

After collecting his bag he jumped on a local bus into Georgetown, the main town on the island and from where he was dropped off he found his way back to the New China Guest House, where he had stayed before.

There was another British traveler staying in the dormitory who had also just come from Australia and they decided to both go to a local traveler hangout to see what they could find out about a good way of getting from Penang to Koh Samui in Thailand.

[Koh Samui is an island in the gulf of Siam. It is the largest of three inhabited islands in that group, which includes Koh Pangan and Koh Tao. At that time there was no airport on the island and the only way of getting there was to travel to Surat Thani, which is half way up the Thai coast, between the Malaysian border and Bangkok and from there take the ferry to Nakon which was the largest village on the island].   At the café they met another traveller, a New Zealander who was also on his way to Samui so they decided to travel together, but first each had things that they wished or needed to do in Penang.

The next day Gypsy who was still wearing clothes that were falling to pieces, went out to the market and bought himself new jeans and T-shirts and after having the three pairs of fake Levis adjusted (for shorter legs) returned with them to the guest house where he changed into his first set of new clothes for eight months. Dropping his other new clothes in his bag, he returned to the street with his camera. The other two had gone off to see the snake temple and a beach so he rented a trishaw for the afternoon and asked to be given a tour of the different temples and views of Georgetown.

The trishaw rider, a middle aged man of a quiet nature first took him and showed him a number of Chinese temples. One such temple was the Temple of Heavenly Peace where local Chinese would go to burn giant two meter tall incense sticks and toy money as offerings to dead relatives, to help them on their way in the afterlife. The temple was a small, old looking building and did not have the same high roofed structure that many of the other temples had. In the center of a stone courtyard surrounded by incense, flower and charm shops was a large metal contraption with clouds of incense and other smells wafting from the burning embers within. The temple itself sat behind a high metal railing with large metal gates. It's roof was made of traditional, rounded, Chinese, red terracotta, roof tiles. Clouds of incense drifted out through its main entrance and the place gave the impression that not much had changed there in a hundred years.

Next was a visit to the local Thai Buddhist Temple that was surrounded by statues of yogis, dragons and demons. The place looked like some sort of weird 'Asian Disney land' with its bright colors and weird animal sculptures.

Next was a ride to the sea to see the view from George Town across the strait to Butterworth on the mainland and the hills beyond. It was raining lightly but that made for an even better view, with the low hanging monsoon clouds giving another dimension to the photos that Gypsy was taking with his new camera.

The Penang trishaw was different from the Indian Rickshaw in that on the Trishaw the passenger seat was at the front and set low, also the driver nearly always had an umbrella set on a short mast, to keep both the sun and the rain off of him.

Having had an interesting afternoon, Gypsy paid the trishaw driver and headed back to the traveler café to find the other two.

Their journey to the snake temple had been interesting too. The snake temple was a temple where snakes were honored and served food by temple servants. Apparently the creatures were slithering around everywhere within the inner temple compound and appeared to be slightly drugged and slow.

Speaking of drugs, the Kiwi had managed to arrange some weed via the trishaw rider who had taken them on their tour. He had rented a room in an ageing and dilapidated traditional style Malaysian house and they all went around there and smoked a couple of joints on his terrace.

The next couple of days were spent relaxing, eating and strolling around the markets. It was the Kiwi who was the first one to spot a very interesting phenomena. The traffic was incredibly well mannered, with larger vehicles making way for smaller and slower ones and no one cutting them up or honking their horns at them. This set Penang in a very different light compared to the rest of South Asia where the rule of push and shove, bully driving in a never ending game of chicken was the norm.

Penang was a truly nice place to be, with the exception of their drug laws of course. But that did not stop Gypsy and his new found friends finding a smoke or two. Gypsy had suggested that it would be safer to only smoke with the trishaw riders, as for one, if they were smoking it with them, then they couldn't also be informing the cops about who they had sold it to. And for two, they would be more likely to know the faces of any plainclothes cops who operated in the area.

So through the next two evenings they sat under some low bushes near the local courts and smoked weed with the trishaw riders.

After four good days in Penang it was time to leave. Early the following morning they jumped on a mini bus to Samui. It was mostly Thais and Malays aboard the bus.

The bus drove onto the ferry for the short crossing to the mainland. The ferry was single leveled and open-decked, with just enough room to get out and stand between the cars. Once off the ferry they were driving along the main highway to the border, past rice paddies and the coconut plantations and past old farmers walking along in traditional clothes and lampshade hats. Everything was damp and green as the monsoon was not yet over and there was the occasional downpour as they rode along the northbound highway to the Thai border.

ROAD TO SAMUI

OCTOBER 1984.

They came to the border after a drive of an hour or two and got out of the mini bus, firstly going through Malaysian passport control and then the same procedures of form filling on the Thai side of the border. Gypsy had got himself a proper visa for Thailand at the Thai consulate in Penang, as opposed to the two week transit visa available at the border. Now he would be able to stay for a month or more if he wished to.

Once through the border formalities another mini bus, this time a Thai one came and collected them. First the luggage was loaded onto the roof and then everyone got aboard for the ride to Surat Thani. Heading north they reached the small and somewhat scruffy town of Hat Yai. The mini bus stopped outside of a cafe and everyone got out for something to eat. Twenty minutes later they were back in the vehicle and on their way again. Leaving from there, the mini bus drove inland, north and towards the other coast, on the Gulf of Siam. The land looked far poorer than either the land in Malaysia or that of north and central Thailand. There were at that time, no towns and only the occasional village, on the highway north.

Gypsy got talking with the other two travelers and soon they were all talking about what they had heard or read about the island.

At about three o'clock that afternoon, they reached Surat Thani. The mini bus drove through the town and eventually reached the small harbor from where the ferry to Samui left from. The bus dropped them at the ferry and left. They boarded the boat, a medium sized and somewhat modern car ferry, with a glazed and air conditioned viewing deck, complete with a snack bar that also sold beer.

The boat pulled out through the narrow estuary lined with fishing boats and headed out to sea, passing as it went, small rocky islands covered in jungle. There were three older men who were expats onboard.

They worked in Bangkok and had come down to Samui for a short vacation. One was British, another was Australian and the third was an American. They had been to Samui several times before. Gypsy got talking with them about the island. "So where's the best place to stay on Samui?" he asked. "Well what do you want?" asked the Australian. "Sex, drugs and rock and roll and in that order", said Gypsy. "Ah that's easy", they all replied at once. "Joy Bungalows at Chawang Beach". "When you get off the ferry you'll find a row of pickup trucks that act as buses on the island, just ask for one that's going to Chawang" the Australian explained. Gypsy went back and joined the other two and told them what he had found out. "sounds like a plan to me" said the Kiwi, "yep that sounds like just the ticket" said the other Brit.

The boat pulled in at Nakon, the small scruffy town on the west of the island that acted as the main harbor. They got off and carried their bags to the waiting line of pickups and were soon riding along the narrow, single lane road through the coconut plantations in the direction of Chawang. At that time tourism was not a big thing on the island and most of the small population of the island made their living from either coconut farming or fishing. There was no airport at that time and the few tourists who made it there, were either hippies, backpackers or expats who worked in Thailand.

SAMUI (CHAWANG)

After a drive of fifteen minutes or so they were at Chawang. There were maybe seven small resorts and Joy Bungalows was easy to find. Even before they had checked in and thrown their bags in their respective bungalows they sat down at a table in the bar for a drink. Before they quite knew what had happened they were descended upon by a crowd of young Thai women. One came along dressed in a white miniskirt and ultra low slung top and promptly sat down on Gypsy's knee. "Hello, my name Sulie you like live with me?" she asked. "Sure", said Gypsy. Within ten minutes each one of them had been grabbed so to speak by a woman and in turn, was buying them drinks and food.

The next priority was to find some weed, which turned up at almost the same speed as the women had. There was a disco at Joy bungalows, the only one on the beach and after a couple of hours of drinking and dancing, they all ended up in their bungalows with their newfound girlfriends.

The next day, Gypsy awoke early and after a walk along the beach, decided to move to a more quiet and more drug oriented set of bungalows. The resort next door was called Munchies bungalows and apart from being cheaper, at forty baht per night, [which at that time was the equivalent of one dollar and forty cents]. It was less intense than Joy bungalows as it didn't have a disco or hoards of desperate young women. It also had a large notice out on the beach, proclaiming "Magic mushroom we have every day".

Gypsy's new bungalow was between ten and fifteen metres from the sea and had a wooden terrace around three of it's four sides. Inside it was just a hut with a bed, a fan and a light, there were communal showers and toilets in a concrete building some twenty metres behind the bungalow and a restaurant up on a wooden platform with a palm thatched roof, it looked as the beach did too, as if it had come straight out of the Bacardi advert.

Sulie wasted no time in following him and moving herself in too. The other two came to visit and were impressed with the restaurant's menu of magic mushroom dishes and other interesting herbal products that were used in the making of cookies and also sold loose in bags across the counter of the restaurant.

The beach had a rocky outcrop to the south about a hundred meters along the white sands from Gypsy's bungalow.

The resort next door on the south and thus on the outcrop side was more fancy and had bungalows that could cost up to ten dollars per night, but they were big enough to accommodate a whole family and had A/C. Again that resort looked like the photo for an advert for some high end product. North along the beach there was not much at all with just one more resort after Joy bungalows and after that just white sandy beach and thick jungle like coconut plantations. However one morning while walking north along the sand, after about a kilometer, he saw a small cluster of more primitive looking bungalows. The owner came out and got talking with Gypsy and said he would offer him and his friends a free bungalow each if they would eat at his restaurant at least twice a day. It was a nice offer but with no electricity and primitive huts with no mosquito nets Gypsy was more than happy to be in the Bacardi advert than in some jungle Jim, hippie masochist camp, getting the shit bitten out of him by mosquitoes all night and eating food cooked in questionable hygiene.

Back at Munchies or more to the point on the beach in front of Munchies in the warm shallow waters that stretched far off the beach, Gypsy relaxed for the first time in a very long while. Sulee who was three or four years older than him would look at him at least three times a day and ask, "You want fuck? We go bungalow now, yes?" and so some days passed by as he relaxed into a life of sex, joint smoking, drinking and lying on the beach. There were other backpackers at the resorts too. One evening while walking up off of the beach to his cabin he noticed a young German man who was staying in the next cabin who had practically tied himself around one of the two upright pillars of his cabin's porch. He was hanging on to it as if it was his last grip on reality before he disappeared off into his own mad hallucinations, never to be seen again. He had a big silly grin on his face and was almost one hundred percent motionless. He was still standing there when Gypsy returned from the shower block some ten minutes later, even his facial expression had not changed, he still had that mad, manic, big silly grin on his face. Fifteen minutes later after Gypsy had changed and gone out to eat, the German was still there, his legs and arms tied around the post in a tight embrace and he had still got that mad grin on his face.

Gypsy sat down to eat and Sulee came and joined him for some food and drink. The other two came over with their girlfriends and they sat around getting bombed on the local weed and drinking beers. Later Gypsy wandered over to his bungalow to get his spare bag of weed and as he came back out of the cabin in the dark he could still see the German wrapped around the pillar with that same mad silly grin on his face. "Those must have been some super strong mushrooms he ate, either that or he ate too many of them" thought Gypsy to himself.

The next day, the German was back down from his trip and Gypsy asked him how many mushrooms it had taken to fuck him up like that. "Ah it vos just ze vun small magic mushroom omelet on ze restaurant menu card", he replied. "I voz not expecting it to be so strong." "Mad", thought Gypsy to himself. "and that was the smallest one that they made!!!". That afternoon Gypsy and the other two were sitting in the restaurant at Munchies. The other two ordered a magic mushroom omelet each, two of the smallest and cheapest ones on the menu. But when Gypsy told them about how fucked up the German had been on one of the small ones, the night before, they both decided to donate a portion of their omelets to Gypsy.

Soon after, at least for Gypsy, the sky began to turn to all sorts of weird and strange colors and things like posts, plants and trees began moving around, all the while, while staying still. Dimensions blurred and changed and he was having a hard time trying to remember who he was or where or how. They all ended up sitting on the beach and staring at their own weird hallucinations as they looked out to sea.

Sulee came along and seeing that Gypsy was tripping, looked at him and said, "You do magic mushloom you clazy maybe you poison self and die". Gypsy got pissed off with her for trying to put a downer on his trip and told her to fuck off and not to come back that night.

The next day she came around to his bungalow to say "velly solly" for trying to fuck up his trip and admitted that she had been tripping on mushrooms a few nights previously. She insisted on washing his clothes and tidying his bungalow. But Thai women are among some of the most jealous and insecure females on the surface of this planet and as things went Gypsy was starting to feel a little bit claustrophobic. She would never leave him alone and if he did manage to escape off for an hour or two he would be met with accusations on his return.

"My flend say she see you talk with other woman in lestalaunt, who this other woman?" "She was the waitress I was ordering food and a drink", Gypsy would reply in all honesty, at which point he would be treated to a most suspicious stare. Gypsy was also starting to feel restless. He did not have huge cash reserves and wanted to make it up into North East Asia before he ended up spending all his money in Thailand.

He took a trip with Noi, out to see the big Buddha that was atop a small hill on a peninsula jutting out from another beach. On the journey of between seven to ten kilometers in the back of one of the pickup taxi/ buses they saw maybe five or seven other four wheeled vehicles on the road, either farm vehicles or pick up taxis. Noi told Gypsy about how she had worked as a hooker at a bar on Sukumvit road but had moved to Samui in the hope of finding a more permanent and maybe younger man to live with. Her mother had died some years before and there was nothing for her back home in her village, so she had moved to Bangkok. The choice of work was limited if she wanted to get ahead. She had very little in the way of education and was left with a choice of a factory job, domestic helper or working as a hooker. At least if she went on the game she would have enough money to live reasonably well and would have some freedom.

She was at Samui looking for a younger man to live with and to better her life.

They reached the big Buddha monastery area and got out of the pickup and walked through the area to the hill and up the steps to the giant Buddha at the top. Noi burned some incense and kneeled and bowed to the image three times and then placed the incense at the shrine at the Buddha's feet.

Walking back down the steps Gypsy noticed some small shacks on stilts in the sea around the base of the Buddha hill. "What are the shacks for?" asked Gypsy. "That were monk live", Noi replied.

Gypsy was the only tourist at the site at that time. Other than him there were only locals and an occasional Thai or two from Bangkok or elsewhere who was working nearby or living on the island.

Back at the beach again Gypsy was starting to feel bored and his feet were getting very itchy. Noi's conversational skills revolved around food, sex and alcohol and the occasional tirade of jealous, insecure ramblings. Also she was costing more than he could afford to keep, as she ordered ever more expensive things on the restaurant menus.

SAMUI TO BANGKOK

Gypsy went and booked himself onto a boat to the mainland, he made his excuses and promised to be back in a week, to stop her from trying to cling to him or hitch a ride north with him. Even then he had worked out that Thai women had an adhesive quality about them and if they got their claws in deep enough, they would never let go.

The other two who had travelled up from Penang with him were staying for longer before making their journeys north to Bangkok and onwards. But eight days of tropical paradise was quite enough for Gypsy at that time. He was bored and craved some real adventure. Any fool could lie on a tropical beach and get stoned with a jungle bunny all day and fuck his brains out with her all night.

He said his goodbyes and headed for the ferry at Nakon. Crossing to the mainland he had decided to take the night train to Bangkok. He made his way from the harbor to the railway station and bought a ticket and sat down and waited for his train.

The train arrived and he boarded. Although the train was not overcrowded, each seat except for his own was full, which meant that the ride would be anything but comfortable.

BANGKOK

NOVEMBER 1984

After a night stretched out under the seats, Gypsy awoke at 6 am, climbed out of the small space where he had slept and sat back in his seat. Three hours later the train pulled into the station at Bangkok. Gypsy grabbed his bag, jumped off the train and out of the station. He got into a taxi and directed the driver to take him to the Kaowsan Road.

Leaving the taxi at the entrance to the road he wandered on down to the alley where Bonny Guest House was located and checked in to the dormitory.

The Baht (local currency) had been devalued by ten percent that morning and so knowing that he had no time to lose, he headed into town and hunted around for an air ticket before anyone had had time to up the ticket prices.

From one of the ticket offices near the Malaysia hotel he purchased a return from Bangkok to Tokyo via Hong Kong, for three hundred US dollars and took a motorbike taxi back to the Royal Orchid hotel boat pier. There he was sat on the back of a small but fast motorbike being driven at breakneck Kamikaze speed through ten lanes of traffic. It had been a somewhat scary form of transport but at least it got him there quickly and alive. Then he took the river taxi back up the river to Bang Lam Po and walked through the side roads back to the Kaowsan Road. His flight was leaving the next evening to Hong Kong so with his main mission completed for the day he relaxed with a bottle of Thai whiskey and some weed that he had managed to score at the snooker hall further along the street.

There was another traveler there who was much older than him and who was from Australia. He was sitting outside his room at a concrete table in the courtyard of the guest house, getting drunk on a bottle of Mekong whiskey. Gypsy sat down and joined him for an afternoon of drinking and listened to his descriptions of the lawless zone up in the golden triangle. He described how the people up there thought and what it was like living in their villages and smoking opium regularly. Eventually, late in the night Gypsy staggered off and found his bed and went to sleep.

The next day he awoke early and after some breakfast in a local café, went out looking for music tapes to take with him on the trip. Then he wandered over to the jetty at Sunam Luang were he had taken his dragon boat ride from before and jumped aboard one that was rapidly filling up with people. This time he had his brand new Minolta SLR and he wanted to take photos that would show how life was for those who lived on the river. The boat left it's mooring and reversed out into the river, then turned and took off at high speed diagonally across the river, weaving in and out of the other traffic as it raced towards the canal on the other side. The river and canals that came off from it were treated like roads and instead of cars, motorbikes and scooters the people who lived on the river had small boats, many of them motorized and some even customized to give a bit of a dragster look to them. There were children swimming in the canal and old men and women washing themselves in it. There were people washing plates and dishes in it and others washing clothes and still others brushing their teeth and spitting the contents of their mouth into it. There were people fishing in it but it's most important function seemed to be transport. The canal that the boat was traveling on was lined with houses built up on stilts, above the water. Many of them had boats parked next to them. There were traders with boats loaded with all sorts of produce from fresh fruit and vegetables to rice and soft drinks, rowing their way from house to house as door to door salesmen. There were also convenience stores and petrol stations that faced onto the canal. Then there were the boats loaded with produce heading down stream towards the river and the centre of the city. There were many dragon boats loaded with anything up to forty people aboard them, heading past them in the opposite direction, at high speed. There were also dragon boats loaded with goods cruising along the waterways. They passed houses, temples, monasteries, businesses and the like as they zoomed along. There was not one dull moment all the way to the final stop on the boat's route. The boat had made several stops along the way, dropping people off and picking others up. Some people, it appeared, had been picked up or dropped off from the front deck of their own homes. The Boat came to a stop at the end of it's run and everyone got off.

Gypsy took a short break to buy some food then was back on board another boat heading back into the city. He used up more than one roll of film on that journey as there was so much going on that was worth getting pictures of.

When he got back to the jetty on the river he wanted to take some photos around the area of the Emerald Buddha but it was late afternoon by the time he got there and it was already closed inside so he was restricted to taking his shots in the twilight from outside of the high walls. Never mind, that area would have to wait for another trip to Thailand before he could photograph it properly. He had photographed much of what he had seen along the banks of the rivers and canals and that would do for now as a record of Bangkok.

At around seven thirty in the evening, he headed out with his bag to find a bus to Don Muang airport. At that time the airport was well outside of the city on a northbound highway. Gypsy took a succession of local buses that eventually got him there.

He checked in at one of the Air India desks and made his way through to airside and found a bar. Chatting with a backpacker who was in transit from Hong Kong to India, he was told the same as some other travelers had told him in Bangkok. That the best place in Hong Kong, if on a tight budget was Chungking mansions on Nathan Road, at the tip of the Kowloon peninsula.

After a few more drinks at the bar and a briefing on smuggling work that was available in Hong Kong, Gypsy headed out towards his gate. Next he was riding on an airside bus, past a long line of jumbos that were parked along the perimeter fence, until it reached the Air India plane. He climbed aboard and found his seat. The plane was only a quarter full and though the flight would only last for some three and a half hours he was happy that he would at least be able to get a bit of sleep.

BANGKOK TO HONGKONG

NOVEMBER 1984

The plane was pushed back from its parking space and they were on their way. It taxied out to the runway and after a brief pause there was a huge rumble from the engines as it started to speed down the runway, it gathered more speed then rotated and took off into the darkness.

After the seat belt sign had been switched off Gypsy stretched out on three seats on the window side of the isle and went to sleep. He awoke after the plane had started its descent into Hong Kong. It was coming light outside in the early morning. He sat up and buckled in and watched as the plane ducked down between the island and the mainland, still with no land in sight in front, it looked as if the plane was going to land in the water. Then came the thud of the plane hitting the runway. Looking absolutely straight down Gypsy could see the narrow strip of runway that they were landing on. He came out of the airport with a standard two week transit visa stamped into his passport. He walked out to the main street of that area and hopped on a local bus in the direction of Nathan Road.

It was early morning between 6:30 and 7.00 am as he got off the bus at an intersection with Nathan Road. He had nothing that he needed to do urgently so sticking his arms through the hand hold loops of his holdall as so as to carry it as a backpack, he walked along Nathan Road and watched the early morning goings on of its people. The best way to describe the place would be to say that it looked like it was just waking up from an exceedingly heavy night of partying. The placed lacked the general colorful vibrancy of Bangkok. It was buzzing but it was a heavier less happy vibe. It was a place where a hippie or backpacker would feel a bit out of place.

Insert image file name "12.....page 192.......Sunam Luang, Bangkok, Thailand" here full page.

HONGKONG

Nevertheless, Gypsy wanted to see the place and also he wanted to travel across China, which had opened to independent travelers just a couple of years before. He walked for what felt like two or three kilometers, until eventually he found Chungking mansions, an ageing, somewhat scruffy and degenerate shopping mall, populated mostly by Indians, Pakistanis, Bangladeshis and Nepalese. The backpackers stayed in dingy hostels in apartments, on various floors of the building's four, seventeen storey towers.

"Travelers hostel" was on the sixteenth floor of 'A' block whose elevator was at the near end of the shopping centre, in relation to Nathan Road. Gypsy checked in and threw his holdall onto one of the scruffy bunks in one of the hostel's cramped and depressing dormitories.

He felt not the least bit sleepy and so took his camera bag and his walkman and headed out to the street. Heading to the end of the road and turning right he walked past the famous Peninsula Hotel before arriving at the Kowloon terminal for the star ferry. Purchasing a ticket, he boarded one of the green boats that cross between Kowloon and the island.

On Hong Kong Island, he walked into the centre of the city and watched the people hectically running around. He eventually saw a sign for a funicular that ran to the top of the island. He bought a ticket and rode up to the top. After shooting some photos of the panorama, he found a path leading down to the Chinese harbor at Aberdeen, on the other side of the island. He had no idea where he was going or how far it was, but he wasn't worried and hoofed the seven kilometers down through the jungle park to the quayside and watched the goings on there for a while. There were junks, fishing boats and all manner of small and medium sized craft both moored and on the move.

He shot off more film there, before heading back to the other side of the island on board a local double decker bus.

He walked around "Central" for a while, but the vibe was so hectic and unfriendly that he took the ferry back to Kowloon and walked back to Chungking mansions to get something to eat at one of the Indian cafes. By the time he had got back to the hostel it was six thirty in the evening, he stretched out on his bunk and fell asleep.

He awoke early the next morning and after a quick shower got dressed and headed down in the lift in search of some breakfast. He found a café on the ground floor that did eggs and toast and sat down with some other travellers who also wanted to travel to China. They knew where to go to get a visa. And so after breakfast Gypsy joined them for a walk along Nathan road past the big white mosque to the travel agent.

Like them Gypsy filled out the forms, paid his money and handed over his passport and was told to come back the next afternoon to collect it.

Back at Chungking mansions Gypsy's first thought was about finding something good to smoke. While chatting with some of the other long term travelers he was told to go and see a certain Chinese man on one of the lower floors, which he promptly did. The deal was small and not so cheap, but it was good gear, so he wasn't disappointed. Climbing up a ladder from the seventeenth floor and through a hatch, onto the roof, Gypsy found the perfect place to smoke and relax in this hectic, uptight and claustrophobic city.

From the rooftop he had an incredible panoramic view of Hong Kong island and not just that but if the cops ever were to come and try busting him, he had a perfect place to throw his stash, in any direction. The roof was also the largest space that he had seen on Kowloon that wasn't full of people. The one place where he could hear himself think and have some peace and privacy.

The dormitories of the hostel were crowded, claustrophobic, scruffy and dirty but were the only truly affordable accommodation for a backpacker in all of Hong Kong. The lift entrance down in the shopping center would more often than not have a queue waiting outside of it. The lift descended and rose so slowly, often taking between seven and ten minutes to make the journey down and back up. The other travelers who were staying there for the most part weren't real travelers who lived on the road, or even expatriates. Many of them were people who had gone on a one to three month adventure having finished university. If they had travelled to anywhere else on the trip it would have been Australia, New Zealand or the U.S.A. Places that their parents would have approved of and now China was to be their "real adventure".

Some of them who were a little bit more adventurous had come via the Trans Siberian Express, which was a journey that took ten days from Berlin from where another train was taken to Moscow to join the Trans Siberian. Again in Siberia it was necessary to change trains to get to China, otherwise the Trans Siberian carried on to Vladivostok on the Russian North Pacific coast.

Russia was under Soviet communism at that time and travel in all of the states of the Soviet Union was extremely restricted. As such the Trans Siberian Express was a chance to get a more extensive view of the place without having to deal with too much of the beaurocracy in the process.

Also it was an extremely cheap way of getting to Asia by overland route. At two hundred and fifty dollars for a one way ticket from East Berlin to Beijing. Trains in China were exceptionally cheap as long as they were paid for in local currency. So it would not have cost more than fifty dollars to get from Beijing to Guanzhou and then the five hour luxury train to Hong Kong also was not expensive.

So many of the occupants of the hostel dormitories where not much more than low budget tourists and were generally unfriendly, po faced party poopers. who gave the appearance of having a large cucumber stuffed up their rear orifice if the expressions on their faces was anything to go by.

However there was also a loose collection of misfits and hardcore travelers hanging around the shadows of the hostel. Some of them had found jobs around Hong Kong and were looking to stay for longer.

One man who though he gave off the impression of being Mr Normal, had lived on the same dorm bed in the hostel for the past four and a half years. He was out at work for much of the day but would return back to his dorm bed in the late afternoon. He would then lie there until the early hours of the morning reading paperback novels, only getting up occasionally either to go and get himself some food or for trips to the toilet. He was from England and his name was John Catchpole. It appeared that he had a teaching job as he would be up and out early each morning, dressed in quite smart looking clothes.

Then there were the smugglers, mostly hardcore travelers and expats who had grown tired of slaving for meager amounts of cash on dead end jobs and were now having fun and making money at the same time. Gypsy got to know some of them and asked what he needed to do and who he would need to see to get in on the "Milk Run".

The milk Run was an eight day smuggling run through Taiwan, South Korea and Japan, carrying all sorts of strange things from point to point. From Hong Kong to Taipei the goods included much in the way of electronics, jewelry and watches. One of the customs gates would have been paid off at Taipei and the group of between six to eight smugglers would pass through unhindered. The group would then spend the night in Taipei before leaving on the following morning. From Taipei to Seoul the cargo was women's fashion clothes (which could leave a male smuggler red faced and lost for words if he got pulled for a search). From Seoul to Tokyo it was women's cosmetics (ditto if he got pulled with this lot too). From Tokyo to Seoul it would be a cargo of electronics and bananas (yes that's right, 'Bananas', apparently they were in short supply and sold for top money in Korea). From Seoul back to Taipei, apparently it was women's cosmetics again. Each of the runners would then get paid in Taipei and also would be given an open ticket back to Hong Kong. The pay for the week's work would be approximately two hundred U.S. dollars plus a ten dollar bonus for each stop where the goods were cleared successfully. The milk run was what was known as a low risk operation, as the goods were not viewed as serious contraband. As such, the most that the authorities could do was to seize the goods and let the culprit go. Thus the low pay!

One of the travelers took Gypsy to meet one of the Chinese men that he worked for. But when Gypsy was told how low the pay was (a maximum of two hundred and sixty dollars for an eight day run) and not just that but was told that he would have to cut his hair and wear a suit, he started to back out of the door. That was definitely too little money for the time and the work involved, besides, Gypsy viewed wearing a suit as akin to dressing up in drag, which was something that he would never dream of doing. Also there was a rumor circulating among the travelers at the hostel about one or some of the Chinese smuggling gangs filling the handles of some of the bags with gold, which had resulted in some unwitting smugglers getting busted and locked up while trying to clear customs at Seoul. [At that time South Korea was reputed to have some of the most harsh and sadistic prisons on Earth]

Gypsy went and collected his passport from the travel agent's office, it had a new visa in it printed entirely in Chinese, except for the dates.

Hong Kong was like a spiritual vacuum and Gypsy was reading his way through some Hare Krishna books at the time as so as to help him keep the light burning within. He had noticed in the back of the books that there was a list of all of their temples and centers around the world. He noted that there was a small set up in Hong Kong and not just that but it was on Kowloon, not so very far from where he was staying. So using his map he found his way to the right street and then looked at the address again to find, first the block and then the apartment where they were.

The devotees were a mixture of Americans and Chinese, maybe ten or fifteen of them in all. It was by contrast to the busy streets outside, a much more relaxed vibe. It was a world apart from the heavy materialistic nature of the rest of Hong Kong. For the first time since he had arrived he felt comfortable in the company of the people around him. The devotees at this temple were a much more special group than any of the Hare Krishnas that he had met before, in that they seemed to spend far less time tripping over their own egos, and more time demonstrating the way by example. There was a great maturity and great humility in their approach to their chosen spiritual path and Gypsy could not help but admire them and wish to emulate them. Most of all he wished to be able to devote some of his time in service to them and their temple. The devotees had a much more peaceful nature about them and there were no zealots in the place. It was a breath of fresh air that Gypsy had been craving for the past few days. He was invited to stay and join them for some food, which he did.

Feeling partially recharged he made his way on foot back along Nathan Road to Chungking mansions and back up to the travelers hostel.

Later that night he sat up on the roof of the tower block, smoking a joint with some of the other travelers. He spoke of his unease about working for the Chinese on the milk run. Another traveler, a man from Holland, had been cheated at a camera shop that afternoon. When he took the camera that he had purchased earlier that day back as it did not work and asked for an exchange, the owner of the shop, a Chinese man, shouted at him and told him to get out of his shop. The Dutch man called a cop who was standing nearby and showed him his receipt and told him what had just happened. The cop, instead of helping him, started to attack him and threatened him with arrest if he pursued the matter further. So with that Gypsy decided that there was no way that he could risk working for the Chinese. They were obviously a generally dishonest group of people who had no idea what words such as accountability or reasoning meant. He had already encountered Chinese dishonesty and rudeness first hand and didn't wish to have the experience of working for them. It seemed that unlike the Indians, Malays or Thais, that they really did not like foreigners one little bit.

"No problem", said one of the other travelers. "I work for the Manangis and they pay good money for not too much work, I can introduce you to them if you like". "Who are the Manangis and what does it involve?" asked Gypsy. "The Manangis are from Nepal and the job involves running gold to Kathmandu", another traveler cut in. "Isn't that just a little bit fucking dangerous?" Gypsy asked.

"No one has been caught on that run for a couple of years now, besides, it's rumored that an in law or relative of the King is the financier and benefactor of the route and with the power that he has, he protects his cargos. Besides no one in Nepal mind's as most of the Gold is smuggled over the border into India to be sold on their black market", the other traveler continued to explain. (India at that time was socialist or at least the government and administration were. Things were controlled and rationed. Gold was not only taxed at exorbitant levels but was also extremely hard to come by. Expatriate and travelling Indian business people would always bring some gold in with them when returning to India from a trip abroad. An Indian wedding always involved gold, even among the poorest of people. As such India had an absolutely massive black market in smuggled gold and Nepal with its long porous border made good money supplying it into India). "I don't know, I'll think about it", said Gypsy "Ok. I'll be around tomorrow, come and let me know", said the other traveler.

At the back of the shopping mall at Chungking mansions, through a labyrinth of alleyways, was a Chinese spit and sawdust style café. Gypsy would go in there for just one dish that they had that he liked. It was noodles, steamed or boiled with Chinese cabbage and oyster sauce. It was simple but it tasted so good. He was doing his best to stay vegetarian but it was hard if not close to impossible without his own kitchen.

Back upstairs in the hostel, one of the more decent of the travelers, Dutch Eddie who had come via the Trans Siberian Express to Hong Kong with his wife and two children had just got back from a Kathmandu gold run. "Yep, it's no problem!" he said.

On the eleventh floor of 'A' block existed, at that time a scruffy but extremely good Indian eating house come restaurant, called 'Nanak Mess', it was run by Sikhs and when ordering from the menu one only had to pay for the curry itself, the chappatis and rice were given for free and that meant that you could have as much or as many as you wished to eat. The place had more than a slightly homely feel to it with the sort of scuffed tables and chairs that you would get in a British greasy spoon café. But the food was fantastic and Indians are a more relaxed lot than the Chinese, so the vibe was more conducive for talking.

Gypsy was sitting in Nanak Mess and talking with Dutch Eddie and a couple of other travelers who had just done the run. "You've got to go and see that place", said Eddie. "It's mind blowing, the rainbow's end for all hippies". "Sounds good", said Gypsy. "And there were no problems either at the airport or in getting paid afterwards?" "No", they all replied.

After finishing and paying for his meal, he took the elevator back up to the sixteenth floor with the others and went and found the other traveler who had offered to connect him with a Nepalese smuggling gang. They headed on down to the ground floor and walked to the back of the shopping center. From there they took another elevator to the twelfth floor of 'D' block and entered a small, dingy apartment where he was introduced to the gang.

"So when can you go?" asked the chief. "I'll do it the day after tomorrow, if that suits you too", Gypsy replied. "Ok that will be fine", said the chief.

The others explained that he was only to bring hand luggage and to be outside Chungking mansions at 5:30am on the morning of the run. The pay on completion of mission was to be six hundred dollars (which at that time was a fair bit of cash, especially in Asia). The other traveler who introduced him was an Iranian refugee who having got an American passport preferred the life on the road in Asia, to going, as many of his compatriots had done, to the U.S.A.. He was also into making extra money for himself and would do the run as often as twice a week, Saad was a brave but mad so and so, but one had to admire his enthusiasm. He knew Asia better than any of the other travelers and for the most part kept his cool, even when those around him were losing theirs.

Gypsy got his clothes washed at the laundry at the back of the shopping centre and put them in his bag, along with the film that he had been shooting as he had travelled. Locking it in, he then placed it in the left luggage room at the hostel. Then with only a small bag as hand luggage, containing a couple of changes of clothes, his camera, walkman and some cassettes, he was ready to go.

He went out for a couple of drinks at 'Ned Kelley's Last Stand', an Australian Jazz Pub, two or three blocks over from Nathan Road and watched the band play. Another traveler from the hostel had wandered in and they got talking. He was also from England and was out on a wilder sort of trip than most and was also looking for work.

He was interested in the smuggling and wanted to find out more. They moved to a less raucous pub and Gypsy briefed him about the options that he had been offered in Hong Kong. The weirdest thing was when the other traveler showed his passport to Gypsy to prove that he wasn't a cop, before Gypsy would point him to any specific contacts, it showed that he was born on the same day of the same year as Gypsy and in the same country. Now here they both were in Hong Kong at the same time and both trying to do the same thing. "Weird or what?"

"I don't believe you", said the other traveler. But Gypsy could not prove it as the Nepalese gang he was about to work for were holding his passport, which at that time was his only form of identification.

He wandered back to Chungking mansions and up to his bunk at the hostel and crashed out. He awoke at 5 a.m., had a quick shower and put on fresh clean clothes. Then with his small shoulder bag, he headed down in the lift. It was a cool morning as he stepped out into the street, in the predawn, at 5:30 a.m. The lights were still on and flashing and the street was not empty. There were taxi drivers, hookers, pimps, drunks and people on their way to work. And there was also a group of small Nepalese mountain men, sitting on the metal railings by the street.

Their eyes lit up when they saw Gypsy coming towards them, they knew now that they would be running on time.

Most of the gang did not speak any English at all and they looked more out of place in Hong Kong than even a hippie traveler did. That is to say that they were like fish out of water in this city of sky scrapers and probably only left the confines of Chungking mansions when they were on their way to or from the airport.

HONGKONG TO KATHMANDU

NOVEMBER 1984.

They signaled to him that they had to wait for the boss, so they stood around and waited in the early morning cold for him to arrive.

After a couple of minutes he wandered out of the front entrance of Chungking mansions, clutching a coffee in a plastic cup. They hailed a taxi and all piled in for the ride down through Kowloon to Kai Tak airport.

It was still dark when they got out of the taxi at the airport. Going inside Gypsy and his "minder" took a seat while the chief and his number two went and checked them in for the flight at the Royal Nepal Airlines desk. After returning with the boarding passes the gang's number two who spoke some English gave Gypsy the names of the two pick up men and the hotel where he was to meet them in Kathmandu. Then Gypsy and his minder, who was at that time in possession of the gold, headed to passport control and went through to airside.

Soon they were riding the bus out to the plane, an ageing Boeing 727 of which this was one of the three that made up Royal Nepal Airlines's jet fleet, which were used exclusively on their international routes.

Gypsy felt nervous, yet he was outwardly calm. When he was aboard he looked around and to his surprise, realized that he knew almost half of the people on board, either from Chungking Mansions or from cafes and pubs in the surrounding area. The only faces that he did not know were those of the Nepalese, one of whom was sat next to each of the western travelers on board. "So the only purpose of this flight to exist was for the clandestine movement of gold from Hong Kong to Kathmandu and onward to India" thought Gypsy to himself. There were no straight tourists, businessmen or returning workers on this flight, this was the bullion express!!!. . The plane taxied out to the runway and made a long lumbering take off, using the entire length of the runway, it's engines roaring at full power. It then climbed slowly skyward above the hills of Hong Kong as if either heavily over loaded or flying on old engines. It was probably a bit of each.

The jet lumbered and climbed with great effort and then turned and headed out on its route across Southern China, to its next stop at Dhaka in Bangladesh..

Looking down from the plane window, Gypsy watched as they flew for an hour or two across a landscape of ridged and steep hills, with sugar loaf peaks and weird formations. He had never seen a landscape like this before and certainly not on this immense scale, it seemed to go on forever. These were the limestone hills of southern China, an area that he was planning to visit in the near future.

Breakfast was being served and Gypsy was glad when the trolley reached him. He was hungry and a fried breakfast like the one being served would suit him just fine.

Later, after the drinks trolley had done its rounds, he got up and was standing around chatting with some of the other people that he had been hanging around with in Chungking mansions. Saad was on board and seemed to be well known by the others, it was a bit of a party that was going on in the gangway as people stood around with whiskeys and beers chatting. A couple of the other travelers had been to China, where they had travelled across the southern part by train to Kunming in Yunnan province, which borders onto Laos and Burma. They spoke about how they had seen ganja growing down the streets of Kunming and about the stone Forrest and the ancient walled town of Dali with its pagodas and fancy gates. Gypsy was interested and put it in his mind to go there when he got to China.

Eventually the flight started its descent into Dhaka and everyone sat back down and buckled in. they landed and taxied to their allotted parking space on the apron and the plane was fuelled up again. No one got off or on the plane, this was just a fuel stop before reaching Kathmandu.

The plane took off again and all through the cabin, each of the western travelers were handed a small but extremely heavy package by the Nepali seated next to them. As soon as the fasten seat belt sign was turned off, there was suddenly a line of westerners queuing at the toilets as so as to hide the goods with no one looking as to where it was being stashed. Saad was such a crazy so and so that he would just stuff it in his boots or in his pockets while making no attempt to conceal his actions.

As the plane started its descent into Kathmandu it was a clear day and Gypsy from his window seat could see Mount Everest and two other massive peaks towering above them, it looked so very close indeed. This was the closest that he was ever likely to be to the peak of Everest. He could see it clearly and it felt not so very far away. However when he looked straight down, the ground was so far away that he could make out few details at all, yet the peak was way above them. It was a spectacular and breath taking view. There was the world's tallest mountain looking like it was only a stone's throw away. He could see the peak clearly but also had a wonderful panorama view of the entire mountain. Unfortunatly he was too busy staring at this incredible view to think to get his camera out and take a photo of it, also his mind was concentrated on clearing customs.

The plane then started its final descent into the Kathmandu valley. The undercarriage was down and as Gypsy looked out of the window, he could see mud brick houses with thatched roofs and men ploughing with water buffaloes and heavy bulls in the fields below. The women, who were dressed in colorful clothes, were either carrying water in ceramic jars on their heads or washing clothes in buckets on the ground.

The wheels touched the runway and as the reverse thrusts kicked in he could see tens if not hundreds of men in traditional Nepali clothes squatting down or standing, on an earth mound by the side of the runway, watching the flight land.   If there was a security fence it was no more than enough to keep animals and children off of the runway and to stop people from using it as a short cut.

The jet stopped, turned around and taxied back along the runway to the apron, where now all three of the Royal Nepalese Airlines jet fleet were parked.

They disembarked into the cool pleasant mountain air and Gypsy's pulse was racing but outwards he was totally calm as he walked across the apron, to passport control and customs. Apart from the inner nervousness that his work was causing him to feel, he was excited to have finally reached the hippie rainbow's end. Even the air felt like it had magic within it. He filled out the visa form and paid his ten dollars and was issued a visa on arrival stamp.

Customs stopped him and took a look in his bag, but seeing just clothes, a camera and walkman they let him go straight away.

KATHMANDU

He came out of the airport and jumped into a taxi and told the driver to take him to Asia guest house in the Thamel district of the city.

The driver turned around and gave Gypsy a sly grin and said, "Ah, so lucky this time yes?" it was obviously an open secret that this particular flight was the contraband bullion express. As the taxi drove into the city Gypsy looked around at the view in wide eyed disbelief. The place was like another realm and looked like it had been built by and for Elves and hobbits it was a truly magical realm with earth brick buildings with plants growing from the roofs and walls. There were Hindu temples and pagodas, streams and waterfalls and clean fresh air. The people even looked somewhat elf and hobbit like. They were short but quite stocky and wore their own quite practical style of clothes.

The taxi reached the guest house and the driver asked for five dollars, it was supposed to cost just one or two dollars for the ride but with the driver already knowing too much of his business he didn't waste time arguing about such a trivial amount and just paid it and went inside to find the pickup men.

"Mr Green" and "Mr Brown" [just like something from the movie "Reservoir Dogs] were inside waiting with their own personal gang of minders. They went over to a quiet corner and Gypsy handed over the gold and was paid his six hundred dollars.

Some other travelers were sitting around a table in the courtyard drinking beers and smoking joints. They invited Gypsy to join them. He felt so very relaxed having got through and having just been paid. As they sat there some of the others from the flight started trickling in and made their way to the toilet were the noise of a heavy thud followed by a groan of relief could be heard emanating from. Soon there were many travelers sitting around and talking, the recent arrivals looking far more relaxed than they had done just an hour before.

He was now at the Rainbow's end of Hippie travel, the legendary Kathmandu and it was more mystical, colorful, and magical than he ever could have imagined. Now he knew why the place had such a reputation among the hippies, it was like Shangri La.

He checked in at the guesthouse next door. It had a homely feeling, with its low ceilings, worn carpets and old world nature about it. For the first time ever while on the road he had a room with a bathroom and hot water, to himself.

He spent the rest of the day smoking joints and drinking with the crowd next door. All of them had been on the road for a long time and one of them, an ex-merchant seaman from England, even had a Hong Kong passport.

Outside the gate, in the street a cow stopped outside the grocery store opposite and mooed! The owner threw it a large chunk of bread, apparently according to the other travelers the same cow stopped every day, at the same time, at the same shop for its mid afternoon snack.

The next morning, Gypsy joined up with some others who were going out to get breakfast. They stopped at a café called "KCs" and went inside. The place was full of people who were going trekking and climbing. They sat down and ordered a fried breakfast each. The breakfasts arrived on sizzling Chapatti pans [like a small flattish sort of wok] with a thick straw mat underneath each one, to stop them burning the table. Jimmy Hendrix was playing on the stereo and with the décor and the music, it felt as if the sixties was still alive in Kathmandu.

Later Gypsy took a look around the city, wandering down through the markets to Durbar Square and Freak Street (so named because it was the hippie and traveller area before Thamel became the main hangout).

Around Durbar square was an assortment of wattle and daub, pagoda temples, dedicated to different Hindu deities and a house built in the same style, with carved wooden circular windows. This was the house of the living goddess that was constantly occupied by a young girl under the age of puberty and before her time of first menstruation. A different young girl was chosen each year to be the living goddess, to occupy the house and perform the ceremonies.

Gypsy spent the next two weeks exploring Kathmandu and Bodhanath, [a Tibetan area close to the city]. Saad came and went several times in that time and the other travelers laughed at how blasé he was about it.

The cow continued to make her mid afternoon stops outside of the grocery store and on at least one occasion brought another cow friend along with her. The travelers continued to sit, drinking beer and smoking joints each afternoon as old ones left and new ones arrived, all to be met by the Nepalese gold recovery teams. Apparently, one of each team would be waiting at the airport at least an hour before the flight was due to land, casing the joint and making sure that there was nothing and nobody around that could disrupt the smooth flow of the operation. The gangs were all from the Manangi tribe who originated from the village and district of Manang, high in the mountains behind the Annapurna range and just near a particularly high pass. To reach the road from their village was at least a ten day hike for a westerner.

Ten to fifteen years, previous to the time that is being written about Manang was in the grip of severe famine. Nepal was under the reign of the father of King Birendra who was on the throne at the time that is being written about.

The people of Manang sent representatives to Kathmandu to explain their situation to the king and ask for help.

The Manangis have always been a tribe of traders and in days before, had sent Yak caravans to other parts of the Himalayas, on many occasions to trade. On one such occasion they had heard that glass beads that they particularly liked were being made in a land to the west called Czechoslovakia, so they dispatched a yak caravan to go off and find the place and trade something for the glass beads. They were eventually stopped and turned around in Soviet Kazakhstan by a bunch of humorless communist party poopers.

Kazakhstan is several thousand miles from Nepal and these people had travelled the whole distance on foot, trading as they went, for food, etc.

With this in mind, the king did something never done before. He gave them all passports and licenses to make international business. Since those early days, when they were just trading bags of clothes and jewelry on the streets of Bangkok, Hong Kong and Singapore, they had graduated to gold smuggling and were now in the process of buying up as much of the property in Kathmandu as possible, to the point where they were making the local tribe, the Newari nervous.

If a Nepali was doing business in any other country you could be pretty sure that they would be Manangis and they were a large factor in filling seats on flights in and out of Kathmandu.

Gypsy shot off several reels of film around the city and was relaxing into an easy routine. But then he got itchy feet again and packed his bag and took a bus to Bhaktapur, thirteen kilometers away. Another country had donated a trolley bus system to Nepal and its only route was from Kathmandu to Bhaktapur. So Gypsy took the trolley bus.

Bhaktapur was the capital of the old kingdom that was centered around the Kathmandu valley area.

The ancient legends say that the Kathmandu valley was originally a lotus filled lake. There is geological evidence to support this story's authenticity, according to some sources. The lake was obviously breached at some point and thus became the Kathmandu valley.

Bhaktapur, Patan and Kathmandu were the three main centers of population in the valley and each one was full of ancient buildings and temples. But there was no place more beautiful than Bhaktapur.

Gypsy got off of the bus just outside of the main square, and walked through a gate into the large red brick paved area.

Kathmandu Valley, Baktapur;

If being in Kathmandu had been like a journey to another time, then Bhaktapur was like another time in another dimension, more akin to middle earth from J.R.Tolkien's hobbit stories. There were beautiful temples and pagodas and a palace with a golden gate. There were few if any motor vehicles present within the gates of the city and the houses and shops all had low ceilings and doorways. The houses were made of wattle and daub and red ceramic bricks of a similar color to those that paved the streets. The windows and doors of many of the buildings were often made of ornately hand carved, black stained wood.

Around parts of the square were shops selling Tibetan and Nepali religious paintings and religious implements, e.g. prayer wheels, mantra beads, special ceremonial trumpets, incense, etc. In the area where the temples were Gypsy asked some local people if there was a guesthouse in the area.

He was directed to a nearby side street, he walked along it and someone pointed and showed him where it was, without him even having to ask. It was up a flight of steps, one floor above the street, so he walked up the steps and in.

He was greeted by a really friendly receptionist, a man by the name of Raj, who sorted him out with a small single room for around US$0.75, the room was small but it was homely and clean and anyway, Gypsy didn't have such expensive taste, for him it was luxury enough to have a private room, even without an on suite toilet and shower.

He put his bag down in the room and went back down to the restaurant which was also the reception area.

He was the only westerner in the place, all of the others, eight in all, were locals. They were very friendly and he sat down and talked with them. He ordered some dahl and chapattis from the restaurant. As he waited for his food to arrive he was chatting away with these friendly locals and they were telling him about their wonderful town.

Apparently, the money to pave the city roads and square had been donated by the German government in order to help to enhance the place. This was good in itself as it did make the place look good. But the most incredible thing about Bhaktapur was the almost total absence of motorized transport within the town it's self. It made the place peaceful, especially after dark, with no noise pollution, the place had a special feel to it.

The other thing that caused Bhaktapur to be so special was that people were still living and working in much the same way as their ancestors had done for perhaps the last two thousand years and all this without any colonialists ruling over them. They by and large seemed like a happy and friendly people. They lived hard and simple lives, orientated around their family, their land and their religion and shamanic ways.

It is a truly wonderful thing about Buddhism, Hinduism and its many offshoots that as they grew in both popularity and influence, that they did not try to kill off the shamanic paths that predated them. As such they worked side by side. For example, in Buddhism there is no such thing as a marriage ceremony. Marriage is not even encouraged in Buddhism as it is just one more distraction (a big one at that) from finding one's way to the ultimate truth.

As such, in Buddhist countries a wedding will more likely be a form of shamanic ceremony. Likewise, when ceremonies for the start and completion of a building project are conducted, first of all the shamans are called in to choose the starting date for the project. Their decision will be based on astrology and vision from an oracle. Then on the day of starting, first thing in the morning will be the shamanic ceremony, which will then be followed later by a blessing from the Buddhist monks. This order of ceremonies is followed also on completion of the project.

With Hinduism, it is so all encompassing that the shamanism got absorbed within it and even got written down into a language that can still be understood to this day.

The oneness of the people with their religion kept the people happy and the place peaceful. Mysticism and nature held greater sway in this area than the pursuit of western materialism. With their belief in reincarnation and a group conscious awareness of the short and temporary nature of life, these people were in some ways richer than any others on earth.

Gypsy finished eating and Raj and the others invited Gypsy to join them in going to a local Nepalese pub. "That sound's like a good idea," Gypsy replied and soon they were walking along the brick paved alleys and roads of Bhaktapur, it was well after dark and the streets were almost deserted.

The pub was on the main street and was in a small cavern like shop space. It had three tables and sold Chang and Rakshi, but no western style drinks. Chang was a beer made from rice. White in color and opaque like milk, it tasted slightly vinegary and was made on a small scale by farmers and local people in their backyards and houses. Rakshi was the local moonshine in Nepal and was possibly produced on a larger scale.

They sat down and ordered a Chang each and then another and another and another and then it was time for the rakshi. There was a man in the corner of the room, busy with a paraffin stove and a wok, frying potatoes with a hot chili massala seasoning. So they sat getting drunk and munching curried potatoes, then later that night they piled out of the pub and all staggered off home, drunk.

The next morning Gypsy awoke early. There was the usual early morning mist over the town when Gypsy got down to the restaurant, which made the place appear even more other worldly. The air was cool and fresh and there was a rural aroma, mixed with the smell of spices and incense, wafting gently through the air.

"I'm sorry about last night," said Raj to Gypsy. "I hope your head is not too bad this morning." "I'm fine," said Gypsy "there's no need to apologize, I really enjoyed my evening. I'm up for going there again tonight." "Great!" said Raj, "we don't normally take our guests out drinking at places that we use, as most of them are a bit distant and standoffish, but you are more friendly and open, so we thought you would like to see a bit of how we live."

"Thank you, I really am grateful, it was a good night and I enjoyed it," said Gypsy. He spent most of the day exploring Bhaktapur and finding good angles to take photos from. It was like being in an enchanted realm, there were very few tourists and the place functioned for the local population and not for any big tourist operations, which at that time thankfully did not exist.

In the afternoon, while relaxing at the guesthouse, a procession came past below, down in the street, with men playing trumpets and drums leading the people. At the back of the procession, being led on a rope was a most reluctant and nervous water buffalo. Further along the narrow street in the middle of a crossroads was a small Hindu shrine made of carved stone, the procession stopped there and started to perform a ceremony.

Later, when Gypsy went back outside, he found out why the water buffalo had been so agitated and nervous. There in front of the temple lay the head of the poor creature, surrounded by flowers and incense. They had used it as a sacrifice to their god and were now obviously at home cutting up the meat and cooking it.

That evening Gypsy and Raj headed back to the pub, but this time the drinking was more subdued.

The next morning Gypsy paid his bill and headed for the bus stop. He took a bus out of Bhaktapur that was going up to the village of Nagrakot, which was at a high elevation at the very end of the Kathmandu valley. It's main attraction was that it was possible to see the peak of Mount Everest from there.

Kathmandu Valley, Nagrakot;

The bus went along the valley floor and then started to climb and climb and climb.

When Gypsy got off of the bus at the top of the ridge, the air was decidedly colder.

Nagrakot, like many mountain villages, was just a sparse collection of small houses up on a ridge. The guesthouse that had been recommended to Gypsy, was called "The Restaurant at the End of the Universe" after the book by Douglas Adams. It was a cold austere place with a restaurant with the most basic of menus, at that time it also had no electricity. But the view at sunset was stunning. There was a distant line of snow capped peaks and Everest was among them. It didn't look particularly big from where he was standing and was a great distance away. It was in no way comparable with the incredible close up view that Gypsy had seen from the plane during the approach into Kathmandu, but never the less, it was still an incredible view.

The next day Gypsy took a bus back down to Kathmandu. After checking back into the same guesthouse that he had stayed in before, he went down to the Royal Nepal airlines main office on new road and booked himself onto a flight back to Hong Kong.

A couple of days later he was at the airport waiting for his flight out. There were actually two people checking in for the flight who were not gold smugglers, an American couple who had just been on holiday. "They looked so squeaky clean that if they were running anything at all then it would have most likely have to have been guns or smack", thought Gypsy to himself. The airport, for all intents and purposes resembled a small regional railway station more than it ever did, an airport, even the food at the snack stand was grotty enough to have been of the same quality as that that used to be found on British Rail.

Kathmandu – Hong Kong;

A Thai airways A300 Airbus landed and taxied back down the runway to the apron and parked. Gypsy watched the passengers walking across to the terminal building. There were a couple of faces that he knew from among the crowd coming down the steps. One of them was an Australian called Greg that Gypsy had spent time drinking with at the Hotel Asia. He was dressed in a suit and tie, so it was obvious what he was doing. But to his surprise and disbelief he could tell by the strange slow way that people were walking, that a large number of the westerners on this flight too were gold smugglers.

The flight back to Hong Kong was uneventful and after the stop in Dhaka, and the evening meal had been served and cleared away, many of the smugglers were standing around in the isle and chatting. Many, including Gypsy, were thinking of going again during the following week. It was well after dark when the plane started it's decent into Kai Tak and soon everyone was back in their seats and buckled in. The lights of Hong Kong came into view, then the plane made it's final approach down between the buildings of checkerboard alley and landed.

With only hand luggage, Gypsy was out of the airport at record speed and in a cab back to Chungking mansions. It was a world away from Kathmandu, being back in the fast paced up tight Hong Kong. Gypsy checked back in at "travelers hostel," he had brought a piece of Nepalese hash back with him and he and two of the other smugglers headed up the ladder and on to the roof for a smoke. At least there was the roof to relax on.

The next day Gypsy visited the Hare Krishna temple at the apartment on Ho Mantin Street. He had asked them if there was anything that they would like him to bring for them from Nepal. Each of the women had asked for a new sari, so he had a bag with him with four new cotton saris in it.

They were very happy with them but asked "why did you get them all in the same color?" "Ah, that is as so that none of you get jealous or start fighting over them for one and for two, you are devotees, these can also help your humility in front of God." Gypsy explained.

They gave him books to read, including one that was a biography of the life of their guru, Prabupada. Gypsy took them with him on his return to Chungking mansions. He spent the next two days reading some of the books while he contemplated doing his next run. The labyrinthine dormitories of the Travellers Hostel were a bit like the streets down below, in that they were both full of hyperactive, unfriendly people, running here and there, all the while encased in the tiny world of their own sad and lonely thoughts.

However, amid the mindless bustle, Gypsy somehow managed to find the space to read, shutting out the disturbance, as he put his awareness inside the book. It was as if he was in a cocoon and all the others in the room where not there, being just background noise and flickering light. Now he knew how John Catchpole coped with living on a dormitory bed for so many years. He too was always reading, his life existed inside of the pages of other peoples' stories, all else was an illusion to him.

The biography was an interesting read. Prabupada had been a shop keeper in Bengal but had always been deeply religious, following the path of vaishnavism, which means devotee of Vishnu. Of the Hindu trinity of Brahma, the creator, Vishnu, the maintainer and Shiva, the destroyer. Vishnu is viewed as the highest and the root of all conscious and unconscious awareness. Brahma is the deity of creative energy, as in living beings and is ultimately the same as all other trapped beings within this universe. Shiva, the destroyer, the saver of the fallen, the God of the animals and fallen spirits, he has long hair and sits in deep meditation. Shiva is time. Time destroys everything. It saves the fallen and animals, as without time there would be no opportunity to purify the soul by paying off debts of bad karma and as such, time liberates all souls from this world of suffering.

Vishnu is ultimate, in that Vishnu is the source of everything that we know, and is existent outside of the dream bubble of illusion that is this universe.

The Vaishnavas, (which is the name given to devotees of Vishnu) claim that Vishnu has taken birth several times on earth in pure form. The two times that most will have heard about were as Krishna whose exploits and thoughts are recorded in the Mahabharata and the Bhagavad-Gita and Ram whose story is recorded in the Ramayana. These books along with the four Vedas make up the backbone of Hindu philosophy. The Vaishnavas also claim that Gautama Siddhartha Buddha was a pure incarnation of Vishnu. As such, deities of Buddha can often also be found within Hindu temples. Hindus have a lot of love and respect for Buddhists on account of this. They view Buddhists as being a very special type of Hindu. It is also not uncommon to find Hindu deities within Buddhist shrines and temples, as there is such mutual respect between the two paths.

At a certain point in his life Prabupada made sanyas, which is something that many of the more deeply religious of the Hindus do. In fact the instruction is to do it if at all possible before the age of fifty, in order to give one's self at least twenty years to find spiritual liberation, before death.

Sanyas involves giving up everything. All wealth must be given away to family and others. The man will then go off in search of spiritual liberation before his death. His wife may accompany him for the first few years as he travels to the four most holy of the Hindu shrines but then she must return home while he carries on on his own it is recommended to give oneself at least twenty years for such a search. He must say goodbye to his family and friends and then with just one change of clothes in his bag and a thin blanket, a small food bowl and a staff, he will hit the road as a holy man, staying no more than three nights in any one place but an ashram and even then, not sleeping under the same tree more than once.

In his dreams at night Prabupada saw himself on a boat, going to America. He contemplated the dream and decided that it must mean that God wished to take his particular spiritual path to America and spread Vedic understanding there.

Someone that he knew, who was also a Vaishnava, brought him a passenger ticket on a freight steamer from Calcutta to New York. On the journey he read his books and also had many dreams that showed him his path and what he had to do.

He arrived in New York with nothing but his books and a change of clothes. He was then invited to stay in the house of a local Hindu family who lived in the city. It was the middle of winter and freezing cold when he arrived. Inside he felt lonely and wondered what he was expected to do in this cold, materialistic place. To get some peace he would spend a lot of time both sitting on a bench and walking in central park. The year was 1965 and soon he was approached by some curious young beatnik/hippies.

He got talking with them and told them about who he was and about his spiritual path. They became interested and would go to the park regularly to meet with him and listen to him explaining about Vedic philosophy and spiritual understanding. They were very open and had also started to understand the futility of material existence, even before they had met him.

Soon they were asking to become devotees, at which point he set out a very strict set of rules that were to be adhered to rigorously, before he would agree to take responsibility for their spiritual training. He explained that he must do this as he would be taking on a portion of their karma, as their guru and he did not wish for them to screw up along the way. Some of them agreed and so the Hare Krishna movement was started in the west.

In India, it has existed in its' present form for around about five hundred years and was started by a Hindu saint by the name of Lord Chaitanya Mahaprabu who was most active in Bengal, where Prabupada came from.

They made their first temple and ashram in New York and from there it spread out across America and around the world, as more and more people became interested. Because it was started by an Indian and some hippies, these types of people made up the largest percentage of the devotees and friends of the temple.

The Indians would come to all of the temples in great numbers as many of them were already Vaishnavas. That is to say that a deity of one of the forms of Vishnu would take the place of prominence in the shrine/ temple that these Hindus would keep in their houses.

To the Indians, the Hare Krishnas, far from being a cult, where living by the highest of Vedic moral standards and were true holy men and as such to be respected and supported with donations, service and attendance at the temple, in much the same way as devoted Christians support their churches, enthusiastically.

The Hare Krishnas appealed to the hippies for many reasons. For one; many of the hippies were already vegetarian and others just needed to be presented with the facts to move that way. The Hare Krishnas served fantastic, tasty vegetarian food for free at their temples (notice the word free, hippies were often penniless), also Hare Krishnas believe in reincarnation and karma, and are deeply into Vedic mysticism and science [yes, you did hear the word science].

Vedic and mystical Hindu books speak of man's history on earth in terms of millions of years. They also speak about life forms on other planets, they even speak of souls occupying bodies of fire on the stars and on our sun.

Their description of how the universe was born is remarkably similar to that of Steven Hawkins and many others in the astrophysics community, all be it, in a different language and using a different angle to describe it from. But never the less, they are both describing the same thing, except that in the ancient Indian scriptures is also described what is outside of this universe, (it is said that there are many universes of illusion outside of this one).

And the third main reason that the hippies liked them was that their teachings came from India, a place where many of them wished to travel to. The Hare Krishnas represent the highest level of idealism for India's ancient ways, where people lived simply, not because they could not make wealth but as so as not to get distracted from their primary task of staying spiritually focused.

The Hare Krishnas would turn up at pop festivals and set up a temple and canteen made from tents where they would feed thousands of people for free and give away free books including their own translation with commentary of the Bhagavad-Gita, which is to a Hindu, what the New Testament is to a Christian.

Soon they had many people reading their books and coming to their temples. George Harrison of the Beatles gave them a large old manor house in a village somewhere north of London where they started an Ashram and a Vedic style farm where animals were treated with dignity and had rights too. Such as the right not to be killed and eaten, at least not by humans that is. The Beatles, especially George Harrison and John Lennon, got very interested in the movement and one song that George Harrison made and recorded is played in temples around the world during part of the morning devotions (which would go on for hours). He also helped them record and release a single that went to number one in the British music charts.

In America, some of the cult icons of the time would turn up at the temple and ask to meet Prabhupada. One of these was the poet, writer and musician, Alan Ginsburg, a man who had associated with Jack Kerouac, Timothy Leary and Ken Keasey [of "The electric coolade acid test" which can be read about in the book by Tom Wolfe]. Ginsburg hung around for quite a while and possibly helped draw in more people by his presence around the temples and the endorsement he gave of the Group as a whole.

Gypsy was disturbed from his book by one of his acquaintances in the smuggling fraternity. "Do you fancy doing another run?" he asked. Gypsy sat up feeling slightly disturbed as he entered back into the world around him. "When?" asked Gypsy. "In three days time" said the other traveler "sure" said Gypsy "put me down for it." However Gypsy didn't feel one hundred percent easy about it, unlike on the first run when he knew deep in his soul that he was going to get away with it. He went up on to the roof and smoked a joint, to relax.

Through the next day Gypsy lay on his bed, continuing to read his Hare Krishna book.

Then in the evening when he was relaxing in the communal area, another traveler came in, he had just come in from Kathmandu on the evening flight and was speaking so fast that no one could keep up with him. Apparently there had been a big bust at Kathmandu customs. Fourteen smugglers had been caught, it was heavy, the sentences would be severe. What had gone wrong? Apparently the man who organized the whole set up, a man who according to rumor was either from the Nepalese royal family or else married to one of their women, was either assassinated or died under mysterious circumstances in Switzerland. Also two American suits (who most likely were from either the CIA or DEA) were seen talking into phones and radios at the airport shortly before the flight landed.

In terms of international policies it added up. America under Ronald Reagan was in the process of an anti drug, headless chicken moral crusade, under the wise guidance of Nancy Reagan, who incidentally wouldn't know what a joint was if you blew the smoke in her face. During the time of the greatest frenzied madness and arrogance, While these idiots ran their war on drugs, they got to hear that India had thousands of government licensed shops where hashish, ganja, bhang and opium where the specialty products on sale. (Hashish and ganja are used by some Hindus, especially the babas and holy men in much the same way as Christians and Jews use sacramental wine for ceremonies) Because of India's close proximity to the US, i.e. on planet earth, Nancy Reagan and her fellow retards wanted this practice stopped before all of the American youth went to India and got turned into junkies by the "evil cross eyed snake charmers" there.

So the Americans in their great tradition of sticking their noses where they do not belong, wanted India to close its dope shops down. Never mind that this was not just an Indian tradition but deeply embedded in parts of the Hindu religion.

India, now under the westernized Prime Minister Rajiv Gandhi was willing to do a deal. They wanted the vast quantities of gold coming across the border from Nepal which was an American ally, halted, or at least curtailed somewhat.

Shortly after the big busts at Kathmandu, hashish, charas and ganja where outlawed in India and suddenly, instead of being able to smoke freely, people were getting busted and locked up for a long time for possession of just small quantities of charas i.e. five to ten grams.

So the deal looks like it was done. Gypsy cancelled his plan to do another gold run and decided to use his visa for China instead.

Guangzhou;

The next day he went to the Hare Krishna temple and told them of his plans and asked if they had leaflets in mandarin or Cantonese that he could take and distribute for them in China.

They explained to him the dangers and told him that it was best to just leave the leaflets somewhere were someone might find them and pick them up and have a look, a park bench for example.

He took a large bundle from them that he later hid in the bottom of his bag.

Back at the hostel that evening, word came back of a second bust at Kathmandu. All runs were cancelled the next day as the gangs wondered what to do.

The next day Gypsy took a taxi to the international railway station on Kowloon and boarded the train to Guangzhou. Off they went across the new territory to the Chinese border, where the train stopped and the passport teams came aboard and stamped everyone out of Hong Kong and into China. The train was decked out to look smart but in a communist old world sort of way. As such it looked more like a set for a railway based vampire movie than like anything that could be described as luxury. Several uneventful hours later the train pulled into the station at Guangzhou. Gypsy left the station and tried to follow a map that someone had given him that led to a hostel that accepted westerners. China was still very much communist at that time and very controlled.

There were not many hotels or hostels and foreigners were limited to only one or two of them in any one city.

Guangzhou was simply the foulest ugliest most depressing and unfriendly shithole that Gypsy had ever had the misfortune to step foot in. Bombay with its vast foul smelling shanty towns and thousands of homeless people sleeping on the streets paled in comparison to the misery and depression of Guangzhou. There were few if any sleeping on the street but the pollution was disgusting and the roads were full of thundering large trucks being driven badly and at speed. All of the signs were written only in Chinese script and the people were so unfriendly as to put Londoners, New Yorkers and Parisians to shame. Apparently, according to local superstition, it would bring bad luck to help a stranger in need.

After a long time feeling lost in this strange environment, Gypsy by chance spotted another foreigner (there were very few indeed, in China at that time) he asked him for directions to the hostel. "I'm going there myself, you can come with me if you like" said the traveler.

The hostel was a bland concrete building but it was a place to stay at least. From there he was able to find people who knew how to move and get things done in China. The next day he was able to join up with some other travelers who were going to the railway station to buy tickets to Guilin, which was in the same direction as Gypsy wished to travel, he tagged along with them and just copied what they did.

After a long wait in a pushing and hassling scrum of a queue, they all had tickets to Guilin. Gypsy would be leaving after the others, on a train that would be leaving after three days.

Gypsy's Chinese visa had almost expired during the three weeks that he had spent in Nepal so he went to the immigration office and got it extended and also got himself a permit to go to Tibet. "There must be something good, something worth seeing, something photogenic in this dump", Gypsy thought to himself. He got a city map from back at the hostel and went out to a local park that had an incredibly beautiful Chinese water garden. He was able to take some good photos there and catch the place in a good light.

Guangzhou was definitely a shithole with very few redeeming features and their taste in food was definitely not one of them, nor their table manners. The front of the restaurants resembled not so much places to eat as they did pet shops, featuring a variety of different live animals in cages that could be chosen for breakfast, lunch or dinner. There were tortoises, dogs, cats, snakes, rats, monkeys and a host of reptiles and birds to choose from. "Meet your lunch then eat your lunch," could have been their advertising slogan. Gypsy got one of the workers at the hostel to write him a note in Cantonese, stating "I am a vegetarian, please do not put any meat in my food". Never the less, when he went to a café to eat and showed them the note, they pointed at the meat and started laughing derisively.

After two more days in this shithole Gypsy was more than glad to be getting out of the place. He boarded the train with some other westerners who were heading north. He would be changing trains a few hours up the track.

It needs explaining, that China then was a very different place than it is today. Many of the people still wore chairman Mao outfits for one. Foreigners were not much known about and where ever the few foreigners that were travelling in China at that time would go, the locals would all stop and stare at them. Gathering around them like a crowd of mannerless zombies, they would not try and make contact or greet the foreigner, as an Indian would do, regardless of difference of language. They would just stare as if the foreigner was a TV set or an object of entertainment. It was more than a little tiresome after a few hours of it each day.

Guilin, China;

Also in China at that time, communication was the hardest thing imaginable. The Chinese would refer to foreigners as "Gwailow" which in the local dialect meant foreign devil. They would more often than not, be rude and hostile too. It would probably have helped however, if the British had not in the past, sailed up the river there and fought a war with the locals to force them to buy opium. After all no one like's drug pushers, especially not ones who force people to become junkies at gun point. Gypsy could understand their point of view, however he resented having to pay for the crimes of others in such a way. He had come across the crimes of the British in other parts of the world too and resented them for the troubles that it caused him, an innocent party. The mess that they had made as they went around the world, robbing people and shitting on them was totally shameful and unforgivable and made Gypsy wish that he could travel on either an Irish or Swiss passport.

On the train, Gypsy hung out with the other foreigners, it was good that they had their own set of seats to gather in, as in the Chinese area there was not a moment when the sound of at least ten people hawking and spitting in cacophonic symphony could not be heard. Kkkkkhhuuuuckkkk thwapppp, ggggarrrrrrrg thwaaaatttt! Cuuckh thwwwippp! Non stop. Every ten to fifteen minutes a man with a bucket and a mop would clean the floor of the carriage with hot soapy water. Disgusting was not the word for it.

Eventually, Gypsy reached his stop and got down from the train and waited. The crowd gathered around him jostling and pushing for a view of him like a zombie mob from "dawn of the dead" or some other "B" rated horror flick, except that they were not biting (well not at that time at least,..... they had probably just been fed).

After half an hour Gypsy's next ride came along the tracks and stopped. He got on board and placed his bag in the overhead rack. Luckily he had the company of another foreigner who was sitting opposite him, which helped keep the nearest Chinese spitter far enough away that their saliva was not hitting his shoes. The train rumbled on through the night and other foreigners boarded into the same carriage, they were also going to Guilin. The next day the train stopped at Guilin station and they all got off and walked through the town to the guest house. It was easy to find and not so far away. It was a much better place than the one back in Guangzhou and the food in the local cafés and restaurants was actually quite edible, never the less, they still looked like pet shops.

Guilin was a city set among the limestone sugar loaf hills and gorges of southern China. Gypsy had flown over the area and looked down on it on the flight to Kathmandu. A river ran through the area, sometimes forming lakes on its way. The natural beauty was stunning, with the hills and their reflection in the still lakes and slow running river making up an incredible panorama.

Also at Guilin were caves with their formations lit up by a multitude of Technicolor lamps, Gypsy visited them and took some photos. He stayed around Guilin for a couple of days taking photos and looking around.

Then he bought a ticket for a train that was going from Guilin to Kunming in Yunnan province. It was to be a two day ride. He packed and left the guesthouse and walked to the station and waited for his train.

At this point it is necessary to give some more background on how China was at this time. There were two types of money. There was the normal local currency known as renminbi and there was tourist money. Luxury goods such as Coca cola and other western consumables were sold only at a small number of shops where goods had to be paid for in tourist money. There was super high demand on the local black market for tourist money, which was sold by the travelers at massively high profit, thus making a trip through China at local levels of comfort, extraordinarily cheap.

As mentioned, there were few if any western brands of soft drinks available at that time. They had their own brands but even they could be hard to find.

When a Chinese person was thirsty, unlike most other people in the world they would rather drink hot water than cold. As such, on the train rather than having a water cooler from which to fill a glass, they had a large, solid fuel fed earn built into the end of the carriage with a tap on it and people would stand around, drinking mugs of hot water.

The train rolled on through the ravines and passed the impossibly steep sugarloaf hills. The area seemed to go on forever.

There were two jovial old men in their carriage who though they spoke no other language but mandarin, took the time and trouble to communicate. They were dressed in blue chairman Mao outfits and also wore Russian style bearskin hats. They were going home to their area near Kunming. As the train rolled on, they also passed by ugly factories pumping out noxious smoke and fumes from their hidden locations among the hills. The train rolled on through the night and the bunks were folded out and lights turned down. All the while with the sound of the cacophony orchestra, hawking and spitting through the night.

The next morning came and the carriage was hot. Gypsy was desperately thirsty but all that was available was boiling hot water from the earn. He drank a few cups of it but it just didn't hit the spot. He made his way to the buffet car and had to wait in a queue for a place to sit down. There were bottles on the tables that looked like they contained an orange drink but when Gypsy eventually sat down, he was informed by one of the other travelers that they were only for show and contained water with orange colored dye. The only drink available was hot Chinese tea.

The day rolled on and so did the train, through the gorges and tunnels, with a constant view of sugarloaf hills. The next night came and the bunks folded down again. Then came the morning and sometime around 10:30 am the train pulled into the station at Kunming.

They all got down and headed to one of two places in the city where foreigners were allowed to stay. It was a large looking hotel, all be it in dull, totally unimaginative communist style. On the roof of the hotel were two very large dormitories. Gypsy, along with the other travelers checked in to the dorms.

Gypsy saw a couple of Japanese travelers smoking a joint and asked them where they had got the weed from. They pointed out of the window to a huge ganja plant growing in a flower bed next to the street alongside other cultivated shrubs. Gypsy took the elevator to the ground floor and practically ran out to the street. The plant was covered in huge buds and Gypsy got picking, filling all of his pockets. Some of the Chinese stopped and stared in puzzlement, they obviously must have thought of the plant as either just ornamental or as something to make rope, fabric or paper from.

But one old man with a wrinkled face and grey hair, started to laugh when he saw what Gypsy was doing, he obviously knew what Gypsy wanted it for, even if the others didn't.

The dormitory contained a mixed crowd, there were some travelers and some decent friendly budget tourists who were having a nose around and then there was a bunch of uptight po faced wankers, the so called intellectuals. They came from universities in the west. Some were students and some were lecturers, travelling on tight budgets, on a limited time frame, from as short as three weeks, to two months.

These people would be going back to their uptight rat race existence in a short while. A short trip to China, unfortunately, was not going to help them to open their minds or break their conditioning. How could it? China was the land of Confucius, the grand master of all uptight wankers, no doubt some of this crowd had come to worship at his shrine.

The Chinese would have done better to have had Lao Tzu as their great hero, he was an enlightened master. One who was not afraid to name the game.

The intellectual types, though they were staying in the common space of the dormitory, were not a friendly lot and tended to do a lot of complaining about the activities of the travelers. They didn't like music being played or dope being smoked or even people sitting around and socializing with a couple of beers.

Gypsy went off the next day with his camera and started to explore Kunming, he had had a dream when in his early adolescence about being in this place, he remembered the dream most vividly and was looking for two places. There was the Golden temple and there was the Dragon Gate temple. In the dream he was looking for the house of the golden dragon, but when he got there he had found that it was just a low quality slot machine arcade inside.

In real life he took a bus to the Golden temple with a stack of Hare Krishna leaflets in his bag.

The temple was practically a museum with no active services being performed there. It was just a tourist attraction. The architecture was beautiful but with no devotional ceremonies, the place lacked much of its energy. Gypsy put leaflets down on benches and low walls around the gardens and then made his presence scarce.

He took another bus up to the Dragon gate temple, which was on a hilltop overlooking a large lake. Again whatever had given the place any spiritual significance had long since left. There were no monks, no ceremonies and no worship. Instead there was a snack bar and a well tended walk way through a garden. It was just as he had seen in the dream, all the wonder and energy had gone from the house of the golden dragon and the place was now a place of second rate entertainment.

The workers in the hotel had their own routine when it came to serving breakfast to the hotel guests, Gypsy had observed by his third morning in Kunming. First they would bring a plate with fried eggs on it and then they would wait for them to get cold before bringing a knife and fork, regardless of how many times any one asked for them, immediately brushing of the request with arrogance and bad language. They then would bring cold toast and then maybe ten minutes later they would bring butter and jam followed by cold tea or coffee. It was hard to imagine that they were not doing it out of hateful jealousy and outright racist spite. The word Gwailow (foreign devil in English) was in constant use in China at that time and the locals were often rude and unpleasant. By the third day Gypsy had noticed where the knives and forks were kept and worked out how he was going to deal with the breakfast situation.

That morning he sat down to eat with an old American who sported a beard and glasses and was dressed in a suit. He looked like a professor or academic of some kind. Gypsy was pleasantly surprised to find that the man was well versed in Hindu philosophy, which they chatted about for some time. Gypsy ordered his breakfast and they started talking about Vaishnav concepts and philosophy. "Yes, many years ago, I used to hang out at the Hare Krishna temple in San Francisco. I knew Prabupad well and used to join in the chanting and prayers," said the man.

"What do you do now?" Gypsy asked. "I'm a poet," said the man. "What's your name?" Gypsy asked curiously "Ginsburg" said the man. "Alan Ginsburg?" Gypsy asked. "Yes," said the man.

Gypsy's eggs and toast turned up at the same time, for once. He jumped to his feet and went over to the counter and helped himself to a knife, fork and teaspoon from the drawer. The waiters started shouting, snarling and gesturing unpleasantly at him. And even gestured at him to put the eating implements back. At which point Gypsy lost it and snarled back his displeasure at their bad service and told them to fuck off.

"Yes, I'm tired of their game of giving everyone a cold breakfast, from what it looks like, they don't like us very much," said Gypsy. "Are you still into the Hare Krishna take on the philosophy of Vaishnavism?" Gypsy asked "I've became much more interested in Buddhism these days," said Ginsburg. "How does it differ from vaishnavism and the Hare Krishna way?" Asked Gypsy. "Well, Buddhism is more about how you see things and how you deal with life. Take for example how you responded to the waiters when they shouted at you." "What would you have done?" asked Gypsy. I might have helped myself to the eating irons, but I would not have wasted energy by responding to their protests." said Ginsburg. "Right," said Gypsy. This was the first time that Gypsy had ever thought about having a read on Buddhism.

Ginsburg then asked Gypsy where he might find some weed and Gypsy explained about the giant Ganja plants growing in the flower beds along the road outside. "What are you doing that bring's you to here in China?" Gypsy asked. "I've come to a writers and poets convention." Ginsburg replied.

Breakfast finished, they got up to leave. "I would recommend that you take a look at Buddhism, the Hare Krishnas are OK but Buddhism has something else Again" Ginsburg recommend, before walking away.

"Wow, I've just had breakfast with Alan Ginsburg," thought Gypsy to himself maybe he's right maybe Buddhism is also worth looking at. I'll have to go find a book that explains it in a way that I can get my head around."

At the back of the hotel was a bear in a cage, he was black with a white "V" on his chest. Not only was he in a cage but he had also been tied up with wire. The cruelty of how he was being kept was breathtaking. Gypsy unable to watch such barbarism reached through the bars of the cage and untied the bear, leaping back in time to avoid a swing from one of the bear's paws. After that he would visit the animal regularly and take it fruit and cakes, (bears really like sweet things like cakes, honey fruit, etc). The funny thing to watch when a bear eats a cake with a filling, at least this bear was the way he would open the cake and lick out the filling before munching the rest of it, a bit like the behavior of a small child.

He told some travelers from Sweden about the bear and they too went and visited it and took it some food. One of the Swedes returned to the dormitory having also just fed the bear and said, "you may not believe this but I was standing in front of the bear's cage and I had bought it a load of bananas. I took one out of the bag and held it out and moved it around once in a circle. The bear then got down and did a summersault on the ground and then stuck its' paw out in a begging gesture, as if to say I've done the trick now give me the treat." Wild huh!. "It must have been a circus animal" said one of the others what's it doing in a cage at the back of the hotel?" Gypsy asked. "Bear paws are a Chinese delicacy" an American across the room interjected.

Gypsy, even after that went and had a look at the zoo. Inevitably many of the animals were being kept in entirely inappropriate surroundings. There were giant pandas being kept in a cage with a concrete floor with no plant life anywhere near them, it wasn't a small cage but it also was not what you would call a generously sized space either. The animals were ill tempered and would take out their frustration on each other, fighting and snarling as they battled for space. And they wonder why it is so hard to get Giant Pandas to breed in captivity?.

There's not enough space in the cage would be one reason. For most of the time they have a bunch of voyeuristic hairless creatures staring at them, would be another. And thirdly, you can hardly call a concrete floored cage with not even a privacy curtain, a romantic venue. I mean you would have to be some perverted exhibitionist to want to get your rocks off in such a place, and everyone knows that pandas are introverts.

The night market was the best place to eat in Kunming. It was set up each day in the late afternoon, in a big square in the centre of the city under tents and tarpaulins on poles. The great thing about the night market was that people could choose what they wished to eat in its raw state, from containers on a table. Putting it on a plate, they would hand it to the stall holder who would fry it up in a wok with some sauces and bring it to the table along with a helping of rice. It was possibly the cheapest place to eat in the city and the food was very fresh and always tasted good.

Gypsy and the three Swedes plus one Australian traveler, would eat at the market every night. Gypsy had now seen all that he wanted to in Kunming and the others were talking about taking the bus to Dali, a village, one day's bus ride away. It sounded like an interesting place, being on the edge of the tribal area, near the Burmese border. Gypsy decided to join them for the trip, it sounded like a nice place to spend Christmas, which was fast approaching.

The journey there was along a narrow two lane but paved road. There was not much traffic on the road at all as they passed a truck or a bus coming the other way every few minutes (private cars in China were as rare a rocking horse shit at that time). But every five or ten miles they would see a freshly crashed truck or bus, a testament to the wonderful excellence of Chinese driving. ["Honestly officer the tree did step out in front of me but now it's stepped back where it was again, it's playing tricks on me, it's a conspiracy"]. One can only wonder at what sort of excuses the drivers would give for crashing a truck on an empty, relatively straight road in broad daylight. One also could wonder at the incompetence of a system that allowed such untrained people out on the road in such large vehicles.

Dali, China;

Eventually at around the time of sunset, the bus reached the walled village of Dali. There was one guesthouse, a government run one that foreigners were allowed to stay in. It was basic, as in very very basic indeed, five of them shared a room. It had a cold concrete floor and the beds and that was it. The showers were cold and the toilet cubicles which were outside in a very long line had neither doors nor proper partitions. What partitions there were ended at waist height. So everyone could talk with each other as they were taking a dump, Gas masks would have greatly helped, as the stench was absolutely overpoweringly vile.

They went out to a café where they had seen other foreigners eating. There was a menu card in English but the owner of the place turned out to be a rather rude and aggressive little man who would curse and swear at his foreign customers in the local dialect if anyone asked for anything more once they had made their order. He even started shouting and threatening when an innocent mistake was made over currency while paying the bill.

The next day was Christmas day. Gypsy and one of the others went off for a wander with their cameras. Not only did the village have walls, it also had arched, gates with single level pagodas on top of them, they in turn were painted in red, white and gold, they were truly stunning and looked as if they had come out of a Chinese movie set. Outside of the walls of the village were two multi level pagodas, and a large long lake with hills behind it, it was a most picturesque place. Gypsy and the Swede walked out across the farmland which was being tended in the most primitive of ways, by subsistence farming without the use of machines. On the other side of the farms they climbed halfway up the hill, but as it was, it was covered entirely in forest so they could not find a place to get a good view to take photographs from and so they headed back down to the village.

Back in the village they met the others who had been on something of an expedition with a map that someone had drawn for them.

They all headed up a sloped alleyway to a garden café that one of them had found, found a table and sat down. Then the Australian and the two Swedes who had been with him produced about a kilo of weed from their pockets and a small aluminium cooking pan which they put a bit of ganja in at a time, then heated it over the candle that was on the table, in order to dry it.

"So that was what the map had been about" thought Gypsy to himself. It. was Christmas night and they were in south China, in a village that belonged in a period chop sockey movie. They were sitting in a beautiful walled garden, eating spring rolls and drinking beer while drying out a huge pile of local buds. It was all somewhat surreal.

The owners of the café, an old man and his wife, were doing the cooking at an outdoor kitchen in the corner of the semi paved garden. When the old man brought the food and saw the huge pile of weed on the table his eyes lit up as he exclaimed "Ah marijuana". He went running off to his house and came back with a brass hashish/ganja pipe with intricate designs on it, he then put it on the table for all to use.

It was strange how only the old people knew about ganja in China. Anyone who did not have a head of grey hair and a wrinkled face just stared in puzzlement when they saw foreigners picking or smoking it. The evening wore merrily on, as they smoked their way through a small quantity of what lay there on the table. They had Chinese munchies and beer as their Christmas dinner. Gypsy knew that this would be a Christmas that he would never forget.

The old man sold his pipe to the Australian for the equivalent of three US dollars in local Chinese money. That was the last that Gypsy could remember of that very stoned evening.

Dali was beautiful but the guesthouse and its toilets (which even to this day Gypsy maintains were the worst in the world. Even super ceding those at the old Glastonbury festival, for foulness and discomfort) were just too bad to live with.

The next day they all went and booked places on the bus back to Kunming for the following day.

So they all spent one more day sightseeing and relaxing. Being that Gypsy was on a super tight budget, he used his camera film sparingly and waited until he could find a good position to get the format that he wanted, with the light working for him before he would click the shutter. He had Fuji slide film and it would prove to be a good choice later when the film was processed. Sometimes he would change lenses and put on the bulky 70 to 210 zoom to capture long distance and detailed shots. Gypsy would rarely take more than 15 to 20 shots in one place but would aim to use the film carefully as possible to capture the feel of the place.

After one more cold depressing night in the government run guesthouse they were on the bus for the all day ride back to Kunming. On the way back they saw a fresh, brand new display along the roadside of bus and truck crashes. The ones that they had seen on the way to Dali having already been hauled off for repair. Now there was a fresh lot of drivers, standing by the road. Some of them were looking at the truck that they had either just rolled over or rammed into a tree, a post or something, standing with their hands on their hips and no doubt thinking "Oh shit how the fuck am I going to explain this one to the boss."

Gypsy and the others all wanted to go to Hong Kong from Kunming. Gypsy had a permit to go to Tibet but the land route would involve a two week or longer journey and he did not have enough money for the flight. He had also wanted to see Beijing and Shanghai but the money was not there to do it.

Kunming, China;

Back at Kunming one of the other travelers had bought a guitar from a supermarket for three US dollars. Gypsy had a quick go on it and then went out and found the supermarket and bought one also. It was hardly a fender or even a cheap Italian jumbo folk guitar but it played, just about.

That evening Gypsy and the other traveler were jamming. They were out on the roof and a crowd had gathered around. Someone else was using a chair as a drum and there was a bit of a party happening, with people sitting around drinking beer and singing along with the songs. Then this highly tactful and diplomatic German woman appeared at the door of one of the dormitories and ragefully screamed "vil you fucking bastards shut up vee haff to take zee train early in zee mornink und now it is eight thirty in ze night und vee vont to get zum sleep." Due to her wonderful manners and relaxed and thoughtful nature, Gypsy and the Australian on the other guitar, serenaded her with a rendition (a bad one at that) of the Rolling Stones song "Satisfaction."

Then they played louder than ever for five or ten more songs just to make sure that she was listening.

The food at the night market tasted good, like really good and one night Gypsy had two plates of it.

The next day he awoke feeling sick as a dog with heavy stomach cramps. The Australian who he had been jamming with explained that the reason the food tasted so good was because they shovelled heaps of monosodium glutamate over it while they cooked it and if he ate two plates of food, he probably had M.S.G. poisoning. He told Gypsy that he was in China to complete an Acupuncture training course. He offered to give Gypsy a free treatment. Gypsy willingly if nervously, accepted. And so for what felt like a large part of the afternoon, he lay there on his bed with needles sticking in him feeling much like a pin cushion.

Kunming is known as the place of eternal spring, as the weather all year round is always mild. Even then at the end of December it was not particularly cold and flowers were in bloom, there were certainly no frosts but the air would be a bit fresh in the morning.

The three Swedes were going to take the train to Hong Kong but Gypsy and the Australian had had quite enough of China and wanted to get the hell out of the god forsaken hell hole as fast as possible. What with pictures of mass executions on the public notice board, the cruelty to animals and the tiresome experience of going into shops and pointing to a stack of goods behind the counter and asking for one of the items, just to be told by the sullen shop assistant "No have", just out of hateful laziness. Gypsy had met one Chinese man at the night market who spoke fluent English. They got talking and after eating Gypsy invited the man to come to the hotel and meet some of the other travelers (a Chinese person who spoke such good English was an extreme rarity in China at that time and would thus be a valuable link by which to understand the local culture better).

However, when they got to the hotel steps a plain clothed man came up to him and said something to him in mandarin. The blood drained from the face of the one who could speak English, he turned as white as a sheet and started trembling before taking off at a run. The plain clothed man obviously worked for one of the state agencies tasked with enforcing oppression and fear into the population.

> "How sad and pathetic that such a huge country with such a massive population could allow itself to be led by such cowardly cynical and frightened little men, who in their hysterical terror of other people, found it necessary to micro manage, control and oppress its people in such a way. These so called leaders were the same murderers and criminals who later ordered the Tiananmen square massacre in Beijing in 1989. May the fruits of their acts return on them wherever their low dark fallen souls may be now".
>
> Gypsy

Gypsy was so disgusted by China that he used up some of his precious resources on a flight from Kunming to Guangzhou. There was only one airline in China at that time, The government run C.A.A.C. [which at that time due to their terrible safety record and frequent vertical prangs was reputed to stand for "China Airways Always Crashes"]. The

Australian also booked himself onto the same flight, he too had seen more than enough of China. The beautiful China that any of them had hoped to see had been defaced and oppressed almost to the point of complete extermination, firstly by arrogant acts of western colonialism and then by a large pile of foul smelling shit called the communist party.

They got to the airport which was also a military area, checked in and waited for the flight to arrive. The plane was a British made BAC Trident (The Chinese government had done a large deal with the British Aircraft Corporation in the early 1970's to by a quantity of the aircraft. At one point, tridents made up the large part of the Chinese civil aviation fleet).

Hong Kong, January, 1985

They boarded the plane and it was soon taxing out to the runway, past a long line of old Russian MIG 17 fighters. Even then these planes would be more commonly seen in a museum than in the sky. Gypsy wondered how many if any of them would still be air worthy. They took off and the plane then turned and headed east. It was a bit like flying on Ryan Air or Easy Jet, in that there was no in flight service, but they did come around giving out tins of dried black tea. What use that might have been in a plane with no hot water or sugar is anyone's guess.

An hour and a half later the plane touched down at Nanning and everyone got off, took a piss and smoked a cigarette (nearly every adult male in China smoked at that time). They waited for half an hour before being told to reboard the flight. The plane took off down another runway lined with antique Migs and was now heading directly for Guangzhou. After two hours and another blue tin of Chinese tea leaves, the plane made a bumpy landing at Guangzhou.

Gypsy and the Australian grabbed their bags and practically ran out of the airport, jumped into a cab and headed off at speed to the railway station. There was only one or two trains a day going to Hong Kong and they had tickets for a train that was about to leave in minutes. They jumped from the cab and ran into the station and boarded the train just as the whistle blew to announce it's imminent departure. The train started to roll within a minute of them sitting down. As the train rolled away Gypsy breathed a huge sigh of relief, he never thought that he would be glad to see Hong Kong but after China anywhere barring north Korea or Saudi Arabia would be a breath of fresh air. There was something fundamentally wrong in the collective psyche of the people as a whole it was not just the government.

The mindless unspeakable cruelty that they would inflict on animals. Their cravings for some of the foulest and cruelestly harvested foods e.g. rat embryos in chilli sauce, monkey brains while the monkey was still alive. Beaten and tortured dog (apparently beating the dog and breaking all its bones while it was still alive made the meat taste better).

Not only did the people in general lack any form of compassion for animals, but also for each other. They were rude and aggressive and would put a monkey to shame in bad table manners. These were some of the most savage, uneducated, unenlightened beings that Gypsy had ever had the misfortune to be in the company of.

India was even poorer and suffered chronic problems, partly caused by iodine deficiency in the diet of a large segment of the population, causing many of them to suffer from cretinism. But in India there was kindness and compassion towards animals and a large part of the population as such, were vegetarian. Even the non vegetarians for the most part would eat vegetarian food. In India there were hospitals and even retirement homes for animals. The people of India were a far happier people. Even if they were not happy, they would do their best not to spread their misery to others. They were also friendly, sometimes dare I say, too friendly. They were hospitable, generous, free and chaotic and in that freedom and chaos everything still worked, all be it by different methods but people were far happier than the Chinese, with their strictly controlled regime.

It was after dark when the train crossed back into Hong Kong and rolled across the New Territories. It was New Year's Eve and Gypsy was glad to be in crowded, congested Kowloon for it. He headed back to Chungking mansions to get a bed and drop his bag. He then went out to Ned Kelley's last stand for a beer.

Then after buying some hash from his connection on a lower floor of "A" block, he went up to the roof for a joint and to take photographs of the lights. He had bought some 1600 a.s.a. night film and wanted to capture the lights of Hong Kong with his camera.

It felt just so good to be out of China and in the international atmosphere of Hong Kong. That said, he didn't want to be spending too much time in Hong Kong either with the uptight anal attitude that permeated the place at that time. Hong Kong was the ultimate rat race city, even more so than New York. New York might have a rat race but it was built for people to live in and enjoy in liberty, with great museums, parks, theatres, etc. New York is filled with culture and good eateries, it has a soul that feels. Hong Kong, that last significant piece of the British Empire, was concerned with business and commerce only. Acting not only as a centre for shipping and banking but also as a giant sweat shop and proxy by which Chinese goods could reach the world market.

Hong Kong had a soul too, but of the dark variety that can more commonly be found in a snake or other hostile reptilian predator.

At the hostel Gypsy got chatting with some of the former smugglers. Some of the Gangs had moved to Bangkok and were doing the run from there, some were doing business as usual, though there had been several more busts at Kathmandu. A couple of gangs were running it across China and Tibet to Nepal. Going first to Guangzhou then flying to Chengdu and then changing onto the Lhasa flight before then taking the bus to the Nepalese border. It was paying a lot more but the smugglers were expected to carry a lot more gold.

Gypsy had seen all that he needed of areas under Chinese government control. To have to see the Tibetans under their nasty repressive thumb would just have pissed him off too much.

He had not much money and it was not yet the right time to go to Japan. They would not be looking to take on new English teachers until April and anyway it was freezing cold in Japan in January.

Gypsy missed playing guitar. The three dollar guitar he bought in China was so bad that it had not even been worth the effort of carrying it back to Hong Kong. Besides, right now having a guitar was not just a hobby it was going to have an economic angle too. In Japan he planned to busk until he was up on his feet with a job. He was going to need a bit of time to practice and build up a repertoire of songs. Also it would be a better idea to buy the guitar in Hong Kong where it was tax free and much cheaper.

Gypsy had noticed a guitar shop on Nathan road on previous visits. He made several visits to the shop trying out several of the guitars in his price range and then going away to ponder which one was going to be the best for him.

In the end he made up his mind, went back to "Tom Lee's" guitar shop and bought an Aria jumbo folk guitar for one hundred and ten US dollars.

Back at Chungking mansions he got asked to play it and did his own raging versions of "Jonny B. Goode" and "House of the Rising Sun" where he belted the lyrics out at the top of his voice almost at scream pitch, a bit like Noddy Holder of Slade. It was raw energy and people liked it. Well at least the travelers did. The uptight wankers who had come out for just a few weeks to go see China. pulled faces that night as if someone had farted right under their nose. A look that could best be described as a sodomized stare.

They seemed to feel threatened and frightened of the hippies, freaks and misfits that characterized the most of the travelers. It was as Jack Nicolson said in the movie "Easy Rider" people can talk about freedom all day and about what it means, but if you show it to them they'll try to kill you.

Yes, they were going to see another country, but only as voyeurs, looking from the confines of the prison of their intellect and conditioning, they would never feel the place that they were in. They would never understand the culture, energy or direction of a place as they would never have touched it from the inside.

It wasn't long before the cucumber in rectum club was out, complaining about the noise, even though it was early, e.g. 7:30 p.m. And so Gypsy and some of the crowd including some who had been jamming along, headed up the ladder onto the roof and carried on playing.

The thing that really got Gypsy the most about the complainers was that these were the very same arseholes that made Gypsy dislike his visits to the West so much. He was in Asia at least partially to get as far away from the mother fucking creeps as possible. These were the types that always made him feel unwelcome in England and now the twats were out here. Not just that but out of pure meanness they had invaded a traveler bastion and now wanted to arrogantly dictate the terms by which the place should be run.

The next day a German in his late thirties who had just arrived from the Philippines loudly and angrily voiced his displeasure at the miserable nature of the people staying at the Travelers' hostel.

"Look at zees miserable vankers zey have no idea, zey are not travelers zey are all a bunch of miserable sorry losers not friendly, not real. I just come from Philippines now I live zer for five years. In zat time I never see one person so stupid and miserable as zees people." Gypsy had to agree, he felt the same way.

He went by to the Hare Krishna temple a few more times and they suggested that if he would like, he could try living in a temple again, as he had done in Australia. The ashram that they had on Cebu Island in the Philippines might be worth him going and checking out.

He got thinking about it and went and checked out what he could buy a return to the Philippines for. It worked out cheaper getting a one way via Manila to Tokyo than buying a return to Hong Kong.

He took the ferry over to Hong Kong Island and took a bus to where the Philippine embassy was located, off the lower level road several kilometers from the star ferry terminal, and applied for a visa. He paid the fee and was told that he could collect his passport after two days.

Back at Chungking mansions the wait for the lift going down got to be so long as to be unbearable. The lift would go up and down several times from lower floors to the ground before finally making it up to the long agitated queue outside of the travelers hostel. Gypsy on several occasions ran down the emergency stairs at the back of the building, to the ground floor. Thankfully the wait to go up was never so long. Walking back up the sixteen flights of steps would probably take more than half an hour and be a somewhat tiring exercise.

Gypsy was chatting with Dutch Eddie about his plans to go and stay at the Hare Krishna ashram in the Philippines. "I don't like these religions with so many beliefs and too many books," he said. "I like Buddhism it deal's with much more tangible and real experiences. You must know that you don't see the world how it is, you see it how you are. Until you get rid of conditionings everything is subjected to them."

Gypsy remembered these words but he still wanted to check out the Hare Krishna Ashram.

He was going up to the roof to smoke a joint and invited another misfit traveler from England to join him. The guy had been busted and locked up on a gold run into Seoul. . There was another gold smuggling run that used to go to Korea, but it was too dangerous to be considered by all but the clinically insane, as the Koreans did not have much of a sense of humor about people breaking the laws of their country. In the prisons people were reported to be housed in cages that gave so little room to move about that it would have driven a battery hen to insanity. Lights where kept on the whole time and there was absolutely no privacy. Harsh punishment was meted out for the most minor of infractions. In America there is even a clinical name, given for the post, trauma, stress from suffering such an ordeal, it is known as "Post Korean syndrome. He had spent nine months in the lock up before being released. Whatever can be said about it, this guy was not quite right. He could have been like it before he got banged up or he could have just been a fragile quiet type and the Korean experience pushed him over the edge. He was a harmless enough person but he seemed to live partly in another world, unable to comprehend all that was around him in this world.

They were both playing music but this guy was off in a world of his own and his harmonica accompaniment was just a nonsensical cacophony. He could articulate his thoughts but his general field of vision in life was too close in for him to be anything but vulnerable like a child, as he travelled on the road. However, if he went back to England he would probably end up being made to feel like a loser and dying of depression, so in the absence of something better, life on the road was possibly his best choice.

They met, smoked joints and shared travel stories on several more occasions and Gypsy figured the guy must have a spirit watching over him, as most of people as naïve and innocent as this guy would not be able to travel and be housed in sheltered accommodation while being patronized by ignorant care staff. The interesting thing is that Gypsy met him many years later on another continent, but that is another story.

He collected his passport from the Philippine consulate. It had the brightest Technicolor visa that he had ever seen. He didn't know so much about the Philippines but judging from the people that he had met from there so far, he figured that he was going to like the place.

He went and bought a one way ticket via Manila to Tokyo for one hundred and fifty US dollars and headed back to Chungking Mansions. He had been given directions by devotees at the temple on how to find the place when he got there.

At the temple he met another American Hare Krishna devotee who was just visiting Hong Kong. He was the chief of their Taiwan operations and worked from an office come temple in Taipei where he was involved in the publishing of Hare Krishna books. He and Gypsy chatted for some time and then he said "listen, the Philippine temple isn't everyone's cup of tea for many reasons. If you find that you don't like it there, you would be welcome to come and stay with us in Taiwan if you would like".

Hong Kong was too uptight, grey, miserable and claustrophobic in January when it is cold and the beaches and parks are not such a good place to hang out. Even the roof of Chungking Mansions "A" block was not such a pleasant place to be with the fog and rain blowing around.

Gypsy got a stack of films back from processing, the Fuji chrome had been a good choice. Gypsy was amazed and very pleased with the results. The camera too had worked exceptionally well, giving him good sharp focus and depth. The Fuji chrome gave water, as in seas, rivers and lakes an extra vivid richness to the blue. The sky too would also be of an extra vivid shade of blue. He had used the camera carefully and sparingly, not wasting the film on shots that did not help to tell the story about the local ways, of the places that he had visited. Temples, panoramas, life and habitat shots were what he wanted. He wanted shots of people too but not just their faces he wanted to get candid photos of them in the midst of attending to their occupations or casually relaxing, he certainly did not want them posing. He may not have liked China but he was more than happy with the photos that he had taken there. He had managed to catch it in a most flattering way on film. To look at the photos he had taken one might have imagined that the place was some sort of oriental wonderland.

A camera never lies, well almost never, but its greatest trick is to show only one facet, one angle. If the photographer can find that one or maybe two or three good angles, anywhere including a dump or a sewage works can be made to look good.

He reckoned that he had done well to get so many good interesting shots from each of the films that he now had processed onto slides.

With his bag heavier from the boxes of slides and now a guitar over his shoulder as well, he took a cab to Kai Tak Airport and checked in for his flight, then went through the gauntlet of formalities to airside. The wonderful things about Kai Tak Airport was that the bars were so close to the airbridge gates that you could be sitting on a bar stool until the very final call, knocking back the gin and tonics before casually walking over to the gate after the last other remaining passenger had run gasping and stumbling down the tunnel to the plane and walk down to the plane and find ones seat without having to stand in the usual snail's pace queue.

To Cebu City, Philippines;

The Philippine Airlines DC10 taxied out to the runway and took off in an easterly direction, out to sea. The plane was full of miniature Philippina women who worked in Hong Kong. They were going home to visit the family for a couple of weeks. It was a happy feeling on board the flight, also the plane was clean and modern and the service was both good and very friendly. Lunch was served and then an hour and a half later the wheels hit the concrete at Manila. After the usual immigration and customs routine Gypsy was out of the airport in a taxi for the two kilometer ride to the domestic terminal.

At the somewhat small and cramped domestic terminal (which resembled a postal warehouse and packing station more than it did, an airport terminal) he bought a one way ticket on the afternoon flight to Cebu City for $30U.S. and went to the bar to wait.

At the bar he met another westerner waiting for the Cebu flight. His name was Fred and he was from the American Virgin islands. He lived and worked in South Korea and was going to Cebu to join up with an American friend who also lived and worked in Seoul.

They were planning to hit the town and party, something that for them was not so easy to do back in Korea. The problem was, that although they were best of friends they never got to see much of each other back in Korea, on account of Fred being banned from Doug's house by Doug's wife, because of the jokes he liked to play. Koreans do not have such a boisterous sense of humor as some people. One of Fred's favorite jokes was to wait until no one was looking and then sneak into the marital bedroom and stuff the filthiest, most perverted porno fetish magazine that he could find, under Doug's pillow and then wait until his wife would find it and go crazy at Doug, who hadn't got a clue as to what had just happened or why his wife was screaming at him.

Right at this particular moment what was transpiring was this: Doug had been on holiday in the Philippines for a week with his wife and two children at a resort. He had then sent them back home to Seoul, making excuses that he had to stay on in Cebu for business, which was true if you count the monkey variety too. Fred was booked to fly in the next day which, was the flight that he was presently waiting for. Fred then told Gypsy another story about a joke he had played on a professional con artist from England who was a work acquaintance of his. The man was going on holiday to the Philippines but Fred was there two weeks before him having his regular bar and brothel crawling vacation. He placed an advert in a Manila based newspaper saying:

Mr. Richard Leary will be visiting the Philippines on March 3rd to 18th and seek's a young local lady to show him the sights of Manila for the duration of his stay, his flight will be arriving from Seoul at 2.30 pm on the 3/8 flight no……….. please meet at airport.

The man spoke English with a posh colonial style about him and Fred said of him "You could almost imagine him in a pith helmet and jungle jims."

Anyway when he returned to the office after his holiday Fred asked him in an innocent tone if he had had a good holiday. This was what Fred had been waiting for. "You'll never guess what happened to me at Manila airport," said the man. "I came out of the arrivals gate and there was this huge crowd of women all holding up signs with my name on. When I told one of them that I was Richard Leary, they mobbed me as if I was a rock star or movie actor or something. Then this little fat one just barged through the crowd pushing all the other girls aside and bundled me into a taxi and started gibbering something about me being in the paper.

Most of the other westerners in the office had figured it out and knew that it fitted with the pattern of Fred's humor, but Richard Leary was convinced that it was because he must have a famous namesake who by chance was inbound to Manila that day.

The topic of conversation changed, to talking about cameras and then about the rude, aggressive Chinese who sold fake items, then called their corrupt cop friends to intimidate or even arrest people who came back and complained when the item didn't work. Fred told Gypsy a good way of dealing with such people. The "Piss Pistol", which involves pissing into a water pistol and then going to the camera come electronics shop and giving its owner and his stock a good squirting. This course of action of course, requires having a good exit strategy e.g. a waiting taxi on a clear street, a fast bicycle or a good pair of running shoes.

Fred told another story about how he had recommended this trick to a friend.

His friend was looking in shops in Penang for an 80 to 200 zoom lens for his camera. He was in one particular shop looking at one particular lens. He asked the price, but when he was told how much, he looked at the shop owner and said "look, I know how much they cost in Vancouver, I want to know how much they cost here, I'm not prepared to pay that much for one."

The Chinese shop owner exploded "look I know you Canadians look, look, not buy, get out of my shop go on get out fuck off." It was at this point he remembered about Fred's piss pistol idea and decided that if there was someone in the world who deserved to be sprayed then it was this particular Chinese shop keeper.

He went to the market and found a children's toy stand and bought a water pistol, from a distance it looked like a real gun. He found a toilet and loaded his weapon, then he went back to the camera shop. Bursting through the door robbery style, brandishing the toy as if it was a real gun and shouting "right mother fuckers, now it's time for revenge." The shop owner and his staff of four hit the tiles so fast that they knocked over the shelf stands behind them on the way down, causing them to wobble severely and rain cameras, lenses and other heavy delicate and expensive items on to their heads and the hard tiled floor.

At this point the Canadian got frightened that he would get into serious trouble for this, so he threw the water pistol on the counter and ran. He then went back to the guesthouse that he was staying at and hid for the rest of the day, trembling in fear, as Malaysia had a reputation for it's draconian rules and harsh punishments. He re-emerged that evening and went to a local café where other travelers went. Even then he disguised himself behind a hat, dark glasses and a newspaper. However a group of Australians that he had been sitting chatting with several days prior to the event came wandering into the place and immediately recognized him despite his disguise.

"Struth mate was that you, making that ruckus at that camera shop this morning?" they asked "Shhhh!!" the Canadian replied with a finger crossing his lips, "I'm hiding, I don't want to get into trouble here in Malaysia."

The Aussies carried on in loud exuberant voices. "You'll never guess what happened next mate" one of them said "no sooner had you taken off like a bat out of hell, than some cops came down the street and the shop keeper called them into his place and told them what had just happened, while pointing to the gun on the counter. The most senior of the cops picked it up and realized straight away what it was and cursed the shop owner for being so stupid. Then to demonstrate, he squirted some of the content into his mouth. It must have been something pretty bad that you put inside of it fella! Because the next thing he did was spit it out, his face went bright red with rage then he pistol whipped and shouted at the shop owner."

"Of course if you want the absolute smelliest revenge ever, on a shop owner" Fred started to explain with an evil grin on his face "then you will have to make a katusha" "What's that?" asked Gypsy. "You will need an egg a turd and a tomato" Fred continued "you put them all in a polythene sleeve, tie up the ends and then put it to steam in the sun for a few days. When ripe take to chosen target, untie one end of the sleeve, place in shop doorway and jump on it. If you get it right you should be able to spray the whole shop in one move. It makes such a stink that it will take an age before they can get rid of it"

"You'd want to wear old clothes and have a fool proof, quick getaway plan for that one." Gypsy commented.

The flight was called so they each ordered one more drink at the bar and waited for the queue to subside before going outside to board. The plane was an old British built jet, a BAC one eleven and the flight was already one hour late due to a heavy monsoon thunder storm over Cebu. It was overcast at Manila too as they walked across the apron to the old jet. There were many other old planes parked on the apron too. They had a variety of different markings from a range of airlines that Gypsy had never heard of. There were old 707s and 720s, there were 727s and a range of different twin engined prop planes, some marked in the colours of Philipine Airlines and some with no markings at all bar for their numbers. Some of them looked as if they were freighters and others just looked as if they were being used for spare parts. The Philippines being a chain of islands, there was only two choices by which people and goods could move over large distances, one was by sea and the other was by air.

It was around five thirty in the afternoon when the plane started its descent into Cebu. They descended at a normal rate before they reached the layers of cloud but then the plane was placed into a sharp dive through the clouds. It was still diving at a sharp angle as it came through the last layer. It was still raining quite hard and Gypsy looked out of the window onto a warm, green, tropical paradise that looked very third world indeed, as drops of water streaked across the small windows of the plane.

The plane leveled out at the last moment then landed onto a very wet runway and taxied to a parking space near the terminal. After collecting their bags Fred suggested to Gypsy that he might like to come and meet Doug and join them for a night on the town. Gypsy agreed and so they jumped into a cab and headed across town to the guest house that Doug was staying at.

It was after dark when they crossed the bridge from Maktan island to Cebu city (Cebu airport was on a small island off of the coast of the main Cebu island). It was some ten or fifteen minutes later when they finally made it to the place where Doug was holed up. It was a cheap and run down doss hole of a guest house with an institution style feel about it. It had dull yellow walls, was made of concrete and was what could only be described as soulless. Gypsy and Fred both checked in and got Doug's room number from the man running the reception counter.

All though they knocked hard and continuously, It took a while for Doug to open the door. When he did, he opened it just a crack and looked out nervously, as if expecting trouble. he looked somewhat sheepish even as he invited them in. He explained how his wife and kids had taken off the previous afternoon, they had been staying all together in a resort on Mactan island which was not only where the airport was located but also where a few reasonably fancy resorts were operating. It's two claims to fame were that, one; it is where the famous Spanish navigator, Magelan met his end in a battle with the locals as he sought to control and impose Spanish colonial domination on them. And two: it was the home to a large quantity of good luthiers (people who make guitars) many of whom had their own shops on the island and in Cebu city. Maktan island was known in the Philippines at least as a place to buy a good guitar. Doug had immediately checked into the cheap guest house after seeing his family off at the airport and then gone out on the razzle.

As he poured the beer and whiskey down his throat in a wild celebration at getting his wife off of his back for a week he started getting drunk, and obnoxious with it. He got brazen with some Australians and took the piss out of them in a most insulting manner.

Later while sitting at the bar and drunkenly slobbering over one of the in house resident hookers, the Aussies saw their chance for retribution and seized upon it with both hands.

They went up to Doug at the bar who was now barely coherent and said "well done Doug, you've got the best hooker in the place, we all wanted to take her but you beat us to it. Tell you what, just to show that there are no hard feelings we'll treat you"

They paid his bar fine for him (house pimping commission for taking a hooker out from the bar) and put him in a taxi back to his hotel.

The next morning Doug awoke to the sight of a man in woman's under wear lying next to him in the bed. He couldn't remember what had happened the night before and was worried about what might have happened or what he may have caught.

All day he had hidden in the room out of shame and self disgust. Now it was after dark so he got himself sorted out and they all went out to find a place to eat.

They ended up in a place that was almost a street stand but in a private garden. The food was nothing special but was moderately edible. They then took off to a club.

Gypsy hadn't seen anything like it before. There were perhaps three or four hundred local men sitting around, drinking while watching live sex shows on a large low set stage. Lesbian performances etc. At one point before Gypsy got his wits about him a girl grabbed him and pulled him up on to the stage but there was no way that he could have got an erection with so many men watching. It's a shame that women wern't the main clients at such events as that would have just added to the stimulus, he would have had no problems putting on an acrobatic performance if that had been the situation. The crowd let out a sigh of disappointment when Gypsy turned around and said "sorry folks but there's no way I can get it up with your ugly faces all staring at me," he slunk off to the bar and ordered another drink. Fred came over and asked Gypsy "hey man what happened? you could have become a famous star of the stage." "Could you have got it up with three hundred Philippino midgets leering in your direction?" he asked in return. Fred laughed and Doug suggested they go and do a tour of the girlie bars, so they drank up and went out and walked a couple of blocks down to the first one. It had loud music and was full of hookers dressed in gaudy outfits, sitting around drinking and prancing about on the dance floor.

The latest music from the west was blasting out of the stereo as they entered the place and sat down at the bar. First it was Bruce Springsteen's "Dancing in the dark" followed by Robin Gibb's "Boys do fall in Love" then Madonna singing "like a virgin" which was taking the piss in a joint like this.

some women came over to them and introduced themselves, then one sat down next to each of them and tried to extract a "lady's drink" which is anything that she might ask for but at a fixed hyper inflationary rate. It was the bar's way of getting the best value and highest returns on their hookers, who also got a commission for each drink that was brought for them.

They moved from that bar and took a cab to another bar were the clients were mostly men from Germany. The place was owned by a German and was in a large stand alone building, it was a smart looking place, both inside and out. There was a high set stage with girls queued up waiting to take a turn dancing on it. The place was full of mirrors and decorated in a high quality way, but the best thing was watching the girls dancing. Each one had the most beautiful well proportioned body that Gypsy had ever seen and their faces were not what anyone could call ugly either. They had obviously been selected by one of those legendary German quality control inspectors. The Germans who attended the establishment were even known to fight each other over which one of the hookers each one got to take for the night.

Finally they ended up at an Australian run bar and Gypsy met one woman that he liked. She was three or four years older than him with a fine body and an attractive face but unlike many others that had done the chat up on him this one genuinely gave off the vibe that she liked sex. She was bigger boned and stronger that the other girls in the bar. Yes it is always about money in Southeast Asia but as with any profession you are always better off employing someone who's enjoys their occupation.

"Tell the taxi driver to take you to Queensland," Fred advised as Gypsy paid the bar fine to take the woman out. "What is it?" asked Gypsy. "It's a hotel that you pay for the room by the hour, but believe me it's worth it." Fred replied. "Well I'll take your word for it and give it a try." Said Gypsy as he left the bar with the woman, who said her name was Marilyn.

They jumped in a taxi and told the taxi driver to take them to Queensland.

They drove for a couple of kilometers through Cebu City before pulling into a drive way and entering a 60ft long tunnel of pulsing multicolor lights. As they entered, the clerk handed them a key, from the window of his office to the window of the cab, then he set a timer for the room. The taxi dropped them off at their room and they went inside. If someone couldn't get the feel in this room there would have to be something either wrong with him or with the woman he brought with him.

There was a giant king sized double bed with mirrors set at all sorts of different angles, totally covering the hood canopy that went up the wall and over the top of the bed. There was a porno playing on the in house TV monitor and Diana Ross gently wailing on the stereo. On the table where condoms, towels and tissues and the shower had two heads, with one pointing from above and the other pointing up from below.

They both wasted not a second in throwing off their clothes and getting in to the bed. they were both feeling pent up and horny as they had both been winding each other up back at the bar. Gypsy held back as long as he could, causing her to climax first, before allowing himself to release. She stayed for a few hours and then after another session they got dressed and after Gypsy had paid both the "fuck palace" and the woman they both headed off to their different places to sleep. She asked where he was staying and said she would visit him later.

After he eventually awoke at about mid day and feeling tired and hung-over he stumbled to the bathroom to get himself cleaned up. He thought to himself, "isn't life bizarre in its contrary nature|? all the time that I'm looking to meet a woman, none is there that is available. The moment that I'm about to go and live in an ashram then I'm taken on a tour of girlie bars where I meet a really horny one who gives me hot passionate sex, all be it for money, but that was not her only motivating factor". He got dressed and went and found something to eat.

When he got back Marylin was outside the room in the corridor chatting with Fred. She kissed Gypsy on the cheek on his arrival and they went inside. Gypsy still had a hangover and wasn't up to much at the time. Never the less they chatted and she got him to play her a couple of songs on his guitar. But he was worse for wear that day and also apart from this getting in the way of what he came to do on Cebu, he also did not have the money to support a woman. So they parted as friends having had a very good night together.

It needs to be explained that in both Thailand and the Philippines as many people know, there are many women who are working as hookers. They often do this in order not to be in absolute poverty. Many, in fact the vast majority of them just want to meet a man who will be kind to them and stay with them. In the Philippines were many of them are catholic, they often are simply looking for a man, preferably a westerner, to get married to.

In both countries there is a higher ratio of women than men and even then a higher ratio of the men are either homosexual or sex changers than in other countries. If they do have a local man then there is a good chance that he will give them a couple of kids and one day just leave, sending her nothing with which to look after them. She would often find herself broke, if not destitute and have to fend for herself and her children. Working in a factory, indeed if she could ever get such a job would see them living in grinding poverty and working hard, long shifts, as would any manual job that she could likely find. So she gets a job working in a bar and having sex with a mix of mostly old men and American sailors. With the old men she would just have to close her eyes and think of something else. With the American sailors she would have to take care of them when they were too drunk to fuck and paralytic, staggering around and speaking incoherent shit. But she would be prepared to marry one if they would only lift her out of her grinding poverty and help her. Gypsy was at that time still only twenty two years old, making him younger than many of the women working in the bars, which meant that sometimes he would get it for free just because they liked him.

Gypsy stayed another night in the city and went out drinking with Fred and Doug again, but he was hung over and didn't have the same energy as the night before.

The next day he said his goodbyes to Fred and Doug and took a jeepney ride in the direction of the ashram (jeepneys were like large minibuses and at that time were made from converted American military jeeps. they were the number one most used form of land transport in the Philippines).

The Ashram was out of town among fields and scattered houses and shacks. Gypsy walked down a rough track from the road several hundred meters, went in through the gate and into the walled compound of the ashram.

The temple president was a tall muscular American who was an ex-Ohio state wrestling champion. He looked at Gypsy and said "this life is not for everyone and also even if it is for you it would be better for you to find out slowly. I've seen people who have jumped straight in, shaved their heads and start wearing robes only to go crazy and run off and do something stupid. Like injure themselves or even attempt to commit suicide. It's great that you're interested in learning more and it would be good if you would like to come and eat with us, give some service and come and join the ceremonies in the temple, but for your sake as well as ours, I think it would be better if at first you live outside of the ashram."

"Ok" said Gypsy "but do you know somewhere close where I can rent a room." "Yes, there's a house just back up the track just two hundred metres from the ashram gates. The lady in that house has rented rooms to us before." The temple president told him.

Gypsy went back up the track and found the house. It was a modern and clean house, unlike the shacks and hovels that most of the locals were forced by circumstances to inhabit. The woman's husband worked in Saudi Arabia and sent cheques home every month. She had a daughter and son who were both at college in town and yes she would be happy to rent a room to Gypsy.

Early each morning Gypsy would go into the ashram at any time between 4:00 to 5:30 am to join the prayers that would last for between two and three hours and then eat with the monks, before helping to clean around the temple.

They were building a special and elaborate hand pulled cart for the Hindu festival of Ratha Yatra, otherwise known as the festival of chariots. The festival celebrated another of Vishnu's incarnations on earth as a being known as Sri Jaganath. The festival apparently originated in the eastern state of Orissa in the town of Puri, which is famous for its Jaganath temple. Gypsy got on well at the temple for the first couple of weeks. The temple president was a descent easy going type who had no axe to grind with anybody and gave cheerful encouragement to everyone, as well as good lectures on Vedic philosophy that really made sense. Gypsy got on with painting the chariot and was starting to spend more time mantra chanting as he had been instructed. The food was nothing special for the most part, but it was vegetarian and reasonably edible. In the late afternoons before sunset Gypsy would get his guitar out and go and sit under a mango tree near the house that he was staying in and practice for an hour or two. He knew that when he eventually reached Japan that he would have little or no money and if the guitar was to help him make money then he better be able to play it well.

He would make the occasional trip into town and would sometimes even visit the girlie bars. One time when he was feeling the need just too much, he took a younger girl from a bar. She was a woman of maybe nineteen or twenty years old who had been all over him in the bar. But when he took her to Queensland he found out that he had made a big mistake as the woman was a frightened little mummy's girl. She had very little sexual experience and a lot of prudish attitudes. She had not a clue about enjoying sex and was only doing it to make a buck. Gypsy felt a bit like a pedophile with this one. Being a decent type Gypsy gave her a reasonable sized tip even though she had not pleased him in the least. But unlike Marilyn she started giving Gypsy an ear load about giving her more. At this point Gypsy told her to get away from him before he got angry, she had wasted his evening, not performed, had caused his pockets to be empty and now she wanted more money – for what?

At the village area near the temple the place hopped with life, there were huge booming stereos set up even in the most basic of huts and even through the early morning mist, the sound of rock music could be heard throbbing from one direction or another. Up on the paved road, even in the early morning, old men would be sat around a makeshift table made from a large cable drum that had been laid on it's side. They sat on makeshift chairs, made from logs, upturned buckets and planks of wood laid across piles of semi stacked bricks. They would invariably be drinking "Toddy" which was the local homemade alcoholic drink of the area. It smelled more foul than rotten eggs, it was truly amazing that anyone could bring themselves to drink anything that smelled that bad, it was so gross that even the local dogs probably turned their noses up at it.

Also through the early morning haze could be seen the occasional farmer riding to work on his water Buffalo. At the road, the jeepneys would be collecting people and driving them into Cebu City to go to work.

While this was all happening, Gypsy as often as not would be sitting under the mango tree across the track from the house where he was staying, strumming his guitar practicing, as so as he would sound his best when he got to Japan. The locals would see him and always laugh.

At the temple there were many devotees from the local population as the people were naturally religious, so when the Hare Krishna monks explained the ways and wherefores of their spiritual path they attracted a lot of attention from the people, especially on Sundays when they put on a free feast for all comers.

There was also an Irish Hare Krishna Monk who had been with ISKON [International Society for Krishna Consciousness] for many years, living in their temples around the world. But he had spent the majority of his time in the |Philippines (Well in the Philippines what is a spiritual organization without a resident Irish priest, just the Irish accent alone probably did its part in convincing the locals of the organization's authenticity).

The organization had obviously thought this one out well in placing him at this particular temple, as this individual was someone who had obviously been to Blarney castle to kiss a certain stone. If he wasn't in the Hare Krishna movement he would have no doubt been either in some mission or the other, spreading the word of God in some remote, far flung part of the world or cloistered up in a catholic monastery somewhere on Ireland's northwest coast. It is truly a sight to behold, how an Irishman in a dress can inspire so much confidence in people when pertaining to matters of religion and spirituality.

February, 1985

The American temple president was only in the job as a temporary. He had been sent to clean up a bad mess of a situation that had apparently been created by his predecessor who had fallen from his spiritual path and served the temple and the devotees badly. The Hare Krishna monks and even the laity live by very strict codes of conduct regarding everything in life, especially strict were the laws concerning celibacy.

Prabupad, the Guru had laid out very strict rules regarding sex, even between married couples if they lived or worked within the temple area.

Apparently something had got very out of order, according to their rules it was also something that they did not wish to talk about. Anyway the American had done his job and the new, hopefully more permanent temple president had just arrived. He was British, a short stocky man with square head and glasses. He was not nearly as at ease with himself as the American had been, he had a dog like aggressiveness about him. He did not make himself popular with the other devotees either. In his first few days he made no secret of his intentions to run the place as if it were an army camp. He treated the other monks in much the same way as a sergeant treats, and speaks to rookies at a boot camp. There were soon loud complaints being made about his manners and his demeanor towards them. The other devotees sent a request to the main local branch of the movement in Manila begging them to replace this unfriendly, hostile individual as quickly as possible. The request was denied and this canine individual got wind of what was said about him.

During the morning discourse, he berated everyone for complaining about him and set out to justify his manners and behavior. The man should have been a lawyer but even so his words did not ring true.

There was a German Hare Krishna too, who lived at the temple with his wife, they were both in their mid twenties. he had a dirt bike and one day Gypsy hitched a ride with him into town.

They took the back way through the forest on local tracks, dropping down the sides of steep ravines, riding through streams and creeks and then up the other side. Gypsy was amazed at how the bike handled, he had expected to die on several occasions as his new found German friend performed "Evil Kaneval" tricks with him, sitting on the back. It was most definitely the most memorable ride into town that he ever had had. The distance was only a few kilometers but it was obvious that this muddy path was where the German got his kicks, dropping down through ravines and riding up and down impossibly steep cliffs, along fast flowing stream beds and through all manner of undergrowth. Doing jumps off of rocky crags etc, treating it as a motor cross track. Feeling somewhat exhilarated Gypsy got off the bike in the middle of Cebu city and made his way to what had become his favorite bar. The place was owned and run by a retired Australian plumber. He had married a local woman and set up his own girlie bar to help him finance a decent lifestyle. Many of the expats would gather there and shoot the breeze through the afternoon.

The owner of the bar was telling a story about when he took a short trip with a hooker and a male friend to a resort on the other side of the island called Maul Baul in his beach buggy.

He phoned his wife to say that he was guiding a tourist and his girlfriend and would be staying over in Maul Baul for the night. The truth of the story was that the tourist was married and did not have a girlfriend, as he did not wish to cheat on his wife. The bar owner on the other hand had no such scruples, as long as he did not get caught. The tourist agreed to pretend that the girl was with him if the bar owner's wife did show up. He spent the night with the girl and then the next morning as they were putting their bags in the back of the motor and were preparing to leave, his wife showed up looking pissed off and jealous. The tourist and the girl put on a fine act and the bar owner berated his wife for not trusting him. The car was full, what with three people and their bags (beach buggies don't have a hell of a lot of storage space). His wife asked for a lift back to Cebu City with them. "You've got to be joking," he told her, "and besides you got yourself here so you can get yourself home." "But I've got no money with me," she said. "Well, I guess you'll be walking then, won't you? That will teach you not to trust me." He retorted before driving off and leaving her standing there by the side of the road.

March, 1985;

"This is the Philippines and you have to understand how it works if you want to stay on top of things," he explained. "Take my wife for example, she is educated and has been to college and university, this already gives her one large step up in society. She is a school teacher, this gives her another step up. She is married to a foreigner, this is another step up in society and to top it off, I'm a successful business man, never mind that all I'm really doing is acting as a glorified pimp.

Anyway, this all gives her a very high place in her community so every now and then, it's a good idea to play a trick on her to bring her down a peg or two to stop her getting too full of herself. You have to understand that behind the arrogance and nagging they are all highly insecure. This easily works to your advantage. For example, my misses she starts nagging me and picking fights over little things, trying to see how far she can push me. So what I do is to turn around and say "please be more quiet I've got a headache, you are causing me pain." She shuts up immediately and goes and bring's a wet towel and start rubbing my forehead with it. They all like to test the boundaries a bit but most of them know how lucky they are when they can catch a foreign husband. There are a hell of a lot of good looking women on these islands and they are for the most part, poorer than poor and their men rarely get their shit together to do anything. So we westerners are their best chance that they have for a good life. Besides, they are also catholic, which mean's that once one of them has caught a westerner, she will do anything to avoid losing him."

There was a young American man of about the same age as Gypsy sitting at the bar, and it was primarily to him that the bar owner was directing this story and advice.

The man used to visit the Hare Krishna ashram quite regularly. He was about to get married to a particularly beautiful young Philippina woman of about the same age as himself. So after the bar owner had finished, some of the others at the bar started gently winding him up, all be it with sound warnings of the nature of the game.

"You wait," said Gypsy, "she's all sweetness and honey today as she get's you lined up into the trap. But you just wait for the morning after, what with a catholic wedding and all, she's got you on a leash, at least in her view of things. You will find that your little sweetheart has turned into a bossy nagging monster. My bet is you will feel the change by the next morning. Tell me, why do you want to get tied up like this at your age? There are plenty more beautiful women out there to meet and have fun with." Gypsy was wasting his breath, the young American was totally besotted and lost in it, he had not travelled outside of North America before and was not quite used to the way that Philippine women come on to men. She made him feel like no North American girl ever had, to him she looked like heaven on earth in all ways.

Later in the week he was at the Hare Krishna temple visiting friends who were American Hare Krishna monks. They looked at him and said much the same as Gypsy had. "Are you really sure that you want to get into this mess?" The Irish monk asked him. "Look, it all look's like roses now but in a few years when you've got two or maybe three, four or five children or more then you will find yourself running on a racetrack of types, it's called the rat race and you will find yourself running on it just in order to stop the ground from moving under your feet. If you are lucky any children that you have will be people who are relatively free of problems, remember that in this regard there are many options. And to feed them, cloth them, and send them to school you will be working hard and long hours. So who will be at home entertaining your bored and frustrated wife when you are not there? If you are lucky then all of your children will grow up to be good people who choose to follow a spiritual path, but again in this regard many things are possible. And all of the time you will be running just in order to stay still and believe me, she will not become more beautiful as she gets older, are you quite sure that you want to screw your life up so quickly?" The young American argued that he did and anyway it was a bit late to chicken out now, he had booked everything for the wedding and it was to be in two days time.

His wedding happened and with a speed that was comical to watch and so very predictable it was, she turned from being a sweet demure beauty into a little miss bossy control freak, literally overnight.

He was at the bar complaining about it several days later. "Since the morning after the wedding, she's been trying to boss me around and has been complaining about everything and anything just like you all told me she would, how did you know?"

"It's pretty obvious when it is staring you in the face," they all told him in one way or another. Gypsy was laughing about it too, but even he was a little surprised that it had happened quite so quickly as it did, he thought that it would take a few days to really kick in and had been exaggerating slightly on what he thought would happen.

Back at the temple, Gypsy was giving the Hare Krishna form of meditation a go. It involved holding a set of rosary type beads in one hand and chanting a mantra while holding one bead, then moving on to the next bead and chanting the same mantra again and so on. The beads were known in Sanskrit as japa beads, there is one hundred and eight beads on a "japa malla" (one hundred and eight is a magical primary number according to Vedic traditions, some say it is the number of basic primary meditation techniques that there are in existence). In the centre of each japa malla was an extra bead, like a toggle, this was as so as a devotee could know when he had reached the end of one round of chanting. The idea was to chant sixteen rounds of the japa everyday.

At the ashram, an ovalesque shaped path of some length had been constructed. This was as so that the devotees could get some exercise while chanting. They would walk around the path quietly chanting the mantra, it would also help them to avoid getting a numb bum from sitting in a lotus position while chanting.

Gypsy gave it a go through several evenings. Then one night while walking around the dimly lit path, from a distance, at the other end of the oval he was sure that he could see the figure of a man standing and looking at him, but when he got around to the other side of the path, all the while watching the figure, it just seemed to vanish.

Though he was slightly disturbed by this strange happening he figured that he was OK as he was meditating on a name of God and in such a state, nothing was going to cause him harm. So he carried on walking around the path and the figure kept appearing and staring at him but always from a distance, still he was not worried as he walked slowly around the path chanting the mantra.

Hare Krishna Hare Krishna Krishna Krishna Hare Hare
Hare Rama Hare Rama Rama Rama Rama Hare Hare.

As all of the monks made their way to where they slept, Gypsy slightly warily made his way back up the track to the house. He had chanted nine rounds on his japa beads and now he was tired, the weather was unbearably humid and hot and his clothes were stuck to him.

That night he had the most vivid and harrowing dream, so harrowing was it that he first saw what he saw as symbols on sign posts so as to prepare him for what was about to come.

It was the nineteenth century and he was in the Crimea as a soldier. He wore a tunic and one of those strange bucket shaped hats with a small peak on the front. They were court-martialing him for something. Something to do with a chipped china cup. There was an officer screaming and shouting in indignant rage about it, it carried on for what felt like a long time. Then he found himself with some other men, being led out to a hilltop overlooking the Black Sea, where a line of gallows had been built. His heart was beating fast as they led him up the steps and placed a noose around his neck, there was a roll of drums and then ....

Still in the dream, the next thing that he knew, he was flying on something similar to a bedstead alongside a young boy, they could have been supported by a hot air balloon but Gypsy couldn't be sure of this, they were fifty to one hundred and fifty feet off of the ground and moving at some speed. They were being pursued on the ground by a group of angry snarling horsemen. However, they were laughing as they made their escape, knowing that the horsemen could not get them up there in the air.

The next morning Gypsy awoke shaken from what he had seen in the dream. It felt more like an old and deeply buried memory than it did a dream. He had recognized the face as his own and he knew that what he had seen was his death from his last human incarnation. The flying on the bedstead with the child felt more like it was in another dimension, what the Tibetans call "the bardo," the space between lives in this dimension.

That evening Gypsy again walked around the japa walk chanting on his beads and again the figure appeared in the distance.

Again that night he had a vivid frightening dream. He was at what looked like a medieval village with wattle and daub houses. It was high in the foothills of the Himalayas, it looked like Nepal but it wasn't, it was west of the Nepalese border.

He was in the village square. The square was full of people and there was a gallows in one of the far corners where they were hanging an old woman with long gray hair, her tongue was sticking out grotesquely as they choked her slowly to death. Gypsy ran for the exit to the square, which was the last thing he remembered before waking up. Again it felt like a deep past memory and Gypsy was sure that he had seen something that was connected to a life that he had had two human lives back. He was puzzled as to why he had died such horrible deaths in the past.

The following night, he was in yet another dream, but this time he was in the present age in a high school, he was in a country full of east Asian type faces but the place was super modern and full of machines. It felt as if he was on the set of a science fiction movie, but in real life. He was travelling on different under grounds trains and overhead urban railways, he was running, just like all of the Asian people around him, as they all rushed to be on time. Also he was doing something at a school and was surrounded by people in navy blue school uniforms. Also he was feeling very stressed out.

When he awoke, at first he thought "that's strange I stopped having nightmares about school, three or four years ago, what was all that about?". But then he stopped to ponder it further and then realized that what he had seen was the future yet to come. It had been a very vivid dream and he suspected that what he had seen was Japan.

Still he would sit out under the mango tree playing his guitar each late afternoon and still the locals would walk past and laugh.

It was not until Ronaldo, the son of the owner of the house asked, with a grin on his face if Gypsy sat under the mango tree and played guitar that Gypsy thought to ask why all of the locals laughed when he played there.

"Ah," exclaimed Renaldo, "you don't know?" "Know what?" asked Gypsy.

There is a hobgoblin living in that tree, we were wondering if he was going to play tricks on you for disturbing his peace." "No" said Gypsy. "I'm pretty sure he likes the sound I make, I always get a good feeling under that tree."

That night Renaldo took Gypsy with him to meet his friends, they turned Gypsy on to some really strong Philippine weed. Sitting under the trees up by the paved road, they smoked two very small and skinny joints, it was the first smoke that he had had in several months. He had never smoked anything so strong in his life and the others had to help him get home, as he was barely able to walk.

In the ashram the next day, the new temple president was bitching to Gypsy about how no one in the temple liked him. Gypsy asked him, what he had done before he joined the Hare Krishnas. "I was a biker," the man told him. "I was a Hell's Angel." He rolled up his sleeve to show Gypsy that he still wore a Hells Angel tattoo on his arm.

So either the guy had got religion in a big way and got fully into what he was now doing, as it very much appeared he was, or else he was in deep deep shit somewhere and was using the organization as a deep cover place to hide. However, this option was highly unlikely as the Hare Krishna lifestyle would not seem in the least bit compatible with that of the Hells Angels, and apparently he had been in the movement now for several years. Of course there were a couple of other options too. One being that he had pissed off the Hells Angels themselves and was hiding from them, in which case a Hare Krishna temple would make for a pretty good place to hide. After all it would not be the sort of place where either Hells Angels or their friends or acquaintances were likely to visit. The second, other option being that he had pissed off one of the chapters so badly that they had made him join the Hare Krishnas under threat of death, in order to inflict some real suffering upon him. Just imagine, no sex no drugs no rock and roll, no meat no fish no eggs, can't, shouldn't, mustn't, And all this time while wearing a carrot top hairstyle and a pink or orange dress.

Gypsy was now running very low on finances and needed to do something about it in a hurry. A Philippino friend took him into town and tried to help him get a job playing guitar in one of the beer bars. But at that time he was just not good enough and there were many Philippino musicians who were exceptionally good, so he was not in with a chance.

April, 1985

Back at the Australian bar, he was sitting and drinking a beer when one of the girls came over and started talking with him. She was beautiful and slim but quite tall and muscular. She had two children, so in order to feed and cloth them she worked two jobs. She was not only very strong but also had a blackbelt in karate and so through the day she worked as a security guard. At night she worked as a hooker at the bar and in what little spare time she had, she was doing an open university degree in architecture. She was like some sort of Amazon super woman. She offered her services to Gypsy for the night, but apart from the fact that he had no money he had no desire to get eaten alive black widow style or have his balls crushed by those super powerful thighs. He could not help but admire and like her as a person but he had no desire to get into bed with her.

Gypsy was back at the ashram when two American Hare Krishnas who lived outside of the temple came by to visit, he had met them several times before. They were both married to Philippina wives and jointly owned a factory making jewelry for export, from local sea shells.

They invited both Gypsy and the young American who had just got married, and was also hanging out at the ashram that day, to join them on a trip to the factory. They drove across town in their SUV and then entered a factory compound of substantial size that was surrounded by a high, spike and barbed wire topped wall, with security guards patrolling the perimiter. At the gate was a small guardhouse and standing outside of it dressed in a security guards' uniform was a tiny petite and beautiful woman. Gypsy took a double take and said "do you just keep her on the job as a mascot? She looks like she would have a job dealing with an obstreperous eight year old child."

"Don't let looks deceive you," said one of the men, "she's a third dan black belt in taekwondo she could put just about anyone on the ground before they would know what had happened."

As Gypsy got talking with one of the men the man told Gypsy how he had been the first Hare Krishna monk sent to the Philippines to get the order started there. His job had been to set up the first ashram and temple on the islands.

"So what happened, why don't you live inside the ashram anymore?" Gypsy asked him. "Look around you," said the man, "this is the Philippines it's full of some of the prettiest sexiest most scantily clad young women on this earth and their all smiling at you and you know what they want. I fell down I couldn't maintain celibacy in a place like this, not when tit and bum was being flashed in my face all day every day. So I moved out of the ashram, started this business and looked around for a good woman to get married to."

He was exporting his jewelry products mostly to America and much of his profits he donated to the ashram. He also helped them in other ways, bringing their books in for them and helping sort out anything to do with ashram finances and accounts.

In town was another group who could not make it within the ashram's strict code of rules but still wished to follow the Hare Krishna path. They had a somewhat watered down set of teachings but were far less uptight with themselves than the bunch out at the ashram. Gypsy was starting to wonder if the ashram had got something wrong in how they perceived the teachings that they were attempting to follow. They were not a relaxed bunch and since the Hells Angel Hare Krishna has arrived as temple president a pall of unhappiness seemed to have descended over the ashram. Faces weren't smiling anymore and Gypsy noticed that when this tiresome man was smiling it looked totally false. Gypsy wondered if he had pissed the Hells Angels off so badly with something that he had done, that hiding among the Hare Krishna was the only safe option that he had in order to escape with his life. It would certainly be the last place that anyone would look for a fugitive outlaw biker on the run. And besides he would get a new name in his passport that most westerners would be hard put to pronounce, let alone remember. Also he would have a group of people who would fight next to him to defend him from any attack [though the Hare Krishna monks are generally non violent by teaching, they are allowed to defend themselves and others most vigorously from attack. As to tolerate violence is violence itself, according to their teachings]. Apart from this many of the monks were young and being celibate and young can make people very uptight and aggressive indeed. The testosterone of youth would send them almost crazy, deep down under all of the teachings of love and peace that they learned about they were more uptight than a compressed spring and just spoiling for a fight, even if they weren't consciously aware of it.

The temple president made it clear that he didn't want Gypsy around the temple. Gypsy as far as he could see had done nothing wrong and got on well with everyone at the temple. It was either just a personal dislike or he was worried about Gypsy blowing his cover. Gypsy suspected the latter.

In the event Gypsy was not upset to be leaving. It was the excuse he needed to get out and on his way. He went and booked his ticket back to Manila. He had heard that sometimes it was possible to get a job as a bar manager at Angeles City, north from Manila and next to the huge American run "Clark Air Base". The whole place was wall to wall bars, catering to the massive quantity of U.S. service personnel on the base.

To Angeles City, Philippines

Gypsy packed his bag (a ten minute process) and headed for the airport via a number of different jeepneys. He made a brief stop in Cebu

City to visit the grave of Magelan and then took another jeepney across the bridge onto Mactan island and to the airport. The flight was a one hour hop to Manila, he had booked his flight from Manila to Tokyo for the following week and figured that if he did find a job in Angeles, he could always cancel it.

Getting off the plane in Manila at the domestic terminal and grabbing his bag he walked outside and found his way to a bus going to the central bus station. At the central station he got on a bus going to Angeles City. On the bus he met some other European travelers going the same way and sat down near them and got talking with them, asking if they knew a cheap place in Angeles to stay. One of them said "yes, there is a cheap one that's good, called the Far East Guesthouse, try that." "Thanks" said Gypsy. "Is it easy to find?" "Yes, it's right around the corner from where the bus stops" he was told.

In Angeles city Gypsy checked into a room at the Far East Guesthouse. Though the room only had a high frosted glass window for light, the room was cool and had an ensuite bathroom, a luxury that Gypsy had rarely had in all his time of travelling.

He was so hungry and went out looking for something to eat, he had very little money left and so when he saw a noodle stand on a hand cart in a side alley with many people standing around it eating bowls of noodle soup, he figured that it looked like a good bet. He went and bought a bowl of noodle soup and was standing there eating it when a beautiful slim woman come up and asked in perfect English "excuse me but what are you doing eating here? You're a westerner, westerners don't eat in places like this." "I've got no money at the moment" Gypsy explained. "What do you mean you've got no money? You're a westerner" the woman exclaimed. "I'm not the same as the other westerners" Gypsy explained, "I live on the road like a gypsy, when there is work I work but sometimes I find myself in a place like here were it is almost impossible to find a job. At the moment I am waiting for a flight to Tokyo where I need to find a job, desperately."

"Look I'm working in a bar tonight, I need to make money but tell me where you're staying I want to come and meet you tomorrow" she said

Gypsy told her his hotel name and room number. She said "I've got to go now but I'll be around at your room at 10 o'clock tomorrow morning by the way my name is Yolanda."

Gypsy went out and did a tour of some of the bars and tried to find out if there was any truth to the rumors that he had heard about work, managing bars.

After several games of pool in a bunch of bars with names such as "Thunder McGraws" and "Mississippi Bar" Gypsy ascertained from what he was told by the old expats hanging out there that the rumor was just that. There were no paid jobs for westerners here outside of the airbase unless you were some sort of qualified engineer working for a foreign company.

The next morning at 10 o'clock on the dot there was a couple of loud knocks on his door. He opened it to find the beautiful Yolanda standing there and smiling at him. He invited her in and they spent a while talking before jumping into bed together. The Dictator Ferdinand Marcos was in control of the country at that time and people were scared to speak badly of him even in their own homes for fear that someone would report them to the secret police. They were like all instruments of repression, and only employed the most sadistic, self hating miserable humorless cowards and bullies that the place had to offer.

However this did not stop Yolanda describing the wife of the dictator Imelda as "The Mother of all pigs". Gypsy liked Yolanda she was bright and intelligent and had spirit, she always spoke her mind. If she had been raised in a western or first world country she would have gone to university and got herself a highly paid job and commanded respect from people. She would always be regarded as a bit of a rebel and would probably do part time volunteer work for something like "Amnesty International" or "Medicines sans frontiers." She would be married to another high earner with high ideals and would enjoy reading and learning in her spare time.

As it was, she was born into a very poor family in the Philippines, they lived in a shack that was constantly on the point of falling down, food was in short supply but family members weren't. She was one of nine children (which goes some way to explaining why the chief Catholic bishop of the Philippines at the time - a man who expressly preached against the use of condoms on the overpopulated islands with scarce food resources was called Cardinal Sin. His full name was Cardinal Jamie Sin, it was a most appropriate name for a man who caused so many unwanted and unloved children to be born on islands that didn't have the resources to take care of them.) Her father had become a violent alcoholic who was always beating her and she had left home at a young age to get away from it. With only the most basic of education it left her with not much option other than to work in a bar as a hooker. It was truly sad as this woman was worth so much more to herself than this. But what could she do. She was four years older than Gypsy and only the wisdom that she had gained from living her hard life gave that away.

She looked younger than Gypsy and was delightfully childlike and innocent in some ways all the while, while verbally articulating what she saw in her life with the vision of a totally fine tuned state of the art bullshit detector.

After a most pleasurable afternoon in bed together she offered to take Gypsy out to dinner.

They went out to eat but no matter how poor he was at the time, he couldn't let this lovely beautiful woman who was also poor, pay for him. She would need all the money that she was making to help herself and two of her younger sisters who were staying with her. Gypsy insisted that he at least meet her halfway with the bill even if he couldn't afford to pay it all.

Yolanda had to go off to work at the bar after they had finished eating. "I'll see you tomorrow, same time," she said. Gypsy was too tired and too broke to go out bar crawling much that night. He spent much of the evening smoking joints and chatting with a Vietnam veteran who was also staying at the guesthouse. He had come around and knocked on Gypsy's door and asked him if he would like to smoke a joint.

Gypsy invited him in, his name was Saint and he was staying in the next room with his American wife and two children. He had cancer and he had come back to East Asia to die.

He told Gypsy about many crazy things that had happened in Vietnam and how ashamed he was to have been fighting in that war on the American side "Not just were we wrong to be there in the first place but then we committed terrible atrocities on those people and our CIA was running heroin back to the US in body bags and selling it to fund other wars or whatever. I wish I could go to Hanoi and throw myself on Ho Chi Min's grave and beg for forgiveness for being there fighting on the wrong side. Our governments in the states are always such a bunch of corrupt shit, first they get involved in someone else's war, fighting for the wrong side then when we got our asses kicked by a bunch of peasants fighting from holes in the ground but then our government, military and populace go into denial and sulk while vilifying the Vietnamese and refusing to speak to them. I am ashamed to be an American it is truly embarrassing having to travel on an American passport."

Gypsy learned a lot about the Vietnam war from Saint that night as they sat there smoking.

The next morning at 10 o'clock on the dot once more there was a knock on the door. Gypsy opened the door to find Yolanda standing there smiling at him and holding a bar of clothes washing soap.

On entering the room she grabbed Gypsy's small pile of dirty clothes and took them to the bathroom. "please" Gypsy said "you are my friend you don't need to do this." "it's because I'm your friend that I am doing this" Yolanda replied.

Gypsy could see by the determined expression on her face that it would be useless to argue further and gratefully let her do what she was doing, even if he felt somewhat embarrassed to let this lovely woman do such a job for him.

After finishing that task she made Gypsy sit down and insisted on manicuring his nails.

Gypsy didn't even know what a manicure was until that point and would have rather have foregone the treatment, but she was so insistent and enjoyed doing it so much that he couldn't bring himself to say no to her.

She told him about her previous night in the bar when a group of completely drunk U.S, service personnel had staggered into the place, one of them had treated the pool table as a bed while others had staggered around repeatedly falling on the floor and vomiting everywhere.

"They were in such a bad way that we thought that we were going to have to call an ambulance for them to take them either back to the base or even to hospital".

"I'm a hooker, a bar hostess not a drunkard sitter" she complained, "they were disgusting and we had to treat them like children, they chased all of the other business out of the bar, none of us could make any money with them there and it took such a long time to get rid of them."

They spent the afternoon in bed and then went out to eat. Gypsy bought a set of shoes as he didn't have any and hadn't had anything but rubber flip flops for the last several months, since his last pair of shoes fell to pieces. He was booked on a flight for the following evening to Tokyo and wanted to be prepared.

They went out to a restaurant in the market to eat and then Yolanda had to go to work.

Gypsy spent much of the evening smoking joints and talking with Saint and his wife. Yolanda came around later and introduced Gypsy to one of her sisters. They got to sit and talk for a while and Yolanda wrote her address down in Gypsy's book and gave him a photo of her with a message on the back.

The next day Yolanda came to see Gypsy before he left and accompanied him to the bus stop. She looked stunning in a miniskirt and tight t-shirt. Gypsy was one hundred percent sure that he wanted to see her again and wondered if he would be lucky enough to make money quickly in Japan and come back quickly and see her. Anyway he intended to write to her. They kissed goodbye and Gypsy got on the bus to Manila.

After a couple of hours on the bus and after passing a large imposing volcano the bus entered urban Manila, a chaotic, ill designed, polluted, urban sprawl with overhead flyovers and countless anonymous glass edifices.

Manila had the reputation for being extremely dangerous. Foreigners were the main target of many of the city's armed muggers. There were apparently a lot of guns kicking around and many pistols among them.

There were apparently fake jeepneys cruising the streets looking for westerners to pick up and take around the corner, then hold up and mug them at gun point.

Back in the Aussie bar in Cebu, one of the regulars recounted a story that explained how things worked in Manila.

A group of male Aussie tourists were out on the razzle on one of their first nights in the Philippines. They spent most of the night drinking in a bar on the third floor of a building. The bar had nonstop sex shows running on a stage. Anyway as the Aussies got a little bit drunk they also got a wee bit bold and looking around at all the miniature people around them they figured that they could do a runner without paying their tab.

They bolted down the two flight of stairs at Olympic speed, only to be met at the bottom by a four foot nothing sized Filipino man squat with legs apart silently pointing a 357 magnum at them. At which point they ran back up the stairs and paid their bills and nothing more was said of it, and they were allowed to leave in peace. But there is no question about what would have happened if they had failed to cooperate at the time that they did. Life is cheap when there are such a high number living in such extreme poverty. Cops on low wages can be easily bought as can heavies and assassins. Then there is the natural hot headed ways of the locals, remembering of course that they have smaller, lighter bodies that do not handle alcohol well. The fact that the Philippines has the largest brewery in South East Asia located on one of it's islands does not help the situation. Guns and alcohol are the joint cause of many of the murder and manslaughter deaths in the Philippines.

Gypsy had almost no cash and no desire or reason to be in Manila and so he took the local bus out to the airport.

He was surprised at how modern the airport was, and how busy. He checked in and went through to the departure lounge. From the flight announcement boards and by looking out of the huge windows at the parked and docked aircraft all around, he could see that Philippine Airlines was running a fleet of jumbos to destinations around the world with flights being announced for London, Sydney, Tokyo, Los Angeles, Paris, Frankfurt, etc. Gypsy wondered how such a poor country could afford to buy and run such a fleet of aircraft and have such a modern well run airport, it was a paradox if ever he had seen one.

He got chatting at the bar with an Aussie who was also carrying a guitar with him. He had just been denied entry to the UK and been put on a plane back to Australia. He was waiting for his flight to Sydney that was due to leave in twelve hours time.

"So what happened' Gypsy asked him.

"Well it was like this" the Aussie started to explain "I met these poms back in Sydney and they had a band back in England. Well to cut a long story short they came and saw a gig that I was playing in. After the gig they approached me and explained that they had a band back in England and invited me for a jam around at where they were staying in Sydney. One thing led to another and they invited me to fly to London and join their band and all was well until I got to immigration. They asked me what I had come to England for. When I told them that I had been invited to join a British rock band, they deported me for not having a work visa in my passport. No one told me that I needed one of those, this has been a right pain in the arse, and it's still not over."

Manila to Tokyo;

An hour or two later Gypsy's flight was called, it was a Philippine Airlines flight to Los Angeles via Tokyo. The flight, a Boeing 747-200 series, was full but that was not such a problem for him as it was only a five hour flight to Tokyo. He was more worried about clearing immigration and surviving in the world's most expensive city with only a hundred dollars, a guitar and his wits.

He had not a clue as to how to speak or read the language but he knew that it was his only chance if he wanted to make the money to stay on the road. Besides that, he loved Japanese art and design and wanted to fully experience life in Japan. Back in England before leaving he had bought himself an album by the Title, Silk Road, by the Japanese musician Kitaro [pronounced Ki Ta Ro], it was a complete turn on and could best be described as Zen music. It was the Zen take on perfection through simplicity that had him so very interested. In this regard the Japanese seemed to have their own magic about them and had taste and refinement that left the rest of the world far behind.

The flight took off and climbed up over the paddy fields that receded far below. Gypsy was more than a little sad to be saying goodbye to this warm sunny nation of miniature people who seemed to suck helium before they spoke. He hoped that it wouldn't be long before he returned, but sadly his gut feeling was telling him something different, deep down he could feel that it would be a very long time before he ever got to return to the Philippines.

The plane flew on into the evening and soon it was dark as they sped towards Tokyo.

CHAPTER 8

April, 1985

Tokyo, Japan;

T he plane was flying along the coast of Hon Shu and occasionally through a gap in the clouds it was possible to see the bright lights of a Japanese town or city. Then the plane started its descent into Tokyo.

As the plane came down through the clouds Gypsy could see the urban sprawl of Tokyo off in the distance all brightly lit up and buzzing with movement. The plane touched down and taxied along the massive apron to the terminals. This was a very busy and super modern, first world airport. The plane docked at the new and as yet not fully completed Narita airport, sixty kilometers from downtown Tokyo. He had disembarked and had walked along the passages that led to immigration control when he looked around and noticed how very modern everything was.

"How am I going to be able to make it here?" thought Gypsy to himself, "the place looks so modern that it must have been made for robots, to live in."

Gypsy breathed a huge sigh of relief after he had cleared immigration without being asked any awkward questions. He collected his bag, changed up one hundred dollars, virtually all of his last money and went and found a bus to Shinjuku station.

After an hour or more the bus arrived at Shinjuku railway station, the busiest station in the world. Gypsy wandered through the vast corridors of the station, it was after midnight but there were still plenty of people around, though the place was not packed. Gypsy had the phone number for a hostel that was apparently only three stop away on the Yamanota line.

He stopped by a public phone and put his bag and guitar down while he rummaged through his pockets looking for his two small pocket address books, one of which contained the number for the hostel. He found the books and then took a dig in another pocket for where he had put his yen coins.

He phoned the number but got no reply, it was not surprising it was late, everyone at the hostel was probably asleep.

Gypsy picked up his bags and strolled on through the station wondering where he was going to sleep. There were groups of men in suits walking through the station in all directions. Every so often a group would stop. Then they would form into a circle and all bow to each other several times, almost as if they were spring loaded, then they would split up and go to find their respective trains home. Everyone was very well behaved and there was no loutish or yobbish behavior that was common at this time of night in any other first world country that Gypsy had visited, baring of course Singapore.

The station though massive was exceptionally clean and well organized. The vibe from the people was different to any other place that he had been to.

Here was first world but very much an Asian first world. There were some signs and instruction by the phones and ticket machines in English but for the most part everything was in Kanji (the modern adaption of classical written Japanese – it only has some nine hundred or so characters as opposed to classical Japanese that has at least some four thousand to eight thousand different characters or maybe even more).

Then to his horror Gypsy suddenly realizes that he has left one of his address books, back at the public phone. He turned and ran back while still carrying his bags. When he got there he found that it had gone, he searched his pockets, his money belt, his bags, the surrounding area and the route he had walked but all to no avail he had lost it. It was gone and to make matters worse it was the one with Yolanda's address in it. Gypsy was heartbroken, the nicest woman that he had ever had the pleasure to hop in the sack with and what happens? Of all of the things that he could lose why this and why so soon after arriving? It felt like a bad trick had been played on him by forces unseen. This was Japan, a land where people don't steal, at least that is what he had been told about the place.

Gypsy pulled himself and his bag back together and wandered off back along the huge wide underground walkway in the direction that he had been heading in before this enraging distraction diverted him. As he came out of the tunnel and onto the street there were two Europeans selling paintings on a makeshift street stand in front of him. They turned out to be French as Gypsy found out when he asked them if they knew a cheap place to stay for the night. "At this time of the night the best place to go is the sauna" one of them said, "no it's not a bordello it's just a sauna but there are beds there were you can sleep it is only $10.- to use it for the night."

The French man pointed Gypsy to the other side of the wide sets of railway trucks and told him to take a left down into Kabukicho which was one of Tokyo's biggest red light areas.

The place was well lit up and soon he found the building that housed the sauna. It was an ultramodern, ultra clean looking white edifice of some eight or ten floors. There were well lit pictures of the facility laminated to a back lit glass case. He went in, paid ten dollars and was given a locker key. He went and found the locker, much to his relief it was big enough as to be able to accommodate both his bag and his guitar inside.

Hanging up inside the locker, was a large clean white towel. Gypsy did as all of the others were doing and stripped off his clothes, placed them in the locker, wrapped the white towel around himself and headed off down the stairs. There were two saunas, hot and hotter Gypsy went in to each for a while and sweated. When he came out he saw a strange looking shower cubicle and a few people queuing to use it Gypsy went and joined the queue and watched. When someone went in they hung their towel outside and hit a large button on the wall. When it was his turn he did the same, it was a sensation to behold, the chamber was circular except of course for the entrance. In the wall were tens if not hundreds of jet nozzles that water was firing out of plus there was an over head device also shooting jets of high pressure water. The pressure of the water got more and more intense until he felt like he couldn't stand it anymore and then, as suddenly as it had started, it cut out.

The next area had a large swimming pool and two very large Jacuzzis, also there were tanks of water with rounded relatively smooth pebbles making up two or three layers on the bottom, people were in the tanks walking on the pebbles with the water coming up to their knees, apparently it was natural D.I.Y. foot massaging Japanese style. There were also such strange phenomena as humidity rooms that people were going into to sit down in as they would do a sauna.

The next area contained lines of mirrors on walls with plastic stools in front of them. Each area contained a stainless steel, wall attached basket with fresh supplies of soap, shampoo, shaving foam and disposable razors. There were many lines of people sitting down and washing themselves. After this was a room with a big long mirror and baskets containing disposable toothbrushes with tooth powder already in the brush next to each of the basins lining the counter in front of the mirror. So this room was set up for the sole purpose of brushing teeth.

Next was a basket to deposit the used towel into and a rack of freshly washed [and no doubt sterilized] bath robes to change into.

Next came a room dedicated to hair and face manicuring, with hair dryers, combs brushes bryll cream (of which the Japanese used a lot), scissors, tweezers and other implements stationed in front of each mirrored sitting area. All of the reusable items had been placed in a sterilizing machine on a recessed shelf in the wall after having been used. Further down the corridor on the right hand side was a large massage hall where many people were getting the treatment all at the same time. The massages were not included within the ten dollars so Gypsy decided to give them a miss. The next room was full of cots and people sleeping on them. At the end of the corridor was a lounge with many lie flat, reclining chairs in front of a large television set. In the corner behind a screen was a Japanese style cafeteria with low Japanese tables and cushions on the ground. Everyone wore their locker key on a cord around their neck and the key holder on the end that slotted over the key contained the locker number written on in large figures. Payment for food and drink was taken from the cashier at the front desk upon leaving the sauna. (The front desk held everyone's shoes as a deposit.) Gypsy sat down and ordered a bowl of noodles. It tasted different to any that he had eaten before in East Asia. They were thicker noodles but also the soup tasted not only of fish but in some way also of the ocean. It could have been the seaweed but also something else, maybe other extracts or sea vegetables that they had put in.

After eating he went and took two blankets from one of the piles placed against a wall for customers to use and found a quiet and darker corner of the large lobby to bed down.

He awoke early the next morning and like everyone else he went through the treatment again before going to the lockers to get changed, pay his bill and leave, it was surprisingly inexpensive for the food, with no hidden extra costs.

He stepped out into the cold air outside, it was shiveringly cold and it was trying to snow with a small quantity of snowflakes blowing around.

"Wow, what a welcome to Japan" he thought to himself, "that sauna was incredible and cheap too".

As he walked through the streets he saw noodle bars and restaurants with plastic models of the food that they sold in showcases in the windows. He went up and looked in the windows of several of the noodle bars where they had prices next to the noodles. To his surprise he found that he could get a bowl of noodles for as little as a dollar twenty five ($1.25). There was only one thing for it, he was going to have to learn to like Japanese noodles.

A short time later he had found his way to the hostel that he had been told about, three stops north on, the Yamenota line. The place was a working man's hostel that now also accommodated not so rich Gaijin (foreign) travelers.

It was run by an old couple who were well past retirement age. There was also another man who also wasn't so young who worked there, possibly a family member or an old friend.

There were other westerners, staying at the place but they were either on back pack holiday trips or just passing through on short stopovers.

That late afternoon Gypsy went out with his guitar and returned to Shinjuku station where he set up and started busking. It took him quite a while to find a good position but when he did, the money came flowing in. When the Japanese had time to stop on their busy schedule they could be very generous indeed. Gypsy went back to the hostel several thousand yen richer than when he had left. He had to be back at the hostel by ten thirty as that was when the doors were locked. on the way he stopped at a soft drinks machine on the street and put a one hundred yen coin into the slot, to his delight he found that it also had hot drinks within it. He selected hot tea with sugar and milk. Out it popped in a tin, just like a can of pepsi or coca cola, except that it was hot. Gypsy was amazed he had never seen hot drinks come out of a machine in this manner before

The old fellow who ran the hostel was clearly from another time that had long since gone, as every night at lock up time he would come

357

through the hostel with a clockwork music box in his hand chiming away as he slowly chanted "time for bed" in English. Behind him walked his tall old friend who would be spraying air freshener from a can as they slowly paced around the hostel like two Walt Disney cartoon characters.

There were some Aussies and kiwis staying in the same dormitory as Gypsy and they were falling about laughing in hysterics about the nightly ritual of the two old boys.

However in that dorm there was also a Canadian man who was so pleased with himself that he thought that he didn't need a sense of humor and he got angry that the others in the room dared to laugh three minutes after the 11:00pm lights out. At this point Gypsy joined in with the Aussies and Kiwis and they all started taking the piss out of the po faced Canadian instead, making him wish that he had not bothered to open his fat wingeing mouth. "You need to go down the doctor's in the morning mate and get that cucumber removed from your arse" one of the Aussies commented at him. "With attitude like you've got why don't you go and stay in a hotel or something instead of coming here and imposing your bullshit on us travelers who live out of places like this, which clearly you do not" Gypsy said to him.

Realizing that he had picked a fight with the whole room the Canadian shut his mouth and went to sleep and left the hostel early the next morning.

The next night Gypsy returned to Shinjuku station and once more sat down near the exit turnstiles and started playing his guitar. He was doing well and had taken over two thousand yen by the time the railway police turned up. They looked down at him sitting on the ground playing his guitar then pointed at the nearest exit and just shouted "OUT". Gypsy couldn't complain, he already had enough money to live for another day and he had been more than a little bold in his choice of busking spot.

He wandered around the station until he found a less obtrusive place to set up. Then in one of the exits on the east side of the station he found a spot that was to be his regular evening busking spot for the next few weeks.

He put his soft guitar case down as his collection bowl then sat down behind it and started to play his guitar. The position was good and he did take money but not as much as at the prime position that he had used previously.

He eventually finished for the night and headed back to the hostel to witness the nightly ritual performed by the two old men.

The next morning he got chatting with a British man who had just finished a degree course in literature at Adelaide University. Gypsy asked if maybe he had a spare photo copy of the degree or at least a letter from the university saying that he had passed. "No problem" said the man and handed Gypsy just such a letter from his bag. "Thanks" said Gypsy "with a bit of alteration this should help me get a job. "Good luck" said the man "I hope it get's you what you want."

Having to be back in at 10:30 pm, each night was cramping Gypsy's ability to make money and also this hostel was not where Gypsy was likely to meet people who would know where and how to find work here. So he, started looking around for another hostel. He eventually found one near by a station on the Marinota line which sits inside the Yamanota circle line that rings central Tokyo.

The hostel was more relaxed than the last one with a kitchen for the guests to use and no curfew or lights out. Gypsy moved in immediately. There were other people there who were either looking for or had already found teaching work and that boded well for Gypsy's plans. But first he would have to continue playing his guitar on the street until he had made enough money to buy some smarter clothes as so he could at least go to a job interview without feeling like a clown. The person who ran the hostel voz a German voman and she voz very small but she had ze uptight attitude Jah! Und voz very strong.

She certainly made sure zat zee cleaning roter voz done.

The first person that Gypsy made friends with was a young American called Jim who had been studying Greek philosophy in Athens. He had attended a Greek university for a year and a half before hitting the road to Asia. He had been on the road for a few months before arriving via China, to Japan and also was looking for work as an English teacher.

Then to Gypsy's surprise a face that he knew from Jerusalem appeared. Avigdor had been around at Fagin's place on several Shabbat evenings prior to Gypsy leaving the Yeshiva. And now here he was in the same hostel as Gypsy. He was working as a movie and advert extra. He was a good thirty years older than Gypsy and there he was, still travelling and working while on the road. He had decided back in Jerusalem that the Yeshiva was not a good idea, then left to travel to East Asia. However his reasons for not wanting to stay around at the Yeshiva were most different. Gypsy was to find out later.

Every night without fail Gypsy would take a couple of metro rides to Shinjuku where he would always busk at the same pitch in the east exit. Sometimes pickings were slim and he would get worried as he was living almost hand to mouth but then he found that if he started work after 9:30 p.m., then he could generally do better as many of the salary men were drunk by that time. Having spent their after work time in a bar with their immediate boss and other work colleagues, they were then drunk and emotional. The sight of Gypsy sitting there on the ground playing his guitar reminded them of the time in their lives when they were most happy i.e. when they were at university back in the sixties and seventies when they also might have sat on the ground and jammed on a musical instrument. Not just that but Gypsy was playing music from that time, playing songs from Bob Dylan, The Stones, The Beatles, The Who, Simon and Garfunkel and many others.

It was not that uncommon to have up to fifteen salary men and their bosses all sitting on the floor in a cross legged position in their business suits and clapping along and even trying to join in the singing. For a brief moment they could dream that they were once again free like Gypsy was. On one occasion after they had clapped along through several Beatles and Stones songs the boss of one group got up and put a one thousand yen note into Gypsy's guitar case, then all five people with him did likewise. Gypsy had taken over ten thousand yen that night and decided to treat himself to a night at the sauna as it was very late when he finished.

The next few nights were not so prosperous but Gypsy was still ahead. He spent a good part of his free time exploring Tokyo with his camera, looking for temples, Japanese Zen Gardens and other examples of Japanese art. Of course he wanted to capture modern Japan as well in his photographs it was such a mind blowing place, the total lack of cultural conditioning from lands that contained Semitic religion as the corner stone of their beliefs was most refreshing indeed.

In some ways there was a beautiful innocence about the Japanese and how they viewed things that allowed them in some ways to think in a less inhibited way. By western uptight Christian thinking they would be considered possibly a nation of sexual perverts. As in this regard there was not so much of the can't shouldn't, mustn't or the guilt that follows such inhibitions.

Yes they still made jokes about sex but it was out in the open rather than loitering about in the corner, waiting to be disapproved of by self appointed, so called moralists. Men in suits would sit on the underground metro trains openly reading some of the most hard core sadomasochistic, pornographic, comic books imaginable. And nobody would say a word about it. Men would have a wife and a mistress and the wife might have a lover, both might think nothing of visiting hookers, the woman hiring a male one.

Japan at least sexually was liberated. However Gypsy had heard, from other travelers with Japanese experience, that the women most often liked it rough. Back in the Philippines, one of the expats said that they liked and expected to be virtually raped, which put Gypsy off somewhat besides many of the Japanese women had baby doll faces and that was a big turnoff to him, also they behaved somewhat like small children too. Gypsy was turned on by more mature looks and behavior than he saw among most of the Japanese women.

He carried on playing his guitar in the subway and eventually built up his cash resources a little and bought one set of smart clothes. Also he now had enough money in his pockets to allow him not to worry so much about where his next meal was going to come from. He had enough that at a push, could be stretched to last for at least a couple of weeks. He had become adept at living in Tokyo on the very cheap, learning where to find the cheapest food anywhere that he was and the route on foot to many of the places that he wanted to go to.

There were no English channels on the television networks of Japan at that time as satellite television was either only just on the horizon or not yet thought of. But that did not matter, Japanese television was brilliant for comedy and it was so visual that you did not need to speak Japanese to understand what was going on. All of the people at the hostel would crowd into the lounge to watch the "11p.m. show, "this was everyone's favorite. It was presented by this goofy fellow with a big evil grin on his face and big glasses. During the show, it would turn to footage of him out with the camera team on a previous night. It would start with him out on the streets of one of the main red light areas of one of the major cities of Japan then with microphone in hand and evil grin on face he would start running and enter a brothel at speed, then still running as he went down the corridors inside he would be talking about where they were as he faced the camera they would burst through a door into a well lit room where typically there would be a sadomasochistic scene going on. For example, a woman dressed in a dominatrix outfit who was beating a naked man who was tied upside down with a leather mask over his face.

The show compare would thrust the microphone into the face of the woman after asking her about how much she charged for this sort of service. Then she would stop and give her cute service smile and explain how she had special long term customer rates, and a rate for couples and special group rates etc.

On one such program just to show what high taste show they were running, they had one of the men who had been found tied up in a compromising position, in the television studio giving an interview with a leather mask with eye and mouth holes over his head. He look like a sadomasochistic Ned Kelly, and to top it off they even got him up on stage in front of the studio audience to sing or should it be said moan a song about sadomasochism while still in his Ned Kelly mask and with the studio band playing along.

There was an American man who had recently checked in at the hostel and was also looking for work he was brooding and uptight and didn't really get on with anybody. He was too in love with himself to have a sense of humor and so Gypsy, Jim and Tim who also was from England, gave him a wide birth. But one day he had an appointment for a job interview that he couldn't be bothered to go to. He had a college degree and thought that he should be getting more than the job was offering. He offered the interview to Gypsy who jumped at the opportunity and went and got his newly purchased smart clothes from his bag and put them on. After collecting the address plus directions and phone number from the fellow he rushed off down to the metro station around the corner and jumped down inside. Two train rides later he came out of a subway in front of a huge American style baseball stadium and amusement park with shriek provoking rides.

Gypsy looked at the directions that he had been given and realized that the office was in the stadium building.

He walked around the building until he found the right entrance, right by the ride with the most feminine shrieks and squeals coming from it. Gypsy had to stop and check himself to make sure that he was not hallucinating. Right there in the middle of the wide walkway around the circumference of the stadium was a free standing coin or note operated machine that served hot burgers in a bun.

He was used to the sight of machines that sold hot and cold drinks in cans and machines that sold cigarettes, beer, whisky, sake etc. but hot burgers that was a new one. He wondered how it was made to work.

He found the office on the third floor, it had a long window facing out towards the scream park. There were several other westerners also applying for jobs. The chief of the business was a man of short stature who had a bald head. He was the Japanese equivalent of a wheeler dealer not unlike a certain character from a British television situation comedy except of course for the fact that this man was more cultured, educated and intelligent. Never the less he was a jammer and bodger, which was why things worked out for Gypsy on that particular day. The man had a considerable wit about him, he asked Gypsy for his resume "What's that?" Gypsy asked. He had never even heard the word before, let alone knew what it meant. One of the other interviewees explained to him and Mr. Oneida gave him a sheet of paper and said, "Here write it on this." Gypsy then set about the creation of a work of fiction that would rival any for audacity and speed. He then handed it back to Mr. Oneida. Mr. Oneida was a sharp one, he asked Gypsy about the one thing on the resume that was not fiction. He was interested that Gypsy had worked as a volunteer with difficult children and asked more. It was fortunate as this was the one subject area where Gypsy was competent to speak. Besides he had been one himself so he knew the problems from the inside. Mr. Oneida told him that that was why he was being taken on board. This pleased Gypsy as he always liked the rebels and outcasts the best, and he knew that he would be the best one to work with such students.

He was told to meet Mr. Oneida at a certain train station in two days time, for a Shinkanzen (Bullet train) ride up to Sendai which was 500km from Tokyo and half way to the Hokkaido tunnel to Sapporo.

They were going up there for a job interview at a high school.

When Gypsy got back to the hostel and thanked the American for giving him the chance for the interview and told him what had happened and how well it had gone, the American flew into a rage and stomped off to his room. He then put on some smart clothes and returned to the lounge and kitchen area, snarling "if he can get a fucking job so easy then I'm going to go and get something sorted for myself" he then stomped out of the door having a satirically textbook gringo fatty tantrum. The German woman (we will call her Helga for now) also had a self righteous wobbly, "how dare you go and get a job like zis you are not kvalified vot do you know about zee teaching. You are cheating zem." "Wait a minute there," said Gypsy "zo you sink zat it is goot zat zee Japanese learn to speak zee Inglitch language vith zee tick Deutscher accent and zee mispronunciations ja? you sink ziz iz goot ja. Zee British, zee Aussies, zee Americans vill not understand a vord zey say as zey vill be too busy pissing zem selfs laughing. If you can teach English vith your tick Deutscher accent then vy can't I vith mine Britisher accent? Ja you understand? Now zer vouldn't be any hypocrites in zis room vould zer?." Besides this barrage of piss taking that he dished out on her he said. "I am going to do this job well. The fact that I don't have any qualifications from the fucking system that you believe so devoutly in does not mean shit. I left school with no qualifications because I didn't see why I should perform a bunch of doggy tricks to win approval from a bunch of cunts with cucumbers stuck up their arseholes. I am self educated and I honestly don't see that I need to prove myself to someone like you, do you understand?"

At this point she shut her mouth and stopped giving Gypsy dirty looks as she looked down at the ground then said "OK, if you are intent on doing zee job properly zen I have no problem vith zat".

The American came back from Mr. Oneida's office. He had also been promised a job but being an asshole he was still angry, mostly at the fact that Gypsy looked like he was going to get a job instead of having to busk in the railway station every night.

A British fellow, a tall bullying cricket and rugby playing type had just checked in to the hostel and tried to push his way around, using his modulated posh accent and arrogant demeanor to talk down to everyone. He was told to shut the fuck up by Jim who being American was not in the least bit impressed by the twat.

Tim came in as well and on hearing that Gypsy had likely found a job both he and Jim congratulated him on his success. For the last three weeks they had watched Gypsy traipse off down to Shinjuku each night with his guitar, coming back many hours later with just enough money to subsist on for the most part, as he saved slowly to buy smart work clothes. They admired his determination and persistence and were happy for him that it looked like he had hauled himself up and out of the bottom echelon of a dignified existence.

In his new smart clothes Gypsy met Mr. Oneida at the station where he was waiting, not just for Gypsy but for a whole group of other Gaijin who were also hoping to get a job at the school in Sendai.

The others all arrived and Mr. Oneida handed out the tickets and they boarded the Shinkanzen to Sendai. At that time the Shinkanzen was the most super modern and fast train in operational existence anywhere on earth. They were taking the slow train that made three or four stops along the way. It was scheduled to take two hours to cover the five hundred kilometers from Tokyo to Sendai.

The train left the station and cruised out of central Tokyo before hitting the accelerator. Gypsy was saddened to see as they cruised north that for the most part, the whole of the coast north from Tokyo to Sendai was built up and industrialized. Every bit of flat land was occupied with no open countryside to be seen until just before Sendai. This was one very crowded place. The Honshu north east coast megatropolis, there had been no break, no fields or parks to separate it from Tokyo it just sprawled everywhere. The buildings were not high, going up to a maximum of just four or five storeys,   this being due to Japan's vulnerability to earthquakes. Indeed Tokyo only had three or four sky scrapers at that time, built at great cost and designed to withstand the most heavy of earthquakes. All of the other buildings were much lower.

Inside the train the carriage had been spotless when they had left Tokyo but now that they were close to Sendai the floor and empty seats of the carriage looked like the inside of a semi full skip at the end of a pop festival, it was gross. Although the people of Japan for the most part were always very clean and well presented, and though their houses, their streets and their businesses and gardens were kept in immaculate condition, this did not extend to their manners while on intercity transport. In this way and in this way only, it was akin to China in that their behavior displayed a lack of respect for their immediate environment and the other people co occupying the space around them.

The train stopped at Sendai central station and the group stepped down into the crisp cold air of northern Japan. The streets of Sendai looked similar to what he had seen in some of the more suburban areas of Tokyo. Japan had a whole different feel or vibe to it than any other place that he had ever been to. The Japanese people looked at life through a whole different set of angles to that of Europeans, Americans, South Americans Africans or even other Asians.

The religions that had influenced their culture were Shinto which was based on shamanism and ancient legends and Zen which some might describe as the flowering of Buddhism.

However, like others around the world they did something with their slice of the truth that had not been intended, they ritualized it. The influence of Japanese Zen teachings still permeated through much in Japan, perhaps going deeper than Christianity ever went into the psyche of the people.

Some of the vibe he liked, but the uptight and unseen goings on always had him a little bit on his guard. Japan had strict codes and different customs, he wanted to get it right and not unintentionally cause offence to anyone or put a foot wrong in any other way. They walked through the streets until they reached the high school where they entered through the main front doors. Inside as is customary in Japan, they took off their shoes and placed them on a rack, replacing them with the slippers that were provided.

Mr. Onida had spoken with Gypsy on the train on the way from Tokyo.

"Don't worry, if this job doesn't work out and you don't get it, then I'll get you a job back in Tokyo, It's because you like working with difficult children, I have a hard time finding people for these sorts of posts no one wants to do it." This pleased Gypsy, why would he wants to have a bunch of well behaved do goody robots to teach when he could have the monsters? Crazy? Maybe but working with the types that he understood would ultimately be easier and also more rewarding for him.

He went for the interview but didn't get the job. He was not so worried as he would rather have a job back in Tokyo where there were other travelers to mix with rather than getting cabin fever in Sendai.

Upon leaving the building he found his shoes were missing. "Try on another pair and see if they fit" Mr. Oneida advised. "Though the Japanese were famously honest and theft was something too shameful to even be considered by almost anyone of Japanese nationality this rule did not apply to umbrellas, bicycles (which are just borrowed and left in another place) and occasionally shoes where the absolute rule of the jungle applies.

Gypsy could not find another pair that fitted so Mr. Oneida took him to the shoe shop around the corner and got him a new pair of shoes.

Then those who had not got jobs at the high school went back to the station for the ride back to Tokyo.

It was dark when they got back into Tokyo and Mr. Oneida asked Gypsy to come to the office after two days to set up his teaching schedule in Tokyo.

Back at the hostel the angry American had been told that his teaching post would be on the southern island of Shikoku and he was to fly there in three days time.

Jim and Tim had both found some work though none of them could find that elusive yet reportedly lucrative job of being a male prostitute servicing bored Japanese house wives. Most of them who used the service were apparently very horny and not so old, being perhaps in their mid thirties and not just that but they were reported to tip well too. Oh well another day, but for now they would all be English teachers.

Susan was a British woman staying at the hostel, she was a professional teacher and had been living outside of England and for that matter Europe too, for many years. She was certainly no good looker but that was a shame because in every other way she was beautiful. She was refreshingly straight up with an earthy sense of humor, she was highly educated and not just that but she was naturally intelligent and inquisitive which meant that when she gave an opinion on something, then she would have taken it and looked at it from many different angles first before passing any kind of judgment at all.

The only reason that she had worked within the confines of anyone's system at all was to change it from within. She liked hanging out with Gypsy, Jim and Tim, going out to bars with them and chatting about previous adventures.

Gypsy started at his new job. It would not be unfair to say that he was more than a little bit nervous. He had never done the job before and wasn't a hundred percent sure that he knew how they wanted the job done or to what level he would be required to teach at.

The school was some distance from central Tokyo. Mr. Oneida had set him up with work at three very diverse locations around the city that made him circle Tokyo on the metro almost every day.

First he had to take a train on the Yamanota circuit where he would ride to Ikebukoro on the northwest corner of the line. Then he would take a train on the Seibu line that ran diagonally northwest out of the city to Tokorozawa and then onto another train to his final destination at a small suburban station. The school was not even half a kilometer from the station.

He was not the only new teacher. There was a whole line of them including one other foreigner, an Australian, he really did have the education and spoke fluent Japanese. The new teachers all got up on to the stage where they stood in a long line before introducing themselves to the pupils who were gathered at the morning assembly meeting. The Japanese teachers were all dressed in suits with greased back hair and glasses and each one was carrying an attaché case.

The Australian was in smart trousers and a sports jacket, sweater and tie. And at the end of the line stood Gypsy in a new pair of blue jeans and a Nepalese hand knitted hippy style sweater.

The children looked along the line and saw Gypsy at the end and started laughing. Gypsy didn't mind, he didn't take himself too serious anyway. This would work in his favor when it came to teaching them, in as much as Japan was too uptight. If he could help them to laugh and relax a little then maybe he could help them to learn to speak some English in such a way as to be useful to them in the future.

At his introduction to the school principal, a woman in her fifties, it was explained to Gypsy that the school was a Zen based school for under performing students. There was to be a three minute period of meditation before every class and it was to be timed and controlled by the teacher.

Gypsy was very happy about this as he also believed, as they did, that meditation could help the students relax and thus perform better. He communicated his thoughts back to the school principal via his interpreter. He had become more and more interested in Buddhism since his meeting with Allen Ginsburg back in China and after witnessing several bits of wobbly behavior with certain members of the Hare Krishnas he decided to look at both the Buddha teachings and the Hindu/Vedic story told in the Ramayana.

He was very happy to be working in a school that adhered to the teachings of one of the branches of Buddhism.

The Australian had figured Gypsy out and could see he was new at the job so he invited Gypsy to watch him for a session and see how it was done.

The man was formidable, barking orders at the children in Japanese, he was more strict with them than a Japanese teacher at his worst. He sent several students out of the class to kneel in the corridor in disgrace within the first fifteen minutes of entering the classroom. The students were aged from sixteen to eighteen years old and had to wear uniforms based on those designed for the Japanese navy. The school and the classes were mixed, with the girls also having to wear a navy based design off uniform but this was standard throughout Japan,.

Gypsy knew that he could not use this style by which to teach, he was relieved to see that it even made the Japanese, English teachers wince.

In the classroom after the role call, where Gypsy's mispronunciations of their names caused great amusement to the students, it was time for the "Mukso" as the meditation session was known in Japanese. After that had been completed Gypsy picked up the text book and opened it to the page that he had been told that they had reached.

He started to teach from the book, picking each student out, one at a time for a session of book based interaction. But by the end of the class he was frustrated, as all that the book did was teach them how to parrot the language without the true interaction that was necessary for the teaching to stick. It got him thinking, he would have to devise his own method for them.

He carried on working from the book for the next two lessons until he had to leave to go to his next job which was at a far flung suburb by the name of Omiya on the northeast side of the city. There he had to teach a class of young children who had lived with their parents in other countries, mostly America where they had attended local schools. They all spoke fluent English and the purpose of the class as far as the parents were concerned was to make sure that they did not lose their ability to speak, read and write in English.

After several long train rides and an hour and twenty minutes later, Gypsy found his way to the correct building and in turn the right room on the right floor.

It was set up as a classroom and by the time that Gypsy arrived, was full with seven to eleven year olds.

Their parents had sent them to the class to learn but the children had other ideas, as far as they were concerned the class was there for them to let off steam after being hemmed in all week within the Japanese system, which was not only highly restrictive but also alien to the ways that they had become accustomed to in America, England and Australia.

Try as he might there was no way that he was going to get them to learn anything, it was as much as he could do to keep a modicum of control.

He had asked for monsters, well these were them, as they ran around treating the desks and furnishings as an obstacle coarse. Of course there were a few well behaved little girls who tried to learn as they sat at their desks writing, but Gypsy's time was mostly taken up trying to curb some of the more wild excesses and actions that were being perpetrated by a segment of the pupils who viewed the class as the "anything goes hour".

The battering hour had finished, and Gypsy ran back to the station to catch a train to Tamachi which was a station on the southeast side of the Yamanota circuit and near some of Tokyo's extensive port facilities.

There he was to teach two classes in a room at the back of a hall dedicated to ten pin bowling.

The first class that Gypsy was to teach was a cram school class for two eight year olds. It was clearly cruel and insensitive of the parents to be sending their children to such a class when they were so exhausted that they kept nodding off as they tried to keep their eyes open as they tried to write. The final class was for a group of three professionals who wanted to perfect their English, as they were constantly travelling the world, troubleshooting and setting up new installations for their company. All three men were engineers and their grasp of English was very good already and Gypsy wasn't sure that they needed any more help. Their written work for their job was perfect and they even seemed to understand English and American slang. But the company had sent them to the class, so here they were.

The job finished at 8pm and Gypsy headed home to the hostel. He and Susan went out for a drink shortly after he got in and Gypsy asked for her advice as to how to make the class at the high school more dynamic and interactive. What she told him got him thinking and he visualized something like a board game in his mind that he was going to use as a teaching aid.

Jim's new job was working out and Tim was getting by on some teaching work that he had found. Gypsy upset Avigdor's delicate sensibilities by telling him that he was going to play a song that he should remember from a time when he was not so old. He then played The Tennessee Ernie Ford song "sixteen tons".

Avigdor instead of laughing and letting the joke be on him stomped off to his room in an angry chewing sulk.

This was a new phenomena to Gypsy, The "self-centered American adult baby tantrum. He saw it first with the other American who had got him the job and now here was Avigdor behaving like a wanker too, it had Gypsy somewhat confused.

When Gypsy was at work in England on his father's plant nursery and again in both Israel and Australia, people used to play jokes on each other and boisterously take the piss out of each other all day as a form of D.I.Y. entertainment, not out of aggression but as a form of comradery and affection for each other. Gypsy couldn't understand why most of the Europeans, all of the British, Australians, New Zealanders and white South Africans and most educated Hindus could get it, yet the people of the Americas had a tendency to read it the wrong way and get offended.

He kept on using the text book to teach from at the high school for the next three weeks while he developed the ideas for his English learning game. He didn't like using the text book as not only was it deadly boring for him and the students, but it wasn't going in, and even if it was it could hardly be deemed as useful English.

He got his first pay packet and looked to move to a Gaijin house several stops outside of the Yamanota circuit on the west side but it was run by a cosy little clique of uptight Australian women who took themselves far too seriously to be the sort of people that Gypsy wanted to share the company of.

The next day he found his way to a much more welcoming abode at Oyzumi Gakoen on the Seibu line, out from Ikebukoro which was on the line that took him to his work at the high school. Gypsy had found a place that specialized in accommodating foreigners on a medium to long term basis. Yoshida house was a Gaijin house with two long, wooden buildings, two storeys high with outdoor, roofed, walkways providing access to the ground and the area between the two buildings part occupied by a single storey wooden structure that was like a vastly overgrown and over engineered garden shed that acted as kitchen, dining area, television lounge and telephone point.

Gypsy had to share a room with someone else for the first couple of weeks until a single room of four and a half tatami mats in size became available. Four and a half tatami mats made up an eight foot by six foot floor space, plus there was a small internal porch with a stainless steel wash basin off to one side.

It wasn't the largest space that Gypsy had ever seen but it would at least give him some privacy to sleep in. Something that had been most lacking for a large part of his travels thus far.

As he arrived with his bags, to move in he was met by squeals of delight and laughter by two very earthy Australian women.

"Ooh look it's the hash cookie man" one of them squealed with laughter, the other one turned around and on seeing Gypsy, giggled and said "have you come all this way to sell us some more hash cookies, we could certainly use some." Here were two of Gypsy's former customers from Goa who had also come to Japan to tank up on cash before disappearing back down into cheap and cheerful third world Asia. They were working as hostesses in Japanese bars that catered to business men and were only expected to pour drinks and light cigarettes. There were Japanese Filipina and Thai women at other venues if the men require other services.

Gypsy's new roommate was a Bangladeshi man by the name of Faizal. He was a quiet man, who was studying at a university in Tokyo.

He wasn't in very much of the time, but neither was Gypsy, the place was used strictly for sleeping only. Both of them had busy schedules that didn't allow much time to relax, apart from when either of them came in and crashed out in their respective side of the room on the thin futons that were provided by the management of the place. The room was eight tatami mats in size but would have been too expensive for one of them to have rented on his own. Absolutely exhausted from the day's work, Gypsy would come back at ten oclock, eat and then go and crash out. He would then sleep until it was time to wake up for the morning shift.

Gypsy and Faizal, on the odd occasions that they did speak to each other, spoke mostly about the Hindi/Urdu pronunciation of words as compared with the Bengali pronunciation. Gypsy had become very interested in how things worked in India. From his time on the streets of Bombay to the stays and visits he had made to Hare Krishna temples and ashrams, plus the many books he had read he had learned more Hindi than perhaps he had realized.

He also was starting to understand the essence of what made the cultures of India what they were. Since his meeting with John in the railway station in Bombay his view of life had changed and he now looked at things from a Hindu Vaishnav perspective. He was vegetarian and primarily interested in matters spiritual. Life was to be a conscious effort to lift the soul through hard work and the pursuit of knowledge and wisdom. From Faizal, Gypsy learned that Bengali was almost the same as Hindi, often it was just that the first letter of some of the words would be different and other than that it was just a question of a different accent and a few local quirks. A bit like the difference between English and Glaswegian.

After ten days or so he got his own room, the size or smaller than a monk's cell. It was comfortable however, with its slightly sprung, tatami mat floor and a thin roll up futon against one wall.

He was also now ready to introduce his coarse at the school, he had spent much of his spare time thinking how it could be simplified down from the much more elaborate vision that he had had when he had his "eureka" moment.

His first ideas all had impracticalities that would stop it from working properly, but after two weeks of brainstorming it alone, he had his solution. We must remember that Gypsy had never done any full time work of this kind up until just three weeks prior to this moment.

The first part of the course involved the use of four sentences and a map that he would draw onto the black board. This was some of the only writing that he made them do. Their coordination in English was not good and they could not speak a sentence in the language. So Gypsy had designed them a game to help this. He explained that one at a time each one of them would be required to give him guidance around the map, using the four sentences and some alternating words.

He would put his piece of chalk onto the map and move it to follow their instructions. If they gave a wrong direction then he would take it and then they would have to guide him around the block again.

The students in all of the classes took to the game like ducks to water. It was truly interactive like a primitive video game. Soon almost all of them were becoming proficient at giving and understanding directions, and the great thing was that they didn't even release that they were learning.

In the staff room even though he only taught part time at the school, he had his own desk to sort out anything that needed taking care of. On certain days when he was teaching a later class, he would join the other teachers in ordering lunch from a certain café in the locality. The food would be delivered by a scooter driver who had a free swinging box on the back of his machine, which meant that he could deliver such things as noodle soup without spilling it.

"Ted" who taught in the next classroom to gypsy also had the next desk in the staff room. He was Japanese but had studied in the United States and spoke fluently in English. He was a decent and friendly type who helped Gypsy to understand some of the subtleties of Japanese thinking.

There was a woman teacher at the next desk who was a seventh day Adventist, and like Gypsy, she was a vegetarian. She was the one who helped him to order vegetarian food from the café. She also spoke some English and used to talk with him about different things. She was tiny in stature, coming up to Gypsy's armpit only. However, many of the students were taller than Gypsy and well built. The younger generation were obviously getting far more protein in their diet than generations past had done.

One day when Gypsy got to his desk there were two male students who must have both been over eighteen years old who were kneeling in front of the desk of the tiny woman with sheepish expressions on their faces. The woman must have been teaching a class at the time as she was not at her desk. Gypsy was preparing for the two classes that he was about to teach when the woman entered the room she didn't hesitate to go straight to work berating the two boys knelt on the floor and then set about bashing them around the head with a large and thick hard back book whilst shouting and screaming at them. In England or another modern country the students would most likely have bashed her back or at least held her in a restraining posture until she had calmed down, but this was Japan where elders were given respect even when they didn't earn it, one can only wonder if these two students later in life were destined to become leather masked participants on "The 11pm Show".

On other occasions he had also seen other teachers beating students in the staff room. The teacher with a desk across the room from Gypsy's had a haircut and style that would suggest that he had once been in the military. He was a teacher of science and classical Japanese but his main purpose no doubt was to be the school's 'bogey man' and was probably responsible for most of the adolescent nightmares and bed wetting that may have occurred in the immediate locality. He was forever disciplining and caning students. On one occasion Gypsy was working at his desk marking test papers when he was startled into looking up by the sound of a loud thwaking sound and a loud feminine scream. On this occasion he was beating two girls across the shoulders with a strap. . . Gypsy had very much his own style of how he kept discipline in his classes. He was more prone to using a practical joke to make his students behave. He used to time the three minute meditation with an old clockwork alarm clock with a handle and two bells on the top. Some of his students would not be so interested in the class and would sprawl themselves over their desk and go to sleep. The other students would giggle and chuckle as they watched Gypsy, tip toe across the room whilst winding up the alarm lever then placing the clock right by the students ear, he would release the alarm and watch, as the student shot bolt upright with a totally shocked expression on his or her face. "Good afternoon welcome to the English class" he would say with a grin on his face. It worked he didn't have to do it too many times. It didn't cause any nightmares or bed wetting but it almost caused a number of students to piss themselves from shock.

For the most part Gypsy had no problems with any of his students. Some of them were a bit slow witted but that was no problem as he would endeavor to find the time to sit down with them and give them some slow, patient one on one tuition. Watching the students actually learn something from him was a very rewarding experience. He liked the students and though he was not formally trained to do the job that he was doing, he did it with sincerity and spent much time thinking about how to benefit his students in the best way possible. His course was working much better than he could have ever imagined, he had somehow got inside the Japanese collective psyche and found a way of teaching that was custom made for them.

Jim and Tim had both got themselves out of the hostel and into private rooms. All of them were racing around the city all day, teaching at different locations. Jim had located a good expat bar near Ikebukoro station, at least that is to say that it was a bar where expats, would meet. 'The Red Onion Bar' was large in floor space for Japan and had a pool table. A ginger haired Canadian traveler who Gypsy knew from Chungking Mansions in Hong Kong was there, he had come to Japan also to find teaching work.

Back at Yoshida house where Gypsy liked to relax the most, he found, via Jim a source of hashish and if he was very careful he could smoke it and blow all of the smoke out of the sliding screen window and no one would smell a thing.

It was very dangerous and highly against the law to smoke hash or weed in Japan. It was a subject that was never even discussed with anyone of Japanese race or nationality, even if they did smoke. That was because, if the cops ever collared them for anything at all, even if it was not concerning drugs, they would squeal faster than a parrot on amphetamines about what 'the Gaijin was doing, not out of maliciousness but out of sheer terror of their cops.

So dope was dealt strictly between the Gaijin and smoked that way too.

On Sundays Gypsy and the others would go out on beer fuelled photographic explorations of the city. One of Gypsy's favorite places that he would return to on many an occasion was the Yasakuni Shrine. At the time he didn't know the significance of the place but it always made him feel good being there, as if it gave him some sort of inner peace.

Of course they checked out all of the main Shinto Shrines in the city but another thing that they enjoyed was Harajaku on a Sunday. Harajaku was for Tokyo what Carnaby Street was for London or Greenwich Village had been for New York, a place which contained the most bohemian of fashion and behavior.

Every Sunday a main road would be closed to traffic and young high school students would do their thing, whatever their thing was, in the middle of the road. There would be groups dressed up in teddy boy outfits and dancing to music by Elvis Presley and the likes that would be blasting out of huge ghetto blasters. There would be punk bands, street theatre plays and dramas involving Kendo and other martial arts, there would be groups on roller skates and so on. It was the one time in a week when the Japanese youth were allowed some freedom of expression. Jim had bought himself an electric guitar and had got friendly with some students who had started a band at their university. They would meet at Harajaku on the weekends and use a studio nearby to practice in. One day he invited Gypsy along to the session and lent him his new guitar to play. Gypsy stayed for the whole session but it really was not his kind of music. If there were two things in Gypsy's way of thinking that rivaled opera for outright hideous, nausea causing, cacophony then one of them must be the standard "oh wow is me broken hearted" lame ballads and the other must be the sound of men singing sugar sweet love songs. The band was playing them both so Gypsy did not bother going to another session. However on listening to the recording of the session it was Jim that pointed out that Gypsy was starting to sound OK on lead.

Via friends, gypsy had got himself some easier but lower paid work at an English conversation lounge. It meant that on his way back from Tamachi on some nights he would stop at Omoto Sando. It was inside of the Yamanota circuit and near an area that specialized in retailing guitars, stereos and other electronics. His job was just to be there and talk with people in English.

The people attending the lounge were all Japanese who were fluent in English and wanted to improve further. Although for the most part the clients were business men, salary men and secretaries there were also some more interesting types who would come by from time to time. There was one who was a freelance photographer who had travelled much of the world pursuing his profession. He was the rarest of rarities in his country, a man with a free life and a free mind from which he was not afraid to speak. (It need's mentioning at this time that the Japanese system was much more self restrictive than anything known in any other part of the world. Everyone was so afraid to stand out that for the most part, it stifled freedom, even the freedom of thought, which thus stunted inventiveness.

However, though they were few in number as far as percentages went, the Japanese who had broken free, made up for it in terms of sheer creativity and bottle. If they decided to go for adventure it would be something ultimately hard, wild and most of all, masochistic. like tobogganing down the Everest ice fall, or riding a motor cross bike across Antarctica for example. But occasionally there was a balanced one among them, like this photographer, who though he travelled to many different places in a short time, had developed a good understanding of the places that he had visited, even or should it be said, especially, the photographs that he took showed this.

Back at Yoshida house, Gypsy and just about everyone who was around at the time was crammed into the television lounge watching some absolutely priceless Japanese television at it's very best "Japanese Candid Camera."

They had dressed a man up in a Buddha mask and put on heavy layers of make-up then a layer of black paint, then a layer of bronze paint.

Then they had sat him out in a market. As he sat absolutely motionless they built a shrine around him, and waited for their first victim.

An old boy came by and seeing a Buddha shrine, went and put some money down and put his hands together in a prayer motion. At which point the Buddha statue snarled "wrah" and sprung his arms and torso forward. You could almost see the shit flying out of the old boy's trouser legs. He lifted off of the ground at least a foot and had gone as white as is possible for a yellow man to go. Who says there's no humor in Zen Buddhism?

They had a few more hapless victims with the same trick and no doubt provided each one with access to a bathroom and a fresh charge of underwear.

The look on people faces was priceless, they were in absolute confusion.

Then the team moved on to their next trick.

They had dressed another of the show's presenters as a monster that looked as if it had come straight out of the pages of a "marvel" comic book.

Then they buried him under the pavement and waited.

A group of young women, either in their late teens or early twenties, walked along the road, on the pavement. As they walked over the place where the man in the monster outfit was buried the ground started to wobble and the monster popped out, "wragh!!!!" he roared and then chased the screaming women who were moving in the other direction at Olympic speed as they screamed and cried. Once again there was strong reason to believe that a fresh pair of underwear was provided to the victims of the prank. . . . Finally to give a full demonstration of how very gullible some people can be, they dressed up yet another show presenter. This time it was in a gorilla suit. They then put him in a small transit cage, out on a Warf by a batch of cargo that was waiting to be loaded onto a freighter of some description. As a group of women passed by and looked at the grunting gorilla in the cage, the cage broke open and the gorilla suddenly burst out. There he was, grunting, and beating his chest as he ran, chasing the screaming women as they took off at high speed in the opposite direction. Yes it was funny, the whole show seemed to focus on just one thing and that was to cure any problems that their victims may have had with constipation. "And the winner of this week show get's a one year supply of clean underwear and dried figs.....heart medicines and funeral expenses paid for on request".

In the Japan times or maybe it was the Tokyo journal, it was reported that the police in England had rioted on a group of hippies who travelled and lived in buses and trucks and called themselves, the "peace convoy". According to the article and accompanying photos of women and children with blood splattered faces, the cops had gone on the rampage when the hippies had pulled off the road into a bean field. Then the cops had rioted on them, much like a gang of traditional English football hooligans on a Saturday afternoon. In their violent frenzied rage they had rampaged around the field, smashing the windows of the busses and trucks and bashing and beating anyone who had the misfortune to encounter one of these loutish thugs. The music scene from the west that was at that time new and fresh had Madonna, The talking heads and The Clash at the forefront with ACDC and Bruce Springsteen contributing a couple of tracks to the mix. However Gypsy was more into a cassette that he had been given with John Martyn's "bless the weather" on one side and Jim Cappaldi's "Fierce heart" on the other. Another good tape that he had been given was Robert Plant's album "Now and Zen." Those were what he used to listen to on his walkman as he travelled the Tokyo metro each day.

The other conversation lounge that Gypsy worked at was at a suburb well outside of the Yamanota circuit, The area was called Kichajoji.

The owner of the business was one of those goofy toothed gregarious and humorous types of character that were more common in Asia than in the west. He would have probably been right at home running a dating agency. He reminded Gypsy of the presenter of "the 11 p.m. show."

The only problem with it was it was a Sunday job which left him not one whole day off in a week. However he needed to make money and he had not managed to find himself any private work teaching so he had to be contented with the lower paid work at the conversation lounges. It was longer hours but it was more relaxing than full on teaching jobs.

The people at the lounge were a more interesting bunch of characters, plus also there were many attractive women that would attend. Some who were there were obviously looking for men, possibly Gaijin men too. But gypsy had a strict rule for himself that he used in order to keep himself out of unnecessary trouble. Never fuck around at your place of work – keep any sex life away from place of work at all costs and for the most part, keep it away even from place of abode if seeking a quiet life.

After the lounge had closed one Sunday evening the boss and some others suggested that as Gypsy had been talking about India that maybe it would be a good idea to go out to a nearby restaurant called 'The Silk Road' that had Indian food on it's menu.

The restaurant was in a basement under a shop and had been made to look like the cellar of a building in the Middle East or Central Asia. On the right hand side, inside the entrance was an open sided small room with a glass cabinet taking up one entire wall. Inside was a collection of highly exotic musical instruments that had been collected by the owner when he had travelled along the legendary Silk Road that went from China to Europe. The collection had everything from Lutes, Balalaikas and Bazookis to Indian Sitars, Sarods and Santoors. There was also a whole range of instruments the like of which Gypsy had never even seen or heard of before. Apparently the owner of the restaurant had learnt to play them all.

The food too was from along the Silk Road. There were Turkish dishes and dishes from Iran, Afghanistan, Pakistan, India, Nepal, Tibet, China and Korea not to mention dishes from areas north from India and Pakistan in the Turkic republics. Gypsy ordered an Indian vegetarian thali and the others mostly ordered either Chinese, Korean or Turkish dishes, as most of the Japanese do not like so much spices or chili in their food.

The owner of the restaurant was a Japanese traveler who on travelling to each county along the Silk Road, had both learned to cook the local food and play the local stringed instruments. There was a small stage set up against one wall where on Saturday nights and special occasions he would perform concerts with his huge collection of instruments.

The food came out and each dish was a work of Japanese perfection. The only thing was, the different subjis (curries) in Gypsy's thali had been spiced only to Japanese tastes. The chilli wasn't in it. It was indeed strange that the Japanese liked wasabi so much and that was a flavor that could take your head off for burn power, but they didn't like chili and spices.

At Yoshida house there were a lot of young Israeli women staying. They had just finished their army service and were in Japan working as bar hostesses to earn enough money to go travelling further. They did nothing to make themselves popular with the other residents. If someone phoned in with a job, even as an English teacher, they would post the message up on the board in Hebrew as so that no one but one of them would get the job. When as anyone of any other nationality would put it up in English for all to see. They behaved without sensitivity to anyone but their nasty selves and were despised by all. When people confronted them about their foul behavior they would stick their arrogant king sized snouts in the air and say "so what" as they argued some twisted lame logic to try to justify themselves. When confronted by everyone and told collectively as a group to start fucking well behaving like adults, they turned on the crocodile water works and accused everyone in the place of being anti-Semitic.

Unfortunately this hideous dodge worked on a couple of the Germans who lived in the place, setting them off on a guilt trip that really shouldn't have been put on them. None of them had even been born at the time that world war two ended. Gypsy had no such guilt trips however and gave the nasty foul bitches a piece of his mind. "I'm not anti-Semitic I'm Jewish and I don't like people like you getting the people who I am from a bad name" he berated them. "My family helped build your country, my great grandfather worked with Herzl (Theodore Herzl was the founder of the modern day state of Israel) and my grandfather and his two friends founded one of your towns, my family donated a brand new high school to the people of Israel. I myself have not only lived and worked in Israel but have also spent time studying at a yeshiva.

My great grandfather would be turning in his grave if he saw the foul way in which so many of you young Israelis behave, please desist and stop making me ashamed to be Jewish."

They tried reaching to grab something from the air with which to defend themselves. "But if someone does this what's wrong with it?" one of them tried in a defense of pure chutzpah. Their lame defenses came out of mouths that appeared to be on automatic pilot because all that was really coming out was a load of writhing noise.

"You are wrong and deep inside you know that you are wrong, now shut up I don't want to hear your justifications I just want you to change your behavior, as so as you stop upsetting everyone else who lives here."

There was some chuckling and quiet grins as Gypsy returned to the lounge. He had been able to beat all of their underhanded defenses and talked down to them like no other from the guest house could, as from a great height. Whether it would have a lasting effect remained to be seen. Gypsy had no time for them he did not find any of them to be attractive in any way. He could read them so easily and totally despised their self centered, manipulative behavior. Here was a further example of the type of attitude that was a root cause of anti-Semitism.

The television was on and it was another piece of priceless Japanese sick humor. This time it was a game show where the contestants had to eat ever more weird and disgusting things before moving on to the real hard core masochism.

It started with things that the Thais and Vietnamese would think nothing of eating, like deep fried whole snake or fried whole scorpion in garlic and ginger etc. Then it was time for Cantonese whole rodent recipes. Then came flied lice and flied cockloach if you get the point. The Japanese certainly had a sense of humor, a very goofy, geeky, twisted, sadomasochistic one at that, which made for great television viewing. They would do things that would be unimaginable in the west.

Their comedy sketches too would have been way past the edge for most western television censors of the time. If a program had much speaking then sometimes one of the travelers who had learned to speak Japanese would translate for the others.

The next program on, that evening was a show featuring a series of comedy sketches that at that time would probably have got a station closed down in the west if they had dared to air such a show. And this was mainstream television in Japan, what's more, the country was reported to suffer from far less cases of rape than almost anywhere else on the planet. The Japanese attitude towards sex was very liberated compared with other countries and cultures.

What little free time Gypsy now had was normally spent resting, but he did still get out with his camera, taking pictures of things that made Japan unique and totally different from anywhere else. Gardens, streets, temples, shrines, buildings, people and events etc, and he would always make time to visit Yasakuni shrine.

At the conversation lounge at Omoto Sando he would sometimes be invited out after work by the owner and his friends, to a Japanese pub to drink sake and shochu. The floor of a traditional style pub in Japan would be made of tatami mats (which were large block like mats, either made from bamboo or from rice stalks) so everyone had to take off their shoes before entering. Inside a simple almost empty room would be many small Japanese tables and small, flat floor cushions. For groups such as the one that Gypsy was with there were areas with extra long tables.

The sake and shochu were brought out in small ceramic jugs and were served into traditional style ceramic sake cups. It was always served warm at around about, body temperature. Plates of snacks started to arrive and Gypsy got to try a whole load of things that he could never have imagined before could be turned into a snack. Seaweeds and raw fish of many types, fermented plumbs, fermented beans etc. it was a new experience, different from the pubs and bars of any of the other places that Gypsy had ever visited before. It was very cultured and refined. The food although weird and different, tasted very good and the shochu crept up on everyone from behind. It had tasted so warm and smooth that Gypsy couldn't believe that he was totally shit faced on just eight or ten cups of the stuff (a favorite game for Japanese who had contact with Gaijin was to take the Gaijin friend to a bar and see if they could get him or her drunk before they were rocking about, themselves). The Japanese do not have a great physical tolerance for alcohol on the whole (of course there will always be some exceptions). After two moderate glasses of whisky most of them will be red faced and rocking. As such they were curious to know what a westerner looked like when they were drunk and how much whisky would be required to do the job.

As such, Gypsy, Jim and some of the others were forever being invited out for drinks with their Japanese friends.

One day the conversation lounge people from Omoto Sando invited Gypsy to come and watch a Sumo tournament with them at the Meiji shrine. The temple was dedicated to Emperor Meiji who one hundred and fifty years previously had started a fast paced reformation of his country. Turning it in a very short space of time, from a feudal society under the control of the Samurai, into an industrialized western style nation that could hold its own with the powers of Europe and America. He was considered a very big man in Japanese history, perhaps the biggest. Thus a shrine and temple were dedicated to him.

It was a Sunday and throngs of people were around the place.

A traditional opera style performance was going on on an open air stage. A small crowd were watching as women done up to look like Japanese dolls sang and performed. But what everyone had all come to see was the sumo wrestling that was going on in the make shift stadium next door. The wrestlers were absolutely huge and contrary to popular belief outside of Japan. They were not only massively tall but covered in muscles rather than fat. The reason that some think it is fat is because they literally have muscles on their muscles and looked as if they could give an elephant a run it's his money in a boisterous wrestling game.

Before each tournament was an elaborate ceremony where among other things, salt was spread on the ground. The rules of the tournament were that each had to try to throw the other out of the large circle Marked on the ground, and in which they were standing, by means of force. They were also allowed to distract their opponent, which is what some of them did. If one managed to throw another one out of the circle in such a way that he landed horizontally, it would make the ground shake.

It was an incredible spectacle to watch, even though each tournament would on average last for only seconds, not even minutes, as the two legged, pink elephants danced.

Apparently they could only do the job when they were in their teens and twenties, after they retired from the sport, they would go to a specialist health farm to lose some of the weight before it turned to fat and eventually killed them. Wrestlers who did not drastically lose weight after their retirement from the sport had a very low life expectancy. Often dying in their early to mid thirties, however they were all the rage for many of the women and teenage girls. For some reason, these guys turned them on.

It was coming up to the school summer holidays, a four and a half week break.

Gypsy was planning in his mind to go back to the Philippines and see if he could find Yolanda and maybe help her also to get to Japan and find work. However destiny had other plans for him. He phoned his family and told them what he was doing and what his plans were for his summer vacation. Then they said "we haven't seen you for nearly two years, please, would you come and visit us?" "I haven't got the sort of spare cash sitting about that would pay for me to make a trip to England and get back to Asia in a financially secure position" he explained "the Philippines is cheap from here and living there is cheap too."

"OK, if we pay your ticket will you come then?" they asked. They had him trapped now. It would have upset them if he had said no. "OK" he said I'll go and look for a cheap flight.

What with the schools all having their summer holidays at the same time in Japan, there was no such thing as an available "Q" class ticket out of the place. The only effective way out would be to buy a ticket to Hong Kong on full fare economy and hope that he could get a cheap ticket from there to London. At that time, full fare economy meant business class.

When he saw the list of airlines from which to choose his flight to Hong Kong he chose Swissair. He had had a good flight with them before and not only that but they had his favorite drink in the onboard bar "Williams". He like schnapps and hadn't had any for a long while. The flight was expensive but it was the only way out of Tokyo at that time. Gypsy's flight was booked for two weeks time. One way to Hong Kong and then......?

At work the Australian, English teacher was pissed off at the other teachers in the staff room. They could not get their heads around the fact that he spoke fluent Japanese and understood most of everything that they said. "Do you know what they are saying about us as they stand around talking in the staff room?" he asked Gypsy "No" Gypsy replied. "Well they call us things like white monkeys and even the ones who teach English, don't talk about us with respect, they do not view our role as essential. To them we are just like performing animals that are put out front to attract parents to send their children to the school. I want to play a trick on the bastards to shut them up and put them in their place, will you help me?" "Sure" said Gypsy. "If you've got a good idea then I'm ready and willing."

The Australian explained his idea "look most of the Japanese English teachers can hardly speak a word of English maybe you've noticed. "OK, yes, apart from Ted and the woman at the next desk" Gypsy pointed out "well yes but that's two out of ten yes?" "Ok so what's the idea for the trick?" Gypsy asked.

"Even though they are not competent to do the job, they don't want anyone else to see it". "Right" said Gypsy "so we set an oral test that is to run in the assembly hall, and require the services of each one of them to help us judge it.

It is my belief that at the very least it will put each one of them in a particularly nervous state for a few hours."

So they set an end of term test. The Japanese teachers used Ted to try on their behalf, to talk Gypsy and his Aussie work mate out of it, but all to no avail.

"If you are to teach spoken English seriously then at the end of each term the students must be tested for proficiency and the only competent method is to test their oral pronunciation and grammar." Gypsy explained to Ted with a sincere look on his face. "Couldn't just you two do it in batches? Ted asked "we don't have enough time on our own we both teach classes at other schools in central Tokyo" Gypsy explained.

So with their balls pinned to the wall and nowhere to back out to, especially with the school principal in favor of the test. It was a highly nervous and agitated group of Japanese English teachers who were standing there twitching and snapping angrily at their students and each other in the assembly hall on the fateful morning. Poor Ted, he was getting subtle undercurrents of hostility from the other teachers for failing to stop the Gaijin from carrying out their plans.

As it was the Aussie had set what Gypsy thought would be a pretty damned easy test for them. He knew that his students would be able to go for a more complex test, but that would have totally fucked the teachers and the aim was to cause them a little bit of discomfort but not so much as to have them reaching for the sepeku knives or taking one way bus tickets to places with high bridges or steep cliffs.

The test ran easily for Gypsy, the Australian, Ted and the small woman. Almost every student passed. It was the sort of test that might be set for children at primary/ elementary school.

However it had most of the Japanese English teachers in a bit of a state. When the test was over they looked particularly drained and couldn't wait to scuttle back to the staff room to catch their breath, get their bearings back and hope that their absolute inability to speak a word of English had not been noticed.

Gypsy and the Australian spent the rest of the morning trying to suppress smug grins from their faces. It had worked perfectly and hopefully now it would be a while before the other teachers had the nerve to think of bad mouthing them again in the staff room, where the Australian could hear them.

The Australian was grinning as he and Gypsy left the school "That will teach them" he said. He had lived in Japan for several years and understood their ways and their culture quite well. However, like most expats who had lived there for too long, he was often full of contempt for them. But he saved his worst venom for the school at which they both worked. He viewed them as fools who would hire anyone. He had sussed Gypsy to be someone who had bullshitted his way into the job, on his first day. But Gypsy had kept his head down and endeavored to do the job properly, so he had kept his mouth shut.

He warned Gypsy about Mr. Oneida's Scottish wife and how if she sussed him he would be out in a heartbeat. So Gypsy did what he could to avoid her and on the few occasions when he couldn't, he was friendly and polite but got out of the office as quickly as he could. As it was, he normally only went to the office at the stadium once a month and then only to collect his pay packet. Normally there was only Mr. Oneida and his assistant present, but occasionally his formidable Scottish wife was there. Gypsy did not need questions being asked about the time he had spent at university, what university????, he could not even remember a time when he had even visited a university campus.

The Australian explained a lot to Gypsy about how Japanese people think.

To anyone from outside of Japan, except for maybe the Koreans and possibly the Chinese, the Japanese way of thinking was completely alien. Emotions however were just the same and what with the constant work and social life based, backstabbing and the silent stress that it generated it would occasionally cause someone to go off pop. At the more passive end of the spectrum there were the drunks and dropouts who lived in the underground passages of some of Tokyo's metro stations.

Many of them were people who had had a profession before but had collapsed under the constant load of social pressures and were now destitute. At the other end of the Japanese nervous breakdown scale were the ones who went off with a bang. Some were highly respected professionals in the intellectual or business world who until the moment that they went Kaboom, everyone looked up to as pillars of their society. Then one day the stress of showing a smiling mask to the world while silently suffering inside got to be just too much to live with.

The SKUBA EXPO which was a huge international fair was happening somewhere on the outskirts of Tokyo at the time. Groups of school children were constantly being taken there, and shown around by their teachers. In one tent was a display of different models of hair dryers all of which were plugged in. So one male student pick's one up and tries it. His teacher beat him to death with it literally, accusing the boy of being effeminate. Also one night, some of Gypsy's friends witnessed an unprovoked attack on an old man by some youths while on their way home on the metro. By all accounts it was reminiscent of a scene from the movie "A Clockwork Orange".

Everything was very uptight in Japanese society, people maintained false facades to greet the outside world with. People hid and buried their true feelings. Very few people in Japan dared voice an individual opinion. They would normally just parrot what they had been told was the right way to look at things. No one would dream of ever speaking badly to someone's face but would think nothing of backstabbing them with the boss at work.

Most people's wages including the salary men in their suits, was far lower than that of someone in the same job working in Australia, the USA, Northwest Europe or Canada. Their official annual holiday was just five days. Most of them would not take it for fear of missing a chance of promotion.

After they finished work, which could be as late as nine or ten oclock at night, they were expected to join the boss going to a bar where they would drink until paralytic. Not to go was extremely bad form. Not just that but they were generally expected to get drunk before the boss did.

There was an unwritten law in Japanese society that stated that what someone did when they were drunk was never to be spoken about the next day and from then onward.

The one pressure valve that they had was alcohol. Their houses were small and crowded, their work environment was hyper stressful and the journey to and from work on the overcrowded metro trains was not what one could call pleasant. It was something truly remarkable about the Japanese that they could live in such a way without far more of the population either dropping out or turning into psychopaths. It might also go some way to explaining why suicide is treated by some in Japan as a national sport. "Is it a bird? Is it a plane? No it's Kenji from the office, he's just jumped off the railway bridge", SPLAT!!!!!!!!!!!!!.

Gypsy had his small bag packed and also his guitar as he headed for the station at Oizumi Gakoen.

He took a ride down the line to the final stop in the city, Ikebukoro and from there took another train on the Yamenota line to Shinjuku which was several stops to the south. From there he took a bus to Narita airport and checked in at the Swissair business class counter.

He had never been in business class before and he was looking forward to it.

He was paying for the ticket rather than being upgraded so he had his most favorite old clothes on. A pair of jeans with holes and signs of heavy use about them, and the psychedelic T-shirt that he had bought at Glastonbury festival several years before with the ripped armpit.

The airport was still being built which meant no business class lounge at the time, so business class passengers were given vouchers for the bar.

Gypsy was already in his seat when the steward entered the business class section. He saw Gypsy sitting there and gave a startled look and went running to find the purser. Gypsy could see him talking in an animated way and pointing to where Gypsy was sitting. Gypsy was quietly amused by the spectacle as he sat back and read the Tokyo journal. He couldn't understand Deutsch and certainly not Swiss Deutsch but he could read people's eyes and he could imagine that the conversation was going something like....

STEWARD: Vot iz going on on ziz flight, zer is zee longhaired hippy vith zee psychedelic clothes sitting in zee business class section, did somevun upgrade him? Vot is going on?

PURSER: Don't vurry he haz zee ticket he has paid zee money he is OK jah?

STEWARD: You are certain ja? I do not see zee business class travelers like zat before.

PURSER: Jah! I haf checked his boarding pass. Maybe he is zee rock star. If he vos zee criminal he vould be dresses smart, like zee vuns zat come to svitzerland to stash zer dough. Jah? You be nice to him zis vun has his own story.

The steward came back into the cabin, and from that moment on he gave Gypsy exceptionally good service. The flight took off out of Narita and headed south as it climbed. Gypsy relaxed back in the big comfortable seat as the steward brought him his first shot of Williams Krist in a very long while. He ordered another, then sat back and read the paper. He was wondering how it would be trying to get a flight out of Hong Kong to London, what with most first world countries having their longest school holiday at that time of the year. He hoped that he could get out by the next night but was concerned that it could take much longer. He hoped that he wouldn't have to hop further south to Bangkok to get a flight to London.

Looking down through the window Gypsy watched as Taiwan came into view as the dinner was being cleared away. The trolley with the fresh fruit and Swiss cheeses came by and served him, then he relaxed and looked out of the window as he got his first look, all be it from a great height, of a place that he wished to visit in the near future.

He had been in mainland China and he had been in Hong Kong a few times and he liked the people in neither place, he hoped that Taiwan would be different. Hong Kong was a nasty rat race and mainland China was a land of oppression and poverty. Taiwan housed the free Chinese, he hoped that they would be a happier people.

Forty minutes after the coast of Formosa had disappeared from view the plane started it's descent into Hong Kong's Kai Tak Airport. It was after dark when the lights of Hong Kong came into view. The wind was blowing the other way that night and the plane was going into its final approach via checkerboard alley (the notoriously dangerous final approach into the old Hong Kong airport. This was where 747's and other large aircraft would fly between narrow gaps between apartment blocks with the wing tips on either side of a jumbo being only a few metres away from the buildings on either side at times.

It was known as the toughest landing of any major international airport on earth. Pilots had to do extra training and take tests of all kinds, before being able to get the extra license that was required by law, for a pilot to be allowed to fly in or out of there).

The plane flew down towards the chequer board until it's markings came into view then banked hard right and flew down between the buildings. As Gypsy looked out of the window he could see the inside of many apartments flashing by as they passed building after building, he could see the washing hanging out to dry and people taking care of their daily lives as the jet rushed past. Then the plane leveled its wings as it made its final approach and then touched down on the runway at Kai Tak.

The steward equipped Gypsy with a doggy bag full of miniature bottles of Williams and then Gypsy disembarked from the best flight that he had ever had.

He went through passport control and picked up his case from the relevant carousel. Then after changing a Yen travelers cheque into Hong Kong dollars he was out of the airport and in a cab heading down to the end of the Kowloon peninsula.

Getting out of the cab at Chungking Mansions, he took the lift up to the sixteenth floor of "A" block. He checked in at Traveler's hostel and was allocated a bed in the overflow dorm on the fourteenth floor.

He dropped his dirty clothes that he had not had time to deal with in Tokyo at the twenty four hour laundry at the back of the ground floor shopping mall. Then he disappeared out through a labyrinth of alleys at the back of the mall to his favorite Chinese café, for a plate of his favorite steamed Chinese greens on a bed of egg noodles, topped with oyster sauce.

Then it was off to 'Ned Kelly's' for a few beers. The Jazz band was really giving it some that night, playing a non stop repertoire of raucous Dixieland jazz. Most of the people in the bar that night were people who did not live in Hong Kong but visited the place regularly. The thing that brought people to Ned Kelly's was the fantastic jazz band that played there. You had to like trad and Dixieland jazz to be there as it was blaring out loudly all night.

The next morning Gypsy headed off to the star ferry for a trip to the island. He had been given the name of a travel agent on Hong Kong Island and had been told by a friend that she was very good at her job. Gypsy found her office without any problems. Teresa Pang on the eleventh floor of the Dragon Seed Building on Queen street. He told her that he required a ticket to London for that night. She arranged it on the spot and got him on a Cathay Pacific flight leaving out of Kai Tak at nine thirty, that night. After taking the deposit she told him to come back and collect the ticket in the afternoon. So Gypsy took a bus to Stanley and spent much of the day swimming and relaxing on the beach. He had bought nice high quality gifts for the family at a shop that had been recommended to him in Tokyo. It sold only things that were traditionally Japanese.

In the late afternoon he took the bus back to central Hong Kong and collected his ticket, then crossed back to Kowloon, collected his laundry and went up to the fourteenth floor to collect his bags.

Taking a taxi to the airport shortly after dark, he checked in and went through to airside. He went and propped up one of the bars for the next hour and a half, and chatted with other expats and travelers while he waited to board his flight. It had been his best trip in and out of Hong Kong. Partly because it had been short and practical, partly because he now knew his way around and partly because he now had money and a good job and was not so stressed about such things as survival.

One thing that he liked about Hong Kong was that it felt like everyone was on the move. Even the ones who lived there seemed to travel a lot by air to other countries and many people he met, even the older ones gave the impression of being up to date on global current affairs and had on the ground experience in many counties.

It was mostly the older ones at the bar who were the most interesting to listen to. They had been travelling to and fro between many countries frequently over a long period of years and had deep insights to share about the undercurrents that moved events and phenomena in general. There was nearly always another story or stories underneath the so called information that was sold to the masses as news.

There were unseen hands that moved things for their own advantages and news services that willingly and unwilling covered for them. In Hong Kong though, people got to know about the layer upon layer of self interest that made up some of the facets of a news story.

Gypsy learned a lot by sitting and listening and asking questions of these people. Of course there was nothing quite like listening to a foreign office diplomat from one of the English speaking countries when one arrived at the bar, probably still jetlagged from the flight and now waiting for their onward connection.

Having just witnessed some act of international diplomatic madness, based solely on the geographic and cultural ignorance of the elected leaders of his country. The fellow would normally be seen sitting at the bar knocking back whiskeys or G and T's and cackling like a mad man as he rocked back and forward on his bar stool. Then he would start telling all who wished to listen about what he thought of the imbeciles that were the elected government in his country and their recent affronts to intelligence and common sense. His worst venom was usually saved for the "incompetant wanker" who had been put in charge of the foreign office. After a few drinks more the fellow would start to spill the beans on the background stories that made up the news. And as the fellow got more and more oiled so his tongue would loosen further. It was at these times that Gypsy got to find out what a filthy group of degenerates most politicians are and how many layers there can be to any one story.

At the very last minute before the gate was to be closed to his flight, Gypsy walked the approximately ten meters from his bar stool to the gate and headed down the tunnel to the plane.

The flight took off into what was to be a very long night. The airline was a super luxury one, even in economy, it was good and it had beautiful women from most of the different counties of East Asia, as it's hostesses. They had taken off at 10 p.m. but it was still very dark when they landed in Bahrain eight and a half hours later, to refuel. Very few if any people left or joined the flight. It was a fuel stop only. The first Generation 747, 100, - 200 and 300 series, could not make the hop from Europe to East Asia in one go without some serious modifications. It was obvious to Gypsy from what he could see as he looked out of the window that Bahrain was the gas station of choice for many airlines. At that time, of night it was like a who's who of East Asian and European flag carrier airlines. There was a line of air bridges with a plane parked at each of them, and there were yet more planes parked out on the apron. Not just that but as one left for the runway, another landed and came in to park. The only planes there were either 747's, DC10's or L10/11 Tri-Stars.

It must have been very cheap fuel there, as why else would everyone from Alitalia to British airways, KLM, Air France, Japan Airlines and Singapore airlines be landing 747's on a small barren desert island with not much of a population and nothing special to do there? Unless of course you were working at the rough end of the oil industry or in commercial services that were connected to it.

The flight took off again with the next stop being London Gatwick Airport.

"England couldn't be as lost and ridiculous as I remembered it as being", he thought to himself "my memory must be playing tricks with me. Nowhere else that I have been comes close to the level of pompous, ridiculous, madness that I remember the British as being so full of". In Asia there was always method in any madness that he had witnessed and the Europeans, Australians and the Kiwis always seemed like a decent, well balance friendly lot, on the whole. So why was it that he remembered the people of his country of origin as being such a bunch of frightened, insular uptight wankers with a propensity towards either snobbery or great ignorance which they wore like a badge of honor. The frightened little members of the aspiring classes all huddled together in their little England terrified of difference and change while trying to climb the social ladder by whatever means. They were a bit like the salary men of Tokyo but without the underlying wisdom and liberation of Zen Buddhism permeating their culture. "Nah it couldn't be that fucked up or ridiculous, my memory must be playing tricks on me" he reasoned. He lay back and tried to get some sleep as they sped on through the night towards London.

Dawn came as they were looking down on Austria, then an hour and a half later, after breakfast had been served and cleared away, the plane started its descent as the English channel came into view.

Gypsy was looking down on the rolling chalk hills of South East England and the villages that lay in their folds. The memories came flooding back, "Oh no, he thought to himself it is as crazy as I remember it being, the villages are more how I remember them than I remember them. It was as if somewhere over the English chanel they had passed through some sort of weird cloud that had transported them all into another dimension which had its own independent reality and where many people's grip of what constituted as truth or reality was severely challenged. Even some of the ones that had travelled seemed to see everything through the prison of their British upbringing. Part of the problem was the media, which worked twenty four hours a day to keep them uninformed, brainwashed, greedy, dissatisfied and arrogant. You couldn't tell them anything, they knew so much. After all they had read it in the papers or seen it on the television, here in the land of Murdochstan.

The plane touched down, taxied and then docked at the terminal. Gypsy was soon off the plane and heading with the crowds through the tunnels towards the emigration desks.

At the carousels there was evidence to suggest that the baggage handlers had been visiting the free take away again. Locks had been busted off of some of the large trunks that expats favored when shipping home. It most likely happened at Gatwick as Kai Tak was more heavily watched and patrolled in that area of the airport.

Gypsy's bag looked far too rough for any self respecting, thieving, luggage handler to want to break into it. So he collected it and wandered out of the controlled, area to go and find his father who had come to the airport to collect him. Even then, they gave him a pull at customs and asked him all sorts of questions even after he had got his haircut in Hong Kong and bought new jeans and a new t-shirt for the trip back to London. He hardly ever got pulled in Asia so why did they always pull him at London? Could it be that it was a criminal offence to be under the age of thirty five and not have that brain washed stare in his eyes that so many of them had, on this bizarre, sad little island. Indeed, it was somewhat scary to think, that in the not so distant past this nation had controlled the biggest empire to have ever ruled on earth, it didn't say much for the rest of humanity.

He met his father at the arrivals gate and Gypsy started to recount his travels, and adventures as his father drove them to the family home on the south coast. When he had been younger his father had had a go at him for not getting a formal education. Now he showed his father his work contract for his job in Japan, stating that he was a senior high school lecturer at a Japanese high school.

He had been disgusted by what he had experienced in the name of education when he was a child, growing up in England and didn't want to be around the likes of such narrow minded and ignorant people again.

They arrived at the family home and after greeting his mother he brought out the presents, that included, a set of lacquer food bowls, chopsticks and holders, Japanese dried food products a kimono dressing gown for his mother, plus a couple of jade lions that he had bought for them while in Kunming in China.

He had never seen his slides projected onto a screen at that time so he borrowed a projector and screen from his grandfather and gave the whole family a slide show with a narrative about the journey.

The quality of a good portion of the slides was good and clear and well focused. To look at the photos of China you would think that he had even liked the place.

The slide show was a hit with the family and they asked him to give a showing to other members of the family and to their friends.

There was a party in the garden, either for the staff on the nursery or to raise money for some local village cause.

One of his brother's friends from when he had been at school was D.J. for the event. And even he could not resist taking the piss out of the lame naivety of the mainstream public who were attending the event. People would ask Gypsy what he was doing and what he had been up to and where he was living. Some got it and possibly wished it was them that was out there having adventures. But most of them looked at him as if he was speaking Swahili or Chinese when he answered them. He could sense by the look in their eyes that circuits inside of their head were blowing as their programming wasn't formulated in such a way as to be able to hear stories of this nature. It was too frightening to imagine for most of them.

Gypsy had shown them that outside of the confines of little England there were places where he too could succeed in ways that they could not begin to imagine. Not just that but his on the ground geographic, historical and political knowledge was growing rapidly.

One day shortly after arriving in England he was speaking with his father over lunch and saying how he would be reluctant to fly with a Japanese airline as the Japanese approach to things did not bode well for a good aviation maintenance and repair regime. Things would be done by the book but only by the book. The Japanese were a nation of yes men and none of them wanted to get the blame for pointing out a potential problem. In the field of aircraft maintenance that is a very unfortunate and potentially fatal character trait to have.

Later that afternoon on the news well after the conversation had occurred. It was announced that a Japan airlines short range 747 had crash into mountains outside of Tokyo. It soon came out that the accident was as a result of poor maintenance procedures in the parts replacement department.

"See what I mean" would not have been the right thing to say at such a time, had he been in Tokyo. But he was in England and was glad that he had flown to England via Hong Kong on a non Japanese airline.

Not much else happened on the trip to England and apart from a foray into London to get a Japanese one year commercial visa, he stayed mostly with the family.

Everything looked different to him now, he was looking at everything through different eyes. He had discovered much on his travels, not least the inner teachings of Hinduism and in some ways felt like he was looking out at the place that he had come from with the eyes of an Asian. He felt, thankfully disconnected from it and tried to keep it that way.

The three weeks soon passed and it was time to hop on the plane back to Hong Kong.

His parents had told him that they were planning to take a walking holiday in Nepal and Gypsy said that he would see what he could do in order to join them for it. He had already spent three weeks in Nepal and knew that although it was a charming beautiful and enchanted land it also had a dark side to it too. He had been aware of heavy undercurrents while there and thought it would be better if he joined them as he already had a better knowledge than them of the local ways and customs.

As he waited in the departure lounge at Gatwick for his flight to be called, he felt deeply sad for his family, being stuck in such a limited society with it's pompous idiot views. It was hard to imagine that anyone could find their way to spiritual liberation while their head was stuck in the psyche of little England. He was really happy that his parents were going to take a holiday in the subcontinent, but also a little apprehensive for them. As far as he could make out, no one who ever went to the area was ever the same when they returned to their homeland. The sort of changes that could occur to someone on a visit to the Subcontinent tended to be of the permanent kind. The most common way that such changes were induced often involved deep emotional trauma, and who could know what kind of awareness raising tricks the spirits of the place may have in store for some one. Though he wanted his parents to be able to see the world with a clearer and wider field of vision, he was worried for their safety, none the less and wanted to be in Nepal with them as so as he could watch out for them.

He felt empty and without direction as he waited to board his flight. He had some money in his pocket that he had saved from working in Japan and most of all he had proved that English mantra of "Oh you can't beat the system" to be totally wrong. He was doing just that as he worked in Japan. He viewed it as his unpaid job to try to help free the minds of his students from the fear of standing out or of being a unique individual. He was a living example that freedom does not need to be seen as being in the way of success. He did things in a way like no other teacher and was friendly and understanding when asked to help or explain something. He knew that for some students it could be difficult to grasp and memorize some things. He knew because it had been the same for him at some subjects when he was at school.

He boarded his flight and soon they were taxi-ing off out to the runway. The plane took off and headed out in a south easterly direction towards Bahrain. Again it was a comfortable flight. Just across the Isle from Gypsy was sat the most stunningly beautiful ex air hostess and her two boisterous young children. Gypsy got chatting with her then one of the children piped in "our daddy is flying the plane today" the woman looked quite embarrassed and said "yes, it's true but they are not meant to go around telling everyone" "well it makes me feel all that more safe knowing that the captain has got his family onboard with him" Gypsy replied.

Seven hours later the plane began it's decent into Bahrain airport, it was just after mid day. The airport apron was almost empty except for two L10/11 Tristars, one with British Airways markings and the other being in the colors of the local airline, Gulf Air. The outside temperature was somewhere in the mid forties and the terminal was almost deserted apart for the Hong Kong bound passengers. An hour later they reboarded the plane and were joined by eight Philippinos, each one carrying a huge, brand new ghetto blaster over his shoulder. They were heading home for their annual holiday having just done a year's hard labor in the deserts of Arabia. The refueled plane with a fresh crew operating it, taxied out to the runway and took off in the direction of Hong Kong. It had been the longest night on his way to England. Now on the way back it was the longest day as they flew in an easterly direction.

Seven hours later the plane started it's descent into Hong Kong and once again descended into checker board alley for a low level close up tour of the Tower blocks. they rounded the turn straightened up and touched down smoothly.

Gypsy was soon once again riding down Nathan road in a cab, back to Chungking Mansions.

At the hostel John Catchpole was still occupying his same dorm bed that he had been sleeping on for the past so many years. Not just that but Gypsy found out that in the 14th floor dorm the old Danish fellow who had occupied the bed in the corner had been there for some eight years and there was a young Irish woman who also had been occupying a dorm bed for the best part of a year. Either it was that Hong Kong had some strange effect on some people and made them feel that there was nothing wrong with living in such a way for a period of years, or they were part of some strange coven who maybe used the roof of Chungking Mansions 'A' block for their wild, debauched and sexually depraved, meetings. The cult of the Hong Kong dorm sleepers, it would be the sort of thing that maybe Steven King would write a horror story about.

The weather was muggy, heavy and overcast the next day as Gypsy went out to find some breakfast. Well that put paid to any idea of going to the beach.

His dope connection on the lower floors of "A" block had been busted and the gold smuggling work into Kathmandu had become too dangerous to even contemplate.

However, there was the Indian Restaurant "Nanak Mess" and "Ned Kellys last stand" to enjoy.

The queue at the lift on the sixteenth floor of "A" block was at its level worst, so once again Gypsy got some exercise, running down some sixteen flights of steps of the emergency exit.

He had a ticket back to Tokyo that included a three day stop in Taiwan. He had a boring, uneventful three days in Hong Kong and then he was back at Kai Tak waiting for his flight to Taipei.

As dusk fell the passengers were bussed out on to the apron to board the "China airlines" flight. They taxied out to the runway and took off. A quick dinner was served then An hour later they descended into Chang kai Chek airport some sixty kilometers outside of Taipei.

The massive airport had been built some years before when America treated Taiwan as one of it's best friends in East Asia. It was now something of a white elephant since the government of the United States had down graded it's diplomatic relations with the nation and started sucking China's cock instead. Taiwan had since become the land that diplomats and governments liked to try to forget existed. It stood like a thorn in their side, as a reminder of their rank hypocrisy every time a western politician got up for a good old rant about how much they valued freedom and democracy.

Gypsy took a bus into the city. He had the address of a cheap hostel in Taipei that he planned to stay at. After a one hour ride from the airport he dropped off of the bus several blocks from where it was located. All of the signs were only in Chinese and so it was difficult to find his way. As he walked he passed by several different barbershops. There were things about these barbers shops that had Gypsy thinking "now what's going on here then? Something just not right"

The chairs were just that little bit too fancy, the floor was covered in a thick pile silk carpet and there were heavy velvet pull around curtains for each chair "That was a strange way for a barbers shop to look" thought Gypsy to himself, "looks more like a pimps palace than a barber's shop."

At the hostel the other travelers were a much more relaxed and laid back crowd than the ones that he had shared space with in either Hong Kong or Tokyo. Some of them were working in Taipei and some were looking for work. Though Gypsy was going back to his job in Tokyo he wanted to know what options were available in Taiwan for teaching work.

It looked like a promising place with plenty of well paid work and a low cost of living. Not just that but the foreigners living and working there were a different crowd. For one they were less stresses than the Tokyo crowd but had the good sense to realize that there would be less competition from other foreigners in a less obvious country to travel in like Taiwan.

Since China opened up to the rest of the world in the nineteen seventies Taiwan has been treated by most Asian and European countries as a political non entity allowing only a diplomatic interests office to be opened in their countries by Taiwan, in their slobbering lust to lick up to China and get their hands on that huge market of potentially 1.3 billion consumers to sell their respective national products to.

Never mind that Taiwan was at that time heading rapidly towards democracy, becoming a fully fledged democracy in the late nineteen eighties. It became so democratic in fact that their parliament featured such entertainments as politicians resorting to fisticuffs and brawling in the lower house, in their passion to get their message across. It is indeed nice to see politicians doing physical damage to each other, rather than getting the Police or the armed forces to do it to some hapless minority group or the people in general, as what happens still to this day in mainland China. In this regard Taiwan leads the world in sane and balanced politics, being at times like a real life punch and Judy show.

Gypsy asked one of the travelers who had been in Taiwan for a while about the curious looking barbershops that he had seen. A big grin spread across the traveler's face. Go on what's the joke? I mean the places do give the impression that they are set up for sex, it's just the fact that they are so damned public and the barber shop set up that I don't get" said Gypsy.

"They are hand job and blow job centres" said the other traveller. "You can go in and get a hair cut and shave and get a blow job or a wank while you're sitting there getting it done."

The traveler said that he had also worked in South Korea and they also had the same kind of barber shops that also had young women providing extra services. He recounted with mirth an incident when another traveller came back to the hostel complaining about how Koreans view things and what they think of as normal.

He had gone for a visit to one such barber shop for some stimulation and been welcomed in and requested to sit down in one of the luxury, velvet, barber shop chairs. A curtain was pulled around the area where he was sitting, the chair reclined right back and a wet towel placed over his eyes. He had ordered a head massage and a wank. But then he felt a particularly rough hand around his prick and so had pushed the towel away and opened his eyes, to see the owner of the establishment, a man in his mid fifties, with his hand around his cock. Pushing the man away in total disgust he asked him what the hell he thought he was doing. The owner apologized, saying "very sorry, all woman busy now, I think you not want to wait."

The food that Gypsy found in Taiwan was not much to his taste but he liked the people. They were busy, just like in any other first world country (Taiwan was becoming or had become a first world country by that time) but also they were friendly and polite, even though many of them spoke no English. Most of all they were, from what he could make out, generally a happy people. Certainly when compared with the people of mainland China with their oppressed, no hope lives, but also when compared with the Hong Kong Chinese, who lived in cramped overcrowded apartment blocks and worked long hours in factories with Dickensian ideas about how to treat their employees. In Hong Kong at that time, some of the people's extra foul moods could be accounted for by the fact that there were several tens of thousands of people who lived close by if not right under the second aerial approach into Kai Tak (The first being over the sea). Which meant that every time the wind was blowing the wrong way there would be a stream of thundering great metal monsters passing by their windows and balconies at a rate of up to one every three minutes, they were that close that they could possibly throw a stone from their apartment window and hit the wing of a passing plane, the ground would shake below and the apartment would feel like it was being hit by an earthquake every time a plane went past, no one could hear themselves think, let alone hold a conversation. Imagine trying to sleep in such circumstances.

Though it was also very industrial, Taiwan was not overcrowded and the quality of life was in many ways much higher than that of Hong Kong. The international airport was sixty kilometres out of Taipei. So there were no people being sent crazy from living in housing estates near by it.

The interior of the island was mountainous, which made it unfit either for agriculture or industry and as such it was treated more like a national park than anything else, indeed some of the area was devoted to national parks. There were also several indigenous aboriginal tribes who lived in the jungles in the centre of the island.

Taiwan for those who don't know, became a separate country from China when the Nationalist Ku Min Tang government under their leader Chang Kai Chek fled from China and took all loyal troops and their political followers with them when they fled to the island of Formosa in the late nineteen forties. The island, located roughly one hundred kilometers from the cost of mainland China was then renamed Taiwan. They had been totally routed by the communist peasant hordes but they still had one very good trick up their sleeve.

They had taken with them almost the entirety of China's national gold reserves. Now, with a vastly smaller country and a reduced population with a high percentage of educated people among them, they first used the gold to equip their armed forces, turning the island into a fortress. Then they spent large amounts of the wealth on developing a strong business friendly infrastructure, which in turn set the ball rolling for them to become the manufacturing hub that they are.

In the time after the communist revolution when Taiwan was a nationalist dictatorship, America viewed Taiwan as it number one most trusted friend in the region. Which was why such a huge airport had been built outside of Taipei, in anticipation of the coming hordes of Americans. Also the nationalist government, gave their small nation the official title of 'The Republic of China.' Then in the early nineteen seventies Mao invited Nixon to a meeting in Beijing or Peking as it was known then. After the meeting and the setting up of diplomatic relations, with George Bush senior as the first U.S. ambassador to communist China, Taiwan was dropped like a political hot potato and the massive airport at Taipei looked like it did not belong. America was forced to down grade its diplomatic ties with Taiwan, in order to open full diplomatic relations with mainland China. Under huge pressure from the massively powerful business lobby in Washington who wanted access to the huge untapped market in China the American government were tweaked into behaving in a most dishonorable way to a very staunch ally.

Obviously there were still deep military and trade ties between the U.S and Taiwan but all deals were then done in a covert and quiet manner. Taiwan still had deep ties with the Americans which could be seen by how many flights leave out of Taipei each day destined for cities in North America. However one thing that all U.S presidents would climb mountains to avoid would be a joint press conference on the white house lawn with the leader of "The Republic of China" which would cause much wailing and gnashing of teeth in the great hall of the people in Beijing.

It was indeed unfortunate that China chose Confucius as the one who's teachings they took to heart the most.

They might have been very much better served by Lao Tzu, the founder of Daoism which at its core is very much the same as Buddhism. Though Buddhist teachings state that life is pain and suffering and that there is no hope of making much in this world, as everybody dies, it's adherents have a tendency towards far greater happiness and contentment than the followers of Marx or that silly old fool Confucius, could ever dream of.

Well there's the rub, because in Taiwan much of the population were Buddhist and Daoist so much so that there were a number of vegetarian restaurants that did brisk business, as even the most casually observant Buddhists would take the family out for at least one vegetarian meal in a month.

Taipei was like many other bustling cities in East Asia but unlike most of the other cities it had not much in the way of defining features apart from the Chang Kai Chek memorial which although it was pleasant with gardens around it was new and not so spectacular in any way like the Hong Kong Skyline or the incredible temples of India, Thailand or Japan. Nor was it's geography and natural landscape anything special not like Quilin or Singapore or Penang.

The buildings were modern and shabby. The city was essentially a concrete jungle with everything written in Mandarin.

Gypsy decided to go and visit the Hare Krishna temple in Taipei and see if the temple president who he had met in Hong Kong and who had extended an invitation to him, was around.

He took a taxi, armed with a piece of paper with the address written in Mandarin. Though the driver could speak no English he was friendly and helpful as were most of the people he had met so far on his short visit.

The temple was several kilometres out of the city in a pleasant suburb where people more commonly had houses rather than apartments. It was in a house in a side street.

He was welcomed in at the door by a Chinese devotee. The American that he had met in Hong Kong was there and they sat and talked. Gypsy told him what had transpired at the ashram on Cebu.

He turned to Gypsy and said "yes there has been some trouble at the Cebu ashram with the new temple president." Apparently, everywhere that he had been he had ended up in conflict with everyone. So in order to keep everyone at the Australian and New Zealand temples and farms happy they had bought him a one way ticket to Manila (and of course Cebu), put a glowing report in his top pocket, merrily gave him a lift to the airport and went home and got out the balloons, cakes and ice creams.

Gypsy could not help but wonder if it was a sister Josephine game that was going on (sister Josephine Was the name of a song by the British guitarist and singer/songwriter Jake Thackery. The song was about a burly bank robber who on the run from the forces of Laura Norda disguised himself as a nun and went to ground in a convent. The song was sung from the angle of the police telling the mother superior that the nun was in fact a male bank robber in disguise, and she in her innocence, having a hard time believing it, while all the time wondering about little things she had seen the fake nun doing, such as leaving the seat stood up on end after using the toilet). After all he still had his Hells Angels tattoo, he hadn't had it covered up. Of course he may have pissed off his local chapter as badly as he pissed off everyone else who he had met.

It would be a pretty comical sight to imagine them telling him that in order to survive with his life unscathed he would have to go and join the Hare Krishnas for three years, that would be to really take the piss out of someone, but it was not past credulity to imagine him pissing off the 1% biker fraternity enough for them to vent their humor on him in such a way.

The temple had only five or six monks in residence and specialized in the translation and printing of books. It was the more mature and sober approach to their spiritual path that Gypsy noticed the most about the monks at the temple. They weren't a bunch of manic street preachers and instead did what a person is meant to do with their religion or spiritual path and internalized it. Gypsy also noticed that Buddhism also played a part at this temple and apart from images of Krishna and Rahdarani and Lord Chaitanya Maha Prabu there was also a Buddha diety in the Temple room.

He thought that it was the Buddhist influence that he liked the most about the temple. They were certainly a more balanced and serene group than any that he had encountered in either the Philippines or Australia.

All of this was fuelling his growing interest in Buddhism. With the Hare Krishnas the vast majority of what they were saying could be seen to be true, but when they wanted to talk about descriptions of the heavenly realms and planets in the higher heavens or in the spiritual realms, it put Gypsy off.

Buddhism had less writing on such subjects and concerned itself instead with giving people instruction on techniques for stilling the mind as so as the adherents could reach such a point of clarity and objectivity that the truth could find space enough to reveal itself to them. It did not require the adherent to believe in some second, third, forth or umpteenth hand account of someone else's story. Just they need to have faith enough that the techniques themselves are an effective way in which to be able to reach a point of clarity and balanced objectivity. The truth cannot reveal itself to a cluttered mind.

Gypsy's thoughts when he had time to stop and think, normally turned to matters spiritual, he was intensely aware of life's impermanence and desired more than anything else to get a glimpse beyond the clouds of illusion that brought such great sadness to both human and animal (and no doubt plant) existence on this planet. What didn't make sense at all in his mind was the incredible weeping, wailing and sorrow that so often accompanied someone's death in so many of the societies of this world.

Everyone has to die it is guaranteed, just like breathing, eating, sleeping and shitting so why the great sorrow?

Tribal societies tended to view a funeral as a send off and a birth whether human or animal as a welcome back. Western societies make much of their progress in matters material, with their advanced technologies. But they still cannot stop death. They can delay it but not by so many years and even if they could still do more and increase life expectancy up to say a thousand years it would still be as nothing in the great scheme of things and life could still be viewed as a bird flying through a barn and our lives being the time the bird took to fly in through the front doors of the barn and out of the back doors.

For this reason most of all he was intensely interested to find the ultimate truth. He knew that a part of him, the most important part, his awareness was eternal, he could feel it as could anyone if they stop what they are doing for long enough to truly still their minds.

No one ever, deep down inside has ever felt that there was a time that they did not exist or that there will be a time in the future when they do not exist. The two concepts are unimaginable. Yes, we may cease to exist in this dimension just as we cease to exist in a room when we walk out of it. But no one cries on the whole when we leave a room, even if we return dressed in different clothes and new haircut.

The three main religions of the west are of the Semitic kind. Which is to say that they are not based so much on a personal journey to the truth as they are on a mass forced belief system that leads to making its adherents feel guilty and disempowered. It makes their brain go into contortions to accommodate the somewhat stretched and twisted stories that their priests lay upon them. Guilt is laid upon them for the unstoppable natural cravings that their bodies have, especially sex. If it is so terrible then why would a god make it in to such a totally unstoppable force?

Celibacy was not something that many people could achieve. Even the one's who had maybe got there were sometimes grouchy and bad

409

tempered it didn't look so much like a tool that worked for people so much as an easy stick to beat them with.

Though Gypsy prayers to know the truth had been answered by "Hare Krishna John" he could see that the followers of the Hare Krishna path were possibly missing some of the facets that made up the whole picture. The beautiful logical and simple uncluttered path of Buddhism now had Gypsy more than a little interested

Here in Taipei, was the most relaxing of all the Hare Krishna temples that he had ever been in and he liked the Chinese devotees for the deep and sincere humility that they demonstrated but there was still this one thing bugging him. He imagined for just one moment that he was god looking down upon the earth. He could see large groups of people dancing around statues of himself in order to grovel up to him as so as to be freed of their horrible earthly existence. Then he listened to their constant prayers asking for things. Why would a god want this? If they were to do something to truly make him happy rather than making him feel like vomiting then he would rather that they go and demonstrate kindness, compassion, empathy and understanding to all of the other suffering beings around them and got on at turning their habitat into a fitting place to invite him to. A place where fear, loneliness, arrogance and snobbery had been replaced by love, kindness, wisdom and compassion. He certainly wouldn't want them building temples, churches, mosques and synagogues in which to go and make mass hypocritical grovellings within.

For one thing people who grovel in such a way are rarely sincere and would put a knife in the back of who ever their god was, the moment his or her back was turned. The argument for the worship of a god in a temple was already lost as far as Gypsy was concerned.

If someone really wished to serve a god, they would do it by showing kindness and compassion to their fellow beings as it is only when everyone takes this attitude that people can even begin to know what it is that would make a god of goodness happy. There would be no time for prancing around idols or singing songs in disempowered voices. We would all be far too busy giving real service as everyone becomes concerned with making sure that no one is lonely or being left out or excluded. It would be the one thing that might help to turn the lights on, so to speak.

Gypsy left the temple and headed back to the hostel. Yes he had liked the vibe at that temple, but it had been the Buddha vibe that had set it apart from all of the other Hare Krishna temples that he had ever visited.

The next day Gypsy headed back out to the airport for his flight back to Tokyo. He had liked Taiwan, even though it was an industrial country with no great sights to visit and photograph and not so much to do if you weren't working. However, it had something that he had not seen before and wanted to see. It had happy and generally pleasant people living in it which was living proof that the majority of Chinese people could probably be happy and centered if they had both education and freedom possibly also having their lives grounded in a good practical spiritual path like Daoism or Buddhism would also help.

He checked in and walked through the massive and almost empty airport to the departure gate where a china airlines jumbo was parked and waiting.

It took only three hours for the flight to Haneda, which was Tokyo's domestic airport. The only international airline to use this airport was the Taiwan national flag carrier "Air China" due to Chinese sensitivities and infantile temper tantrums. The only way that the Chinese airline was going to agree to a reciprocal flight arrangement with the Japanese carriers was if the Taiwanese airline was not invited to move to the new international airport at Narita.

The flight landed and after the usual routine of form filling and rubber stamps Gypsy was out and on his way to Yoshida house. The good thing about Haneda airport was that it was hooked up to the Tokyo metro system, so getting back to his abode was an easy and relatively short journey.

He went to the school a few days before the start of the new term and used the duplicating machine.

In England he had chatted with a neighbor who was an English teacher who worked with foreign students. From the ideas he had gained in that conversation he had got to work on a new course that was to run through the next term, and now he was busy printing it up, ready for the new term to begin.

At Yoshida house others were also returning from their summer breaks. Heidi, a German woman who had been partly raised in England and Northern Ireland and spoke absolutely perfect English with a mixed, English Irish and Deutsch accent, had just come back from a break on the Philippine island of Palawan. She had got to make friends with the local pirates and would spend time both with them and alone on an uninhabited island that she had found and liked.

Heidi had worked for the press, both in England and Northern Ireland. She told Gypsy and others about how very censored the British press was. On one occasions she had been reporting and recording events as some trouble erupted in front of her. She faithfully recorded what she had seen, where a group of innocent non combatants had got caught in the crossfire of a gun battle between the police and the IRA. She then dispatched the report to her paper. She had been at a vantage point which allowed her to see everything but she had done one thing wrong. She had not waited for the official police version of events to be posted. Her version of events differed from theirs and so they took her to court and sued her. This goes some way to explaining why the police in not so great Britain and Northern Ireland are called Cuntstables.

She spoke about how Prince Charles and Lady Diana's marriage had been an arranged one (this was seven years or so before it came out in the British press) and spoke about the inside stories that made up much of the news and about the kind of restrictions on reporting there were in the UK.

Another of the characters that lived at Yoshida house was Ken, he was a dealer in Japanese art antiques. He was covered in oriental tattoos and had served in the American army in Vietnam. He told of a time that he had found a recent newspaper at a place that he was temporarily based at. On the front page there was a picture of President Nixon, part of a speech that he had just given was printed beneath it.

In the speech, he had given his absolute word that he would never send American soldiers into Cambodia and there was Ken standing reading the paper at a fire base in Cambodia.

Ken knew his way around in East Asia and had been in the area for a long time. He told a story of an incident that had happened to him recently at a water park in Tokyo.

The only people in Japan who would commonly have a tattoo on their body would be a member of the Yakuza. So at the water park, dressed in only his swimming trunks and with his body covered in tattoos Ken kind of stood out and no doubt attracted some curious and maybe frightened stares. Everyone in Japan it would appear was frightened or should I say terrified of the Yakuza. For very much the large part they were above the law, even to the extent that if two rival gangs were having a battle in one area the godfather or their spokesmen might get up on a local television channel and warn the public to stay out of the area until it was over.

Emperor Meiji may have gotten rid of the samurai rule during his reformation one hundred and fifty or so years before but the Samurai lived on as the Yakuza who also lived and worked within a strict code of honor.

Ken was standing in line behind some twenty thousand or so others waiting to use the showers when some Japanese men who were also covered in tattoos came up to him and started talking with him. They were part of the local branch of the Yakuza. They liked his tattoos which were mostly intricate copies of designs from Japanese antique objects de art. They invited him to join them and together they walked to the front of the massive queue. At the front everyone stepped aside to let them through, other people got out of the shower quickly and no one else came in until they had all finished.

The Yakuza it was said had little respect for most of the people of Japan as everyone was so frightened of them. But they seemed to like many of the westerners who were a people with a big enough set of balls to sit down and drink with them and speak with them in the same manner as they would speak with anybody else that they might meet along the way. However, it needs to be said that, a foreigner in Japan is often someone who has been travelling for a while, Japan is not viewed by many as a country for tourism due to the fact that it neither has tropical beaches nor cheap beer. The travelers that had made it to Japan were a hard core bunch on the whole. They were there to work or trade and they were generally people of an open minded nature who were not easily shaken.

Ken made friends with some of the Yakuza men and was invited by them to their night clubs. Other westerners had recounted similar tales of Yakuza being not only friendly with them but also taking them along drinking with them.

A good looking Japanese woman moved into Yoshida house, her name was Yoko, it was pretty obvious what she wanted and soon it was Ken that she wanted it from. She was soon to be seen with him everywhere that he went until she just plain and simple moved in with him. Lucky Ken he couldn't have found a better looking or sweeter natured woman if he had gone out looking. Prior to meeting her he said that his plan for retirement was to move to the golden triangle to an area that had no roads. There he would have his own harem of Shan hill tribe women who would also be his body guards and he would have his own private ganja and opium patches where he could grow enough for personal consumption.

Now no doubt if Yoko was planning to stick around with him for any length of time his plans for old age may have to change.

Two members of the nasty Israeli bitch association had pissed off the other non Israeli residents of Yoshida house yet again.

There was just one Japanese resident at the place other than Yoko. He was based in Tokyo temporarily while he worked at the SKUBA EXPO which was still on going at that time. He had brought two complementary free tickets home with him for one Swiss guy who had asked him if it was at all possible to get such a thing. The Swiss guy got on really well with the Japanese fellow and it would be safe to say that the two of them had become good friends.

When the two nasty bitches got to hear that he had two free tickets for the expo to give to his friend they went to his room and bullied, cajoled and nagged him until he gave up the tickets. He was a shy Japanese man from a polite culture where no one could dream or even imagine that someone could behave in such a thoughtless foul, selfish and invasive way. He had been stunned and shocked by their manner which was how they had managed to wrestle the tickets from him.

One British couple lived above a room containing an Israeli bitch infestation and so every afternoon when the bitches were sleeping before going to work the British man would do his exercises skipping with a rope, which would cause the room below to vibrate and shake, stopping the nasty little tarts from being able to sleep. The more they would complain the more he would Endeavour to give them a headache. When they came up to his room knocking on the door complaining he would open it and tell them straight to their faces "While you all have been living at Yoshida house you have behaved with an arrogance and total lack of regard to anyone else but yourselves, you have pissed everyone else off to the point that everyone here hates you all. When anyone dares to complain about your behavior you have the audacity and cheek to accuse them of being anti-Semitic and now you want me to respect your sleep time when you have failed to respect my sleep time by having your stereos on and blaring loud rock music into the early hours of the morning when I asked you to turn it down you told me to fuck off. So now you can fuck off because I'm going to keep on jumping up and down until I'm sure that I've given you a nice big headache like the one you gave me, the other night."

Back at work Gypsy had his new program up and running at the high school. Still he would leave either just before or after lunch each day and run to the railway station. He would then head on down the Seibu line to the final stop at Ikebukoro, where if he had not had time to eat at the school he would stop at a "stand up and eat" noodle stand and have a plate of iced noodles and a tempura before running along to catch his next train. It was his very favorite Japanese dish. Iced noodles served on top of a bamboo mat in a square shaped lacquer bowl, with slices of Nori, spring unions, a dollop of wasabi and a dip made up of soy and Worcester sauce, then he would have a vegetable tempura with it. It tasted so good that he would have had an extra plate of it if indeed he had had the time and not been in such a hurry.

The next journey would take him ten stops down the line where he would change to another train for the ride to Omiya, where he taught the monsters. Actually to say he taught them much would be a bit of a lie. He tried, in fact he tried really hard but some of these kids had not only lived and learned in America but seemed to have also learned a lot from watching Tom and Jerry, Woody Woodpecker and beep beep Road runner cartoons. It was all that Gypsy could do to try to keep a façade of order in the classroom in the absence of the parent's permission to dangle them upside down outside of the fourth floor windows by one leg.

Even in England he had never seen such ill behaved brats. The trouble was that their parents were paying for their kids to be there, this was Japan, a place where it does not pay to rock the boat. There was nothing much Gypsy could do except to try to stop the little terrors from hurting themselves, each other or somebody else and to make sure the room and its equipment did not get damaged.

After this extended torture session he would jump on a train back to central Tokyo, the train would after some fifteen stations, join the Yamenota line and Gypsy would get down after another eight or ten stations at Tamachi.

He would then walk to the bowling alley and teach the little girl her English. As ever she would fall asleep as he tried to teach her and after some time he just didn't have the heart to wake her any more, the poor kid was knackered. He needed to tell someone that this poor kid was being over crammed and that trying to teach her in this state was inhuman, but who could he go to? In the end he decided that he needed to pass a message back to Mr. Oneida about this.

His next class was the salary men. They had taken to taking Gypsy to their favorite bar where they all kept their own personal bottles of whisky on the shelf with their names on them.

Then they would start trying to engage Gypsy in that favorite Japanese game of "let's see it we can get the Gaijin drunk."

So the class with the salary men would be more enjoyable now that they all wanted to pour whisky down his throat. But Gypsy couldn't afford to let it go too far as his working day was still not over. To the consternation of the salary men Gypsy would sometimes revert to soft drinks to stop himself from getting pissed and then he would walk out of the bar in a straight line while they would stagger and wobble out of the door and wait until they thought that he was not watching before wrenching up in the gutter.

Gypsy could not afford to waste time and would head back to the station and take a train in the direction of Omoto Sando where he had to be by 8 p.m. to work in the conversation lounge.

He got there early one day and the owner asked him about a troubled teenager in his family, up north in Hokkaido and said that they had found a special school for children with special needs that they were thinking of sending him to. He asked for Gypsy's opinion.

Gypsy said that if he was that troubled then it would probably be better for him to be somewhere other than his present school and maybe this other school could possibly do him good, but until they see the new school and are sure that it is a good place it would be good to keep all the options on the table.

After an evening of discussing everything and nothing he would leave the conversation lounge at around 11pm at which point he had seen enough of the Tokyo metro system and would walk the two or three kilometres to Ikebukaro and go to the Red Onion bar for a couple of drinks with Jim, Tim and the others before heading back to Oyzumi Gakoen to go and crash out. He was running like a Japanese salary man with virtually no full days off of work. The stress was starting to take it's toll on him.

He made friends with one of the Americans who also worked for Mr. Oneida's agency. The guy was friendly and Gypsy figured him to be a stoner even before he made Gypsy an offer to supply him with some top quality Hawaiian weed. The price was unbelievably cheap for Tokyo and at first Gypsy was suspicious. But after the first deal proved to be sweet Gypsy bought more and started to supply a few friends with it. He was scoring at ¥1000 per gram, which at that time amounted to four U.S. dollars. He passed it on to his friends at eight dollars, which was still below the wholesale rate in Japan, but still Jim bitched about the price and thought Gypsy was screwing him.

The process of picking the stuff up was intricate, as in the crammed confines of Tokyo eyes could be watching from anywhere and it was extremely heavy for those who got caught. People also would have no hesitation about calling the cops if they knew what was going on.

So they would meet down a dark alley in a non descript part of the city, far from where either of them lived. They would step into the shadows, scan their surroundings quickly then without anyone being able to see them they would quickly exchange packets and then each leave the alley by a different exit.

Gypsy would then quickly jump into the first taxi that he could find and go to a station somewhere on the Seibu line. It was only when he was sure that the coast was clear that he would jump onto a train back to Oyzumi Gakoen and walk home.

Some of the western women who came to Japan to make the fortune that they needed for their next great adventure where of the wildest type. Even though some of them were ultra beautiful, like Heidi, they were strong and could hold their own on the road, just like the men who travelled. And just like the men they also conducted their sex lives mainly with the locals in the places where they were living.

There was a Canadian woman who Gypsy had met somewhere along the way, either via a female friend or at a bar where the expats and travelers hung out. She had hitched rides across Tibet on local trucks. Entering Tibet via the northern overland route from China via Golmud, she had made her way down to Lhasa and then had travelled on further, south to Shigatze and from there she had made her way west and then eventually north and up into the Uigher region around Kashgar. She had travelled on her own but said the Tibetans had been most kind and helpful.

She had had affairs and one night stands' with a few of them along the way and spoke of the journey fondly. She also travelled in other areas of the world and was more at home on the road than ever she was in the place where she had come from.

One Saturday night she and Gypsy decided to do an all night bar crawl covering many of the areas that they liked, around the city.

Starting at 'Maggie's revenge' which was an Australian bar in Akasaka and then moving to Kabukicho, which was Tokyo's version of Soho in London or Pat Pong in Bangkok, before ending up at some place on the other side of Shinjuku. In between this they also went and saw a midnight showing of some new horror flick called "Phenomena." It was just to prove that Tokyo never sleeps, it never rest's it buzzes twenty four hours a day, not during one moment through the night was there nowhere open. There was always a good choice of eateries that would be open including Japanese pubs, also entertainment of many and varied kinds was always there and available 24/7 Tokyo buzzed like nowhere else. Hong Kong couldn't come close, boring Singapore only had Bugis street to go and sit down and have a beer at while cynically laughing at the local goings on. Possibly the only other city to match Tokyo for twenty four hour buzz was Bangkok. But Tokyo was cleaner and un-spoilt by tourism. The Japanese had their own ideas about what constituted good night life and much of it made for a much better night on the tiles than he could ever hope to get in any other city of the world.

The Japanese culture made for many enjoyable experiences when going to eat and although some of their ideas, about food may sometimes have seemed weird, the food normally tasted incredibly good, and was so well presented and in a way that made it look very tasty. There were also the hot baths and saunas that were open throughout the night and could be used for a quick freshen up before heading on to the next venue. On top of all of that, if cigarettes were required, or a snack, a hot or cold drink of almost any description, a can of beer, a half gallon can of beer, a bottle of whiskey, a bottle of sake, etc, it was all available from machines on the streets.

Back at work and Gypsy is at Mr. Onida's office to collect his pay. Mr. Onida being the wheeler dealer that he was had got himself a job to supply women to dress in funny outfits and hand out leaflets and persuade people to by a certain product. He asked Gypsy if he knew anyone who would like to do a day's work for him. Gypsy asked him how many he needed. "About twenty should do it, if you can get me all of them then, there will be something in it for you." He replied. "OK," said Gypsy "I'll see what I can do."

Back at Yoshida house Gypsy went and had a talk with Heidi and the Australian women, of whom there was four, and asked them if they wanted a one day job on that coming Saturday, working for his boss. They were all up for it now they just needed another fifteen women to make up the crew.

They found another seven western women but could find no more. So it was with great trepidation that they contacted the association of rabid Israeli psycho bitches in the rooms above.

They thought they could control it by just talking to the few who had been conferred the title by the other residents of honoree human being, instead of bloodsucking vampire bitch. But it didn't work. The moment the sweet well behaved ones were spoken to by the group, the rabid werewolf and vampire variety of the Israeli females were shouting, 'Ma Ze' at her, (which means "what is it" in English). The ghouls had total domination, of the sweeter of the Israeli girls and they would feel forced to tell the blood suckers what was going down.

The moment that word got out that there was some daytime work going that was paying reasonably well, they came flying out, of the woodwork like a plaque of banshees rapidly dribbling "did someone say something about money?"

All of a sudden they were surrounded by these salivating monsters and Gypsy wished that he had brought a very large can of "Pedigree chum" with him. That he could use to distract them while he made a speedy get away.

They were not a pretty sight and were enough to have both the Munster and the Adams familys running for sanctuary. "Oh shit," thought Gypsy to himself, now that the cat was out of the bag there would be no putting it back in. Anyway, this collection of money hungry, manipulative and aggressive females couldn't behave badly all the time could they? Maybe they would behave well seeing as it was about their number one most holy sacrament, Money!!!!!!!!!!!!!.

After all, if they didn't behave well at work they would not have been able to keep their jobs.

Again that was something else about them that Gypsy did not understand. How the fuck had some of these monstrosities managed to get jobs as bar hostesses in the first place???

Some of them were so ugly that they would even have had Afghans, Turks and Greeks running in the opposite direction.

Indeed there must be some really twisted Japanese perverts out there but it was indeed hard to fathom how anyone even the most seriously twisted deviates amongst humanity could gain any pleasure from the company of one of these creatures. It would be a bit like going on a date with Jabber the Hut, or the rejects from The Hound of the Baskerville.

Gypsy had seen prettier Rottweiler's than some of them. Maybe they wore latex masks to work or dressed up in a Burka or Hijab.

At Mr. Onida's office instead of twenty there was more like 35 women waiting for a job for the day. A third of them, may have been what could be described as attractive and the rest well…. We can be sure that their mothers found them attractive but other than that the only other admirers that they were likely to have had, would have been some drunk perverted salarymen who had left their glasses at home.

Gypsy had been most apprehensive as to whether Mr. Onida would take on this horde that descended upon his doorstep and hoped that he would still be getting a kickback for his troubles. To his relief, the ghouls behaved and there was no Israeli bad behavior in the office. Also Mr. Onida seemed happy with the result, but with the Japanese you never could tell. But he told Gypsy that there would be more times that he would be requiring similar services and there would be money in it for him.

On the way to one of his jobs later in the day he was in one of the big stations of the Tokyo metro system when he saw someone's wallet fall out of their pocket and on to the ground. He picked it up and ran after the woman who had dropped it and gave it straight back to her. She wanted to give him a financial reward for it but Gypsy would have none of it, he had his honor too. He made his excuses and got on his way, he had a job to go to

Soon it was out of his mind as he was contemplating how it might be best to conduct his next class.

The weekend came and Mr. Onida's promotional team went off to work. There was Heidi and her team who were all attractive European and Australian women of pleasant disposition. They were all quite good at charming people into being interested in the product, and then there were the ones who ate kosher pedigree chum for their breakfast.

It wasn't that they were naturally physically ugly, it was their attitude, the way they held themselves, their nasty manipulative behavior and their bad dress sense that made them so very unpleasant. The sound of their voices wasn't a nice sound either, but that could have been more to do with the shit that they were speaking..

If any of these women had been raised in Europe or Australia, New Zealand or many other parts of the world they would most likely be just as attractive, if not more so than any in Heidi's team and with a balanced personality that would make them a pleasure to be around (unless of course they were raised in France, in which case they may have run away from home at aged fourteen to make an early career choice of becoming a junkie at Calangute Beach in Goa).

But they were raised in Israel and even if their immediate parents weren't Ghetto survivors you would not have to go back through to many generations to find Ghetto dwellers within the family tree.

Only the very toughest could survive in the ghettos and every trick would have to be used in order to get through their daily lives. The less manipulative, more passive and decently behaved of the community tended to fall by the wayside and die off. The Russian and European Jews who made it to Israel were a hard and determined bunch. Also they had learned every nasty trick imaginable in order to survive, but now the tricks had become an ingrained habit that became part of everyday subconscious behavior. Their children picked up the tricks at an early age from both their parents and the society around them which was populated by people who also were descended from Ghetto dwellers.

At the age of eighteen they were drafted into the army to help protect their country from the very real threat from both the Arab bogey men outside of Israel who constantly had been threatening to drive them into the sea, and constant attacks that were being made by Arabs living within Israel's borders.

What's more, on the news they watched as their country was attacked and the Europeans just sat on their hands and said and did nothing. But when Mossad or the Israeli armed forces went and caught or killed the perpetrators of the atrocity there was great wailing and gnashing of teeth to be heard coming from many quarters within Europe, as if the only thing that the Jews were allowed to do as far as they were concerned was to lie down and be killed. They could be very much forgiven for resenting the vile hypocrisy and the retarded under handed aggression that still came at them in such a cowardly manner from so many quarters within Europe. It had not just been the Germans who had persecuted their ancestors and as far as any Israeli was concerned if someone in Europe didn't like it when they defended themselves or took retribution for previous attacks, then they had every right to fucking shut their cowardly anti-Semitic mouths and fuck off. Jews were not there to be scapegoats for every nasty humanoid microbe who on waking in the morning, got angry with the retard staring at him from out of the mirror and deciding that something must be done about it, took it upon themselves to go and start a crusade or a Jihad against the Jews.

Of course the other thing that screwed up the Israelis was their language and their interpretation of their religion.

The language was never designed or meant to be used in everyday conversation. It was specifically designed for use in dealing with matters of religion, law and science.

Aramaic was the spoken language of the Israelites. Hebrew has no nouns not very much in the way of politeness and also no such thing as swear words (Israelis have to revert to Arabic or Yiddish when they want to turn the air blue). The trouble was that when Hebrew was translated directly into English, then it could sound very rude indeed.

Hebrew was turned into a modern everyday spoken language in the mid to late nineteenth century by a man called Benyahuda. He was a great man even a hero to the secular Zionist settlers, but because what he had done was viewed as a terrible transgression by the orthodoxy, when he died, they refused permission for his body to be buried in a Jewish graveyard.

The religion did not help one little bit either. The idea that God has his favorite chosen people and all the others are nothing special shows that either they or their God needs some serious psychological help.

God had just made the world and its people and he was wondering if there were some of them who would like some commandments.

So firstly he went to the British and asked them if they would like some. "No thank you," they replied "we are quite capable of making all sorts of silly ridiculous rules for ourselves," they told him.

He went next to the Germans, but they said "Nein danke vee already have made too many rules for ourselves, so much zat vee can give you some rules if you like".

Next he went to the Italians but they said, Noa we eez notta lika a lot ofa people tell us whatta we can do, noa bad feelings huh?"

Then he went, to the Jews and said "hey Jews would you like some commandments?"

"How much do they cost?" they asked "they're free" said God.

"In that case we'll take ten" they replied.

All of this however did not excuse them from what the nasty bitches did next.

Gypsy got back from his Sunday afternoon and evening job late after 10 p.m. "Oh Gypsy I am so sorry about what happened on the job today" said Heidi. "Oh what's that?" Gypsy asked. Then Heidi explained while the Australian women all sat around nodding in agreement and occasionally interupting to mention other things that had happened.

The long and the short of it was that the man who had contacted Mr. Onida to provide the team had taken exception to the fact that most of the team (meaning most of the Israelis) were not well turned out and not what he had asked for. He had asked for good looking, attractive women. This of course only came out at the end of the day when he refused to pay Mr. Onida.

Mr. Onida was planning on using the cash payment to pay the team and had only enough cash on him for the day's expenses. He had stood up and explained the situation to everyone and apologized that he couldn't get the money that day to get them all paid. But he gave his absolute Japanese word of honor that if they would come by to his office on Tuesday then he would pay each and every one of them from his own pocket, but today there was the slight problem of the banks being closed and ATMs if they were in existence at that time were not able to dish out the amount of cash that he would need. The other women meaning Heidi's group were happy with his promise and his explanation. They all knew were his office was and knew that he could nearly always be found there, but most of all he was Japanese. The chances of getting robbed or cheated in Japan were very much lower than just about anywhere else on planet earth. When a man like Mr. Onida gave his word it was unbreakable, despite his wheeler dealer ways.

However the Battersee Dogs Home rejects did not agree and swarmed around him shouting and getting aggressive and generally behaving worse than a gang of British gutter snipe football hooligans on a piss up after their team had lost.

They had been physically pushing him and telling him that they did not believe him and no doubt they must have had the man quite frightened, despite the fact that he lived with his formidable Scottish wife. He must have wished that he had her by his side that afternoon, she would have sorted them out better than anyone, the Scots are known as remarkably good dog handlers.

Gypsy felt crushed, his new budding carriers as a labor recruiter had just come to a very premature end and all thanks to the hyenas upstairs. Not just that but if all that Heidi and the others had told him was true and he had no reason to doubt what they said, then Gypsy had lost face in a big way with his boss, a man who he liked and who had essentially helped him. This meant one thing to Gypsy deep down he knew it but at that time did not want to admit it, he had done what he had come to Japan to do, at least for now. His cash reserves were replenished and he now had four thousand dollars worth of yen, with some as cash but most as travelers cheques. It was time to pack his bag and head to Kathmandu and watch out for his parents on their walking holiday. They weren't streetwise to the ways of Asia and he would feel batter if he was there in order to keep them out of unintentional trouble.

However he had wanted to be able to stay on in Japan until he had saved ten thousand dollars. And then he had a dream to go and set up his own guesthouse, somewhere in the Kathmandu valley. (it is perhaps a good thing that such a thing did not come about as it would have prematurely curtailed his freedom).

He went raging up the stairs and found three of the nasty salivating creatures sitting outside, they reminded him of the Lee sisters, beastly, ugly and ghastly. Gypsy was beyond anger or rage he was furious. Why oh why were these ugly creatures so incapable of behaving like humans. Why did they always have to let themselves and everyone else down so very badly at every opportunity possible? it wasn't just childish, it was damned right infantile.

He let out his rage at them. "I've just been told about what happened at the job today and how you misbehaved with my boss, you fucking pigs you make me ashamed to be Jewish, you have now made me lose face and I will have to think about moving on because of this. You are shit or something lower, do you still not get why everyone here hates you?" "But he wasn't going to pay us" they bleated and whined. "He said that he would pay everyone on Tuesday after he had had a chance to go to the bank. He's Japanese, it would be too shameful even to contemplate the idea of ripping any of you off for him, don't you fucking get it. You have all been here almost as long as I have, have you ever heard me complain about him. He's a good man and never fails to pay anyone and anyway I asked you to behave well with him. I did you a favor by letting you in on a day's payed work but I should have known that it was totally beyond your abilities to even behave moderately like human beings. You're an embarrassment, the lot of you, instead of working as bar hostesses why don't you do something more fitting and see if you can get yourself in the movies. I'm sure that Hammer house of horror would have some great openings for you, why some of you have got such unique features that they should be able to get some ideas to create a whole new range of monsters for their stories just by looking at you."

They went automatically into defence mode and tried to argue but just a load of gibber came out, they did not have their ace card when confronted by Gypsy.

They could not even turn up the tear ducts and claim victimhood and anti-Semitism. Gypsy's Jewish credentials were every bit as good, if not better than theirs and he truly hated what they had done to Heidi by making her feel guilt for something that had happened before she was born. Yes, she may have had blonde hair and blue eyes, but she was one of the most nonracist, informed, educated, straight up, intelligent and decent people that Gypsy had ever met. She had travelled around Africa on her own and also Tibet plus many other regions of the world and concentrated on making friends as she travelled. The very last thing that this lovely woman could be accused of was either racism or anti Semitism.

Gypsy was left in disgust, he really wished that he could once again meet some decent Israelis. But as everybody on the road knows, the decent ones don't travel in packs. They will either be on their own or maybe temporarily travelling or living with a multinational crowd, or maybe travelling as a couple.

Back at work, a letter arrived at the high school addressed to Gypsy, it was written in Japanese and had a thousand yen note inside. That's very strange thought Gypsy to himself and showed the letter, written in Kanji to Ted who was also sitting at his desk in the staff room. He asked him to translate it for him.

"It says thank you for picking up my wallet and giving it back to me when I dropped it" said Ted "you did that?" asked Ted. "Oh yes I remember now" said Gypsy, "it happened in one of the stations on the Yamanota line, I had forgotten about it, what puzzles me is how she found out where I work and what my name is. If I had told her anything of my name or where I work it must have been too quick for her to write it down. I was running to my next job and didn't have time to speak much with her other than to wish her good luck and remind her to be careful with her things and then I was gone. Anyway it's a very nice gesture on her part and I'm grateful but I did tell her that I didn't need, want or expect anything for it as it is what any good person would do."

The course was starting to run at the school in Gypsy's class and was starting to work. He was, as always a dedicated anarchist and had put something into the course to help try to free the students minds up and get them expressing (which to an average Japanese adult at that time was like heresy and blasphemy all at once and a rather frightening idea to put it mildly) what they really thought was never spoken so Gypsy put his spanner in the works to see if he could change that, at least for a few of them.

Jim had made friends with another American rock and roller, a man from Florida who was in Japan to do work for the Hitachi yacht racing team. He was a boat builder and worked on making the hulls of the boats, as a member of an American yacht construction team. He would come by to Jim's place and he, Jim and Gypsy would get their guitars out and jam out a few cacophonies together and drink a few beers. Gypsy was always tight for time as he had jobs that he would have to run to seven days a week. So he could never stay more than a couple of hours and always had to limit his drinking.

However one day the fellow from Florida invited Jim and Gypsy to a party to celebrate the completion of the boats and also their contracts in Japan. It was being hosted by the Hitachi bosses to honor the Americans for their dedication and hard work.

The party was at a function room up two wide sets of stairs in a non descript building in a commercial and office district in the southwest of the city.

The Hitachi bosses were sitting there in their suits and the boat builders from Florida in jeans T-shirts and long hair. It was a bit of a sterile affair even though there was good food and plenty to drink. People were sitting around, chatting and relaxing. For Gypsy it was good to meet westerners who weren't either school teachers or businessmen. Then after the food and a couple of rounds of drinks their friend got his guitar out and started to play a rude song about his boss.

"Hey shut that up, you're out of order" one of the team told him. But he carried on playing, so they pulled the lead out of the amp and that's when it kicked...... The place exploded into a wild west style saloon bar punch up and people were fighting and flying down the stairs they were fighting over the tables and all around, it was like something out of "the Dukes of Hazard" or an old Hollywood western. It wasn't the kind of thing that you would expect as a live event at a polite farewell party in a commercial area of Tokyo. Taiwan or the Philippines, yes it could happen quite easily, but Japan.... The Hitachi bosses stared on in total disbelief. They had probably had no experience of Gaijin but now must have been thinking "shit they really do behave like in the movies."

The only thing that was missing was the sound of banjos, guitars and fiddles playing a fast southern jig.

The expression on the Hitachi bosses faces could have been confusion as maybe they thought that the Americans were doing it specifically to entertain them, with a real live wild west show, a bit like Buffalo bill's Wild West Circus. But if that was the case why weren't they dressed up in the cowboy gear as well? and anyway where were the props and the music?

Jim grabbed Gypsy by the arm and pulled him out of the way of a couple of flailing fighters and they got down to the street and out of the way.

"That's what's known as southern crackers" said Jim "they can be the most easy going friendly types but they can explode in a heartbeat just like you saw there." "I just thought we should have helped our friend out" said Gypsy. "No!" said Jim, "we wouldn't stand a chance against those guys, they are built like brick shithouses did you not notice? And our friend got himself needlessly into that mess so leave him to it, I'm sure that that is not the first time that something like that has happened in that team, it's not our business and I'm happy to keep it that way".

427

At the conversation lounge at Omoto Sando an interesting crowd had gathered on one particular evening. There was a Japanese man who travelled a lot and was self employed, there was an artist, a writer and a Sri Lankan businessman who made his money by selling gems stones. Each one of them had their stories but most interesting of all was the Sri Lankan. He pulled a packet from his top pocket and on opening it, took out a small stone of dark green complexion that had a moving line across it and told everyone that it was a called a cat's eye and that it was a two carat stone and that it was worth $2,000 per carat. Gypsy was totally astonished, why would someone pay so very much money for that? It didn't even look that good. It was useless, unless you wanted to set it into something. Even so Gypsy was intrigued, why would someone spend so very much money on something so frivolous and useless? it was a deep mystery to him.

After going to Mr. Onida to both collect his wages and apologize for the ordeal that he had to endure at the hands of the Israeli 'rent a werewolf' service Mr. Oneida told him what had happened. "The trouble was I needed good looking, well behave women, that is why I did not get paid, these women were neither, they weren't even nicely dressed or sweet smelling." Gypsy explained how he had first recruited the good looking non Israelis but when unable to get the numbers had gone and discreetly asked some of the nice looking and well behave Israeli girls if they wanted to work, but how it then got translated into Hebrew, thus causing the stampede of ugly females to turn up for the job.

"I'm deeply sorry, I did not expect anything like this to happen" said Gypsy. "It was just that I was at work until just before the audition so I gave one or two of them your address to make sure that they found the office in the event of me being late. It was not my intention to bring monsters to your office.'

He lost one of his classes the next week, the salary men. Gypsy was not surprised, they did not need the classes. He had read part of some of the technical papers that they had written in English and even a British writer would be hard put to write better grammar, they really didn't need him.

However on their last meeting he had told them what he could see.

"Yes your country has incredible economic growth at this time based on manufacture of technologies but when this boom dies down as the factory ownership outsources manufacturing to other countries where the labour is cheaper, then what is going to happen in Japan without a new wave of technological development? And even if there was a new wave and the market expanded, what about power? The world is already becoming dangerously polluted so power might need to come from a far cleaner and more renewable source. So my conclusion is that the only way that Japan can avoid its' long running boom from running out of steam in the very near future is to become the leading player in the field of clean energy generation? Without it what are people going to run their ever increasing collections of gizmos' with? If Japan does not get into clean energy generation then it is going to have a long recession in the next few years."

They laughed at him and from the look in their eyes Gypsy could tell that they did not agree with him. At that time such opinions were viewed by the mainstream of the world's population as being from the outer limits or beyond. They tended to think that they were going to use ever finite resources of fossil fuels forever.

One night it all got to be too much. The seven day work week the claustrophobic living conditions and the constant running. He didn't even had much time for himself in the evenings when on at least two nights a week, he wouldn't get free from work until after 11 p.m. He couldn't get out of Tokyo to go to the mountains as there was only hours between each job, it had all got to be too much. The stereo went flying at high speed towards the ground and disintegrated. He let out a roar and finished off what was left of his small Ghetto blaster. He had had more than enough he looked at his cramped lifestyle and wondered if he was not starting to turn into a Japanese workaholic salary man. All he would need other than a grasp of the language would be a suit, some bryle cream and a pair of glasses.

It was at that moment that Gypsy knew that for his own sanity he would have to leave Japan and quickly.

He had reached the point where he could not do his job and phoned in sick. He still had a ticket with Air India that would take him as far as Bangkok via Hong Kong and thought that first he would use it to go to Hong Kong. He booked his ticket as far as Hong Kong, to leave in five days time. He then set out to find a replacement for himself at the teaching job. Mr. Oneida had been good to him and he didn't want to leave him in the lurch, it would be far better for all if he could just make a smooth transition to a replacement. He phoned Jim and a couple of other friends to ask if they knew anyone from an English speaking country who wanted a readymade full time job doing his rounds. They all said they would ask around and put the word out the next morning.

Kitaro was to play a gig at the Buddakan (which was Tokyo's biggest and best known concert hall) the day after he was due to fly out. He went to the travel agent and asked if it would be possible to change the date. All flights after the one that he was booked on were booked solid for a month so it was not possible to make it to the concert. It was very much like a kick in the balls, he had waited the whole time that he had been in Japan for the chance to see Kitaro in concert. He had bought a double album entitled silk road while in England several years before and the music just blew him away. He would sit up through the night listening to it and drawing. It had been something that he had dreamed of so much to see this, one of his favorite musicians playing a concert.

Like a Japanese one man Pink Floyd, his music was reflective of the Zen art and design that Gypsy enjoyed so very much. The music reflected deep inner peace and gave meditative vibes to the listener. And he was playing at the gig hall of all gig halls in Asia and Gypsy was not going to be able to go.

That night a British traveler came by. He had been sent by Jim and wanted a job. "This is your lucky day" said Gypsy, "all you have to do is step into my shoes, the job is yours and ready to roll. You will have to convince Mr. Oneida that you can do what is required, don't worry he won't take much convincing. Here I had better show you the course that I have designed for the high school classes and if you like you can use it instead of the textbook."

Gypsy showed him the course and explained it and then got out a map of the Tokyo metro and briefed him on the daily grand tour of Tokyo city. He warned him about the monsters of Omiya, explaining that he would most likely be used as a human climbing frame by the little gremlins and that the best option was just to view it as a twice a week penance session "it doesn't feel quite so bad then" Gypsy added.

It was one very happy British traveler who then left Yoshida house with Gypsy's job, and Gypsy was happy too. He could now phone Mr Onida and tell him that he had had to quit the job but not to worry as he had found a replacement for himself who would come to the office in the afternoon or who would phone in.

Gypsy went to Mr. Onida's office and collected his final pay pack and said goodbye. He went to Akihabara and bought a new, much smaller stereo that would easily fit in his bag and then he made a visit to the Tokyo branch of the Hare Krishnas. They were talking and one of them said "the problem with explaining the path and the stories to the Japanese is that they have no concept of a God in their culture or religion we have been writing books to first explain the God concept. Also it is very difficult to stay vegetarian here as they put fish oil into everything including the milk".

With everything done, Gypsy went for a couple of drinks with his friends at the Red Onion bar and headed back to Yoshida house and started packing his bags.

The next day he was ready to go, he said his goodbyes then headed out to the station at Oyzumi Gakoen. As he got on the train with his bag and guitar a wonderful sensation of freedom swept over him. He always felt good when he was leaving a place that he had stayed at for too long. It was his favourite place to be, on the road between places with nothing particular planned and no one waiting for him at the next destination. An hour later he was at Shinjuku station waiting for the bus to take him out to Narita Airport and he was dreaming about his future travel plans.

At the airport a voice from behind said "Hello Gypsy what are you doing here? "He looked around to see a familiar face, a traveler that he knew from both Thailand and Tokyo. "I'm booked to Hong Kong but I'm going to ask if I can book straight through to Bangkok. The flight to Kathmandu will be cheaper from there and anyway Bangkok is a better place to hang out" Gypsy replied. "That's where I'm going, it would be cool if you can book through then we can both hit the Bangkok nightlife with a pocket full of yen tonight."

Gypsy was able to book straight through and now had a boarding card for Bangkok. They went through to airside and found the bar and sat talking about what each had been doing in Japan until it was time to go and board the red and white, head wobbling express.

The plane left the terminal and taxied out to join the queue. After a few minutes of waiting and watching other aircraft start their take off run it was their turn. The plane turned onto the runway then stopped for several minutes before the engines were revved and they were on their way. The plane lumbered and bumped its' way off the ground and headed out over the pacific ocean as it turned and headed south towards Hong

Kong. This being Air India there were no free drinks but the vegetarian food was very good and served in large portions. However, those who had ordered meat suffered. Gypsy was sitting next to two angry looking old men with beards who looked remarkably like a pair of geriatric goats. They had ordered non-vegetarian. It came as a really small portion of mutton and even then most of it was bone which caused the two old goats to look even more pissed off.

After three and a half hours the plane started to make it's descent into Hong Kong and thankfully the wind was blowing the right way and they were approaching Kai Tak from the sea. Landing through checker board alley with any airline from the subcontinent, with the exception of Royal Nepal who have skilled mountain pilots, was to be viewed as an adventure of kinds.

Across from the runway which jutted out into the sea, it was rumored that there was a bar at the aviation club, where many of the American, European, Australian and New Zealand pilots would go for a drink after landing and finishing their shift for the day. There was a list on the wall of the scheduled arrival times of all the major airlines of the subcontinent and of any Arab or African airline that used their own local pilots to do the Hong Kong run. When the wind was blowing in such a way as to necessitate a chequer board alley approach and a flight on the list was due in, they would congregate on the deck outside and wait and watch, for the shear entertainment. From the aviation club deck they could get a clear view of the plane both going into and coming out of checker board alley, wing tips wobbling wildly, the planes attitude, offset and watching as still wobbling it tried to touch down bouncing and doing a hop skip and jump before getting its wheels on the ground, then the engines screaming as they deployed near total force possible on the reverse thrust.

Sniggering they would wonder what was being said on the flight deck of the aircraft and wonder how in the hell the pilot got his Hong Kong license. (Even though the land side approach to Kai Tak was the most dangerous approach to a busy international airport that there has ever been, by the time it closed and was replaced by the new airport at Chep Lap Kok there were no accidents within checker board alley and never a serious accident causing fatalities at the airport. However, the Taiwanese flag carrier, Air China christened the runaway at Chep Lap Kok by landing an MD 11 down it upside down).

The plane landed with a hop skip and jump and screaming of reverse thrust. When the plane turned off the runway to taxi on to the apron Gypsy could see that there was barely a hundred yards between where they had finally stopped and where the runway ended

Off they got from the plane for a quick stretch and a few drinks at one of the bars, It was dark and out through the huge windows, Kai Tak could be seen to be buzzing at an even faster rate than normal, all that was going on was visible straight in front. There was just one long line of air bridges and every aircraft that could not get on to a gate was placed in a marked area on the apron. The Apron was large, with great lines of Jumbos parked almost wing tip to wing tip. Kai Tak, because of its location on the ultra congested Kowloon peninsula was extremely limited for space and had to accommodate both a huge airfreight operation and an aircraft maintenance company within its grounds, along with the passenger terminal and other services. The place heaved twenty four hours a day. If ever they designed an aircraft carrier that was big enough to land and park jumbos on it's deck then it would probably look a bit like Kai Tak Airport.

Soon they were back aboard the flight and the plane taxied out to the runway and took off for Bangkok. Three hours later and they were touching down at Don Muang airport into a hot tropical night.

CHAPTER 9

OCTOBER 1985

It was sometime after 9 o'clock at night as the taxi sped along the highway into the city. Gypsy and the other traveler were heading to the old traveler's area off from Rama IV and near the Malaysia hotel, which had been a favorite R&R hangout for US soldiers during the Vietnam war.

They checked into the Boston Inn, a guest house with a swimming pool, and after dropping their bags they hit the town to party.

At long last Gypsy felt free again. He had a little over $4,000 worth of Yen in his pocket and had far less burning ambitions for travel than before, he could afford to kick back and relax for the winter as long as he stayed in third world countries, which were the sort of places where he would rather be anyway.

Some other travelers joined them and off they went and took a taxi to Pat Pong. They had all heard about the banana show and various other sex shows of a decidedly sleazy nature and decided that they just had to go see one.

They got called over to one club entrance and shown a whole menu of different bizarre acts that the girls in that club would perform. They went in and watched. They never saw a girl fire a banana up in the air but they did watch one woman opened a bottle of beer from between her legs and another pull out a string of razor blades. "Please remind me in case I forget but I don't want to have sex with either of those two, they look far too dangerous" said Gypsy to the others. "What! you mean you don't want your dick severed or cut off?" one of them shot back.

They drifted out into the street wondering what to do next, so someone hit on the idea of going to Soy Cowboy (another of the red light areas of Bangkok). So they all piled into a couple of tuk tuks and headed to soy cowboy. They stopped for a few beers in a few bars, where they stood around while the hookers groped and leched them, but none of them was ready to take one back for the night yet. Then after a few more drinks in a couple of different bars they jumped into yet another taxi for a ride to the Grace hotel. Many of the signs on the surrounding buildings were written in Arabic and obviously there also were a lot of Arabian people out and about on the street in the area too.

There were a lot of street stands. It was the first time that Gypsy had seen a stand selling assorted fried insects, in much the same was as a stand in India might be selling roasted nuts and seeds.

It gave "flied lice" a whole new meaning, these guys were selling flied cockloach and flied locusts, beatles, maggots, etc. it was like something from an army jungle survival training course but with added sauces and a wok.

Inside the bar, down stairs it had not begun to kick off yet as it was not yet 11 p.m. at that time, so they went back to Soy Cowboy and did a grand tour of the bars before eventually at half past midnight with just three of them left they took another cab to the Miami Hotel. Around at the back of the building was a set of toilets. The entrance to the disco was between the men's and women's blocks, looking for all the world like it was an entrance to just another convenience. The disco was down in a basement and was large and packed with hundreds of people. "The girls who work here are freelance, there is no bar fine" said the traveler from the flight.

A track by a singer called Murray Head, called "one night in Bangkok" had come out on the charts in western countries several months earlier and though it was officially banned in Thailand, it was blasting out after every third or fourth song played and hundreds of hookers were there dancing along to it. The night was warming up, this place was electric. As the evening wore on Gypsy spotted one woman that he liked the look of. She came over to where he was sitting and they negotiated the price and then took a taxi to the Malaysia hotel.

The next morning Gypsy felt very much more relaxed as he left the room with the woman and went down to pay his bill.

She took off home, sitting side saddle on a motorbike taxi and Gypsy crossed the road and walked up to the Boston Inn. He felt very much relaxed, as he had not been with a woman in Japan, while his efforts had been focused on survival and making enough money to go back to Nepal and India.

Relationships complicated things and made life messy and restrictive and relationships at work were always a big No No for Gypsy.

When it was time for making money then it was time for making money and he would not let a stupid thing like a quick fling get between him and his livelihood. Gypsy lived on the edge by being on the road as he was. There were no welfare offices he could go to, there were no free medical services. Staying alive required a very conscious effort and in order to survive he had to work to make money. A regular girlfriend was not a luxury that Gypsy could afford, besides what free time did he have? One night in Bangkok can make a hard man slightly less horny, it is also less complicated and less full of woe than a relationship and cost a damned site less money too.

Gypsy slept for most of the day, getting up in the late afternoon to walk down to and across Sathon road and then through the side alleys ("soys") he reached Silom road, (a large commercial shopping area in the centre of the city) then he turned left and walked along to the end where he turned right along new road and past the post office until he took a turning on his left, and walked down a side street that led to the Royal Orchid Hotel. From a place near there he took the river taxi to Bang Lam Po and the Kowsan road where he looked for Ronny's travel agency.

Ronny's had gone but now there were many more guest houses, shops, travel agents etc. The Kowsan road had changed. There were many more travelers and now most of everything in the road was there to cater for low budget travelers.

It was not relaxed anymore, Israeli accents could be heard everywhere, fighting over the price of every and anything, from an air ticket to a cup of tea.

Street stands were springing up all over the place and Gypsy was glad that he was not staying there. In the area surrounding the Malaysia hotel, there were far less travelers around, just a few of the hardcore ones who had been on the road for years.

He went into a travel agent's office and bought a one way ticket on Royal Nepal Airlines to Kathmandu for the next evening and then took a motorbike taxi back across Bangkok to the Malaysia hotel area. Sitting on the back of a crackling two stroke machine while being rushed across the city by a kamikaze rider as he weaved in between eight lanes of trucks and cars was a total adventure in it's self and also the fastest way through the traffic, but it would be no way for a cat to travel as they would burn up at least one of their nine lives with each journey.

He and the traveler from the flight went to the bar at the Malaysia hotel that night. They were both tired from what they had been doing and screwing the night before and couldn't be bothered to go out on the razzle for another night. They were sitting in the bar drinking beers and talking about adventures on the road that they had had and how very good it felt to be out of Japan but with large pockets full of yen. They had both made a few thousand dollars which was going to pay for the winter, living and travelling in third world countries. The other traveler was planning on staying mostly in Thailand and then travelling down through Malaysia and Indonesia to Bali and then flying to Australia and finding work there.

Gypsy planned to joined his parents on their walking holiday and then stay on in Nepal while he figured out what he wanted to do next. He knew that he wanted to go back to India as he had not seen nearly enough of that place. There were still many, many things there which were yet to be explored. But other than that he had not an idea of what he wished to do. He thought of maybe going to Taiwan and doing some English teaching there, but the idea really did not leave him feeling that motivated or inspired.

Two hookers wandered over to their table and introduced themselves, "sorry ladies but we're not up for any business tonight, we're still recovering from last night," Gypsy said "no wully" said one of the women "we sit and talk we just want be fliendly." The women were a few years older than them but still good looking. The topic of conversation moved on to the highly intellectually stimulating subjects of;

What your name?

Where you flom?

You like Thailand?

You like Thai lady?

How long you stay?

Where you come flom now?

You work there?

You have lady there?

Why you not stay longer in Thailand?

Thailand velly beautiful yes?

And so on….

However when these two young men got talking about travelling, working and living in Asia the women got to see that they were both extremely street smart across the region and stopped talking to them as potential customers and gave them respect enough to ask them about their travels and stayed quiet, listening intensely as each of them spoke of what they had been doing on recent journeys and in Japan.

After that round of storytelling they could have probably had the women for free, or at least at a knock down rate (after all everyone has bills to pay and life especially in the city is not free). But they were both too knackered to even bother and also Gypsy had to be ready for his flight the next evening. Walking back up the road to the Boston Inn the other traveler said that he was going to do another week of Brothel crawling in Bangkok and then head back down to where he had been before on Koh Phan Gan. Gypsy told him about Chawang beach on Samui and recommended it for good weed and mind blowing magic mushroom omelettes, not to mention the women at Joy Bungalows disco.

The next evening, equipped with new fake designer jeans and a bag full of new T shirts and other items available in Bangkok but not in Kathmandu he got into a minibus with a bunch of other travelers and headed out of town to the airport. At the Royal Nepal Airways check in counter There was an older American man who was travelling with his son to Kathmandu. His son was in his mid to late twenties and both of them had travelled in business or first class all the way from the American west coast to Bangkok, on Singapore airlines. The man worked in the air cargo business, running his own midsized company. Later on airside when he saw the ageing Boeing 727 of Royal Nepal airlines pull up at the terminal, he shuddered. "Oh shit" he said, he obviously thought that he was now either entering a Tin Tin comic adventure or a real life Indiana Jones story.

Gypsy wasn't too worried Royal Nepal only had three jets to maintain and probably contracted the work out to Dragon Air at Hong Kong. Also its' pilots had started their flying careers as twin otter and Dornier pilots flying much lighter prop aircraft between the mountains to remote and short, high altitude, unpaved landing strips. If these guys could land a severely over loaded twin otter at Lukla then they were certainly fit to fly a jet from Bangkok to Kathmandu.

(The airstrip at Lukla was a one week walk from the end of the road and the start of the Everest trail. It is approximately a five day walk from Namche Bazaar and nine days from Everest base camp and is also the closest airport to that region, other than a miniscule air strip at Namche Bazaar that it would only be possible to land a small Cessna on. The airstrip was set running up a hill and it was not very long. It was just about the only thing that has managed to blemish Royal Nepal's safety record, as there where the carcasses of several aircraft that either didn't make it into the air on the way out or else landed too fast on the way in, lining the runway).

"Do the planes from this airline crash a lot?" the older American asked. "No they only ever do it once" a British fellow in the queue to board replied dryly.

The plane lumbered off down the runway, its old engines struggling for power as it lifted slowly into the air. They climbed up to an altitude of twenty eight thousand feet and were flying past a huge, multilayered tropical thunder storm over the Burmese jungle as the plane flew through the darkness. Gypsy watched out of the window. He had never seen a thunder storm from this perspective before as the plane flew through a narrow passage between several storms, lightening crashing away on either side of them.

The food on Royal Nepal was also something rather good and to add to the pleasure of course there was the free bar. The evening dinner included nice crispy samosas, a most tasty, spicy, vegetarian curry and chapattis plus a gulab jamun for dessert. Then glass after glass of brandy to wash it down with.

As Gypsy was wandering up the gangway in order to make maximum use of the free bar on this short two and a half hour hop, to his surprise he saw Saad, the Iranian traveler who had introduced him to the gold running gang back in Hong Kong. They got chatting, the subject of conversation was mostly about the ones who got caught.

Next to Saad was another Iranian traveller who had also been involved in the scam.

They all resolved to meet and go and visit their friends who got caught and were now all in the Dilli bazaar prison on the outskirts of Kathmandu, and take them some food and other basic supplies. There also were other seasoned travelers on the flight who also had been in India and Nepal before. Gypsy felt happy to be in the company of such people as they sped through the darkness towards the ultimate hippie Shangri La.

The plane descended into the blackness as it made its approach to Kathmandu which could not exactly be described as one of those cities that looked spectacular from the air during a night landing. There was an occasional light here and there but otherwise it was about as picturesque as a black cat in a coal cellar.

They landed and taxied back down the runway to the apron. Stepping out into the cool night air felt good. He was back in a place where he truly felt at home. He had a Nepalese Visa and was set for a long stay. After clearing immigration collecting their bags and clearing customs they were out through the tiny airport quickly.

Gypsy, Saad and the other Iranian traveler all shared a taxi to Thamel and Gypsy checked into the Hotel Asia while Saad and his friend went around the corner to their favorite guesthouse.

Gypsy was happy to be back in this homely place again as he climbed up the stairs with it's worn, thread bare carpets and low narrow passages. He put his bag down in his room and then the room boy arrived and handed him a five gram chunk of Nepalese hash and said "that is free on the house, welcome to Kathmandu have a great stay." "Thank you very much" Gypsy replied. I'm sure I will.

He ordered a pot of massalla chai, then sat down on the bed and skinned up a joint and smoked it.

Sitting there in this basic but comfortable room with that luxury of all luxuries, an en suite bathroom, with hot water, with a cup of hot massala chai in one hand and a joint in the other, he felt like he had arrived home. Everything was very cheap and he could afford to hang out for the entire winter here living in relative luxury.

The next few days were spent getting reacquainted with Kathmandu. He got together with Saad and his friend, they then went and bought a large bag of groceries each and took an auto rickshaw to Dilli Bazaar prison to visit their friends. One of the people who Gypsy had spent a lot of time talking with was inside the bars, he was also a good friend of Saad and they spent a while talking. Each of them got sentenced to between four and a half and five years in this shit hole. Food rations for them consisted of seven hundred and fifty grams of rice a day plus one rupee with which to buy vegetables. Gypsy, Saad and his friend all knew that they were lucky to be standing where they were and not inside with the others. They had all been ready to run on the following day from the bust until of course, it had happened.

Gypsy's parents were due in in a couple of days and so he went and found a guest house that he thought would be suitable for them and booked them a room. He then went and asked some questions about hiking permits before ending up at the Pumpernickel bakery in the centre of Thamel. He spent the rest of the afternoon sitting in the garden behind the bakery, smoking chillums with a group of hippies and freaks who had taken up more or less permanent residency in Kathmandu. These were the people who Gypsy knew that he needed to meet if he was to be hanging out there for a while. Not just did they know the place well but were also his kind of people.

He felt relaxed and at home in Kathmandu, there weren't the stresses there that were part of everyday life in Tokyo, Hong Kong or even Bangkok.

The place looked like it had been designed and set up as a sanctuary for Hippies, misfits and dharma bums. Most people moved on foot, there were all sorts of highly colorful shrines and temples of all sorts of shapes. The cafes' looked like they had been designed by refugees from Woodstock.

Everything was cheap and affordable and there were many bookshops that sold the kind of books that Gypsy liked to read and that were extremely hard to find in the west. Gypsy at last managed to find a copy of the Ramayana in English, a book that he had been most interested to read. It was the second most important book to the Hindus after the Bhagavad-Gita. While the Bhagavad-Gita was a lesson on enlightenment that was given to a great warrior on a battle field before the battle began, the Ramayana was a story about when God incarnated on earth as the oldest son of a powerful king in north India in order to position himself well to kill a demon so powerful and well protected that no human on earth could kill him. The story's underlying theme was honor and the code of the warrior.

There were shops selling gemstones and some had huge pieces in their windows. Gypsy became interested when he found out that they were not all massively expensive. They looked interesting, especially some of the ones with marks inside of them.

Gypsy had met some Kashmiris of the rare and more honest variety. Unlike many of the other people from that particular state, They weren't always trying to sell him something or offering to score hash or smack for him. He would stop by at their shop each day and join them for a cup of tea and a chat.

One evening he was sitting around a table with Saad and his quiet friend when because Saad and his friend were both Persian, the topic of conversation drifted onto the nature and method of manufacture of carpets. Gypsy mentioned that he had made friends with some Kashmiris who had a large pile of silk carpets in the corner of their shop. Saad was immediately interested and wanted to go and see them.

Around at Jahan the Kashmiri's shop, Gypsy walked in with Saad and his friend.

"Ah you are from Iran, I have some real Persian carpets, would you like to see them?" Jahan asked. "Yes please show them to me" said Saad. Jahan and his assistant moved maybe ten large carpets out of the way before pulling out several four foot by six foot intricately designed silk carpets. Saad knelt down and inspected them closely and turned them over to inspect the work from the back side. "Yes I can see that it is very good work, six hundred knots per square inch and good Persian classic designs." Then he looked up at Jahan while grinning and said "very clever," these are the best copies that I have ever seen but they were not made in Iran I can see that and guarantee it. The stitch and knot work is not quite the same but they would fool most people who are not from Iran. "Where were they made?" "In Kashmir" Jahan replied, you are the only one who has ever caught me out, no one else knows."

They all sat down and chatted over a cup of tea. Jahan explained how his family had a carpet factory outside of Srinagar and that every month they would send him some new stock. Other family members had shops in Delhi and Goa and he was a part of a big extended family who all did business together, but over long distances. He was happy to be away from the fighting and troubles going on in Kashmir at that time and enjoyed his life much more in Kathmandu.

Saad spoke about Iran, he had left before the revolution and as such stayed away from the troubles. He had been on the road for over twelve years. He would go back to Iran from time to time to visit his family and what friends he still had there but after a visit he would be back out on the road again.

He was what Gypsy was becoming in some aspects. He was someone who was globally streetwise. He could get off the plane in the middle of the night in any of a number of destinations, dodgy ones included and be sorted with a room, a meal, a drink and hash or ganja within the hour, the world was his home. Yet just like Gypsy, he was a refugee of kinds, who could not bear to live in the society in which he had been raised. Even without the revolution, it had been too restrictive for him. Gypsy's main motivation for travelling had been different, in that he had been focused on his quest to find out the truth about what happens to the soul after death, and most importantly to find out what part of a living being is the soul, and what is not. Saad was not what anyone would call an atheist but his interest in matters spiritual was more casual as other things took centre stage in his life at that time. Gypsy liked him, he was someone who was straight up and lived by his own code of honor. He had seen Saad help other travelers and people that he did not know. He knew other people's pain having been there himself. Come to think about, it all of the Persians that he had ever met had all been good company and were often very interesting to listen to, also he had never been ripped off or cheated by any of them.

Their train of thought would often come from an entirely unexpected angle and as they spoke people listening would be able to perceive what they had been talking about from a whole new perspective and often make more sense of it all. It was a total irony to Gypsy that a country that had given birth to such a multitude of intelligent people, who were for the vast majority, a cultured, decent well mannered and attractive race was viewed as a pariah state by the majority of western countries. They were more similar to northern Europeans than the Turks or the Arabs. By all rights their country should be a major world player in many different fields, including space exploration. The country had given birth to two pacifist religions, the Zoroastrians and the Baha'i, both of which were non proselytizing paths that forbade violence from their followers.

Within Islam, Iran has been the home of many enlightened Sufis and celebrated for it around the Islamic world.

Iran has for centuries if not millennia, been a home to writers, thinkers and artists, a place of culture and tolerance. In short it was the great jewel of the Middle East.

What happened with the Islamic revolution and the response of many other countries of the world to it did not make even the tiniest bit of sense to Gypsy. From what he could understand, the way the Islamic law was applied in Iran was a damned sight more progressive than in other Islamic countries that the west was deep in bed with. The friends of America and Europe at that time included such notable pillars of freedom and democracy as Saudi Arabia, Iraq and Pakistan, which at that time was under the control of the brutal military dictatorship of General Zia. The west was happy to sign all sorts of military contracts with these highly questionable regimes, supplying them with copious quantities of the latest high tech ordinance, guns, ships, tanks, and planes etc. Pakistan under general Zia had introduced his brand of Sharia law as both a popularist move and as a vicious tool against his enemies. Iraq was under the dictatorship of the mad, vindictive and somewhat mentally and emotionally unstable megalomaniac, Saddam Husain and Saudi Arabia was a brutally oppressive medieval, misogynist tyranny.

Pakistan was an American ally and was armed by the United States. While America chose to conveniently look the other way the country set about constructing a collection of nuclear warheads to attach to their missiles. It was clear that the only reason that Pakistan was a U.S. ally was as so that the Americans could use it as a stick with which to beat India, who they despised for limiting access to foreign (namely American) companies to their huge domestic market.

India was and is of course a democracy. However the people had repeatedly elected socialist governments and in Bengal and Kerala they had committed in America's eyes the most heinous of heinous capital crimes. The people had repeatedly elected a communist party to govern the state. Even worse than that was that in Kerala they had been highly successful in improving the daily lives of the people and achieving outstanding rates of literacy. And not just that but people around the world were getting to hear about it. America couldn't be seen attacking India directly, after all despite India's poverty it was an extremely well behaved democracy and by any law more than entitled to choose it's own ways by which to live and didn't need to seek America's approval to do so. However some in Washington chose to have gringo fatty tantrums about the fact that India refused to be dominated and bossed around by them and set about setting up clandestine contacts with Pakistan's – I.S.I. (Inter Services Intelligence) and started stirring shit. When war started against the Russian invasion of Afghanistan America was deeply involved.

The war judging from the circumstantial evidence was being funded on the sale of smack (heroin). Across India at that time and also in Nepal, there were so many junkies of all nationalities desperately hooked on "brown sugar" (which was the name given on the street to the brown heroin from Afghanistan) that it was frightening. In some traveler hang outs there were so many fucked up smack heads that it felt like a real life zombie adventure going there, and you were relieved when you got out without anyone ripping you off or biting your leg.

The fight in Kashmir had gone from being full confrontation to being a guerrilla war, with the Pakistan army officially taking no part in it. However it was obvious that ISI had got some funding from somewhere and was training and arming terrorists and sending them across the border along with the smack that was traceable back to the Kashmiri community.

It was obvious that someone with a lot of money and a lot of power was attempting to destabilize India by covert means, possibly thinking that in so doing it would bring about a change of government and then said person could get his businesses into the massive Indian market.

As far as Iran was concerned, the U.S. government had been in there, supplying the Shah with every and all kinds of help including tools of oppression which the Pahlavi regime used unsparingly on their own people. When the revolution happened, the people were angry with the Americans for aiding and abetting their oppressors. When they took the workers in the US embassy as hostages they just wanted to show them just a little bit of what it felt like to be taken into custody by the US armed and trained Iranian secret police.

But the Americans chose not to understand this as it would mean apologizing, taking a bit more responsibility for their actions and committing themselves to better behavior on the world stage in the future. If America's response had been different at the beginning of the revolution the outcome could have been very different.

But America's leaders rather than try to learn to understand what they had done that had caused such very deep offence to the people of Iran chose instead to storm of for a good old collective sulking, gringo, fatty tantrum after which they decided to back their own worst enemy up until that time, the raving megalomaniac dictator Saddam Husain. This was another sad reason that Saad could not visit Iran easily, as he was not above the age where he could be drafted into the military. Every day that he would spend there with his family he would be living in mortal terror of getting press ganged into the army.

Gypsy had taken a cab to the airport to meet his parents who were arriving that afternoon. The airport was perhaps one of the most basic that you could imagine. Consisting of a runway and an apron where there was parking space for a maximum of 5 to six medium sized regional jets and a smaller area for the helicopters, Sky Vans, Twin Otters and Dorniers that covered domestic flights. The international terminal was a single storied scruffy looking building that was no bigger that the size of the building at a railway station at a small regional town in England or Europe. The domestic terminal was yet smaller again. There was also a small maintenance facility for the choppers, sky vans and twin otters. Then other than the essential fuel storage, control tower, and fire service and ambulance there was not much else. In short it was basic. However, their national airline covered one hell of a route network from there with their three jets flying to Hong Kong, Singapore, Bangkok, Dhaka, Calcutta, Colombo, Delhi, Bombay Karachi, Dubai and more.

It was mid afternoon and the apron was empty when the landing lights appeared over the brow of the hill and slowly came down lower as the plane made its final approach until the plane and its exhaust trails were visible. The plane touched the runway and brought its front wheel down then shot past where Gypsy was standing and waiting on the big earth mound that was set back from the runway behind the apron. It turned and taxied back down the runway and pulled up on the apron. The flight, a Biman Bangladesh airways 707 from Dhaka turned off its engines, the steps were pulled in and the doors were opened as the generator was plugged in and services of all kinds swarmed around the plane in order to get it turned around and back out to Dhaka before the sun was down.

Although the Kathmandu valley is only 3,000 feet above sea level it is surrounded by large hills and high mountains. The take off exit route in at least one direction involved pulling the plane around in a relatively tight spiral, looping around the valley twice in order to gain enough altitude in order to climb out. The clouds have rocks in them in Nepal and with avionic navigational equipment in that country being of the most basic kind needed to operate, the Bangladeshis wanted to make sure that they had got their plane up and back out of the Kathmandu valley while there was still light to see. Only a seasoned local Nepali pilot could ever feel comfortable putting a plane down or lifting it back out of that airport after dark.

His parents were in the crowd that was slowly descending down the steps and he went and waited for them at the arrivals exit. They were both carrying large back packs.

He found a taxi and negotiated a local rate for them all to go into town.

They both look out of the taxi in amazement as they drove into what to them looked like another century, several hundred years in the past, mixed with its exotic religions and strange temples.

Plants were growing over old mud brick buildings and just like in India, cows were free to wander.

He got them to the guesthouse that he had booked them a room at and then took them up to their room. He left them to relax and sleep, it must have been a very long flight via Dhaka.

In the next room, a long but not so large reception room, a talk was being given by a Nepali man to a group of westerners.

When Gypsy saw a young woman coming up the stairs to go in to the room he asked her what was going on inside and what the talk was about.

"Oh he's a living god an enlightened living Buddha "the American woman gushed. "Yea sure" thought Gypsy to himself. If he was that special he would have felt it and gone in to listen to him himself but Gypsy felt no such urge and left swami Numb bum to speak with his audience of gullible westerners.

He went around to the Pumpernickel bakery and joined the expat residents in the garden for the daily chillum session.

The next morning Gypsy went and collected his parents from their guest house and took them out to have breakfast, giving them a quick tour of Durbar square on the way with it's pagoda temples, Giant Durga image and the house of the living goddess.

He took them to "the Lunch Box" a large eatery on Freak street.

They went in and sat down to order when his father said in a loud voice" It must have been terrible here in the seventies when all the hippies were here."

The place was crowded with people in psychedelic costumes with long hair and beads around their necks on. It may have been 1985 but there was a sizable number of hippies, travelers and freaks, even then that treated Kathmandu as their permanent refugee camp.

A large of number of eyes turned around to stare at them and it was at this moment that Gypsy regretted not having brought a pair of dark glasses, a hat and a newspaper with him. A false beard would not have been unwelcome either.

It was for precisely this sort of reason that he had decided that he needed to join them for their first trip to Nepal.

With his growing knowledge of the Hindu religion and customs and his streetwise ways in Asia he intended to keep them out of trouble to the best of his abilities and get them streetwise as fast as he could, in the most painless way possible.

Breakfast came and they ate. Gypsy had advised them not to do a guided tour or guided walk and not to book it in England. So they had done as he had suggested and just bought their flights in London. Now before going to look for a porter they needed to decide which walk they wished to do.

Although they had walked in the Alps on numerous occasions and they had no problems in achieving ambitious objectives, the Himalayas was different.

What was considered a reasonably high mountain in the Alps, would be considered a foothill in the Himalayas. The Himalayas were far far higher and there were very few roads amongst them. People in Nepal often had no choice but to move on foot. There were villages and even towns that it could take up to a month to reach from the nearest road if you didn't fly to an airport in a district part way there.

Gypsy recommended that they take a bus to Pokhara and go and walk the Jomsom trail which would be less demanding than either the Annapurna circuit (which was a three to four week hike around the north side of the Annapurna mountain range) or the hike to Namche Bazaar, (which was the last main village before the five day hike to Everest base camp and also was a one month hike there and back).

The Lang Tang trail that went north out from Kathmandu along the Lang Tang valley was not known to contain as much picturesque scenery or history as the Jomsom trail and so they prepared to take the bus the next morning to Pokhara. Gypsy gave them more of a tour of Kathmandu and also showed them where he was staying.

That evening to Gypsy's extreme consternation, he went down sick with the flu and a fever. He was going to go and see doctor Chai, the Ayervedic doctor and get himself sorted by that route but his parents were both telling him to use antibiotics. Gypsy knew a bit about Ayurvedic medicines and knew enough from experience that it was effective, but they didn't. Gypsy had a headache and couldn't bear the noise they were making over it and the wide eyed western panic syndrome they were exuding and so reluctantly took the antibiotics that they handed him from their bag.

The next day they took a bus from the muddy unpaved central bus station in Kathmandu. Gypsy felt rough and the bus journey was certainly not going to help his day to be any better.

There were two seats on one side and three on the other. The seats were much smaller than on any other bus in any other country that he had travelled in, and to add to that, the rows were closer together thus giving less leg room.

They shoe horned themselves into their tiny seats and soon the bus departed for Pokhara, bouncing along the road and giving a ride that would make a camel seasick.

Gypsy stretch back as best as he could and tried to sleep. The bus left Kathmandu and drove through the valleys and over bridges as it headed west to its first stop at Mugling.

The bus stopped at Mugling just after mid day and everyone got down and went and found something to eat at one of the numerous food stalls and chai shops. Half an hour later they were all back on board for another bone jarring ride through the afternoon.

Eventually after a stop some seventy kilometres outside of Pokhara to drop off the hikers and locals who were going to be walking along the Annapurna circuit, the bus bounced its way into Pokhara and they got off and looked for a place to stay.

They found a place by the large lake that Pokhara is famous for.

Gypsy still felt as sick as a dog and crawled off to his room to sleep. By the next day he was already starting to feel better and was eating properly again. In the afternoon he took a walk along the lakeside and found a hippie area that was full of makeshift shops and cafés. One of them was run by a long haired Italian by the name of Slim. His cafe had a vegetarian, health food menu, also he was a master of speaker cabinet designing as was evidenced by the large stereo that he had set up with his own design of speaker cabinets connected to it. Gypsy sat down and talked with him for a while, listening to what he had to say about cabinet design. Slim had been about on the road for many years and at the time had been based in Nepal for some while. He was a well known face amongst the travelers.

There were many other cafes that looked like they had been designed by and for the hippies and travelers too.

Gypsy walked on along the road occasionally bumping into people that he knew, either from Kathmandu or elsewhere on the road. He would stop and chat with them and they would speak of journeys and adventures that they had recently made and give each other relevant news from the road.

He ended up back at the guesthouse. A family of rich Indians from Bombay had just checked in. They were sitting in the restaurant trying to show off to the other Indians and everyone else by speaking English between each other. They had servants with them who they treated in the most demeaning of ways and also they tried to treat the Nepalese waiters in much the same manner.

Gypsy was walking to the restaurant when one of the waiters came out carrying a tray "these Indians are no good" he said to Gypsy as he went past fizzling and crackling with rage.

It is worth mentioning that at that time at least, there was a very good rapour between the Nepalese and many of the westerners and many friendships were thus made. Gypsy for his part had told the waiters how he remembered when he had worked in kitchens and served food to people for the most miserable of wages back in Israel, so knowing that, they felt safe to speak with him about it.

Soon it became like something out of a comedy movie as the Indian family continued unknowingly to embarrass themselves and everyone else who was in the restaurant at the time. The waiters were all outside swearing, hissing and spitting and taking it in turns to go in and serve. They would if they got called to the Indian table end up leaving the room with their teeth bared in an angry snarl.

As this was going on, the manager of the hotel came and saw Gypsy and his family and said "I hear that you are looking for a porter, is that true?" to which Gypsy's family all said "Yes" and nodded in unison. I have a very good man who I have sent with people before, would you like to meet him" "That sounds like a good idea" said Gypsy's father.

The guesthouse although it was basic and simple was also one of those few places that can be found in that part of the world that just oozed with integrity.

The menu was basic and simple, but the kitchen was very clean, no one in their right mind would complain about the prices of anything there and they survived on their good name that was printed in one or two of the low end travel guide books. The place had been given most favorable write ups.

They also operated low end but solid, value for money, tourist services.

The next day they met Nima who was to be their porter, he didn't speak much English but he knew his way through the mountains and although he was tiny in size, would think nothing of carrying a pack of thirty five to forty kilos on his back for the whole day, from sun up to sun down.

Gypsy was better now and they were ready to leave early the next morning. If the guesthouse was making a commission on Nima's pay then it couldn't be very much as what he asked for as his pay for each day was miniscule.

Early the next morning they took a bus to the end of the road and then started walking. They had two packs between the three of them and Nima had a small bag that he tied on the top of the pack that he was carrying. Gypsy and his father split the work of carrying the other pack between them.

Some people took rides on decrepit old pickups that bounced along the rough stone strewn dirt tracks to the base of the first large hill. But Gypsy and his parents thought better of it and used the walk out to get themselves exercised and warmed up in order to be ready for the climb.

After a couple of hours hike they were at the base of the hill, then they started the climb up. The path was mostly steep and it brought everyone but Nima to a point when they were really sweating. In any other part of the world but the Himalayas and possibly the Andes such a hill might be called a mountain, but in Nepal this was just a hill. Up and up and up they went until eventually they were on the top. They then walked along for a while, as they still climbed but at a more gentle angle as they walked up through the forest. Eventually by the end of the first day they had reached a large village and looked around for a chai shop at which to spend the night. As they got further into the village they saw other westerners sitting around at a chai shop and drinking beers and so they wandered over and got themselves fixed up with beds in the chai shop's upstairs dormitory. There was an Australian man in his late thirties to early forties chatting with another westerner as they reached the chai shop.

"Yea my son tells me that here in these mountains, they grow some really strong whoopee weed, I'm hoping that I get a chance to try some of it" he said. Gypsy grinned, you didn't see so many people of his age, who spoke about it in such a straight up manner.

They got talking later with another hiker, he had just done a trip up into the Annapurna sanctuary (a place that is ringed on all sides by the Annapurna mountain range). He had his own personal guide, cook, and porter with him and other than them was travelling alone. He was an American who worked in Switzerland as part of a team who managed investments for a small group of extremely wealthy clients. When he was on holiday however he liked roughing it in far flung lands while he walked, climbed and explored.

The next day they were up and out of the door before the sun was up.

Just as they had hauled themselves up the hill the day before so they had to drop back down on the other side that morning. In the distance at the bottom they could see a river, a bridge and a large village.

It took only an hour to make the descent and reach the bridge, which like most bridges in these mountains, was a narrow rope, Wire and plank suspension bridge, wide enough to get pack mules and people across but no more.

On the descent they had passed mule trains going in the opposite direction, the lead animal always had a bright colored plume attached to it's head. The people of the mountains got most of if not all of their supplies of out of district commodities either via porter or from the multitude of mule trains that were run up and down all of the main paths of that area of the Himalayas.

They crossed the river into the village, a pleasant place with paved walkways and large Hindu shrines. On they walked, passing numerous chai shops along the path that followed the valley floor, then they started to climb again. Going up and up and up until by the early middle of that afternoon they had reached a village that was just below a huge forest of Rhododendrons.

They stopped and got sorted with beds for the night and then relaxed for the rest of the day as the next day was going to be a long hard hike, going uphill only.

There was a crowd of young Americans staying at the chai shop who were on a three month adventure, travelling in Asia. Also there was a group of educated young Indians from Calcutta. Gypsy had made friends with some Anglo Indians from Calcutta before and from them had learned a bit about the life and the ways of the Bengali people. He immediately hit it off well with this crowd and soon they were all sitting around talking animatedly about everything from religion to what are the greatest current problems in India and how to get to the root and solve the problem.

They all spoke English exceptionally well, all be it with a Bengali accent and a good deal of head wobbling. They were the kind of people that were the hope for a new dawn in India.

They were Hindu, but they were as against the misuse of the caste system as a tool of abuse as anyone. They were university educated and also had sharp and fast thinking minds to compliment it. Gypsy sat chatting with them until late into the night. It was one of them who explained to Gypsy how there were two types of time in India. "There was Indian standard time, by which all of the institutions of state and commerce operated and there was Indian stretchable time which was what most of the Indian people worked by" he explained. Everyone laughed because they knew how very true it was. It was the best and truest description of the situation.

The next morning, again before sunrise they were out on the trail with their packs, climbing up through the Rhododendron forest. It was reported to be a dodgy and dangerous area with bandit attacks against foreigners having been reported on several relatively recent occasions. They walked with a group of other travelers for the few hours it took to reach the top of the forest. Then they were out and walking and climbing up and up. Eventually in the early afternoon they reached Gorapani on the top of the pass. They were at twelve or thirteen thousand feet up and the air was thin but the view of the valley below was spectacular.\, they could see almost to where they were to walk to the next day, at the far end of the valley

All the way up they had seen the constant stream of travelers and trekkers and also multitudes of mule trains and porters. Gypsy had run into another traveler who he knew from both Hong Kong and Bangkok. He stopped to talk, telling him briefly about what he had been up to in China, the Philippines and Japan and then listened as the other traveler told him about what had been happening to the other travelers who they both had been hanging out with in Hong Kong. Two of them had moved to Bangkok where a couple of Thai hookers had moved them in with them as their regular boyfriends, while taking care of them financially as well as in all other ways, (sounded like a pretty good deal to Gypsy and sadly reminded him about Yolanda). Two of the others had had a bit of a misadventure in Bangkok. They were two British likely lads out on a journey across Asia without much of a clue about or much respect for the cultures within which they were travelling.

One of them had gone missing completely and the other had turned up in such a state of shock that he could not speak. So no one knew at that time what had happened to them or whether the one who was missing was still alive or laying face down somewhere in one of the clongs (canals) around Bangkok.

In the mid eighties there were far less travelers around than there are today. Life was different from today in that there were no mobile phones to call home on or credit and debits cards that could work through an ATM. Anyway travelers were not the sort of people who would have access to such things. If you needed to get money wired in in an emergency there were twenty four hour services run by Thomas Cook and American Express (meaning that they would Endeavour to get the money to you wherever you were in the world within twenty four hours). Everyone travelling carried a mixture of cash and travelers cheques and maybe jewellery or just gold for selling. This would have made the two lads who had had the problems in Bangkok, attractive targets for Thai criminals to roll, especially if they had been doing smuggling runs and were loaded with cash.

Gorapani was a quite large village with a multitude of chai shop guesthouses.

The one that Gypsy and company had chosen even offered private rooms. A rarity and special luxury on the trail. It was cold up there on the pass and there was a permanent fire burning in the hearth of the chai shop's hall. An old man was crouched down beside the fire smoking a chillum, 'Charas?', Gypsy ask him as he pointed at the pipe. The old man smiled and nodded and gestured for Gypsy to join him for a smoke. Gypsy crouched down and joined him and they passed the chillum back and forth between each other as the more straight travellers around looked on in shock. They had all made many suppositions when they had seen Gypsy walk into the place with his parents and now here he was doing a session of Boom Shankar (praise Shiva) with one of the old locals, billowing huge clouds of hash smoke into the room while his parents looked on nonchalantly. They had all made many assumptions that had now been blown so far out of the window that they were practically gibbering as they asked Gypsy "do you always smoke in front of your parents?" "Look I don't hide it from them if that's what you mean, I've been on the road on this trip for over two years and I've been travelling for a long time before that. In my last job that I quit just two weeks ago I was a senior high school teacher in Tokyo. I have done many other things too in the last few years. They were coming out here for a holiday and I know the area and the culture a little so I thought I'd better join them in order to make sure that they are safe on the journey. It's not quite the same as a walking holiday in the Alps as you can see. As such I live by my own set of rules. I don't stop them if they want to drink and they don't give me a hard time when I want to smoke Ganja or charas, I'm going to do it anyway so why hide it?"

Gypsy's mother took a hike along with Nima before dawn to go and watch the sunrise from a nearby peak just over one hours climb from the village.

Neither Gypsy or his father bothered, as it was going to be a very full day's walk down and along the trail to Tatapani (which in Pali the local language of Nepal, means hot water) by The Kali Gandaki river.

The Kali Gandaki river originates up past Mustang, [the hidden kingdom on the border with Tibet] on the Tibetan plateau. It flows on down through the Himalayas, joining with other rivers before eventually joining the Brahmaputra, which winds its' way through both India and later Bangladesh and then reaches the sea at the most northern point of the bay of Bengal.

With Gypsy's mother and Nima returned from their early morning climb, they started down. To Gypsy's surprise the path was paved for the most part with well worn flagstones set into the mountainside in many places in order to make steps. The path was quite wide and needed to be as there was a lot of traffic moving on it. There was a constant stream of porters, mule trains, hikers and locals, walking between villages. It could best be described as a pedestrian highway. Two Tibetan Kampa nomads went racing past, they were walking but at a pace that no one else could imagine doing in such terrain. They were dressed in traditional outfits and looked as if they had come from another world.

Through the day Gypsy, his parents and Nima dropped down and down and down. Each time they saw a ridge below them and expected to see a clear view down to Tatapani after it, they were disappointed to see yet another hill or ridge blocking the view.

Eventually on the last light of day they reached the rope bridge across to Tatapani and reached a chai shop before it was completely dark.

The place had a fantastic menu. There they were, several days walk from the nearest road, in a land that looked like it had not changed much in the last two thousand years and not only could he order local and Indian food and the usual western things like a fried vegetarian breakfast, sandwiches, burgers and the like, but also they had both a full Italian menu and a full on Mexican menu. Gypsy ordered an enchilada. It could have been partly due to how hungry he was after the hike but the enchilada tasted wonderful and he would have been surprised if there were better ones in Mexico.

The Nepalese have proved themselves to be highly adept at learning how to cook many different types of food from many other cultures and counties and were probably the most versatile of all chefs on the subcontinent. This explained one part of why this restaurant was so good, but how the devil did they get the ingredients up there? they didn't have such things as refrigerated mule trains. The only explanation could be that most of the ingredients were grown and made locally.

The next day they relaxed and went to the hot springs, which were immediately next to the fast flowing Kaligandaki river.

Outside the guest house stood a lone mule that was fed regularly. Gypsy asked the owner why this mule was always there. The owner of the chai shop explained that one of the mule trains passing through had asked if this mule could stay and rest for a few days as he had a sore on his back. They had left some money to feed him and would collect him on their return back up to the higher villages in a few days time.

Nepal was a Hindu country, in fact it was the only country that was run entirely by Hindus and in a manner that accorded with Hindu ways. (India had many minority groups within it and even though Hindus made up the vast majority of the population, they had a secular constitution in order that all sides had a chance to be represented).

This meant that there was no death penalty in Nepal and you could be locked up for twenty years for killing a cow.

All life was sacred and animals as such were treated with more respect than in most other third world countries. This however did not mean that they were vegetarian, as occasionally they would make animal sacrifices at their temples for special occasions like weddings and religious festivals. However part of the aim of such a thing was to re-elevate the soul of the animal back up to human level or higher.

There was an understanding and compassion towards animals in the people, as they knew that animals have souls and personalities too, they saw it as if to say "that could be me stuck in that body, I had better work to make good karma to make sure that I don't end up where that poor soul is". As a result, it would be a very rare and strange sight to see an overloaded pack mule. They would never dream to treat their animal in the same manner as in China or the Middle East. They would overload themselves before they would ever over burden their mules.

In the mountains, many facilities that most other people now can take for granted, (not just in first world countries either) things like basic education, access to basic health care and medicines, electricity and public transport were all missing. Most people were illiterate and knew nothing about medicines, either the old systems like Ayervedic and herbal or western modern medicines.

They knew that westerners had modern "miracle" medicines in their packs, often in generous quantities. As such, locals and villagers along the trail would often approach foreigners and ask for help with ailments, some of them serious.

On the way through the mountains Gypsy's family was approached by a young man who was escorting his mother on her way to Pokhara to find a doctor. Her foot was swollen and desperately infected, she had a fever and was going to die it she didn't get help soon.

Gypsy's father got his medicine pack out and dug out an extra course of amoxytetracycline that he was carrying and gave it to the son, explaining via Nima (who it turned out did speak and understand some English) how many to take each day and when to take them, and told them that they should also continue to Pokhara as the infection would need more than just this to be fully cured, it would also possibly need a poultice of barley to pull out the poison. They explained as best as they could that whatever happened, she must take the medicines at roughly the same time each day and that she would need to make sure that she finished the entire course, even if she felt better before she finished it. Hopefully it cured her enough that she reached Pokhara safely and got treatment.

There were a few clinics that had been established in areas high in the mountains but they could still be several days walk from the outer high altitude villages that dotted the more remote valleys. Often by the time a person realizes that they needed to go and see a doctor they were already too sick to make the journey.

The level of poverty that these people suffered was unimaginable for those who have not seen it. It was not outwardly obvious like it was in the slums of Bombay. It was hidden behind the walls of beautiful, picturesque villages with thatched roofs and painted walls.

Being without even the most basic of infrastructure that even the most backward of countries would endeavor to put in for their people they were very much reliant upon themselves. There were stories of villages that had had famines and that most of if not the entire population of the village had starved to death when their crops failed. There was great beauty in the mountains but also there was great sadness too.

No wonder they so eagerly and warmly welcomed the hikers. They really did, for the most part put on an exceptional effort to make their guest's stay as enjoyable as possible.

This was an area of the world where tourism really caused substantial benefit to a large swathe of the population.

From the chai shops and convenience kiosks and shop owners to the porters, mule train operators, farmers and the likes, tourism helped alleviate some of their poverty.

A holiday in Nepal even then could be considered very much as an eco holiday, as for much of the time there a person would not be using electricity or motorized transport of any kind. They would be eating locally produced organic vegetarian food and contributing just by spending a little money there to a better life for the impoverished locals.

The owner of the chai shop at Tatapani had gas lights that ran at night. The gas was generated from the organic waste that the guesthouse produced. This was a concept and a rather good one at that, that was being promoted by some of the charities that worked within the subcontinent. It was likely that he had got some help in making the device from a charity expedition to the mountains. Either that or he had heard about it and applied to have the parts or the whole apparatus brought to him on one of the mule trains.

The next day Gypsy took off up the trail with his parents, they were following the river up the valley. Then Gypsy's mother said that his father had not been feeling at all well that morning. "Then what the hell are we doing hiking to high altitude if one of us is not feeling well? it really won't help, he needs to rest another day before going up again." "Gypsy exclaimed, "he wants to do it" said his mother. "If we are going to be climbing back up and possibly to higher altitudes than at Gorapani then we all need to be fit before we start as it will just aggravate the problem to walk all day in bright sunlight and then to sleep at altitude" Gypsy replied.

Finally after a bit more persuasion they agreed to return to Tatapani and rest another day. It turned into two days rest as his father recovered.

After this there was not enough time to make it up to Jomsom and back before his parents had to fly out. So they decided to drop down through another trail that reached the highway thirty five kilometers south of Pokhara. The trail dropped down along the Kaligandaki River and passed through the towns of Beni, Baglung and Kusma, reaching the road just after the village of Karkinet.

They followed the trail down early the next morning as it wound along the river valley. The walk was relatively easy as most of it was in a downhill direction. There were far less hikers and chai shops on this trail as they walked along. Nima would stop occasionally and chat with porters going in the other direction. Being as few of them could read or write this was the substitute for a newspaper as they passed information back and forwards. They passed through poor but highly picturesque villages where the locals had built big toys on the village green for their children to play on.

The favorite design and the one to be seen in most villages was a mini **ferris'** wheel with bars to hang on to and space for four children. It would invariably be made of wood and stand about ten to twelve foot in height (3 ½ to 4 meters).

The people lived from subsistence farming and there were terraced fields on the hills around the villages. Up much higher on the sides of the mountains in the far distance other smaller and no doubt poorer villages could be seen perched precariously in places that did not look so inviting to live at. How they had managed to make terraces in such places was hard to imagine, life must have been tough in such a place.

Some of the villages, even on the trail were so poor that it would be hard even for a seasoned traveler to imagine just how hard must be the life of its inhabitants. This area of the world suffered cold weather including frost and snow at times during the winter. The need for firewood as well as food would mean that they would have to work even harder than the poor people lower down the trail.

They stopped in a village to eat but as there was no chai shop Nima went and spoke with a woman at a nearby house.

She was more than happy to make a little money by making Dahl Bahts for them all. (Dahl Baht was the staple Nepalese meal similar to a south Indian rice plate or a very simple vegetarian thali – it would typically consist of rice, dahl a vegetable curry dish and a dollop of achar, which was a hot pickle.).

They sat down on the rope mat in her front room, while she cooked. All of the houses were painted white and brown in the village and it appeared that the mud bricks had been lined with clay that had been baked by the sun before thatched roofs had been placed on top. Some of the houses were bungalows and some were two storied. In essence the houses resembled the type that people in England were using several hundred years before. However, the inhabitants of these dwellings appeared to be a damned site more enlightened and peaceful than our own savage ancestors.

The food came out served on spotlessly clean stainless steel plates and although the food was simple, it tasted really good. Absolutely no ingredients had come from a packet or tin, in fact most of it if not all had come from the surrounding fields. It was the first time that Gypsy had ever tasted a freshly made achar. It was made with slices of muli [giant white raddish] with lime juice and sesame oil mixed with different spices. It was the best achar that he had ever tasted in his life. It was not however the sort of thing that you could buy in the local supermarket or order in the local Indian restaurant back in England.

When they went to pay her she asked surprisingly little money and it could be assumed that Gypsy's father left her a tip that made her day. So once again they headed on down the trail.

In the late afternoon, they reached the town of Beni and stopping for the night, checking in to the one chai shop that was set up for westerners. It was not big and it was almost full. Just about everyone who had come down the trail from Tatapani that day was staying there.

It was not such a well known route and as such there were only ten to fifteen other travelers and hikers in the place.

Gypsy pulled out his small portable tape player from his bag and put a tape of John McLaughlin's Mahavishnu orchestra "from nothingness to eternity" album on. His mother complained and Gypsy was about to turn it off when all of the other travellers said "no leave it on we like it". There was a young British woman in the corner smirking with assumption, obviously thinking that Gypsy had flown in to Nepal with his parents.

Gypsy went over and sat with her and pulled out his piece of charas, his cigarettes and his rolling papers as he asked her casually "so how long have you been travelling then?" At this point she stuck her nose up in the air in a gesture of arrogance and said "Oh I've been on the road for a year now."

"Really?" said Gypsy "so where have you been?" "Oh I was living in Amsterdam up until when I came here a month ago" she said "you didn't go anywhere else but Holland?" Gypsy asked incredulously. "No" she said. "What about you?" she asked, "Are you on holiday?" "No, said Gypsy. I'm also on the road, my parents were coming here for a holiday, it's their first trip to this part of the world, so I thought that it would be better if I was here to keep an eye out for them and make sure they stay safe. Up until two weeks ago I was working as a senior high school teacher in Tokyo"

Gypsy had finished rolling a large spliff filled with Nepalese charas and put it in his mouth and lit it. At this point the woman looked at him with a shocked look on her face. There he was smoking a spliff in front of his middle class British parents and no one was saying a word. It was almost possible to see the cogs ticking around in her head imagining what would happen if she tried the same thing at home.

Gypsy continued to puff on his joint as she asked "so how long have you been travelling?"

"I've been making long journeys and living in other countries on and off for the last six years now" said Gypsy "but I started this particular journey exactly two years ago give or take a couple of weeks."

"Where have you been then? She asked Gypsy took a couple of hits on his joint and then handed it to her, then he started to tell her about his travels.

It was a somewhat less uppity set of eyes that was looking at him after that. The dope had also helped.

Beni had no roads in or out but there were several vehicles that had either been carried in by hand or else lifted in by plane or helicopter. There was an airstrip that was serviced with a daily flight to Pokhara. The vehicles could only be used in the town and parts of the valley and were operated by the local municipal and emergency services. The Town of Beni was set up on a rise of the valley floor and was a centre for local services including medical. It had pharmacies and a small hospital plus of course a police station, local government offices and a small army garrison.

The next day they walked on down the trail then climbed high up on to a plateau where the town of Baglung was located.

Baglung was surrounded by lush green fields, except for where the wheat had become ripe, where it was a golden brown color. The local farmers were threshing the grains from the stems by bashing bunches of wheat heads on a large rock and catching the grains with a reed mat screen propped up a meter from the rock.

Ploughing was done using water buffalos and there was not a machine to be seen.

The town of Baglung looked similar to Beni, except that it looked a little bit richer, probably due to its good soil and lush crops.

Gypsy had taken to walking with the English woman as they chatted about travelling and Gypsy gave her a briefing on what to expect in India, her next destination after Nepal. They stopped for lunch at a chai shop shortly after Baglung and then carried on walking, dropping back down to join the trail along the Kaligandaki to Kusma.

By the later afternoon they had reached Kusma, a far more developed town with stone paved streets and a larger population. Again it had no roads in or out but at that time one was under construction and destined to reach them within the next few years.

The chai shop was bigger but not so comfortable a place as the ones that they had stopped at on previous nights. There were quite a few guests and they had a better menu than the one at Beni. There was electricity in Kusma, at least at the guest house there was. However it was a boring evening and Gypsy was glad to crash out early.

The next day as they walked it was cloudy. They stopped at a chai shop along the way for a tea break. The woman in charge of the place first made them a cup of chai each and then came out and indicated that she had toothache and asked via Nima if they had some medicines that could help her. They gave her a bottle of oil of cloves and some pain killers and advised her via Nima to go to Pokhara and see a dentist quickly before it got any worse.

It was poor along the trail to Karkinet. There were porters carrying goods up the trail in bamboo baskets, taking supplies to Kusma, Baglung and Beni. They were overloaded and many didn't even have proper trousers, they were wearing just loin clothes, shirts and decrepit old sandals. They were staggering under the weight of their loads and much pain showed in their faces.

There were other porters who were carrying building supplies including corrugated iron sheeting with each one carrying two or three sheets on their back and walking bent over and side ways to avoid hitting the side of the mountain or other walkers on the path. The job looked like pure torture. It was hard to imagine how must be the life of someone who had to earn his living in such a manner. Certainly none of them had a smile on their faces. It looked like the sort of work that should only be performed by particularly heinous convicts when it was necessary to break their spirits in order to reform them, but not the sort of work that a normal decent human being should have to perform.

They eventually reached Karkinet early in the afternoon and although they could have reached the road by sunset, they decided to stay at the village just in order to have one more night in the mountains without electricity or the sound of motor vehicles.

They had climbed up to Karkinet from Kusma and were now at the top of the pass. The main street of the village ran along the ridge and the houses were built on either side of the hill. The houses were painted brown at the bottom and white on the upper part. The walls were made of sun baked clay stuck on like stucco. Gypsy was told that the amount of white on each house indicated the caste of the inhabitants. Karkinet was a poorer village as there was not so much good available farm land around it. It was at the top of a steep pass and any fields that did exist were small terraces. However, the village did well by trading with porters, travelers and a small number of foreign trekkers who would passed by each day. There was quite a large Hindu temple in the centre of the village and a shop selling Indian style sweets such as jalabis barfi, ras gula and gulab jamun.

Gypsy went and bought a piece of barfi and sat down for a cup of chai as he watched the procession of porters as they made their way through the village. The woman who ran the guesthouse was a good looking woman and appeared to be in her late twenties. She was lively and constantly making earthy jokes with her foreign guests, especially the young male ones. She was a character. The food at her guesthouse was particularly good and the females of the family worked and ran the place while the men worked in the fields.

The building was of the same most basic style two storied design as the other houses in the village and they were all joined together in a terrace. Accommodation consisted of an upstairs dormitory and a shower consisting of a bucket of cold water outside the house, on the backside of the building and slightly down the hill.

The next morning they walked on down the hill, passing terraces of poor soil where the meager crops had just been harvested and only broken stems remained.

Eventually in the early afternoon after a descent downwards that had started just after dawn, they reached the road. They had passed on their way the area where the road to Kusma was being constructed, however it had been on the other side of the river from the track on which they were walking. It looked set to miss Karkinet, thus depriving it in the near future of much of its chai shop money.

The road was a side road, leading to a small village, but eventually it would lead up past Kusma to Baglung. However if it was ever to reach Beni it would need some very serious money put into the engineering, as to drop the road down from the plateau at Baglung to the river would be no small task.

They rode on the roof of a local bus to Pokhara as inside the bus was full. Sitting and bouncing and rocking along with the locals who were also up there. While the bus was bouncing along the road the ticket collector climbed out of the back door of the bus and hauled himself up onto the large roof rack and went around taking money and selling and checking tickets. Job done on roof he did his movie stunt trick again as he climbed back down into the bus. They reached Pokhara before dark and went back to the same guest house that they had stayed in before.

Nima was paid and judging by the expression on his face he was more than happy with the tip.

It had been an easy few days work for him, working for the most part for what to him were half days, carrying a pack that was well under thirty kilos and having chais bought for him along with his food, through the day and sometimes a beer in the evenings. But then he had done his job well and without any complaint. He knew the paths and sometimes guided them and had always guided them to where the best food was. He was a quiet relatively happy individual who had been a pleasure to have around on the walk.

The next day they relaxed in Pokhara taking the bus back to Kathmandu the following day. Back in the Kathmandu valley Gypsy gave his parents a tour of Bhaktapur and two Buddhist stupas at Bhodanath and Swayambu.

Swayambu was also known as the monkey temple as thousands of monkeys lived in the forest that covered the hill on which the stupa was located. They were well fed from the visitors who bought food for them. however if they didn't have fur they would most likely all have gotten busted for gross public indecency for what many of them were getting up to. It is possible that whoever had written and illustrated the karma sutra could have learned a thing or two from them. However what many of them were doing would have been deemed far too perverted for such a book and would have been much more likely to feature in some depraved pervert magazine from the sewers of Soho or Dam square area in Amsterdam.

One such furry pervert ran along and jumped on Gypsy's shoulder and demanded a free ride to the top. Gypsy was in no position to argue with this hairy bag of teeth and claws as it showed its teeth aggressively. So he walked to the top and the monkey jumped off as he got there.

Later they descended among the masturbating and butt fucking monkeys and walked back into town. Gypsy wondered whether they behaved like that every day or whether they had inadvertently picked the day of some special religious occasion to visit the Stupa, when the monkeys throw an orgy and outrage public decency as a way of honoring their God.

The next day they visited Patan to see it's Durbar square, which is lined with some of the largest and most beautiful Hindu temples in Nepal. After this as Gypsy's mother was a potter they made visits to several small villages where ceramic items such as water pots were made. A local potter spun a large pot to demonstrate how it was done. He worked crouched over a large stone wheel that spun in a notch in the floor. The sheer weight and velocity kept the wheel spinning well without too much attention as he shaped out the large roundish dollop of clay that he had thrown on it. It was incredible to watch this guy spin out such a large and perfectly spherical water jar with such basic tools. He showed the firing technique where a large pile of rice husks were placed over a six foot high pile of water jars then just set on fire. Teracotta fires at a relatively low temperature but Gypsy had no idea that you could generate the heat necassery with something as light and fast burning as the husks and stems from a grain crop. Gypsy also took them by to the local Hare Krishna temple to show them a bit about where his spiritual interests had taken him.

The temple was far more laid back than many he had been at and was run by an ex hippie from America who explained about the movement's roots in classic Hindu Vedic culture. And how far from being a cult, it was a deep and respected part of the Indian religious ways.

The next afternoon his parents were flying back to London and so Gypsy accompanied them to the airport and saw them off. He had been sad to see them go and thought about returning to England to live there for a while during the following spring and summer. They had also brought a form with them that they asked him to sign. Apparently, at the time when Gypsy was born his grandfather had placed some sixty four pounds into a trust fund for him, now it was time for it to be released to him and it was worth over two thousand five hundred pounds.

"Waow" thought Gypsy to himself, "I've got over four thousand dollars to last out the winter on and now I've got this too. Grandad would wish me to use it wisely and besides it would be a good idea to think long and hard about how to spend this money."

Gypsy headed to the Pumpernickel bakery straight from the airport to join the expat and Indian afternoon chillum circle in the back garden. All the regulars were there and Gypsy sat down and joined the group. He had hit it off well with a group of Anglo Indians from Calcutta and some of the Germans, Swiss and Austrians who were hanging out there too.

The big news at that time, and had been for a while concerned what had happened to Bhagwan Shri Rajneesh at his 'spiritual' commune in Oregon. He had just come out of three years silence and denounced Ma Sheila, the Indian woman who set the place up and ran it, as a dangerous megalomaniac.

She in turn along with a small group of cronies had fled in two aircraft and had made it to Switzerland before being arrested and deported. Almost every day was bringing fresh news either of statements from Bhagwan or of actions taken against him by U.S. authorities.

His disciples at that time, all wore orange clothes and a malla of black beads with a picture of him set in a round frame or laminate in the centre, around their necks. People of all walks of life including the hippies and travelers tended to avoid them as they were sometimes infamous for their totally outrageous behavior.

He was known as the Guru of drugs, sex and rock and roll on account of some of the techniques that he recommended to his disciples to help them develop spiritual clarity. The thing that he was perhaps most famous for other than his collection of ninety three Rolls-Royces that had been given to him by his disciples, was a talk that he had given on Christianity. At the end of which he read out a complaint from one of his disciples, who claimed to be upset by Bhagwan's regular use of the word fuck. At which point He said "why are you so offended by this word" and told the person that the English speakers of the world should be proud to have such a versatile word in their language.

He then, to everyone's amusement listed off a myriad of different uses for the word:

the last question ...

Bagwan, I feel shocked when you use the word "*fuck*"

what to do?

sargamo, it is one of the most beautiful words. the english language should be proud of it.

I don't think any other language has any such a beautiful word. One of the most interesting words in the english language today is the word "*fuck*".

it is one magical word: just by it's sound it can describe pain, pleasure, hate and love.

in language it falls into many grammatical categories.

it can be used as a verb, both transitive: "*john fucked mary*"

and intransitive: "*mary was fucked by john*"

and as a noun: "*mary is a fine fuck*"

it can be used as an adjetive: "*mary is fucking beautiful*"

as you can see, there are not many words with the versality of "*fuck*".

besides the sexual meaning, there are also the following uses:

- fraud, *"I got fucked at the used car lot"*
- ignorance, *"fuck if I know"*
- trouble, *"I guess I am fucked now!"*
- aggression, *"fuck you!"*
- displeasure, *"what the fuck is going on here?"*
- difficulty, *"I can't understand this fucking job"*
- incompetence, *"he is a fuck -off"*
- suspicion, *"what the fuck are you doing"*
- enjoyment, *"I had a fucking time"*
- request, *"get the fuck out of here!"*
- hostility, *"I am going to knock your fucking head off!"*
- greeting, *"how the fuck are you?"*
- apathy, *"who gives a fuck?"*
- innovation, *"we need to get a bigger fucking hammer"*
- surprise, *"fuck! you scared the shit out of me"*
- anxiety, *"today is really fucked"*
... and it is very healthy too.

if every morning you do it as a trascendental meditation just when you get up, the first thing, repeat the mantra: "fuck you!" five times ... it clears the throat.

that's how I keep my throat clear!

enough for today.

Gypsy got invited to move in at the house of some of his Indian hippy friends. He was often around at their place and had passed out on a couch after long chillum sessions on several evenings. "Come on Gypsy you may as well just move in with us, you're always falling asleep around here as it is" one of them said.

So after a time he moved in with his Indian friends. He was also spending some time over at the Hare Krishna temple. However he was spending a lot of time alone, reading. He had rented a small cheap room with no attached bathroom at the peace guest house that was near to a river on the west side of the city. Even though he was staying at the house of his Indian friends, he needed somewhere to go and get peace, a place where he would not be disturbed. He was deeply engrossed in the Ramayana and was planning to read the story of the Buddha next. The story of Ramayana had two authors Valmeek who was the original author and Tulsi Das who was a poet and was born long after Valmeek had died. To be fair, all he did in actuality was to take Valmeek's story and embellish it. Valmeek had his own story too. He had been a bandit in the woods who robbed and killed people.

One day a holy saint and his small group of disciples were walking through the forest and Valmeek and his gang pounced on him and his followers. They became angry when they found that the saint and his follower had nothing to steal.

At this point the holy man looked at him and said "tell me, why do you do these terrible deeds?" at which point Valmeek said "it's my job it is how I feed my family, I'm a professional bandit, if I don't do this my family will not eat." At this point the holy man asked another question. "Tell me would your family take responsibility for what you do to feed them?" At this point suddenly Valmeek felt puzzled and confused "I don't know" he replied at this the holy man advised that maybe it would be a good idea to go and ask them. Valmeek at that time was not the most trusting of people and so he tied the holy man and his followers to trees while he went back to his village to ask his family if they would take responsibility for his actions.

"No" said his father "I am old now it is your responsibility how you choose to feed the family it is no longer my responsibility". His wife said "looking after the house and all who live in it is my responsibility, but bringing food and other materials that we need is your responsibility I cannot take responsibility for what you do to bring home the food." Then he asked his children, they said "we are not old or strong enough to work yet you brought us into the world it is your responsibility whatever you do to bring home food for us."

Valmeek returned to the forest and untied the holy man and his people and said "none of them will take responsibility for what I do." "So what do you want to do now?" asked the holy man. "I want to find spiritual liberation and be free of this world of suffering" said Valmeek. The holy man advised that Valmeek should sit down and chant the names of Vishnu over and over again. "How can I do that? I am a bad person I have robbed and killed many people, how can a person such as me even say the name of God without bringing dishonor upon it, I am damned."

The holy man looked at him and said "well, sit down and chant 'I am damned' over and over and over again and eventually this will lead you to spiritual liberation." So he did, he sat down and chanted 'I am damned' over and over again. Eventually as he was chanting, the sound became Ram Ram Ram etc. Which is one of the names of Vishnu. He stayed there chanting for so long that eventually an ant hill grew over him and still he was sitting there chanting.

One day Ram and his brother were walking through this particular forest when Ram stepped on the ant hill and then out from it stepped Valmeek. Valmeek actually means 'he who step's out from an ant hill' in the local dialect of the area from where he originated.

He is famed throughout India for recording the story of Ram, Lakshman, Sita and Hanuman.

The story of Ram starts with a demon king performing great austerities in order to gain mystic powers. He had gained a great boon, being that no mortal man or even demi god could kill him, and was getting ready to do unstoppable bad deeds.

The demi gods, led by Brahma journeyed to the edge of the universe where they called across to Vishnu, the ultimate God who resides outside of the bubble of illusion and asked for his help to kill the demon before he destroyed the planet and possibly more.

Vishnu incarnates in pure form as Ram, the eldest son of a powerful king in northern central India. He forgets' that he is Vishnu but lives by the highest possible warrior code, thus setting an example for all to follow. His father had four wives and each one had many children. However Ram and his younger brother Laxshman were his two favorite children of his favorite wife. When Ram and Laxshman where teenage boys a well known highly accomplished Rishi (saint) came to the palace and demanded from the king that he lend him his two eldest sons for a spot of demon hunting in the forest where he was living. The demons had been desecrating his daily prayers and offerings to Vishnu.

The king was more than a little upset by the request as he was worried for their safety. But the Rishi was very powerful and also known for having a ferocious temper which was his one downfall. It had stopped him from reaching full liberation, he had even successfully cursed Indra the god of rain, on one occasion.

The demi gods had played a trick on him to test him. They had sent one of the women of great beauty from one of the heavenly realms within this universe to seduce him and get him to stop performing his daily and continuous austerities that he performed in order to try and gain spiritual liberation.

She walked into his life and for ten years he forgot his practices as he was totally infatuated with her.

One day he woke up and realized what had happened. He asked the woman who was now trembling with fear, who had put her up to this trick. When she told him that it had been Indra, the Rishi cursed him, causing his testicles to fall off. However the other demi gods could not allow Indra to remain with no balls so they cut the nuts off of a goat and sowed them onto Indra. The Rishi had been made to fall down in using his power in such a way and had to start his austerities all over again. Reluctantly and out of fear of what this Rishi could do if he lost his temper, the King agreed to let Ram and Laxshman go and help him.

So after a spell of demon hunting in the forests Ram and Lakshman returned to Ayudya, their home city. Shortly after, Ram got married to Sita (who's name in the local dialect meant 'from the furrow'). The story tells of how she had been found alone lying in the furrow of a field as a small baby and no parents had been found or seen near her.

Then later the king wanted to hand over power to his highly popular older son and go into the forest as a sadhu (holy man, ascetic) and find his way to spiritual liberation. Preparations were made for Ram's coronation and no one wanted anything different from this, except for one old hunch back hag who went to one of the kings' other wives and cajoled her out of her happiness for Ram and into a state of anger and envy for her own son.

She had been promised a boon by the king, of anything that she wanted that was possible for him to give to her, after she had saved his life on a battle field many years before. At the time she had told him that she would save the wish for later.

Now she was going to the king to call in the favor.

She demanded that her own son be placed on the throne, instead of Ram and that Ram be banished to the forest for seven years. Then to cut a long story short. Ram moved to the forest with Lakshman and Sita. His father died from grief and the brother who had been placed on the throne went to the forest to beg Ram to return and be king instead of himself. Ram refused, saying that he could not as he first had to keep his word to his father and stay in the forest for seven years. The half brother then asked Ram for a pair of his shoes as so he could hang them on his wall to remind him that he was just a caretaker King until Ram would return after the seven years to take up the throne. Sita was captured by the demon whom Ram has incarnated in order to kill. His name was Ravenna and he had a multi engined flying machine and lived in Sri Lanka.

On the way down through the forests of India to Sri Lanka, Ram and Laxshman met Hanuman the king of the monkeys who offered Ram his service including that of his monkey army. So Ram, Laxshman and hundreds of thousands of monkeys and bears headed on down through the jungle to the southern tip of India.

When they reach the coast they build a causeway across the shallow waters to Sri Lanka and marched across. A battle ensued between the demons of Lanka and Ram, Lakshman and the monkey army.

It sounded more like modern warfare that was being described in the book with missiles being launched that had all sorts of capabilities including ones that sounded like they were armed with some kind of nuclear device. There were stories of flight taking place not only with Ravana's flying machine. Hanuman is described as flying to the Himalayas to bring a certain medicine for Ram to cure him of the slow, deadly effects of one of Ravenna's missiles.

I'll stop telling you any more in case you wish to read the book yourself. It is one of the two most relevant Hindu books that are the basis of the religion. The most important and largest Hindu festival, Dewali is in celebration of certain events that happened within the pages of the Ramayana.

It is also to be noted that in all Hindu tales of God incarnating as a man on earth that he always has a close friend and brother that walks next to him. With Ram it was Laxshman, with Krishna it was Gopal (in Sanskrit 'Gopal' mean's 'the keeper') and with Guatama Buddha it was Ananda (Hinduism and Buddhism are so intertwined that it is impossible to see where they separate, Buddhism could be described as the crown of Hinduism. The Hindus view the Buddha as a pure incarnation of Vishnu and would be happy to put an image of him either inside a Hindu temple or on their private shrine room in their house.

Equally a Buddhist would not hesitate in using images of Vishnu or any of the Hindu demi gods to help emphasize points to any lesson that they teach, to do with the path to enlightenment.)

It is said by the Vedic teachings that when god incarnates as a man, then his effulgence his aura incarnates next to him as his protector. In statues of Vishnu his aura is often portrayed in the form of a multi headed cobra that is arched up around his head.

Gypsy enjoyed the book which was a mixture of both Valmeek and Tulsi das. Next he picked up a book about the life of the Buddha. He also picked up a book of Tibetan folk tales and several other books on Buddhist and Hindu themes.

Every afternoon he would go and join his friends from the house at the chillum party in Thamel. In the garden at the bakery he made friends with one German and his wife, who both used to dress like Tibetan

Kampas (tribal nomads from the high plateau) and would often smoke with them.

Also in the group was one Indian hippie who had a large but very peaceful dog called Barry. Barry's collar was a japa malla doubled or tripled up. (a japa malla as I explained in chapter 7 is a necklace of 108 beads that Hindus and some Buddhists use for counting how many mantras they have chanted. Just like a set of catholic rosary beads is used for counting prayers).

It was always an interesting crowd at the chillum circle and all sorts of news and information that could not be found in any newspaper on earth was exchanged.

Many of them had previous firsthand experience of heroin addiction at some point in their lives and so the topic of conversation moved to the 'brown sugar' pandemic around the world and its root causes.

"Look" said one of them "when I was young back in the sixties there were the hippies and the anti war peace demos and all that. Someone, maybe from the arms industry maybe from the CIA saw that the demonstrators were fond of trying different types of mind altering drugs and started putting people among the crowd selling bags of China white(East Asian heroin from the 'Golden Triangle' i,e, Thailand, Lao and Burma). No, one knew what the stuff was or what its addiction rate was like until it was too late. It did a lot to discredit the hippies and the peace movement, it also killed a lot of people. So isn't it strange when a new peace movement springs up in Europe against American nuclear missiles being stationed there and when another war in an area of the world that grow's opium where the Americans have gotten themselves involved, suddenly smack starts flooding western Europe and India, a country that refuses to bend over for America. They sell them low grade cheap heroin. The thing is that this it isn't working against the peace movement as the backbone of the movement now is made up of mothers and grandmothers".

A voice from the corner that will go without a name in this book said "Me and my friends have been doing business with the Afghans for years and used to deal in the mujahadeen hash, you know the stuff with the gold seal embossed on it like the stuff they used to sell in Kabul back in the seventies with the government quality stamp on it. Anyway there has not been so much of it around recently as everyone is starting to turn their main crops from ganja to opium. Some of them say they need the extra money that the smack bring's in to pay for the American weapons systems and guns. They are better than what the Russians have but much more expensive, but others have said that the Americans had actually refused to take hash money for guns and had set them up with smack laboratories instead. There are also stories coming from people in Pakistan about tracks through the dessert to the coast that only the smack runners use. They say that they have seen them moving in heavily armed convoys with the Smack being transported in eighteen wheeler trucks with machine gun nests on the roofs and they are surrounded by armored cars and heavily armed militias riding in four wheel drive pickups."

"Yes there are many dirty hands at work in this business but the circumstantial evidence points to the involvement of a right wing cabal in the American arms and intelligence community pushing and cajoling things along, Apart from the use the stuff has to them in attacking their perceived enemies [of which America always has so many] but also the business can generate billions of dollars that can be put aside to start other wars and fund things that their government has not given them permission for, with the invisible funds that the smack is generating for them" said another of the crowd.

"Never mind what is going on in Afghanistan, this place is crawling with spooks of all kinds" said the shadow in the corner. "There are CIA, DEA, Interpol and all sorts nosing around. The CIA have a listening post at Mustang where they monitor the Chinese from. Kathmandu is crawling not just with DEA but with drug cops from across Europe, Australia and Canada. I would be surprised if you haven't been tailed by them yet" he said while looking at Gypsy "after all you don't look too much like Mr. suit and tie yourself." "If I was a cop it would be the ones in the suits and ties that I would be watching the most" said Gypsy "hippies might move a little bit of hash and acid but it's suits that move pills and powders and besides anyone in a suit in Kathmandu would stand out and look dodgy anyway."

There were some quiet chuckles and smiles at this remark as everyone tried to remember if they had ever seen a westerner in a smart suit on the muddy streets of Kathmandu. Nepal really was not the place for such clothes. Even the staff at the embassies did not wear suits and the Nepalese parliament wore traditional Nepalese clothes. Gypsy for his part wore jeans with embroidered patches a Nepalese thick rough cotton white shirt and a highly embroidered waist coat. The chillum crowd were a colorful lot, with many people wearing both traditional Nepalese clothes and stuff that had been made by local tailors with the hippie, freak and traveler market in mind. Kathmandu was a hippie paradise. Everything was cheap and the local temples and houses were beautiful and colorful. The religions were all laid back and very mystical and as far as Kathmandu was concerned, Jim Hendricks, Janis Joplin and Jim Morrison had never died. Their music was to be heard, regularly blasting out from the stereos in many if not all of the myriad of locally run cafes around the city. City was perhaps the wrong word to describe Kathmandu.

It was more like a large overgrown village or a small town. Pokhara was certainly no more than a village even though it was one of the most important places of trade in Nepal. But Kathmandu was only deemed as a city on account that it was the seat of royalty and government.

Another place that Gypsy would go on more than just a few occasions was to the temples of Pashupatinath (which is the multi headed aspect of Shiva). No person who was not born as a Hindu of caste was allowed to enter the actual temple compound. But around the outside of the temple were many other temples and shrines and places where holy men lived. Down by the small river that flowed near the temple through a ravine there were small man made platforms where often (meaning a few times in a day) dead bodies would be placed on a pile of firewood and set alight, while the immediate family performed purification rites for both the deceased and for themselves in the river beside the funeral pyre.

It was all so very different from other parts of the world where death and dead bodies are a no no subject even for discussion in many circles. It being kept locked in the closet like a bogey man that keeps banging on the door while everyone tries to ignore it, while feeling subconsciously terrified of it. So terrified of it in fact that many of them will choose to ruthlessly ridicule anyone who brings the subject up or dares to say that there is more to the story than either the atheist or the Christian approaches care to acknowledge.

Every now and then the bogey man break's through and takes one of them. So for the next few weeks they all run around clucking and crying and those who spoke about death before and were ridiculed by the frightened ones is welcomed in and if they have any powers of vision they may be called upon. But after a few weeks or months when the trauma wear's off, it's back to the same old routine until the next time.

In this part of the world however death is out in the open every day. When someone dies in India or Nepal straight away they will find or make a stretcher and then place the dead body upon it and carry it openly through the streets to the local burning ghat. The family will purchase fire wood and possibly dried cow dunk also. If it is a man who has died and if he had sons then the sons would be required to have all the hair shaved from their heads, this applies to grandsons also if there are any.

In Hindu and Buddhist societies it is known that the soul is eternal and travels on and so even though there is nearly always sadness when someone dies it is as nothing compared to the fearful grief that Atheists, Christians and Jews feel, over death. The Indian and Nepalese newspapers at that time would often feature articles about children who could remember who they had been in their last life and had insisted on going to visit their previous family on the other side of town or a bus ride away across the countryside. Often they had taken their new parents around to their old home and after explaining who they were to their old family, introduced their new parents. In Tibet lamas who had died were actively searched for and their reincarnation would be brought back to the monastery that they had lived and practiced at before. Another activity that was also reported on regularly at that time in the local and Indian papers was that of Indian holy men would have themselves buried deep in the ground and be there for up to two weeks at a time before being dug back up. Then they would slowly come back to life and then speak of the oneness of all souls and speak instructions about compassion, non violence and tolerance to their disciples.

Gypsy always tried to make sure that while he was in Kathmandu that he made regular visits to the crowd in Dilli Bazaar taking them regular food parcels. It couldn't be much fun being locked up in that place.

Also he liked to go to Bhodanath where many of the Tibetans lived and sit around there eating Tibetan vegetable momos and drinking rakshi.

It was on one such visit while accompanying his German friends and their children that all hell broke loose. It had started in a relaxed enough way when they had stopped by at the house of some of the friends of the Deutschlanders. They had sat on the floor with them eating yak cheese and drinking Rakshi as the German man explained to Gypsy how the yak cheese was made at such high altitude that the milk did not ferment before separating. It was hard and required a lot of chewing.

After an hour or so at the house of their friends it was time to go and do what the German had come here for. He had put up an antique Tibetan Thanka (Tibetan religious painting) as collateral against a loan of some twelve thousand Nepalese rupees and now he had the money he was going to go and repay the loan and reclaim his beloved painting. However, when they arrived at the man's house the man invited them in but then told the German man that he had sold the Thanka. At this the German man exploded with rage and pulled a knife as both he and his wife attacked the man. Gypsy did the only honorable thing that he could given the circumstances and got the two young German infants out of the room while their parents did there psycho thing.

This had caught Gypsy completely off guard. It was not his fight and he wanted no part of it but he had to at least try and make sure that these two small children were safe even while their parents were doing the Freddy Kruger over a $500 painting.

The fight broke out into the street where Gypsy had taken the kids. They had to leave the area in a hurry as the whole community came out and started throwing stones and rocks at them. So they took off across the rice paddies following the elevated paths between the fields, but soon a police Vehicle arrived and the police came running and walking towards them. The German and his wife could not have easily made an escape as they were both dressed up like Fu Man Chu in their colorful but totally impractical Tibetan silk ceremonial outfits.

Before they arrived at where they were all standing, the German turned to Gypsy and said "you're safe they won't arrest you as you were not involved in the fight. When they arrest me and my family I want you to go into Kathmandu and find a certain restaurant and ask for my friend, he is the owner, tell him that I have been arrested and I'll need him to get me out.

The sun had been down for over two hours now and the evening was getting cold as the police approached them. They immediately let Gypsy go as the locals had told them that he had done nothing wrong. But they arrested the two Germans and also took their small children along.

Gypsy wasted no time and took the first auto rickshaw that he could find back into the city. He quickly located the restaurant and went running up the steps and found the owner and told him what had happened to his friends. "Come with me" said the owner. They went outside and got on a motorbike that the owner steered across the city and out some way into the country on the other side. They stopped at a house in a large garden and knocked on the door which was opened by a servant who led them into a living room on the backside of the house. They were greeted and asked to sit down by the chief of police for Kathmandu.

The Nepalese man spoke with the chief briefly and then turned to Gypsy and said please can you explain what has happened, to the chief here?"

So Gypsy explained what had happened including the events leading up to the fight. No one had been seriously hurt, so the chief picked up his phone and dialed the station and spoke briefly in Pali to whoever it was on the other end.

He then put the phone down and turned to Gypsy and said "please ask your friend to be more careful in his behavior in the future."

Then Gypsy and the Nepalese friend of his German friends thanked the chief and left. They rode back into the city and pulled up by the police station in Durbar square just as the German family were walking out towards the compound gate. They smiled and thanked Gypsy and their Nepalese friend. Then they all headed out of town to the house of the Germans, for a chillum session and some food.

At times in Asia, especially the subcontinent, corruption could be right in your face and blatant. But at other times it could be most subtle. But at times like this, though it may have been considered corrupt by the so called standards of western countries, what had just happened would not have been viewed that way in Asia. If you were living in a place like Kathmandu or any other similar sized town in that area of the world and you were a small businessman, you would by necessity have many friends. Problems were normally worked out in a friendly way within the community, often without the police being called upon. However, even if they were called upon, they generally only tried to keep the peace and were not much interested in arresting people or bringing charges. If someone had damaged something of someone else's or caused similar troubles or light injury to another, then the police would often, just force the culprit to pay some suitable compensation to the victim and stay there until the deed was done. Maybe later the victim would quietly give the police a tip or a nice gift for their troubles.

In the case of the Germans it was not too complicated. Thankfully no one had been injured and no one was vindictive enough to pursue the matter further. It had been purely a heat of the moment event. Their Nepalese friend was either a close friend or a blood relative of the chief of police and Gypsy got the feeling that maybe the Germans had put up the initial investment and helped with the design and the running of his restaurant with him.

One of Gypsy's Indian friends one day explained to him about how it worked with the Indian police.

"Never treat them as if they are stupid" he said" if they ask me if I smoke dope I never say no to them, as they know that I do, they can see it. It is always good to be polite with them even offer them a chai, but always watch their hands in case they decide to put something down that could get you into trouble. If they wish to search your place, always insist that you search them first. The small local cops don't want to make trouble for anyone. But Nepal gets a lot of aid money from abroad and of course most of the money ends up in the back pocket of corrupt local officials. So every now and then the Americans and Europeans demand that they do something to stop the flow of drugs. So the local cops are put out there to make some token busts just as so that they can turn around to the foreign governments and say "you see! we're not soft on drugs, we've just busted a load of people from your countries." It is obviously good to be on friendly terms with the local police and it is certainly not a good idea to keep too bigger stash in your own place."

His Indian friends had the top floor of a large house and the owner and his family had the lower two floors as their residence. One of the family was getting married and so down in the garden that for most of the year was a vegetable patch, they were preparing for the feast. They had baskets of live chickens that they were slaughtering and at one point a large part of the ground was covered in headless, flapping chickens.

By the evening the feast was prepared, bamboo mats had been laid across the empty vegetable patch and hundreds of people were sitting down to eat. Bottles of Rakshi were being passed around Gypsy and his Indian friends had been invited and were sitting amongst the locals. It was cold but everyone was well wrapped up in warm clothes and a good night was had by all.

Gypsy could still not think of a good idea of either what to use the money from his grandfather for or what to do in the spring. So he just drifted across Kathmandu each day, ending up in the mid afternoon at the Pumpernickel bakery for the chillum session.

Sometimes sitting there they would play a game of spot the Interpol foreign agent. Some people didn't fit the tourist mold. There casual clothes were a little bit too straight and smart for a tourist or a trekker. Their eyes and facial demeanor were neither relaxed or of a pleasant nature and from the sides of their eyes they would be watching the chillum circle. But it was the way that they did not fit into their surroundings that made them stand out the most, their body language was all wrong. They looked like people who were looking for someone to hate and victimize. There was nothing good in their eyes. Gypsy's Indian friends pointed a table of them out to Gypsy who eyeballed them hard. After that he found it easy to pick out other nasty narcs that came to the bakery.

It was the cheek of it that got to Gypsy the most. It was disgusting enough that alcohol and tobacco were actively pushed in the west, while ganja and hash, which are far less noxious were banned. But here were these vile, sleazy dollops of shit out in Nepal, the hippy Shangri-La trying to enforce their depraved ideas on another culture for one reason and one reason only and that was to control everyone and make them live how they wanted them to. Such behavior portrayed the collective insecurity and fear that was at the heart of western society.

Was it not indeed pathetic that someone who controlled enough ordinance to destroy the world umpteen times over felt disturbed by the fact that a group of people who were some six or seven thousand miles away from them were sitting down and happily smoking some hash together?

Ronald Ray Gun was president of the United States at that time. He was no more than the puppet of big business and the lunatic "Christian" right. The lunatic Christians were perhaps the most dangerous group as they believed some of the most retarded hogwash that had ever been spoken and all of them felt guilty and were looking around for someone to feel morally superior to. As such Ronny's obnoxious wife Nancy had gone on a moral crusade against drugs, even as the spooks were flooding India and western Europe with smack.

Some say the United States is the greatest and oldest democracy in the world, but it would be more true to say that it is the world's greatest hypocrisy.

One thing is for sure and that is when the right wing is in power it will always be the latter. At that time America had got itself involved in a war in El Salvador where the U.S. sided with the fourteen families that controlled the country like a bunch of mafia thugs and were committing terrible atrocities against the rest of the population. In Nicaragua where a peasant uprising overthrew a brutal and savage dictator, they sided with and armed the dictator's thugs and henchmen and sent them back to wage war on the population. In Guatemala, a country that was largely made up of indigenous tribal villages, they gave the evil dictator there humanitarian aid in the form of helicopter gunships which were used to murder close to half a million people, nearly all of the victims were tribals. It was genocide. They were involved in the conflict in Angola and the one in Afghanistan too.

They refused to deal or even speak with Cuba since Batista, their local friendly murdering dictator had been removed. They had no dealings with Lao and Vietnam and were sulking about the fact that their mighty war machine had received a hard slap on the nose from a peasant army who told them to fuck off and get out of their country. Never mind that they had been the aggressors the peasants had been expected to lie themselves down and willingly allow themselves to be napalmed. The Americans could not forgive them for refusing to do so. Never mind that America had murdered hundreds of thousands if not millions of them and fouled and poisoned their land with unexploded ordinance and Agent Orange. Never mind that it was still causing loss of limbs and life, not to mention horrendous birth defects to the local population. As far as the American government, it's military and it's arms industry were concerned they were in the right and the Vietnamese peasants were in the wrong. Never mind that Ho Chi Min and the Viet Min nationalists had helped them to defeat the Japanese in South East Asia during the second world war only to be betrayed by President Truman at the end of the war. They refused to even apologize, let alone pay any compensation for the damage that they had caused.

Now here they were in Kathmandu causing shit for the hippies while all the time moralizing at everyone.

A few months prior, Bangladesh had banned four American made drugs that were also banned for sale in the United States due to their highly dangerous side effects.

Ronald Ray Gun was then reported in the papers to have threatened Bangladesh, one of the world's poorest and most vulnerable countries, with serious consequences for refusing to import the American death medicines and administer them to their people. As such there was a lot of anti American feeling amongst the peoples of not just Central and South America but also amongst the Asians and Europeans. In Europe there were many demonstrations and campaigns against various aspects of American foreign policy and in Asia there was just quiet resentment at the behavior of the U.S. administration and big business.

The time was going by and Gypsy still had no idea what he wanted to do. He was watching the same things going on day after day and he was getting bored. He would have liked to have something to do some work or creativity or the likes. He had taken all the photos that he wished to take. He had got to know the place well but now he was bored. Every day he would do the same thing getting stoned and talking and listening to his friends. He was thinking of going to India for a trip around that country. He had only just scratched the surface on his previous trip there and wanted to see, feel and experience much more of it. Besides he now had a camera and he wanted to catch the place on film.

His room at the peace guesthouse was only used sometimes as it was costing him only $1.00 per day but sometimes he liked to go to the Manangi run café across the road.

The café looked totally out of place in the semi rural third world suburbs of Kathmandu, it was totally modern and hyper clean with a brand new, high quality espresso machine and other state of the art kitchen implements. But to Gypsy's surprise most of the customers were young locals. There was always good music inside and the customers were sitting at bar stools and skinning up large joints with generous chunks of top quality Nepalese charas. The only other westerners, who came to the place, were people who had been invited by Nepalese friends. The place from the outside did not look hippie cool, it was just too smart. However if a cop or a spook had the audacity to enter the place he would most likely have got a chunk of hash covertly dissolved into his coffee or a micro dot, or two in his ice tea. That of course was if he wasn't a regular customer, protector or supplier. This was one cool cafe full of young moderately well off Manangis, many of whom had travelled abroad. It was a well kept secret, it looked so expensive from the outside that not many people ventured inside.

A Nepalese girl had been giving him the eye, so they went out and about together for a while. But she didn't speak any English and he hardly spoke any Pali other than greetings and numbers. It was another world that she had come from in the villages high in the mountains around Gorka district. There was no point at which they had much in common.

A Canadian woman who Gypsy knew from Japan turned up in Kathmandu and was talking about making a journey around India, so they talked about making a trip together.

Just after Christmas, Gypsy suddenly felt hyper energy running through him one night and couldn't sleep.

As usual he had fallen unconscious with the rest of the crowd at the Indian house after a long chillum session. But suddenly he was wide awake in the middle of the night.

The downstairs door was locked so he jumped from a first floor window to the ground and headed off into the night.

He walked until he found his way to the five star Yak and Yeti hotel where he headed for the casino and bought a small quantity of chips and wandered over to the roulette wheel.

He played the one to eighteen and eighteen to thirty six alternately. He lost the first two goes but doubled his bet on the third and fourth and won. He had now won enough to pay for his drinks and so he stopped and cashed in his chips and went to the bar, passing on his way a Japanese tourist who was holding his head in his hands, he looked totally devastated. No doubt he had been considerably richer just prior to entering the establishment.

Gypsy on the other hand was not a natural gambler. He didn't normally gamble at all. This had been a strange one off affair and as such he had set himself a low and strict limit on how much he was prepared to lose. When he had won enough for his drinks he did not want to be greedy or push his luck.

After a drink or two in the hotel bar he took off on foot and walked down the road to Patan and spent some time sitting amongst the temples in the main square. It was now 3 o'clock in the morning and he was still feeling hyper. So he walked to Bhodanath which was a few kilometers away and waited and watched the sunrise from there before walking back to Kathmandu and having breakfast. Now that he had cleared his head he knew what he was going to do.

He was going to buy and have products made that he could take back and sell in England and Europe. That way he could both see his family regularly and spend some of each year living and working in India and Nepal.

After breakfast he started looking amongst the shops for products that he thought that he might be able to sell.

The next forty eight hours were the first time since Japan that he had had some time when he wasn't stoned, as he looked at various products for making business with.

The jewellery, gemstones and clothes looked like the best place to start and so that's where he concentrated his efforts.   He also looked at Tibetan products, especially thanka paintings, knifes and objects connected with spiritual practices. He was going to take his time and plan what kind of stock he wanted to buy during his coming trip around India.

He said goodbye to his friends and took a bus to Pokhara where he had arranged to meet the Canadian woman, Sally. Getting there late in the afternoon he found his way to a rather good but cheap guesthouse called the ANZUK. It was owned and run by a man who had served in the British Army Gurka Regiment for twenty six years, rising from the rank of private up to that of captain. He was very friendly and especially liked people from Australia, England and New Zealand. He was very proud of how he ran his guesthouse and employed the very best chef that he could find. Every now and then he would stop a waiter who was carrying food to the guests and pull out a spoon and take a small sample from the plate. If he was not happy with the taste and quality of the food he would send it back to the kitchen and make the cook do it again until it was up to the standard that he was happy to serve to his guests. Captain Kim ran his staff as if they were an army unit, the place was spotless, the staff looked clean and presentable and the quality of the food was second to none.

Gypsy was doing a little bit of business with a Tibetan refugee and Captain Kim warned the Tibetan seriously, not to consider cheating Gypsy or any of his other guests.

Gypsy ended up at a Tibetan refugee area up on one of the hills above Pokhara, where he traded his bulky sleeping bag (the one that he had bought in Sydney a year previously for A$50.00) for a multi colour striped Tibetan blanket and a couple of other items that he could either use or sell. He stayed for a cup of Tibetan butter tea but it was not his favorite of drinks, he wasn't so keen on tea that was salty instead of sweet. Then he headed back to the guest house.

There was an American woman that Gypsy knew from the chillum circle at the Pumpernickel who had rented a house facing onto the large lake. It was set up high above the lake, giving a good view and was a nice place to spend an afternoon smoking joints and playing guitar while in good company.

On the subject of music, Gypsy had listened to two young Nepalese musicians playing a single stringed bowed instrument and a drum and also singing with it. They were busking around the cafes along the lake side. They sounded so incredibly good that he not only gave them some money on the spot but also invited them to visit his guest house the next day as so as he could record them on to a cassette.

As it was they went and sat in a field and played while Gypsy recorded them and took photos of them framed by the fantastic peaks of the Annapurna mountain range that tower high above Pokhara. One of the peaks is known as Machupuchare in the local language and is a sacred mountain. It was strange and interesting therefore to know that on the other side of the world in Peru that there was another sacred mountain called Machu Pichu, Gypsy wondered if therefore there was some kind of connection, after all the peoples of the two different countries looked more than a bit similar and made similar types of handicrafts with the same exact choice of colors as each other. Also both nations had landscapes that were mostly made up of high mountain ranges.

Sally arrived after a brief few days trekking in the near by mountains. She had been taken to visit a Tibetan family by one Tibetan man that she knew. He had brought a small puppy back from his trip into the highlands (Pokhara is only 2,500 feet above sea level) The puppy stank so he gave it a bath. The puppy was most definitely not amused by the dunking that he got and was snarling with rage and even started growling angrily when the Tibetan man touched the dog with a towel to dry him. He was taking the dog to his uncle in Kathmandu as a present before returning to his home on a Tibetan refugee camp in Karnataka state in the south of India.

Sally and Gypsy left the following evening on a bus to Sonali which was down on the plains and was one of the main crossing points between India and Nepal. The bus trundled down through the mountains throughout the night. They reached the plains just after dawn. It was indeed a strange sight to see, looking back out of the rear window of the bus it was as if the Himalayas had no foot hills.

There it was, first the plain and then suddenly there was a wall of huge, massively tall and steep mountains. Of course, these massive mountains were the foot hills, as the true highlands lay at formidably higher altitudes than these mountains, but it was indeed a dramatic panorama just to see this massive natural wall.

Mist was rising from the land as the sun made it's appearance and the bus trundled on across the Terrai, as the Nepalese plains area is known.

After an hour or perhaps less they were at Sonali and checking out of Nepal at the passport control office. Gypsy had to pay a small fine as he had overstayed his visa but that had all been factored in before leaving Kathmandu where he had found out what the procedure was before deciding that it would be cheaper and easier to pay the fine than to get a new visa.

There was certainly no shortage of hustlers and harassers at the crossing. People were trying to literally grab the bags forcibly from travellers hands as so as they could carry it across the border and then try to demand an exorbitant tip. This kind of ridiculous and outrageous behavior was a symptom of the huge deficit of iodine in the diet of the people. Iodine deficiency causes cretinism and as such India at the time was overloaded with cretins. They could normally be found in the greatest of numbers around anywhere that there were many strangers passing in large numbers. They would pester and make themselves a nuisance to the passers by and do uncalled for deeds and then demand ridiculously huge tips even though the person had neither asked for or wanted the deed to be done.

Gypsy fought off the scrum and walked across to India carrying his own bags. A group of four Indian officials were processing the foreign passports while eating their breakfast of chai and jalabis (jalabis are a type of Indian sweet made from fried non egg based batter coated or dipped in sugar syrup – disgusting -)

The old 49 year visa on arrival had gone out of the window since the assassination of Indra Gandhi by her sikh bodyguards in the previous year. Now her one surviving son, Rajiv was prime minister and he or his immigration minister had decided that foreigners be given a visa for between three and six months, regardless of whether or not they were from commonwealth countries. So Gypsy had had to go and pay for a visa at the Indian embassy in Kathmandu before leaving the city.

Soon they were both through the border and boarding a bus to Gorakhpur. The bus bounced down the road across the Indian plains for several hours as they passed poor agricultural lands and equally poor villages. They bought fruit and cold drinks from vendors who surrounded the bus each time it stopped for anything, including traffic jams.

Eventually the bus dropped them at the bus station in Gorakhpur in the early afternoon and they took a rickshaw to the railway station and waited for their train. It was there shortly after they arrived. The first train took them to Lucknow, the capital of Uttar Pradesh. They reach there at 7:30 pm and waited for an hour until the night train to Agra arrived. They had bookings in the second class 3 tier sleeper section of the train, and so set about finding their carriage.

Soon they were on their way and after sitting and smoking a couple of joints they threw their bags onto their bunks and used them as pillows as they slept for the most part of the way.

The train pulled into Agra central station at 7 a.m. and they got off the train carrying their bags and found their way to a guesthouse.

Of course the first thing that they did after checking in and dropping their bags was to take a cycle rickshaw to the Taj Mahal. They had both seen so many pictures of it that they were excited to be seeing it for real for the first time.

It was still early when they got there and paid their fifteen rupee entry charge and went in.

However nothing could have prepared them for the onslaught of aggressive, pushy cretins who suddenly descended upon them from out of nowhere like a swarm of agitated flies and mosquitoes. They refused to leave them alone and hustled and pushed no matter how many times they were told to fuck off. All the way through the garden until they were inside the Taj itself they had to wrestle and push this iodine deficient mob of zombies away. It was not what anyone would expect to find when visiting one of the greatest wonders of the world.

The tour of the inside of the building was limited but interesting. The marblework was a wonder in itself. The Taj looked just like it did in the picture postcards in the early morning mist and the view across the Yamuna River behind it was also enchanting.

Then they fought back through the cretin hoards to the exit, managing to take a couple of photos of the Taj when the zombies had turned their backs for a moment. Otherwise they would leap about trying to pose themselves' into the picture, which was more than a little annoying.

They were given a tour of the red fort which was just down the road from the Taj and then went back to the guesthouse.

They both had upset stomachs from something that they had eaten and so the owner of the guesthouse suggested that he could make them a cup of opium chai which would calm their stomach ache and make them feel good for the day. They readily accepted and each had the most pleasant day, lying on chairs in the garden and feeling like they were floating in the air.

In the late afternoon they went for another look around in the town. They took a rickshaw into town but the rider only went a few blocks and then hustled them into a jewelry and gemstone shop.

The owner offered them a chai and then chatted explaining about gemstones for a while, before launching into an aggressive sales pitch. Each time they said now wait a minute he pushed on as he tried to convinced them that they could make a lot of money if they bought his stones and short of being extremely rude and aggressive there was no way they could get out of the shop.

He carried on and on with his sales pitch until he had them convinced that he was not lying. However, they both had an uneasy feeling about this humorless little man. No matter how hard he tried to ensure them of his sincerity, he had pushed and pushed so hard to sell them the deal that they pushed back hard and said wait we want to think long and hard about this. "What is there to think about" he said with his Indian bullshit sales shpeel which just made them more wary of this snake. They told him "look whatever happens we're not doing anything today and we really don't like the idea of parting with three hundred dollars each of our hard earned travel money on a chance". But still he latched on and tried to convince them that they were fools for turning down his offer and insisted on taking them for breakfast in the morning. At that they managed to wrench themselves free from this sticky persistent individual. They were both green to India even though Gypsy had been there once before could not have prepared him for the sleazy tricks of Agra.

There had been cretinism present among some of the people from out of state in both Goa and Bombay but nothing on this level - a symptom of cretin behavior is when someone is constantly trying to trick people using really dumb tricks and thinking of themselves as being very clever. However when the trick didn't work, if the person who they tried to trick did not get immediately aggressive with them and chase them away like a bad dog then they would most likely get aggressive and angry with their intended victim for refusing to be cheated. It was as if a few wires to do with logic were rattling loose and unconnected within their brains. There must have been plenty of others who suffered from the syndrome also but without menacing the public. But it was always the "ner do wells" that stood out, as these ones would fight their way through a crowd in order to harass a foreign tourist.

They got back into the rickshaw and carried on, but they didn't get more than a couple of blocks before the rickshaw pulled over again.

This time it was a marble shop. Their products were beautiful and incredible but there was no way of getting this stuffed shipped to England or Canada on the cheap and the product wasn't cheap in the first place. However, one does not expect a gemstone inlaid, marble chess or backgammon table to come cheaply.

The owners of the shop had distinct Persian faces so Gypsy asked them about it. It turned out that they were the descendants of people who had migrated from Isfahan in Iran to work in India centuries before and they had kept heir stonemasonry skills and passed them down through the generations.

When these men heard about their visit to Shalim gems, they said "Oh no" and asked anxiously "you haven't given him any of your money yet have you?" "No" they replied. "Thank goodness for that" they said "he is an out and out con artist, he specializes in ripping off tourists and young travellers such as yourselves. The stones that he want's to put in a parcel and send to you are worth a fraction of what he say's they are worth, you will only lose money dealing with him."

"Thank you very much for the warning" they both said "he was the most persistent snake that either of us has ever met. Short of hitting him we weren't going to get out of his shop without saying that we would think about his deal."

The next day they didn't bother going to join the rip off man for breakfast, instead they stayed in the guesthouse and had another cup of opium tea instead. However the arsehole turned up at their guesthouse at about lunch time and threw a huge great tantrum when they told him the reason that they had not come was that they had no wish to be ripped off.

He went red in the face and started shouting at them as if he was within his rights. Gypsy would have got up and thumped him if he had not been too stoned to move, which was just as well. In a country like India, if you thumped a local, no matter how deserving of a thump he was, then you would normally find yourself dealing with an angry mob. Eventually after almost giving himself a cardiac, ranting and raving his anger at them for refusing to allow him to rip them off, the piece of dog shit and his Quasimodo assistant slithered off in a state of rage and disgust. They had certainly disgusted Gypsy with their obscene behavior he had not seen such foul disgusting and dishonorable behavior since he had been at school in England.

That night he and Sally went and had dinner with the marble wallas. Gypsy would deeply have loved to have made business with their fantastic and beautiful products but he could not see how he could ship them safely without breakage and in a way that was economically viable. The price of the product was not out of the way, especially considering both the cost of the ingredients and the fine painstaking labor and skill that had gone into the making of these works.

The dinner was fantastic and their hosts were good company too. Everyone was so hungry that the plates and serving bowls looked like they didn't need washing by the time they had all finished.

The next day they took the train to Delhi, passing the stop for Vrindavan, [which was reputed to have been the birth place of Krishna] on the way at Mathura station.

Gypsy would have liked to have seen the place, however his experiences in the Philippines had somewhat diminished his interest in the Hare Krishna movement and right now he wanted to get to Delhi which was just four hours north on the train. The train arrived in Delhi and the two of them got down and carrying their bags, they fought their way through the scrum of rickshaw wallas and assorted hustlers' that were trying to grab at them and their belongings. They then found a quiet man sitting on his rickshaw minding his own business, so they got him to take them up through the Pahar Ganj market to the hotel that they had read about in the guide book that one of them was carrying.

The Hotel Chanakya was a basic but honest establishment that catered mostly to small Indian businessmen on tight budgets. The rooms had ensuite bathrooms but the floors were plain concrete and there was just one or two lights plus a fan in the way of amenities' but it was clean and reasonably priced and they had a balcony with a third floor view of the street below.

Pahar Ganj district starts at new Delhi railway station and runs south for perhaps two kilometers. In the mid area of the main street of the market was where most of the foreigners gathered, in the multitude of cafes and guesthouses that catered to them. However after a kilometer or so there was a main turning to the right that led past the Imperial Cinema and along to where a group of Sikhs ran tandoori chicken daburs (a street café in India is known as a darbur), it was always deemed as wise to look around for one that was crowded with people, as the food would be hot and fresh and if so many people were interested to eat there then it probably tasted pretty good too.

The Chanakya was after the Imperial Cinema but a long way from the chicken stands that were up on the corner with the crowded four lane highway that cut it's way through the area.

To sit in a café in Pahar Ganj and watch the street life go past while the flies, beggars, shoeshine boys, fake babas and all manner of others pester the shit out of you is an experience to behold, as anyone who has been there knows.

In those days there would be a slightly different traveller scene sitting in the one particular café that most of the older hard core travellers would gather at. There would most typically be a French or German junkie gouching out across the table from you nodding backwards and forwards a little. He would mumble something occasionally in English and want to scrounge a few rupees off you. Zen zer vood be zee German hippie (there were a lot of them there then) and he would look at you and say "Jah I voz in India ten years ago it voz goot zen now it is sheet" zen he vood continue "Jah I haf my baba in ze mountains ver I go and smoke my special chillum zat ze holyman haz made special for me in Pushkar (Pushkar is a special holy village built around a lake on the edge of the Rajastan dessert. It is said to be the birth place of Brahma on this planet. apparently each planet has a Brahma according to Vedic scriptures and as such It was the only place in India with a Brahma temple. Brahma does not hold the same rank as Shiva or the ultimate God, Vishnu on the Hindu trinity. Pushkar was also famous along with Pondicherry,- an ex French colony in south India,- for its chillums).

Then there would be the stoned Italian hippie with a big silly grin on his face and little comprehension of what was going on around him and even less comprehension of how to speak or understand English.

Then there would be the English or European woman in her early to mid twenties who had heard about an ashram and had flown out to find it. She would either be dressed very plainly or in hippie/tribal psychadelics.

Then if the day was a typical one, there would be two analy retentative students from a British university who were doing a Bachelor's degree in becoming yuppies who would be sitting, terrified and agitated in the corner.

They had come to India because they had heard that it was a cool thing to do, but they were not cool enough to handle India, as scenes from their worst nightmares walked past in the street not even two meters from where they were sitting.

This was the first of what was to become countless visits to Delhi and Pahar Ganj for Gypsy. One day he would come to know this area as one of his many homes on this planet.

He liked Delhi, especially the people, they were a bit of a gruff bunch but they were ok, they had nice food and were the sort of people who told it as it was.

Outside of the hotel was a stand that sold chola batura (greasy chappatis and chickpea curry). There would be a long queue each day at about lunch time in front of the stand and many people would be standing around on the side walk eating the product. Gypsy grew curious one day and decided to give it a try. Then he understood why the long queue, it was both super tasty and filling, it was good enough to rival a Bombay vegetarian Thali and even better than a plate of samosas with baji.

Delhi was much cleaner and better managed than Bombay, it had also been better designed and was not so overcrowded. Connaught place was the heart of the city with its large roundabout and outer circular roads that were lined with shops. Off from the circle was Barakumba Road, that housed many international banks and airline offices. Then there was Jan Path which started with Palika bazaar, a large Indian style, underground shopping mall on one side of the road and a large Wimpy (England's answer to McDonalds) on the other side. Along the right hand side of the street ran a large market that showcased the best of

Indian handicrafts. After that came the Tibetan market, selling Tibetan handicrafts then after this came the entrance to Delhi's finest hotel, the Imperial. The other side of the road was lined with travel agents and money changers.

The road continued on down as a wide four lane avenue for two or three kilometers to the Gateway of India, a large arch set in front of a huge parade ground that in turn was directly in front of the Lok Saba which is the Indian parliament building.

The area including the nearby diplomatic quarter was huge and spacious, well planed and clean.

To take a journey in the other direction across Connaught place would lead down to Old Delhi. The best way to get there was on a very strange vehicle that could be caught from the inner circle of Connaught place. The vehicle was best described as a three wheeled motorbike with seating for somewhere between ten and fifteen people. The engine was a large agricultural style diesel but the rest of the kit including part of the frame, looked like it had been taken from an ancient Harley Davidson motorbike. It would cost just two or three rupees for the ride all the way from Connaught Place to the Red Fort in Old Delhi, which was a journey of several kilometres.

The vehicle would start off by leaving the circle and then go through an underpass and then continue past a crowded Muslim neighborhood and a large field put aside for events and walled off from the road. They would then pass the tourist camp, where vehicles that had either just arrived or were just about to leave on the overland route to either Europe or Kathmandu would be parked.

Then it would continue past the Delhi gate that was just a relic in the middle of the central reservation and down another large road that was lined with all sorts of hardware and electronics shops until at the end by the traffic lights, the Red Fort came into view on the right hand side of the street (Both Delhi and Agra have famous red forts that were designed and built by the Moguls who invaded and colonized much of northern India before the British got there). Then as the vehicle continued past the lights there would come into view a huge mosque known as Lal Masjid on the left hand side, also designed in traditional Mogul style. The walls of the red fort were set back from the road in a grassed area on the right hand side. Then on the left after the mosque was the huge sprawling Chandi Chowk market at the heart of old Delhi. It was a scruffy and overcrowded area but full of interesting shops and stands selling all manner of things. This was where the strange contraption would finish its run before loading with people again and heading back to New Delhi. The main gate to the Red Fort was across the road.

After a few days in the cool January air of Delhi it was time to think about heading south. They took a walk through the market to New Delhi central railway station and waited in a queue to book tickets to Bombay.

Eventually they were served and bought tickets to travel in the second class, 3 tier sleeper section of the express train that was scheduled to leave at 6.30pm on the following evening.

They relaxed and enjoyed Delhi for another day and then went to the station the following evening and joined in the usual scrum to get into their carriage.

They found that they had been booked into a compartment with a bunch of other westerners. Anyway that would save on answering a number of favorite Indian questions a dozen or more times e.g.

"what is your good name sir?"

"where are you hailing from?" or "what is your country?"

"How many family members are you having?"

"are you having a jolly time in India?"

"Is it true that things are very costly in your country?"

After this question and answer session, normally the abilities that they had attained during their English lessons at school were mostly used up and there would be not much to talk about and everyone would just sit there wobbling their heads with big goofy grins on their faces.

However, this time, with so many travelers in one area it was going to be a good journey. As the train pulled out of the station the joints, chillums and tolas of Himalayan charas started coming out of peoples' pockets (a tola in case I hadn't mentioned it before is an Indian measurement unit which translated to ten grams when relating to hash or opium and a measure of eleven point sixty six grams when relating to anything else).

The other travelers were mostly first timers in India except for an Austrian junkie and a couple of older travelers who had been coming to India for a few years. Also there was an old Australian man among them who lived most of his time in India and spent a good deal of time travelling around it.

Windows were usually left open in the second class carriages on Indian trains and the doors were also mostly left open. With the natural ventilation that this gave it was no problem to smoke a chillum in the compartment as it would not bother anyone else in the carriage.

The train rolled on through the night and everyone fell asleep on their bunks. The next morning people were woken at 6 a.m. as so as the middle bunks could be folded away.

Breakfast was served to all of those who had ordered it. It cost the equivalent of $0.50, it came as all Indian railway meals did, served in an aluminum foil disposable container and consisted of rice, curry, chapattis and hot pickle, as usual it was most tasty.

The train rolled on through the day as it made occasional stops at major stations along the way, eventually it made one last stop at Surat before heading for Bombay V.T. station. Gypsy went and had a chat with the old Australian and asked him if he knew where to find some cheap accommodation that was cleaner than the shitholes of Colaba (Budget accommodation in Colaba with the exception of the spotlessly clean Salvation army hostel that was not so very cheap was in tiny airless cubicles that had no natural light and only enough room to shuffle into and drop a bag on the floor and climb onto the bed. In any prison in the west there would be many laws against putting even the most vile and depraved of criminals into such a cell but in Bombay they actually charged for this form of torture).

The old Aussie gave him a couple of names and addresses of cheap guesthouses near to V.T. station to check out.

The train pulled in and Gypsy and Sally rushed off to find a room. It was late in the afternoon and they needed to move quickly if they wanted to find a room, rather than sleeping on the floor in the station along with twenty thousand other people. Some twenty minutes later they had found a room at one of the guesthouses that had been recommended to them. It was on an upper floor of a building that faced toward's V.T. station.

The room was tiny but it had a window facing the street and it was relatively clean and secure. Gypsy only saw one or two small rats running around inside of the guest house, as opposed to the giant, dog sized ones that reportedly infested many of the shithole, guest houses in other parts of the city. Land in Bombay was so very expensive that decent accommodation in the city was unaffordable to all but the very wealthiest of travelers. They stayed for a couple of nights in Bombay and Gypsy gave Sally a tour of some of the good eateries that he had found in central Bombay, when he was living in V.T. station two years prior.

He wanted to give his family a phone call and so he went to the Central Telegraph Office but it had moved to a new building. He had some food, some bottles of water and a couple of novels with him and was prepared for a wait of several hours, so imagine his surprise when he was told on completing the form, to go to cubicle number two and pick up the phone when it ring's, he was stunned, it was incredible. Two years prior he had waited for over eight hours to make a call from the old telephone office and now there was no wait at all he felt kind of silly holding his two books, a newspaper and a large bag of cold drinks and snacks.

Other things had also changed since he had last been in the country. Dope and opium were both now most strictly illegal for use by anyone but the "holy men". Japanese motorbike companies had set up shop in India turning out large quantities of 100 cc bikes and scooters from factories that they had set up inside of India. Suzuki had gone into partnership with an Indian company called Maruti and were producing cheap small mini vans and cars. Also now at long last, clean bottled water was available for sale everywhere, so gone was the soda water with sugar or salt in it and the foul taste from the purification tablets that some people used to put in their drinking water.

However the range of soft drinks available was still limited to the usual Indian made Limca, Campa cola, Thumbs up and Gold spot, all of which tasted distinctly second rate. Early on their second morning in Bombay they headed off in a Taxi to the terminal for the Goa steamer.

They were there a little early and after buying their tickets, relaxed and had a chai and some breakfast. The boat pulled in and disgorged its passengers and Gypsy told Sally how things worked and suggested that they get themselves positioned in front of the gates for the mad frenzied scramble up the gang plank.

After the dust had settled they both had managed to find a good space each, close by each other. Sally had stretched herself over three seats and Gypsy had found a place on the deck.

The steamer honked it's horn then pulled out of its birth and headed out into the large bay, on its way to the open sea. Gypsy had not had a working camera with him on his last trip and so was now making up for it as he took shots of the Bombay skyline as the boat pulled away.

The freaks, hippies and hardcore travelers had gathered at a point on one side of the boat and were having a chillum and music party while a group of young women from an assortment of western countries who had just started their first ever journeys to India looked on with disapproving, nervous expressions on their faces. India must have already been a big enough shock to their systems but watching a group of westerners who felt relaxed and at home in India while they partook of a local brand of intoxication must have been a truly frightening sight for them to see.

It has to be said that at that time there were getting to be less hippies and hardcore travelers on the road and more and more spotty faced herberts on their gap year from college or university and also there were the arrogant, frightened, unfriendly, narrow minded uptight, yuppie types on a three month break from their nasty jobs in London and elsewhere.

Gypsy awoke the next morning to see the coconut fringed beaches in the distance and felt happy to be truly back in the tropics. He went to the canteen and joined some of the other travelers who were having breakfast.

By nine o'clock the boat had pulled up at the pier in Panjim. Gypsy and Sally headed straight to the bus station and jumped on a bus to Margao, one hour south.

At Margao, they negotiated a reasonable rate for a ride down to Colva village with an auto rickshaw walla and piled, first their bags and then themselves into the back of the small vehicle and took a bumpy twenty minute ride to Albert Musquita's house.

We haven't had a hash cookie salesman at the beach since you left" said Albert, smiling warmly as Gypsy walked up the path. This time Gypsy had more spare cash than he had had the last time that he had been there, so they rented one of Albert's nice private rooms, with marble floor and comfortable bed. It was good to see Albert again he was such a very decent man. He and his sister were always so friendly, helpful and trusting. Staying at his house was like staying at the house of a very good friend. Gypsy felt truly at home as he relaxed in one of the two chairs on the front veranda that had long arms on them that could be used as leg rests.

He was back at a place that he felt truly familiar with. Across the road at Umatis restaurant Gypsy got another warm welcome. The family had been doing well with their business and now had a weather proof building to live and work in, it was no bigger than the hut that had stood there before but it was strong and secure and could keep the worst of the monsoon out. Also they had made enough money to buy themselves a television. This also was a new phenomena in India since Gypsy had been there last. Two years prior televisions were only used when hooked to a video player. Now there were television stations and poorer members of the community were now able to afford locally made television sets.

Gypsy sat down and ordered a rice plate and a lime soda and chatted with the restaurant owner, who told him about some of the local news since Gypsy had last been there.

Later he took Sally for a wander down to the beach where they wandered along to Gypsy's favorite late afternoon hang out, at the Sunset café up on the dunes above the beach.

The owner of that establishment also had improved his lot and instead of the old structure of plastic and hessian sacks tied together and suspended above on bamboo poles, he had a new concrete and corrugated iron structure for the kitchen and a concrete and crazy paving floor with a smart palm thatched roof for the sitting area. It offered the same wonderful panoramic view of the sunset over the sea as ever, but now it had a more comfortable and less crowded sitting area.

Gypsy got a welcome back there too from the owner. And again he wasted no time in using his camera to collect a record of the place including the fantastic sunset. Now he would have something more than just his memories of the place.

Sally took a bit of a dislike to Colva and wanted to move on quickly. However, Gypsy wanted to stay another few days and relax.

After three days Sally jumped on to a train from Margao to Hubli and then took a bus to Hospet in Karnataka state while Gypsy spent a few more days relaxing among old friends in Goa.

Sally to him was just like many of the other western women who he had come across on the road in India. She would flirt at him, but when he came close she would push him away, it was getting to be infuriating. Gypsy did not like this game.

The next evening he was sitting out on the terrace off to one side and quietly relaxing when two good looking British bitches with foul personalities, pulled a train of young men out from the house and out to near where Gypsy was sitting. They were flirting and deliberately winding the fellows up until they were slobbering like a bunch of horny dogs around a bitch on heat. Wiggling their noses and their asses too while posing semi provocatively. They had the young fellows agreeing with every bit of manipulative shit that came out of their mouths. It was a truly embarrassing sight to watch and made Gypsy feel somewhat ashamed of his own species as he watched silently from the shadows.

Then one of them stuck her nose in the air and turned to the panting hounds and said "don't you just hate people who have lived in another country and have picked up the accent from that place?" "Oh yes" they all groveled and slobbered all at once at the feat of these two prick teasers.

Then one of them turned to Gypsy who had been watching the charade with a mixture of disgust and quiet amusement and said "which country are you from ?" At which Gypsy looked them straight in the face and put on the thickest Australian drawl that he could muster and said "where do you think I'm from can't you hear it I'm from Sussex, England." At that they gave Gypsy a weird guilty look as he stood staring and grinning at them coldly.

The canine pack went silent then "urrr yyyesss" and quickly left the terrace and went to play their games elsewhere.

What pathetically lame and small lives some people must live that they have so much time to be annoyed by anything as trivial as someone's accent" thought Gypsy to himself.

The only thing that mattered to Gypsy about other people was where their heart and spirit were at, everything else was unimportant. He had finished his first read of the Ramayana, but he had also found a pure Valmeek translation of the book in a shop in Delhi and so was in the process of reading it all over again but in pure form.

It was such a wonderful story but here in the Valmeek and original version it sounded often like a poem or the words to a song. It was the way that it portrayed honor at it's highest warrior form that Gypsy liked the most about the story.

The story was of fearless dedication in the face of death, the truest of true warrior codes at a level that most humans would never dare imagine.

Gypsy could not understand why many more people were not pursuing a spiritual path in life or at least having a look. After all life in this dimension when truly examined is most frail and we live but a short time and are then dead. It was a vital thing to do, to take a deep interest in a spiritual path or a search for the truth as far as he was concerned.

After a couple of days he was on his way again. That evening he went to the railway station at Margao and boarded a train to Hubli. At three or four in the morning he was awoken by the guard when the train pulled into Hubli station and he got down from the train with his bag. He made his way to the bus station that was nearby and found a bus going to Hospet. He boarded and soon it was pulling out of the station for the bouncy bumpy ride into central Karnataka state.

After an hour or two the sun came up. Gypsy was sitting on the back seat of the bus and the door in front of him to his left was open, giving a welcome and refreshing breeze. There was a fat man with some equally fat women in colorful saris sitting next to him.

The countryside was different to what he had seen so far in India. The plants and trees were different, the language was different and the way of life was different. It was much hotter than either Goa or Bombay.

However, the roads were the same, potholed, disintegrating and bumpy and the cars and administrative system were also the same. Not just that but also they wobbled their heads in a similar manner.

At about 9 a.m. the bus pulled into Hospet bus station and Gypsy grabbed his bag and made for the rickshaw stand.

Three rupees got him a one and a half kilometer ride to the anonymous concrete building that was the hotel where Sally was staying. He found her room and knocked on the door. She opened it and let him in and as he dropped his bag by the bed she started telling him about the deserted city of Hampi.

Not long after, they were on a bus over the hill and around a few bends to see the place. It was only eight or ten kilometers from Hospet. Even the bus journey there was among weird and vivid landscapes, dotted with ancient ruins.

Hampi itself was spectacular, with many large stone temples and other structures all made of stone. The backdrop to this setting was a bunch of huge rock formations that looked as if they had been put there by giants. They looked, actually like the ruins of a super giant's house or temple. But these stones would dwarf the biggest rocks ever used for construction ever or anywhere on this planet that is known about.

There was a street full of darburs and chai shops in the middle of the ruins that catered to the pilgrims tourists and travelers that visited the place.

Their stands were also popular with the flies that swarmed around them. However one of the Darburs that was there, the one that they had chosen to sit down in, had a very kind notice on the bottom of it's menu. It said "if you have no money then I will feed you for free for three days."

It was a very kind gesture by a good man who was doing his bit for humanity in his area. It made Gypsy happy to know that there were others in this world who also got joy from sharing and giving, if only more people were open to others in such a way, the world would be a different and better place.

The main temple was well maintained and still in use. A small number of Babas where hanging out in different parts of the compound and around the inside of the actual temple. Up on the solid stone hillside were a number of Jain temples that were smaller but each was made of a large single piece of carved stone. The Jain religion started at about the same time as Buddhism. The founding patriarch of this particular path was called Mahavira and like the Buddha, had gone off on his search of the truth at a young age. However the Buddha, on his search had tried the practice of extreme austerity and had backed away from it, seeing that it caused an equal and opposite effect that got in the way of objectivity, he chose what he called the middle path as his way.

Mahavira from the beginning veered more towards extreme practice on his quest for self realization. He started by plucking all of the hair from his head and eyebrows. The Buddha just shaved his.

Then he went off to the forest and performed extreme austerities for a long time.

He must have attained some level of liberation as the Jain religion has many followers in India. They are all extreme vegetarians who will go to great lengths to avoid using animal products. The ultra-extremists among them even wear nets over their mouths to avoid accidently swallowing insects.

The followers are also banned from partaking in drugs or alcohol and many other things. Many of them are successful in business and are known even amongst the most skilled of Indian business men as vegetarians who suck blood. When they name a price it is hard to get them to even give the smallest of discounts even when buying in serious quantities. No other group in the market is so heartless and unyielding not the Sikhs not the Muslims not the Tibetans or any other groups from the minorities and not the Hindus, not even the Marvadi or Banya casts in their hardest deals could ever be as stubborn as a Jain.

Further out across the stones and around the side of the hill was a giant deity standing some fifteen to twenty foot high and carved from stone. It was a representation of the lion god Nasringa Dev, who is said to have come and sorted out and killed a bunch of badass demons tens if not hundreds of thousands of years ago and was also revered as a pure incarnation of Vishnu upon earth.

It is also interesting to note that when Vishnu in one of his earthly incarnations kills a demon, he doesn't send it to hell forever, he absorbs it back into himself.

> To a Hindu, Vishnu is everything, including all conscious and unconscious awareness. In short, everything is Vishnu including all life forms and all energy and matter. So this is where the corrupted teachings of Christianity fall down. Can anyone in their right mind really think that their god is going to send a piece of himself to hell for eternity? He would have to be pretty twisted to do such a thing. So before anyone who reads the Bible and believes in it's teachings, goes running off to flagellate themselves and pray for forgiveness for being such a terrible person it would be pertinent to ask. What is it that you think you are praying to, it doesn't sound much like such a loving, whole and compassionate god to those of us that watch your actions and see the fear in your eyes.
>
> Gypsy

In the Hindu teachings, the background to the story of why Demons appear on planets within the universe originates in the spiritual sky far beyond the bubble dimensions of the various universes. Here is a brief description of one such story.

Two servants of one of Vishnu's godhead presences on a planet in the celestial dimensions were clumsy and screwed up what they were doing due to lack of concentration.

Vishnu gives them a choice, they can either incarnate within one of the universes five times as followers and friends of Vishnu or three times as his enemy.

They chose to go as his enemy as so as they could return to the spiritual sky more quickly.

509

One of the terminologies for describing the activities of Vishnu in an earthly incarnation is the Sanskrit word "Leila" which translates into English as the word "past time" as if it is what Vishnu does to keep himself entertained and it is all just a game. Hell to a Hindu only exists within the universe, especially on this planet. However this planet is described as being one of those, somewhere in the middle between the hellish realms and the lighter heavenly dimensions.

The statue of Nasringa Dev was incredible and a group of Indian archeologists on a field trip were also looking at it in wonder. The skill of the stone masons who had carved and shaped it, no doubt with the most primitive of tools was truly impressive.

Late in the afternoon after stopping for a rest in the shade of one of the abandoned structures that over looked the Jain temples and the main temple compound, they headed for the bus stop and went back to Hospet.

The next day they took a bus to Mysore, arriving in the afternoon, they found a cheap guesthouse and dropped their bags in their room before going out to explore their new surroundings.

Mysore was a beautiful city with a large elegant and well maintained palace that used to be the residence of the Maharaja of Mysore. Apparently he used to say that he was an earthly incarnation of Shiva and to prove it, once a year he would stand on the upper balcony of his palace and pull out his prick and stand there in front of the watching crowd, showing off his errection for all to see.(Just try to imagine prince Phillip trying the same stunt from the front balcony of Buckingham palace!)

The next day gypsy and Sally went exploring Mysore again, this time going to a Shakti temple on the hill above the city. (Shakti in the Hindu pantheon of gods is the wife of Shiva and also has other forms such as Sati, Parvati, Kali and Durga).

Shiva could be taken to be a representation of time. Shiva is the savior of animals and other fallen souls he is also the great destroyer.

Shakti is the Hindu goddess of power and their son Ganesh,(the one with the elephant head) is the god or deity of endeavor. Thus a Ganesh shrine will be found within the offices and homes of all Hindus.

After a couple of more days in Mysore that included a trip to the movies to see "Ghost Busters", which had hit the cinemas of the world, several months prior, they jumped on to a bus to Kosindaghar. It was a two hour journey from Mysore, there was a Tibetan refugee camp there where Sally's Tibetan friend and his family lived, and they had invited her and Gypsy to stay there for Tibetan new year (Tibetan New year and the Chinese new year occur at the same time as each other, each year).

A quite smart if casually dressed, well built man came running up and jumped through the back door just as the bus was pulling out of the station. He sat down on the back seat next to where Gypsy and Sally were sitting. He introduced himself and then told them what he had been up to that morning. He was a cop who worked in the drug squad. They had been staking out a smack dealer from Europe and today was the day that they sprung the trap, catching him with over two kilos of heroin on him. "He offered us money but we all said no thanks" said the cop, "I don't mind when people want to smoke some charas or ganja but heroin destroys lives and communities, you can't pay me to turn a blind eye to that." "Why are you on this bus now? Are you going home?" asked Gypsy "No" said the cop "our car broke down and we still haven't finished the job. I got on the bus while the others try to get the car fixed as so that at least if they can't make it I can round up some local help to go and catch our other targets."

They didn't get time to talk further as the cop car had now been repaired and had just overtaken the bus and forced it to a halt. The cop said a quick goodbye as he hurried from the bus and jumped into the waiting ambassador car. They then sped off down the road in front of them, at high speed. "So he was telling the truth," thought Gypsy to himself.

A couple of hours later the bus stopped at the entrance to the camp. Far from being a place of overcrowded squalor as most refugee camps around the world were, this place was made up of four or five clean and tidy villages that each had land on which to grow their own food. It was cleaner inside the camp than it was outside of it's gates. There were Buddhist monasteries and great efforts had been made to make it feel like Tibet, culturally. The buildings in the villages were strong, smart and clean and there was not a slum or hovel to be seen. It is a testament to how much love and respect the Indians have for the Tibetans that they had given them good places to live as neighbors and equals next to them like this. The Tibetans in turn spoke of the huge gratitude that they felt towards the Indians, for their generosity and kindness of spirit and for taking them in in their hour of need, and for treating them as friends rather than as a bunch of unwanted refugees. Indeed maybe other countries of the UN could learn a thing or two from this in how not to make Ghettos when it comes to housing refugees. It put the rest of the world to shame to see a country as poor as India, that had done such a good and selfless act, while the countries of the UN fought and bickered over who was going to help the Palestinians, Afghanis, Vietnamese boat people etc.

Sally had been invited to stay at the house of her friend and they also arranged for Gypsy to stay nearby.

Tibetan New Year celebrations had started and a huge old parachute had been set up on a frame, as a tent for the dragon dancers and other masked performers to do their acts in. New prayer flags were being prepared and large cooking pots with wooden straws were being passed around. Inside was a sort of reddish brown grain or pulse and under that a liquid. Gypsy asked what it was as it was passed to him "chang" they told him "Ah, I know what that is" said Gypsy before sucking up a large swig. They, then all watched the festivities throughout the day and the evening.

The next day they visited the monastery where a monk explained about the ceremony of killing demons for the New year. He showed them around the monastery and then gave them each a prayer flag, a prayer written on rice paper in Tibetan script and a special fringed small red and gold embroidered flag to put on the front of any meditation shrine that they might have. Of course they put some money into the donation box on the way out but while they had been there at the temple no one had asked them for anything. Tourists as a rule were not likely to stumble across this temple and it was very real and unspoilt in its practice. The monks had come across as most genuine. The monk had spoken with them in English with no help from a translator and had explained about their particular branch of Buddhism in a way that could be comprehended. Earlier Gypsy had noticed a black man who he presumed to be an American, in Buddhist monk's robes and with a shaved head, he wondered if the man was learning from this particular monk.

They stayed for one more day and then left, taking the bus back to Mysore. They stopped for a couple of nights more in Mysore and then took a train to Bangalore.

A few hours later they arrived, got off the train and went and found a café and sat down.

Bangalore was busy and bustling. It was modern with wide streets and glass fronted office blocks, but it was not the kind of place that they were looking to hang out in so they went back to the station and booked onto the next available train to Madras and then waited at the station for two hours, until it arrived. There had been nothing in Bangalore that either of them wished to see, but at the station there were good food stands and all the hot and cold drinks that they could wish for, and the prices were cheap too. The food in south India was different from anything that they had tasted so far, on this journey. Gone were the chapattis, Nan and parathas, and instead there was a lot more rice and dishes and snacks made from rice flour.

Gypsy's favorite of the southern food that he had tried so far was tomato and onion utapam which was like a pizza made from rice flour but with no cheese and instead it would be served with different types of chutneys. Other foods that were new to him included "massala dosa" [which was like a large crispy pancake made without the use of eggs that was filled with an ultra spicy potato curry], and "idli wada" which was rice flour dumplings in a thick curry soup.

The train arrived and they found their carriage and hopped aboard. The train rolled on through the late afternoon and into the evening and night. They climbed into their bunks and went to sleep.

They awoke as the train pulled into Madras main terminus station and stopped. It was 3:30 am. It was incredibly hot and their clothes stuck to them as gallons of sweat poured from their bodies.

Outside of the station, even at this ungodly hour, they were approached by the usual scrum of grubby rickshaw wallas and taxi drivers. They did not know their way and so they got ripped off by a taxi driver who over charged them for the short ride to the bus station which unbeknown to them was easily within walking distance.

After an hour's wait they were on a bus rolling out of the station for the five hour ride to Pondicherry. The bus had no glass in the windows, just safety bars. It was so hot even late in the night and in the early morning, that closed widows would have made a non air conditioned bus with closed windows a coffin on wheels.

They were sat at the back of the bus. The road was not particularly smooth and so every twenty to thirty seconds on average they would hit a pot hole that would send them flying two or three feet up in the air, it was a very bouncy journey. The smartest thing about the Indian highways however was the way that many of the roads and highways were lined with large trees that for the most part kept the road shaded and relatively cool.

Five hours later they got down at the small bus station in Pondicherry and found a rickshaw and negotiated a price to Serenity beach which was between two to three kilometers away.

When they got there they found that there was a small crowd of westerners living in the place, some of whom had been hanging out there for months.

There was a group of totally friendly and laid back Brits who liked drinking beer, smoking joints and playing scrabble. There was a British junkie who sat with his coconut hubble bubble pipe smoking brown sugar all day. However he never caused trouble and never stole from or cheated anyone.

There also was a pleasant assortment of other misfits from around the world.

Gypsy found a room for five rupees. OK it only had a string bed that was more like a hammock than a bed, and an electric light but for $0.30 per night, who would complain?

Pondicherry had been a small French colony back in the days when the British controlled India. It still retained much of its French character in the town itself. There were louvre shuttered windows on the French style houses and there were still bakeries where they made croissants and French bread, also there were some French style cafes serving coffee.

Insert image file name "24.....page 343....hampi, india' here full page.

An interesting story that happened and continued to this day to unfold in the Pondicherry area concerned a mystic, philosopher and freedom fighter called Orobindo.

At the time of the British Raj about eighty years prior to the time being written about, give or take ten years, Orobindo spoke out against British rule and tried to get resistance to it started. When the British came after him for the trouble he was causing them, he crossed into the French colony of Pondicherry. While in exile in Pondicherry he started writing on spiritual matters, which in turn attracted a following.

A French woman came and joined him in his work. She was much older than him and was known to the group as the mother. An ashram was founded in the name of Orobindo and the Mother.

He had a dream for a new kind of city that would have a spherical temple at its' centre. Inside the main meditation chamber, would be blank white walls and no writing or symbols.

Instead, in the middle of the circular room would be the biggest clean quartz crystal that could be found and nothing else. The town was to evolve in it's own way without influence from outside pressures or unusually wealthy individuals.

It was the aim to let it work by anarchism, where by the people would be so aware and responsible about their own actions that no rules would be needed. If policing was needed then the whole community would have to be a part of it.

The community was actually brought into existence after the death of Orobindo with the help of his followers, the Indian government and possibly a couple of other international organizations.

It was located on a huge tract of land a few kilometers from Serenity beach.

It was one of the reasons that Gypsy had been keen to travel to Pondicherry. He had heard about this place years before, back in Israel from Chai, the old traveler who had given him such good briefings on traveling in Asia. Now he was enthusiastic to go and see it.

Sally had decided that she wanted her own room. Her behavior was starting to wind Gypsy up. She would flirt at him and then back right off, pushing him away if he responded, it was starting to send him into a state of anger and confusion. He rented a bike and went off for a ride. He followed the signs to Oraville and then cycled around the place.

It was so huge and spread out that he hardly saw anyone apart from what looked like a team of engineers who were working on the huge spherical temple at the community's centre. the structure had allready been built and now they were getting ready to start preparing it for it's inside and outside coatings. Gypsy cycled on but still did not see anyone or any place where it looked like people gathered at. It was a bit like one of those weird sci-fi movies were all the people have gone or disappeared, leaving one person wandering around on an empty planet.

Gypsy rode back to Serenity beach and returned the bike. "Well that was one illusion shattered" thought Gypsy to himself.

He and Sally took a rickshaw into Pondicherry and went to a typical south Indian darbur. It was very different to a northern Indian darbur. It had stone tables and benches. Washed slices of banana leaves were place in front of them as plates, then rice and different types of curries and pickles were placed on them. Each time that they finished one of the types of curry a man came over and put some more of it on the banana leaf. They had to tell him when they had had enough otherwise he would keep filling them up all day. When thoroughly bloated, they went to pay their bill they were staggered to be charged just two rupees each ($0.15). It must have been the cheapest meal that either of them had ever eaten.

Sally had been flirting at Gypsy again and gave a nonsense of a reason for not just pulling back but acting pissed off as well. Her behavior was thoroughly insulting to him, and now she was pissing him off really badly. Either she didn't know what she wanted and was confused, or she was doing it as a game, just to make sure that she was protected by a man as she travelled around India. Anyway Gypsy was deeply pissed off by it he deeply despised being abused in such a way. He was young and it was playing hell with his testosterone. She had a good looking figure and was cute, too cute.

He was so very pissed off that he went and sat down for the afternoon with Don the smack head. He threw in thirty rupees for a small bag of brown sugar and sat there smoking the coconut hubble bubble with Don and another European partaker for the afternoon. Other than the opium tea that he had had in Agra it had been over two years since he had last partaken of an opiate.

It felt really good as all his thoughts and all his pains disappeared. However, he knew exactly what he was doing. It would be for this afternoon and only this afternoon. If he felt rough in the morning then he could always smoke a joint but with smack the rule that he used for himself was straight. Never use it for more than an afternoon and evening at one time, smoke it or chase it, never snort, eat or bang it. And never let the times that it was used get to be too close together. It was for uses on certain occasions when the pain, either physical, mental or emotion had got to be so bad that it needed to be killed off, at least for a while until the worst of it had passed.

Of course Sally was too freaked out by this to even say anything and disappeared and hid for the afternoon and evening. There were only two or three chai shops in that area of Serenity beach and she went and found a different one to go and sit at.

Serenity beach was not such a popular place amongst travelers as the beaches in Goa, Karnataka or kerela, on the west coast of India. This was possibly as it was not a good beach to lie on or go swimming at.

This was on account of the local habit of shitting on the beach and waiting for the tide to come in and flush it away. Thus treating the bay of Bengal as a giant flushing toilet, just like all of the other peoples whose coastline faced onto this part of the Indian ocean. The Ganges, Brahmaputra and Irrawaddy each would carry untold amounts and types of human waste, including dead bodies and raw sewerage not to mention industrial pollution into the bay each year and it can be a sure fact that along much of it's coastline it was used as a toilet. Thus, the bay of Bengal was probably a very good place for microbiologists to go exploring for new and exotic species but perhaps not the cleanest of waters to go swimming in.

Sally was still shaken and scared the next morning and had decided that she was going to leave on her own. No doubt thinking that by having his smoke of smack Gypsy had in one fell swoop turned himself into a zombified, shaking, money thieving junkie.

Gypsy had woken up that morning feeling fine and had no great urge to go and stick a smack pipe in his mouth. He was far more interested in a cup of chai and some breakfast. After he had eaten and chatted with the others, he went by to Sally's room and asked her what she was doing. She gave him a strange hurt look and said she was leaving and didn't want to travel with him or see him again.

It was his birthday and she knew it. She had been winding him up and leading him on the whole way from Pokhara. "What did she want? Ohh for the straight up no nonsense of east Asian hookers" thought Gypsy to himself

The endless flirting and drawing him close but then pushing him most firmly away. It was either a case of psychological issues or deliberate manipulation. Of course she probably, despite her travelling experience, also believed all the bogey man scare stories about people getting addicted to smack the moment that they touched it. Maybe it was true for some people but not for Gypsy and he certainly was not going to do it again for a long time.

Gypsy was sitting smoking a joint in the café where the other British and Australian travelers were hanging out when one of the crowd came and told Gypsy that Sally had left on a bus to Madras and was heading for Delhi.

"Oh shit" said Gypsy, his other bag was stored in the same locker as her extra bag in Delhi.

Gypsy went back to his room, packed his bag and paid the landlady. He then took a rickshaw to the bus station. When he got there she had already left. He caught the next bus to Madras and thought about what to do as the bus bounced along the Pondicherry to Madras section of the east coast highway.

Five hours later the bus was going past the airport at Madras. He couldn't get the driver to stop and drop him off so he had to ride into the city and get a taxi, back out. There had been an Indian airlines A300 airbus parked at the domestic terminal that looked like it could be Delhi bound. He slipped the driver an extra 20 rupees and asked him to pull out the stops and put his foot on the floor. The driver duly obliged and Gypsy got a crazy James Bond style ride through the crowded streets and alley ways of Madras, to the airport. He was right, the flight was to Delhi. There were seats available but first he would have to change some of his Yen Travellers cheques into rupees. There was a special discount rate on air travel, available at that time for young foreign travellers and Gypsy qualified for it.

He was made to jump through hoop after beaurocratic hoop however, in order to get it. By the time that he had got done dealing with this pedantic bunch, and had reached the final counter, where he was eventually given his ticket he was almost in a state of despair. It had been a bit like some sort of wind up from a Monty Python sketch to the power of twenty. The BBC could save themselves a lot of money on their comedy budget if instead of having sitcoms and shows with paid actors, they just set up a few hidden cameras in places of great Indian beaurocracy and had the goings on translated to English when necessary. It would make Monty Python and just about ever other comedy act that they have, totally redundant.

Ok it was costing some money to do this but he had enough and after all it was his birthday and he didn't fancy a thirty six to forty eight hour train ride, especially if it meant sitting there being glowered at by Sally for the whole journey.

Eventually he boarded the flight and the plane taxied out to the runway in the last light of the afternoon. The plane took off on the first leg of the flight which was to Hyderabad. Gypsy felt better, he knew that he had done the right thing. He was still fuming that he had wasted time with this prick teaser but now she was on a train rattling and lurching its way to Delhi, far below. He was going to be in Delhi well before midnight.

The plane was not up at cruising altitude for long before it started its descent into Hyderabad. The sun had still been up and visible, above the clouds but now they descended into the darkness.

The plane landed and pulled up near to the terminal. People got off the plane and others got on. There was not much to see out of the window as it was not exactly the best lit airport on earth, but that didn't matter as a short time later the doors were closed. The steps and various service vehicles were pulled back and they were on their way again for the two and a half hour flight to Delhi. Once up at cruising altitude, dinner was served. It beat the meals that were served on the railways by a long way, not least because the food was served hot.

He had turned the situation around and now was enjoying his birthday. Time for some new adventure without any impaired company getting in the way.

The plane landed at Palam airport and pulled up and parked next to an Air France jumbo that was just preparing to depart. The steps and generator had been taken away and it was being pushed back.

It was the first plane that he had seen from a western country since back in October at Bangkok. It made him think and wonder how it would be on his own return to the west that he was planning to make within the next two months or so.

By the time they were down the steps from the airbus, the jumbo's tail lights could be seen as the plane taxied off into the distance. There were no other planes parked at the small international terminal that stood next to the larger domestic terminal.

After collecting his bag he jumped onto a bus into the centre of Delhi.

Getting down in Connaught place he found a metered auto rickshaw and got the driver to take him to tourist camp at Delhi gate (There were two tourist camps in Delhi. The other one was in Old Delhi but it was the sort of place that only the thieves and junkies used. It was near the Kashmir gate and not far from the interstate bus station).

The air was decidedly cool when compared to the sweltering tropical heat of Tamil Nadu. Gypsy would have found it refreshing if he was not still boiling with rage over what had happened in the last few days.

The auto rickshaw pulled up at the gates of the tourist camp and the auto rickshaw walla got out his table chart and looked at the meter Gypsy paid him and gave him a healthy tip but the driver started shouting and yelling demanding more. Gypsy had had to deal with too much unreasonable behavior recently both from Sally and various assorted cretins who had done their best to piss him off with lame tricks and dishonest and dishonorable behavior. He was at the point where he was not going to put up with anymore. He told the rickshaw walla to fuck off in no uncertain terms, which he duly did, at extremely high speed, and Gypsy went inside the gates.

Gypsy got into the reception just in time. The next arrival after him was told that the last room had just been taken. Gypsy turned around to see that the new and disappointed arrival was an older hippie in his forties. Most of the so called travelers at the time were up tight types on short breaks and the only ones amongst this group that Gypsy could stand the company of were Germans, Swiss and Australians, who were generally less uptight, frightened and insecure and far more open minded.

He turned to the old hippie and said "look mate it's after midnight you're a traveler like me there's an extra bed in my room you're welcome to use it if you would like." The old hippie looked at Gypsy and said "thank you, I'll take you up on that offer I'm tired and I've been travelling all day."

At the room, they got talking. Gypsy told his story of what had happened to him that day and why he was in Delhi. The old hippie was from Italy and his name was Luigi.

He had just flown up from Goa where his wife and child were still on holiday.

He had some hash so they smoked a couple of joints, while Gypsy told him briefly about what he had been doing during the last two and a half years while he had been travelling. When Luigi heard that it was Gypsy's birthday he reached into one of his pockets and pulled out a gem stone and gave it to him and said "Happy Birthday, this is for you"

The next day Gypsy awoke and wandered over to the shower block with his towel and soap.

The tourist camp consisted of a bunch of single storey red bricked windowless rooms, each with electric light, fan, power outlet and two single beds. The rooms were set in a garden where they also allowed camping. At the front wall of the compound were two parking areas for buses and trucks. The parking area immediately inside of the gate, on the left hand side was used once every couple of days by one of the Delhi to Kathmandu buses which used to make grueling three day runs from Delhi to Kathmandu. Also there were several companies that did overland guided tours, from Europe to India and Nepal that would park there. There was "Top Deck," who ran old London "Route Master", double decker buses on the route from London to Kathmandu. They were especially popular with the Aussies and kiwis.

Where the destination sign on the front of the bus was, instead of a destination sign there was a name on each bus. Names such as Bollocks, Scrotum, Tadpoles, Vomit etc. Another company was 'Han Overland' who ran old coaches, and were more of a bare bones basic operation that offered cheaper prices and less bullshit. They seemed to attract the best of the tourists, such as the older, quietly unconventional, free thinking kind. Then there was 'Exodus travel' and 'Encounter Overland' who both hauled their tourists around in ex British army Bedford TK four wheel drive trucks. Their customers used tents when staying anywhere. Something that made many of the other travellers laugh at them. "Why use tents when the rooms are so cheap?" was what they would say.

In the other parking area would be the private overland vehicles, mostly old and battered Mercedes trucks, being driven from Germany to Kathmandu to be sold by German hippies and adventurers to pay for further travels. There was also one bus company called Royal Tur and they were by far the dodgiest company of the lot and would always park up among the travelers.

They ran regularly from Istanbul to Delhi at speed, completing the journey in anywhere from seven to nine days. A lot if not all of the money from their runs came from hauling cargo for themselves. Selling and buying things along the way. They offered the cheapest ride to Europe for anyone who could get a visa to cross Iran. However that was not an easy task, as the Iranian embassy in Delhi did not give visas to westerners easily. Often the bus would leave Delhi empty except for cargo and crew.

Gypsy was sitting in the open air cafeteria having a cup of chai when Luigi came over from the shower block next door. (The shower block and cafeteria were at the other end of the walled compound from the car parks and reception). "I've got some work to do today in Delhi would you like to join me? you'll get to meet some good people" said Luigi. "That sounds like fun and anyway I've got not much else that I need to do" said Gypsy.

They started off at the chai walla across the street, where they had another chai

And some breakfast. Then they took a rickshaw ride to Jan Path road (pronounced as Jan Pat) and the Tibetan market. Gypsy was looking for things to take back to the west and sell and could not believe how cheap things were there. He was eyeing up products that he could buy at the last minute, before leaving to go to the west.

He made a friend at the second shop that he still like's to go and visit, when he's in Delhi, even to this day. The shop was called "Doma" and was run by an old Tibetan woman by the same name. She had left Lhasa two years before the Dalai Lama's group had left on the long march that brought them to safety in India. Luigi had done a deal with Doma's son but he had pulled a rip off and Luigi was trying to get the matter sorted. Doma apologized again and again to Luigi and told him "I don't know what is wrong with my son, all of his life I have tried to teach him the value of honesty and then he goes doing bad things like this. If I see him I will do my best to get your money back for you but I haven't seen him for weeks and don't know for sure where he is. My guess is that he is at Mussoorie, where my ex husband's family is from. I'm afraid that I can't help you as I don't know any of what has transpired between you and him but I will do what I can, and if I see him I will have very strong words with him about it".

In her shop was a mix of items, she sold wooden block prints and copper and brass work of all kinds and she also had a large display of cheap gemstones and crystals. Everything in her shop was basic, simple and primitive but also very attractive. It was a nice shop with a homely feel to it and she sold nice things at cheap prices. Also Gypsy could see that she was an honest person, her eyes were steady and clean and she did not make any excuses for her son. Gypsy made a mental note of where the shop was and planned to returning to England.

After several brief stops at other shops in the market that ran along Jan Path road and a brief stop for cold drinks and a plate of chola batura, they jumped aboard one of the three wheeled motorbike contraptions that ran to old Delhi.

Getting down at the final stop they disappeared into the labyrinth of alleys that was Chandi Chowk market.

There were all sorts of shops selling all manner of items from 22 carrat gold chains and bangles to Indian musical instruments and Indian sweets.

One of the most amazing sites that Gypsy had seen while in the place was a shop where a man was hand making gold bangles. The bustling crowd was no more than two feet away from where he had put down the bangles that he had finished, there were five in all. There was no barrier of any kind between the people and the gold yet no one tried to steal it.

Luigi explained that if someone tried to steal here in the narrow alleys of old Delhi that they would not stand a chance. Eyes were watching everywhere. A thief would make it most likely no more than two or three metres, before the crowd would descend on him, giving him a kicking that he would be lucky to escape with his life from.

After making stops at several jewelry shops along the way, they headed back out of the market and went across the road to the Red Fort. Inside of the Red Fort were lines of shops selling jewelry and handicrafts.

First, they went into an antique shop that contained items from both Europe and Asia, including a collection of carved jade perfume bottles from either China or Tibet. Gypsy asked "how can you be sure that the item is genuine and not a recently made clever fake?"

"It is very hard and we can never be one hundred percent sure" said the man behind the counter.

That answered Gypsy's question and now he knew that he did not want to deal in antiques whatever he did.

The next stop was at a jewelry shop run by a strong, intelligent Indian woman, she had a staff of five or six and was without a husband for whatever reason, and ran the shop in order to feed her children and send them to good schools. She was hard working and had good well chosen, stock and fair prices. She also had a good eye for stones, of which she had a large stock. Gypsy also took note of that shop too, taking a business card with him to help him find his way back.

"I'm meeting my wife and son in Jaipur tomorrow, would you like to come with me?. I can teach you a bit about Gemstones if you like while we are there, that's what I do for a living. There are many other hippies in Jaipur who make their living that way. I think that you will like the place," said Luigi.

"Well I've got no plans and it sound's interesting, yes please" said Gypsy.

They went to the Kashmiri gate, bus station and bought tickets on a Haryana Roadways deluxe bus to Jaipur for the following day, then went back to tourist camp. Gypsy took an auto rickshaw to Pahar Ganj to collect his other bag. He figured that Sally would still be on the train, several hundred kilometers south of Delhi at that time so he had not been in a hurry all day, to go and retrieve his kit.

Their stuff was in one lot and it was at this time that he did something that he was later to regret. He took Sallie's bag too, leaving a note for her telling her to come to Jaipur to get it, or tourist camp, if she got into Delhi early enough. He wanted to see her one more time to just put things straight between them. It was a stupid idea but she had pissed him off with her behavior and he wanted to give her a taste of what being wound up could feel like.

He headed back to tourist camp, taking the bags with him. He stored his big bag in the locker room, taking his normal travel bag, guitar and sally's bag with him for the trip to Jaipur. That evening they went outside of tourist camp again and walked around until they were at the back wall, then crossed the road.

There was a line of darburs in a side street. They looked rather scruffy but Luigi had a favorite one were they went and sat down. It was owned by a man called Ram. His place was open fronted. The cooking pots where on rings on the front counter of his stall, each contained different types of either curry or dahl. There was a long table with benches in the narrow space inside and a man cooking rotis at a tandoor at the back of the shop.

The food tasted incredibly good and was also cheap. It was to become Gypsy's regular place to eat in Delhi for the next few years.

Sally had not arrived by the time that it was time to leave for the bus station so he took her bag along with him. It was not locked so he had checked to make sure that she had not left anything important in it and was relieved to find it only contained some ethnic clothes and cheap nick nacks.

They got an auto rickshaw to the bus station in old Delhi and boarded their bus.

The bus then rolled off out of Delhi, past the international airport and on across Haryana towards Rajasthan. After three hours the bus stopped for a break at the Government run road house at Midway. They had lunch and got back on the bus for the rest of the journey. They were now already in Rajasthan. The land was drier and there were camel carts going slowly along the road. People wore colorful clothes and many of the men wore large turbans.

The land for the most part was flat, and although it was quite a dry area, healthy crops were growing in the fields.

About 15 kilometers before Jaipur ruins started to come into view on the hillsides.

As they got closer to the city the ruins got more spectacular, with fortress walls running up and over the dry rocky hills, and then the spectacular Amer fort, set midway up a hill came into view. They passed countless pavilions and many palaces, one of them in ruins in the middle of what looked like a man made lake. Then the bus drove through a large gate and into the pink city (as the old city of Jaipur is known).

The place was heaving with activity and the streets were lined with spectacular old buildings that for the most part were painted an orange to red colour.

Eventually the bus made it through the chaotic crowded streets to the other end of the old city and was soon pulling into the main bus station at Sindi camp.

They got off and found a rickshaw walla who took the two of them and their bags to the guest house.

It was a place for hippies and travellers. It had some rooms in a courtyard then three large dormitories with a further four rooms built on it's roof. The rooms were primitive and not exactly what you could call clean. But the place was full of hippies and hardcore travellers, a large group of whom were gathered around a stone table smoking chillums, dressed in psychedelic clothes with long hair and beads around their necks.

All the rooms were taken so Gypsy ended up with a dorm bed. He put his things in a locker and got his guitar out and went and joined the chillum party. The others were keen for some music so he played a load of songs from the Who, the Stones and led Zeppelin. Luigi brought his wife and child over and introduced them.

Then they partied late into the night as Gypsy kept playing and the chillums continued to do their circuits of the table.

The next day Gypsy went with Luigi to look at a massive pile of cut and polished pieces of Lapis Lazuli, at a nearby shop. Gypsy had already got a little bit familiar with gemstones and their names from his time in Nepal and his experiences in Agra, and so had some idea of what he was looking at. Luigi helped him further in knowing more about what the jewellers in the west would be looking for. So much of the stone looked good to Gypsy's untrained eye that he did not know where to begin.

He joined Luigi for the next two days and then went out for a look by himself.

The streets of Jaipur were crawling with people trying to make a buck from a tourist and one of the favorite ways of doing it was by taking a tourist or traveller to a gem, Jewelry or handicraft shop.

The owner would pay a small commission to whoever could get such a person through the door and into his shop, and then pay further commission on anything that that particular person would then purchase. The commission could range from five to ten percent for wholesale then jump up to forty or fifty percent for a rich tourist. Gypsy did not have much street knowledge in Jaipur at that time and one such hustler came and approached him.

It was pretty obvious that Gypsy had not just stepped off the plane from London. Just by how he was dressed showed that he was a little bit experienced with India and it's ways. So the hustler said "I know a really good wholesale office where many other westerners have started their business from, seriously I am not wasting your time." "OK" said Gypsy "show me". A short walk later and they were going up the steps at '44 Gangoori Bazaar, to the first floor, where in a tiny courtyard there were entrances to two homes. They entered the door straight in front of them to the residence of the Birla family.

In a room with two mattresses on the floor sat some hippies who were choosing and selecting different types of Gemstones from large trays that they had in front of them. The owner of the business and tenant of the house was a mister Hem Birla. He was a somewhat large man with an even bigger personality. He was telling people stories about gem stones, and about the culture and ways of the people of Jaipur and the rest of Rajasthan. He was gregarious and clearly enjoyed educating people about the gem trade and how to tell a real stone from a fake. Also he was obviously a very generous person, he was constantly ordering food and hot and cold drinks for his customers and staff. In the next room his wife was taking care of their young son as she helped him put his tie on as she got him ready to go to school. Their two daughters had just finished their school day and were helping in the kitchen. As Gypsy listened to the conversation in the room it was obvious that some of the hippies present had been doing business with Birla for some years, this gave Gypsy confidence that he was in a good place to both learn and to buy stones. He asked questions from the other travellers about which stones were most popular among the jewellers back in the west, before starting to look at both moonstones and black stars. Some time in the late afternoon he took a rickshaw back to the guesthouse were he was staying, near to Chameli Walla market and went looking for Luigi to ask his advice about what he had just seen at Birla's office.

He also wanted to ask if Luigi knew if it would be possible for him to trade his camera and zoom lens for gemstones. India had very strict import controls at that time and as a consequence, good cameras were not easily available.

Luigi was not there at the time as he was still out buzzing around the market getting his range of silver jewelry made and buying stones and necklaces. The other travellers seemed to think that there would be no problem with selling the camera for a good profit as many of them had sold second hand western electrical goods at a profit to local Indians in the past.

The evening chillum session had started so Gypsy went and got his guitar out and came to the table and started to jam. Luigi turned up after dark and Gypsy went and had a talk with him about what had happened that day and asked if he knew were he could find a taker for his camera. "Don't worry I'm sure that one of the people that we have done business with will be able to help you" Luigi said.

A week later a deal was done and Gypsy had traded his beloved Minolta for some packets of lapis lazuli, peridot, amethyst and garnet. Luigi and his family left Jaipur with two huge metal trunks full of silver jewelry and headed back to Delhi, ready to catch their flight back to Rome. Gypsy hung around Jaipur for a couple of more days before also taking a bus back to Delhi, he was planning to go back to Kathmandu and see if he could find Sally and return her bag to her, he now really regretted what he had done and wanted to put it right. He was not a dishonest person and had no wish to dishonour himself by keeping her bag. Also he wanted to see his Indian friends again and also have some silver jewelry made by some of the good Nepalese silversmiths who worked in Kathmandu.

Back at the tourist camp in Delhi he looked around for a way to get back to Nepal, first he went to the Nepalese Embassy to get a visa, then he went and made enquiries about a comfortable way of getting back to Kathmandu. He really didn't fancy the grueling three day ride on the bus.

Back at the tourist camp the Turkish bus was still there, waiting for permits and visas to return to Istanbul, the drivers were sitting around getting bored and had taken to throwing fire crackers around the tents of the encounter overland and exodus travel tourists at two or three o clock in the morning for a laugh. It had many of the seasoned travelers who were still sitting around smoking chillums amused too as they watched the spotty faced herberts on thier adventure holiday, peering out of there tents with shocked expressions on their faces. None of the seasoned travellers had the least bit of respect for these apprentice yuppies who obviously did not have the balls to travel on their own and needed someone to hold their hand in order to move about in Asia.

Gypsy asked about amongst the German trucks to see if anyone was leaving for Kathmandu in the next couple of days. There were two large German hippies who had two motor bikes in the back of their truck, a Yamaha Tenere and a BMW touring bike and were planning to ride via Thailand, Malaysia and Indonesia to Australia, once that they had sold their truck in Kathmandu. They weren't going to Nepal for another month or so but they smoked Gypsy out with some wickedly strong Afghani hashish and wished him luck on his journey.

By the next day he had his new Nepalese visa and headed back to tourist camp to look around to see if there had been any new arrivals from the west among the trucks. There were two trucks that had turned up that morning with German plates on them, Gypsy went over and asked one of the drivers if he was going to Kathmandu in the next few days. "Yes we are both leaving tomorrow, if you would like a lift and you can make a small contribution towards fuel then you will be welcome to ride with us" said the driver who's name was Chris. "There are going to be two other travellers riding with us as well, they are both from Austria, my girlfriend is driving the other truck so one of you can ride with her to keep her company". "Great" said Gypsy "what time are you planning to leave at? "oh not until the afternoon" said Chris "even better" said Gypsy "I'll be ready by mid day then".

The next afternoon the two trucks left from tourist camp and headed east out of Delhi, on the road towards Sitapur. Gypsy and the Austrian man were in the first truck, which Chris was driving, and the Austrian woman was riding in the second truck with Chris's girlfriend. The road was not the normal route that was used for the journey to Nepal by most people, but Chris said that he preferred this route as there was far less traffic on it. He had done the journey many times and treated it as a business, taking trucks to Kathmandu, and had several other people driving for him at that time. He said that he had another four trucks that other people were driving from Dusseldorf to Delhi for him. He would collect them from Delhi and take them to Kathmandu where he had a house and lived for much of the year. He had short hair and would not have looked out of place in a suit working in a city in Germany. He could have passed as Mr Normal if he wanted to and was running the business like a Mr Normal. It was just that he liked getting stoned and going on wild adventures and also liked living in Kathmandu.

They rode through the afternoon across the north Indian plains on bumpy roads towards Sitapur. In the late afternoon they arrived at the outskirts of the town to be greeted by the sight of a large bull trying to rape a cow while the cow's owner tried in vain to fight the horny beast off. The man was shouting and waving a big stick about, but the big black bovine was having none of it and just kept pursuing the pair of them but it was most obvious which of them he was interested in, in this way at least the man was fortunate.

Sitapur like many Indian towns, was a scruffy and dirty place with not much in the way of redeeming features. They drove on through and found the road to Nepalganj, which was the most westerly of the road crossings into Nepal with road links to Kathmandu. There was another crossing even further to the west, but the roads from there did not connect with the main highway grid of the rest of the country. The truck that Chriss's girlfriend, Tessa, was driving kept having problems, and they had to stop on numerous occasions to fix it, as such it was decided that that she should drive in front of Criss's truck as so that that she didn't have to keep hitting the horn each time that she broke down.

That evening they stopped in a small, cheap guest house in a village, maybe thirty kilometers east of Sitapur. Both Chris and Gypsy had been on the road for quite some time and the Austrian man and his girlfriend had been travelling in India for over six months and were planning to continue on to Thailand if they didn't use up all of their funds in Nepal. So it was a well experienced group of globe trotters that sat down for a chat over dinner that night. Each had something to share with the others and much in the way of information and ideas was shared that night. Gypsy had grown to like his own generation of German speakers since he had started to travel. They were a bright, competent and friendly bunch on the whole, and not just that, but they tended to be far better adjusted to the world around them than their British counterparts, who seemed to get themselves into trouble for stupid reasons as they travelled. Also they often were involved, as Chris was, in interesting projects of their own that they seemed to execute well.

Many of the British would come across as either yobs or snobs and also often would have a post colonial arrogance about them, which made it hard for them to make friends among the locals in the countries in which they were travelling.

The German speakers and the Italians however, often not only made friends in the countries which they liked to travel but also it was not uncommon for one of them to start their own business there, either on their own or in partnership with a local friend. If it was a German doing it then the business would always be either doing something highly innovative and cutting edge or else it would be doing something that already existed but to a level of Deutsch quality. For this Gypsy admired them considerably. He always seemed to get on well with not just these people but also the locals in many of the countries in which he had travelled. He, like the young Germans was also endlessly inquisitive and eager to learn all that he could about the many different aspects of life. But still his number one focus was about matters spiritual. He had a deep and growing fondness for India and was growing more interested by the day in Vedic/Buddhist literature and teachings. Many of the Germans who travelled in Asia also shared this same interest with him, when as many of the British and French gave the impression that they were in India solely for the drugs and a cheap place to hang out or to make money from dealing in Indian products which at that time were incredibly cheap.

The next day the journey took them further across the north Indian plains towards the border with Nepal. The road, in places was just a dirt track but Chris seemed to know his way. The area that they were travelling in was wild and primitive with only poor and basic villages but no towns to be seen for many kilometers. They passed through areas were it was just jungle. The land there could not have been very good as even the jungle was not looking that lush or healthy. Still there were villages amongst it but god alone knows what the people who lived there did in order to feed themselves. The one thing that India definitely did not suffer a shortage of was people, they seemed to crawl out from everywhere even in the most desolate of places. You could stop in a place in the middle of the most desolate of wildernesses and think that you were all alone…. But then they would start to pop up from either behind trees and bushes if there were any, or else from behind rocks or small hills and piles of boulders or sand. You could never be totally alone in India, it was impossible.

The three of them in Chris's truck, through out the day spent a lot of time talking about their different experiences traveling and about world current affairs and the real stories behind the bullshit that the media fed to the masses as news. Being that they were all seasoned travelers they had between them many experiences and insights into what was really going on in the world. As such they often found themselves in agreement with each other on what it was that really made things the way they were.

Tessa's truck kept breaking down and they had to make many road side stops in order to fix it and get it running again. By that night they were not so far from the border crossing at Nepal ganj. Once again they stopped at a cheap guest house by the side of the road and went out to a local darbur for a plate of dahl and chapattis with curd and hot pickle. Chris and Tessa were both very tired from the concentration that driving in the mad chaos of Indian traffic and on bad roads in semi knackered old trucks takes. So they went to bed early, leaving Gypsy and the Austrian couple to sit smoking chillums and talking, as Gypsy briefed them on Kathmandu and Nepal in general.

The next morning they were up and out on the road early, driving along some of the roughest roads imaginable even by India's low standards. They were, at times reduced to speeds of no more than ten to fifteen kilometers an hour. Never the less they reached the border at around nine thirty to ten o clock. The Austrian couple did not have visas and so had to find a way of changing money to pay for visas on the border, the trouble was that there were no banks for many miles on the Indian side and they couldn't reach the bank in Nepal ganj until they had Nepalese stamps in their passports. Eventually it was agreed that Gypsy and Chris would cross over into Nepal in the first truck and go to the bank and change some of their own travellers cheques into Nepalese rupees and come back and lend some to the Austrian couple in order that they could get their visas. While Tessa would wait with them as so that at least they could sit in the other truck while they waited. There was not so much as a chai stand on the Indian side of the border as far as any of them could make out so at least with Tessa there with the truck, they would have access to clean drinking water if nothing else.

The customs and emigration officers were very friendly and helpful as they processed Gypsy and Chris through. Theirs was not the busiest border crossing in the world and very few westerners even knew that it even existed and even fewer of them used it, so seeing a westerner at all was a rare occasion for them. The town was just two or three kilometres from the crossing and so Gypsy and Chris headed there in the truck and found the bank (there was just one in the place) then waited in the queue to cash the cheques. They were back at the border within the hour and then the others were cleared through.

Soon they were on their way again and driving in an easterly direction through the jungle in the direction of Sonali. The road was much better than it had been on the Indian side of the border and there was not much in the way of traffic save for a few trucks and the occasional small, decrepit and tatty old bus that would scream past, over taking them at kamikaze speed. Also there were far less people about and fewer villages than there had been in India. The villages however looked much poorer and the houses were made of rough sawn wood and branches, with roofs either made from thatch or corrugated iron. They were mostly set up on stilts, obviously as protection from the monsoon rains and from insects, snakes and animals. The other thing that was different from India was that in Nepal women would often give young men from the west, the eye, when as in India they would not dare out of fear of deadly reprisals from the Indian men of their own

caste. So as they drove along the road often they were leered and winked at by beautiful young women in colourful tribal clothes.

About an hour into the journey on the Nepalese side of the border they were treated to a sight that none of them had been lucky enough to have seen before. A wild leopard ran out of the jungle on the south side of the road and briefly stopped to look around while standing in the middle of the road, before taking of at high speed into the thick jungle on the north side of the road. Chris had to brake hard in order not to hit it but then he stopped the truck and they all got out to watch as the creature bolted off into the distance (don't try this at home folks). Gypsy had never seen such a fit and healthy animal as this in his life before. It moved almost effortlessly at a speed that would have even put many motor vehicles to shame, it was a truly amazing sight. The other truck with the two women in it had also stopped but they had only got the briefest of views of it as their line of vision had been blocked by Chris's truck. After a couple of minutes they were back in the trucks and once more on their way. It was a pleasant temperature under the canopy of the thick jungle as they drove through the afternoon towards Sonali and Narain Ghat, passing the occasional village along the way. The area was so poor that there were not even many places that they could stop at for a soft drink or even a cup of chai, so they had to make do with the bottled water that they were carrying on board.

They stopped that night at a small guesthouse close to the crossroads with the Pokara to Sonali highway and after eating a plate of sabji and chapattis each and smoking a couple of joints they all went to bed. It had been a long and tiring day and the next day was also going to be long as they were planning on making it to Kathmandu by that night.

The next morning they awoke early and after a quick cup of chai were out on the road, rolling towards Narain Ghat, at the foot of the mountains. The landscape had now changed from thick jungle to open farmland and they were in an area with a larger population, also there was more traffic on the road.

By late morning they had reached Narain Ghat and stopped in the town for some lunch at a smart looking darbur. Then they were on their way again as they drove up through a valley into the mountains towards Muggling, which is situated roughly half way along the highway between Kathmandu and Pokara. They reached Muggling at about 1.30 pm and stopped for a chai at one of the numerous scruffy chai shops that lined the road there. Muggling could only be described as a dump with no redeeming features bar for its daburs and chai shops that serviced the numerous trucks and buses that passed through, en route to Kathmandu, Pokara or the Terai.

They rolled on through the afternoon towards Kathmandu, eventually arriving there in the late afternoon at around five thirty or six o'clock. Chris dropped Gypsy and the Austrian couple off near to Thamel before he and Tessa drove the short distance to their rented house in the Swayambu area, at the base of a hill that housed the famous monkey temple. Gypsy went and found himself a cheap room at one of the many guest houses that he knew in the city and then went to the Pumpernickel bakery to see if the afternoon chillum session was still in progress. It was so he sat down and joined in as he caught up on the local news. The same old crowd was there as before he had left, the only one missing was Prem's dog Barry. Gypsy asked Prem were he was and was told that when they had gone for a trip to Pokara, Barry had gone of for a wander in the woods on his own and been killed and eaten by a tiger. Everyone had been saddened by it as everyone liked Barry, he had been so well behaved that he was regarded as an equal member of the crowd. The German in the Fu Man Chu outfit who hung out with the chillum circle had not been seen around for a long time and everyone wondered where he was. However, he turned up late that night dressed in his weird Tibetan styled clothes and told everyone who was still there what he had been up to. He had trekked high up into the mountains for several days on paths that were never used by the tourists and found a poor village where ganja was the main crop under cultivation. He had then employed the whole village to work for him to make hashish. There are two ways of making a good cannabis resin for smoking. In India and Nepal they generally do it by taking the ripe buds and rubbing them in their hands and then scraping the sticky resin off their hands with a knife. They then slowly build up a pile of the stuff on some sort of shiny non stick surface. The product that is made by this technique is known as charas. In the Muslim world they use another technique to make their version of the smoke, which involves taking the buds and breaking them up and drying them a little before putting them in a bag and shaking them to extract the pollen, then the contents of the bag is run through a sieve. The refined product is then taken and heated gently and not to a high temperature before being pressed into a bar. The product that is made by this technique is known as hashish. The German wanted to see if it was possible to teach the locals to make hashish instead of charas. From inside his Tibetan silk coat he pulled several large bars of semi pressed hashish and broke off a piece from each bar and asked the people sitting around to skin up with it and try it." This is from the first shake" he said "it should be pretty good" he said "it took almost a hundred kilos of ganja to make just one kilo of hashish. This bar is from the second shake and this one is from the third shake" he continued while pointing to each of the bars. He was all fired up and full of energy, having just trekked for several days, down from the village. He wanted to make some quick sales and then get back up there. "You cant believe just how poor these people are" he continued to explain "they cant even afford blankets to sleep under, they sleep under a pile of hay and straw, they don't even have shoes to wear. I need to sell this stuff and then buy blankets, shoes and medicines and head back up there. I've got a hundred and thirty of them working for me and their in desperate need of basic essential supplies. It is truly painful to see people living in such intense poverty. I've got to try and do something to help them so I'm hoping that some of you will help me by buying some of this excellent product from me". To Gypsy it didn't taste much different from the charas that they all smoked in their chillums each afternoon at the bakery, however it did have a rather nice effect and was lighter in it's buzz than the charas.

The next day Gypsy set about his work, he had a collection of gemstones from Jaipur that he wanted to put into some silver designs that he had in his head. So he went off down to freak street to find a certain silver smith that he had been told about.

Then after placing his order and handing over the stones that were to be used, he headed back up towards Thamel to find some of the tailors that he had noticed that did hand embroidered waistcoats. He really liked their products and wanted to make up a bunch to take back to England and sell. He found a shop that had good designs and where the people were friendly and honest and sat down with them.

Over a cup of chai he explained to them what he wanted and how much time he had to get them done in. Then they agreed a wholesale rate for the work and Gypsy then gave them a deposit and went on his way to get on with the next part of the job. He then went to the Tibetan area at Bodhanath to look for Thanka paintings. But they were too expensive there, so he headed back to Thamel and scoured the area to see what he could find. Then in the mid afternoon he headed over to the pumpernickel bakery to join the chillum circle. He explained to the others what he was trying to do and how he planned to do it. They were all very helpful and gave him advice about which shops and dealers that he should take a look at and how to recognize a good quality product.

Then looking around at the people sitting at the other tables in the garden, he was shocked by what he saw. The faces did not resemble tourists at all even though it was obvious that they were trying to. There was the distinct smell of INTERPOL PIG emanating from most of the groups huddled around their tables. They were slyly eyeballing the chillum circle with thin soulless eyes, full of hate and malevonance. Though some of the more anally retentative tourists would give them the odd disapproving or frightened stare it was not like the vibe that was emanating from this particular group of reptiles, this lot were giving off a thoroughly predatory and hostile vibe and try as they might they couldn't hide it. "The place is full of Interpol pigs" Gypsy said quietly to the others, look at them they are sitting at almost every table in the place. I've never seen so many of them here, we better warn everyone who needs to know. They must be planning to make some mega sized busts. Look carefully those aren't tourists sitting there, their eyes are dirty and they don't look relaxed like the trekkers and tourists do and some of them are giving us really dirty looks too". Some of the others stole a glance at them and agreed. So word was passed around the city to all the friends and brothers to keep their heads down and their charas well hidden.

The next day the busts started and reports came in from around the city of people getting hauled away by squads of local police, accompanied by Interpol. Gypsy was worried about the safety of some of his friends when they didn't turn up that afternoon for the chillum session at the bakery. They were always there and virtually never missed an afternoon of smoking and chatting. The next day he went and hired a 200cc motorbike as so he could get around more easily and if necessary he could help a friend make a quick getaway. He went searching around the city to see if he could find some of his friends at their houses, but they were nowhere to be found and so he took off to Baktapur to go and see Raj to see what he might be up to.

In the main square near one of the temples he found a shop that was selling one of the products that he had been searching for. Cheap thanka paintings. The owner of the shop was very honest and explained that they had been painted with water colours and not the paints made with ground gemstones and metals like the expensive ones were made from.

But gypsy was happy with this. It would be too hard to try selling the good ones to the British, these would be fine. Gypsy bought a stack of the paintings and then headed around to the guest house to go and find Raj and tell him what he was up to and see how well he was getting on as the proprietor of the guest house. Raj was more than happy to see him and when Gypsy told him that he had rented a motor bike Raj suggested that he come and stop at the guest house the next night and they could go out for a ride on it on the following day when he had some free time.

Back in Kathmandu there was still no sign of some of his friends and he was starting to get worried for them. He just hoped that they hadn't been grabbed by the reptiles or their accomplices. Never the less, the chillum circle continued as before and some of the old faces that had nothing to hide at the time were there. But the ones that were the heart and soul of the circle were conspicuous by their absence. The next day with a small bag over his shoulder he headed out to Baktapur. He spent the afternoon and evening relaxing then the next day they got on the motorbike and rode up into the mountains, it was the first time that either of them had ridden on a motorbike for any distance. Gypsy had been so busy travelling that he had still not got around to sorting himself out with a license for any kind of motor vehicle but in Kathmandu he didn't need one to rent a bike and so he was taking advantage of the situation to indulge in it. He certainly enjoyed the freedom it gave him. They took turns at doing the riding and ended up at a village somewhere on the road to the border with Chinese occupied Tibet.

The next day back in Kathmandu he was back to work as he did his rounds, checking on the workshops that were making his products. The embroidered waist coats and bags were almost finished and he sat and talked with the owner of the shop and his brother over a cup of chai. They told him that they were from a family of Muslim Tibetans. Gypsy had no idea that there were anything but Buddhists in Tibet up until that point. Anyway he liked them as the people that they were, they were descent and honourable and as such he liked doing business with them.

Down at freak street his silver rings and earrings were also coming together well and he knew that he would be travelling back to India soon. He went around to Chris's house in Swayambu to see what he was up to. He was still waiting for his convoy of old Mercedes trucks to reach India, but he seemed very relaxed about it as he sat back drinking a beer in an easy chair in his garden. He had a very nice lifestyle living in the quiet surroundings of Swayambu and didn't seem like he was in much of a hurry to go anywhere.

Much as he had tried, Gypsy didn't have any luck in finding Sally, he wanted to give her her bag back but no one had seen her or heard from her. He got a pleasant surprise however when one of his closer friends re emerged from the woodwork. "Thank god you are safe, I was worried for you when you disappeared as all the busts were going on, I was worried that the pigs had got you". "Oh no I was fine" he replied, "some German friends of mine got wind of what was about to go down and got a whole load of their friends together and took us out of town in their trucks. For the last three weeks we have been up in the mountains having a bit of a party. Anyway the pigs have fucked off now and everything is back to business as usual".

By the next week Gypsy had his load together and it was time to head back down to Delhi to go and find a flight to London. So once again it was time to say goodbye to his friends and jump on a bus to the border. He still had found no trace of Sally and being that he did not have her address anywhere and had too much luggage of his own, he left her bag behind and forgot about her.

That night he rode the bus down to Sonali and early the next morning, crossed back into India. He was carrying three massive bags and had to get a rickshaw walla to help him haul it all across the border. From the border he took a bus to Gorakhpur, which was three hours to the south and from there he had a train ticket to Lucknow and another ticket that would take him from Lucknow to Delhi. He had bought the tickets from a travel agency in Kathmandu as a Kathmandu to Delhi package.

Getting from the bus station to Gorakpur central railway station and safely onto the train with his three huge bags had been quite a business in it's self. But he was young and strong and most enthusiastic about what he was doing and luck at that time was on his side. Once on the train he was able to relax and skin up a joint as he watched the view out of the window. That night at eight o'clock his train pulled in at Lucknow central station. He got off hauling his elephantine load of clothes and handycrafts. He had it in two massive super sized holdalls and an over sized back pack, all together it must have weighed at least seventy kilos. When he carried it all at once he could only just manage to walk.

Half an hour later, his train to Delhi came in and after finding the carriage in which his berth was located, he staggered aboard hauling his load with him. However, once on board he was informed that he did not have a booked bunk. The travel agent back in Kathmandu had cheated him. A man of roughly the same age as himself who was from Calcutta came forward and offered to help him and soon, after having paid the guard eight rupees, he had a bunk sorted on the first tier and put his bags under it. Then he got chatting with the man who had helped him. The man had a book shop back in Calcutta and was travelling to Delhi on business. "I rolled a joint to smoke on the way before I left Calcutta, would you like to share it with me?" the man asked "yes please" Gypsy replied that sounds like just what I need right now". So they sat in the carriage smoking it as they talked about Vedic philosophy as the train rolled on through the night. Eventually Gypsy drifted off to sleep. When he awoke in the morning he saw the man sitting there, wide awake. He had stayed awake all night, in order to guard Gypsy's bags for him. Gypsy felt most humbled by this and he knew that he had just met a saint.

The train pulled in at new Delhi railway station and they said their goodbyes and headed out in their respective directions to get on with their businesses. Gypsy found a cycle rickshaw and headed over the road bridge towards Delhi gate and the tourist camp. He got a large room and dropped his bags in it and went and had a shower. Later, outside of the gate on the road a young bearded rickshaw Walla came up to him and introduced himself "hello Mister Gypsy my name is Jeet can I be your rickshaw walla for the day?" "Ok" said Gypsy but how much do I need to pay you for a whole day's work?" "as you like" Jeet replied "Ok your on" said Gypsy "let's get started" They started by going to Jan Path road to the Tibetan market where Gypsy had seen a range of pill boxes that he thought would be easy to sell back in England.

Then they went on up to Connaught place to find a travel agent where he could buy a ticket to London. The woman at the travel agent arranged a ticket for him at a cheap rate but it had a strange routing, he would be taking a Thai airways flight from Delhi to Amsterdam and from there he would be taking a British Caledonian airways flight to London Gatwick airport. He was booked to leave in ten days time. Meanwhile he was going to be busy getting ready. Not only did he want to buy more different types of stock to sell but he hadn't been in the west for a long time and figured that he was going to need clothes and other things in order to get by.

Through the next ten days Jeet became his exclusive organic chauffer. He would turn around and talk with Gypsy as he peddled and they started to become good friends. Most days Gypsy would eat both lunch and dinner around the back and across the road from Tourist camp, at Raj's scruffy dabur. The staff got to know him well by his frequent visits there. Jeet also had his favourite daburs that he took Gypsy to on several occasions. They were made from old sheets of corrugated iron and had dirt floors but the food always tasted good. Gypsy's favourite food was and still is dahl and chapattis which was always in plentiful supply in such places.

The other thing that Gypsy wanted to make business with was natural Ayervedic medicines so he went to Pahar Ganj market and visited an Ayervedic chemist who he had been introduced to before and bought a quantity of different remedies that he hoped that he could find a market for.

Jeet helped him by taking him to shops where he could get things at the local rate. He got his photographs developed in this way and also got some new clothes. Later he scored four tolas of good charas and set about hiding two tolas in a cistern of one of the toilets in the shower block at Tourist camp. The other two he planned to take with him back to England as he had been away for so long he figured that it might take some time for him to find a good reliable source back in UK.

At tourist camp there was a small crowd of travellers that Gypsy was hanging out with. Along with them were the Iranian refugees and Turkish bus drivers who would also hang out with them. They would sit around each night into the early hours of the morning smoking chillums and drinking chai or beer or maybe even rum or whiskey. They would all get a buzz out of watching the Turks getting up to their favourite trick of placing fire crackers around the tents of the apprentice yuppies that were travelling on organized package tour "adventure" holidays. It was nice to see that some one cared enough about these po-faced, gap year emotional retards that they took it upon themselves to cure their collective constipation and also it was good for the travellers if these arsehole yuppies in training went back to the west and told their nasty friends nightmare stories about travelling in India. Hopefully this would keep India protected from them. After all many of the travellers had come toIndia, at least in part in order to get away from such creeps.

Almost all of the Iranians had heavy smack habits at that time. That having been said, not one of them once ever tried to pull a rip off on any of the travellers, they were cool and gave no problems and were good company to hang out with.

All too soon it was time to head for the airport and take his flight back to England. He took an auto rickshaw out to Palam airport and waited for his flight to London. He had three massive bags and the guitar that he had bought back in Hong Kong before. He had taken it with him everywhere since he bought it and it had been all around India with him.

He had to fork out an extra one hundred dollars in order to get his load onto the plane but get it on he did. The international terminal at that time was small and crowded and right next to the domestic terminal. Unlike the airport at Bombay there were no air bridges and there were also very few international flights running through it at that time.

They walked out across the tarmac to the plane which had arrived from Bangkok thirty five minutes previously and walked up the steps and into the cabin of the Thai Airways DC10, which was full of Dutch tourists returning from package holidays in Thailand.

The plane was readied for take off, the doors were closed and the plane was pushed back. Then they were taxi-ing out to the runway, Then there was the familiar sound as the engines reved, then the plane moved foreward and they took off into the darkness.

Every seat in the economy section was taken and there were lots of women with crying babies, so it was a long and tiring, sleepless night that Gypsy had as they sped westbound through the darkness. Eventually morning came and soon after breakfast had been served and cleared away they started the descent into Sciphol. The plane landed and pulled up at an air bridge. When Gypsy got off of the plane and looked around he felt very strange. It was cold and the sky was grey and people were racing around looking stressed. He was starting to feel the culture shock. Gone were the easy going Indians with big goofy smiles on their faces and relaxed attitude to life and here were stressed unfriendly northern Earopeans with their sense of self importance, running at sprinter speed, in the rat race. He had felt very at home with the vibe of the people in Asia but among westerners who had not lived in that part of the world he felt like a space alien.

He found a bank kiosk and changed some money into guilders and went to the bar and downed a couple of whiskeys to steady his nerves. Then he went and found his flight to Gatwick. The flight was full of gray faced businessmen and people dressed in grey, navy blue and black. He couldn't have felt more out of place if he had tried. The topics of conversation that he could over hear, the clothes that they were wearing, the expressions on their faces. He must be crazy for even stepping into this place, how long would it be until he could get back to Asia, he wondered.

Forty five minutes after having taken off the plane was descending down through the thick, multi layers of cloud into Gatwick.

Though he was from England he couldn't of felt less at home there. However he put a brave face on it as he got off the plane and saw the security men staring at the people getting of the plane with up tight malevonant looks on their faces. Back in Delhi he had gone to the British embassy to check with their customs book to find out if there was anything that he needed to declare on arrival.

As it happened there was, so after collecting his bags he took himself to the red channel and declared what he had in his bags. He had travelled in Asia for over two and a half years without being pulled for a search, with the exception of when he got pulled at Penang and searched for looking too straight, before he headed into Australia. So he had not thought about what he should look like before flying back into England. He was wearing a pair of jeans that were covered in embroidered patches that he had bought in Kathmandu and a black silk waist coat that was also similarly covered in exotic oriental embroidered designs. Under this he was wearing a tie dyed purple and blue T shirt. Around his neck was an assortment of silver chains with different exotic charms on them, his hair was long and his belt was just a tied length of thick silk with exotic patterns on it. He made the average western hippy look pretty dull in comparison. However he had not reckoned on the reaction that he got from customs. Although he had come to them and honestly declared all that he had, they decided to take him to pieces. They started with his bags, while listing all that they could screw V.A.T. out of him for. Everything and anything in his possession was listed. Then they made him turn his pockets out then, they made him strip and performed a full cavity search on him. they took about two hours over the whole procedure. Gypsy had a tola of charas in his mouth, split into several pieces and another tola wrapped in plastic and two condoms up his arse. Needless to say they found neither of them. But while the tiresome procedure was progressing the pieces in his mouth were starting to dissolve and run down his throat. By the time that they were through with him he was practically tripping from the effects of the mega dose of charas that he had ingested.

His mother had come to collect him from the airport along with a friend of the family who was a retired copper and a freemason too. When he finally walked out of the arrivals gate they were nowhere to be seen and so he stood there waiting for them as he swayed about in his altered state of consciousness. He stood out a mile in his psychedelic, semi ethnic clothes. People were staring at him with hostile, hateful, anal expressions on their faces as if to say "who's that cunt? how dare he dress like that, I didn't give him permission to", he then started to wonder if he hadn't made a terrible mistake in travelling back to this miserable country with its abundance of aggressive up tight yobs and snobs who seemed to be either cold or confrontational at all times. How he had been treated at customs was ridiculous to put it extremely mildly. If he had been carrying serious quantities of any form of contraband he would have been dressed in a suit and tie or in expensive but demure designer clothes. He certainly wouldn't be wearing bright colours or ethnic clothes. By the way he had been treated at customs and by the way people were staring at him he could have been forgiven for thinking that there had been a law against wearing hippie clothes introduced through the British parliament while Margaret Thatcher's government had been in power. He had been away on his travels for more than two and a half years and things appeared not to have improved any during the time that he had been gone.

Eventually his mother and the friend turned up to collect him and they headed off to the car, and not a moment to soon. He pretended to go to sleep on the back seat of the car as so as he didn't have to join in the conversation. He was still tripping out of his mind and knew that he would not be able to comprehend where they were coming from if they asked him any questions about his journey or anything else for that matter. Back at the family house he sited jet lag as the reason that he looked so rough and quickly disappeared off to his old bedroom and after retrieving his other piece of charas, lay down and relaxed.

The next day he showed his family what he had brought back with him to sell. There was all sorts of everything from ayervedic medicines to clothing, gem stones bags, silver jewellery, pill boxes and religious, ethnic artefacts. That weekend they went up to London to stay with some of his cousins for a couple of nights and Gypsy went to Camden market with some of his stock. To his surprise he found it quite easy to sell the jewellery wholesale to some of the stands there, also they seemed quite interested in buying loose gem stones from him. The next day he and one of his cousins rented a stand at the market to see how it would work. However the takings were so meagre that Gypsy resolved to make only wholesale business in the future. He had in effect actually lost money by renting a stand and he could not afford to do this again. He still did not have a driving licence and so his mother said that she would help him by buying an old H,A Viva telecom van for him and he could pay her back for it later. Gypsy was apprehensive about this as he quite liked the peace and freedom he had by not driving a vehicle. He would either hitch hike, walk or use public transport when he wanted to go somewhere and didn't miss what he had never had, but he went along with it none the less.

He would take off in the morning with one of his ethnic bags over his shoulder, full of handycrafts, jewellery and gem stones and walk down to the highway and stick his thumb out. He would often get lifts from the most interesting of people. On one occasion he was given a lift by a retired Concorde pilot and on other occasions he got lifts from people who had got around by hitching when they were younger.

When he reached the town of his destination he would go and find shops that he thought might be interested in the products that he had. He tended to do best around market areas and so would gravitate to such areas if there were any in the towns that he was visiting. Someone who saw the waist coats said "I don't want any but I know someone who would go nuts over these" so Gypsy gave her his address and telephone number.

The next afternoon a most strange creature with long purple dyed hair, colourful clothes and dripping with silver jewellery turned up at his house on a skate board. His face was painted in psychedelic colours and he looked more weird than anything that Gypsy had ever seen on his travels. But he talked quite normally and he proceeded to look through the waist coats, choosing three to purchase on the spot and a further selection that he said that he would like to buy on the following week when he had some more money. So Gypsy put them aside for him and then he was gone, riding back down the road on his skate board.

Within three weeks Gypsy was getting low on stock and so went to London to the Indian consulate to get himself a new visa. Then finding an Indian travel agent in the centre of the city, just off from Picadilly Circus, he bought a cheap ticket on Thai airways back to Delhi. Four days later he was sitting on a jumbo, whizzing off down the runway at Heathrow.

Arriving late in the evening at Delhi he was pleasantly surprised to find the plane pulling up at a brand new terminal on the other side of the runway from the old airport. This was the brand new 'Indra Gandhi International Airport' that had just been completed or I.G.I. as the locals called it.

He took a taxi from there into the city and went to tourist camp and got himself a room. After dropping his bag in his room he went to the shower block and found the toilet in which he had hidden his stash in the cistern of. He took the lid off the cistern and put his hand down inside the water and was happy when he put his hand on the carefully wrapped package. Obviously no one else had thought to stash their dope in such a place, otherwise his hand might have come up empty. Then after cutting it out of its double condom and cling film packaging, he went off to see if the Iranians were still staying at the place. They were so he asked if they had some rolling papers or a chillum as so as they could all have a smoke. They then all sat around outside their room smoking chillums and joints into the early hours of the morning.

The next day after breakfast he grabbed his bag and headed off to Bikaner house which was the seat of the Rajasthan government in Delhi. It was also were the best and cheapest of the deluxe buses that went to Jaipur left from, which was why he was there. He bought a ticket and sat and waited for forty five minutes until the bus was ready to load up and leave. Six hours later he was riding past the Amer fort on the outskirts of Jaipur as they headed towards the main bus station at Sindi camp. From Sindi camp he took a cycle rickshaw to the hippie/traveller guest house that he had stayed at before and got himself a room.

Glastonbury festival was due to start in just under a month and he was planning on fly pitching a stand there so he had no time to spare if he was going to get his job done in time. He took off into the market almost at a run and made his way down to Birla's office at Gangoori bazaar. It was as usual, full of western travellers, buying gems and jewellery. Gypsy sat down on one of the mattresses and picked up a tray and joined them in selecting stones. Later in the afternoon he headed over to Chameli walla market and took a look around for some silver jewellery to add to his collection.

Then he went back to the guest house to see if there was a chillum session going yet. There was so he sat down and joined in for half an hour before taking off into the markets again. He again started searching for cheap and reasonably priced gemstones and silver. He didn't get finished until late into the night. He then he headed to M.I. road to find a dabur to eat at before going back to the guest house to join in the chillum party with the Italian travellers who had just arrived from Goa. It was late in May and it was blisteringly hot in Rajasthan, so much so that it made it hard even to sleep at night. There was only a fan in his room, which at twenty rupees [£0.85p – there were twenty four point something rupees to the pound at that time] a night was the cheapest room available. It was basic inside with just a fan, a light and two beds and walls covered in graffiti from the other travellers that had passed through. Also it was on the roof and exposed to the sun on two sides, so at night it would still be hot inside. For three more days Gypsy searched his way through the market looking for good stones at cheap prices. Truth be told he didn't have much knowledge about what he was doing and had to be careful, Some of the locals were like a nest of snakes at times and were constantly trying to scam him and would try hassling him whenever he went out on the street. It was very tiring and tedious dealing with them, he didn't want to be rude to them but it was sometimes the only way of getting free of their company.

After four days in Jaipur he took a bus ride back to Delhi and made contact with Jeet. The next three days were spent travelling around Delhi in Jeet's rickshaw as he rounded up the different things that he wanted from old Delhi and Jan Path road.

He went and got himself a Nepalese visa and an air ticket at the Indian Airlines office. Then the next day He went to the domestic airport, checked in and eventually boarded his flight back to the hippie Shangri La. It was like a local bus in the air in that it stopped at Agra, Kajaraho and Varanasi before hopping over the mountains and into Kathmandu. After every stop when the plane had taken off he was brought a new box of Indian snacks such as Samosas, pakoras and ladhu, accompanied by cups of tea and each flight lasted for around about fourty minutes. So by the time they reached Varanasi he was full. A large group of elderly American tourists had boarded the fight at Varanasi. Some of the women were behaving in such a strange way that Gypsy realized that it would be better not to communicate with them. When he asked one of them a question regarding which was his seat the woman virtually went into a screaming fit complete with wild frightened eyes. He had a little experience of Americans and their tantrums but this was completely off the wall. No doubt the woman had been traumatized by what she had seen in Varanasi, beggars, junkies, hustlers, filth and the burning ghats with their conveyor belt like funerals running twenty four hours a day. No doubt, this precious little soul had never seen a human body being burned out in the open before, let alone ten or more of them being toasted all at the same time. With legs and arms sticking out of the pyres, the smell of burning flesh and dogs finishing off the parts that the fire had failed to burn. The experience had no doubt had had quite a profound effect upon her. And now here was this hippie asking her something about seat numbers.

The plane once again Taxied out to the runway and took off for the final leg of the flight which took it over the mountains and down into the Kathmandu Valley. The plane landed and taxied back down the runway to the scruffy terminal and soon Gypsy was walking across the apron to the arrivals hall. A short while later he was riding in a taxi into the city.

Once he had got checked into a guest house he went strait out to find the shops were he had had things made before and over a cup of chai he put his new orders in. Then he went to rent a motorbike and then rode off to find his friends and catch up on local news. This time he was short for time and as such he could only join the chillum session at the pumpernickel bakery for a short time each day as he raced around the Kathmandu valley on the motorbike rounding up the different goods that he had orders for or wanted for selling at Glastonbury. He spent some time with his favourite of his friends who were the Anglo Indian crowd from Calcutta. They were as ever full of good humour and fun. One of them offered to lend Gypsy his Enfield motorbike but as it had no working brakes on it Gypsy had to decline the kind offer as he didn't want to get into trouble for crashing into someone. Besides, he liked the small Honda chopper that he had rented, it was easy to ride and normally started on either the first or second kick. Within ten days he was loaded and ready to head out back to Delhi. Once again with great big heavy bags full of wares, he caught a bus down to Sonali and crossed back into

India. He took another bus to Gorakhpur, but this time instead of going to the railway station he took an auto rickshaw out to the small airport and bought a one way ticket to Delhi. He had to pay a bit extra to get his huge bags into the hold but it wasn't much and he had budgeted for it. The plane was an old Vickers Viscount turbo prop. This was to be his first flight on a propeller driven plane and he wondered what it would be like. The passenger terminal at Gorakhpur was a small old concrete shed out on a military airfield. It had no amenities apart from a toilet and there was certainly no bar for him to go and relax at. So he was happy when they were eventually called to go out and board the plane.

The plane lumbered off down the runway and slowly climbed up into the sky. It was much smaller inside than any of the jets that he had ever flown in and noisier and slower too, but it beat the shit out of taking the train back to Delhi.

After an hour or so they descended into Lucknow airport and people got off the plane and others got on. Then some forty minutes later they were taking off again, en route for Delhi. The plane touched down at Delhi an hour and a half later. It was late afternoon as Gypsy collected his bags and found a taxi to take him into the city. It was much hotter in Delhi than it had been in Kathmandu and Gypsy was more than happy to reach Tourist camp and be able to go and get himself a shower. Ali who was one of the Iranian crowd that Gypsy hung out with called out to him "hey Gypsy you look like shit, what have you been doing?" "Iv'e been working my arse off up in Kathmandu getting a load together to take back to England and sell" he replied "last night I rode the bus down from Kathmandu to the border and I've been travelling all of today as well and I haven't had a wink of sleep since early yesterday morning" "here, take my towel and go have yourself a shower and get cleaned up and then come and join us for a chai and a joint" said Ali "we'll be waiting for you here at our room". "Thanks" said Gypsy and headed off to the shower block. A short while later they were sitting outside of Ali's room and telling each other the stories about what each of them had been up to in the last few weeks and sharing the local underground news. Ali's crowd were making progress in trying to get accepted as refugees in different countries. Most of them wanted to go to America, namely California where some of them had some family living there.

The next day Jeet showed up outside the gates and he and Gypsy went off down to The Tibetan market on Jan Path road where Gypsy bought a sizeable quantity of stash boxes with agate lids on them. Also he made a stop at Doma's shop for a cup of chai and a chat before heading off down to old Delhi and into The Chandi chowk market. There he bought some solid silver and enamel pill boxes from a man who Luigi had introduced him to.

The next day he went over to Bikaner house and caught a bus back down to Jaipur. It was boiling hot all the way in the non air-conditioned bus (in those days there was no such thing as an air conditioned bus in India). They arrived at Sindi camp in the late afternoon and Gypsy headed back to the hippie/traveler guest house. Being that it was now the second week in June and boiling hot there were not so many people staying there. Gypsy got himself a room and dropped his bag and then went off down to Gangoori bazaar to Birla's office to touch base with him and find out what new things he had been buying. They sat and smoked a joint together as Birla gave him advice about new treatments that were being used to enhance certain types of stone and how to recognize stones that had had these treatments. Birla was extremely Knowledgeable about stones and kept up with events that were shaping the trade. He liked to share what he knew, he took great pride in being both professional and honest in his work. He was a man who had obviously helped many young people like Gypsy to learn their trade well and gain the knowledge of how not to get cheated.

At Chameli walla market the next day Gypsy went and visited a tailor shop and asked the man to make him a very strong waistcoat that was lined with giant pockets.

He was going to use it to carry extra cargo onto the plane at Delhi as he didn't wish to get stung like he did on his last trip back to England.

The whole of the day was spent scouring the city for stones and silver jewellery, he also bought some antique Mogul style paintings that had been painted on the pages of ancient books. They looked good and Gypsy thought that maybe he might be able to sell them to one of the antique dealers in the lanes in Brighton. By the late afternoon his waistcoat was ready. The tailor was laughing as he looked at it "I never thought of making some thing like this to sell" he said to Gypsy. "Maybe I should make some to sell, do you think that some of the other travellers would buy them?" "I think they would if they knew what they were for" Gypsy replied. "Are you not worried that customs in your country will stop you wearing something as suspicious as this?" the tailor asked. "Oh no,

I wont be wearing it when I go through at London" Gypsy explained it's only for getting the load on to the plane without having to pay massive extra charges. I'm hoping to get at least twenty kilos of weight into these pockets, that's why I needed you to make the pockets so strong. Once I'm on the plane the jacket comes off and packs into a shoulder bag that I will be carrying in one of the pockets. They fucked me for a hundred dollars for the extra weight the last time I flew out and I'm not going to give them another chance to do that" The tailor was almost pissing himself with laughter as Gypsy explained this to him "You think like an Indian" the tailor told him "we are sneaky like that too"

Gypsy chose some shoulder bags and shirts from the ready stock in the shop, paid the man and headed back to the guest house and packed his bag before heading back out into the markets for one final forage before leaving.

That night at around twelve midnight he headed out to the bus station and caught a bus back to Delhi. Arriving at six thirty in the morning he took a rickshaw back to tourist camp where he had his big bags stashed in the luggage room. He got himself a room and went and lay down and got himself some sleep. A few hours later he got up and collected some of his bags from the lugguage room. He then headed out in an autorickshaw to the cargo terminal at the airport to ship the stuff back to England as unaccompanied lugguage.

It may have been cheaper to ship it that way but it took all day and nearly sent him crazy. He was sent from one counter to another and made to fill out untold quantities of strange forms that made not the blindest bit of sense to him. And just when he thought he had finished and got the job done, they presented him with another stack of forms and made him go and visit all the same counters again. When by the end of the day at five in the afternoon he was finaly finished and the shipping had been paid for he was at the point where he wanted to strangle some one. What a fucking buisiness it was, it was as if who ever it was who decided on the rules for shipping protocol had designed this system with the specific aim of sending otherwise sane people to an asylum for the criminaly insane. Gypsy wondered how many murders might have been committed as a result of people being put through this ridiculous palava.

The next day he spent rushing around the city, getting the final odds and ends sorted and then that night he headed out to the airport in an auto rickshaw to catch his flight back to London. He looked like a cross between the Michelin man and a crazy bag man with his cargo jacket on, but he didn't care as long as he got his load onto the plane without getting stung for extra cash at the check in again.

Once onboard the plane he took a shoulder bag out from one of his pockets and proceeded to stuff the contents of his jacket into it. After that he was able to relax and sit down.

Through the night as they sped towards London he took full advantage of the free onboard bar as he downed shot after shot of whiskey and can after can of beer until he finally fell asleep. He woke up as the wheels hit the runway at Heathrow where he staggered off the plane and made his way to the baggage hall.

This time he was prepared and had booked a clearing agent to meet him at customs to clear the paperwork quickly and get him through without the bullshit he had gone through on his last arrival back into England. Even so he still had to wait for almost two hours while the man filled out the forms for him.

While he sat in the customs hall at terminal three waiting, several flights arrived from west Africa and Pakistan. There were a lot of Indians working there for British customs and Gypsy watched with interest as they descended on every pregnant looking African woman and many of the Pakistanis who were dressed in religious looking outfits too, hauling them off into small rooms for full body searches. Pakistan had done much over the years to piss the Indians off, not least starting unnecessary wars and sponsoring and promoting terrorism in India. Now this was the chance for some of the Indians to take revenge. Pakistan had been sticking a finger up India's arse for many years, but here at British customs there were Indians literally sticking fingers up Pakistani arses and they took full advantage of the opportunity to humiliate their enemies.

Eventually he made it out from customs, having handed over a substantial sum of cash to both Her Majesty's department of revenue and to the clearing agent. His father had driven up to the airport to collect him and was waiting outside. Soon he was on his way home, he was worried about whether he had bought the right things to sell, after all all of his money was riding on it and if he had got it wrong then he would be screwed. He didn't want to go back to working for his father for the meagre wages that he got paid there as it wouldn't be very easy getting back to Asia on those sort of earnings.

At the house, he immediately set about laying out his stock to see what it looked like in English light (it always somehow looked different in English daylight from how it looked in either India or Nepal). He was tired but he just couldn't sleep until he had looked at everything and had made himself feel confident that he had bought the right things. He phoned up the strange fellow Steve with the skate board, and told him that he had got more of the jackets. Also he phoned some shops and traders that he had made arrangements with, to fix up appointments. He then went and lay down on his bed and fell asleep and didn't awake until early the following morning at 5 am.

He spent some of that morning sorting out his things and loading some of what he had into his shoulder bag and then hit the road on foot out to the highway to hitch a ride to Brighton. In Brighton he had some luck and sold two or three hundred pounds worth of goods that day. Also he made contact with Steve who bought another two jackets from him. They were purple and had large yinyangs set in fire with a set of Buddha eyes above and an Om above the eyes embroidered on the back'.

Gypsy wanted to take his van to Glastonbury but he only had a provisional driving licence, which meant that he couldn't drive there without someone with a full licence sitting next to him for the whole journey. He didn't know anyone who had a licence but no car who was going to the festival, so when Steve said that he was going and he had a licence but no car they made an arrangement to help each other, Steve got a free lift and Gypsy was able to get himself and his stock to the festival.

At Glastonbury he met some people that he knew from Camden market and they all decided to fly pitch together as they all had different things from each other. Each one of them had just got back from a stock buying trip to a far flung third world country. One of them had been in Pakistan buying carpets and killims, two of them had been in Ecuador buying clothes and one of them had been in Thailand buying all sorts of different things. Gypsy's stand looked like a mobile Indo-Nepalese come Tibetan bazaar, with the hugely divergent range of stock that he had bought. They were all dressed in different ethnic, tribal outfits that they had bought for themselves in the places that they had been travelling. They were all jet lagged but due to the fact that they were at the festival, they had not yet suffered from the stark culture shock that they usually got on returning back to England. They were all quite relaxed and had a good time as they were able to keep a bit of the relaxed third world type vibe going for the entire festival and leave the culture shock aside for when they would get home later. Each was hoping to make enough from festival sales to start thinking about leaving for another trip soon after returning to their respective homes.

The remnants of the "Peace convoy" were parked up in the next field and many of them came to see Gypsy to buy Jewellery, clothing, Tibetan knifes and other things from him. They knew what they wanted and were easy to deal with, some of them wanted to trade hash or weed for items that Gypsy had. He was cool with this arrangement too, after all he was at a pop festival and would have to buy some smoke anyway and these guys were honest with him and had good quality goods.

The festival was over all too soon but Gypsy had done quite well and had several hundred pounds in his pocket as a result. Other people had asked for a lift in the direction that he was driving, so the back of the tiny van was crowded out to the max as they drove back to Sussex.

For the next four or five weeks he concentrated on selling in the Sussex area but soon his sales started to dry up as he sold out of the more popular of the goods and found it extremely difficult to sell the other products, they just were not British taste he was told.

He had stayed in touch with Hariklia who he had met on his first trip to Goa back in 1983 and had just received a letter from her. She had got herself a job as a tour guide on the Greek island of Santorini, taking English speaking tours around the ancient ruins there. She wanted him to come and visit her. Gypsy had not been to Greece for a long time, he wondered if he could sell some of the stock that he couldn't move in England in Athens or even out on the islands. Also he wanted to see his old friend Barbara who was now living in the city of Essen in Germany. Over the years he had heard so much about Amsterdam but had not yet been there. So he decided to do all those things in one easy move by buying himself a one month, all Europe rail pass.

So with a large bag that was half filled with silver jewellery and gemstones and the other half filled with his clothes and bed roll over one shoulder and his guitar over the other shoulder he took a train to London and then after crossing the city he took another train to Harwich, from where he caught an over night ferry to the hook of Holland, and from there he started to use his rail pass.

Amsterdam was just how he had imagined it to be but better. He had never seen such a free place in all of his life. He went and found a bed at a hostel near to Dam square, called 'the last watering hole' and then went out to visit some of the coffee shops that he had seen on the way to the hostel. The next few days were spent in a very spaced out state as he toured the alternative scene of the city. But it was all to easy and soon he was bored out of his mind and just wanted to carry on with his journey. He had not been able to sell any of his things in Amsterdam and not just that but the place was expensive.

On the fifth day in the city he packed his bag once more and headed back to the railway station and caught a train to Essen in Germany, where he had arranged to meet with Barbara. She had finished university and was living in Essen and working for a department of the German government. He had stayed in touch with her by letter while travelling and was looking forward to seeing her again. He got off at Essen hofbahnhof and waited for her. She was not long in arriving and they walked the short distance to her apartment. She had not changed since he had last seen her and still looked extremely beautiful. She lived a very different life from the one that Gypsy had chosen for himself, but like him she had a lively mind and could look at things and understand what it was that she was seeing. Gypsy did not feel alone when he was with her as she in many ways had an open mind and he could talk with her about what he had seen and the theories that he had about life without attracting a blank wide eyed 'aaaaagh I'm sitting with a nutter' stare. He most often got that stare in England when he talked with people who worked in the system or who believed in the system. The Germans in general seemed a much more open minded and progressive people than the British in every way imaginable.

They went out to a pub that evening and sat out in the garden. It was full of young people with long hair and the music on the stereo was all from the sixties and early seventies. There were no aggressive yob types or their snob opposites there to screw up the atmosphere and everyone seemed very relaxed with themselves. Also it being Germany which was not renowned for cheap prices, sun or beaches there were no British tourists, which also helped to keep the atmosphere happy and friendly. Gypsy stuck around for a couple of days and tried with little success to sell some of his products in the area. Then after saying his goodbyes to Barbara, he headed back to the hofbahnhof and caught a train to Munich. At Munich hofbahnhof he was able to find a train leaving for Athens within the hour and went to the station bar to have a couple of beers before it departed.

The carriage that he was in was full of students who were also travelling on Eurail passes. The train rolled on towards the border with Austria and crossed through, carrying on towards the border with Yugoslavia. They crossed through that border at some horrible early hour of the morning and were all duly awoken to have their passports checked and stamped. After an hour or so they were rolling on again, towards Zagreb and Belgrade. The train was full and there was nowhere to stretch out and sleep, never the less, some, including Gypsy went to sleep on the floor. It was an uncomfortable and some times painful night as the train stopped at many stations along the way and fat slavs got on and off at each of the stops, stepping on them and some times kicking them. They had no respect for any one but themselves and Gypsy looked at them and observing their behaviour said to some of the other travellers "these people are going to have a civil war soon, they have no respect for anyone and their demeanour is full of hate and loathing, if they don't change the way that they look at things then soon they will be tearing each other apart". The train rolled on through Yugo-hell for the next twenty four hours and then eventually reached the Greek border. Then they were back into civilization as the train rolled on towards Athens. Indeed the one thing that Gypsy always hated about going overland, either to or from Greece was crossing dismal Yugoslavia.

When Gypsy got off the train he headed back down to the Plaka where he had always hung out before. But now there were no cheap hostels anywhere in the area at all and so he had to go searching much further afield, eventually he found one and checked in. However when he sat down in the in house café and pulled out a packet of Indian bidis and lit one up, the Greek workers came up to him and started shouting at him, accusing him of using drugs. He tried until he was blue in the face to explain to them that bidis were made entirely of tobacco and that there was not even the tiniest bit of anything else in them, but they would have none of it and insisted that he not smoke them there. The only other tobacco that he had was a packet of 'drum' that he had bought back in Amsterdam. So he pulled it out and started to roll a cigarette, but at this point the chief 'Malaka'(wanker) came over and not only started screaming and ranting and raving but also threatened to go and get the police. "Look can't you see? It's only tobacco, there's not a drop of T.H.C in the whole bag are you stupid or something? Don't you understand that this is only rolling tobacco don't you have it in Greece? I thought your country was in the EEC". For this grave crime Gypsy was thrown out of the hostel and not just that but there were two snotty bitches from England backing up mister Malaka and joining in at having a go at him. Apparently, in their great wisdom the powers that be in the Greek parliament had decided to make rolling tobacco illegal as well as ganja and all other drugs. Amphetamines were the only exception and at the time could be purchased over the counter of any pharmacy without a prescription and were sold as sliming tablets.

Eventually Gypsy managed to find another hostel and finally was able to relax, bed down and get some sleep. However even this place was not the sort of place that he felt happy to stay at. Gone were the old days when there was a traveller scene in Athens in the hostels.

The next morning Gypsy headed out and back into the centre of the city. He made a stop at Monastraki and went into one of the jewellery and handycraft shops that lined some of the side streets of the area. He asked the owner who spoke English if he would be interested to see some jewellery. The man said yes he was interested, so Gypsy pulled out some of the contents of his shoulder bag. To his surprise the man became very enthusiastic about what he was seeing and started asking Gypsy about prices. An hour or so latter Gypsy left the shop with a large stack of hundred drachma notes and headed to the next shop where he also made good sales. He spent the rest of the morning and some of the afternoon touring the shops and taking their money from them as his bag became lighter and lighter.

In the late afternoon he met some other hardcore travellers who were sitting under some bushes below the Acropolis. He sat with them and rolled up a joint filled with hashish that he had brought with him from Amsterdam. To his surprise one of the crowd that he knew from the chillum circle at the pumpernickel bakery in Kathmandu turned up and joined in. he had just done a run to Germany with goods and was on his way back to Nepal. Unfortunately for Gypsy he was a person who still had an optimistic opinion of other people and thought that most people around him who had opted out of the system were honest, like he was. This he found out to his cost was not the way things were, especially when French people were involved. A French couple among the group persuaded him that if he would share the rest of his stash with them then they could get him sorted with a supplier in Athens. So he spent the rest of the evening smoking them out with the remainder of his stash until it was finished. Later they took him with them to where they were staying, at a friend's apartment. It was well after midnight by the time they got there so they all found their own spaces and crashed out.

The next morning Gypsy awoke very slowly, as he had got so stoned the night before. He looked up to see the girlfriend of the French man rubbing his crotch and asking him to fuck her while her boyfriend slept. "go on do it" a voice said from behind him, "we all have, why don't you give her a go too?".

The very idea made his stomach turn, he wouldn't have minded a fuck, but not with some dirty bitch who had just done the whole house in front of her sleeping boyfriend? Uughhh!!!!!!!!!!!!!!!. What a terrible way to carry on, Gypsy had far to much self respect to do anything that degraded, He was a human being, not an animal, he felt really horny but he just couldn't allow himself to do something that nasty. He didn't know the French man but he knew that he himself would not be very happy if the tables were turned and everyone fucked a woman that he was living with while he slept. Besides, there was also the question of hygiene to think about. If she was so eager to fuck everyone in this house that they were temporarily staying in then who knows how many other people she had unprotected sex with. A.I.D.S. was beginning to make it's presence felt around the world, and at that time with no medicines at all that could even slow it down a bit it equalled a very unpleasant and slow, agonizing death sentence, so that was also on his mind as he pushed her away and declined her offer.

At this point he became very sad that he had smoked all his hash with such low quality people, he just wanted to get out of their company as soon as possible. He could not even bring himself to stay long enough to get them to help him find a hash connection. Regardless of the fact that hash or even ganja was as rare as rocking horse shit in Greece, he would just have to live with out it while he visited Hariklia out on the island, unless of coarse she had a supply. The French man was not going to be awake for a while and even when he did awake it was unlikely that he would be up for going out to visit his connection straight away, if indeed he even had one.

Gypsy grabbed his bag and his guitar and headed for the door. Out on the street he found a phone box and called Hariklia to say that he was in Athens and needed to get directions to were he had to go in Piraeus to catch the boat out to Santorini.

Then he walked for a couple of kilometres until he was back at Monastraki. From there he took a ride on the metro out to Piraeus and went looking for where to catch his boat ride out to the island.

He was, lucky and there was a boat leaving in just under two hours so he bought a ticket and waited around, first for the boat to pull in and then for the call to board. It was a medium to large sized car ferry and was going on from Santorini to other islands. The lower decks were then filled with trucks, buses and cars and then the ramps were pulled up, the chains detached and the boat pulled out of it's mooring and headed out through Piraeus harbour towards the open sea.

Some hours later in the mid evening an hour or so after the sun was down, the boat sailed in through the ring of the old volcano and passing the stumpy island of the smaller but active volcano in it's centre, pulled in at the island's harbour and tied up.

Gypsy like everyone else who was getting down at Santorini, exited via the vehicle deck. In front of him was a massive stone cliff stretching all the way up to Thira, which was the main town on the island and sat up on the top of the island. There was a stone pathway of steep steps leading up to the top. Some people hired donkeys or mules to haul them and their luggage to the top but Gypsy was not so flush for cash and was also more than fit enough to haul his own things up to Thira.

Some while later he reached the top and walked through the narrow cobbled streets of the town as he looked for the place where Hariklia said that she was living at.

The first thing that greeted him was the sight of a drunken British tourist, throwing up in the street in front of him. "Oh great" he thought to himself "no chance of getting homesick with the place full of twats like this, it will be just like the place that I came here to escape from".

Eventually, with some guidance from some of the locals he found Hariklia's digs and after many knocks on the door and a ten to fifteen minute wait was welcomed in by a very tired, sleepy and bleary eyed Hariklia. She looked like she had either been working too hard or had hit the bottle too early in the evening. They went inside and sat talking for a while as Gypsy told her what he had been up to in the last couple of years and Hariklia told him about what had happened with her and her now ex boyfriend after they had returned from India. Hariklia had free accommodation thrown in with her job, but the one problem with it was that she had to share the room with another woman. There was an empty bed that she told Gypsy that he could use and soon as they were all tired from their day's activities were all asleep.

The next day they were all awake early, Hariklia explained after breakfast that she had to go to work shortly, but she gave Gypsy the keys to her tiny moped and told him that he could use it to get himself about on the island. So later with his towel and swimming trunks tied on the back he headed off, first to the local petrol station and then off to where she had directed him in order to find a good place to go swimming. At one end of the main island he found himself at a rocky outcrop where there was a similarly rocky islet. There were people jumping off of a ledge and swimming the short distance out to the rock. Gypsy parked the bike and joined the fun. The water was so clear that he could see to the sea floor some twenty or thirty feet below. He spent much of the day there swimming and sitting on the rocks. However the people there were not of the friendly kind, even though they were on holiday. Gypsy spent the entire time there in his own company only. He headed back to the room in the mid afternoon to find that Hariklia was already back from her job and so once again they sat and talked. Her room mate was also there, she was much younger than Hariklia and a little bit younger than Gypsy. She was a little bit of a smart arse and had too high an opinion of herself for Gypsy to enjoy her company very much. But none the less he did his best to be pleasant to her and also listened to what she had to say. However he enjoyed Hariklia's way of being and liked her bright mind and sharp wit. She, having travelled a little bit had a far more attractive nature about her than her younger room mate. Also she enjoyed Gypsy's dark dry humour. He had found some highly outrageous envelopes back in Sydney while shopping at Paddington market and sent her a letter in one, which had on the front in official looking lettering "MARUJUANA MARKETING BOARD, News letter for subscribers".

Some people would have been most pissed off to have a letter sent to them in such an envelope, especially if they lived in Greece where the authorities took a very hard stand against the stuff. But Hariklia had thought it to be wonderful and highly hilarious, she had a very rounded sense of humour and enjoyed all sorts of mischievous wind ups like that, which was why she had invited Gypsy to come and stay with her.

On another evening Hariklia was going out with friends and work colleagues for dinner. So Gypsy headed up into the town on his own with his guitar to look for a good place to busk or just to play for fun. Some

British smart arsed yuppie type twats saw him there in his phsychadelic clothes, with his guitar over his shoulder and started to mock him. Calling out "hey Bob Dylan play us a song" so he did a full on Noddy Holder screaming version of several Rolling stones songs including Jumping Jack Flash and Brown Sugar and then carried on with a totally hard core rock version of House of the rising sun. Bob Dylan indeed! that shut the barstards up. They looked on with shocked faces, they weren't expecting a Full on rock performance like that and certainly not from someone playing an acoustic guitar.

Though he enjoyed Hariklia's company nothing much could happen between them while she was sharing a room with the other woman who was also around in the room for much of the same time as they were. Also there were virtually no hippie traveller types on the island to hang out with. So after ten days or so he was feeling somewhat lonely and depressed. So he said goodbye to Hariklia and took the boat back to Athens and attempted to knock out a bit more of his silver and gemstones to the local tourist shops around the Plaka and Monastraki, but with very little success.

That night as he sat drinking with some other travellers he managed to sell a silver Buddha to a man from Yugoslavia. But the next day as he entered the station to take a train back up to northern Europe, the man approached him and said "one of the other travellers said this is not silver and I want my money back". "What?" Said Gypsy "of coarse it's silver, don't you know what silver look's and feel's like? it very much is silver and I have no doubt about that. The reason it was so cheap was that I didn't want to charge a fellow traveller more than what I have been charging the shops. I have no wish to cheat anyone and I know what it is that I sold you. And anyway who is this great expert that told you this? I would like to meet him and challenge him over this" "well you can't said" the man "I don't know where he is and anyway I want my money back". So Gypsy in order not to leave a bad feeling in his wake, gave the ignorant cunt his money back, all six hundred drachmas of it, which at the time was about six British pounds or nine U.S. dollars.

He sat for most of the journey surrounded by somewhat straitlaced European students who were returning from backpacking holidays around Greece. It was a somewhat boring and lonely ride back up to Austria, surrounded by people that he shared not one ideal with.

The train divided in Belgrade and Gypsy ended up in the wrong part. Several hours later the train stopped at Zagreb and everyone got off. He spent several hours waiting on the platform at Zagreb central station for a train that would take him as far as Vienna. It was no problem as he was not really in a hurry to go anywhere apart from maybe a coffee shop some where in a city in Holland.

The train eventually arrived and he boarded and sat down in a carriage with some pleasant and quite intelligent young students from Austria and Germany. Well at least he had some relatively good company for the journey up to Vienna. It was early in the morning when he arrived there. As he had never been to Vienna before he decided to go and have a look around. So he went to the bureau de change in the station and bought some Austrian shillings and then went out to explore the city. It was quite an attractive place but far too conservative and genteel for his tastes. So after two or three hours of wandering he walked back to the station and caught a train to Munich.

He got to Munich in the early evening and after taking a brief look around the station, decided that this place also was not somewhere that he wanted to spend much time at. So he went and had a look at the timetable and found that there was a night train that was leaving for Amsterdam within the hour. He went and bought himself a bottle of whiskey and then jumped onto the train to Holland and commenced to neck the bottle.

He got chatting with some young people from the Middle East as he was getting more and more drunk. It must have been a pleasant conversation because when he awoke in the very early morning at Eindhoven station with a throbbing hangover and a bad case of wrestler's armpit in his mouth, he found a letter pinned to him sincerely wishing him a good and safe journey from those same people that he had been talking with.

Two or three hours later the train pulled in at Amsterdam central station and Gypsy sprang from the train and headed into the red light area at almost a run, looking for the first coffee shop that he could find. He was gasping for a joint and wasted no time in choosing a bag, then sat down with a cup of tea and started to skin up. After the end of the first joint the hangover was starting to fade a bit. But after three spliffs it had all but gone. Then he headed out to where the canal boats were moored and found himself a bunk on one that had been converted into a hostel.

He spent the next few days trying to make sales with his goods around the area. He even did a run across the border back into Germany to Dusseldorf to see if he could get some buissiness there. But it was all to no avail and he made absolutely no sales at all. Back in Amsterdam he went into one jewellers shop and showed what he had in the way of stones and silver but the owner of the shop just slagged of his stock and told him rather smugly how he could get the same stuff in Amsterdam for the same price that it would cost in India. Then to add insult to injury he wouldn't let Gypsy get out of his shop to go searching for other buisiness as he insisted on showing him what he had bought and telling him what he had paid for it. By the time that Gypsy had managed to wrench himself free from the company of this obnoxious greasy character he was in a rage and wished that he could have just strangled this smug self satisfied creep.

Back on the canal boat the next morning during breakfast, he tried to at least sell some of the chillum pipes to some of the other guests. But one nasty egotistical cunt from England insisted that he show Gypsy how to "really make a chillum mix" even though he had never been in India. He virtually kidnapped one of Gypsy's chillums and made a mix with no tobacco, just using hash. Of course it wouldn't burn properly, but he insisted that that was the way that it it should be done. Then after that he didn't even want to buy the pipe. There were just too many smart arses and twats like this one hanging out around Amsterdam for Gypsy's liking and their company was not only intensly boring and annoying but they always seemed to want to show off and put others down all the time as well. So he once again packed his bag, grabed his guitar and headed for the station. He took a train to Hook van Holland then took a boat back to Harwich. Then he took a train to London, crossed the city on the tube to Victoria station and took a train home. He spent the next few weeks selling around the Sussex area and managed to get just enough money together for another run to India. His father had suggested most strongly and forcefully that he should concentrate his efforts entirely on the gemstone market, as this was the area where the margins could be higher. He had made friends with a man who worked as a gem cutter and tester in a large local antique market. On being told that Gypsy was planning on making another run to Jaipur, the man made an order for certain types and cuts of stones, mostly garnets and amethysts. While he was planning his trip other jewellers had told him what they were most interested in buying, so Gypsy had some idea at least of what he should be looking for.

He took a train to London one Monday morning and made his way to Holborn, where he joined the visa queue at India House and waited the customary two hours to submit his passport for a visa. Then he had to join another long queue to pay for the privilege, it cost the sum of twenty pounds. By one o clock he was eventually free so he took the tube to Earls court and had a look around the cheap travel agents there for a return to Delhi.

Within a week he was sitting in the departure terminal at Heathrow terminal three waiting to board a Thai Airways jumbo to India [The old 200 series 747s did not have the range of modern planes and so flights to the far east would have to make a refueling stop somewhere along the way. Thai used to use Delhi for some of their flights including the London run]. The plane took off just after nine thirty in the morning and ascended up through the multiple layers of clouds that block the sun from the British countryside for much of the year. Soon after the plane reached it's cruising altitude Gypsy headed for the galley and started what was going to be an all day drinking session.

Some nine hours later he was standing outside the terminal building at I.G.I. waiting for a taxi into the city. Even though it was after 11pm the air was still hot as he rode in the battered old ambassador cab past the end of the runway, the turn off to the domestic terminal and around the bend that took the cab on the road towards the city centre.

The street was unlit but at least it was a wide road without too much traffic on it.

He got dropped off at the entrance to the tourist camp and went in and to his relief was able to get a room. There were no hippie travellers there at the time, just the all to common narrow minded po faced yuppie types that he had encountered all the way across Europe. They had come to India in body only and left their minds, hearts and souls back in their respective countries of origin. The exception perhaps were the Gemans, Dutch and Swiss, who although they looked quite straight, had open minds and were none too quick to discount anything out of hand.

There were two quite friendly fellows from England but from the way that they listened and talked it was obvious to Gypsy that they were a couple of under cover cops, no doubt out on an Interpol assignment, so he avoided them until he was out of the city. [There was a lot of Interpol activity at that time in both India and Nepal. They were easy to pick out but they would sometimes even stay in the traveler haunts to see what they could learn. What was pathetic was the amount of effort that was put in to stopping hashish shipments while they let heroin flood Western Europe by the ton].

The next morning with his bag and guitar over his shoulder he headed out in an auto rickshaw to Bikaner house down in the government and diplomatic district of the city.

Within an hour he was sitting on a Rajastan Roadways bus as it headed out of the city and out past the airport towards the Jaipur highway. He enjoyed the ride as he watched the countryside go by as the bus moved at reasonable speed towards it's destination.

As they drove south the flat lands around them grew more arid until they reached the R,T,D,C, [Rajastan Tourism development corporation] road house at midway and everyone got of the bus and headed hurriedly towards the toilets. The bus, always made just one stop along it's five to six hour journey in order to let people on board go and relieve themselves and get some refreshments. Gypsy went and ordered a vegetarian thali, collected it from the counter and went and found a table and sat down to eat. They were already within the state of Rajasthan and it was hot and dry all around. There were villages along the road and the fields were well tended but the air was so dry that everyone on the bus was constantly drinking water. The stop had lasted for it's customary twenty minutes and then after everyone had been accounted for, the bus left on it's way to Jaipur. Now they were passing camel carts along the road as they rode deeper into Rajasthan on the bumpy two lane highway.

By early afternoon they had passed the Amer Fort and Jal Mahal (lake palace) and were entering the pink city via the lower gate as they headed for the final destination at the Sindi camp bus station. Sindi camp was located just outside of the Chanpole gate on the west side of the city. It was a dirty, dusty, scruffy area full of daburs, chai shops and small, cheap hotels. The bus turned right across the traffic and in through the entrance to the bus terminal and pulled to a stop. The usual mad scrum of rickshaw wallas descended on it's occupants as they disembarked. Gypsy once more had to push them out of the way as they tried grabbing at him and his bag. He made his way out of the station and found a less aggressive rickshaw walla sitting on his rickshaw minding his own business. He asked him how much he would charge for a ride to the hippy/ traveller guest house. They agreed a price and Gypsy jumped up on the rickshaw with his bag and guitar and the man took him at just above walking speed to his destination.

At the guest house he got one of the rooms on the roof of the dormitories, threw his bag and guitar onto the bed and headed out into the market. His first stop was at 44 Gangoori bazaar to go and see Birla.

Birla had had to sack the two men that he had had working for him previously due to their gross dishonesty. He had found out that they had not only been steeling goods from him but that they had also been steeling customers too and conducting clandestine deals with them outside of office hours. He was most pissed off about it and quite rightly so.

There was a German man there by the name of Andrias who was a couple of years older than Gypsy and he also was in the process of setting himself up as a gem dealer. He was heavily built but though he was very strong and had a boisterous and strong personality he was a gentle person with a deep interest in Indian history and spiritual practice. Gypsy took a liking to him straight away, he liked the way that this man, like both Birla and himself was first and foremost interested in his spiritual direction and was extremely honest, even if what he said did not please everyone.

Back at the guest house there were other travellers much like himself and for the first time in months he did not feel lonely, they were mostly misfits from Europe but there were also some Australians and New Zealanders there too.

Some of them had been in the gem and jewellery business for some years and knew the place well. They recommended to Gypsy that he go and check out the dealers on a certain side street called Gopal Ji Ka Rasta which was where the seriously large deals were mostly conducted. The rest of the evening after everyone had stopped talking about business was spent jamming together on different instruments and smoking chillums until everyone had eventually crawled off to their rooms in semiconscious states to get a few hours sleep before it was time to start work again.

The next morning Gypsy walked outside through the market until he reached the main road and looked around for one of the rickshaw wallas that he knew. He wanted one of them to take him down to the pink city to go and find this street that he had been told about.

Ram who was a middle aged alcoholic was his driver for the day and he peddled Gypsy along M.I. road to the third gate to the city and then swung left inside and peddled along Johari bazaar before stopping in front of the entrance to a mud side street. "This is it" he declared "this is Gopal ji ka rasta" Gypsy walked inside through the heaving crowd of people who were all dressed in traditional Indian clothes, complete with turbans and moustaches. It was perhaps one of the most scruffy streets in the whole of this well designed city. Even the shop fronts did not look as smart as many of the other gem dealers that Gypsy had seen within the walls of the city. But this was where it all happened, this was where the big deals were done.

He found his way to where one of the shops that he had been told about was located and went inside. Inside it was just an office with not much to tell anyone that it was a gem speciallist's shop. It was just a stark bare room with a desk and some chairs on one side and a large mattress with a white sheet on it on the other. He was welcomed in and offered a cup of chai, then after a while they asked him what he would be interested in looking at. Gypsy pulled out his shopping list from his trouser pocket and read out to them what it was that he had been asked for back in England. They then proceeded to make some phone calls and told Gypsy that there would be several lots of each stone for him to choose from arriving shortly.

Within fifteen minutes the first of the brokers arrived, carrying a scruffy cloth bag in his hand, which he proceeded to open. He pulled out from inside it a large pile of grubby looking paper packets which he then placed on the table in front of Gypsy.

Gypsy proceeded to open them one at a time until he had gone through them all and chosen a couple of packets that he wanted to take another look at. The broker then took out another bundle of packets and Gypsy proceeded to go through them all. Before too long there were several brokers sitting outside, waiting to show their goods to Gypsy.

The process carried on all day until early in the evening when he did his second inspection of the packets that he had put to one side and started asking about prices. He was most shocked about what some of them started by asking for their goods. Some of them tried to ask more than double what he hoped to be able to sell them for in the U.K., he told them no way and to get the hell out of his sight if they wanted to be as greedy as that. But then the shop keeper explained that it worked very much like the scene from Monty Python's 'Life of Brian movie when he wanted to buy a false beard, "no no youv'e got to haggle" he told Gypsy. But with them starting from such a ridiculously high amount Gypsy didn't even know where to begin and told the shop keeper "look if you want to sell to me then just get me the right price or I'll go to some one else who will". There was never so much trouble over getting a good price over at Birla's office so why should he have to waste so much time haggling at anyone else's office? he thought to himself.

He was still really new to the game and did not know so much about the values of different qualities of stone but he had some idea about the value of the cheaper stones such as red garnets, amethysts, moonstones, lapis lazuli and peridot so he tried to stick with these stones for the most part. The Jaipur gem dealers would try to use every under handed psychological trick in the book in order to make a sale and they would try to convince even someone who knew their job well that they didn't know how to judge quality properly. It was an absolute minefield to work in and Gypsy was more than aware that he had to really keep his eyes on the ball in this rat race. The trickery of these people knew no limits, also they were prone to snobbery and would endeavour to make people feel small for not being big enough spenders by projecting on them that they were doing someone a favour by doing buisiness with such a small buyer. Thankfully not all of them were like this but finding the good ones was going to take some time.

Back at the guest house there were two Germans who were staying in the rooms next to were Gypsy was staying. One of them who's name was Reinhardt was making his own designs in a mix of silver and gold which he sold back in Germany and had been making business this way for several years. He gave the impression of being quite successful at what he did, but Gypsy, much as he liked what Reinhardt was making, knew that he could not sell such things on the British market, it was much too expensive and far too tasteful for the people of England.

The other German was new to the gem buisiness and like so many other fools that Gypsy had met in his life, this guy wanted to start at the top.

By the end of a day's work, the last thing that Gypsy wanted to think or talk about was his fucking work. He was tired and wanted to relax and play his guitar, but this motherfucker who knew so very little would not shut up all night, all he would talk about was gem stones, even when Gypsy told him that he did not wish to talk about it. He would drone on and on trying to persuade Gypsy that he should only try doing top end high quality stones, which Gypsy knew with his limited knowledge was a sure fire recipe for disaster. As far as he could see there were much higher margins to be made on goods that were much lower down the scale. Also in the lower area where he was dealing in more quantity for his money then any mistakes that he did make would be smaller, also he would have a larger range of products which meant that possibly he would not have to search so hard to find buyers for his goods.

The German on the other hand would be spending far more time and money for each sale that he got and at small margins too, so how was he ever going to make any profit? However this plastic hippie just wouldn't shut up until Gypsy said "OK get your high quality stones then come and see me in England and let's see what we can do with them". Gypsy continued to select his stones from around the market and also backed himself up with a large selection of cheap hand made silver jewellry, which he knew that he could sell at retail if the shit was really to hit the fan. He did his best to just stay with the things that he already knew, as he selected. But his knowledge at that time was so limited that he also was going to have to take a chance and gamble a bit on some of the things that he selected. At Birla's office Andrias had decided that as Birla was the only truly decent person that he had met in the market then he was only going to do buisiness in that office and nowhere else. That idea struck Gypsy as a bit dangerous, as he knew that not one person on this planet was one hundred per cent OK, even if their heart was in the right place. He also liked Birla as a person and trusted him more than other people that he had met in Jaipur but he was not going to put all his eggs in one basket as he knew that he would be setting himself up for a fall if he did.

There were and probably still are a lot of hustlers on the streets of Jaipur who would approach people on the street and start speaking to them, especially western travelers, as if they were just being friendly, but then sooner or later they would start wobbling their heads and say something like "would you like to come and see my brother cousin's carpet factory?" At which point it was patently obvious that they were just out to make a commission and were only interested in being friends with that person's wallet. If someone did go along with them then decided to buy something then the hustler stood to make a commission of some forty percent which had already been stacked on the price of the goods. In other words the tourist or traveler had been outrageously ripped off. The travelers or at least the hard core of them knew about such tricks and warned the others about any new variations to the formula, but still the hustlers would try it on.

One night at about nine o'clock as Andrias and Gypsy were sharing a rickshaw for the ride back to their respective lodgings from Birla's office,

Birla and a friend pulled up next to the rickshaw on their scooter and Birla with a big silly grin on his face started a spoof sales rap "hallo yes yes would you like to see my brother cousin's gem shop, I show you carpet factory too, I challenge that you will not find cheaper prices in all of Jaipur yes yes what is your good name sir? where are you from? How many family members are you having? I guaranty you cheapest prices, customer satisfaction is our challenge" then he and his friend sped off while Andreas and Gypsy sat there laughing. He, in just a few seconds had covered the whole of the English vocabulary of the average Jaipur hustler. Birla was the only Indian from Jaipur that Gypsy had met who seemed to have a sense of humor. The others all seemed to take themselves too seriously which made them hilarious to watch but tedious to be in the company of. On another evening he was walking back from Birla's office along the side of the road instead of taking a rickshaw when a rickshaw pulled up alongside him and said "I take you back to the hippie hotel for two rupees". "That's a good deal" Gypsy said "but I want to walk" "OK" said the rickshaw walla "I'll take you there for one rupee" "that's very cheap" said Gypsy "but I like walking" "OK said the rickshaw walla "I'll take you there for free" "that's very kind of you said Gypsy but the reason that I am walking is in order that I get some exercise. While you have been peddling around the city all day getting plenty of exercise I have been sitting down at a table and working and now my body feel's stiff so this is what I do to make myself feel better". "Ok" said the rickshaw walla who was a scruffy young teenager in a lungi and a T-shirt that obviously had once been white but now was a grubby uneven grey color "you peddle" and he jumped onto the back seat. So Gypsy jumped onto the saddle and proceeded to peddle the contraption along the road and around a couple of side roads to the guest house. When he got to the place and Gypsy had got down, the rickshaw walla introduced himself, telling Gypsy that his name was Rais. Then he asked Gypsy if he could introduce him to some good contacts in the business. Gypsy said no and that he had had quite enough of other people's contacts in the market and that he would rather go and make his own contacts than go through all of the bullshit all over again.

Even in mid October it was still too hot at night for anyone to be able to sleep comfortably. So the travelers would party up on the roof of the dormitories until the early hours of the morning, playing guitars and smoking joints and chillums. Then only when the charas had knocked them to a state of semi consciousness would they crawl of to their rooms and get some sleep. Waking in the morning hot and drenched in sweat they would stumble off to the grim and dirty toilet and shower area and get sorted and ready for another day of hard work in the dry and dusty heat.

The month went by and the plastic German hippie who in this book shall be referred to as Hans Burnt became friends with Gypsy, as they were both endeavouring to set up their own gem businesses and both were still rather new at it and inexperienced at the time. Gypsy finally had his load together and was ready to head out back north to Delhi.

He took the night bus that left just after midnight and sat holding his bag of stock on his lap all night for safety. Everything that he owned in the world was in that bag, and he was guarding it with his life. The bus reached Delhi at six thirty in the morning and he headed off to Connaught place to see if he could find a more pleasant and secure place to stay than the dismal windowless cells that were available at tourist camp. He found a quite smart looking hotel in the second circle of the triple circuit roundabout that made up the famous Luchens designed Connaught place that was the heart of New Delhi. He got a room for three hundred rupees (£8.00 at the time) it was smart and comfortable but he was not going to have much time to sleep as he had to go out to Jan path and old Delhi to finish his shopping. He had to be at the airport by eleven thirty that night in order to catch his flight back to London.

He took a shower and then went and lay down for half an hour before going out to get some breakfast and have a quick read of the Hindustan times. After breakfast he went to the Tibetan market to see Doma and one or two of the other shop keepers. Then he took a ride on one of the over sized motor trikes down to old Delhi to go and visit the woman who had the gem and jewellery shop inside the red fort. He was pleased to find that she had a packet of small, high quality emeralds at a cheap price. So with some of his remaining cash he bought a small well picked selection of them. Then he went back to the hotel to get a few hours sleep before his flight.

But when he got there he found that there were two workers fixing something in the room and try as he might he could not get the motherfuckers to leave the room and let him sleep as they argued that they had to do the job or their boss would be angry with them. This was one thing that Gypsy really disliked about some Indian hotel workers, their total lack of respect for the privacy and well being of their guests.

He was extremely tired but he could not sleep until these two arseholes had got their job done, which seemed to take an age, as they continued to do an impersonation of Laurel and Hardy as they fixed a leaky tap. Eventually he got the room to himself and was able to lock the door and keep all other unwanted visitors out, despite their continued attempts to gain entry. It was obvious to him that many of these people had not the slightest idea that such a thing as manners even existed. He got his bags packed and then put his head down for a few hours of much needed sleep.

At around nine oclock that evening, he got up and dressed and headed out with his bags and guitar into the street and found an auto rickshaw to take him out to the airport. So there he was riding out through the city, wondering if the stones that he had chosen would indeed sell when he got them back and showed them to the fussy barstards that owned the jewellers shops in the U.K.

He checked in at the Thai counter and got himself an isle seat in the smoking section of the plane. Then after going outside to smoke the last of his joints, he went through to airside and waited for his flight to be called. The plane arrived from Bangkok and half an hour later they were boarding the passengers from Delhi. The plane took off and climbed to cruising altitude. Gypsy was nervous about his ability to sell the stones that he had bought at a profit and not a loss when he reached England and so was busy pulling his most expensive packets from his pocket and wallet and inspecting them to see if he still thought that he had made the right choices. He was surveying his most expensive lot which was a packet of sapphires that he was taking a gamble on when the man in the seat behind him tapped him on the shoulder and handed him a business card. The name G.F.Williams, gem dealer, was written on it, so he turned around to talk with the man. He was a big sapphire and emerald dealer from Hatton Garden in London and was returning from a business trip to Thailand. He told Gypsy about how he also did business in Jaipur and about how stupid and tricky even some of the biggest dealers in the city were. "I asked them to show me only round emeralds" he said "so they showed me squares, I told them that these are not rounds and gave them back. So the next packet they showed me was full of baguettes so I walked over to the window and asked them if they were rounds, no they said so I turned to them and said, the next time that you show me a packet that is not of the shape that I ask you for I'm going to throw them out of this window, do you understand? After that I had no more problems with them not hearing me". Gypsy liked the idea of treating them like that but knew that he was too small in business to be able to pull such a trick, even though he might have liked to. He had been messed about himself by some of the windup merchants of Jaipur.

Ten hours later he was on the ground at Heathrow, waiting in the customs hall for the clearing agent to arrive. This time the agent was much faster at getting Gypsy out of the hall and through as there was not so much of a variety of goods in his load. It was early morning and once again his father came to collect him from the airport and take him home and once again Gypsy felt absolutely exhausted after having had two sleepless nights. After getting his load sorted into a state where it was ready to sell he went to bed and fell asleep. He slept all afternoon and into the night. Waking at four thirty in the morning with jet lag he sat and sorted his stones some more and waited till nine am to phone the first customer.

Later in the morning he took the train into Brighton, he had very little money in his pocket and so he needed to sell something and quickly.

Once in town he walked down the hill from the station towards the sea and took a right turn at the clock tower and headed down towards the lanes, which was were many jewellers and antique shops were located. The antique jewellery shops were becoming some of his best customers for both the gemstones and the jewellery. They were always needing stones to replace the ones in the jewellery that they had just bought and they liked the jewellery that he was selling because it was hand made and had almost an antique quality about it. This was because the Indians did not have much in the way of modern tooling and still made jewellery in the old fashioned way. Due to their lack of original thinking they still made designs that looked like antiques to an untrained western eye.

He was able to make some reasonably good sales that day and took over two hundred pounds with his brand new, fresh stock, so he was quite happy as he took the train home. Never mind that they had no respect for him and refered to him as the hippie, he would earn their respect by doing his job well. They liked to buy from him because his prices were very good indeed, but they put that down to him not knowing the real prices and thought that he was just ignorant. But Gypsy was not greedy and was happy so long as he made a good profit and could gain enough customers. He didn't want to screw every cent out of someone that he could, after all that would not be a good strategy if he wanted to build a stable customer base for his business.

The gem cutter and tester that he had befriended before came over to see him at his house to see what he had brought back with him and also to collect the stones that he had ordered. "Yes youv'e got some nice things there, I wouldn't say that your prices are dead cheap" he said "but they are very reasonable and will allow me a profit if I want to buy some and sell them on". He went on to select over eight hundred pounds worth of goods and paid Gypsy the full amount in cash.

Gypsy's mother told him that one of his distant cousins worked in the jewellery business in London's Hatton Garden area and suggested that he go and visit him and see if he knew anything that would help him on his way. Gypsy was interested but had to, for the time being concentrate on building up his customer base in the immediate local area. Until he had made all the sales that he could in that way he had no time to stop or do anything else.

After a few weeks he got a phone call from Hans Burnt to tell him that he had reached Germany with his uber high quality, large stones and was having a hard time selling them. Gypsy suggested that he come over to England with them and see if they could move them in London or among the high end jewellers in the smaller towns along the south coast. Several days later Hans Burnt arrived with his stones. It was at this time that Gypsy decided that it would be a good idea to get in touch with his cousin and see what he knew about this sort of quality of gems.

So one Sunday they went over to Hove to go and see him at his house. Gypsy's grandfather had bailed his farther out of deep deep shit many years before to the tune of an extremely large sum of money, so he was very welcoming and friendly towards Gypsy. They showed him the stones that they had and told him what sort of prices that they needed to get for them. He turned to them and said "well it's certainly not out of the way what you are asking for them but it will only be worth that price to someone when they actually need them for a job that they are doing. Stones like these are too expensive to keep in stock on speck unless they have been obtained at well below their market value. I was expecting this to be embarrassing but it is not, you seem to be on the right track within the business and seem to have a reasonable idea about prices too". He recommended that Gypsy also go and have a look at selling his semi precious and cheaper stones in Hockley. Hockley was the huge jewellery quarter in Birmingham where much of England's nine carat gold jewellery was made. He also told Gypsy that if he wanted to make business in Hatton garden then he would have to visit once a week and always on the same day in order that he would get his face recognized and as so that people would wait for him with any job that they had that required a stone.

His cousin worked for the company that his brother in law who was married to his sister owned. Not being the top man in the company he was not able to make any purchases himself but he recommended that Gypsy make contact with his brother in law.

When Hans Burnt returned to Germany, Gypsy took a bus to Birmingham to see if he could make some business. He was standing in Victoria bus station and about to board the bus when a voice behind him said "hello Gypsy" he looked around to see Tim who he had hung out with back in Tokyo, standing behind him. They stopped and chatted for a while. It turned out that Tim had also moved back to England and had got himself settled with a job and was in the process of climbing the employment ladder. Gypsy on the other hand was only making business in order to fund further travel and adventure. He could not imagine anything more terrible than settling in England and becoming domesticated and seeing the same horrible faces every day. Gypsy always had one eye on death and knew that however secure anyone was to make themselves in this world, it was worth nothing in the long run. Death takes everyone in the end, and often when they are least expecting it, so the pursuit of security was a totally futile exercise. It was better to constantly live on the edge of the abyss, but to know where you were standing than to waste time hiding from fear and it's causes in the false security of so called 'acceptable society'.

Three hours later the bus pulled in at Birmingham central bus station and Gypsy got off and went and found a taxi and took a ride to Hockley. He traipsed up and down Vyse Street showing what he had to any of the jewellers who would take the time to look.

Unlike Hatton garden it was a scruffy semi industrial area and was not so well set up for retail sales, although there were quite a few manufacturers that had retail outlets on the street. Most of the work was going on in offices or small industrial units. It was late in the afternoon when he had got there so he only got to visit a few companies before five o'clock came around. One of the shop keepers was kind enough to phone for a taxi for him and he took a ride to the Hagley road in Edgebaston, where he found a cheap bed and breakfast to stay at, at the very far end of the road.

He was still very much a vegetarian and so asked the owner if there was a vegetarian restaurant close by. He was directed to a place through several side streets. The place was called Wild Thyme and was run by two jovial old ladies and to this day Gypsy swears that it was the best vegetarian restaurant that he had ever been to in his life. The food was truly magical, each dish was served with one potion of hot food, two portions of salad and a stack of sliced and toasted, whole wheat pita breads. The desserts were also quite magical and inventive, Gypsy selected figs marinated in cognac topped with chocolate sauce and whipped cream.

After that he took a bus to a pub called the Hagley duck and had a pleasant evening drinking and chatting with some fellow hippie/rocker types before heading back to the guest house to sleep. He quite liked Birmingham, the people were not miserable or stuck up, as they were in the south east of the country where he came from and he noticed that they were actually quite friendly with each other. It was almost like being in a different country.

The next morning he took a taxi back to Hockley and got to work selling his goods. It was hard even there to get sales but by the end of the day he had taken a few hundred pounds. He went back to the bus station and took a bus back to London and then a train back to his home.

He still did not have a driving licence but he had a date for a test, which was only two weeks away, in mid December. A friend had told him about a really good driving instructor that he knew called Tony. So he phoned up and asked if he could book a lesson a day for the next twelve days. The first lesson started that very afternoon and was taken in the instructor's car, but then Gypsy suggestd that it would be better if he had the lessons in his H.A. Viva van as then he could use it for not only practice, but could also take his test in it. He wanted to get very familiar with it's controls as so as he would be less likely to make any silly mistakes on the big day.

Though he was hesitant at first, Tony saw Gypsy's logic and not only agreed but also gave him a discount as he did not have to pay for the petrol or wear and tear on his own car.

For the next twelve days Gypsy had one to two lessons a day and in between the lessons he went out and practiced while accompanied by an older friend who was a retired copper who also knew how to instruct him towards good driving habits.

While Tony was teaching him he would tell Gypsy some of the filthiest gut wrenchingly obscene jokes that he knew to see if he could distract him, but though he could bring a grin to Gypsy's face he could not distract him. So by the end of the twelve days he was confident that Gypsy could pass the test.

On the day of the test Gypsy was as nervous as all of the others who were waiting to take it. He was doing his best to stay focused as he knew that he really needed to pass. The examiner called him out and they got into Gypsy's rusty, yellow van and went out for a drive around the town.

Pulling back into the test center some thirty minutes later Gypsy knew that he had made one or two small mistakes, and turned to the examiner and said I've failed haven't I?. But the instructors said just answer these questions about Highway Code first, so Gypsy did. Then the examiner turned to him and said "congratulations you have passed. If we were as strict as you were expecting then no one would ever pass". Later Tony turned to him and said "well done but I knew you were going to pass, you were so determined too". Gypsy felt most pleased with himself as his brother had taken two or three attempts to pass his test, even though he was meant to be the brains of the family and had been to university. After taking Tony back to the house to go and collect his own car he celebrated his new freedom with a solo drive over some of the more twisty small roads of the south downs, as he went out exploring places that had been too far away for him to be able to get to on foot. However he was going to miss the walking and hitch hiking that he had become so used too. He liked the solitude that he got when he walked somewhere, when he had his thoughts entirely to himself and also he liked the sort of people that he met when he hitch hiked. They were generally the kind, the good and the unconventional members of society and he had had many a good conversation with such people. Anyway a new door had opened to him and now he was going to be able to move around much more easily.

Christmas came and went and then he got a phone call from Hans Burnt asking if his girlfriend could come and stop at Gypsy's house for a couple of days while she was waiting for her flight from London to

Australia. Hans had run out of money so had come up with the ingenious idea to send his girlfriend to go and work in Sydney for a friend of his from Afghanistan. He had the idea that she would send money back to him in Germany that he could invest in more of his hair brained schemes. "Are you sure that you know what it is that you are doing?" Gypsy asked him. "If she is there alone and your Afghan friend is not married then you could very well lose her". "No no it is OK I've known him for a long time he's a good friend and wouldn't do anything like that to me and besides she loves me". So she came and stayed at the house of Gypsy's family for two nights and then took a train to the airport. She was very beautiful and had a nice way about her too. Gypsy very much doubted that Hans had made a right decision in sending her away like this but it was his choice and he was going to say no more until the inevitable happened.

Gypsy had sold some of Hans's expensive stones for him but not at the ridiculous prices that he had first been trying to ask for them. He had agreed that with him before he did it. So Gypsy arranged to fly to Frankfurt and meet him within a couple of weeks. He spent the next two weeks running around the Sussex area trying to build up his cash reserves to what they had been prior to his last trip to England but he was still five hundred pounds down on what he originally had invested and was finding it extremely hard to make any further sales. So he flew to Frankfurt and met up with his German idiot friend and made arrangements to deliver some of his unwanted parcels back to Jaipur for him. By which time the inevitable had happened down in Australia. She had been away for less than a month by the time she had fallen in love with the Afghan, who no doubt thought that Hans had sent her down there as a gift for him.

The idiot had not only lost his source of income but also his beautiful, well mannered girlfriend too. It was a good job that Gypsy had thought to buy a large bottle of twelve year old Highland Park whiskey to share with his imbecile of a friend. He was going to need something to drown his considerable sorrows in.

The next few days were spent staying at Hans's grubby apartment, smoking joints, drinking whiskey and trying not to listen to the dreadful sound coming from the other room as the idiot spent huge fortunes on phone calls to the Antipodes. He made howling, shrieking and bellowing sounds down the line that even made the hideous sound of opera sound quite pleasant in comparison. There was no doubting that the man had committed a grave act of supreme idiocy in doing what he had done, but there was no way now to change it, She was gone. So all he was doing now was wasting time, money and energy with this charade. His apartment was like a rubbish tip and Gypsy was amazed that such a nice clean woman had stayed with this slob of an idiot in the first place. Gypsy was glad when three days later it was time to take his flight back to England. It had been a most unpleasant experience watching this tragic man fall down like this and even then, fail to see what it was that he had done wrong.

He got stopped at customs and searched on his way back in at Gatwick and they found the large bags of stones that he was carrying for Hans. But Gypsy being as he was, managed to talk his way through without any problems.

His father offered to lend him some money to top him up so that he had enough to make another run to India to buy more stock. So a week later and with a new visa he was once again on a plane to Delhi.

Once in Delhi he wasted no time and took the early morning local flight down to Jaipur. It was only ten pounds more than using the bus and got him into the city in time to go out and do a full day's work. One of his cousins in London had a friend who was from Jaipur and had recently moved back there from London and so he had given him a thousand pounds and asked Gypsy to go and see him to see if he could find something in the way of gems that they could make business with.

The first thing that Gypsy did after getting to the guest house and dropping his bag and guitar off was to take a rickshaw down to Gangoori bazaar and go and see Birla again. He got the usual big warm welcome, and sat drinking chai with him while talking about the local news from both England and Rajasthan.

Later he went and dropped off the stones from Hans Burnt at the house of the dealer who had fronted the stones in the first place. He did not even stop for a chai with them as he had no particular liking for them and viewed that they had stitched up the idiot German in such a way that he could do nothing but lose money out of the deal. Next he went to go and find his cousin's friend, a Mr Singh who lived in a compound some way out of the city. He got a friendly welcome and the man seemed interested in getting involved in what ever business it was that both Gypsy and his cousin were interested in doing.

Gypsy spent a few days in the company of Mr Singh and got to meet some of the biggest players in the emerald market of Jaipur but he found that with such people that he could not get any deals worth having as they did not wish to cut such a small player any slack and Gypsy could see that there was no room to do anything but lose money by trying to do business with such people. He didn't want to be rude to his cousin's friend but he was becoming more of a liability than a help with the contacts that he had. They were too big and not interested in players that did not have a large wedge of cash to part with, they were all multi millionaires and Gypsy could not see how he could ever get started, in doing business with them. He felt that the only way that he stood a chance was to stick with the small and medium sized dealers that he was already doing business with. With them at least he was big enough to count for something and that meant that he could tweak them for a discount when he needed to.

Also their prices were already cheaper than the prices that the big boys were prepared to give, which was strange as Gypsy saw it. But then one of the rickshaw wallas told him what was going on, a man by the name of Parilal who was some years older than Gypsy. He explained that his cousin's friend was on a high commission rate and was attempting to take all of Gypsy and his cousin's profit before they had even sold anything.

That night Gypsy paced up and down outside his room like a caged animal as he tried to think of a way of getting rid of Mr Singh without causing any offence. He looked so stressed that one of the other travellers came by and tried to help him chill out a bit. In the end he decided that the only thing that he could do in order to save his business was to cancel any agreements that he had made, to buy anything with Mr Singh's contacts and go straight back to Birla and the contacts that he was developing on Gopal ji ka rasta. When he did this Mr Singh came and told him that as he had done this that he could no longer work with him, which suited Gypsy just fine he didn't need the help of someone like that and was relieved to be rid of him.

However he found that with his main contact on Gopal ji ka rasta he was also hitting a brick wall, the man was a weasel and his word was not good. The man had persuaded Gypsy that a certain packet of sapphires was such a good deal that if he didn't want it then he would take it himself to put into stock. Gypsy eventually bought the packet but later he saw another packet in the market that was both better and cheaper and so spoke to his supplier on Gopal ji ka rasta about it. "Look" said the man "it was such a good deal that I would have been very happy to have bought the packet myself". "Good" said Gypsy "Then I presume that you will be prepared to buy the packet from me for what I paid for it here in your office" and proceeded to pull the packet from his pocket and place it on the table. The man glowered at him in fury but after speaking so boldly from out of his arse he had no choice but to take it if he wanted to save what ever face it was that he still had.

There was no way that Gypsy was going to get a good deal on sapphires in India so he decided to go back to Delhi and jump on a plane to Bangkok where the world's biggest sapphire market was located. He got to Delhi and went and found the travel agent that Birla had told him about, on Jan Path road. His office was not much bigger than a telephone booth. It was called Brook travels and was located in a building called Scindia house. The man whose name was Suresh was both friendly and matter of fact and soon had Gypsy a booking on a Thai airways flight at a very low rate. Gypsy went and got some travellers cheques changed into rupees at the Thomas cook office that was a short walk down the road at the fancy five star deluxe Imperial hotel.

When he got back to the Brook travels cubicle Suresh was waiting with the ticket.

The next night Gypsy was at the airport with one of the other gem dealing hippies that hung out at Birla's office. The other traveller was on his way back home to Norway with his new stock of stones and jewellery. Both of them had quite a long wait for their flights so they went and sat down on the large lawn that covered the roundabout in front of the international terminal. They then both got their bags of charas out and started to make chillum mixes.

An auto rickshaw walla saw what they were doing and so came and sat with them and pulled out his charas and tobacco and also started to make a chillum mix. So for the next hour or so they sat on the roundabout having a chillum party without the security or police giving them even a glance, let alone coming over and bugging them. This was something that Gypsy really liked about India. You could do almost anything as long as you were not causing any problem for anyone else.

The Indian authorities were very easy going in many ways, unlike the control drama queens of England and northern Europe.

Eventually they wandered over to the terminal building, checked in and went through to air side and said good bye as they both went off to find their respective flights. Gypsy's flight took off at two thirty in the morning and he lay back and tried to get some sleep. The flight had just come from London and was full of fat middle aged single men. It was obvious what they were going to Thailand for. Gypsy just let himself nod off and awoke as the plane started it's descent into Don Muang airport.

It was six thirty in the morning when Gypsy emerged from the airport's front entrance. He hailed a taxi and directed the driver to take him to Suriwong road. He found the hotel that he had been told about, which was called the 'New Peninsula' and went inside and asked how much it would cost to get a room there. It was quite expensive, at least by his standards so he went to the travel agent that he had seen next door to the hotel and asked them what sort of discount he could get by buying a hotel coupon from them. They gave him a deal that was so good that he could not turn it down. So armed with a handful of coupons he went back to the hotel and checked in. In all of his travels in adult life he had never stayed at such a place. It had a television in the room, a smart bathroom, a mini bar, air-conditioning, room service and a smart and clean swimming pool down stairs, plus a good, modern and clean restaurant in the lobby. Gypsy was not used to such luxuries and felt strangely un at ease staying in such a place, as he felt that he did not belong. But none the less he enjoyed having a taste of the good life for a change.

Having got himself cleaned up and after some breakfast he went out and around the corner to Mahesk road, which was where he had been told that the main gem dealing area of Bangkok was located. He went from door to door visiting all of the stone dealers in the area to see who he was going to be able to get the best deal from. After a long search he settled on the one that he had heard about from an Australian dealer back in Jaipur, 'Wat Gems'.

The man who owned the business asked him what it was that he was looking for, and so Gypsy explained about which sizes and shapes he wanted and also what sort of colour, shade, clarity and price per carat the items would need to be. The owner got on the phone and arranged for some of the brokers of the area to come around with what they had, that would match Gypsy's description. It was not hard to find what he was looking for and also the prices of saphires were far more reasonable than any that he had seen in Jaipur. Over the next two weeks he found several good packets and also he put in an order for silver rings to be made to his own design.

He took a look at some of the other shops in the area and found one that sold attractive looking display equipment for people who moved around selling gems. They had nice well made glass lidded boxes that were just big enough to place one medium sized gem inside of, and boxes that would hold lines of paper gem wrappers within. So he bought enough equipment to make himself look smart and professional when he would go selling, back in England. Also being that he was in Thailand, the home of the fake everything, he went and bought some smart new clothes that he could wear when he went out selling, and a fake Gucci watch so that when he had to go and deal with some of the unspeakably snobbish idiots that masqueraded as jewellers back in England then at least he could hold his own. People even back then had heard of the fake Rolexes from Bangkok but they did not know so much about the other types of fake watches that were available at that time and so he chose the Gucci because it was not so glaringly obvious.

Most days in the late afternoon or early evening he would go out to the small courtyard that was at ground level and go and have a dip in the swimming pool. It was one of the few places that he could find to relax in this hectic city.

One day, towards the end of his trip he met two brothers who were from Nigeria, who were also hanging out at the swimming pool. He got talking with them and it turned out that they were also in the gem buisiness but in a completely different way from Gypsy. Back in Nigeria they owned a mine that was extracting certain minerals that were used in the manufacture of electronic items such as televisions and computers. As they were digging they came across other deposits that had a completely different market. One of these deposits was clear white topaz which as a clear colourless stone was not so desirable to the jewellery market. But in Thailand they could do tricks with it. By blasting it with radiation and heating it, they could make it turn to a rich dark blue, not unlike the colour of a very high quality aquamarine. This was a popular item with both the British jewellers and their customers who seemed either not to know or not to care that the item was made to look like it did by an extremely dodgy process.

Anyway the two brothers were in Bangkok to arrange some deals with some of the people who had the radiation ovens. They were at that time shipping over four tons of clear white topaz to Thailand every week.

He also took a trip to the Kowsan road to see if any of his previous acquaintances from the road were in town. The place had changed drastically since his first visit there three and a half years before. There were far more backpackers around, there were cafes and restaurants everywhere catering to westerners, there were far more guest houses, travel agents and shops selling souvenirs. Also there were many street stands selling bootleg pre-recorded music, fake designer watches and fake designer jeans. There was a plague of ill behaved Israeli youth who wanted to bargain until death over the smallest of trivial charges and over the price of everything and anything.

The area had lost it's laid back and relaxed oriental feel and turned into a grubby, cheap and nasty international zone where the travellers did not need to adjust themselves to the ways of their hosts in order to stay there. Gypsy no longer felt comfortable in the vicinity and headed back to the river to take the river taxi back to the Bangrak area where he was staying. However on the way to the river, as he was passing through Soi Rambutri, which was the road that passed by the temple at the west end of the Kowsan road, a westerner on a pushbike suddenly stopped "hey Gypsy what are you doing here?" he said. Gypsy looked at him with a puzzled look on his face "you don't recognize me?" said the man "no" said Gypsy "remind me". "I'm the one that you gave your job to back in Tokyo" said the man "ah now I remember" said Gypsy "how did you get on?". Well I followed the course that you gave me and ran it for the rest of the year" said the man.

"No problems?" Gypsy asked, "No it all ran very smoothly for me there and I just left, two weeks ago with a pocket full of cash. Now I'm travelling, I'm on my way to Australia". Gypsy wished him well for his journey and then headed off on his way to the river. He was glad that it had worked out so well for the fellow, which would have also made mister Oneida happy too as he would not have had to run around looking for a replacement at short notice. However when Gypsy had designed that course it was meant to be completed within one school term or less, it was not meant to be run for an entire year, the students must have been bored shitless with it.

With his load together and all shopping done Gypsy packed his bags and headed out to the airport where he boarded his flight back to Delhi.

It was late at night when the Thai airways jumbo left the terminal at Don Muang airport and headed out to the runway. Three and a half hours later they touched down at I.G.I. in Delhi and Gypsy was soon off the plane, through passport control and customs and in a taxi heading into New Delhi, towards Bikaner house to catch a bus back to Jaipur. He had so many display boxes with him that customs had made him leave most of them in sealed storage with them until he flew back out. However they had been fast and efficient about it and it had taken only minutes to do. The storage room was literally crawling with rats and Gypsy could not understand how anyone could stand to work there without laying out poison or taking an air rifle to work.

Soon he was on a bus heading out of Delhi, back out past the airport and on to the road across southern Haryana towards the state boarder with Rajasthan. He was happy with what he had done in Bangkok and surprised at just how easy it had been, however he was nervous as to weather the stones that he had bought would be good enough for his British customers.

Five hours later the bus pulled into Sindi camp bus station and gypsy pushed his way through the usual scrum of over enthusiastic auto rickshaw wallas and found himself a cycle rickshaw outside of the station for the one kilometre ride to the guest house. Through the next two weeks he spent his time between Birla's house, Chameli walla market and various dealers offices on Gopal ji ka rasta as he made up the rest of his load. Eventually he viewed that he had done his job well and was fully loaded and so headed back out on the bus back to Delhi to catch his flight back to London. There was nothing much for him to do in Delhi and also he had an expensive cargo that he could not afford to leave lying around, So he got himself booked onto a flight that was leaving that same night.

Some nine hours after leaving Delhi he was once again standing on the ground in the customs hall at Heathrow's terminal three, waiting for his clearing agent to arrive. It felt weird, he had been at Indra Gandhi International airport just outside of Delhi, just nine hours previously and naturally it had been full of Indians, both as passengers and as operators. Now here he was at T3 London Heathrow and it looked not much different, in fact there were probably more Indians working at Heathrow than there were at Delhi airport. "Namaste, welcome to London". Well it certainly went some way to help lessen the culture shock of arriving back in the UK as far as Gypsy was concerned. However they even had an Indian customs officer who was an expert in gemstones and their values and he was the one who inspected Gypsy's load after the clearing agent returned some forty five minutes later. The fellow obviously knew the rates in Jaipur and other centres of gem cutting around the world too. Gypsy's bills were showing low prices for everything. His suppliers had made his bills up for him and he had not had much time to check them before arriving back and had just handed them to his clearing agent on arrival. Some of his suppliers had obviously decided to do him a favour to help him get started and made things look cheaper on the bill than they had really been. The Indian officer gave Gypsy a look as if to say "I know what game is going on here but you are helping my homeland with your business so I'll let it pass". Gypsy also made it obvious that he liked India as he chatted with the fellow. He paid his tax and then paid the clearing agent and after being collected from the airport, was soon at his family's house in Sussex.

Again it had been a night flight and he was jet lagged and tired. However as per usual, he set about laying his stock out. This time though, he was putting his stones in the new boxes that he had purchased in Bangkok. When he had finished the job, many hours later his kit looked both smart and presentable.

He had brought himself a fifteen gram chunk of charas home with him, so after retrieving it, had smoked a couple of joints, which the effects of, along with the jet lag and a sleepless night now had put Gypsy into a semiconscious state. He fell into a deep sleep and awoke at four o'clock on the following morning. He couldn't sleep and like after previous long flights from east to west he felt wide awake at a time when only the milk man and the neibourhood cats were up and about. He continued to work on the layout and order that his stock was in, but after a time he had it laid out as good as he could get it and there was nothing more to do.

Later that morning, now armed with a driving licence, he put his gem bag on the floor in the passenger side of his H.A.Viva van and headed out to Brighton to see how much he could sell there. He did well on that first day and for several weeks to come. He kept his prices low consistently and people in the trade were getting to know him and liked the fact that despite the long hair and the hippie clothes he was honest, had cheap prices and presented his stock competently.

Some of them were fascinated by where the stones came from and how they were cut, they also wanted to hear stories from his journeys. Others however just wanted a cheap deal on the stones that they used to make their jewellery with. A few wouldn't deal with him because he had long hair, drove around in an old cheap van, and didn't wear a suit or talk with the right accent. Gypsy was not so worried to have their business if that was how there heads worked. It would be painful to be in the presence of such pretentious fools, even for the short time that it might take to take their money. If they were like that, then they were probably not competent at their job and would be difficult to deal with in other ways too.

During this time Gypsy was lent one of the two old static caravans on the plant nursery that his family owned. He was happy not to be in the house of his family and set to work to make his gem business work. He got a very good sale with a local jeweller that really got him going. Then the silver that he had ordered from Bangkok arrived which cost him well over a thousand pounds. But to his dismay, when he looked at it it had all been made for tiny Thai sized fingers, so it was a disaster that he was not going to be able to sell as the design was a chunky man's style of ring.

After a few weeks he was running out of local towns in the area to go looking for new customers in, so it was time to make a trip to Birmingham. One morning he got up at five o'clock, got himself ready then with his gems loaded and headed out on the road. First to the M25 orbital motorway around London and then north up the M1 and onto the M6 to Birmingham (the shorter route from London on the M40 had not at that time been completed). He reached the jewellery quarter at Hockley at nine thirty and wasted no time in getting to work as he went from shop to shop and then office to office, looking for a bite. Out of the hundred or so premises he visited that day he was able to get his bags open in perhaps twenty of them and made actual sales in four of them. It was not as many as he had hoped to sell to and it was not the amount that he had hopped to take but it was a good day. He was three hundred and fifty pounds wealthier and people were getting to know his face. Maybe soon he would be taking more when he visited the area.

Just as the shops were shutting at five in the evening, he put his bags of stones back into the van and drove off around the inner ring road and then out to spaghetti junction. He then joined the M6 southbound for the drive home in his slow, stone aged vehicle (it even had a slot for a starting handle on the front, no joke!!!!!). The van was supposed to do a top speed of sixty miles an hour according to the manual but Gypsy discovered that by slip streaming it behind other faster vehicles he could get it up to eighty miles an hour under favourable conditions. By eight o'clock that night he had driven back down to the south side of the M25. He turned off at Leatherhead, passed Dorking and Box hill and was on a winding two lane road through the hills heading towards Horsham when he followed a Ford Sierra car around a bend at the same speed that it was going at. The van toppled over and spun around on it's side, sparks shooting up around Gypsy's ears for what felt like eternity. Time seemed to slow down as he sat there on his side not knowing what to do. Then the van for some reason bounced back onto its wheels and with two popped tires Gypsy steered it into a layby that just happened to be there, and got out. He was unharmed but a little bit shaken. It was lucky that he had the side window down at the time as at least that had not been damaged and he was able to wind it up and lock the van. Some men came running over from a nearby field to see what had happened. They were relieved when they saw him standing there with no injuries and recommended that he go and use the phone at a nearby pub that was only a few hundred metres down the road to call for some help.

The van, with two burst tyres was not possible to drive but at least he had it locked and off the main road. The wife of a friend of his came and collected him and took him and his gem cases home. The next day, armed with two new wheels with inflated tyres, he was driven back in the car of a friend to where the van was. After fitting the wheels the friend towed him and the van home. His father's company mechanic took a look at the van and decided that he could fix it quite cheaply. It had dents in the side but they could be knocked out to a degree and there was not much wrong with the engine or running gear. Just a few things would need adjusting or replacing. However it would not be done for ten days so he was going to miss going to Glastonbury festival, which really pissed him off. For the next week or so he was back to hitch hiking and using the trains to get around and sell his goods. Already his sales were starting to drop away as he was finding it increasingly difficult to locate places where he could find more customers, it could take days of painful searching to find just one small customer. There were no hard or fast rules but it was normally in the back streets of an old part of a town where he would find the sort of people that he could sell to. However the town itself would need to be old and have people with old inherited money resident there in order that an artist jeweller could survive and thrive within it.

Ten days after having crashed, the mechanic had the van fixed, all be it with some pretty large dents in the side. The hard nature of the gem and jewellery market combined with the uptight ways of those around him in Sussex was giving Gypsy a headache. He needed to get out of the area for a while and be around people who didn't conspire to make him feel like a space alien. He spent the next week converting his tiny van into a space that he could live from. He had seen people doing it with ford falcon station wagons when he was in Australia so he figured that he could do it with his van in order to travel in England.

After a week or so it was ready, the walls and ceiling had been panelled with sheets of hardboard and stuffed behind with old newspaper. The floor had several layers of old carpet and a thick mattress on it. There were several racks and hooks on the wall above the petrol tank that contained his kitchen equipment and on top there was a roof rack containing his water tanks, a tarpaulin and other handy kit. Now he was ready to hit the road. He left in the middle of the night leaving a note behind for his family saying that he had given up the caravan and to let someone else use it. He was looking for a different way to make things work for himself in England and was going off on his journey to find out how.

He drove slowly through the night in a westerly direction. In the morning he found himself on the ruins of the Glastonbury festival. It had finished perhaps eight or nine days prior but there were still many travellers parked up on the site. Gypsy pulled in and parked next to a group of vehicles where the occupants were awake and sitting outside, around a fire. They had some of the weirdest vehicles that he had ever seen. They looked like something from the Mad Max movies. Gypsy was later to learn that they were a group called the Mutoid Waste Company and they made giant sculptures out of old cars and the like at festivals and events.

At first they were wary of Gypsy suggesting that maybe he was a cop. So to test him they handed him a cup of magic mushroom tea and told him what it was. Gypsy knocked it back in one gulp. After that he was in and they invited him to sit down for some real tea and a joint or ten. There were still one or two thousand people still parked on the site.

Most of them were working on clearing the huge quantity of rubbish that was left behind, from the fields of the farm. The festival was run with the aim of raising money for CND (Council for Nuclear Disarmament), a group concerned with saving the world. But here after the festival was over the site itself looked as if it had been hit by a considerably large piece of ordinance. The place looked like an ecological disaster zone. It would have been nice if these people who came here espousing such high and beautiful ideals had taken a turn each to make sure they left their food wrappers and the like in or next to a rubbish bin and not strewn across the fields and hedge rows. It would be better if these people could walk the walk instead of just talking the talk and show that they were sincere about their spoken ideals, thought Gypsy to himself. The site of the mess left him feeling quite depressed. The future did not look so bright if the country only had "Citizen Smith" style hippies leading the call for change.

Later that same day a good looking French woman turned up on the site, she lived in Glastonbury town which was some six or seven miles from the festival site at Pilton. She and Gypsy got talking. She was obviously a good few years older than Gypsy but she was good looking and dressed beautifully. So when she invited Gypsy back to her flat, he didn't need asking twice. Her place was a two bedroom flat on the Windmill Hill council estate, which was situated on the top of a hill overlooking the town. She shared the flat with her thirteen year old daughter. She had been married to the black sheep son of an exceptionally rich family but he had disappeared some seven or eight years before leaving her with the child to raise on her own. She had a university degree but though she had done such things as organize art exhibitions and work in high offices, she had also fallen down on a few occasions becoming a junkie and working in red light areas in Holland and Denmark.

She had been strong and kicked the habit and the bad lifestyle some years before and had been travelling with her daughter and friends in a hippie truck with a group of travellers that had several large vehicles between them. Then after some trouble occurred between the travellers and some particularly violent and thuggish cops, which became known in hippie/traveler legend as the Battle of the beanfield, she was granted a council flat by the local government.

That evening she told Gypsy about her life. It had been rough and hard but also it had had it's moments such as the time when she was in Morocco in the late sixties or early seventies and had scored dope for and got to hang out with the Rolling Stones. She had also been invited to parties and get togethers on the super luxury yachts of her husband's family.

The next night they ended up in bed together and thus started a four month affair.

Gypsy at that time was twenty six years old and she was thirty eight years old. Gypsy had thought it was going to be a one night stand but all of the next day this woman wouldn't let go, Gypsy wasn't complaining, five times in one day suited him just fine and she was kinky enough with it, which also suited him just fine.

Also she was a wild traveler just like himself so he was OK about sticking around for a while through the summer. But he was not the type that liked to be pinned down or trapped by anything or anyone and she seemed to be trying to make long term plans for him that involved her. He liked her and it was fun being with her but Gypsy could not imagine being in a long term relationship at that time in his life. The freedom of the road was far far more attractive to him than anything else. He had left his home in his van with the intention to travel and find something that he really was looking for. She introduced Gypsy to many people that were doing active things in the alternative/green scene. There were people living in tepees in fields and in benders in the woods (a bender is made out of tying willow branches and twigs together to make a self supporting dome then covering it with tarpaulins). some were huge and had sprung floors, all of them would have a wood burning stove inside of them. There were people attempting to live from the land and people who were trying to get started at making handicrafts and the likes. Also they went to parties at the Pilton site while there were still people staying there. Later as the summer wore on the parties happened up on the Tor or in different fields, gardens or houses. Also there was a hall in the town that had been bought by the hippie community and it was used for concerts and other events. Even without the festival the town rocked. There was always something happening. The end of the festival was a bit like the end of the party season in Goa, in that it always seemed to drop some crazy burned out acid cases into the lap of the local community. In Goa it was not uncommon at the end of the season to see an ambassador taxi driving at high speed in the direction of the Christian ashram with a group of westerners trying to hold down another westerner [who might be frothing at the mouth and barking and screaming] on the back seat. In Glastonbury the lunatics were left to walk the streets and harass people.

Gypsy was informed by the woman that on a typical year there would be a good few dozen that had delusions about having been King Arthur, Morgan La Fey, Merlyn, Lancelot or the like in a past life.

It added to the colour on the high street to have the loonies running around in their silly costumes. Sometimes their antics could be fun to watch but it was often better to watch from a distance. Like the time during that summer when one particular fruit cake decided to pursue another person along the pavement at high speed while swinging an unsheathed samurai sword around and screaming like a banshee. Another had engaged the local cops in a thirty mile chase through the back lanes of the district when he forgot to take his medication and turned into Mr Hyde. Many of the loonies would gather on the benches in front of the old stone church, midway up the high street that sloped up in the direction of windmill hill.

In the late summer Gypsy made several brief trips back to Sussex to see his family and sort things out there with them. Also while there in Glastonbury he tried to get his gem business going in that area. He made repeated trips to both Bath and Bristol as he and the woman scoured the area looking for customers. He did his best trades while visiting Clifton above Bristol where he made several good sales but also he made a few good sales to the hippies in Glastonbury and the surrounding area.

However, the woman was getting to be a problem. If he was out of her sight for as little time as twenty minutes then she would seriously accuse him of screwing other women in the neibourhood. This was just not a possibility after she had got him to perform three or four times before he got out of bed in the morning and then again a couple of times in the evening. The woman clearly had no understanding of the biological functions of men. After all, on top of that Gypsy never liked to rush the job and used up one hell of a lot of energy on what he did with her. On top of this if he so much as talked to any other woman but herself then she would fly into a jealous, insecure rage and start shouting at Gypsy when they got home.

Then there were the many times that he wanted to go out selling, as she was on his case to make money. Invariably she would insist on going with him, then would spend so long choosing her clothes and painting her face that it would be late in the afternoon before they reached the town where they were going to go cold calling.

Yes he liked living with a kinky nymphomaniac that kept him satisfied, but she was so insecure that she was doing things that seemed to drain the life out of him. One day he managed to escape out on to the moors for an afternoon and sat in a field with some other hippies. He immediately began to feel his life energy come back into him, The woman was acting like a vampire, sucking his energy from him. He was going to have to get himself out of this situation as quickly as possible, it was definetly a case of black widow syndrome.

When he got back to the flat at just after seven in the evening the woman was not there, but it was not long before she arrived, totally inebriated and shouting wild unfounded allegations about what she had imagined Gypsy might have been doing. Gypsy had had enough by this point and started to gather up his possessions at high speed and sling them into any bag that he could find and then took them and put them in his van. He had everything of his rounded up and in the vehicle and had jumped in behind the wheel locking the doors after himself, planning to make a quick get away. But she came running out of the flat and threw herself on the ground in front of his vehicle in fits of tears to stop him leaving. And all of this in front of her young daughter too. If only to stop her from shaming herself further in front of her offspring, Gypsy abandoned his escape attempt, at least for that night.

On another occasion, a week or so later they drove to a small town close to Bristol called Clevedon to meet with her ex mother in law. The woman lived in an extremely expensive looking apartment surrounded by expensive looking antique furniture. She was dressed in what looked like expensive designer wear clothes and looked like she drank more alcohol than what was good for her. Though on the surface she was polite she was obviously an uptight snob who disapproved of both the woman and Gypsy for having the cheek to be alive on the same planet as her self. Though both Gypsy and the woman did their best to get on with this woman it was still an uncomfortable afternoon. Several days later the woman got a phone call from one of the other members of her ex-husband's family. She was told about her ex-mother in law's disapproval and bad mouthing of Gypsy, who incidentally had done nothing to warrant such an attack. Then she was told that her husband who had been missing for eight years, possibly on a drug fuelled binge was returning to her. She, it would appear had used Gypsy as bait and provocation in order to get her husband back.

She told Gypsy that he was going to come and see her in four days and that he would have to move out before then. Though she was university educated she was not so bright a spark. She didn't understand when Gypsy not only agreed to move out immediately but practicaly ran down the road clicking his heals in the air with joy. She had not so much treated him as a lover as she had a hostage or a prisoner. Gypsy, though he liked her and meant her no harm, was more than glad to be free again. He smiled to himself when he overheard her speaking to a friend "I don't understand it" she said "I asked him to move out and he didn't complain or make any trouble, he just packed his things and started loading them into the back of his van. I thought he was going to make a big fuss about it".

Though Gypsy had enjoyed being around Glastonbury through the summer he had by this point had enough of the procrastinating yogurt weavers of the neighborhood and was now ready for a change of both company and scenery. With his van loaded he drove off in the direction of Bridgewater and the M5 motorway, then took the northbound route and didn't stop until he reached Liverpool. He had an old friend who lived in the city who he had not seen for a very long time and who he wished to see. He took the exit at Runcorn and drove up through the urban sprawl for several miles until he reached the Dingle neighborhood where he found the road and the house where his friend lived. He had known Tony as long as he could remember, as Tony had been the son of the neighbors in the house were he had spent the first four years of his life in Worcestershire. He had joined the navy at the age of eighteen as had many of his family before him but then left as an active objector when he realized that he could not bring himself to kill another human being under any circumstances that he could imagine.

He had worked as a type of voluntary social worker for many years as he worked at various charities helping people that society at large had given up on. At the time of Gypsy's arrival he was working from home as a hypnotherapist and councellor. However he was also a highly practical person and also occasionally worked as a handyman fixing peoples houses for them. He asked Gypsy if he would like to come and help out on one particular job that he had, which involving fixing some rotten window frames at the house of a friend of his.

They drove to the area in Gypsy's van, as Tony did not own a car and did not drive. Gypsy was surprised to see the area had places with the same names as some of the Beatles songs such as Penny Lane and Strawberry fields. Apparently the Beatles had grown up and lived in this area of the city before they had found fame and fortune.

Near to the road where Tony lived was the hippie/alternative neibourhood of Belvedere road. There were all sorts of different spiritual groups active in the area. There was a house full of Ananda Marga devotees and another house where followers of the Hare Krishna path were. Also there were many other groups involved with different Asian meditation practices too, so Gypsy felt quite at home in the area. Tony had invited members of the newly formed green party to come and form a loose knit commune of types at his large old house.

There were six or eight of them in all and just like alcoholics they had many meetings. They were all professionals who worked either for local government or in some other place where they could have a chance to introduce aspects of their ideals to a wider audience. However all though the ideals behind the project were of the highest and most noble Tony was starting to find that the politics of dealing with the others and their disturbing little quirks was interfering with his ability to operate his in house hypnotherapy practice. As such he was wondering if he should dissolve the commune or ask them all to find another house to do it in.

Another house that Gypsy visited had a tepee set up in the living room and parrots and other exotic birds flying and walking around the house. The walls had giant fish tanks built into them and the place was decked out in bright and colourful ethnic/hippie designs.

Even apart from the hippie area around Belvedere road, Liverpool was in many ways a nicer place to be than in Sussex or Glastonbury. The people were a lot more friendly with each other than the uptight yobs and snobs that resided in the south of the country. They even spoke to each other as well as to total strangers while waiting in the bus queue or travelling on the bus. The place was not as materially wealthy as areas to the south and east and the weather was a bit colder too, but the people more than made up for that. Gypsy stayed around at Tony's place for ten days or so while he got his head sorted after his four months with the woman. He enjoyed his time in Liverpool and was grateful to Tony for the relaxing place to stay. Now it was time to go and find a way of sorting out some of the debt that he had run up while making this third attempt to get his business up and running. He returned to Sussex and tried to carry on with his business, even if just to make the money he would need to pay off what he owed.

He arranged to sell all of the rest of his stock to one jeweller for just the amount that he would need to pay his dept back. Then with just a few hundred pounds in his pocket he had to think about what he wanted to do. He was wondering about starting a new business on a low budget, printing T-shirts and the like and his father suggested that he also consider making some items of garden furniture that could be sold via the plant nursery. So Gypsy set to work in an old barn that was on the nursery, clearing a space from old junk and studding up a frame to build a room that could be used for manufacture of whatever. He put one circuit in for lights and another with an ample supply of sockets then got the nursery electrician to come in, check his work and connect the circuits up to the main box. Then with some friends that had helped him to build the room they called in a rep from a company that sold equipment for printing T-shirts. But when they found out what it would cost to buy the machine and equipment to do the job they realized that they were going to have to find a cheaper method of setting up. So they started laying out jigs and patterns for use in making garden furniture instead.

During the time when gypsy was getting rid of his gem stock he had become depressed and disillusioned with how life was and how people in his locality (especially those in the jewellery business) behaved and as so had taken a visit to a certain Buddhist monastery that was within thirty miles of where he lived. The place and the monks there, he found to be inspiring and he promised himself that he would make regular visits to the monastery and learn to meditate. He wrote the phone number and address of the monastery in his pocket address book and went on his way. That was in December of nineteen eighty seven.

At some time and somewhere in the early spring of nineteen eighty eight he mislaid his address book. One day he got a phone call from a man who said that he had found it lying in the street of a nearby town. When he went to collect it, the man said "I hope that you don't mind but while I was looking through the book as I tried to find out who it belonged to I took one address from it. You had the address of a local Buddhist monastery and I am keen to go there and join the meditation". "No I have no problem with you taking that" said Gypsy "in fact I also would like to start going there each night to meditate, if you would like to share on fuel money then we could use my van to get there".

The man enthusiastically agreed and so they agreed to join up on the following evening to make the journey. The man's wife had died two years prior. They had been very happy together and had made many good parties at their house. They had two fully grown sons who took care of themselves so the man now felt free to do as he wished. Without his wife he had no desire to do anything else but to persue his path to enlightenment. He like Gypsy could now see that there was nothing in this temporary world that was really worth pursuing as it always was destined in the long run to bring sorrow, sadness, a sense of loss and ultimately suffering. The only thing therefore that was worth doing was to pursue a speedy route to spiritual enlightenment.

As Gypsy had been untangling himself from his gem business one of the jewellers had asked him if he could recommend a good connection in Bangkok to buy sapphires, rubies and emeralds from. Gypsy had happily given him not only a contact but also a briefing on how to do things in that part of the world in order to get the job done and also on how to stay out of trouble. The man had offered to pay Gypsy for the information at the end of the briefing. Gypsy had refused to take any money for mere information and instead had told the man that if he found that he had bought too much stock on his trip then Gypsy would be more than happy to help him to sell it.

So there he was, that spring wondering how he was going to get a new business ready to start and encountering all sorts of problems as he did so. He had been on unemployment benefit for six weeks and was about to use help from the government's enterprise allowance scheme. Then one day he got a phone call from the man who had been to Bangkok to tell him that he had had a very good trip and also he had brought back extra sapphires and emeralds with the idea to sell them on the local market and he wanted to find out if Gypsy would like to do the selling for him.

Now Gypsy had a pouch filled with packets of expensive stones in his top pocket. He knew that he would need more stock to make this work so he went looking for other people in the trade who had other stock that they might like to have sold for them. His cousin in the trade also suggested that his brother in law might like to get rid of a whole load of packets that had been reduced to the point that there was nothing in them that he could use in his own jewellery. Gypsy went up to London for a meeting with him but was directed to the office of the company buyer instead. He left the office with several large packets that were being fronted to him at very low rates and headed on back to the south coast. But not before first having done a round of the dealers and workshops of Hatton Garden and the Clarkenwell workshop area with what stones he had. For the next few months he ran around the southern part of England trying to get his business started once more. Every evening through the winter and spring he drove with his friend, the older man to the Buddhist monastery to join the monks for the evening meditation. On a few occasions he stayed at the monastery for a weekend. It was an interesting experience and he learned a lot about the way that the mind work's during those breaks. One monk explained to him how it was possible to program the mind like an alarm clock in order to cause one's self to awaken at a certain time, even during hours of darkness. The next night Gypsy tried it and to his amazement he found that it worked. He awoke at the same time as the others, in time for the early morning meditation at four thirty. Also during the meditations it was possible to see the restless and wandering nature of the mind and how most of our lives are so full of the confusion that is caused by the desires and restlessness of this wandering mind. The goal of meditation is to reach a clarity of vision where the ultimate truth can be seen and lived by. This is the meaning of the word, enlightenment!.... At least that's how Gypsy described it.

Meanwhile closer to home Gypsy received a very kind offer from a woman who owned a house in the local town. She wanted a house sitter who was like her, a vegetarian and spiritually switched on, to live in her house rent free and just make sure that all of her stuff stayed safe. It was a very welcome offer and soon he had moved in. He didn't have so much stuff and he was happy to bed down on a mattress on the floor of one of the small upper rooms.

Gypsy's image started to suffer when people who owned shops that he sold to, saw what sort of vehicle he was driving around in. On one occasion when he had a fixed appointment at the house of a jeweller, the man cancelled the appointment when Gypsy turned up in his old yellow van. It had happened in other ways too as he went about trying to sell his stones. Then often when he went out in the evening the cops would pull him over for no reason. It must have been on the third or fourth time within a week that he had been stopped and turned over. As they went through the things in his van he turned to them and said "maybe you can tell me the reason why the hell it is that you and your mates keep pulling me over and searching me when I have done absolutely nothing wrong?". "it's because your van looks like a burglar's van sir, many of the local burglars have been using this type of vehicle for their work as of recently" he was told by a slightly apologetic cop.

"Oh great, my van look's like a burglar's van, no wonder people don't want to make business with me" thought Gypsy to himself. His father had just bought himself a new car and had upgraded from a BMW 520 to a BMW M5. He lent his Old car to Gypsy for a few days when his van was in the garage being fixed. Gypsy noticed how much easier it was to get a sale from a new customer when he parked a BMW in front of their shop instead of a van that looked like it belonged to Trotter Trading Co of London, Paris and Peckham. The BMW was not only a pleasure to drive but actually made normal business look possible to him. He asked his father if he would be willing to sell him the car now that he no longer needed it, but his father refused, saying that it wouldn't help him. Gypsy tried to explain that his sales had improved massively on the days that he had used the car but his father would have none of it and continued to refuse to sell it to him. Gypsy then said that he would have to go elsewhere to find one because that was what he needed to be able to sell successfully. "Why don't you look for something a bit more modest like a Ford or a Vauxhall?" his father asked "because the people that I have to do Business with, drive Mercedes, Porche, BMW and Rolls Royce, I have lost too many sales because of that fucking van and a Ford or a Vauxhall is also equally as likely to cause me not to be taken seriously in the trade" Gypsy answered. "What! You want to start where we left off?" his mother who was present for the conversation retorted at him in an angry tone. "It's what I need if I'm to be able to do my job" Gypsy replied "and besides I'm the one who is going to be paying for it".

Gypsy looked through the adds in the local papers to see if he could find a suitable sort of car for his needs, he even went along with a friend to look at a couple of them. But it was after several weeks that the company mechanic, who he got on well with, said that he had found something that Gypsy could both afford and be able to fix without spending a fortune. They took a trip to a scrap dealer in a nearby local town where the man had an old BMW 520 that worked and he only wanted seven hundred pounds for it. It was silver and had a factory fitted sun roof, alloy wheels and a Blaupunkt stereo. The brakes, suspension and other areas were going to need some attention, not least the body work, including one front wing that was going to need replacing, but with a couple of weeks work it would not be hard to get all of the repairs and replacements done. He was able to drive the car back to the nursery where he left it at the mechanic's workshop ready to start work on it on the following day. He took time off from all his other activities with exception to his daily visits to the monastery with his friend, and set about to service and repair his new set of wheels. The brake pads were the first thing to be done as they were nearly touching the metal. Next came the suspension and after that came a full engine service including plug and filter replacements. The rocker head cover gasket and distributor cap were also shot and were also replaced. After that the rusted out wing and other rust spots were the next thing to receive Gypsy's attention. Then there was a front head light unit that he was going to need if the car was to pass it's M.O.T. test, that was due to be taken within the next six weeks. Also there was both a section of exhaust and a section of the front passenger foot well that needed to be welded, as rust had done some serious damage to them. Some of the parts that were needed were salvaged from old wrecks at local scrap yards. Gypsy climbed up on old cars that were sometimes stacked four or five high, to get bits of trim and instruments from them, it was an adventure in it self just getting the parts alone. Things like pads, filters, plugs, gaskets and the like were available at vastly discounted rates as pattern parts from the local general spares stores. But occassionaly he was stuck and had to go to the local BMW dealer to find out how much an original part would cost. It was a good job that he had taken the company mechanic with him on that first trip to Chandlers BMW parts department. He had been there many times before and knew what the reaction would be when Gypsy was told the price. As such he was there with the smelling salts and the like and also a suggestion of another cheaper way of doing the job.

Eventually Gypsy had a semi respectable looking car that was working reasonably well and was street legal for the next twelve months. There was still a rather worrying but moderate oil leak coming from under the fuel pump and some times the engine just did not want to start. But those things would get sorted as the mechanic had time to help him in diagnosing the source of the problem and as they could find the parts that would be needed for the repair.

The car was as stable as a rock and held the road incredibly well. It was a very comfortable ride but not so very fast, with a book top speed of one hundred and fourteen miles per hour or there abouts. It was built like a tank and would have best been described as a Deutsch autobahn panzer. It was a pleasure to drive and delivered Gypsy to the doorstep of his customers looking reasonably well presented, even if there was the odd bit of trim that was either not there or in serious need of replacement. He had done reasonably well with the first lots of stones that he had taken out with him. The sapphires had been popular and he had done extremely well with a packet of opals that he had taken on sale or return from his cousin's place. He was looking to set himself up as a gem finding service were he could locate cheap deals around the market for people as they wanted. He went and found the office of the man that he had met on the flight back from India a couple of years or so before and asked about getting apro (sale on approval of end customer). He was told that this would be no problem, all that he would need to start an account would be some photo I.D. and a permanent address.

Many of the goldsmiths and jewellers of the area had a problem getting on with each other so sometimes Gypsy was able to make a sale by just being an anonymous runner between the warring parties. He found that the person that he got on with the best among the jewellers, goldsmiths and the like's was the gemmologist and gem cutter. Not only did he test stones and taught an F.G.A. (fellowship of Gemmology] course as an evening class but he also cut stones and could make jewellery by hand with gold, silver or whatever. He was the epitomy of the British garden shed inventor and could put his hand to almost anything. He had built his own rig for casting gold and silver jewellery for the grand total of thirty eight pounds, when the going rate for equipment that would do the same job would cost close to three thousand pounds from the tool shops of Hatton Garden. He was a fully trained chemist and could also teach the subject, but most of all he was one of the few in the trade that Gypsy had met who was not absolutely full of shit.

The man often helped Gypsy in one way or another and on one occasion it was by fronting Gypsy a fifty carat aquamarine, cut stone that a customer said that he in turn would have a customer for. The stone was priced at four hundred pounds and Gypsy saw that he could add at least another fifty pounds to the price as he moved it on. He stopped at the shop of the jeweller on the way home that afternoon and fronted the stone to the man and got him to sign an apro note for it before leaving the shop.

When he returned to the shop a week or so later he was told by the man who was still visibly shaken, that he had been robbed by a man who had come into his shop and held a broken bottle to his throat and taken everything that had been out of the safe at the time. This also included the aquamarine that he had been showing to his customer not half an hour before. "It's not a problem for you" said the jeweller to Gypsy "the shop is fully insured and you will have your money in no more than a few weeks". Never the less Gypsy took off at high speed to Brighton to tell the gemologist what had happened to his stone and to give the man a note that he guaranteed that he would give the man his money within six weeks, weather or not he had collected the insurance money.

This simple act of straight honesty was to earn Gypsy a very good image around the shops and workshops of the Brighton jewellers and Goldsmiths and people got to know that they could trust him. He may be a stoned resin headed hippie and go around in a Davy Crocket style jacket with hair half way down his back and he may prefer to be in the markets and bazaars of the Orient than in middle class England but he was more honest than most of the people in the trade.

The Gemologist had put the good word out on him and suddenly for the first time he was being treated with some respect within the trade and also his trade increased significantly. The jeweller who had done the run to Bangkok was ready to do another run out there and asked Gypsy what his customers were asking for the most. Gypsy told him that he was being asked for bigger stones. Sapphires were the most popular request and the easiest to get in big sizes in Bangkok. So the man returned ten days later with a pouch full of three to six carat stones. Gypsy ordered some glass lidded trays from a supplier in Hatton Garden with which to display these expensive, high quality stones as he went around the jewellers and goldsmiths premises to hawk his wares.

He was having trouble sitting in lotus position for meditation at the monastery and he was wondering what he could do about it.

The ex-husband of the woman who owned the house were Gypsy lived attended a local yoga class and the woman or one of her friends suggested that Gypsy get in touch with him and ask if he could join him one time in going to the class as so he could find out where it was and what time it happened at. Gypsy did just that and went along with the man to the class. It was in a local village hall and the teacher was a woman who was in her late sixties. She was also deeply into the alternative spiritual directions offered by eastern philosophy and also the paths and legends of the tribals and the ancients of the world.

For someone of her age at that time in the British Isles, she was amazingly switched on and aware. As such she had several young students, in their mid twenties attending, aside from Gypsy. Gypsy took an instant liking to her and found it refreshing to meet such a person living so close to where he was staying. From then on through the year he virtually never missed a class. They were held once a week at seven o'clock and went on for an hour and twenty minutes, including a fifteen to twenty minute lie flat let go meditation. Then after the class most of the people from it would go back the house of the yoga teacher for snacks and cold drinks and to talk. Some of them were just ordinary people who were frightened to stick their heads above the parapet of their mundane existences and only came to yoga for the keep fit aspect and to socialize. But others at the class were more switched on and were interested in many things. Some of them including the teacher and her husband were very much devotees of Sai Baba, who was a well known guru from south India. Gypsy had heard about him but had not been interested to go there on account of the Guru's habit of materializing things out of thin air and giving them to people. It sounded like a cheap circus trick. He couldn't believe that someone who did such things was going to have something to show him that he was indeed looking for. However, over the next few months the yoga teacher and some of the others managed to persuade him to take another look at what Sai Baba had to say and what he was doing. There were many people that said that they had never heard of Sai Baba until he appeared to them as a vision or in their dreams in their country of origin and given them spiritual instruction.

Now what with his interest in yoga and meditation being met more close to home, his visits to the monastery grew less frequent. But his friend who went with him started spending more and more time there and was planning eventually to become a monk. But first he wanted to finish renovating his house, sell it and give the proceeds of the sale to his two sons.

Things went sour at the barn where Gypsy had been planning to make the T-shirts and garden furniture after a packet of silver rings (the ones that he had had made in Thailand) had gone missing and someone who was entirely innocent got the blame. Gypsy was stuck by no fault or intention of his own in the middle between the parties and got blamed and vilified by all sides, which somewhat pissed him off. As such he left the project in the barn on ice as so as to let all sides cool off, not least himself as he was angry with all sides for using him as the scape goat.

Through the summer he worked at building up his business and concentrated on building a strong customer base along with grabbing every opportunity available to make a quick sale. The trouble was that some of the people that he had to sell to were not of the nicest or more decent type. Even though they had plenty of money for themselves and lived in big houses and drove fancy cars they got a buzz out of fucking Gypsy's day up for him.

One such individual asked him about a packet of small square emeralds that he had been carrying in his load several weeks before. Gypsy told the man that he would see if he could take them out again the next time that he visited that particular dealer. But the man insisted that he needed the packet that day and told Gypsy that if he went and got them immediately then he would buy the whole packet of some twenty carats for the asking price. So Gypsy made a phone call and then drove some eighty miles through heavy traffic there and back to get the packet.

When he got back to the shop where the man who had requested the packet was, the man opened the packet and then turned to Gypsy and said "I'm sorry but they are not how I remembered them as being, I don't want them". He had just fucked Gypsy and he knew it, as he stood grinning like a smug imbecile as Gypsy left the shop with a cloud of rage almost visible above the top of his head. The arsehole in the shop obviously got his jollies out of playing such tricks on people. Never mind that Gypsy was struggling to get his business started and was running on a micro budget while this individual was stinking rich in comparison. But Gypsy could do nothing if he didn't want to destroy the reputation that he was working so hard to build and this arsehole knew it. Gypsy for his part wanted to strangle the piece of shit, he would have liked to cut the barstard's balls off or beaten him with a large piece of steel until he was a bloody pulp on the floor. Unfortunately the law did not allow for such things and always seemed to be on the side of such arseholes, no matter what they did.

There were other smartarses too among the jewellers of Brighton. One of them had sent a shipment of screwdriver handles to Taiwan where he had them cut, polished and drilled as round beads. Then he had them shipped back to England where he had them strung as necklaces before putting them in the window of his posh looking jewellery shop and selling them as natural Baltic amber.

Another one who had a shop in the same area of the town had said "huh if that hippie can go to Bangkok and buy sapphires and bring them back here and sell them then I'm sure that I can do a much better job of it than him" and promptly went of and bought himself a ticket to the golden east.

Two weeks later he returned to the streets of Brighton with a pocket full of gem packets. He took them to have them tested by Gypsy's friend who after having placed them on the spectrometer and looked at each of them under the microscope merily informed him that most of what he had bought was synthetic and worth bug all. Few if any of the stones that he was sold were what he was told they were. Later he was heard to bitch by one of the people that Gypsy got on well with "I don't understand it, That hippie is selling sapphires cheaper here in England than I could buy them in the big jewellery and gemstone wholesale areas of Bangkok". But even so he would not buy from Gypsy even though Gypsy had done nothing to upset him apart from doing his job well and supplying good stones at reasonable rates. The man had made himself the laughing stock of the local jewellery trade and lost a lot of money into the bargain, also he had indirectly helped to enhance Gypsy's reputation within the trade. It is one thing to know how to be a jewellery retailer in England but quite another to know how to find your way through the labyrinths of the east and work out what is going on around you. This is a job which is much better performed by hardcore travellers than by small minded ponces in suits.

At this time the gemmologist was having problems with the location of where he rented his premises. The owner of the lease on the building had taken to putting synthetic stones into the jewellery that he sold through his shop downstairs. This was a particular problem as it was also the place where the gemmologist hung his F.G.A. certificate on the wall. On the last occasion that he had challenged the owner and his family about them putting synthetics in the window, while advertised as natural, they had turned to the gemmologist and said "oh you think that it's synthetic do you? Maybe you should test it for us just to make sure". "Well I really doubt that it has changed it's self into a natural stone since I tested it two weeks ago" said the gemologist "are you really sure that you want to waste my time and your money this way?"

There had also been other antics with this family that had caused problems in the area. Their name was really quite similar to the word "arsehole" so that was what they were known as in that part of town "the Arsehole Family". The gemologist just had to get out of the place, there was no two ways about it, they were driving away business and soiling his good name with their cynical tricks.

He got himself new premises lined up in a shop around the corner and decided to play a trick on the Arsehole family. He did not tell them what he was doing, not even a day before. Early in the morning one Sunday he and Gypsy went to his Laboratory and workshop in the old premises and through the course of the day they removed the entire setup and moved it to the new premises. They even took the lights and door handles. Also they had the laboratory and cutting set up up and ready to run on the morning after leaving. The Only thing that they had not been able to take was the sink and plumbing and they would have taken that too if it was not such a pain in the arse of a job to do.

Gypsy had agreed to help decorate the shop that the lab had been moved to for the woman who owned it as he had no pressing work on that week. So he was there to see the fireworks. The owner of the shop had gone up the two flights of winding narrow stairs to get the gemmologist to do a job, as was usual. He was even calling out to him to tell him about the job as he was going up the stairs. Then on opening the door and seeing an absolutely bare and stripped room instead of an in house cutting and gem testing service, his jaw just dropped and he fell into silence and just stared in total confusion for a couple of minutes. Then he ran down the stairs to the next floor down where a very high quality diamond and coloured gem setter worked. However, though the setter's work was some of the best available in the trade, no one wanted to have him working at a bench in their shop on account of his attitude and habit of being somewhat straight up about things. Also he was in the habit of singing extremely rude parodies of well known pop songs while he was working, some of which could have been viewed as being sexist and all of them could be deemed as extremely offensive.

The shop owner went running into the setter's room and started to gibber and stutter while pointing up at the ceiling. The man was in his early to mid sixties and presented himself as being upper middle class, posh and educated and was always dressed in a suit. The gem setter who was in his mid twenties and dressed in scruffy jeans turned calmly and looked at the old man having his hysterical rant and asked "what's wrong with you? got a cock stuck up your arse or something?" At this point the old man had gone running out like a chicken and clucked like a madman as he ran back down the stairs into his shop and then on out into the street to see if anyone knew where the gemologist had moved to.

To add to the fun there was a beautiful young woman working in the shop who each day was dressed up to the nines in super expensive looking miniskirt suits. Throughout the day she would be on and off the phone to here lawyer with a very worried look on her face.

It later transpired that her Italian boyfriend had been the one behind a recent robbery that had occurred at a safe deposit centre in Knightsbridge and she was caught up in it. It had not yet come to trial and though she was out on bail she was extremely worried about her future.

Back at the house, a friend of the owner moved down from London and was staying in another of the rooms at the house. He, Like the owner was heavily into cycling and extremely weird diets. He was also into smoking hash and would sometimes source it. Gypsy had made his own contacts in the town now that more people in his part of the country were starting to smoke it, it was becoming easier to find.

The town was not one of the richest towns on the south coast and had more than it's fair share of scallies. In years gone by they had attacked the cops with petrol bombs. On another occasion some of the locals had noticed a police motorbike parked on a footbridge overlooking the harbour and as such had picked it up and thrown it in to the depths, just for something to do. There were no end of fights. On one occasion Gypsy was in one of the local tandoori take aways when a mob burst out of the doors of a nearby pub and proceeded to brawl over the front bonnet of his car. The local cops were being worked off their feet.

Then one of the local lads who had been away on holiday at her majesties pleasure, returned to town. He had learned about dope and got to like it while inside. On his return he started to introduce all of the local hoods that he hung out with to it. Soon after he became the biggest retail outlet for it in the area.

His front room was always packed with people skinning up and listening to everything from Pink Floyd to Kevin bloody Wilson. He even offered a phone delivery service to known customers. During all this time the cops left him alone and never once raided him, even though they must have known what was going on. He had been stopped on the way back from a local delivery on one occasion and the cops had said to him, "the thing that we don't like is people who sell drugs to children". "Good" said the man "neither do I, you do what you can to stop them and you'll be doing me a favour as I can pick up their adult customers when you bust them". "Just be careful lad, that's all" they told him. On another occasion he was sitting on a bench in the middle of the town late one night smoking a joint when two cops walked past on the other side of the road. The older of the two of them sent the younger one to go and wait for him further down the road while he wandered over and said good evening to the dealer before sitting down near him. He then turned to the dealer and said. "It's a strange thing, but in the last year crime has been down in this town, we haven't had to put in the same amount of overtime, we haven't had bottles smashed in our faces or been subjected to other violent crime and all the local hoods look much more mellowed out than before. Well done and keep up the good work lad". The dealer smiled to himself, it was a nice feeling to at last be appreciated for his contribution to society. He had come from an abusive home where his father had been exceedingly violent with him and then he had worked on travelling fun fairs and building sites. He had been locked up on several occasions for burglary among other things. His life had been rough but now he was married with children and made a good living from knocking out large quantities of dope in small amounts. OK it meant that he had a lot of different cars parked outside of his house day and night for seven days of any week but he had the local cops on his side on account of his one man crusade to pacify the town with Moroccan hashish.

Gypsy was around at his house quite regularly and sometimes was around there for hours at a time. Among the scallies, were some who were not so much into money as they were into having a laugh. Two or three of them had felt hungry when they had left the pub at chucking out time. They didn't have enough money with them to get a take away and instead of going home to raid the fridge, decided to break into the local supermarket, not to steel anything like money or alcohol or tobacco but just to have a munch. Inevitably their break in set the alarms off at the local cop shop and a patrol was sent out to investigate. When they got there they found three of the scruffiest residents of the town slouching around on the supermarket floor, in a drunken stupor with a whole array of different types of food from the cold cabinets on the floor in front of them as they tucked into a giant feast. One of them had a giant leg of ham in his hand and was attempting to eat it Henry the eighth style. Apparently it looked like the super market had an infestation of giant rats. These guys were not the cleanest or well presented of people, even by the low standards of this particular town. But funny? It was hilarious, these guys had nothing to lose. Life and society had thrown them on the scrap heap years before and they knew it. The worst that they could get busted for was breaking and entering as they had not taken anything off the premises or damaged anything apart from the food that they had eaten and there was no law against that. It would only be a waste of police time to bust them and it would be a highly unpleasant job to deal with them. Each of them seamed to have an allergy to water, their bodily hygiene was lacking in the extreme. Just bringing them in for questioning would foul up a squad car. So they were let go, the system and the society they lived in had fouled them up and treated them like untouchable rejects so now they had made themselves untouchable in other ways. As such, they could do almost as they liked as long as they knew the law and didn't push it too far.

Another thing about the dealer's house that Gypsy liked was that anyone who was new in town and was cool would turn up there at some point. Most of those who were around in the house had not been out of the town or the area since they had completed their last prison sentence. The new comers were more similar to Gypsy in that they had mostly been on the move before. There were two fellows from sunny Scunthorpe who had been laid off from their jobs when the steel works had been closed down and had come south looking for work. They were straight up and once that they had decided that Gypsy was straight up and did what he said he did they were friendly with him and found themselves trusting him more than anyone else in the area.

The year wore it's weary way on and soon the autumn was there. Gypsy went to the jewellers fair at Earls Court in London and made several new contacts and also sold some stones there. As time went by, he took a check of his business to see how well he was doing. When he did the books for that week he was shocked to find that he had only made twenty pounds with which to live on. He was running around for these jewellers and goldsmiths at high speed and doing his job well. But due to the habit of a few of them to mess him about and fuck him up, sometimes out of thoughtless selfishness and sometime out of malicious spite, he was struggling to make enough to feed himself. This could not carry on.

Gypsy once again decided to quit the business and go off and do something different. His yoga teacher had often spoken about this woman who was an incredible healer and had helped many people to find their way. Gypsy was not feeling so well after another year of slogging it and getting nowhere. So he asked his yoga teacher for directions to the healer's practise. The practise was in a garden shed in a herb garden in a small town somewhere close to the south side of London. He did not have an appointment but the woman agreed to see him anyway. She gave him some dietry advice but most of all she recommended that he go and work as a volunteer at a special yoga facility that taught the path to people who had incurable and terminal diseases.

The place was north from London up the A 1 (M), near the town of Letchworth. Gypsy phoned them to see if they needed any voluntary help and they told him that they were going to need some help in a few weeks time. So he needed something to do for the next few weeks. He had no money in his bank account and so asked his father if he had any work that he could do for the next few weeks as so as he did not arrive at the voluntary job with nothing in his pockets. The only thing that his father would offer him was pushing wheelbarrows of cement for the lowest rate of pay possible at one hundred and twenty pounds a week. It was slave labour for a slave's pay. He didn't want to take it it was a complete insult to him and both of his parents were grinning at him. They had him in a vice, where else was he going to be able to pick up a couple of weeks work at short notice? He was caught in a trap as he was going to desperately need the money, even if it was such a small amount.

So he agreed to go on the concrete laying team. He had moved out of the house in the town and moved up to the house of a local artist woman where other artists also lived and some of them worked. She took her rent in work from each of them, which suited Gypsy fine. The house was up in the hills in a small village and had originally been the local school house. It had since been converted by a very talented artist before he died, he had been the husband of the woman who owned the house. He had built two upper mezzanine floors and a bridge across the open area that entered a bedroom on the other side via the room's wardrobe. He had built very nice round seats, come beds from the cheapest of materials, including hardboard for the seat's base. His giant canvas paintings decorated the walls throughout the place. Gypsy liked them, they were simple but full of texture. He found them very relaxing to look at.

His sleeping space was one of the giant round seats, set up on the second mezzanine in the large hall. One of the residents was a skilled carpenter and was building a wooden spiral stair case to the first mezzanine as his rent for his room. In the back room there was a man and his girlfriend who worked making his own wild and crazy designs of ceramic tea pots. He had made the originals himself from his imagination and was now working to make a quantity of them by slip casting them in molds. The trouble with it was that it took eight hours or more before the casting could be taken out of the mold and he had not the money to buy the quantity of molds that he needed nor the space to store them while they dried. Then there was the question of further time needed to dry the castings and space to do it in and also the question of more kiln space.

He had an incredible product, but in England they expected to get it for nothing. It had to be sold at a "made in China" sort of price, they were in general, too ignorant and spoilt to understand how much work went into this incredible product. Also some greedy shop keepers had no doubt thumped him down through the floor on his prices too. He too, like Gypsy before, was struggling to make ends meet and working his arse off for the privilege as the shop keepers shafted him into the ground.

Also there was another artist who was having some success at selling his work in the local market. He had got several commissions from the owner of a local factory who liked his work and kept coming back to buy more. Also the ex husband of the woman who owned the house where he had lived before lived in the house and worked as a fine artist doing painting work for the antique trade. For company he had a large, over weight and bad tempered cat who would sit with him while he worked.

Several other people at the house including the owner attended the weekly yoga class, the house was a hidden centre of open minded activity of allsorts.

At his job, he was worked each day to exhaustion as he took turns on the mix in between turns at pushing the barrows. They were laying concrete paths through large commercial greenhouses to run trolleys along. The engineers were doing the tamping down while Gypsy and another worker had the job of making and delivering the mix.

There was a café in an old bus just up the road, so every lunch time Gypsy would go there and have a large fried plate of food. The work made him incredibly hungry

And each night he would be exhausted, having spent the day pushing wheelbarrows full of wet concrete along paths stretching up to seventy five metres long.

The two Wednesdays that he had yoga classes during the time that he was doing this job were two of the very best sessions that he ever had. During the relaxation part at the end, he went so deep in that he could swear that he heard bells ringing and music in another dimension.

The more senior of the two engineers went and told Gypsy "you worked really hard for the last two weeks, I'm going to go and have a word with your father, it's a disgrace what he is paying you, you're his son for fuck sake, it's not as if your some kid fresh out of school, you know the job".

For his troubles the engineer was able to get Gypsy's father to part with an extra fourty quid. Now he had one hundred and eighty pounds in his account to last him as fuel and pocket money. The voluntary job gave some twenty five pounds per week as pocket money along with food and accommodation, but he would inevitably need more than that on occasions when he had a weekend off and wanted to visit friends and family.

Next to the house of the artist and still within the area that had been the old school lived a woman who was also very switched on. Years before in the sixties or early seventies she had travelled overland to India on the hippie trail. She had been robbed at gun point when bandits climbed on board the bus that she was travelling on near to the Khyber Pass in Afghanistan and all of her money and valuables had been taken.

Still she carried on with nothing, across Pakistan to the Indian boarder and from there, still with nothing she travelled most of the way across the width of India to the state of Bihar where a friend of her's was living. Bihar was and still is one of the poorest and most backward of all the states in India. The place was and still is rife with poverty, corruption and banditry, not to mention also being a hot bed of Maoist uprising. Anyway the woman made it to her friend's place in Bihar and overland back to England without any cash. She asked Gypsy if he had a track suit to use for yoga. Gypsy told her that no he didn't have one, at which point she told him that he was going to need one as it would be far colder where he was going.

The next day when he had packed and gone out to load his car, he found an envelope on his windscreen. On opening it he found thirty pounds and a letter from the woman saying "buy yourself a track suit and good luck at the new job". Gypsy felt most humbled. This woman didn't have so much herself and she had two children to raise on her own. He finished loading his car and drove off towards the nursery where he dropped his car with the mechanic and got a lift to the local railway station.

The problem with the oil leak under the fuel pump turned out to be a symptom of the engine being totally shagged. The mechanic was going to see what he could do to fix some of the parts and keep it running while gypsy was away at his new job.

After crossing London Gypsy found his way onto a train that was going to a town close to where the place where the job was and spent the next hour and a half watching the flat, green countryside go by. A taxi ride got him from the station to the place, which was an old manor house complete with large courtyard. It looked like the sort of place that Agatha Christie would have used as the setting for one of her upper class murder plots.

Gypsy went inside and found the woman that he had spoken to on the phone and was then sorted out with a place to stay and told to be ready for work at eight thirty the following morning. After dropping his bags in his room he went downstairs and met some of the other staff. Some of them were like him, working as volunteers and others were full time paid staff. The volunteers were for the most part a friendly and constructive crowd who were both interested in yoga and also wanted to do some good for others. Gypsy sat and chatted with some of them and asked what the daily routine would generally entail. They gave him a run down on how things worked and Gypsy got to find out that they all were doing different types of yoga that came with different approaches.

Later that evening however, he was in the dinning hall to join the evening meal when he sat down at a table to eat where two slightly older women were sitting. He introduced himself and they in turn did the same. But then they turned to him in a manner that was not conducive with the attitude of people who were into yoga and works of compassion. Looking down their noses at him, they said, we run this place. Gypsy knew this not to be true as the place was run by it's founder, a man in his early sixties who had made journeys to India and was deeply into eastern philosophy and the practice of yoga. Though one of the women looked fit and healthy the other one didn't look like she had ever seen a yoga mat and wouldn't know what to do with one if it was right in front of her. The power trip that these two were on was so blatant and infantile as to be embarrassing to watch. Gypsy was new at the place and was trying not to make waves, so he let them have their little moment of perceived power and went on his way. But he did wonder why two bad characters like these were working in such a place. Gypsy was latter informed that the fat ugly one was the daughter of one of the yoga instructors and the other one was fucking the old man that ran the place. As such both of them were on full pay.

The next morning after first going to the hall and doing a session of the type of yoga that he had learned in Sussex, he went and found the person that he was going to be working with. They were essentially going to be working as care assistants, lifting disabled people out of bed and dressing them and taking them down to breakfast. Many of the people who came to stay at the facility had multiple sclerosis and other degenerative diseases and needed around the clock care. After getting the two that they had been assigned to ready they got them down to breakfast and then took a short break.

After the breakfast they next took the guests for their morning session of yoga and assisted them in getting into the start position for each posture. Some of them were so restricted that they had problems in moving a limb even an inch or two. The idea of getting them to do yoga was primarily to do with the breathing exercises. As when they breathed more consciously it helped them to focus something similar to will power into their muscles and what it was that controlled them, thus giving them some degree of mobility. Also of coarse there was the spiritual nature of it too but that was mostly only conscious in the minds of the volunteers. The two week trial period went by and though Gypsy had done his best to keep his head down one of the regular staff felt threatened by Gypsy's presence for what ever reason and decided to make trouble.

The trouble was that Gypsy having travelled had a different point of view to that of say a person of limited education who had not made an effort to go and find out what lay beyond the horizon of his town or village.

He knew that with human behaviour, no matter how disgusting that it may be there were no blacks or whites, only shades of grey. He felt disgusted when a large group of people all decided to vilify an individual or even a smaller group as he knew that if an individual or a group were screwing up and doing bad things then there was always an underlying cause. Rather than vilifying that person, it would be more constructive to put the culprit through a corrective therapy course for as long it took to cure them of the dysfunction that was deemed too offensive for the rest of society to be able to live with. Vilifying them and locking them in a cage for five or ten years was only going to make the problem worse when they were released. A group of volunteers had just been to see a movie about rape and returned that evening to the facility with angry expressions on their faces and angry attitudes towards anyone in the house who had a pair of balls between their legs. Gypsy was amused to watch how a movie with single dimension characters had managed to affect them so much. He questioned weather the movie had attempted to show all dimensions to what was happening. Gypsy had witnessed on many occasions both in Asia and the west when young women, just like the ones that were stood in front of him, had acted in a totally inappropriate way with men that they wanted to wind up. As far as Gypsy was concerned he would never even slightly push himself on a woman who had expressed that she was not interested, but all people are different and have different up bringings. If a woman didn't want to attract too much in the way of sexual advances then it would help her if she were to dress more like a human being and less like a sexual object. The outfits that most women chose to wear to work or were instructed to wear, would best be described as overtly sexual in a direction that could be described as sado masochistic bondage. The stiletto heels alone caused them to wiggle their arses in a more exaggerated way, causing aroused disturbance to any males present.

Though most people can control themselves, there obviously is a small minority that cannot. Vilifying and punishing them has been proven not to work, another approach is needed. Gypsy should never have credited such people with the intelligence to understand his argument on the subject. After all it was the eighties and the British were so ill educated that most of them could not even understand the news as it was explained to them on BBC or the other channels. When one of them tried to explain what they had read or watched, Gypsy would inevitably have to correct many of their misunderstandings. So by the time that the conversation had been repeated to half a dozen people, what Gypsy had said had been changed to something like "Gypsy condones rape|", which could not have been further from the truth.

The next thing that happened was some idiot who wanted to play mister good guy coming and threatening him, in a fit that he had worked himself up into, on account of a trouble making bitch who purposefully chose to miss understand his words. The retard who came and had a go was so fixed in his tiny mind that it took ten or fifteen minutes to get him to shut up and listen, as Gypsy explained what he had said previously. Even then the prat was still ranting and trying to threaten Gypsy. He was one of the ones at the place who did not seem to do much in the way of yoga and was one of the incestuous little group from the local village who worked full time at the place and felt threatened by the presence of the volunteers. He desperately needed to feel better about himself but the trouble was that he was doing it in a way that was used by losers and cowards. Finding someone else to vilify cannot bring true happiness.

The boss called Gypsy to his office at the end of the two week trial period and asked him what he thought and if he wanted to stay on and join the team. Gypsy said that he would as it was a chance to do some good in the world and that he would be happy to return after a weekend break.

Back in Sussex he got a pleasant surprise, Gypsy's father had given the mechanic the go ahead to re engine his car for him, so his car had a new block in it that would have to be run in slowly. Now he would have a relatively reliable set of wheels to get around in. At the end of the weekend he returned north to the yoga centre in his car, ready to start work. The boss was away for two or three weeks and an American woman that was a friend of his was running the place until he returned. The woman was in her late fifties or early sixties but had a very open mind in many ways and a vision of what she wished to achieve in the two to three weeks that she was going to be running the place for. She mentioned that it would be nice to have some healing plants such as Aloe Vera growing around the place. So when Gypsy went to Sussex that weekend he visited the nursery and asked his mother if she had any Aloe Vera that she could spare. As it was, it turned out that she was throwing over a hundred plants away as they were excess to her requirements. Gypsy took the plants and put them in a couple of trays and put them in the back of his car ready to take back with him.

It was strange when he got back, as some people at the centre had been trying to paint Gypsy up as a villain as so as to have someone to scapegoat, and now here he was making efforts to help the place outside of work time. It didn't fit the mold that they were trying to push him into. Gypsy could tell from the expression on the American woman's face that she was now a little confused. It would appear that some of the permanent staff had been making up stories to make trouble for him and the American woman was now not so sure about who she believed.

Gypsy had come to the place because he believed that he could do some good for the world by giving some free work to these people and his work did not finish at the end of his shift. So why were these people so intent on making trouble for him? He was not threatening any of their petty little positions or being nasty to any of them.

It truly is a strange thing about some people how when they get an idea stuck in their tiny little minds heaven and earth could not change them, even if there was proof beyond doubt to prove that they were wrong.

They were a strange bunch at this place, about that there could be no doubt. Gypsy found that he had to be very carefull what he said and how he said it amongst this hurd of sensitive souls. It would appear that some of them had had a sense of humour bypass performed on them. There would obviously be none of the prank playing that had been the staple of all the other places where he had worked with teams.

Soon Gypsy found that he had very little time to himself as he found that he was on night bell duty every night, in addition to his work throughout the day. It had curtailed his ability to have a good yoga session each morning as he had to wait in his small cramped room until eight in the morning with the bell, until it was time to start work.

When the bell was rung then he would have to go and find out which of the rooms that it had come from and then go and help the guest either to change their sleeping position or lift them onto the toilet and help them back to bed afterwards. It was not so bad if the person was smaller and still had some mobility left in them, but if it was a tall or heavy person that had rung the bell then he would have to be ultra conscious about how he went about lifting them.

He spent many of his evenings checking out the area within a radius of some thirty to forty miles. He wanted to get the new engine run in as soon as possible, he didn't want to be driving at forty miles an hour for ever. On evenings that the weather permitted he would have the sunroof open, all be it with the heater on full. There would be Either George Benson, Grover Washington jr or Jean Luc Ponty on on the stereo, as they were the tapes that he had in his car and he would be driving out towards Cambridge or Northampton or somewhere else in the area to go and check out the local pubs and the likes.

In the local village near to where he was working he had made friends with a young woman and her mother. They were both very real psychics, as they proved to Gypsy on several occasions. They gave him tarot readings where they got it one hundred percent right as far as predicting Gypsy's future went. Also the mother was a most acutely aware person who could see into almost any situation and understand what she was seeing. Both of them were exceptionally earthy, there was nothing that either of them was too embarrassed to talk about. As such they both had a great sense of humour. The daughter had worked at the centre as a healer and care assistant up until just before Gypsy had arrived there. As such she knew all about the strange politics of the place and briefed Gypsy as to what was going on there behind the scenes.

Back at the centre Gypsy had, after getting permission, put the Aloe Vera out on a window sill with a price notice and an honesty box, with all money going to the centre. Even then one of them found reason to complain about what Gypsy had done.

"It makes the window ledge more difficult to dust" the man complained. This particular old fart was a walking cliché of "I don't know, the youth of today!!" If someone under the age of forty was doing something, anything in fact, no matter what it was he would be standing there disapproving of it and slagging them off. He was a bit like a stuck record. In fact he was one of the more harmless of the po-faced brigade. One of the others, who didn't even work with Gypsy and indeed had very little if any contact with him through the working day, had put in a frivolous complaint against him. He was duly called into an office where a woman started to question him and accuse him of a myriad of slights against others that either were untrue or taken completely out of context. There was no doubt about it, a certain clique at the place had the knifes out for him. The woman even had the arrogance to accuse Gypsy of lying when in a private conversation he had talked about his travels. "I assure you that every word that I tell you or anyone else is one hundred percent true" said Gypsy. "Look, here are some of my old passports, check them out if you doubt what I say" the woman at this point tried to weazle her way out while still trying to keep a grip on the moral high ground that she had thought was her's when she had started this ridiculous fiasco.

Gypsy had not come to the centre to indulge in anything so ridiculously infantile as power games. He had come to give some good from his heart, so he bit his tongue and just carried on, but he was getting a might pissed off with the po-faced brigade and their petty self interests. It was strange that such people would work at a yoga centre, they were not vegetarian and would often return from the local carvery late in the evening dressed up smartly but red faced from drinking, the women in stilletos, nylons and dresses And the men in suits. There were two yoga instructors who also were resident at the centre and Gypsy found them to be much better company than the others. They shared some of the same ideas about life as Gypsy, with their interest in Asian mysticism and alternative life styles. But they also appeared to be a little stuck in the conditioning of the society that they lived in.

One of them was only really interested in the exercise part of the yoga and was too frightened of being called a crank if she started reading about, let alone started practising the philosophy of the east. For her, it had to be a frightened little world where stability was maintained by meat and two veg, "East Enders" and "Coronation Street" and reading the "Daily Mail".

The other of the two instructors was divorced, her children had grown up and she was free to do as she liked and was looking for her own inner peace, she cared far less about what others thought of her and was more at ease with herself.

Back in Sussex he had spent some time at the house of the yoga teacher when the healer came to give sessions to anyone who wanted to come along, which mostly was the people from the yoga class and their friends and families. The healer suggested that in order to bring some colour and clear vibration where he worked, it would be a good idea to get some cheap amethyst crystals and place them in the plant pots and other places around the old house.

Gypsy duly bought a bag full of crystals and did just that on his return, however he made sure that no one saw him doing it as one of them might find a reason to disapprove. He had mentioned to the healer about the strange behaviour that he had come across while working there. She had grinned ever so slightly and said "yes they are a right bunch aren't they?". So now he knew that it was not just his imagination and he did not have a victim complex either.

It turned out that the reason he had had his ears chewed the previous week was that the woman who instigated it had the hots for him and this was her strange way of trying to get Gypsy to notice her. The trouble was that he had noticed her but just didn't want to go there.. He found it totally ironic that someone who looked so very overweight and generally unfit would be getting paid to work in a yoga center. It didn't seem that her presence was a good advert for the benefits of doing yoga, but then she was the daughter of the senior instructor. When Gypsy failed to respond to her veiled advances she had a go at him about something to do with his work which Gypsy knew to be complete bullshit so he snapped at her "will you get the fuck off of my back you have been making trouble for me since I started here, for fucks sake what do you want from me I came here as a volunteer to help, not to be used as someone's punch bag". At this the woman pulled half an onion from her bag and ran into the building howling. Her tears would have put a crocodile's to shame for bogus. Once again he had to endure this wagging fingered old bat, who the crocodile had called upon, as she tried to tear a strip off of Gypsy. However he was having none of it, he was not here to play silly games and he told the woman "look I do my job and every night I have to man the night bell as none of you will help me by taking a turn, but I am not your punching bag as well, give me a break will you". The woman then huffed and puffed a bit but the alternative to having Gypsy working there as voluntary help was to hire professional nursing help from the local agency and that would no doubt cost an arm and a leg. After that incident The underhanded attacks stopped and Gypsy was able to get on with his job without watching over his shoulder so much. He exacted revenge on the one who had started it all by taking the piss out of some of his strange habits in such an observant and dry manner as to cause some people to burst out laughing when ever they saw him, including his own sister, he could say nothing as Gypsy had absolutely nailed him.

There was still however some things that he was still having problems with with the strange stuck attitude of some of the staff. To some of the older people in England even at the end of the nineteen eighties, it was almost viewed as a crime to be under the age of forty and to have an opinion.

Michael Gorbachov was in full swing, dismantling the Soviet Union and turning Russia into a free society at the time and he was making a state visit to China. Suddenly the news was about what was going on in Tienman Square in Beijing, with the students and activists who had gathered there. Gypsy was excited to see the Chinese People rising up against their oppressors, he had been in China and the thing that he wanted to see there the most was freedom coming to the people. The others did not understand why he cared about what went on for a bunch of Chinamen on the other side of the world. But he had been there and knew what a place of suffering it was and cared deeply about what happened for these people.

One day in the dinning hall Gypsy overheard the woman who was in charge of staff recruitment telling some of the others who had gathered for a meeting, that there was a young woman who was going to be coming to work there as a volunteer "she has problems" said the woman in a smug patronising tone. This quip annoyed Gypsy intensely as he had never met anyone on this planet that did not have problems of one kind or another and the person who had just made the statement was certainly no exception. The woman was going to be working with Gypsy so he thought that he would make his own mind up as to weather she was loopy or not when he met her.

Her name was Sally and she was a sweet and friendly, open minded person who very much had her own ideas about things. She was good company and she was certainly not crazy. She was living at the centre too and agreed to share the night bell with Gypsy. However, it was not long before they were having a relationship and sharing the same room so it didn't matter who was on the bell, in fact it ended up with both of them on it. She was nineteen years old and he was now twenty seven years old. Though with all the travelling that he had under his belt he felt far older. She was very psychic and could read someone as soon as she looked at them by the energy that was around them that she could see. She didn't like places that had too many people in them, indeed she did not like crowds at all unless they were spiritually focused. Her mother and her present step father at that time went to a spiritualist church and met in a group of mediums several times a week. Gypsy became interested about the spiritualist church as she told him about what she had seen happen in the one that she went to. Gypsy had noticed their churches in some towns but had presumed them just to be another twisted offshoot of Christianity. However he could not have been further from the truth.

Until very recently Christianity dominated the vast majority of religious and spiritual thinking in England and they would persecute in many ways, anyone who did not tow the line or adhered to a different faith, e.g. Jews. This group were right out on the frontiers and were engaged in something that some members of the Christian faith would have labelled as sorcery or the likes. The witchcraft laws in England have only been repealed since nineteen sixty two, indeed the last witch burnings in the British Isles happened as recently as the beginning of the nineteenth century. This group had been clever to hide themselves so well through the years.

Their building, from the outside looked like a particularly boring type of church, they even called themselves a church. Inside however, it was different. There were no windows in the walls, only in the roof, and the service did not involve any of the old tripe that masquerades as spirituality in so many churches, synagogues, temples and mosques. Instead there were prayers for the living and the dead to the one great god, then a medium would stand up and address people in the audience who she obviously did not know, and tell them that she had messages from dead family and friends. Though everyone who attended the place made a small cash donation to help cover building maintenance, there was no cash incentive involved here and people were gasping with surprise at what this woman was telling them, because short of her having a gift that allowed her to telepathically read the deep subconscious minds of those around her, the only other logical explanation would seem to be the one that she gave. It was that the spirits of the dead were using her to communicate with those that they cared about, to warn them about things that were to come and to let them know that life did not end with the body. The place obviously gave great comfort and help to many people, it is in itself a level of liberation to know that we continue after our bodies die. However it was something that puzzled Gypsy. He knew about reincarnation but was there a spirit dimension? or dimensions? where spirits hung out at while waiting to reincarnate or was that part of a being always available to contact, even when stuck in an incarnation but in a subconscious way? He wondered if we all are truly trans dimensional, but at present are unaware of it, as our eyes and other senses are focused out into this strange and intense dimension. "Maybe when we die it is like awakening from a dream and we find ourselves to be made of different dimensions of energy and light, without a heavy flesh prison to lug around and cause all sorts of problems. Without a material body to get in the way it may be possible to see with intense clarity, all that is in flow" thought Gypsy to himself.

Back in Sussex, his father was setting up a new garden centre and was going to need all the drivers that he could find, to deliver the stock to it in time for the opening.

Gypsy had saved up some days off by working through a couple of weekends and so returned to help for a week or so and to put a little bit of cash in his pocket as so as he could continue with his voluntary work.

He had the company's battered old Bedford TK truck to drive. It would be loaded at the supply nursery and driven the thirty miles or so to the new site where he the driver would have to take care of much of the off loading work.

Gypsy enjoyed the work as he was on his own for most off the day and did not have to interact with anyone, apart from the loaders and anyone who came to help him off load. Other than that he had his thoughts to himself, it was just what he needed after working with people all day at the yoga centre.

All too quickly it was over and he was back at the yoga centre working away. There were a couple of yoga weeks planned with visiting instructors from different schools of yoga and people who were not suffering from diseases or conditions also came to stay while they participated in the course. One of the teachers was really switched on and had his own style that he taught. He would tell some choice jokes during the session to make sure that people were not taking themselves or their yoga, too seriously. Also he would get them to sing and chant together but nothing religious just affirmations to help lift the energy of the group. Gypsy could not help but like this man and his wife, they had it right and were doing a wonderful job for those who's lives they touched.

Gypsy continued to spend all of every day and night with Sally as he was for the most part working with her. Then in the evenings they would go out together in Gypsy's car, as he was still running the new engine in. They slept in the same bed in the same room and even ate together.

It came as a relief when the boss asked Gypsy if he would like to become the publicity manager for the place. Gypsy jumped at the opportunity and set straight to work. There was a doctor from California who was going to be coming on the following week to do a week of talks and sessions of yoga and meditation. When Gypsy read this guy's portfolio he realized that they had someone quite special coming to stay and went to the local BBC radio station and showed them the doctor's portfolio and asked them if they would like Gypsy to arrange an interview with him. "Yes please" was their reply, they agreed that such a person would make for an interesting interview.

Back at base the Doctor was only too happy to have the platform from which to spread his ideas from and readily agreed to do the interview. He was a man in his eighties but he was tall and walked with his head held up. He was amazingly fit for a man of his age and seemed to have something of a glow about him. He was a surgeon and ran his own healing centre back in California where he also would perform surgery on people if there was no other way that he could find to heal them. But before he would perform any surgery on someone he would first have to be sure that that person was at least on the path towards changing their life radically, and adding a dimension to their understanding that previously had been missing. His centre also kept a bursary to help people who did not have the money to pay for their own treatment. The man was switched on in a way that was so rare to find in a westerner. He had, it would seem, internalised his yoga, he seemed to live it and breathe it.

Gypsy drove him to the interview and got to chat with him about how his centre operated and what his approach to healing was. The man saw life and death in the same way as Gypsy had learned to in India. His thinking could have come straight from the pages of the Vedas or the Bohd Dharma. There was no difference apart from the way that he chose to explain it, which was in a way designed to be understood by westerners.

The interview went like clockwork and the doctor blew everyones minds in the studio with his answers to the questions. What he had to say was totally logical but that did not mean that it was not radical and revolutionary to the established British views on medicine and therapy. After all we are talking about a group of people who for more than a thousand years worshipped an infinite god who only had one son who died because of the sins that they had not yet committed as they had not yet been born. Also that god loved them with all his heart and so gave them free will but if they did not do what his child molesting priests told them then they would be cast into hell for eternity with never a hope of redemption. Not just that but they thought that they would get ahead by going to church and simpering up to their all seeing imaginary friend.

To such people any true angle on logic or the truth would seem like a radical and revolutionary idea. Which may go some way towards explaining why the "sun" newspaper was the best selling daily in the UK.

After the interview they went out and got into Gypsy's car for the drive back to the centre. "How do you think it went?" the doctor asked. "You spoke my exact thoughts on the subject but better than I could even hope to" Gypsy replied. "You were a much needed breath of fresh air, let's hope that there were some people listening, who's lives will be changed by what they heard. In this country people take words like you spoke more seriously when they come from an older person, especially when that person is a doctor or a surgeon". The doctor smiled knowingly he knew what Gypsy meant and wanted to help to spread some more advanced ways of thinking, just as Gypsy did. In the course of his work Gypsy got to attend a few of the sessions that the doctor was giving. The man was incredible for someone who was eighty two years old. He had more energy than most people who were less than half his age and gave off an energy that made people feel at ease with themselves. Gypsy was sad when it was time for him to leave for his flight back to Los Angeles. The man was a living advert for the advantages of doing yoga and meditation daily. While he had been there Gypsy had the company of a kindred spirit. Someone else who could see how mankind could make a great and happy future without much effort, if they wanted to, and like Gypsy he wanted to help such thinking along in every way that he could.

Gypsy's promotion to publicity manager and the subsequent interview that he had fixed up had not gone unnoticed by the po-faced twat brigade. When he went and sat down in the dinning room to eat, they would turn around and steel quick but angry glances at him and then turn back to the little clique that they were sitting with and rant with wild eyed angry expressions on their faces while pointing their finger in Gypsy's direction. Now they felt really threatened, a volunteer had been appointed to a position that they all agreed that one of them, the full time, mostly non yogic team should have had. Gypsy had not asked for the job but he had grabbed it by both horns and was putting his all into it. He believed in the work that the place was doing, even if to him it still seemed to be a bit backwards. They could be using colour therapy by how they decorated the rooms. They could look at what sort of herbal hot drinks would help those who were suffering, instead of just giving them the usual fare of tea, coffee and hot chocolate. There could be a wheelchair path to a well tended jungle of a garden where the guests could breathe some freshly, organically recycled air. Diets could be adjusted and more consciousness put into providing healing foods and raw foods. As far as Gypsy could make out, the best way to heal someone would be to make them feel so good or at least hopeful, that they would want to live and introduce them to new ways of doing things that help in the process.

To acquire the full result would in essence require that the facility were custom built for the job and also the aesthetics including the shapes of the rooms and buildings would need to be taken into account in the healing process of the patients and guests.

Bushy but well tended gardens with access and flowing water would also be important in helping. Add to that, careful consideration towards diet on an individual level and then the yoga would have a good chance in playing a significant part in the healing of those who came to stay at the place. But the rest of it would need to be there if the place was to have much effect on the diseases that many of the guests were suffering from. Gypsy mentioned some of his thoughts to the boss and was told "you are right but even what I'm doing right here, now is deemed by many to be too radical. If we go any further right now then no one will come and stay here, they would be too scared". Gypsy kept forgetting that many of the British were still mentally, emotionally and spiritually stuck in the Victorian age and the word change was viewed as a swear word by many of them. The place has changed vastly from how it was then, thank goodness and become far more cosmopolitan in it's understanding of things. This was partly due to the influx of so many people from Asia and other parts of the world.

The eighties was a time when some of the more advanced professionals in the field were trying to bring the alternative approaches to healing out of the closet and get the medical profession to at least take an honest look and see if there were areas where the complimentary techniques could be used in tandem with allopathic medicines to achieve a better result for the patient. It was and still is a hard process, as there are many in the medical profession who are more than willing to taint the findings of experiments, to show favour for their ways of doing things over any others, if for no other reason but to appease their own egos. It goes both ways however as Gypsy knew. He had met his share of crazy, lost cranks who worked in the alternative practices, who would treat evidence in much the same sort of biased lopsided way, in order to try to prove their own theory to be right. It was a shame that so many people chose to behave as such, as it demeaned both approaches to medicine.

So the centre could not even use colour healing techniques without attracting the attention of the witch finder general, it was sad, truly sad.

Back in Sussex on one of his frequent visits, his yoga teacher introduced him to a group of Sai Baba devotees. They came across as a very genuine and well adjusted people. Many told of how they had not even heard of Sai Baba until he appeared before them and invited them to join him on his quest to help the world to find peace and harmony.

The only time that he had physically left India was when Idi Amin was taking it out on the Gujaratis who lived in Uganda. Apparently Sai Baba went there to talk him out of committing another human rights atrocity.

Gypsy became more and more interested in the work that this particular "Holy Man" was doing and read some of the transcripts of his speeches and other people's stories about how he came into their lives and how it brought good changes.

Back at work Gypsy was preparing for a show, where he was going to have a stand, exhibiting the yoga centre and the kind of work that it was doing and also the programs that they ran for relatively healthy people too. He had got hold of a slide projector and a camera and had gone and taken photos of the actual place and also of the activities that went on there. At the exhibition he was planning to have a running slide show on his stand as so when he had people stop and talk, then they would get a view of some of the more attractive parts of the centre. He did not need to produce brochures or flyers as the centre already had plenty ready to supply him with.

He and Sally continued to spend their evenings together, going out in the car to different places in the area. The engine was now run in and he could drive it a bit faster. Sally would talk a lot about her psychic experiences and Gypsy would listen with interest. She was the second person that he had met at this point who told him that he had had past lives in Egypt and Atlantis. The healer that had sent him to work at the centre had also spoken about such things too. Gypsy was quite intrigued by this, he could remember a life maybe one and a half to two centuries previously where he was a soldier in the war in the Crimea and another life where he had been a witch or something similar in a village in the

Himalayas, near to the border with Nepal. Also he could remember being in a pack of canines and looking out through the eyes of a coyote or wolf or something similar. But he had not yet managed to reach the memories of any lives that felt like they had happened thousand of years ago or at least not in such a way that they were fully conscious.

As a child he had always been very interested to learn all that he could about ancient Egypt and other lost kingdoms. However that could have been as a result of a trip to the British museum to see Tutankhamen's death mask when it was brought there as part of a world tour when he was a child or the interesting programs that had been shown on television about Egypt's ancient cultures or maybe even from reading the old testament as a child. But his interest in Atlantis had been sparked since he first heard about it as a child of ten or eleven years old. He had always been interested in history and felt, deep down inside that there was a very large part missing from the history that he had been taught about at school. If man had been around for one and a half to three million years then he must have been suffering from one hell of a case of iodine deficiency if it was only in the last ten thousand years that he had managed to crawl out of his cave and start exploring his environment and it's possibilities. It therefore would not seem illogical to hypothesise that at several times in the last million and a half years man has reached great heights. ....OK so where is the proof?

The greatest most destructive force that is known to man is time, especially If this is mixed with such things as large natural disasters, which happen at local levels with some regularity. Whether they be droughts, dust storms, earthquakes, tsunamis, storms, floods, volcanoes, land slides, subterranean fires, asteroid strikes, naturally occurring subterranean nuclear reaction etc etc, no part of the world is safe from all forms of destructive forces, nature's violence is evident everywhere. So even if something had been made from stone or steel a million years ago and it had not been buried in favourable conditions, the chances are that the forces of nature would have destroyed or transformed it long ago. As for societies that were around twelve to fifty thousand years ago, there was a growing awareness in certain quarters that the date lines given for the original construction of certain ancient structures, might be far older than originally thought.

Gypsy had read every book that he could about Atlantis and felt sure that it must have existed as a large sized civilisation, taking up a significant part of the earth.

There had been so much talk about the level of technological development that the Atlantians had achieved, that it would be hard to imagine that it could have been developed in a small place alone, such as the island of Santorini which some so called historians have suggested. At the time Gypsy was reading a book that placed Atlantis on a large now nonexistent island in the mid Atlantic Ocean, between the Azores, Canaries and Caribbean islands.

Gypsy did the show that he had been planning for. It went reasonably well and many people at the place seemed to be genuinely interested in the work and events that were happening at the centre. If nothing else it made people aware that the place existed and was open and available. It was shortly after this time that a woman called Barbara phoned him and asked if she could come and meet him. Gypsy agreed and they met up two days later when Barbara visited him at the centre. She was a woman in her late forties but appeared and behaved as if she was far younger. She was working for a company that produced gem elixirs. This was a new thing on the healing market and Gypsy was open minded as to weather it actually worked. He knew that homeopathic medicines worked, as he had direct experience of them working effectively on him on several occasions and the theory behind that type of medicine was far out there if anything was.

He was sure that colour healing was a vastly underrated and highly beneficial technique and wondered if the gem elixirs would work some how as colour healing. He wouldn't be able to get the elixirs onto the medicine menu at the centre as they were just too far out there at that time. Though the yoga teachers would sometimes use "Bach Flower Remedies" on people, that had been brought into the fold by the huge number of middle class, middle aged women who used them. However, other techniques such as gem elixirs and crystal healing were still as yet unknown and had not been through enough testing for anyone to be sure of their effectiveness. Despite this a friendship started between them. Gypsy liked her, she was a refreshingly open and intelligent woman to find in such a place as England. She like Gypsy could see through the bullshit, she mocked it with the greatest of panache and Gypsy felt like he was not alone when he was speaking with her. At the yoga centre he had to be so very very careful what he said and how he said it. With this woman it was like being with the women who travelled on the road in Asia, she had open eyes and could see what was going on around her. She was aware of many things and had made trips to parts of the Middle East on her own. She was sensitive enough to be phsychic and spoke about unseen spirits, energy vortexes, lay lines and other phenomena that moved things on other levels around us all, affecting peoples demeanour on subtle levels. About this Gypsy was in agreement with her as he too felt strange things in some places. Upstairs in the old manor house that the yoga centre occupied, on one occasion Gypsy was alone, delivering new bedding to one of the unoccupied rooms. He was returning to the store room when he walked through an open doorway with a wood and glass panel door hanging in it. As he went through, the door suddenly closed behind him. There was no one else in the upstairs of the place and no device on the door that could have made it do it. There were no open windows or draughts that could have done it either. Needless to say this had him unsettled enough to beat a hasty retreat to the downstairs of the house.

But apart from this Gypsy had been aware of energies in other places too. One such place was Jerusalem, which seemed to have an invisible wall around it, which trapped anyone who came and stayed there for any reasonable amount of time and stopped them from being able to leave when they wanted to go.

Then there was India were in places the energy was of such a spiritual nature that it more than made up for the physical degradation of the place. Closer to home was Glastonbury where the energy seemed to change from time to time throughout the year and this by no means was connected to the weather. Sometimes the place would be full of people with glowing faces and the hippie dream was looking like it was in full swing. Then at other times those very same faces would all be long and sad and all good options had left the table. Though some of this could be accounted for by the lifestyles of the residents of the place, the fact that it would happen on such an unconscious group scale pointed to the advent of other unseen phenomena.

Both gypsy and Barbara were too busy to spend too long talking on that particular day but arranged to meet at another time on another day.

Two young students came to work at the centre as volunteers for two weeks and they were put to work helping Sally on the care assistance work. Gypsy meanwhile was trying to think of new ways of publicising the work and courses of the centre. He decided that the best thing that he could do was to take large quantities of leaflets and flyers from the office and tour the other healing centres and clinics and also the health food shops and new age shops and see if he could put up flyers on their notice boards and in their windows. He spent the following week touring every small town between the centre and Northampton, finding places where he could either put up advertising on a board or leave flyers for people to take with them. He used his own car for the job and cracked on with the job with the energy of a good salesman.

Then came the eve of the Summer Solstice and with it Gypsy had the overwhelming urge to go and find a special place to go and enjoy watching the sunrise. A hill top or a ring of stones, a waterfall, a cliff top, just somewhere were he could feel free. He felt trapped and confined at the centre because he was expected to humour so many fools, not only through the day but all the time he was there, which was on average, for twenty one hours a day. He had expected to meet mostly open minded, kind and intelligent people when he had originally come to work at the centre on account of what the place professed to be engaged in, but it had not been like that from day one onwards. He had found himself constantly walking on eggshells wondering what was allowed to be said and by whom. The place as far as Gypsy was concerned would have a far greater success ratio with healing it's clients if the approach that was taken would be more progressive in what was brought in as healing techniques and also if the psychology of the patients was taken into account to a far greater degree. As far as any of the care staff could see, one of the most common things that all patients shared was a chronic fear of change. Also their speech was often a string of clichés strung together with a few conjunctions and adjectives. These were people who were trying desperately to be average, not daring to step out and be seen standing on their own as an individual. It would appear that some of them spent a large part of their waking hours in pursuit of sanctuary from their fears and insecurities, rather than facing them.

As Sally had been working with the students all day, she brought them along to meet Gypsy after work. Gypsy told Sally about his urge to find a good place to go for the sunrise on solstice morning. Maybe it was the call of the wild as it were

Or maybe he was turning into a werehippie that transformed only on the eve of the solstices and equinoxes, suddenly growing long hair and beads.... And getting urges to do such things as going and living in a tepee in a field and claiming the dole.

Naa, it wasn't that, he was just getting claustrophobic and needed a night away from all the bullshit. He suggested to Sally that they drive to Stonehenge for sunrise and if there was no way of getting in due to police cordon then they could drive to Avebury, which was not so far from Stonehenge.

Sally was up for it and asked Gypsy if it would be OK to take the two students as well. Gypsy agreed and so with minimum fuss, they all jumped into his car and drove off towards Hampshire and Wiltshire. The roads were relatively clear and they reached Salisbury in less than two and a half hours. They were soon at Amesbury which was less than two miles from Stonehenge. However, there was a cordon of cops around the place, blocking all access routes. They could not even get within view of the stones. The cordon started at the edge of the village of Amesbury. The funny thing though, was how the cops treated them. They were in a BMW and not a clapped out old bus or some other hippie looking clapped out antique on wheels. Instead of "get out of here before we arrest you you fucking hippie" it was "we're very sorry sir but this road has been closed and no one is allowed within the vicinity of the stones. If you need any assistance to find directions to a detour route we can help you". It was certainly very different to how he had been treated when he had dealings with the cops when he had the viva van.

It was still dark and there was time to make it up the road to Avebury before the sunrise. So Gypsy turned the car around and headed up the road towards the other stone circle. They got there some time before sunrise and after visiting the stone circle headed over to nearby Silbury hill, which is the largest man made prehistoric earthworks in England. They climbed to the top and waited for the sunrise. They were not alone, there were many others who had come to Avebury rather than wasting their energy confronting the cops at Stonehenge.

There were people on top of the hill and also people down in the stone circle that surrounded the village. But here, as opposed to what was going on at Stonehenge the vibe was both peaceful and friendly and there were no king Arthurs or Merlins or other assorted losers trying to prove that they were something. There were no Brew Crew or other troubled types seeking to spread their misery as if it were some sort of gospel. There were just people like Gypsy and Sally who wanted to watch the sunrise on solstice morning from a sacred place. The sun came up and they hung around for a while before heading off back to Bedfordshire. It had been cloudy so they had all had to rely on their watches to know when the sun actually touched over the horizon.

The others had to start work at nine in the morning and so Gypsy instructed them to catch some sleep while he drove them back. He was, by the time they reached the M25 so tired that he had to concentrate just to keep himself awake while he drove.

When they finally got back at seven in the morning, Gypsy went straight to bed and fell asleep. He was working on the publicity job, if he got started a bit late that day then no one would know and he could make up the time by doing some extra work in the evening. He had been planning to and given notice to the centre that he would be cutting his time at the centre to three days a week to work for them as a volunteer as he needed to get back to making some money for himself, otherwise he would be trapped and not be able to go travelling again. He wanted to go back to India and visit Sai Baba's ashram at the village of Putta Patti in the south of the country.

Suddenly there was a loud knock on his door. He woke up and got up and answered it and was told that the boss wanted to see him immediately.

When he got down to the office he was told that the others had been too tired to work on account of their trip to Avebury and it was all his fault. He was even told that he shouldn't have taken them near to Stonehenge as there could have been trouble there. If there had been trouble Gypsy would have avoided it and anyway there wasn't and besides who was this pompous old man who he worked for as a volunteer to think that he owned Gypsy's soul.

In the last five months he had been on the night bell permanently for over two months because the other staff and volunteers had refused to do it. He had been patronised and spoken down to, he had been both verbally abused to his face and backstabbed and connived against and generally used as everyone but Sally's emotional punch bag. The boss then told him that he would not be welcome in the place anymore and to pack his bags and go. Gypsy then went and told Sally what had happened, then headed back to his room and packed. He was not in the best of moods and made sure that he left the room in as bigger mess as he could. Then he went to say good bye to Sally, they exchanged phone numbers and Gypsy promised to come back to see her.

It was kind of ironic that by sacking him the boss had actually done him a favour. Though he had tried hard to fit in and get along with all those that he worked with, it had been a futile effort, some people were determined to be miserable pieces of shit, no matter what anyone else did. It was part of being British as far as they were concerned and they could damned near make a religion out of it. They had never accepted Gypsy in the place and had a hard on against him as soon as they saw him, maybe they were jealous, but of what?

Gypsy drove back to Sussex and went and stayed at the house of the lady, up in the hills with the artists. She offered him a short time job to work for her and redecorate parts of her huge old house. So for two weeks Gypsy swung a paint brush and spent his evenings visiting friends or chatting with the assorted misfits and creatives that lived at the house.

Then one day while visiting a friend who owned a bookshop and was secretly interested in Indian spiritual paths and knew more about the subject than Gypsy, his friend asked if he had a connection anywhere where he could get hold of Tibetan Thanka paintings. As it happened he did, He had a contact in London who also travelled to India regularly and also was into such things. The painting job was drawing to a close and he had nothing else in front of him in the way of work, so he made a trip up to London to go and see if his contact had the sort of works that his friend had asked for. He did, he had a reasonably large selection of them too.

Gypsy asked for and was given the paintings on a sale or return basis but while he was at the House of his contact he saw an amethyst crystal carved into the shape of the Elephant headed deity, Ganesh and some silver rings that he also thought that he stood a good chance of selling. So he took these on sale or return too.

the next day when he saw his friend he not only took all of the paintings but also took the amethyst Ganesh too. His friend was delighted and bought everything including the Ganesh carving. Then he took the rings to a jeweller in a nearby town to show them to him. To his delight the man took all but two of them.

Now he had a little bit of money in his pocket but he still did not know what he was going to do in the way of work or for making money for his next trip. He need not have worried, before he had even had the chance to go to London to pay his contact, he got a phone call from the jeweller, asking if Gypsy could lay his hands on any more of that type of jewellery. So the next day Gypsy was on the train to London to pay for his last load and ask for some new stock to run. His contact was more than happy to front him, he knew Gypsy well enough that he could trust him not to pull any tricks. So this time Gypsy took a serious quantity as so as he could run wholesale for a week to ten days without needing to top up.

Since leaving the centre he had stayed in touch with Sally by phoning on a daily basis. Since they had thrown him out, they had turned on Sally and had taken to using her as their scape goat and emotional punch bag. Though Gypsy knew that she had done nothing to warrant it they had tried all sorts of tricks and power trips on her, even trying to restrict her movements as if she was a child. Over the space of a week they had made her progressively more depressed, until Gypsy suggested that she come and live with him in Sussex. She readily agreed, so they arranged that Gypsy would come and collect her with the car but also they set it up in such a way that they could give the miserable management of the place a good slap in the face in order to teach them a lesson.

Gypsy drove up to Bedfordshire the next day and went by to the home of a woman that he had befriended who had worked at the centre previously. As they had such a hard on against both Gypsy and Sally, the woman phoned the centre for him and asked for Sally, just to make sure the call got through. When Sally was on the line she handed the phone over to Gypsy. "I'm here" he said "grab your bag and walk out to the road I'll see you there in five minutes". He then thanked the woman and her husband and drove off to the centre. He did not wish to even set foot inside of the place, which was why he had insisted that Sally walk out down the long drive with her bag. He did not want to give them the satisfaction of having anyone else but themselves to blame for Sally's sudden departure.

As he reached the front gate, which was nicely out of sight of the centre, Sally was just reaching the end of the drive. Perfect timing! It meant that there was less chance of anyone seeing him there, if they could make a quick departure. Sally put her case on the back seat and they drove off. "You should have seen their faces" Sally said with a mischievous grin on her face "one minute I was working and then the next I just turned around and said 'that's it I'm leaving, goodbye' their jaws just dropped and they just stared, not knowing what was happening. It was priceless just to see, revenge is sweet, they'll have to get help from the agency and that will cost them considerably. They are understaffed as it is, now they are really screwed. Without outside help the place will grind to a stop".

Back in Sussex Gypsy was staying at the house of his parents, so he had to find a place for Sally to stay, on a long term basis. He had some German friends living in the nearby town and so he asked them if they knew anywhere that she could find a place. They were a couple with children and like Gypsy they had also travelled on the road. The woman took an instant liking to Sally and offered to let Sally stay at their house in return for helping out with their children, also they helped to find her a job as a care assistant for old people. This arrangement worked out well as Gypsy was starting to spend more and more time out on the road, selling the jewellery.

A short while later Barbara, the woman who sold the gem elixirs got in touch. They got on so well that they agreed to try making joint business trips to places for selling purposes. Though she was older than him by more than a decade she turned him on. It wasn't what she looked like, though she certainly was not ugly by any standards, it was her mind and her demeanour. When Gypsy was with her he did not feel like a space alien, she saw things in a similar way to him. She was open to all ideas but like Gypsy she knew bullshit when she encountered it. She was a free spirit in her thinking and actions and carried herself with dignity, elegance and panache.

Gypsy did not want to cheat on Sally, she was such a very good person and he loved her from his heart but the truth was that he felt like he was with a child when he was with her. She was very intelligent and in some ways very mature and responsible for her age, but after all she was only nineteen years old and Gypsy had to teach her about almost everything. It was very tiring and also he felt lonely with no one who he could talk with that understood where he was coming from. Sally knew all about certain aspects of mysticism but as far as understanding what was going on around her, or being able to understand and decipher the news, she didn't have a clue. Gypsy had to teach her everything, it was too big a responsibility. It made him feel like a cradle snatcher.

The jewellery was starting to sell really well and everyone who saw it commented on how very attractive it was. His contact in London was bringing it in from both India and Bali. Both types were selling well but it was the Balinese work that gave his collection the edge. He seemed to move it faster and in more different types of shop than the Indian stock. He was making twenty percent on the silver and anything up to two hundred percent on the few loose stones that his supplier could put with him.

He was able to make a lot of money from this as the stock was selling so fast. Once every ten days, he would drive to London and hand over what he owed, return any stock that had not sold and choose an entirely new load. His supplier was very happy with how well Gypsy was doing and as such was getting ready to do a new run to both India and Bali, to pick up more stock.

Barbara came to join him for his sales trip, she had her own stock of samples with which to get orders from. Sally said that she was not worried about Gypsy working with her as she was so much older than him. When Barbara heard from another source what Sally had said, she waited until she was alone with Gypsy and said with some indignation "huh I'm not old I've a good mind to prove her wrong about not having anything to worry about". "Well if you want to I'll let you" Gypsy replied with a grin on his face. She may have been a fair bit older than him but she turned him on like no other woman that he had spent time with. She was married to a man who worked as a broker in the city and they had two teenaged children and lived a very middle class life.

She was so very very bored with both her husband and the type of life they lived. She knew that there had to be more to life than the media fed mundainity of thought that seemed to dominate the British middle class dream.

She had become very interested in mysticism of all kinds and like Gypsy she could consciously remember some things from previous lives, she was also better than most at bringing all these things down to earth and making some sort of realistic sense of it all. All too often people who claim to be interested in understanding such things are too subjective and try and mould everything into what they with their limited understanding, wish it to be and would never let anything as trivial as facts get in their way. Most of the new age crowd seemed lost and spent ninety nine percent of their time off with the fairies. It was rare to meet such a person who was into the esoteric, who was also very real. Barbara was such a person. The more he got to know her the harder he found it to understand how such a person could have stood to live so long trapped within the confines and bullshit of the British middle class cage. It would have suited her far better to have been a hippie or adventurer on the road like the solo traveling women that Gypsy had met in such places as India, Nepal and Japan. To her, being with Gypsy was like an escape to a place were she belonged, unlike her husband he did not put her down for her ideas and would not only listen but also sometimes add some thoughts of his own on the subject.

They set off in Gypsy's car and headed to Stratford on Avon for their first round of the shops. They got there a bit late in the day, never the less Gypsy was able to get his foot through the door of a couple of shops and got a rather good sale of several hundred pounds in one of them. This would more than cover the fuel to get there and their guest house bill for the night. .

The next day after breakfast they went out and hunted the shopping areas of the town, looking for potential customers before giving up on the place and heading on up the M40 to Birmingham where Gypsy had a few customers for his stones in Hockley.

They spent the night in a guest house on the Hagley road in Edgbaston before heading out to Hockley in the morning. He got a few sales but it was not the best place to sell the ready made jewellery. So in the late morning they drove out to the M5 and drove south. At Barbara's instigation they headed off the motorway and into the Cotswold hills to several villages where there were some craft workshops where she thought there might be some jewellers. But though the villages were very picturesque and there were plenty of tourists, there was no one selling jewellery or making it. So they headed on down to Bath and Bristol to try their luck there. Gypsy got to make a couple of sales in Clifton and Barbara got to show her goods to several potential customers, but Bath was a bit of a waste of time for both of them. They stopped the night in a guest house on the outskirts of Bath before heading off the next morning towards Wells and Glastonbury. They both produced a result from Wells that morning before heading off towards Glastonbury at lunch time. Both of them had sold in Glastonbury before and so when they got there they both headed off in different directions to see how much business they could catch. If Barbara could not sell her gem elixirs in Glastonbury, home of the yogurt weaving space case, then there was nowhere on earth were they would sell.

After a look at a couple of shops that seemed to have potential, Gypsy found himself in a large hall like cavern of a shop that was full of weird and wonderfull things, including jewellery. He wondered whether he was trying to go too big in approaching the proprietors of such a huge shop. After all ninety percent of his sales came from small businesses, with no more than two people working in them.

He need not have worried, the shop was in the hands of a hippie artist called Peter, known in town as "Peter the painter". He was dealing with another person who was selling him raw gem crystals, when Gypsy found him. Gypsy listened as the sale proceeded, the man knew a lot about stones and liked them and could see them for their beauty more than for their value, though he appeared to know about that part too. He knew far more about gems than almost all of the other people that he had met in the British jewellery trade. The attitude in the shop was one of total positivity and there was none of the pinch faced meanness or snobbishness that so often permeated the trade in objects of beauty. Gypsy felt totally at home and relaxed in the shop as he waited for his turn to show his goods. He was going to enjoy this sale, this was only the second or third time that he had met someone outside of Jaipur or Kathmandu who had such knowledge about stones and who didn't have a cucumber up their arse about it.

The sale got off to a flying start as Peter was looking at each piece that Gypsy pulled out from his bag in wonder and also he liked Gypsy's reasonable prices for things. The only problem was what to choose? He would have liked the lot if he could have afforded it. As the sale progressed Gypsy noticing the bright colours, looked up. There around the walls were some of the most incredible airbrush paintings that he had ever seen, all with totally psychedelic colours. He had always enjoyed the works of Rodney Mathews and Roger Dean who had done the paintings for many a rock band's album cover. This was very similar but instead of space themes it was themed on ancient British mysticism.

There were paintings of Stonehenge, Glastonbury Tor, witches, wizards, unicorns and themes from the tales of King Arthur. "Who did these incredible paintings?" Gypsy asked. "I did" Peter replied "wow they are good, I like them and the themes" Gypsy said.

By the time that they had finished, Peter had spent nearly a thousand pounds on new jewellery and gemstone stock for his shop. He obviously knew the prices in the trade well and he could see that Gypsy knew his job well enough that he could trust him. Most of all, he was happy with both the variety of goods and the consistently low prices. Gypsy had never seen anyone who enjoyed looking at gemstones so much in his life, he had been an absolute pleasure to do business with. As they got chatting after the sale, it turned out that he had also been the lead guitarist in several of England's most respected underground rock bands of the nineteen seventies. However there had been none of the ego tripping arrogance that was so common in people who had done such things. All in all he was one of the most decent and straight up people that Gypsy had ever met. As such a friendship started that lasts to this day. At last he had a good customer who he could sit down and smoke a joint with and either chat about music or jam with who was also into the mysticism and all. It was nice to see another hippie doing well for himself.

It seemed that most of the hippie fraternity in England at that time were a bunch of dole bludging wasters who seemed to have turned procrastination into a profession. This was what made Gypsy so very lonely when he was in England. The German and the Swiss hippie crowd were for the most part, pursuing a direction where they could actively bring the positive changes to the world that they believed in. But in England something had gone wrong and this was not happening. That said, Pete was like a breath of fresh air, He was the first hippie that Gypsy had met in England that was going places on the back of his own hard work. There were plenty who had been hippies but had given it up in order to become yuppies and pursue the rat race. But there were very few who lived by the ideals and were successful in being able to make a living from their own creativity.

Gypsy and Barbara spent the night in a guest house in Glastonbury and then left the next day for the drive back to Sussex. Barbara was happy for him that he had made such a good sale and made a new friend at the same time.

She had attracted some interest from a couple of shops and was hopeful of getting an order from at least one of them in the not too distant future and was happy with that.

Back in Sussex Barbara collected her car and headed off Back to Bedfordshire, she had to get home, otherwise her husband would wonder what was going on.

Gypsy spent the next ten days selling in the local area and also he made a trip to his supplier, who when he arrived, was having the biggest television on the market and a satellite T.V. system delivered and installed. "You see that setup there?" his supplier said "well you bought me that with all those sales that you've been making". "That's good" said Gypsy "I'm glad that you are happy with how fast I've been moving. I've not done badly myself. If I can continue like this for another few weeks I might be able to make enough for another trip to India" His supplier had just got back from a lightening fast trip to Bali and had an entirely new stock of silver. It was some of the very best silverwork that Gypsy had ever seen and he had every confidence that he would be able to move it. It was beautiful and also cheap for what it was. The detail was so fine and the finish was high quality, unlike the rough work that the Indians made.

So with a large fresh new stock in his bag, Gypsy headed on back out of London.

He had not been spending enough time with Sally so he went around to see her at the German house. She was totally at home where she was staying and really got on well with the German family, they had been kind to her and made her feel like she was one of the family. Also she had a job that she enjoyed, where she was allowed to get on with her work without someone taking it out on her. She liked the old people that she looked after and no doubt they liked her too. It showed in her face and also in the enthusiastic way she talked about the work and the people that she worked with. Gypsy felt a bit guilty for cheating on her but what could he do, she was in many ways a child but with very prim ideas about things. It was not that she was wrong for being like that, but Gypsy sometimes needed some time out from it. Barbara allowed him to be himself and liked him for who he was instead of what she thought she might be able to turn him into. In many ways Barbara was more youthlike than Sally but in all the right ways. Barbara enjoyed her sexuality and accepted herself for it but Sally was uptight to quite a degree in that respect. Gypsy had to teach her everything and that made him feel weird. She was just too young for him.

It was not long before Barbara called him and asked him when they could make their next trip together, she was missing him. So the next week he drove up to collect her from her house. She insisted that he stay for the night at her place, an idea that he was more than a little unhappy with, he did not want to end up getting shot by her jealous husband if by chance he found out what was going on. However she made a good cover story for him and told her husband that she was just working with Gypsy because he worked in a similar field of activity to herself. He bought the story and everything was cool.

Gypsy awoke early the next morning to hear a blazing row going on between the two of them. Then there was the sound of the door slamming violently, followed by the sound of his car starting and driving away. Even before his car had passed in front of the house she had opened the door to the room that he was staying in and launched herself on him. She looked beautiful in her colourful Indian dress but her face looked so sad as she hugged him. It was not as if she did not love her husband but for sometime now he had bored the shit out of her with his total lack of interest in exploring anything new. Not just that but he had slagged her off for being interested in the mysteries of the world. He was a typical British middle class ex grammar school boy type, almost to the point of being a parody of himself.

He drove a BMW seven series and no doubt had beer and barbecue sessions on the patio in his back garden with other suitably boring types and talked about current affairs, cricket and where they had their holiday last year, but not much else.

Barbara had told Gypsy that the only reason that she had not left him yet was because she really did not wish to hurt him by just walking out and instead was trying to edge out of the door slowly. When he started to have an affair with a woman at work she was happy and hoped that he would grow attached to this woman and then she could leave without causing him pain.

Though he was more than happy to be in bed with her he felt decidedly uncomfortable about it being in a bed that was located in the house that she shared with her husband. He did not want to find himself hiding in a wardrobe or naked out on a window ledge. So after the heat and passion had cooled down a bit they headed out on the road on their sales trip. They headed through much the same route that they had on the previous occasion, as that was the area where the most lucrative of sales were to be had. They enjoyed each other's company and felt so attuned with each other that they did not need to speak in order to know what the other was thinking, as if they had known each other for a lifetime or more. Barbara said that this was because they had known each other and been lovers in a previous life, which she said had been in Spain.

There was no doubt about it they were uncannily familiar with each other for two people who had only met for the first time in this life a few weeks previously.

The summer carried on and the only thing he had to worry about was Sally finding out about Barbara and what was happening on their sales trips together.

His presentation was the only thing that lacked as he went from shop to shop through the day. He had beautiful things for sale but he carried it all in supermarket carrier bags.

this had two distinct advantages as far as Gypsy was concerned, the first being security, he was carrying many thousands of pounds worth of someone else's stock and he could not afford to get rolled or loose any of it. People don't expect other people to carry items of high value in crumpled old supermarket carrier bags. Thus Gypsy could pass under the radar of anyone looking to do an opertunist mugging. The second advantage was the element of pleasant surprise when he pulled his huge stash of high quality items from the old bags, the contrast factor really played it's part in this. Also the shop owner would figure that if Gypsy wasn't using fancy displays, then the price would be more in their favour and so they would be more than interested to check out his full load.

While Gypsy went off visiting his clients Barbara would go off looking for herbalist shops and the likes. In the late afternoon they would meet up and discuss their day and go out for a drink and then dinner. They enjoyed the same music and so would choose places that would play it to relax in through the evenings. Jazz funk was what they both enjoyed and Gypsy had a good collection on tape cassettes in the car, including extensive collections of albums by Grover Washington Jr, George Benson, Stanley Clarke, Earl Klugh and Jean Luc Ponty. Of coarse he still enjoyed his rock but he had been introduced to jazz funk in the last few years by friends and people that he had met while travelling. Another band that he had taken a strong liking to was Clannad, he liked folk music too when it was rocked and techno'd with. He was a fan of Bert Janch, Steeleye Span, Alen Stivell and Fairport Convention to name but a few.

Speaking of Gypsy's favourite music Wishbone Ash were coming to play a gig locally, so he persuaded Sally and their German friends to join him in going to the gig.

The band was back to their original line up of the early seventies and they played brilliantly. There was very little in the way of special effects apart from the coloured lights and a mirror ball that was used for one track. It was all about the music. Instead of having a rhythm guitarist they had two lead guitars and this helped in making their brand of rock somewhat unique. Their take on rock was somehow off on it's own, with reliably good riffs on each track. The gig hall was not that big and still the place was not one hundred percent full. The band were not so well known to the public and relied on a core group of fans who would turn up for the gigs and buy the merchandise. It would be fair to assume that many of their fans were musicians themselves and as such enjoyed the originality of the riffs and lead licks, they definitely could be described as a guitarist's band. Gypsy was having the time of his life but when he turned around to see how Sally was enjoying it, he saw her standing there stiff and looking frightened. She had never been to a rock concert before and the loud music, flashing lights and large crowd had her terrified. Gypsy felt sad that she could not enjoy the gig like everyone else who was there. He felt a bit like he had just taken a nun to an orgy, it was most different to going out with Barbara who would have been up there rocking and dancing like the rest of the crowd. He loved and cared about Sally and would never do anything to deliberately hurt her and would not have brought her along if he had realized before that it would induce this sort of reaction from her.

However it was starting to become apparent to him and possibly Sally as well, that maybe they were not right for each other. They had very different tastes and he could not now imagine that Sally would enjoy travelling in the same way as he did. Indeed, she would be terrified from the very first day.

Gypsy was starting to build up his capital and now had two thousand pounds put aside for his next trip. If he could find two or three customers who wanted Indian goods and would front the money, then he would be there for a business trip to Jaipur.

He spoke to all of his main customers to see if they were interested and was pleased to get two reasonably decent sized orders. His friend who owned the bookshop and had started his run of good fortune, by ordering the thanka paintings also was interested to make an order for more of the paintings. Now Gypsy had enough orders to go on his trip. He wasn't just going to make it a business trip. He would have enough spare cash to fly from Delhi down to Bangalore and make a visit to Sai Baba's ashram, to see for himself what was going on there and see if there was something there to learn.

His relationship with Barbara was starting to attract some unwanted attention, both from Gypsy's mother who had noticed and from the German woman. Gypsy wondered how long it would be before Sally found out. And at Barbara's house when Gypsy was visiting, her son came home from university and took one look at Gypsy, then turned to Barbara and said "what's this? Got a new toy boy mum?"

It was definitely time to hit the road back to India, he wanted to be a long way away when either Sally or Barbara's husband found out about what was going on and he sensed that it would not be long before the cat was out of the bag at one end or the other. Gypsy had continued with his yoga classes and Sally had joined him at them. One of his customers was also a Sai Baba devotee and joined Gypsy on one occasion at the yoga class. He was not the sort of person that anyone could imagine to be spiritually turned on to such things. He had worked among the barrow boys, fences and scam artists of the Brighton back lanes. These were not the sort of people that seemed to gravitate towards spiritual activity. However, this man had an incurable disease and an extended family that ran him ragged trying to keep them out of trouble with the law.

His family was one of the rougher families on a particularly rough council estate and he had done well to pull himself up and out from it. He drove a big, new Mercedes

And no doubt lived in a nice house. But his nephews and brothers back on the estate were always getting into trouble and he invariably would get the job of bailing them out. He had already been to Sai Baba's ashram and wore a gold ring that he said Sai Baba had materialised in front of him and then given to him. It appeared to be made of gold and had a picture of Sai Baba on a ceramic cabochon in the setting.

His connection with Sai Baba had been a totally life changing experience for him and had given him something important to live for. Unlike many of the other people in his trade his eyes were clear and he was of a good heart. He also made an order with Gypsy and fronted him the cash for the goods.

Gypsy bought himself a ticket on British Airways to Delhi and four days later he was boarding his flight at Heathrow. He had done it!, he had made enough to go and buy a new stock and try his luck again. He had been stuck in England for two and a half years, it was an experience that he wanted to make sure never ever happened again. Yes there were nice people too on that miserable rain soaked island but there were so many that seemed to want to give some one else a bad day in order to get their jollies. The place was full of uptight people who totally resented anyone having a good time and it was still rife with class divides that made the Indian caste system pale in comparison.

He had been so content with his life in the last few weeks that he had almost managed to quit smoking. As such he asked for a non smoking seat on the flight. Part of the non-smoking section in economy was placed on the upper deck of the jumbo and Gypsy found that his seat was up there. It was nice, there was one steward for twenty eight people in this area, making for really fast sevice and Gypsy found that he was sitting next to a middle aged Indian couple who were going to India to stay at the ashram of their guru for a few weeks.

Sometime after eight in the evening the flight took off. As the plane climbed up through the darkness Gypsy looked out of the window at the lights of London receding far below and felt as if a huge weight had just been lifted from his back. He didn't mind visiting the place or even staying around for three or four months at a time but he thoroughly resented being trapped in the place. In fact he resented being trapped anywhere and always maintained that the best place in the world, was the space between places, the journey was always the best place to be. He used to enjoy the whole experience, the airports, the flights, the after dark taxi rides to the scruffy guest houses in the cities that he landed in. It was freedom of the best kind, especially since he had been getting to know his way around so well.

It was so nice and quiet on the upper deck of the plane, the engines could barely be heard and there was just the sound of the rush of the wind against the fuselage. Gypsy had ordered Asian vegetarian food when he booked his ticket and so a tray with a full vegetarian thali was placed in front of him, complete with gulab jamun and lime achar. So he had a good dinner and then tried to catch some rest. He found it too hard, trying to sleep in the small seat and got up and wandered to the galley and asked for a drink and got talking to the steward about what went on behind the scenes in the aviation business. This was how he learned interesting things, he was always interested in how the whole thing worked and learned a lot by listening to people who worked on a daily basis in aviation. It appeared that there were sometimes frictions between the pilots and the cabin crew, as some of the pilots wanted to be treated as if they were some sort of gods. The steward said that his main task on the upper deck during night flights was to check on the pilots and flight engineer and make sure that they had not fallen asleep due to boredom. "It is not as bad as it sounds" he said "the plane is flying itself for most of the way and can even land itself with the push of a button, but they do need to be awake in case of an emergency and to communicate with the air traffic control stations along the route".

"The trouble is that night flights are so boring, the only thing that keeps them busy is doing their regular checks of the systems and the instruments. For the most part the plane takes care of itself, there is nothing for them to look at out of the window except blackness and this is not a major route that we are on, so there is little chance that we will be asked to change direction or altitude, the whole way to Delhi".

Gypsy got offered a look at the flight deck. When he walked through the door the two pilots were doing their regular checks and were ticking their charts. The flight engineer was sitting looking relaxed and obviously did not have much to do for a while. It always interested him to see how these machines worked, he knew some of the instruments but on the flight deck of a 747 there are so many different instruments that he wondered how anyone could get their head around them all and operate the thing with the coordination that was obviously necessary. They were flying somewhere over Russia or Kazakhstan and it was pitch black down below.

Gypsy was finally able to get a couple of hours sleep before they were awoken for breakfast. An hour and a half later the plane descended down through the dust into Delhi and landed into the dawn. Gypsy got through the formalities, collected his bag and jumped on the bus to Connaught Place, then took a rickshaw to Tourist Camp. After getting a room and taking a shower he put his head down for a few hours and slept until mid day. He then found where Jeet was hanging out, by way of some of his rickshaw walla friends. He was happy to see Gypsy after so long. He now had a German girlfriend who would fly out to see him regularly and wanted to marry him and take him back to Germany with her. He was very happy with her and enjoyed having some one from so far away coming to see him. But he was extremely worried about leaving India, he liked his country despite what had happened to his people in nineteen eighty four when Indra Gandhi was assassinated. – [Jeet was from a Sikh family and used to dress accordingly. But when Indra Gandi got shot and killed by her Sikh body guards after having ordered Indian troops to storm the Golden Temple, the Indian masses went mad and rioted against the Sikhs. They had pulled whole Sikh families out of their houses, doused them with petrol then set them on fire, women and small children included. Thousands were killed just in Delhi alone. Even at that time Jeet had many European friends. During the rioting they hid him and kept him protected but even so, he needed to cut his hair if he wanted to survive, Sikhs never cut their hair, so essentially he was now outside of the Sikh community.] - He enjoyed his job as a rickshaw walla as he did not have to answer to anyone but himself and he enjoyed the company of the foriegners who he had targeted as his customers. They came from all around the world and he liked listening to the stories about their country and also showing them the wonders of Delhi. He had certainly done that for Gypsy. Now thanks to Jeet, Gypsy knew his way around central Delhi and enjoyed being there. The city had a real heart and soul about it. From the water vendor and the man selling cholla battura in disposable bowls that were made from pressed leaves from a small table on the side walk to the Sikh rickshaw wallas, shop keepers, cops, retiring intellectuals and porters in the market they all looked so very human. Each one of them from the highest to the lowest of them were believers or followers of some pretty exotic religions which gave them the same spiritual outlook as most of the hippies in the west. In fact at that time the only people who lived in the west who did not think of the hippies as being crazy for being interested in reincarnation and alternative religion, where the Indians, they understood about the yearning of the spirit to find it's way to the light.

Jeet said to Gypsy "I like the woman and it sound's like a big adventure, but I am Indian and I like my life here, I'm not sure if I will like it over there in Europe it's cold and I like it when it is warm. A part of me want's to go and a part of me want's to stay and enjoy my life here riding a rickshaw". (Delhi in those days was a very different place from how it is today in 2015, there was not so much traffic on the road for one and that that was was often organically propelled by either horse, bull, elephant, camel or human. There was very little in the way of imported goods available and there were a lot of government run food outlets where things were available at low, fixed prices. There were not such large quantities of beggars and hustlers on the street and night life, other than dining out did not yet exist. There were a couple of bars at some posh hotels if someone wanted to spend some serious money. Other than that, night life consisted of a chillum party at the chai stand, with a whole load of hippies in fancy dress costumes and the local rickshaw walla union membership sitting down for a smoke together, sometimes being accompanied by a Hindu baba or the occasional and I mean very occasional Indian or Nepali freak or hippie.

At such meetings the topic of conversation would drift between spiritual, politics and travel with an occasional foray into world history. Occasionally musical instruments would be brought out and played or someone would start juggling or fire dancing, it would always be spontaneous. This was another thing that Gypsy liked about Delhi, he would always meet interesting people and the chances were that he would bump into someone that he knew from among the travellers.

However he didn't have much time to sit and shoot the breeze if he was to do what he had set out to do. Jeet carried on talking about his situation with his woman as they headed for his rickshaw and he turned around and talked about it as he peddled Gypsy to the Indian Airlines office on Barakumba road. At the airline office he had to take a ticket and wait in a long queue before he was eventually served. In those days as far as domestic aviation was concerned, Indian Airlines was the only show in town, so they had no real incentive to give fast service.

Gypsy bought a one way ticket to Bangalore for the next day. He figured that he might take the bus to Hyderabad to fly back to Delhi from, on the return. It was a special trip that he was going on and it even turned out that the old man who sold him the ticket was a Sai Baba devotee. Everywhere that he had been in Delhi he had seen images of Both Satia Sai Baba and Shirdi Sai Baba. (Shirdi Sai Baba was his last incarnation according to what all around him where saying and what he himself had declared).

The next day early in the morning he took an auto rickshaw out to the domestic terminal at the airport and checked in. It was not long before they were boarding an Airbus A300 for the three hour flight south. The plane took off and lunch was served, then three hours later the plane landed into the lush tropical green of south India. It had been raining just before they had landed and the runway and apron were still wet and covered in large puddles. Gypsy took a bus into town and asked people along the way if they knew if Sai Baba was at his Residence at

Whitefields in Bangalore or at his ashram at Putha Pati. Everyone said that he was at Putha Pati and so Gypsy looked around for a way of getting there.

Time was the thing that he was most short of on this trip and so he opted for a taxi for the five hour journey north. It was not expensive and he could afford it.

His driver was of the same age as himself and was curious to know how life was in Gypsy's country. He was a friendly fellow and asked Gypsy if he would like to have a go at driving the ambassador.

So for some ten or fifteen kilometres Gypsy did the driving. It was like driving a two legged elephant with a mind of it's own. Gypsy had never driven such an unwieldy vehicle in his life, it was like a wobbling jelly every time that he took it around a bend and he was worried that if he did not drive it extremely slowly that it would roll over on one of the bends. The road was paved but it had plenty of potholes in it, but luckily there was not so much traffic on it so for the most part they could swerve and miss them. It was the end of the annual monsoon and everywhere was lush and green and the local ponds were full to the brim. The air was relatively cool and pleasant and Gypsy was so happy to be back in India and making this journey. He was also happy when he finally gave the controls back to the driver and once again went and sat in the back seat. It was not a pleasant car to drive but it was comfortable to be a passenger in so he sat back and relaxed and looked out of the window for the rest of the journey, as the rural Indian countryside rolled by.

As the sun was setting low in the sky they eventually reached the village of Putha Pati and the driver dropped Gypsy off at the gates of the huge ashram that seemed to dominate the most of the village.

Inside, he found that he had to register at the main office, where he was allocated a space in a huge hall to go and put his bed roll at. It was close to the Hindu festival of Dewali at the time and there were thousands of people staying at the ashram. Most of them were Indian but there was also a significant number of westerners there too. In the main hall where darshan and lectures were given, Hindu monks were sitting and chanting the Ramayana in shifts through the entire day and night.

Putha Pati was the village where Sai Baba was born and grew up. He had been born into one of the families of the village and during his early life he had lived and played like the other children. The only noticeable difference happened on the odd occasion that his family ate meat. On such occasions he would go and eat at the house of a neibour or relative, where they were eating vegetarian food.

Then at the age of thirteen or fourteen he got stung by a scorpion and went into a coma for several days.

When he awoke from the coma he declared that he was Sai Baba of Shirdi, reincarnated. Shirdi was many hundreds of kilometres away and was a small town in Maharashtra state where they spoke an entirely different language from that spoken in Putha Pati which was in Karnataka state. Most people in the surrounding area had never even heard of Shirdi and if they had, they did not know where it was and they certainly had never heard of a holy man called Sai Baba. So the family and everyone who lived in the village where puzzled about what had happened to the boy and what he was now saying.

Then one day an old woman came by who had moved to this area of Karnataka from Maharashtra some years before. When the people in the area asked her if she knew anything about Sai Baba of Shirdi she told them that he had been her guru but that he had died some fifteen years before. She explained to them how he had been a teacher for many people and how he had brought peace and harmony between the Hindus and the Muslims of the Shirdi area, by having devotees from both communities and spending alternate nights in Hindu temples and Muslim Mosques. He was very well known and loved and respected in that area of Maharashtra. But because of the poor state of transport and communication links in that part of India at that time, no one in the rest of India knew much about him.

The woman went to the boy's house in the village. The moment she arrived the boy called her by name and started asking her intimate questions about her family, asking about her husband by his name and her children too.

After half an hour or so of this conversation the woman was in absolutely no doubt that this was her guru Sai Baba reincarnated. India being as it is, the local population was delighted to have a reincarnated holy man in their midst and others from the locality would come to hear him speak. Soon an ashram started to grow up around him that was sponsored by his disciples, some of whom had money. However, Baba stayed in a small room at the temple in the ashram and took only the minimum of what he needed for himself, giving all excess away to the local poor. Some of his disciples from his life in Shirdi moved to Putha

Pati to be close to him once more and the ashram continued to grow. Money flowed into the place from his disciples and he put it to good use by building high schools and paying for good and competent teachers to come and staff them. When Gypsy got to Putha Pati there must have been at least five thousand children attending the schools in the village and then there were more schools close to his ashram in Bangalore. The children all wore spotlessly clean, white uniforms and would turn up in great numbers to all of Baba's lectures.

A portion of the donations was also directed to a project that specialised in helping local villages to set up small handicraft industries as so as to help the poor farmers to be able to work their way out of the crushing poverty that they lived in. The most visible contribution to life that Baba was giving was to empower those around him, The children with education and the rural poor with both ideas and the means to carry them out, and he empowered everyone with spirituality. The symbol for his movement was a lotus flower with the symbols of all of the main religions marked in the petals. There were people of all faiths and religions staying at the ashram. Baba did not ask any of them to change religion. On the contrary he said that all religion at it's essence was the same and spoke of unconditional love. So he just asked that everyone follow their religion as it was meant to be followed and love everyone regardless of which religion that they followed.

In the ashram everyone was asked to wear white clothes only, as it helped in creating a good energy field between the people and it also worked as an equalizer. Also people were very much discouraged from giving to beggars or talking with the non ashram people outside of the gates. Most of whom were hustlers or greedy shop keepers from out of state who had come there for no other purpose than to make lots of money from the pilgrims who had come to the ashram. It was explained that money given to the poverty alleviation programs run by the Sai Baba trust would do far more good than giving to a beggar on the street who anyway had access to free food that was given by the ashram to all of the needy of the area and was probably only begging in order to feed a drug, gambling or alcohol habit.

The shop keepers who had come from as far away as Kashmir had not heard or understood Sai Baba's simple message of the universal brotherhood of the soul. They where not at the level of consciousness to do anyone any good with their company, least of all themselves. So these types were best avoided, especially while charging one's spiritual batteries at the ashram.

The village itself was a strange place what with it's large well kept high schools,

A large, modern planetarium that had been donated by some of Baba's American devotees and the huge ashram with it's temples, sleeping and living halls and rooms and canteens. Everything in the village was focused around the home grown phenomena of this great holy man who had incarnated in their midst. There could have been no one in the area who was unhappy about it. Every farmer in the area was able to sell his excess crop to the ashram at a fair price. Their children were given access to good education, which along with spiritual teachings also taught mathematics and sciences to a high level. Access to clean drinking water for the village had been provided and adult training and education was being implemented. No one was rich from it but no one was poor either, unless they chose to be by way of their habits. There was scant chance of not realizing that the village was special on arrival. There were large white arches at the entrances to the village that were adorned with deities and the name of the village written on them. Being that it was the end of the rainy season the fields all around were a lush green color, with crops that were close to ripe and the river was at the top of it's banks. There was a hill that overlooked the village that had a large tree on it which Baba had climbed on many occasions as a child and it was recommended as a good place to go and relax and meditate. So Gypsy went for a wander and found himself up on the hill and then he climbed the tree and joined two others who were sitting there. Sure enough it was a nice place to sit and without the sounds of traffic or even people's voices it was a truly peaceful and tranquil place and there was a great view over the village to the farmlands and hills beyond.

There was a wonderful vibe between the people at the ashram. Never before had Gypsy seen so many people in one place who regardless of any differences between them, wanted to get on well with each other. It was like an energy field of goodness that seemed to permeate the place and grow as more people arrived. There was no room for any sectarianism in the place and people of all faiths were not only there, but treating each other as if they were family too. There were not much in the way of rules in the ashram other than the wearing of white clothes and keeping strict personal hygiene. Of coarse there were the obvious basic rules of being in an ashram but they were for the most part unwritten as people who attended the ashram knew what was considered as reasonable behaviour in such a place. But unlike the other groups that Gypsy had encountered so far in his life, there was no strict regime or masochistic practices. Baba would give a lecture and everyone would naturally want to be there to hear him, he had wise insights to give that could help in everyday life. For some, they enjoyed the way he would materialize things out of thin air in front of them and give it to them. Gypsy had met many people who had gold rings with either perfect gemstones or a picture of Baba on what appeared to be ceramic. Others had other charms or amulets that he had materialized in his hand, so they claimed.

Their stories were all consistent and no one was trying to sell anything, least of all a second hand religion. The only thing being encouraged at the ashram was to be intelligent and aware enough to treat all beings, especially one's self with kindness compassion and respect. To do kind deeds for others and to stay focused on high thoughts concerned with finding one's way to eternal bliss.

Baba was viewed as an Avatar by his followers, meaning one who is born as God. In Baba's case this meant a being who had totally given himself, in mind, body and soul to the supreme energy, the Supreme Being, God or what ever anyone would choose to call it in their language. It was a bold claim but from what Gypsy could see at the ashram there was nothing there but good. No one had sought anything from him while he was there. The accommodation was most basic but free. Though they were obliged to pay for their food, it was extremely cheap and certainly was not making anyone a profit, also it was prepared in hygienic kitchens and tasted very good too. No one had ever come and told him that he had to do something. Unlike the other so called "spiritual" groups that Gypsy had ever come across, it was all rather mature and sensible and not just that, but it worked, it brought out the best in people. There was no chanting of mantras or sitting in meditation with a numb bum for hours on end, there was just awareness, compassion and good deeds. Many people who Gypsy met told of how they had never even heard of Sai Baba until he appeared in one of their dreams and asked them to come and visit him in India. There were other stories too of miracles that had happened to his friends and followers how their lives had been saved by something unexplainable and how Baba had appeared in front of them at the time. Baba had joked with them about it when they went to visit him later at the temple. He had not left the temple during that time but he knew exactly what had happened to them in such great detail that he must have been there.

He was known to berate his followers among the Indian Airlines staff, about their sloppy maintenance practices, complaining that it took up so much of his power stopping their planes from constantly falling out of the sky. Many of the Indian Prime Ministers had made trips that were either public or private, to see him, including Indra Gandhi. The prime Minister who was incumbent at that time who was Narmasingha Rao was even a devotee and would make regular visits to the ashram. Indeed later he was to commission the building of an airport at Putha Pati, which Indian Airlines used to fly a regular route to.

Though the stories sounded too incredible to be real, there were many compelling reasons to believe them, most of all the integrity of how the ashram was run and the behaviour of the people who attended it. There had been some bad stories about Sai Baba put out by certain quarters of the Indian press over the years but now that he was at the ashram Gypsy could see that they could not possibly be true. And even if the magic tricks and materialisations were not for real it would not diminish his greatest miracle, which was to bring people of all races, languages and religions together and put their differences aside and start being nice to each other without precondition or evangelisation of any kind. Everyone there regardless of their status in life was equal when in the ashram. Baba himself lived in a small room in the upstairs of the temple where he would invite people who wanted to meet him personally to seek his guidance. He would spend a considerable amount of time guiding the education of the children in the schools as this was where the future would lie, in continuing his work and ideals and communicating them out to the world at large, all be it in a quiet and subtle way. Teaching by example was what he encouraged his followers to do as it was the most effective way to reach people, or at least the ones that were ready.

All too quickly his visit to the ashram was coming to it's end and Gypsy had to think how he was going to get back to Jaipur to do his work. So he booked himself onto a night bus to Hyderabad for the next night. He planned to fly from there back to Delhi and then take a bus back to Jaipur. The vibe around the ashram was unlike that of any other place that he had ever been in his life and he was going to miss it, but he had no choice but to leave and go and do his job, he had other people's money in his pocket and he was expected to do their buying for them as promptly as possible.

The next evening as the sun was setting he boarded the bus to Hyderabad. He was a little sad to be leaving so quickly but he knew that it was what he had to do and that said, he was looking forward to doing his job and getting the stress and worry of it out of the way. The most of the passengers aboard where Baba devotees from the ashram and so there was a very warm and friendly atmosphere as the bus rattled northward through the night. The road, though it was supposed to be a highway, was not so busy, nor were it's surfaces what could be described as smooth or level. The bus was an express super deluxe but it still bounced around the road as it swerved around some potholes and went straight through others, every hour or so it would pull into a bus station in a small town along the way. Many people including Gypsy would pile off of the bus and after having visited the rest room, which in most cases consisted of the wall at the back of the station, they would all head for the chai stand. The stations that they stopped at all invariably absolutely reeked of piss and it would be fair to say that there were kennels and dog pens in the west that stenched less foul. However the company of the friendly and helpful devotees who were heading home to Hyderabad more than made up for it. They were a warm and kind group of people who took Baba's message to heart and made Gypsy feel at home amongst them.

Eventually at six thirty in the morning the bus reached Hyderabad central station and Gypsy said goodbye to the other devotees and headed off to the airport to see if he could catch the morning flight to Delhi. When he eventually reached the airport he was told that it had taken off fifteen minutes previously and there would not be another flight until the evening and that he would have to go into town, to the airline office to buy a ticket. He took an auto rickshaw back into the city and found himself a room at a cheap hotel to bed down in for the day, he was tired after his bone jarring nocturnal journey and got himself a couple of hours of sleep before the office was to open at ten o clock.

By 10 a.m. he had found his way to the Indian airlines office and booked and paid for his ticket for that evening's flight to Delhi. Then he returned to his room and slept until the early afternoon. When he awoke he realized that he still had at least seven hours to wait until his flight would be leaving, so he decided to hire a rickshaw walla's services to give him a tour of the sights of the city. The first place that he was taken to was a fortress outside of the city that was strategically located atop a large hill. It had obviously been built by one of the maharajas that had ruled the place within the last seven hundred years. But Gypsy had seen too many ruined old fortresses in his life and there was nothing particularly special about this one. So after a quick nose about he got the rickshaw walla to take him back into the city and went and had something to eat. Hyderabad obviously did not have so much in the way of tourist attractions or ancient historical sights to see. So after another short nap in the room he grabbed his bag and headed out to the airport and waited for his flight.

He had a while to wait before he could check in, so he wandered up on to the observation deck and watched as a trainee pilot was put through his paces lifting off and landing a Boing 737 repeatedly. Hyderabad was where Indian Airlines had it's flight training school and the main runway at the airport was used as the training ground. The plane took off then flew around and landed again, then before it had come to a stop the pilot gunned the engines and lifted off once more. This same manoeuvre must have been repeated over a dozen times as Gypsy watched.

Eventually the check in counters opened and the queue was slowly all checked in.. There were, in those days at least, no bars at Indian domestic airports so Gypsy had to be happy with a bottle of Himachal apple juice and a cup of chai instead of a beer with a whisky chaser.

The flight boarded and Gypsy found himself sitting next to an educated young local man from the city. He spoke English fluently and worked in the computer software business. He was flying to Delhi to do some work for the company that he was employed by and was going to be there for some weeks. It was the first time that he had travelled alone so far from his home and he appeared to be a bit nervous about it. He didn't know anyone in Delhi and he had never been there before so it was understandable that he was feeling a bit like a fish out of water. The plane taxied out to the runway, then turned around and went back to the terminal while the pilot came on the intercom and said "I'm sorry about this". With no other explanation they sat and waited for half an hour and then the plane left the terminal and headed out to the runway once more. This time they took off and the plane climbed through the darkness, in a north westerly direction towards Delhi. The usual meal of vegetarian curry, dahl, rice and chapattis was served and then after an uneventfull two and a half hours, the plane touched down in Delhi.

Once inside the terminal Gypsy grabbed his bag from the carousel and headed out to find a taxi into the city. He stopped the night at a cheap guest house in Pahar Ganj and the next morning he took an auto rickshaw to Bikaner house, where he bought a ticket on the Rajasthan Roadways express bus to Jaipur. Then he sat down and waited for the bus to arrive. Six hours later the bus pulled into the bus station at Sindhi camp and Gypsy, like the others on board, got down and elbowed his way through the usual scrum of rickshaw wallas, touts and hustlers. After finding himself a rickshaw outside of the station he set off towards the Pink city Guest house, which was where he was planning on staying on this particular trip.

After checking in he dropped his bag in the room and headed out to M.I. road to look for a rickshaw to take him down to Gangoori bazaar, to go and see the Birla family.

When he got there he found that things had changed a bit. Hem's father had died and out of respect for his father Hem had given up drinking. Also he had made enough money to buy himself a piece of land and have a house built within the walls of the old city. A lot of business was going on around his table and the office was no longer doubling as his residence and so had expanded into all of the rooms of the property.

The biggest part of Gypsy's orders, were for emeralds, so he informed Birla of what sort of sizes, prices, cuts and qualities that he was looking for. There was a young German man of a similar age to Gypsy who was buying expensive high quality precious stones to sell in his home market in the Dortmund and Dusseldorf area of Germany. He and Gypsy struck up a conversation and exchanged notes on prices of stones within the Jaipur market. The German man's name was Frank and though Gypsy did not realize it at the time, the two of them were destined to be good friends for many years to come.

Because of the size of the emerald order and the very particular shade of green that was sought along with the price that was required, Gypsy decided that his only chance of finding the quantity of such stones was to go and see one of the bigger players in Gopal Ji Ka Rasta. There was one particular dealer called Gordan, who was, despite the small size of his shop, one of the biggest dealers on the street. So Gypsy went to see him and ask if he as a broker could line up a suitably large selection of stones of the precise price and quality that gypsy required. Gordan and his brothers were most polite and welcoming and after a brief discussion over a cup of chai Gypsy was requested to return to the office after two days to see samples of what it was that he may be looking for.

Gypsy had over two thousand pounds of his own money to invest and so also went to see some of the other dealers that he knew in the market to see what they had in stock. One of the dealers was called Zail and had a shop in front of the Hawa Mahal (palace of the winds) called Rais jewelers. Another was called Yogesh and he had a shop several hundred yards away, in a courtyard that recessed off from Johari bazaar, close to the entrance to Gopal ji Ka Rasta. Both were jovial and helpful characters who Gypsy knew from experience could turn up some good stones at low prices and they were small enough to treat Gypsy as a serious customer. When as Gordan was doing business deals worth some very serious money even by western standards.

As such, the amount that Gypsy wished to spend was a drop in the ocean to him.

With Yogesh and Zail he knew that they would do a lot more running around to get his business and as such some very good deals were likely to show up.

Another of the hippie gem dealers at Birla's office was an Australian called Steve, He sold silver and loose stones in and around eastern Australia. He had told Gypsy about a good deal to be had on some of the types of stone that Gypsy had orders for.

So one day he and Gypsy went to go and have a look at it. However on the way, they made a stop at the hotel that Steve was staying at. It was a converted palace called Ketri House and had previously been owned by the Maharaja of Ketri district, in Rajasthan. He had died some years previously and while the family fought over his estate, the staff at the hotel kept the place running in order to feed themselves. The place looked as if it could have featured in an Agatha Cristie movie, Where the Indian Butler did it. It had the drawing room with the antique furniture, and a dinning room with an overhead multi arched gallery looking down upon it. There was a central, stone paved courtyard with rooms lining the outside, there was a library full of old leather bound books, there was a small quaint looking gift shop and to top it off there were two executive suites that could be rented for as little as ten dollars a night. The suites had been the private quarters of the Maharaja and his wife the

Maharani. Each suite was made of two large rooms, a dressing room and a bathroom. The palace was covered in beautiful carved stone work and it still looked good. The garden however had been let go and looked like it was turning back into desert scrub. There was the remnants within the grounds of a large and quite deep swimming pool and the garden itself was almost dead, due to lack of water or proper care.

There was a young English woman who was sitting around in the drawing room with two decidedly shady and greasy looking local men. The Indian man who had joined up with Gypsy and Steve for the trip across the city turned to them and said "what is she doing hanging out with those two? they are really bad people and specialize in cheating foreigners. Maybe she doesn't know and can't see it." Gypsy decided to go and talk with her for a short while. At this, the two hustlers melted off into the shadows and Gypsy was able to warn her about the nature of the company that she was keeping. She seemed grateful for the warning and decided to hitch along with Gypsy and Steve for the rest of the day to see what they were doing. It turned out that not only was she half Jewish like Gypsy but she was born on the same day of the same year as him and started her travels at the same kibbutz as he did. Also she had the same natural curly hair and even dressed in a similar style to how Gypsy did, opting for the practical not too noticeable look. It was truly weird, like looking at a female version of himself. She too liked to spend her time on the road travelling and lived a wild and adventurous life.

It was so weird that she decided to hang around for a few days longer instead of travelling on. For the next two weeks she went around with Gypsy looking at gemstones each day. It was truly uncanny how very similar that they were, each felt that they were looking at a twin of themselves. Both were in search of the spiritual but rejected that that was bullshit like dogma and fixed religion with it's absolutes and can'ts, shouldn'ts and mustn'ts.

Gordan came through not only with the emeralds but with a whole load of other things too.

There was a collection of pieces of fine quality lapis lazuli that had been carved in an art nouveoux flower, wings and flow style and were all in perfect matching pairs. They were expensive for lapis but the quality of both the rough material and the work made Gypsy feel sure that he could find a buyer for it. Then there were pieces of aquamarine that had been cut as giant cabochons and pieces of tourmaline that had been carved similar to the lapis but in smaller sizes. Some of them had two or three colours in each piece. Then there were the cabochons in tourmaline, amethyst, garnet and fine quality lapis lazuli. Apart from the orders, Gypsy also was making a very carefully selected collection for himself.

After much work on the selecting and negotiating that carried on over several weeks, The deals were coming close to ready for completion and payment. But before Gypsy parted with such a large wad of both his money and that of his clients, he wanted to take a step back and look at what he was doing with a more relaxed demeanour. However, the last thing that could ever be said about Jaipur was that it was relaxing. It was fun yes but relaxing, never. The place hummed day and night and the hustlers on the streets never gave a westerner a moment of peace. Everyone and his dog or in Jaipur's case his goat, was trying to pull you into a shop or showroom in order to earn themselves a commission. They would get a small commission even for getting you over the threshold and into the shop and then very high rates of commission on each thing that you might purchase. These individuals would bear a heavy resemblance to mosquitoes or flies in both their persistence and annoyance factors. It was due to such annoyances that some of Gypsy's Indian friends were teaching him how to swear and curse in Hindi "you'll need it" they told him.

Also, when Gypsy was in the pink city all sorts of dealers that he had friendly relations with were coming and pestering him to come and see their latest stock. There were not enough hours in the day to do so, but just like the hustlers they would not take no for an answer. Their behaviour was very much similar to that of the rickshaw wallas at the bus station, but if gypsy snapped at them to give him a break and allow him some space to breathe then they would start acting hurt as if he was being rude to them. Some of them were truly impossible people that Gypsy wanted nothing to do with. Even if they had good stones Gypsy knew that it would use up excessive amounts of time to deal with them. They would want to go through the bargaining and haggling rituals and even then, the chances that they would be prepared to sell the stone or stones for what Gypsy Thought that they were worth at local rates was highly negligible.

Anyway it was hugely obvious that there was no way that he was going to be given a moment's peace while in Jaipur. So he, Aussie Steve and the woman who had been hanging out with them all decide to fuck off down to Pushkar for a few days and rest their heads from the Jaipur stress and head game circus. The ride down there was very relaxing and consisted of a two hour ride on a local bus to Ajmer and then a twenty minute jeep ride over the hill to Pushkar itself. The mid morning buses to Ajmer were very rarely full and the door at the back of the bus was invariably left open, with the warm desert air blowing in. it was a pleasant ride across flat semi desert land with scrub bushes and villages where farming was happening. Before reaching Ajmer they passed through the village of Kashingar where huge great chunks of marble were stacked by the side of the road after having just been quaried near by. There were trucks, small cranes and other loading devices and the air was full of marble dust with great clouds of it blowing across the road. This would appear to have been one of Rajasthan's primary sources of marble. A sheet of marble in India at that time was cheaper than a comparable surface of ply wood. Many houses in Rajastan were coated in marble and obviously also had marble floors.

They reached the scruffy town of Ajmer and pulled up at the bus station. Across the road was a line of locally built jeeps that operated as local transport to the villages. They found one going to Pushkar and jumped aboard. The jeep ride over the hill was different from the bus ride. People were crammed in tight and there was a multitude of people standing on the back step and hanging on to the canopy bars for dear life. The vehicle drove firstly through the streets of Ajmer and then up through the hairpin bends and over the large and long hill that separate's Ajmer from Pushkar.

Both Ajmer and Pushkar are holy towns. Ajmer is holy to the Muslims on account of the fact that one of their greatest Sufi saints is buried there. He was the man who first spread Islam to that area of Asia. It was a dirty and scruffy looking town, even by Indian standards, with no real obvious centre, however it was the administrative centre for a large district and contained many government offices and Rajasthan's largest prison. On the other side of the hill and some eight to twelve kilometres away was the Hindu holy town of Pushkar where the Hindu god, Brahma was supposedly born out of the lake. The landscape there was striking and beautiful, there were wild monkeys living on and around the hill and they would either be sitting on the wall by the side of the road or bouncing across the road in front of the traffic to get to one of the trees that they had spotted a morsel of fruit hanging from.

Pushkar was made up of one road that was primarily a pedestrian through way and encircled the lake. There were many guest houses lining the way, but Gypsy having been in Pushkar previously, suggested that they go to the government of Rajasthan official guest house, which was not only highly reasonable, with it's room rates but had nice rooms with hot showers and comfortable furniture, a nice garden with a view over the lake and a relatively hygienic kitchen.

From the garden there was a fantastic view of the buildings that wall to wall, lined over three quarters of the lake, the other quarter of the lake shore being lined with a cause way. The buildings of the town were elegant and often consisted of multi arched structures. Many of the buildings were temples and ashrams. The whole town was dedicated towards spiritual practice and meat fish and eggs along with alcohol, were banned from sale in all parts of the town. As such there were no fried eggs for breakfast in any of the guest houses, restaurants or cafes. However there were plenty of other good options available such as puri baji, stuffed paratha and toasted cheese and tomatoe sandwiches.

The few days that they spent in Pushkar went by very fast as they relaxed in their surroundings. Pushkar was the most pleasantly relaxing place to be, with no rush of traffic and no one so desperately keen to try dragging anyone into their shop. There were a few Braminas hustling people to do ceremonies that they expected to get paid for performing and a few fake babas looking to gouge money from people but it was nothing compared to the hustle of Jaipur.

Then it was time to once again return to Jaipur to finish the work.

Back in Jaipur, he still had to line up a few more packets of stones, both for himself and for his customers. There was also the order for the thanka paintings for his friend, which Birla had promised to arrange but had so far failed to materialize. Tomorrow, he was told, it was allways fucking tomorrow and never today, when dealing with Indians. As everyone knows, tomorrow never comes, as it is always today.

Slowly as in snail's pace, the deal came together. Then there was the problem of getting the lazy bastards to make up his invoices as so that he could pay them all.

Several days of high stress ensued as he tried to get the work finished on time.

Emeralds are an exceptionally hard stone to appraise as they will look entirely different in different lighting conditions, so he was extremely nervous about getting it right for his customer. He wanted to win future orders from this customer, who had set him an extremely hard task, to be able to match the quality with the price and the size. Gypsy was so mentally exhausted by it that he was becoming irritable and found that he had entirely lost his apatite and had to virtually force himself to eat. The jeweller who had made the order had set him an almost impossible task.

Eventually he was finished and he and the woman who had been a great help in helping him stay cool, took a late night bus to Delhi. Arriving in the early morning, they checked into a guest house in the Pahar Ganj area of the city and then went and had breakfast. Despite his promise, Birla had been unable to materialise the thanka paintings back in Jaipur and instead had given Gypsy the address of a shop that belonged to one of his many aquaintances in old Delhi. With only one and a half days to go before his flight was to leave, Gypsy had much work to do in Delhi. He went and found a rickshaw and took a ride down to old Delhi, getting the driver to take the side road that runs up between the huge, mogul style mosque and the Chandi Chowk market. After several twists and turns, he found the shop that Birla had given him the address of. It was a dark and somewhat dingy, medium sized establishment that specialised in Tibetan art and antiques. There on the wall by one of the internal doors, hung a large collection of large sized thanka paintings, all neatly framed in silk mounts. They were beautiful and striking, also the prices were reasonable for what they were. They were not antique but they were high quality and painted in the old way, using paints that had been made from ground up gemstones.

He carefully selected the most attractive and vivid from among them, then paid for them and took another rickshaw back across the city to Pahar Ganj.

Once back in his room, he placed them carefully in his main bag and went out again. He took another rickshaw to Connaught Place. From there he took a walk along Jan Path road to the Tibetan market and went and visited his friend Doma and stopped for a chat and a chai. Also while in the Tibetan market he bought some items from both Doma and some of the neigbouring shops for use as both gift items and also for selling.

Eventually all had been taken care of and early the next morning he took an auto rickshaw out to the airport for the flight back to London.

It was mid morning and the airport was almost empty when they boarded a British airways L1011 Tristar for the ride to Heathrow. [in those days, possibly due to atmospheric conditions, the international terminal at Delhi airport would buzz like a hive of activity between eleven at night and six o'clock in the morning, but was largely deserted through the daylight hours].

The plane took off and lunch was served. Then three hours later the plane touched down at Kuwait for a scheduled stop. Gypsy was too tired to be bothered to get off of the plane and tried to sleep as the cleaners came onboard and fussed around. All that he wanted to do was get back to his place in England and hand over the Emeralds and other goods to the people who had ordered them. Doing this work for others had created an abnormal amout of stress and discomfort in his life, but that was the price of getting himself re established in the jewellery trade.

Arriving in the evening he found the clearing agent waiting for him in the red channel. This time it was relatively quick. It was only the stones that needed declaring as the Thankas were not of a commercial quantity and it was only the VAT that needed paying on them.

Once more he was being collected from the airport and being driven home.

The next day he delivered the Emeralds. The Jeweller was not complaining but neither was he smiling. It seemed that he thought that Gypsy would be able to perform absolute miracles for him. With Emeralds this is just not possible except in very rare circumstances. There is very little profit to be made from emeralds unless you actually own the mines. In certain parts of the world emeralds are used for laundering dirty money and this also messes with the prices in different parts of the world.

Next he had stones to drop off for the friend from Brighton who also was a Sai Baba devotee. He seemed happy with his order and also bought most of the packet of carved lapis lazuli. Around the lanes that day Gypsy got many sales and returned home with a good wedge of both cash and cheques.

Finally there was the friend who had ordered the thankas. He was overjoyed with his paintings. He had originally ordered them with the idea of selling them through his shop but then on seeing them decided to keep them all for himself and used them to decorate the walls of his house with.

The rest of the gems continued to sell well until he had very little stock left. He had a stack of cash that he had converted to travelers cheques and money in the bank too.

Christmas was coming and he had turned his business around and into a success.

Sally had disappeared off when he had left but came back for Christmas. Barbara was still close by and they teamed up for another sales run that once again took in Glastonbury. He saw Peter the painter again who once more bought a load of stock from him and asked him what he may like Gypsy to bring from India on the next run.

He had now sold enough that he had doubled his money, the trip had been a success in all ways.

After Christmas he started to plan for his next trip. The healer had told him that he was meant to stay in England and work but there was just no way that he could do that, he had had enough of being stuck in UK and craved to be back in India. He was not at home in England and still had not found all that he had been looking for. He was wanting to go spend some time at an ashram where he could learn something and take himself further spiritually and was thinking about the BKS Iyengar school of yoga in Poona as a starting point.

In book two the story of what happens when Gypsy gets to Poona is told. He ends up in an ashram but not the one that he was originally intending to go to........this will all be spoken about and more in Gypsy and the guru of drugs, sex and rock and roll which also has more stories of travel adventures, gemstones, mystecism etc.....................

many names have been changed in this story but not all, names of places have also been kept quite vague in order to further help protect identities......England get's quite a slagging in this book. Please understand that it is the England of the eighties that is being slagged off and not the England of today....The country went through a huge transformation through the nineties and into the next decade.....it is now a far more switched on place and the attitudes that were being slagged off have become much rarer..... The UK via the immigrants and the internet has become a much more open minded place......it has lost much of it's ridiculousness and become much more international in it's attitude.

Printed in the United States
By Bookmasters